A GREETING OF THE SPIRIT

A GREETING OF THE SPIRIT

*Selected Poetry of John Keats
with Commentaries*

SUSAN J. WOLFSON

THE BELKNAP PRESS OF HARVARD UNIVERSITY PRESS

Cambridge, Massachusetts, and London, England

2022

FIRST PRINTING

Library of Congress Cataloging-in-Publication Data

Names: Keats, John, 1795–1821. | Wolfson, Susan J., 1948– editor, writer of added
    commentary. | Keats, John, 1795–1821. O Peace!

Title: A greeting of the spirit : selected poetry of John Keats with commentaries /
    Susan J. Wolfson.

Description: Cambridge, Massachusetts : The Belknap Press of Harvard University Press,
    2022. | Includes bibliographical references and index.

Identifiers: LCCN 2022005855 | ISBN 9780674980891 (hardcover)

Subjects: LCSH: Keats, John, 1795–1821. | LCGFT: Poetry.

Classification: LCC PR4834 .G74 2022 | DDC 821/.7—dc23/eng/20220304

LC record available at https://lccn.loc.gov/2022005855

TO JOHN KEATS

*One word more, for one cannot help seeing
our own affairs in every point of view - Should
any one call my dedication to Chatterton affected
I ~~say~~ answer as followeth:*

> *"Were I dead Sir I should like a Book
> dedicated to me –'*

CONTENTS

AUTHOR'S NOTE ON TEXT AND STYLE

Texts. The base text represented in each chapter is specified at the chapter's
end.

The principle of selection is eclectic: sometimes first or lifetime publications;
sometimes manuscripts (Keats's living hand!); sometimes the edition in
Jack Stillinger's *The Poems of John Keats*.

Keats's letters: variously transcribed from holographs; based on my Longman
edition (*K*); or on the edition of Hyder E. Rollins (*L*).

Keats's Books. These editions are "Keats's library" (his copies often marked
and underlined by him), which I have used as my base texts for quotation.

Coleridge, Samuel Taylor. *Biographia Literaria*. 1817. *Sibylline Leaves*, 1817.

Dante Alighieri. *La Divina Comedia* (*The Divine Comedy*), translated by H.F.
Carey, *The Vision; or, Hell, Purgatory, and Paradise, of Dante Alighieri*. Taylor
and Hessey, 1814.

Hazlitt, William. *Characters of Shakespear's Plays*. Taylor and Hessey, 1817.
Houghton Library, Harvard. Cited by page and sequence. https://iiif.lib
.harvard.edu/manifests/view/drs:16001859$205i.

Milton's Paradise Lost. A New Edition / Adorned with Beautiful Plates. 2 Vols.,
Edinburgh: 1807. A little duodecimo edition, online at http://keatslibrary
.org/paradise-lost/.

Shakespeare, William. *Poetic Works of William Shakspeare*. 1806.

Dramatic Works of William Shakspeare. 7 Vols., C. Whittingham, 1813–1814.
Cited by act, scene, and *DW* volume: page (each play starts with p. 1). For
the folio edition, Caroline Spurgeon's transcription.

Spenser, Edmund. *Works of Edmund Spenser*. 6 Vols., Edited by John Hughes.
Jacob Tonson, 1715, including especially *The Fairy-Queen* (so spelled).

Wordsworth, William. *The Excursion*. Longman & c, 1814. *Poems*. 2 vols. 1815.

Style

[editorial insertions: a word, letter, or punctuation mark]

[editorial comment within quoted text]

Disliking swarms of quotation marks, *I may put quoted wording in italics.*

I keep <u>Keats's underlinings</u>, punctuation, and other stylings, including ~~strike-throughs~~ and ‹insertions.

I keep older spellings.

I silently emend printers' errata (especially in the newspapers of the day, where, for example, **u** can get set as **n** or vice versa).

I revise older print styles bearing no author preference, e.g., quotation marks (") at the front of successive lines of poetry and semicolons and colons set within closing quotation marks (;" :").

Keats typically elides the letter *r*, sometimes indicating it with a compact downstroke. I spell it out.

Line numbers are mine, except for *Endymion*, which follows *1818*'s.

Italic titles are Keats's.

"Titles in quotation" use the convention of first words.

[Titles in brackets are mine]

Citations

If no particular edition is of consequence, date of publication only is given.

Short titles and abbreviations are keyed to Works Cited.

Dedication:

— John Keats, to the publishers of *Endymion,* 19 March 1818. Morgan Library MA 209, *Preface,* p. 4. Keats's export-ready quotation I return to him.

ABBREVIATIONS

1817 John Keats. *Poems.* C & J Ollier.

1818 John Keats. *Endymion: A Poetic Romance.* Taylor & Hessey, emended with reference to Keats's corrections (*L* 1:272–273).

1820 John Keats. *Lamia, Isabella, The Eve of St. Agnes, and Other Poems.* Taylor & Hessey.

1848 Richard Monckton Milnes. *Life, Letters, and Literary Remains of John Keats.* 2 vols., Edward Moxon.

&c And other poems or publishing partners.

ALS Autograph letter, signed.

Berg John Keats Collection of Papers. Henry W. and Albert A. Berg Collection of English and American Literature, New York Public Library. Identified by folio.

CR Charles Cowden Clarke. *Recollections of Writers.*

CW *Complete Works of John Keats.* 5 vols., Gowans & Gray, 1900–1901.

DW *Dramatic Works of William Shakspeare.*

f Folio (page): r (recto) or v (verso).

FQ *The Fairy-Queen* [i.e., *The Faerie Queene*], by Edmund Spenser, 1596; in the 1715 edition that Keats studied.

HK Harvard Keats Collection. https://library.harvard.edu/collections/harvard-keats-collection.

MsK Manuscript, Keats's poems and letters, in the Harvard Keats Collection cited by collection, item, and sequence, for example: MsK 1.53.233.

JnD Samuel Johnson. *A Dictionary of the English language . . . illustrated in their different significations by examples from the best writers.* 2 vols., Longman, 1755. https://johnsonsdictionaryonline.com/.

K *John Keats: A Longman Cultural Edition.* Edited by Susan J. Wolfson. Pearson, 2007.

KC *The Keats Circle: Letters and Papers.* Edited by Hyder E. Rollins. 2 vols., Harvard UP, 1965.

KPL Keats's *Paradise Lost,* cited by volume: page; his underlining of the verse and other markings, along with his marginalia (see the Keats Library online images)

KS *Keats's Shakespeare,* by Caroline Spurgeon. Oxford UP, 1928.

L *The Letters of John Keats.* Edited by Hyder E. Rollins. 2 vols., Harvard UP, 1958.

OED *Oxford English Dictionary.* http://https://www-oed-com.

P *The Poems of John Keats.* Edited by Jack Stillinger. Harvard UP, 1978.

PL *Paradise Lost,* by John Milton 1674; in *KPL,* cited by Book and line.

SpW Stuart Sperry, ed. Richard Woodhouse's annotated *1817.*

sq. Sequence in a digital file.

ILLUSTRATIONS

A GREETING OF THE SPIRIT

Introduction

WRITING TO HIS BROTHER and sister-in-law in America, 14 October 1818, John Keats assures them of his resilience after two influential, harsh reviews of his first ventures. "This is a mere matter of the moment," he says, with a poet's undefeated alliterative lilt,

> – *I think I shall be among the English Poets after my death.* ~~The~~ *Even as a Matter of present interest the attempt to crush me in the* ~~Chro~~ *Quarterly has only brought me more into notice and it is a common expression among book men* "*I wonder the Quarterly should cut its own throat'[.]* (MsK 1.39.146; K 209)

The unpretentious *I think I shall,* the temporality of *after my death:* hope tinged with modesty. By 1883, Poet Laureate Alfred Tennyson would endorse Keats's *among the English Poets* with this upgrade: "He would have been among the very greatest of us if he had lived. There is something of the innermost soul of poetry in almost everything he ever wrote." Keats, he declared, "promised securely more than any English poet since Milton" (Hallam Tennyson 2:286, 504).

Promise. Keats is ever this poet, because his career scarcely exceeded four years: from 5 May 1816, with a sonnet in a newspaper, to 21 July 1820, when *To*

Autumn was reprinted in the *Chronicle* (the host volume had appeared a few weeks before). This is the legend of "Keats": flushed early with talent, crushed (but not extinguished) by early abuse, cherished by a coterie, winning posthumous praise in zig-zags, secured in durable fame. The "romance" of Keats is persistence through (by means of; pressing beyond) disappointments, an ability to turn dead ends into back channels, resourceful inventiveness at every turn. Had he been able to attend a university, had there been an "English major" in his day, Keats would have been a star student, pursuing an interdisciplinary program of philosophy, science, medicine, ethics—all the while writing poetry and talking with poets, reading everything. He ached to be a poet.

Poets may be born, but they are also made by the world into which they are born. For Keats, books were vital. His reading included some eighteenth-century writers (Pope's translations of Homer, Ann Radcliffe's gothic novels, James Thomson's retro-Spenserian satirical romance, *The Castle of Indolence*). His chief loves were Spenser, Shakespeare, Milton, and Dryden. "Shakspeare and the paradise Lost every day become greater wonders to me –I look upon fine Phrases like a Lover —" (MsK 1.58.287; *K* 264). Keats also *writes* fine phrases, loving what words can tell and what they can do. An essayist that Keats admired, William Hazlitt, called such energy *Gusto,* "imagination" taking "a double relish of its objects, an inveterate attachment to the things [it] describes, and to the words describing them." This is Keats's energy. With an "instinct for fine words," he "rediscovered the delight and wonder that lay enchanted in the dictionary," said J. R. Lowell ("Keats" 325). Keats's own enchanted word-works live in memorable circulation:

"Much have I travel'd in the realms of gold"
"negative capability"
"the ardour of pursuit"
"diligent indolence"
"A thing of beauty is a joy for ever"
"camelion Poet"
"tender is the night"
"Beauty is truth, truth Beauty"
"Season of mists and mellow fruitfulness"
"Fanatics have their dreams"
"I am leading a posthumous existence"
"I always made an awkward bow"

Some of these phrasings are so well known that we may not realize that their melodies were unheard before John Keats. Charles Lamb praised Keats's talent for "prodigal phrases . . . each a poem in a word" (*Examiner* p. 495). While their contexts are important (inflections, qualifications, and ironies), it says much about Keats's brilliance that these wordings have been so prodigal, so radiant in general circulation.

By the century's end, this was "Keats": "the power of concentrating all the far-reaching resources of language on one point, so that a single and apparently effortless expression rejoices the æsthetic imagination at the moment when it is most expectant and exacting, and at the same time astonishes the intellect with a new aspect of truth," said Robert Bridges (xci–xcii), deeming him Shakespeare's equal this way. Bridges would become Poet Laureate (after Tennyson), and he had been a doctor, a profession for which Keats trained; he could appreciate this visceral fiber in Keats's poetic genius. When, in 1928, Herbert Read argued that word-power is poetry's very definition, he gave Keats automatic honors. "In Poetry the words are born or re-born in the act of thinking" (xi). Whether or not you agree to the distinction Read makes between poetry and prose, what is notable is Keats's legibility in his list of unmarked examples of such power in an "affair of one word, like Shakespeare's 'incarnadine', or of two or three words, like 'shady sadness', 'incense-breathing Morn', 'a peak in Darien', 'soft Lydian airs', 'Mount Abora', 'star-inwrought'" (xi).[1] Like Shakespeare, Keats also invented words as he needed them (as testified by this book's index, which lists dozens).

No wonder Keats is often called "a poet's poet": he writes with an extraordinary sensitivity to the emotional, psychological, and intellectual resonances of verse, achieved through exquisite technical skill. And so I arrive at my title, *A Greeting of the Spirit.* This is a phrase from Keats's letter to a friend, surmising that "every mental pursuit takes its reality and worth from the ardour of the pursuer — being in itself a nothing." Ethereal things, he proposes, range from *Things real* "such as existences of Sun Moon & Stars and passages of Shakspeare" to the *Nothings* which are elevated by that "ardent pursuit." Between these poles is the span of spirited imagination:

Things semireal such as Love, the Clouds &c which require a greeting of the Spirit to make them wholly exist – [.]   (13 March 1818; MsK 1.3.81)

A greeting: a great call to poetic imagination and our invitation for reading Keats. Ever immersed in words, as a means for thinking, as sounds with surprises, and as lettered figures, Keats is a poet for everyone ready to be caught by writing that is challenging and heartbreaking, funny and stimulating, formal and intimate, satisfying in the intelligent pleasures of concentrated analysis and revelatory in wider vibrations.

Life Distilled: John Keats (1795–1821)

"No young man believes that he shall ever die," wrote Hazlitt in 1827, a little more than six years after Keats was no more. "Death, old age, are words without a meaning, that pass by us like the idle air which we regard not."[2] How otherwise it was for Keats, who had seen and endured plenty of death when he petitioned in *Sleep and Poetry,* the capstone of his debut volume, "Oh, for ten years, that I may overwhelm / Myself in poesy" (pp. 96–97). This was written in late 1816, published the next spring. Not granted even half this span, he still achieved a remarkably full poetic life, seeming in brief years to "write old"— so Elizabeth Barrett Browning measures the amazing intensity:

> By Keats's soul, the man who never stepped
> In gradual progress like another man,
> But, turning grandly on his central self,
> Ensphered himself in twenty perfect years
> And died, not young, — (the life of a long life
> Distilled to a mere drop, falling like a tear
> Upon the world's cold cheek to make it burn
> For ever;) by that strong excepted soul,
> I count it strange, and hard to understand,
> That nearly all young poets should write old.[3]

Long life distilled into a burning drop is a perfect conceptual biography, beautifully figured by the embrace of parentheses. A generation on, Oscar Wilde opened his *Lecture on the English Renaissance* (9 January 1882) by hailing in Keats's poetry an epochal force for a modern "artistic renaissance of England": "He was the forerunner of the pre-Raphaelite school, and so of the great romantic wave" (30). Quite an accolade from one who quipped in 1889, "Books of poetry by young writers are usually promissory notes that are never met." He completed this sentence with an admission that every now and then "one comes across a volume that is so far above the average that one can hardly resist the fascinating temptation of recklessly prophesying a fine future for the author" (*Pall Mall Gazette*). Wilde meant twenty-four-year-old Yeats's *The Wan-*

derings of Oisin ("strongly influenced by Keats"), but it could just as well have designated Keats's 1820 volume, also published at age twenty-four, holding *The Eve of Saint Agnes, Hyperion, Lamia, Isabella,* and the "Great Odes" that are synonymous with his fame.

Distilled indeed. Keats's lifetime publications total fifty-four poems, forty-five in his three volumes, others in periodicals, along with a couple of unsigned reviews. The census of a long life would find all these slotted as "early works," "juvenilia." Comparisons are striking. At twenty-five, Chaucer, Spenser, Dryden, and Swift had written nothing about which we know. Shakespeare had racked up only *The Comedy of Errors* and *Love's Labour's Lost;* Ben Jonson, *The Isle of Dogs;* Marvell, some courtly Greek and Latin poems. Wordsworth had one sonnet and two slender volumes of descriptive poetry (thirty-four and fifty-seven pages, respectively), read today mostly by specialists; the landmark *Lyrical Ballads* didn't come until age twenty-eight. The first publication of Victorian sage Carlyle, born just weeks after Keats and surviving him by six decades, came in 1824, on the cusp of age thirty: a translation of Goethe's *Wilhelm Meister.* What if Keats had the gift of even those "ten years," let alone Carlyle's and Wordsworth's decades?

This mystery vibrates along Keats's several talents. Poetry, yes. His eye was also on drama; steeped in Shakespeare, he might have written tragedies for the times, or comedies from his keen observation of personalities and social behavior, not only in deft outlines but also in nuances of action and conversation. Student of history, politics, science, and medicine, he might have become a forceful reviewer and essayist, joining Hazlitt on "the liberal side of things" (*L* 2:14). An astute, disinterested observer of the character of his friends and of public actors, he might have become a modern novelist. To quote a famous ode: *Unheard melodies!*

John Keats was the eldest of four children, their father the proprietor of a suburban London livery-stable. He was nine when this father died from a riding accident. His mother was doting but erratic, and John was devastated when, in the turmoil of a second marriage quickly secured and soon ended, she left the children with her mother. Four years later (four long years in boy-time), she returned, wracked by tuberculosis. John took charge of her care, guarded her door, and in 1810, when he was fourteen, watched her die. This trauma would replay in the adored, adoring, inconstant (sometimes fatally) women in his poetry, early and late. The love of his life, Fanny Brawne, was destined for this sorority, constant as she was. (It didn't help that Fanny was also his mother's name.)

The boys attended progressive Enfield Academy. Bright and appetitive, Keats thrived, reading like a demon, tutored by the headmaster's son, Charles Cowden

Clarke. Boys yearn to run outdoors; Keats's paradise was books: "the quantity that he read was surprising. He must . . . have exhausted the school library," recalled Clarke (*CR* 123). He nurtured Keats's interests in literature, music, theater, and liberal politics. Then the legal guardian appointed by their grandmother, businessman Richard Abbey, intent to train the boys for a livelihood and keep young Fanny (his ward) from their influence, put an end to Enfield. In the summer of 1811, Tom and George went to his countinghouse, and John, not yet sixteen, was apprenticed, for a five-year term, to a brutal Edmonton surgeon in the days before anesthesia. When Keats could, he would walk the three miles back to Enfield to visit Clarke, usually with "a book to read, or . . . one to be exchanged" (125). He kept another lifeline to Enfield, continuing the project he had undertaken to translate Virgil's epic of war and empire, *The Aeneid,* the word-care sharpening his Latin literacy and the poetic rendition deepening his feel for meter and sensitivity to verbal nuance.

He was also moonlighting, writing poetry, and plotting a way out of his misery and loneliness in Edmonton. In October 1815, he persuaded Abbey to enroll him for medical study at Guy's Hospital in south London. He was soon working as a surgeon's dresser, still reading away (Homer, Virgil, Tasso, Chaucer, Spenser, Shakespeare, Milton, Chatterton, and contemporaries Leigh Hunt, Wordsworth, Byron)—and writing poetry: on impulse, as escape, and in fantasy vocation. He was always close to his brothers, often his first readers, always impressed by his talent. He showed Clarke some poetry, hoping for help into print. When this didn't happen, he ventured a sonnet to the weekly paper, *The Examiner,* signed "J K."[4] Editor Leigh Hunt took it. Seeing it published in May 1816 was far more a thrill to Keats than acing the rigorous qualification exam in July for medical practice. Clarke, a friend of Hunt, soon followed up with him with a folder of Keats's poems; in October Hunt invited them to his cottage on Hampstead Heath. "As we approached" (Clarke recalled), Keats was pumped: "there was the rising and accelerated step, with gradual subsidence of all talk" (*CR* 133). This was foreplay to love at first sight. "We became intimate on the spot," Hunt recalled; "I found the young poet's heart as warm as his imagination. We read and walked together, and used to write verses of an evening upon a given subject" (*Lord Byron &c* 410). Coming of age on 31 October (his twenty-first birthday), Keats decided that poetry could be more than a vacation from medicine. It was a vocation.

Hunt introduced him around. Painter B. R. Haydon was quite taken with his talent, and soon brought him to Wordsworth's notice. Then, in a pivotal essay in *The Examiner,* on 1 December, Hunt featured Keats as one of three new "Young Poets" to watch for, printing the sonnet "On First Looking into

Chapman's Homer," Keats's second-only publication. With Hunt, another of the trio, Percy Bysshe Shelley, convinced his publisher to produce a volume. To preview and publicize this venture, Hunt put two more sonnets by Keats in early 1817 issues of *The Examiner*.

Keats designed *Poems* as a presentation portfolio, showing technical skill and versatility (poems long and short, songs, sonnets, verse-epistles). It was also a celebration of great poets and poetic greatness: Keats's bookshelf. He was rushing a Bard Fraternity, full throttle. The title-page features a profile of a laurel-crowned poet, with a motto that tacitly speaks back to Wordsworth's elegy in his "Immortality" Ode (1815), about the loss of "delight and liberty" after early childhood. The motto, from Spenser's *Fate of the Butterfly*, reads; "What more felicity can fall to creature, / Than to enjoy delight with liberty."

Keats would hail poetry's durable gifts, ever present, but Spenser's *Fate of the Butterfly* holds a fuller story: this creature's delight is destined for a spider's web. Keats's epigraph is a slight, grim in-joke, because he knew that his Hunt-fanned debut would be webbed in culture wars. The seemingly incidental word "liberty" was quite potent in the day, byword for opposition to tyranny, especially the monarchal institution. The motto of the French Revolution was *Liberty, Fraternity, Equality*. Hunt's fierce oppositional polemics in *The Examiner* had drawn prosecutorial ire, earning him a steep fine of £500 for "seditious libel" on the Prince of Wales as well as a serious prison term (1813–1815). Keats was not naïve about dedicating *Poems* "To Leigh Hunt. Esq."[5]

Hunt was also everywhere in its pages. The unit titled "Sonnets" held "Written on the day that Mr. Leigh Hunt left Prison" (III), and offered further praise in "Great spirits" (XIV). The volume's first formal poem used a line from Hunt's controversial *Story of Rimini* (1816) in place of a title: "Places of nestling green for Poets made" (p. 1). In such a retreat, the (in)famous adulterous lovers Paulo and Francesca (of Rimini) tryst. Dante's *Inferno* sees them in hell. Hunt weaves a tragic romance of erotic liberty, indulged in secret against the patriarchal tyranny that bartered and tricked Francesca into a loveless, politically advantageous marriage (to Paulo's older brother). "Z" (the reviewer-scourge of *Blackwood's*) was outraged at Hunt's "sentimental" cast on sin: "Many a one reads *Rimini* as a pleasant romance, and closes it without having the least suspicion that he has been perusing a tale pregnant with all the horrors of the most unpardonable guilt."[6]

The Examiner was a voice, *the* voice, for social and political reform. Even the essay on "Young Poets" spoke revolution—in poetry: the eighteenth-century regime of regular rhymes and meters was over! Keats bore this into *Poems* with a panache of liberties: couplets scarcely anchored by lambent rhymes of falling meter (*wandering* / *pondering*), a high frequency of free enjambments (syntax

To Wr Wordsworth with the author's sincere Reverence. —

Poems,

BY

JOHN KEATS.

" What more felicity can fall to creature,
" Than to enjoy delight with liberty."
Fate of the Butterfly.—SPENSER.

LONDON:
PRINTED FOR
C. & J. OLLIER, 3, WELBECK STREET,
CAVENDISH SQUARE.

1817.

Figure 1: Title page, *Poems,* with Keats's inscription to Wordsworth (1817). Wordsworth never replied and left most of the pages uncut (that is, unread). The publisher designed a full coding of the volume as "poetry," from the title and epigraph from Edmund Spenser, to the profile of a Poet Laureate (evoking both Shakespeare and Spenser, England's unofficial first Poet Laureate). Published on 3 March 1817, *Poems* was priced at 6 shillings, and eventually remaindered. Courtesy of Rare Books and Special Collections, Princeton University Library.

running over lines), irregular meters everywhere, demotic diction galore. *Sleep and Poetry* was a Hunt-themed essay on the "new school of poetry," one conspicuously at play in Keats's new poetry, sparked with satire on the *foppery and barbarism, musty laws,* and *wretched rule* of neoclassical poetics (162–206). This manifesto was a brave and risky debut. Haydon hailed it as a bolt of lightning. Hunt loved it. Byron (who loved Pope) did not, despising the smart-ass upstart. The review-Hunters were too ready. *Blackwood's* Z. had taken a first shot at Hunt's "Cockney School of Poetry" (October 1817), his epigraph naming the next target, in a rhyme of mock hyperbole:

KEATS,
The Muses' son of promise; and of what feats
He yet may do.

Cockney was a house-brand slur, class contempt with a whiff of effeminacy.[7]

Even before this jab, Keats's publishers, irritated by low sales, wanted no more of (or from) him. The third of Hunt's "Young Poets," J. H. Reynolds, introduced Keats to his publisher, the entrepreneurial firm of Taylor and Hessey. Keats soon had a contract for *Endymion: A Poetic Romance,* the longest poem he would ever write, ever publish. It was a credentialing project sparked by a compact with Shelley to finish "4000 Lines" by the end of 1817.[8] Eager for *a test a trial of my Powers of Imagination* (MsK 1.13.42), Keats fired up and finished on time. While he awaited page-proofs, he was thrilled by the debut of Hazlitt's lectures on the English poets on 13 January 1818. Speaking "On Poetry in General," Hazlitt hailed a "universal language which the heart holds with nature and itself":

> Many people suppose that poetry is something to be found only in books, contained in lines of ten syllables, with like endings: but wherever there is a sense of beauty, or power, or harmony, as in the motion of a wave of the sea, in the growth of a flower that "spreads its sweet leaves to the air, and dedicates its beauty to the sun,"—*there* is poetry, in its birth.
>
> (*Lectures* 2)

Hazlitt's quotation riffs on Romeo's worried father comparing his love-bitten son to an infected bud thwarted of blooming (*Romeo and Juliet* I.i). Weeding out the pathology and turning Shakespeare's lambent iambic pentameter into natural prose, Hazlitt replants the words for fresh, liberal poetic harvest. As the packed houses at his lectures made clear, it was a good time for poetry:

publishers' lists were growing, success paid handsomely, and everyone was reading it.

Yet for all the excitement, as Keats proofread *Endymion* through this winter, he saw immature fever, and said so in his Preface, stating his intent for better endeavors. Instead, the candor primed the anti-Hunt reviews. Out in May 1818 and quickly into reviewers' claws, *Endymion* was ridiculed for its frou-frou fable, its extravagant rhymes and conceits, its lax meters, its obscenities (which reviews still quoted), and the low-hanging fruit of a gratuitous anti-monarchal rant at the top of Book III. Z. mocked an "imperturbable drivelling idiocy" (*Blackwood's* III:520), and the more widely read *Quarterly* branded it as "unintelligible . . . tiresome and absurd . . . nonsense" (205). Keats shrugged. "My own domestic criticism has given me pain without comparison beyond what Blackwood or the Quarterly could possibly inflict," he told publisher James Hessey. He was independent: "no external praise can give me such a glow as my own solitary reperception & ratification of what is fine" (8 October 1818; *K* 206–207). Keats coined the word *reperception* for this self-discipline. It would come to characterize his poetic way.

Keats, writes Ernest de Selincourt, "is the most striking example of a poet self-educated and disciplined by his own severe and strenuous mental effort. . . . he continually reviewed his art in the light" of his growing ideas; "his mind is continually reacting upon his art, diagnosing its weaknesses, . . . and strengthening its natural growth" ("Warton" 4–5). *Review, reacting, reperception*: Keats's next plan for a long poem, conceived in 1818, was just such an effort. This is *Hyperion*, named for the last Titan to be defeated by the ascendant Olympians. The plan was to hail the rise of Apollo, Hyperion's successor, a gorgeous new-generation god of knowledge, poetry, medicine—a portfolio dear to Keats. Yet for all this investment, there were evident problems. The determined main course of Apollo-poetry served a lot of Romance candy. Far more compelling, strengthening for sure, was Keats's poetry of the Titans' pained bewilderment at their lost divinity, with sustained intensity in yet unfallen Hyperion, knowing the doom of his brothers. When Keats's own brother Tom, wasting from tuberculosis, died in December, the master plan for Apollo's victory thinned into evaporation. Or reperception.

Keats recharged with other genres, and across 1819 blazed out the poetry that would claim him fame: *The Eve of St. Agnes, La belle dame sans merci, Ode to a Nightingale, Ode on a Grecian Urn, Ode on Melancholy, To Autumn*. It is surprising to discover that these "Great Odes" (so called in Keats's renown today) were no feature in the volume titled *Lamia, Isabella, The Eve of St. Agnes, and Other Poems* (1820)—by "John Keats / Author of *Endymion*" (no less!). The three title-poems took up 104 of 199 pages, another 31 pages went to "Other Poems." To Keats's dismay, the last 57 pages held *Hyperion, a Fragment,* with an Advertisement at the front of the volume that excused him from responsibility for this inclusion, explaining its incomplete state as the result of the discouraging reviews of *Endymion.* Keats was furious (see Figure 9). It wasn't the reviews; it was reperception. In fall 1819, he attempted a recast of the project as *The Fall of Hyperion: A Dream.* The dream is a poet's, and this, too—his last major project—remained unfinished.

I must choose between despair and Energy—I choose the latter, Keats wrote to a friend in May 1819 (*K* 256). Energy fuels life as well as writing. *Talking of Pleasure, this moment I was writing with one hand, and with the other holding to my Mouth a Nectarine – good god how fine – It went down soft pulpy, slushy, oozy – all its deliciousness embonpoint melted down my throat* (September 1819; *K* 269). Writing and living, both with intensity. Early in 1820, this energy was felled by a major pulmonary hemorrhage. Medically literate, Keats saw his death warrant.[9] By July, his doctors were advising winter in the warm south, Italy. Self-cartooning, Keats tells Haydon in mid-August, "I am affraid I shall pop off just when I [*sic*] mind is able to run alone" (*L* 2:320). He had just sent John Taylor his "Testament," still pausing for a name-pun – *pay my Taylor the few pounds I owe him* – before rendering a last sentence with a formal flourish of inverted syntax and perfect iambic pentameter: *My Chest of Books divide among my friends—* (2:319).[10] Hoping to be *among the English Poets,* Keats would place his books among his friends. No pun, *My Chest* was sadly double bound. *My dear Taylor,* he had written just the day before, *My Chest is in so nervous a State, that . . . writing a Note half suffocates me . . . every line I write increases the tightness of the Chest* (13 August; ALS Morgan). Ten days on, a last letter to dear friend William Haslam (23 August 1820) tells the tale again: "I could say much more than this half sheet would hold, but the oppression I have at the Chest will not suffer my Pen to be long-winded" (*L* 2:331). He could barely breathe, let alone write. He was losing everyone in England, not least his beloved fiancée Fanny Brawne: "I have coals of fire in my breast," he wrote to his dear friend Brown about her on 1 November 1820, from Naples, a thousand miles away from both of them (*L* 2:352).

In a last letter to Brown (30 November), Keats describes his life as a "posthumous existence," and muses wryly about living in contradiction to his prized poetic value: "the knowledge of contrast, feeling for light and shade, all that information (primitive sense) necessary for a poem are great enemies to the recovery of the stomach." In the best energy of friendship and poetry, he signs off with a witty self-regard, in briefer tetrameter: "I always made an awkward bow" (*K* 433). This is ruefully gracious. Another bowing out is the despairing pentameter epitaph he dictated on his deathbed: *Here lies one whose name was writ in water.* Not even *on* water (ephemeral enough) but *in* water, the very medium invisible. Ironically, these words were engraved on an oft-visited tombstone.

The 1820 volume was praised, but it was no hit, remaindered and sold for pulp. Except for coterie admirers and the fable of Shelley's *Adonais: An Elegy on the Death of John Keats* (1821), which railed against the reviews for killing off a frail flower of genius, Keats was nearly forgotten for a quarter of a century: *snuffed out by an Article* was Byron's wry epitaph in 1823 (*Don Juan* XI.LX), more widely quoted than any line in *Adonais.* Hunt did his best, and on St. Agnes Day 1835 (21 January), printed *The Eve of St. Agnes* entire, with a "loving commentary." In 1848, R. M. Milnes's *Life, Letters, and Literary Remains of John Keats* gathered forty new or uncollected poems, and quite consequentially, eighty letters, most for the first time (Hunt's 1828 memoir included a few). So began an appreciation of this sociable archive, as brilliant and lively as the poetry: letters to read, reread, share, *interread one another,* a verb Keats coined for his relay with two of his correspondents (MsK 1.64.313). By turns (often in the same letter), he is playful, ironic, sentimental, funny, thoughtful, passionate, candid, full of comments about poetic style, method, purposes, "flashing phrases which never desert the memory."[11] No surprise that striking passages have a poetic pulse; and no surprise, too, that some of Keats's poetry was first communicated in letters—even as letters. Reborn in Milnes's *Life,* relieved of Regency cultural wars, Keats found a new generation and new influence on the nation's poets.

Yet frail "Keats" was still in the air, swatted at with Victorian gender-cudgels. Even friendlier accounts were dubious help. In 1853 Matthew Arnold described *Isabella* as a "treasure-house of graceful and felicitous words and images . . . vivid and picturesque turns of expression, by which the object is made to flash upon the eyes of the mind, and which thrill the reader with a sudden delight" (Preface to *Poems* xxi–xxii). Yet without the armature of substantive "action," the returns for an iron age in need of sterner stuff seemed minimal. "The dialogue of the mind with itself" (vi) was Arnold's diagnosis of the disease of modern poetry. Diagnosis aside, there is a potency in this reflexive phrasing, a poetic action in the mind's conversation "with itself." For twentieth-century modernism, this would be Keats's brand, his name standing for nexus of sensuous vitality, skeptical ironic modernity, a thrilling intensity in imagery, energy in words—captivating at one turn, elusive, uncertain, doubtful, mysterious in the next. Keats had a wording for this, too: *Negative Capability.*

Energies displayed: dark Passages, Soul-making, Negative Capability, camelion Poet

In any age of "New Poetry," poets like to plant their flags. Wordsworth issued testy defenses in Prefaces, Essays and Appendices; Shelley polished Prefaces and mounted a *Defence of Poetry;* Byron polemicized in public letters and Prefaces; Hunt wrote reams of essays, reviews, criticism; Coleridge produced an epic, *Biographia Literaria; or Biographical Sketches of My Literary Life and Opinions* (1817). Keats? He never drafted, let alone published, any position papers. His résumé as critic was a theater review, a literary review (both unsigned), and that self-incinerating Preface to *Endymion.* Even for what he sensed would be his last volume, he had no "intention . . . to have a Preface" (*L* 2:276), and crafted no "dedication" (as he had for his first two volumes). His thinking about poets, poetry, and poetic practice gets worked out in his poetry, and in lively correspondence with family, friends, and publishers. It is no little thing to hear the first important editor of Wordsworth's epic autobiography, de Selincourt, say about Keats's letters: "in them we can study the growth of a poet's mind even more minutely than in Wordsworth's *Prelude;* and their evidence is more authentic, in that they are less conscious, and are a spontaneous record of the present rather than a careful recollection of the past" ("Warton" 2).

The phrases in my subtitle are "signature" formulations and meditations, durable touchstones not only for Keats's reputation but also for literary criticism over the last century. How striking that all are one-offs, produced in conversations and sociable letter-writing. In two letters, one from spring 1818 and one a year on, Keats presents key figures for his sense of life's trials in the world: *dark Passages* and *a vale of Soul-making.* The first he mapped in a letter to Reynolds, at the end of an extended simile comparing life in the world to a "Mansion of Many Apartments" (3 May 1818; *K* 129–131). We begin in the *infant or thoughtless Chamber* (analogous to Paradise). On "the awakening of the thinking principle," this becomes a *Chamber of Maiden-Thought,* a female-troped "delight" that is "intoxicated," to be sobered and regendered with a "sharpening of one's vision into the heart and nature of Man," with a visceral "convincing ones nerves" that "the world is full of Misery and Heartbreak, Pain, Sickness and oppression." This is not sin-logic, just maturing thought: reperception. This chamber opens inevitably into a labyrinth of *dark Passages,* a metaphor that Keats invests (with dividends) for worldly experience and its reading. In such passages, Wordsworth's poetry proves far more existentially valuable than Milton's theological illuminings: for all the erudition, Milton's "Philosophy, human divine, may be tolerably understood by one not much advanced in years," Keats dares to say to Reynolds (*K* 130).

In Keats's second great metaphor, written out in April 1819, dark passages are no pointless wilderness but a *vale of Soul-making* (MsK 52.261–263; *K* 250–251). If *chrysteain religion* (Keats's reduced respelling) conceives of an immortal soul pent in mortal life's *vale of tears* until its redemption *by a certain arbitrary interposition of God and taken to Heaven*, Keats dismisses this plot as *a little circumscribe*[d] *straightened notion.* If the world is a "Place where the heart must feel and suffer in a thousand diverse ways," this is the existential forge of *Identity,* the process of Soul-*making.* No surprise that a trope of reading is ready at hand. The world is a *School,* its primer is <u>the human heart</u>, the *necessary* agent *to school an Intelligence and make it a Soul.* In his letter of 3 May 1818, Keats insists that book-reading has to pass this test, too: "we read fine — things but never feel them to [the] full until we have gone the same steps as the Author." No help are *Dogmas and superstitions* (especially Milton's) that supply prefab *resting places and seeming sure points of Reasoning* (*K* 131). The "mere wording" of "axioms in philosophy" has to be "proved upon our pulses" (nicely pulsed in this very sounding). Having read *Hamlet* forty times, Keats knows it as a Soul-making experience: "now I shall relish Hamlet more than I ever have done" (*K* 129). How great that his verb for rereading is unreluctant *relish.*

In late 1817 (*Poems* published, *Endymion* drafted), Keats coined his most famous formulation (often reiterated without knowing its actual provenance). "Several things dove-tailed in my mind"—what a great verb!—and "at once it struck me" what to value: "<u>Negative Capability</u>, that is, when man is capable of being in uncertainties, Mysteries, doubts, without any irritable reaching after fact & reason" (*K* 78).[12] Keats saw this in Shakespeare's dramatic power, felt its limitation in a Wordsworth too prone (he jests to Reynolds, February 1818) to "brood and peacock over" his speculations (Keats verbed the bird), leaving his reader feeling "bullied into a certain Philosophy engendered in the whims of an Egotist" (*K* 99). In a letter to Woodhouse, 17 October 1818, he coined this bullying into the *wordsworthian or egotistical sublime,* setting this as foil to his own *poetical Character:* a *camelion Poet of no self . . . no Identity,* no particular philosophy, but *continually in for— and filling some other Body,"* capable of (sometimes, unable to avoid) living in the intensity of a mood, a character, a disposition, the *gusto of light and shade . . . foul or fair, high or low, rich or poor, mean or elevated.*[13]

He could sense this capacity even in severely theological Milton, in a throb of camelion imagination into Satan's sensations as he hides out in a sleeping serpent to evade God's spies.

his sleep

Disturb'd not, waiting close the approach of morn.　　　　(9.190–191)

Theology be damned in this sympathy for a former archangel so confined. Keats's underlining conveys his amazed appreciation (*KPL* II:79–80):

> *Whose spirit does not ache at the smothering and confinement - the unwilling stillness - the "waiting close"? Whose head is not dizzy at the prosiable speculations of Satan in the serpent prison - no passage of poetry ever can give a greater pain of suffocation.*

And no passage of prose can render greater payment to a camelion Milton. Keats greets Milton's sympathy with his own: the agony of Satan's *unwilling stillness,* the noun triple-ached with stasis, silence and slow time.[14] He contributes his own sinuous participles, *smothering, unwilling, waiting,* with his fine echoing of *confinement* in *serpent,* a pun-relay of *pent* into *prison,* and an echo in *pain.* Compare Milton's spirit-aching poetry here to a flat glossing later on (as if he needed to sober up): "the enemy of mankind, inclosed / In serpent, inmate bad" (9.494–495). Keats had no care to underline these lines.

"The only means of strengthening one's intellect is to make up ones mind about nothing—to let the mind be a thoroughfare for all thoughts," Keats said in September 1819 (*K* 276), finding a new kind of poetic "identity." He had put it this way on 19 March:

> *Though a quarrel in the Streets is a thing to be hated, the energiies displayed in it are fine; the commonest Man shows a grace in his quarrel—By a superior being our reasoning may take the same tone — though erroneous they may be fine. This is the very thing in which consists poetry; and if so it is not so fine a thing as philosophy - For the same reason that an eagle is not so fine a thing as a truth.*　　　　(MsK 1.53.233)

Keats is large-minded enough, generous-souled enough, to imagine his own errors, including the liking of energetic debate as such a spectacle, thinking philosophically with poet-gusto. One can envision an eagle, but *a truth,* however finer in vision, is still kind of abstract. Such self-accounting helped Keats think harder about philosophy.

He saw two sides of Wordsworth, in dialectic: a poet reaching for *certain Philosophy* and a poet of *dark Passages* feeling *the burden of the Mystery* (*K* 130).

Keats drew this last phrase from *Tintern Abbey,* where it is lodged, remarkably, in a subordinate clause:

> that blessed mood,
> In which the burthen of the mystery,
> In which the heavy and the weary weight
> Of all this unintelligible world
> Is lighten'd. (38–42)

Keats reads against the grain of Wordsworth's dominant syntax, deep in the grain of his poetry. Lines 39–41 impose twenty words of weighted prepositional clauses against the declarative *Is lighten'd.* Not every poet can pace *unintelligible* into iambic pentameter. Wordsworth did, on the stressed halts of *mystery, heavy, weary.* Keats caught how the argument for "blessed mood" pulses through its antithesis. "We are in a Mist. <u>We</u> are now in that state – We feel 'the burden of Mystery" is his tribute, word-working *Mist* in *Mystery.*[15] As Keats was writing this, his brother Tom, who'd been having a good day, started coughing up blood. It was Wordsworth's *dark Passages,* not his *certain Philosophy,* that held Keats's thoughts (*K* 129–131).

One word more / Words for thought

One word more: so Keats introduces his dedication of *Endymion* to Chatterton. One word stands for many in Keats's reading. It goes wide and deep, always open to new turns. His spirited greetings animate words into poetic phenomena— and his own phenomenal poetry. He is keenly tuned to verbal and aural memories, inventive about new words, new ways of saying old ones. There are verbal felicities that seem like accidents, but in effect are so right that they seem like gifts of quiet genius. What a scientist who was Keats's contemporary, Humphry Davy, said of the poetry of science is fine enough for Keats's science of poetry: "words which are the immutable instruments of thought, are become the constant and widely-diffused nourishment of the mind, the preservers of its health and energy."[16] Keats is a phrase-receptor, a word-witness.

If the plotted trial of *Endymion* thinned in his esteem, its word-work was wonderfully generative. Keats was avant-garde, and it wasn't for everyone, even well-disposed friends. In the summer of 1820, Shelley politely advised him against "treasures poured forth with indistinct profusion." Keats pushed back, suggesting to Shelley that he might "discipline" his political spirit to "the Poetry, and dramatic effect": "<u>an artist</u> must serve Mammon," he insists; "be more of an artist, and 'load every rift' of your subject with ore" (*K* 425–426).[17] Such a fine resounding of *ore* from *more*. Keats is alluding to a passage they both knew, Spenser's Cave of Mammon, a scene of wonder and trial (*The Fairy-Queen* II.7.XXVIII):

> Emboss'd with massy Gold of glorious Gift
> And with rich Metal loaded every Rift,
> That heavy Ruin they did seem to threat.

The aesthetic thrill in the threat of ruin is in the verbal load: "Met*al l*oaded" presses one word into the next along a lettered, sounded *all*. The "sound is unaccountably expressive of the description," writes Keats about a line in *Paradise Lost* (*KPL* I:74). "The sound is the gold in the ore," said Robert Frost in this vein.[18] Word-loading is Keats's mine.

This is veined with what critic and poet J. H. Prynne calls "a heightened sense of the accumulated layers . . . of previous usage" (18). *"Reluctant" with its original and modern meaning combined and woven together, with all its shades of signification has a powerful effect.* So writes Keats, learnedly and subtly, about one weaving for the voice of God in *Paradise Lost* that drew his underlining (*KPL* II:4):

> So spake the Sovereign Voice, and clouds began
> To darken all the hill, and smoke to roll
> In dusky wreaths, reluctant flames, the sign
> Of wrath awaked   (6.56–59)

The Latin root of *reluctant* is *struggle against;* the later branching is *unwilling, averse*. Keats loves these senses *woven together*, with a fine rolling from visual *wreaths* to a sonic awakening in *wrath*. He could suspend his irritation at Milton's theology with keen love of his word-work. In a similar key of appreciation, Virginia Woolf could set aside her annoyance at Milton's "masculinist" view of "marriage and women's duties" to admire the "inexpressible fineness of the style, in which shade after shade is perceptible," compelling one to "keep . . . gazing into it." No settling for "surface business" here.[19] "Deep down one catches still further combinations, rejections, felicities, and masteries," is Woolf's measure.[20] Keats and Woolf show us a theory of reading in the practice of reading. Poetry, not least Keats's, rewards "slowing down the process of reading to observe what is happening, in order to attend very closely to the words, their uses, and their meanings."[21]

Words are the central nervous system of Keats's imagination, wiring his reading, as even his early verse shows. Writing of *Spenserian vowels that elope with ease,* he adds his own rhythmically stressed, mellifluous vowels and consonants. Such a happy figure is *elope.* Better than *lope,* the added long *e* opens up the sense "break loose, refuse restraint" with a subtle phonic chiasmus in the *o el elo* in the span of "*vowels elope.*" Irrepressible punster Keats sounds the vowels of long *e*'s in *ease.*[22] Reading's pleasures become poetry's figures animated: *No sooner had I stepp'd into these pleasures / Than I began to think of rhymes and measures.*[23] Meter-measures rhyme with *pleasures* and figure *I stepp'd,* a coy poet's foot. Keats's word-audits, with a feel for history and idiom, are finely tuned to present play.

He loves the double-play of puns and meta-puns. Flirting with a new female friend, Keats jousts and jests, "You must not expect that your Porcupine quill is to be shot at me with impunity," vowing retaliation "with the armour of words and the Sword of Syllables": *words* anagrammed into *Sword, armour* winking at *amour,* the fun armed inside "im*pun*ity."[24] Punning on *pun* doubles the fun: "As for Pun-making, I wish it was as good a trade as pin-making," he quips on another occasion, exchanging *pun* for *pin,* and not sparing *change:*

> I wish one could get change for a pun in silver currency. I would give three and a half any night to get into Drury-pit—but they wont ring at all. No more will notes you will say—but notes are different things—though they make together a Pun mote—as the term goes. (*L* 2:214)

What rings for Keats is the fun of spinning the Frenchy phrase about language itself, *bon mot,* into the currency of a pound note (as a verb, *pun* can mean "pound"). I'm very glad editor Hyder Rollins refused the tone-deaf tradition of emending *Pun mote* to *Pun note.*[25]

Always ready to theorize language, Coleridge defended punning as no trivial byplay, even imagining a formal "Essay in defence of Punning":

> (Apology for Paronomasy, alias Punning) to defend those turns of words,
> > che l'onda chiara
> > E l'ombra non men cara,
> In certain styles of writing, by proving that Language itself is formed upon associations of this kind . . . that words are not mere symbols of things & thoughts, but themselves things— (*Notebooks* 3, entry 3762)

Apology is principled argument. Turning the Italian words, Coleridge notes how *che l'onda chiara* (clear wave) delivers a sound wave to *E l'ombra . . . cara* (shadow dear), its dark twin. This is word-life. Fatally ill in the shades of Rome, Keats could still rise to words, writing to his beloved friend Brown of having "summoned up more puns, in a sort of desperation, in one week than in any year of my life" (30 November 1820; *K* 432).

Our Passages

The young poet's dream of being "among the English poets" in posterity was the least clubby of ambitions. It was a romance of intelligent, ongoing experiment, as he was trying to balance the effect of bad reviews, on himself and on his supporters. Keats didn't begin by competing with Wordsworth or Shelley or Byron, or by contending with the canonical imaginary of his first tentative homages, or by imitating his early sponsor Hunt. His hunger for poetry, in a career of worded desire, was inspired by reading deep into its English traditions, in a crash course as critical as it was devoted. An ear for the seductive fluency of Spenser and the nativist strain in Chatterton took him through sonnet adventures, the workout of *Sleep and Poetry,* and the expansive experiments of *Endymion,* this "4000 Line" expenditure of verbal panache refreshed by a sojourn again in sonnets with an ever more Shakespearean dexterity and confidence. This readied him for the meta-Romance recoil of *Isabella,* and a high-yield return to Milton's blank verse in *Hyperion,* taking on modern Wordsworthian burdens. Although this epic project hit an impasse, Keats's consolidated powers broke free, formally and thematically, for the opulent narrative drive, darkly edged, of *The Eve of St. Agnes,* the withering ironic balladry of *La belle dame sans merci,* and then, in an idiom now wholly his own, the psychological turns and verbal acuities of 1819's Great Odes, the rainbowed, sweet-acid satire and strange pathos of *Lamia,* the stark, severe passages of *The Fall of Hyperion.*

This was no linear run across six and a half years, from first-love *Imitation of Spenser,* to a matured assurance at the end of 1819, before a horrible hemorrhage in 1820 took over the body of the poet. Keats's ways are characteristically zigzag: sometimes prospective, sometimes forward, sometimes recursive, always hungry, revisionary, self-critical. Re-vise: revisit, review, reperceive, re-see, double-play. *A Greeting of the Spirit* reflects Keats's developing adventures in being a poet, and his use of poetry to discover himself. He progresses less on a master plan (though he has aspirations) than on the pulse and flow of experiment, trial and error, sudden concentrations, dead ends and fresh starts, new turns around tenacious poles. I include best-known short and shorter poems, some less well known gems (jocular, sexy, occasional), and tortured selections from the longer ones. I set some poems in the letters that generated them, often with previews and postscripts. Others are represented by manuscripts that show Keats thinking out his poetry in process. All are here because I love reading them, thinking about them, writing about them, ever enjoying Keats's experiments with words, fueled by his volatile and always remarkable genius. When J. R. Lowell grumbled, "to say a thing is *Keatsy* is to contemn it" ("Life of Keats" 15), he at least got the gambit. The eponym these days is *Keatsian,* an honorific for verbal energy and genius.

No master-argument, then, except the inevitable: what poetry calls for in eliciting our attention to the evolution of this extraordinary poet's language. My aim is to illuminate Keats's ways of imagining and writing poetry, to unfold the lively complexities of the verbal arts of meaning-making (sometimes meaning-unmaking). My method is conversational, meditative, scholarly, critical, brain-teasing, and always heartfelt. Keats imagined readers of *Endymion* treating this long poem as an anthology as well as a developing plot, a field in which to *pick and chose* (*K* 61). *A Greeting of the Spirit* greets you this way: let's follow Keats finding his ways, then pluck your own interests and curiosities in the Keatsian spirit of finding things *new in a second Reading.* "Rereading" is as Keatsian as rewriting: "On sitting down to read *King Lear* once again." Rereading always comes with *rather new* impact: "the following . . . never struck me so forcibly as at present" (*L* 1:133). I greet you with series of connected close encounters across this rich terrain. To summon one of Keats's metaphors for reading, any one point may serve as a starting place, through which various routes wend, wind, converge, intersect, or radiate.

> *I have an idea that a Man might pass a very pleasant*
> *life in this manner - let him on any certain day read a certain*
> *Page of full Poesy or distilled Prose, and let him wander with*
> *it, and muse upon it, and reflect from it, and bring home*
> *to it, and prophesy upon it, and dream upon it . . .*
>
> any one grand
> *passage serves him as a starting post . . . How happy is*
> *such a voyage of conception!*

(Princeton ms. f.1)

So he proposes to Reynolds, 19 February 1818. How appealingly he aligns *Man* and *manner,* the *pass* of *life* in reading and a *passage* of reading as a voyage in life.

In that letter about the *greeting of the Spirit,* Keats suggests that "every point of thought is the centre of an intellectual world" (*K* 114). In the wide orbits are political events, historical markers, personal history and its psychological imprints, literary history and its present scenes and sensations. If *greeting* is a noun in *a greeting of the Spirit,* it is ever a verb in Keats's reading and writing. He always challenges himself, takes the energies of conflict (with others, within himself) as productive, is as capable of witty self-regard as he is of serious self-consciousness. To inhabit his fine iterative coinage, let's read—and read along with—Keats in the voyages, the very passages, of *reperception.*

[1] Keats twice: *Hyperion* 1.1; *Chapman's Homer;* once for Milton (Keats cites his "soft Lydian airs" in *To George Felton Mathew*), Gray, Coleridge, and Shelley (xi). Richards cites Read to complain of fetishizing of words out of context; *Coleridge,* 100–102. My point is not the debate but Keats's crystallized presence in this census of word-powered poets.

[2] "On the Feeling of Immortality in Youth," *Monthly Magazine* 3.15, March 1827, 267. Hazlitt was just shy of fifty, and a defender of Keats against the politically motivated attacks on his poetry by the Tory establishment and its upstarts, who also, always, had liberal Hazlitt in their aim.

[3] *Aurora Leigh* (1856) Book I, pp. 32–33.

[4] Writing later on *Poems* (*Examiner* 1 June 1817), Hunt remarked that Keats was then "anonymous" (345).

[5] On 2 March 1817, the day before *Poems* debuted, the *Examiner*'s front page blazoned Hunt's essay, "On the Proposed Suspension of the Habeas Corpus Act" (Roe, *Culture of Dissent,* 210).

[6] "Cockney School . . . No. II," November 1817, 201.

[7] "Cockney School . . . No. I," October 1817, 38. "*Cockney,* a well-known term of reproach" (glossary, *DW* sq. 3333). *JnD* elaborates: "*Cockney:* A native of London, by way of contempt; Any effeminate, ignorant, low, mean, despicable citizen." Keats's turn came with No. IV, tagged with "the Cockney School of Politics, as well as the Cockney School of Poetry" (3:524). The epigraph credits Cornelius Webb, a poet in Hunt's circle who actually admired Keats, and wrote a posthumous tribute to him in *Literary Speculum* 1822 (2:368; cited by Marsh, 332–333). *Blackwood's* series went on for years. See my *Borderlines,* especially 245–247.

[8] This "rivalry," recalled Shelley's cousin Thomas Medwin, produced *Endymion* and *The Revolt of Islam* (*Life* 178–179).

[9] Tuberculosis was thought to be hereditary because of family incidence (for instance, Keats's). Not until the 1880s was it identified as a bacterial infection, contagious in close proximity. Keats probably got it from nursing Tom; the death rate in London at the time was about 30 percent.

[10] The metrical catch (often repeated, not often credited) is Ronald Sharp's, Bicentenary Keats Conference, Harvard University, 1995 (*Persistence* 66).

[11] I borrow T. S. Eliot's phrase for Lancelot Andrewes (1926), *Selected Essays,* 325.

[12] I follow *1848,* based on the transcription of John Jeffrey (Georgiana Keats's second husband), the only source (MsK 3.9.14). Bate's eponymous monograph (honors thesis, Harvard, 1939) set the hallmark. For the wide iterations (and frustratingly mysterious provenance), see Rejack and Theune, *Keats's Negative Capability.*

[13]To Woodhouse, 27 October 1818 (MsK 1.39.139). I use Keats's spelling, *camelion*, also in *Hamlet* (3.2.90; *DW* 7, p. 56). Seven years Keats's senior, Woodhouse, legal and literary adviser to Taylor and Hessey, became a close friend. Early convinced of Keats's genius, he began collecting letters, drafts, and unpublished poems.

[14]About *prosiable:* editors try to settle a seeming shift of Keats's pen from *prospect* to *probably* to *possible.* H. B. Forman, Keats's first scholarly editor, opts for *possible* (*Poetical Works &c* 1883, 3:30). I think *prosiable* a possible ad hoc Keatsian portmanteau, also packing *prosey* (tedious, wearisome).

[15]Keats's friend Benjamin Bailey recalls his attachment to this phrase (*KC* 2:275).

[16]*Discourse Introductory,* 322.

[17]Shelley to Keats, 27 July 1820; Keats to Shelley, 16 August 1820 (*K* 425–426). For more, see my "Load Every Rift" (Keats Letters Project). Christopher Rovee has a sharp essay on Keats's relays between market-praised trash and poet-valued treasure.

[18]"The Figure a Poem Makes," Preface, *Collected Poems,* 1939 on (2d).

[19]I allude to Best and Marcus's much-cited, superficially flashy polemic, "Surface Reading."

[20]*Diary,* 10 September 1918, 5–6.

[21]Reuben Brower, "Reading in Slow Motion," 5–6.

[22]*To Charles Cowden Clarke* 56 (p. 71); Christopher Ricks's nice catch, *Embarrassment,* 71.

[23]*To Charles Cowden Clarke* 97–98 (p. 73).

[24]To Jane Reynolds (J. H.'s sister), September 1817; Berg f.1 (cf. *L* 1:156–157). In 1825, Jane would marry the master of poetic wordplay, Thomas Hood.

[25]For *pun* meaning *pound,* see *DW* Glossary (sq. 3344). I'm intrigued by editorial resistance to Keats's wordplay. The long train of emending Keats's wit to "Pun note" began with John Gilmer Speed (who had the letter from his mother, Emma Keats Speed, Keats's niece); *Letters and Poems of John Keats* (1883) 1:107. Forman's *Letters of John Keats* (1895) follows this, 421; also a 1901 Glasgow edition, 122, with credit from Sidney Colvin's *Letters of John Keats* (Macmillan, 1891), 316, and H. E. Scudder's Cambridge edition (1899), 405. Even Frederick Page's 1954 Oxford UP edition refused Rollins's restoration (356), as did Phaeton's 1970 reprint of Forman (110). Although Robert Gittings and John Mee (Oxford UP, 2002) allow *pun mote* (304), they feel compelled to say that "pound note" may have been meant (414).

Sonnet Ventures

April 1814–April 1817

KEATS'S CAREER-LONG romance with the sonnet—productive, experimental, accomplished—flexes what can be done with 140 syllables and 14 lines, metered and rhymed. Sonnet-writing is an arena for testing and contesting rules; playing rhythm against meter, syllables against words, line-design against the pause and flow of enjambment (syntax "striding over"). It is a great little experimental field for skill and virtuosity, a poet's poetry. No wonder there is a meta-tradition of sonnets about the sonnet, with finely spun tropes: a scanty plot of ground, a narrow room, a cage and chains, a happy bondage, an arduous model, a hard task, a varied and peculiar frame, an intricate machine, a moment's monument, a little picture, a garland, a woven wreath, a wave of melody, an undulating maze, a simple flow'ret of fourteen, a gift, a precious jewel, a pearly shell, a drop of blood, a gem of thought, a crown, and (of course) the key to Shakespeare's heart.

Sonnets emerged in the thirteenth century as a social recreation in the warm south, said to be initiated by Giacomo da Lentini, one of fourteen notaries in the Sicilian court of Frederick II. Troping this fraternity, Lentini devised fourteen lines out of the troubadour *strambotto, abba//abba,* adding a sestet. This form is often called "Petrarchan," after Francisco Petrarcha, who sequenced it into epic love poetry. Its 8-6 imbalance is primed for drama: an octave situation, with pressure (slight or urgent) toward a *volta* ("turn") with new rhymes (typically, *cdecde*) in response (distillation, qualification, reconsideration, resolution). Discovering the sonnet in Italy and Spain, ambassador and poet Thomas Wyatt took it to England. Wanting more variety of rhyme, English poets (notably Shakespeare) split out two distinct quatrains (*abab cdcd*), the sestet into a third (*efef*), with a couplet finale (*gg*). This design could plot a three-stage drama (sometimes punctuated, Petrachan-style, at line 9), building to a volta at the closing couplet. Milton's sonnets tuned the Italian form to acutely personal subjects (his blindness) as well as broadly public ones on political figures and historical events. He also liked enjambment, not only over lines but also across the stanza units, especially octave and sestet.

As Milton's career may attest, sonnet-writing is traditionally regarded as training for higher endeavors. Dante worked toward *The Divine Comedy,* Spenser toward *The Faerie Queene,* Shakespeare toward tragedies, Milton toward *Paradise Lost.* A mere sonnet-writer could seem juvenile or dilettantish. The long poem, the expansive ode: all these "high" forms drove the sonnet's stock down to a point where Samuel Johnson's *Dictionary* (1755) could dismiss the sonnet as "not very suitable to English language . . . not used by any man of eminence since *Milton*"; a "Sonnetteer" is "a small poet, in contempt." Johnson even excluded sonnets from his edition of Shakespeare! Some loyalists, Thomas Edwards and Thomas Warton, kept the form alive, and in the 1780s, Charlotte Smith found wide popularity with her serial publications of *Elegiac Sonnets,* intricately inventive on the form, and many on subjects that would draw Keats, too: moon and stars, nightingale, solitude, love-ache, melancholy, the allure of death—even social anger.

Wordsworth subscribed to *Elegiac Sonnets* as a school-lad. Hitting the man-marks, he took up public as well as personal subjects. He also leaned into Milton's formal skill. He liked how Milton "lets the thought *run over*" from octave to sestet, a super-enjambment, and admired the "simplicity and unity of object and aim" to be achieved with the "music" so scored: an "energetic and varied flow of sound crowding into narrow room more of the combined effect of rhyme and blank verse than can be done by any other kind of verse I know of."[1] The Italian word for room is *stanza.* "Nuns fret not at their Convent's narrow room" is the first line of Wordsworth's *Prefatory Sonnet* to a sonnet-unit in his 1807 *Poems* (1:101).

With the rise of newspapers and magazines, a space-efficient sonnet was a good gambit for publication. Wordsworth's first publication was a sonnet. So was Keats's (*To Solitude*), his first four, in fact, all in the *Examiner.* The second one (1 December 1816), *On First Looking into Chapman's Homer,* is now among his most famous poems.[2] *Poems* featured a unit of seventeen "Sonnets," including the two published in 1816; it also had an untitled poem composed of three Petrarchan sonnet-stanzas (pp. 47–49).[3] Yet another sonnet is the *Dedication* to Hunt. Keats also likes to set meaningful sonnet-stanzas in long poems: "I stood tip-toe" opens with a 28-line verse paragraph, a setup for a self-referring jest about lingering on a scene for as long as it takes to "read two sonnets" (*1817* p. 69); *Hyperion* opens with a sonnet-stanza of Titanic arrest; a sonnet-stanza in *Lamia,* with Petrarchan satire, hails a newly formed "lady bright" (1.171–184); and a sonnet-stanza halts a late ode ("What can I do . . . ?"), twelve of its lines in neoclassical couplets, to satirize the Pope's view of orderly, "unerring nature" (30–43).[4]

A sonnet was no little thing in Keats's conception. He loved the drama of accumulating phrasings over the formal partitions, describing this momentum in September 1816 in an epistle "To Mr. C. C. Clarke," the mentor *Who read for me the Sonnet swelling loudly / Up to its Climax, and then dying proudly.*[5] Keats hears the sonnet as a heroic actor. The enjambment swells past the line-end to the stressed trochaic inversion, *Up,* a meta-poetic stress on *Cli*max, then *dy*ing. The falling meter of *loudly/proudly* is still pretty proudly said. Rhythm over metrical prescription: this is the spirit of Keats's first poetry. His very first sonnet "O Peace!" greets a new political era with a spirited freedom of poetic form.

---

[1] H. C. Robinson, January 1836 (2:484–485, his emphasis, most likely recording Wordsworth's); Wordsworth, 1802 (*Letters, Early Years* 379).

[2] The other two are "To Kosciusko" (political hero) and an untitled melancholy, "After dark vapors" (both February 1817). With the exception of *La Belle Dame sans Mercy* (*Indicator,* 1820) and three odes from *1820,* all of Keats's poems published independently of his volumes were sonnets, all by Hunt's agency.

[3] Garrod (21–22) and Allott (43–44) actually present these stanzas as distinct sonnets.

[4] For this last embedding, see my essay in *CCJK,* 109–110. Keats had good models. Shakespeare's plays have inset sonnets, and Wordsworth liked to scan *Paradise Lost* with sonnet radar, identifying some "fine fourteen lines" as "a perfect sonnet without rhyme" (Robinson 2:484).

[5] 1 September 1816; facsimile in *Books and letters, collected by William Harris Arnold of New York* (1901), 104–108. In *1817,* this epistle (p. 71) is followed by "Sonnets."

"O Peace!"

O Peace! and dost thou with thy presence bless
    The dwellings of this war-surrounded Isle;
Soothing with placid brow our late distress,
    Making the triple kingdom brightly smile?
Joyful I hail thy presence; and I hail
    The sweet companions that await on thee;
Complete my joy - let not my first wish fail,   7
    Let the sweet mountain nymph thy favorite be,
With England's happiness proclaim Europa's liberty.
O Europe! let not sceptred tyrants see
    That thou must shelter in thy former state;
Keep thy chains burst, and boldly say thou art free;   12
    Give thy Kings law - leave not uncurbed the great;
So with the horrors past thou'lt win thy happier fate.

Keats may have written this sonnet during his apprenticeship, in April 1814, just after Napoleon was captured by an allied coalition, forced to abdicate, exiled to Elba, and the Bourbon monarchy restored. Keats never knew an England not at war with France, begun just weeks after the Republic guillotined Louis XVI in January 1793. By the decade's end, Napoleon was invading Europe's monarchies and republics, soon with world-conquering ambition. A reader of *The Examiner* since his schooldays, Keats followed the events, and was excited by the prospect of better times for Europe and the "war-surrounded-isle" England.

    Keats's sonnet speaks as an *Examiner* house-poet, opening with a national bard's "O," to address a new era, petitioning a classical goddess against the state religion cited to endorse Kings' laws. Keats infuses his poetics with the spirit of liberty against inherited rules. By the second quatrain, he is counterpointing end-rhyme rule with a dynamic chiasmus, *Joyful I hail . . . I hail . . . my joy,* and sound-patterning an incantatory *let not . . . Let . . . let not . . . leave not.* While lines 1–8 mark a Shakespearean pattern, the closely sounded rhymes—*Isle/smile* (2/4); *hail/fail* (5/7)—evoke a Spenserian stanza's interwoven *abab bcbc,* set to anticipate the extravagant Spenserian hexameter of his final line.[1]

    Keats plays against a sonnet's expected pause at line 9, taking a dramatic breath at line 7 to call on "Peace" to "Complete my joy." He propels his rhymes for this call, drawing *thee* (6) into triplet *be/liberty/see* (8–10) into the sestet, then a meta-climax at *free* (12), the very character of the sonnet's forming. At this climax, he supercharges his metrics with nine plausible stresses on an overload of eleven syllables. The injunction, *boldly say thou art free,* is as much about the sonnet's poetics as about the national prospects. The full stop at 9—*With England's happiness proclaim Europa's liberty*—is a heptameter paraphrase of the celebratory banner on Somerset House (home of the Royal Academy and the Royal Society): *Europa Instaurata, Auspice Britanniae// Tyrannide Subversa, Vindice Libertatis* ("Europe's Renewal, Britain's Auspice// Tyranny Overthrown in the Defense of Liberty"). Hunt quoted the banner verbatim in an article on the Peace of 1814 in the 17 April *Examiner* (255–256); a sequel on 1 May (273) coincided with Keats's hopes for milder monarchies, in England as well as France.[2] Keats's poetics are militant on this hope. The percussive lines 12–13 (eight beats in 13 alone) unfurl into that closing hexameter: a sonnet-banner. For a theme of peace, this speaks out loud and bold.

The horrors that this sonnet would declare *past* for *happier fate* (14) proved not to be (as in line 12's surprise reverse when *keep thy chains* is both contradicted and complemented by *burst*). Napoleon escaped Elba in late February 1815, and English Liberty went into reverse. Keats's anti-monarchal temper was a risk for any fledgling poet, especially with an *Examiner* brand. He kept this sonnet out of *Poems* (it appeared 1905, as a curiosity), needing no lessoning on how the tyrannies that wreck national liberty can also hunt down a nation's liberal poets. This is the legend of Thomas Chatterton, abused in his lifetime for both his politics and his poetry.

[Woodhouse's commonplace book; see also *P* 28]

---

[1] Keats's first known poem is *Imitation of Spenser* (*1817*, 44–46).
[2] The liberal hope was that the new French Constitution would restrain its restored monarch from playing "the tyrant."

"Oh Chatterton!"

Oh Chatterton! how very sad thy fate!
  Dear child of sorrow! son of misery!
  How soon the film of death obscur'd that eye,
Whence genius wildly flash'd, and high debate!   4
How soon that voice, majestic and elate,
  Melted in dying numbers! O how nigh
  Was night to thy fair morning! Thou didst die
A half-blown flower, which cold blasts amate.*   8
But this is past. Thou art among the stars
  Of highest heaven: to the rolling spheres
Thou sweetly singest—nought thy hymning mars,
  Above the ingrate world and human fears.   12
On earth the good man base detraction bars
  From thy fair name, and waters it with tears!

* Affright—Spenser

Joseph Addison's essay on "Genius" in his popular daily, *The Spectator* (1711), arrays the subject with two categories, natural prodigies and learned artists. He would vindicate Shakespeare's "natural Genius," "something nobly wild and extravagant," against the French school's "Turn and Polishing" the "Rules of Art" (460). Wild, extravagant, possibly forgery-trafficking is Thomas Chatterton's fatal genius. On 24 April 1770, at age seventeen, broke, discredited, in despair, he committed suicide with arsenic.

"Chatterton" became a byword for such tragedy. In 1790, at age seventeen, Coleridge began a *Monody on the Death of Chatterton,* and reworked it throughout his life, haunted by and identifying himself with this blazing meteor.[1] The legend weighed on thirty-two-year-old Wordsworth, born the very month of Chatterton's exit. Feeling "happy as a Boy" on a fine morning after a night of fierce storms, he can't help murmuring,

But there may come another day to me—
Solitude, pain of heart, distress, and poverty.

It's just a heartbeat to

> I thought of Chatterton, the marvellous Boy,
> The sleepless Soul that perished in his pride.

"Marvellous Boy" became Chatterton's allonym ("pride" has the eighteenth-century sense: prime of life and energy). The stanza's rock-bottom line takes Chatterton as a portent:

> We Poets in our youth begin in gladness;
> But thereof comes in the end despondency and madness.

Better, maybe, to end "in youth" than "in" this "end."[2]

Keats knew both poems well, dear to his fears and tears. "Oh Chatterton!" is his fourth sonnet, written during studies at Guy's Hospital. He didn't mean it for publication; it was a diary entry of tribute, a self-enlistment with the good men who lament and protect. The odic greeting "Oh" unleashes a high-style effusion: prodigal exclamations, mannered diction, lush sentimental tropes. For all this affectation, there's genuine poetic fiber in the wordings. Keats's first line dramatically issues seven percussions, taking one, *thy*, into the rhymes and chimes of *dying/nigh/night/thy* (again) and *die* (6–7). From the double trochee of *dying numbers* that gets downbeat into *nigh* and *night*, he launches *thy fair morning* to rise over undertoned *mourning* into a phonic volta at "*high*est heaven" (10). The sounded *die* in *and high* [debate] is so audible that it has to burst out in *dying*, almost as a metaphor for cadence in *numbers* (meters). His accelerant for Chatterton's acclaim is the rhetorically amped volta, *But this is past* (9). A blunt dimeter hits *past* with a temporality more declarative than any mere lapsing "pass'd." The midline period is the actual pivot, into a present tense redemption: *Thou art among the stars*, the very word *art* giving its letters to *stars*. Keats's ear for intra-word music will become ever more finely tuned in poetry to come—not just poetry about poetry, but in the grain of his own greetings, voiced invitations to his verbal inscapes.

One of "the most interesting aspects of Keats," remarks poet J. R. Lowell, is "intellectual ferment . . . kindled by a purely English leaven" ("Keats" 324–325). Keats wasn't yet there in 1815, but Chatterton's nativist idiom would rekindle him in the fall of 1819, the month he wrote his most "English" ode, *To Autumn*. Chatterton's "purest . . . English Language" stayed in his ear. "He has no French idiom, or particles like Chaucer—'tis genuine English Idiom in English words," he comments to Reynolds on 21 September, out of tune with the Latinate "inversions" of "Miltonic verse," which seem to be written in "an artful or rather artist's humour." This proves a vital pivot: "I wish to give myself up to other sensations. English ought to be kept up" (*L* 2:167). How nice this relay from *give myself up* to the loyalty *kept up. I shall never become attach'd to a foreign idiom so as to put it into my writings,* he writes to George and Georgiana in America, where purest English must have sounded as foreign as Milton's art:

> *The Paradise lost though so fine in itself is a curruption of our Language – it should be kept as it is unique —a curiosity. a beautiful and grand Curiosity. The most remarkable Production of the world – A northern dialect accommodating itself to greek and latin inversions and intonations. The purest english I think – or what ought to be the purest- is Chatterton's – The Language had existed long enough to be entirely uncorrupted of Chaucer's gallicisms and still the old words are used – Chatterton's language is entirely northern –I prefer the native music of it to Milton's cut by feet.*
>
> (Morgan Library)

Chatterton lives for Keats in these present tenses. Milton's English, a curious deformation by *greek and latin* syntaxes and inflections, is a *curruption,* in Keats's onomatopoeic pun-gloss.

Okay, but what "native music" sounds in *amate,* rhymed in Keats's sonnet, with polemical point, to *ingrate?* Woodhouse added the footnote (*P* 543). No wonder; this is the only *amate* in Keats's poetry, and not "purest english": it is really Chaucer-gallic, Old French (from *matter:* "to crush or subdue") on its way, via Spenser, to Chatterton's retro Old English for *destroy.* It comes twice in Chatterton's forgery of a fifteenth-century poet "Thomas Rowley," *Ælla; a Tragycal Enterlude* (1777). Keats, who read and reread *Ælla* and knew *amate* from Spenser, too, rekindles the word for ingrate reception, especially of the "Rowley" poems. What were these? At age fifteen or sixteen, Chatterton gave a Bristol publisher the manuscript, identifying it as a bequest from his father. When it appeared posthumously, its authenticity was doubted. The Preface to the edition Keats had suspends the question for the sake of literary interest: "Whether the Poems be really antient, or modern; the composition of Rowley or the forgeries of Chatterton," these are surely "a most singular literary curiosity" (xi)—Keats's view of *Paradise Lost,* but here with English grammar to defend.

Keats wields the rhyme-chain of *amate* to track Chatterton through sad *fate* to the flash of high *debate* to a voice *elate.* Usually a transitive verb, the adjective *elate* is as conspicuously obsolete (or retro) as *amate,* both words in lexical homage to Chatterton. Keats was "disappointed" by Hazlitt's disparagement of Chatterton in Lecture VI on the English poets, 17 February 1818 (he told his brothers, *L* 1:237). Hazlitt did note Wordsworth's esteem and read it from *Resolution and Independence* (quoted above), but when he sifted the poet-legend from the poetry, he could find little remarkable beyond the fact that they were written by "a boy of sixteen." He suggested, moreover, that Chatterton sensed that this "extraordinary precocity" would not mature into "extraordinary powers of genius," and so "set a seal on his reputation by a tragic catastrophe" (*Lectures* 243). Perhaps hearing of Keats's regret at his judgment, he took time at the start of his next lecture, 24 February, with apologies for any offense, then defended his opinion (245–251), and read out a poem that he thought the "best," one that Keats loved, the Minstrel's song in *Ælla* (252–253). Even so, just shy of forty, Hazlitt would not join the "woful lamentation over fallen genius" (251).

Keats stayed true. Proofreading *Endymion* during these weeks, he drafted this dedication:

> Inscribed,
> with every feeling of pride and regret,
> and with "a bowed mind,"
> To the memory of
> The most english of poets except Shakspeare,
> Thomas Chatterton ~   (Ms p. 1)

The phrase in quotation is from the opening lines of the poem just before the *Monody* in Coleridge's *Poems* (1797), *Ode on the Departing Year,* with relevance to departed Chatterton. Coleridge keeps his "eye fixt of Heaven's unchanging clime" with *a bowed mind.*

After reading the *Quarterly*'s ridicule of *Endymion,* Richard Woodhouse (literary adviser to Keats's publisher) worried about the young poet's discouragement in "the land which let Chatterton . . . die of unkindness & neglect" (21 October 1818; *KC* 1:51). Keats assured him that Chatterton's solution was not his. Even so, "Chatterton" would shade "Keats." When Woodhouse was gathering a loan of £50 to him, he dunned with Chatterton-pathos: "Whatever People . . . regret that they could not do for Shakespeare or Chatterton, because he did not live in their time, that I would embody into a Rational principle, and . . . do for Keats" (*KC* 1:83). What Shelley did for Keats was twin him to Chatterton in the fable of his great elegy *Adonais* (1821), a master-romance of poets slain by life and vindicated in death. A Keats-coded "bloom whose petals, nipped before they blew, / Died on the promise of the fruit" joins Chatterton in the "splendours of the firmament of time," both "inheritors of unfulfilled renown" to be "enrobed in dazzling immortality" (XLIV–XLVI). Keats's friend Bailey had his work cut out for him in an unsigned essay for the *Church of England Quarterly* (1849), trying to unbrand Keats as "another Chatterton" (whom he despised as much as he did Shelley): "never were men or poets so dissimilar. . . . In the heart of one sat the spirit of a burning vanity that would not be satisfied—in that of the other presided the gentle spirit of a gentle love" (140–141). Nonstarter: within a decade *Encyclopædia Britannica* listed him this way: "After Chatterton, Keats is the most extraordinary phenomenon in our poetic literature" (57).

In his lifetime, Keats pledged his heart—and soul and thinking mind—to another fatal fraternity, Leigh Hunt's.

[*P* 32]

---

[1] As the first of *Poems on Various Subjects* (1796), Coleridge's *Monody* (1–12) was a virtual dedication. Keats read this version in *The Complete Works of Thomas Chatterton* (I:xcii–xcvi), which included several poets' tributes; Coleridge and Wordsworth were on the subscriber list. For Keats's love of Chatterton and its influence on his diction, see Penelope Dineley.

[2] Keats read these lines from *Resolution and Independence* in *Poems* (1815), 2:28–29.

Written on the day that Mr. Leigh Hunt left Prison

WHAT though, for showing truth to flatter'd state
  Kind Hunt was shut in prison, yet has he,
  In his immortal spirit, been as free
As the sky-searching lark, and as elate.   4
Minion of grandeur! think you he did wait?
  Think you he nought but prison walls did see,
  Till, so unwilling, thou unturn'dst the key?
Ah, no! far happier, nobler was his fate!
In Spenser's halls he strayed, and bowers fair,   9
  Culling enchanted flowers; and he flew
With daring Milton through the fields of air:
  To regions of his own his genius true
Took happy flights. Who shall his fame impair
  When thou art dead, and all thy wretched crew?

Keats's "Chatterton" elides "political" Chatterton, a satirist who would have jibed with *The Examiner*.[1] And not without peril: Leigh Hunt and his brother John, the publisher, were prosecuted (unsuccessfully) three times between 1808 and 1811 for scathing critiques of the government. Then in 1812, when the assassination of an unpopular prime minister in the lobby of Parliament (11 May) sparked attacks on oppositional journalists as public enemies, the Crown nailed the Hunts for a "libelous" article (22 March) on the Prince Regent's "libertine" profligacy amid widespread social misery. Each brother was fined £500 (a sum meant to ruin them and *The Examiner*) and sentenced to two years in separate prisons.

Leigh's assignment was Horsemonger Lane, Surrey. With friendly influence, payments, and sympathetic jailors who regarded him as a hero, he secured a two-room cell in the infirmary, which he transformed into a bower: a ceiling painted with sky and clouds, Venetian blinds over the window bars, rose-trellised wallpaper, bookcases and busts, a piano, vases of flowers, and an outside garden with flowers and young trees. Charles Lamb called it a room "in a fairy-tale" (*Autobiography* 2:148). Hunt's wife and her sister were allowed long visits. In addition to Lamb, several friends and political allies visited: Hazlitt, Clarke, poets Thomas Moore and Reynolds, and painter Haydon (the last two to become Keats's friends)—and, not least, celebrity poet Lord Byron. Prison enhanced Hunt's political fame. For all the Crown's "wretched crew" of enforcers, he was captive only administratively. His cell was a salon, also an office where he continued to edit the *Examiner* (it flourished in the notoriety, demand exceeding the print run). To acquit the fine, Hunt published *The Feast of the Poets* (which Byron loved) and wrote *The Descent of Liberty* (a political poem) and, with Byron's research assistance, much of *The Story of Rimini,* an indictment of tyranny, which he dedicated to Byron.[2]

On the day of his release, 2 February 1815, Clarke went to visit him, joined part of the way by Keats, quietly hoping to meet his hero. An invitation not forthcoming, Keats faded back, but not before giving Clarke this sonnet. It was the first inkling that his former student was writing poetry (he kept it, thinking it was a gift to him, *KC* 2:154).

Keats's poet-persona indicts the Crown in the voice of an *Examiner* columnist, arraigning Hunt's tyrants, the State, in the carceral tradition of spiritual liberty amid material confinement. Everyone knew the theme of Richard Lovelace's *To Althea from Prison* (1642): "Stone Walls do not a Prison make, / Nor Iron bars a Cage."[3] *To Althea* sets *liberty* and *free* (in spirit) as key rhymes. Keats's first rhyme is *free,* gestured into the figural space beyond the line-end and pressing the bars of rhyme with enjambment. He liberates his Petrarchan pattern. Satirizing the minion-warden's key (7), he dramatically unlocks his volta at line 8: *Ah, no! far happier, nobler was his fate!* His own confinement in lonely apprenticeship, with solace in reading, gives him a fellow-feeling for Hunt's resilience, with his books as mental freedom. *Spenser's halls . . . and bowers fair* sound these *halls* against *prison walls.* Keats felt such elation in his own reading: "In Spenser's fairy land he was enchanted, breathed in a new world, and became another being," recalled Charles Brown (*KC* 2:55). In a sonnet in the Christmas Eve *Examiner* of 1815 (82), Hunt declared that if he could have but one dearest poet, it would be Spenser, for his power "To lay a wounded heart in leafy rest, / And dream of things far off and healing." Poetry, reading it and writing it, keeps alive what the State can't contain.

The "Milton" of Keats's sonnet is prison-tinged. A defender of the regicide of Charles I, nearly jailed when the monarchy was restored, blind and financially ruined, Milton had hell on earth from Charles II, the vengeful son-king who behaved like God, as Milton tried to keep faith with a God who could seem like such a king. He kept true to his political principles. So, too, Hunt: *he flew / With daring Milton through fields of air.* Finely enjambed, *flew / . . . through* finds its medium in *fields of air,* its own lettered uptake from "*of air*" a rhyme against *impair* and into *bowers fair.* Wordsworth found liberty "bound / Within the Sonnet's scanty plot of ground" (*Prefatory Sonnet*). Keats unbinds his sonnet-plot in homage to Hunt's liberty in confinement: his *elate* against the oppressions of *state.* Poetry is freedom, in the company of other poets.

[*1817* Sonnet III, p. 81]

[1] For political Chatterton, see David Fairer, 232–236, 248–250.
[2] Prison "had come to feel like home." N. Roe, *Fiery Heart,* 224–225.
[3] The thematics eclipse the politics (Lovelace was a Royalist in the civil war of the 1640s).

TO SOLITUDE

O Solitude! if I must with thee dwell,
  Let it not be among the jumbled heap
  Of murky buildings;—climb with me the steep,
Nature's Observatory—whence the dell,   4
Its flowery slopes—its rivers crystal swell,
  May seem a span: let me thy vigils keep
  'Mongst boughs pavilioned; where the Deer's swift leap
Startles the wild Bee from the Fox-glove bell.
Ah! fain would I frequent these scenes with thee;   9
  But the sweet converse of an innocent mind,
  Whose words are images of thoughts refin'd,
Is my soul's pleasure; and it sure must be
  Almost the highest bliss of human kind,
When to thy haunts two kindred spirits flee.

J. K

The carceral poetics of the sonnet on Hunt were also personal. The release from his lonely apprenticeship brought Keats to murky London, and work assisting often brutal, unanesthetized surgery. With little time to read and write, he fell to "frequent melancholy."[1] This is the undertone of *deep* in "jumble*d heap*," the sound-enforced base for imagination thirsting for a *steep* climb away. Great effects are to come from this kind of sound-play.

This sonnet is a city-cry to a paradoxically personified "Solitude," companion in a world elsewhere. Keats wrote the sonnet in October 1815, and sent it the next spring to *The Examiner*, hoping for notice. Without knowing anything of "J. K" Hunt took it. When Keats opened the pages of the 5 May *Examiner*, he saw his first publication at the bottom of a column just below a report of a soldier dead from a grievous wound:

> the Sister of the deceased was refused admittance to see the remains, till the body was so changed that she with difficulty recognised it to be her brother's, and the blood was then oozing through the shroud.

Such are the ironic contingencies of print. If the sonnet's theme is a wish for reprieve from such hells into "Nature," its poet also knows the illusion of *fain . . . flee*. In pastoral tradition, a vacation in the country is shaded by its knowing what's being vacated.

Addison's *Spectator* essay "On the Pleasures of Imagination" is so in tune with this double consciousness as to seem an allusion:

> when the Sight is pent up in a narrow Compass, and shortned on every side by the Neighbourhood of Walls or Mountains . . . a spacious Horizon is an Image of Liberty, where the Eye has room to range abroad, to expatiate at large on the Immensity of its Views, and to lose itself amidst the Variety of Objects that offer themselves to its Observation. Such wide and undetermined Prospects . . . (no. 412, p. 96)

Observation in Keats's sonnet is willed imagination. His verbal moods know the score. The dashes are more than punctuation: they are scripts of expansion.

The prepositional title *To Solitude* doubles into an existential sigh in the first line, *O Solitude!* Ace Latinist, Keats knows that *Solitude* speaks "solus" (alone). A sad wit personifies a companion. His rhyme sounds *with thee* into *let it not be*, then *climb with me*, softly chimed in the last syllable of the shared sight, *Observatory.* Such Observatory (the only instance of this word in his poetry) scans rural sights as if ready-made poetry: *flowery slopes . . . crystal slope . . . boughs pavilioned.* You may wince at the artiness, but Keats is being deliberate about this effect. The *O* that marks a "poet" speaking is continuous with this kind of "Observatory."[2] The triple stress of *Deer's swift leap* (7) animates the release and liberty. Its predicate, *Startles,* hits line 8 with six stresses: *startles,* then its object, the *wild Bee* (in the) *Fox-glove bell.* Meter is metaphor. So is sound. Bell is a visual shape that Keats rings into his *a*-rhymes. In its audit is Wordsworth's imagining of how bees, high-soaring in the peaks for blooms, can also "murmur by the hour in Foxglove bells" (*Prefatory Sonnet*). Keats's *wild Bee* hums into "scenes with *thee*" and "sweet" (8–10), on its way to *must be* (redeeming in sound and sense line 1's *must with thee*) and *spirits flee,* the very figure of inspiration and the last word. No bee is bell-bound.

Keats's octave graphs a Petrarchan plan, seemingly ready for a volta at line 9, perhaps a sestet ode to solitude beginning *Ah! fain would I frequent these scenes with thee.* Keats overrides this for the sake of the volta that awaits at line 10: *But . . . ,* a turn from personified *Solitude* to a kindred person, for spirit-sharing. When he revised these lines for *Poems* (p. 85), it was to work a double-volta force: "*But though* I'll gladly trace these scenes with thee, / *Yet . . .*" Jack Stillinger thinks this was the original text, which Keats restored from Hunt's "tinkering" (*P* 546). Stillinger has a good eye, but I won't discount Hunt's good ear. The *Ah!* in the *Examiner* text (9) echoes the first vowel of *Observatory* (4) into a personal sigh, expressed into a meta-poetic pun on *converse:* con*vers*ation and *verse,* a poetry of human company. To put this as *my soul's pleasure* (12) improves the *sole* of Solitude. The call to *human-kind* echoes in *kindred.* This adjective draws on *kind,* an old word, Keats-refreshed, for *Nature* (4) and natural human desire.

How intuitive that the sonnet's most evocative phrase (a figuring Keats will invest and reinvest in his poetry) comes in the rhyme-partner for *human kind: thoughts refin'd.* The language of Shakespeare, Hazlitt said in a lecture that Keats attended, "translates thoughts into visible images" (*Lectures* 107). Keats's sonnet makes language itself a visible image, a reader's Observatory. He packs a rich grammar into *words are images of thoughts refin'd,* allowing the participle *refin'd* to modify all three nouns.[3] When Keats's brother Tom copied the sonnet, he could imagine inscribing himself as this kindred spirit. A kindred greeting of the spirit is what Keats sends, over long English miles, in another sonnet, to his other brother, George.

Both brothers were his soul-mates and always his readiest of readers.

[*Examiner,* 5 May 1816, 282, column 2]

[1] George Keats to Charles Dilke, 23 April 1825 (*KC* 1:285).

[2] The poet-declaring calling of O-apostrophe is finely addressed by Jonathan Culler's "Apostrophe" and in Geoffrey Hartman's *Beyond Formalism,* 193.

[3] William Empson includes double grammar in *Seven Types of Ambiguity* (chapter 2), a term I'll call on again for Keats's poetic physiology.

TO MY BROTHER GEORGE

MANY the wonders I this day have seen:
    The sun, when first he kist away the tears
    That fill'd the eyes of morn;—the laurel'd peers
Who from the feathery gold of evening lean;—   4
The ocean with its vastness, its blue green,
    Its ships, its rocks, its caves, its hopes, its fears,—
    Its voice mysterious, which whoso hears
Must think on what will be, and what has been.
E'en now, dear George, while this for you I write,   9
    Cynthia is from her silken curtains peeping
So scantly, that it seems her bridal night,
    And she her half-discover'd revels keeping.
But what, without the social thought of thee,
Would be the wonders of the sky and sea?

Keats's brothers were often his first readers, his transcribers, and always his champions. This is the first sonnet in *1817*'s unit of "Sonnets," a pride of place in fraternal affection. Keats wrote it in August 1816, vacationing with Tom at coastal Margate (about seventy-five miles southeast of London), having passed his examinations at Apothecaries Hall on 25 July, for a medical practice he could begin on 31 October, his twenty-first birthday. Here is a hybrid of Shakespearean and Petrarchan forms: a Petrarchan octave reports "wonders"; the volta (9) turns a sociable address to "dear George," with a Shakespearean sestet, tuning *dear* from the chain of hoped-for, shared images of the *b*-rhymes (*tears,* etc.). Keats knows George will enjoy this wordplay.

    In this imagination, the wonder-making *sun* and *laurel'd peers* are mythological as well as natural figures. Not named, sun-god Apollo is implied in light and *laurel* (his attribute; hence, Poet Laureate). In *Ode to Apollo* (1815), Keats imaged a throng of *laurelled peers* (20) in the god's temple. These are the only two instances of this phrase in his poetry, in tacit relay. The *Ode*'s temple hosts Shakespeare. So does this sonnet's octave, both in its Shakespearean sestet and Keats's conscious echoes of Sonnet XXXIII (which he marked; *KS* 40):

Full many a glorious morning have I seen
Flatter the mountain tops with sovereign eye,
<u>Kissing with golden face the meadows green,</u>
<u>Gilding pale streams with heavenly alchymy</u> (1–4)

Keats also tips a sociable pen to Shelley: "far clouds of feathery gold . . . gleam / Like islands on a dark blue sea" (*Queen Mab* 2:16–18). Poetry is always a lens.

Keats's survey unfurls a mini epic catalogue, asyndeton-styled, paced from external sights to internal thoughts. Hunt loved the second quatrain's modulation "from the mention of physical associations to mental": *mention to mental*, as Keats shades "the sea-shore like a border, as it were of existence" (*Examiner* 498, 443). The volta turns from this existential interiority to *dear George*. Keats's "I," at first a general reporter, is now personal and fraternal, recovering the temporality of *what will be, and what has been* into this intimate connection, across the miles. To seem to be "thinking of the past and future, while speaking of the instant" is the *gusto* Keats will admire in Edmund Kean's acting (*K* 75). The sonnet time-spans George in his affectionate thoughts, past, to come, and in *now, dear George, while this for you I write* (9). George is so present that Keats can wink a jest about an erotic moon (no virgin Diana) peeping at them both as the brothers voyeurize *her half-discover'd revels* on her bridal night (with Endymion), a fantasy delivered from their shared reading of Ben Jonson's Elizabethan satire, *Cynthia's Revells.*

The affection of the closing couplet is a sequel-volta to the turn to *dear George* at line 9. All wonders dovetail into the *social thought of thee*, the familiar, unmysterious voice that has been and must be. Keats sent George the sonnet right away. Two years on, an ocean with its vastness would separate these brothers, with George far in the American interior. Writing to him there, Keats says, "sometimes I fancy an immense separation, and sometimes, as at present, a direct communication of spirit with you." What joins them, in Keats's fantasy, is reading together, "a passage of Shakspeare" (of course) at "the same time and we shall be as near each other as blind bodies can be in the same room"— physical bodies blinded to each other, but bound in imagination's greeting of the spirit (MsK 1.45.177).

[*1817*, Sonnet I, p. 79]

"To one who has been long in city pent"

To one who has been long in city pent,
    'Tis very sweet to look into the fair
    And open face of heaven,—to breathe a prayer
Full in the smile of the blue firmament.
Who is more happy, when, with hearts content,   5
    Fatigued he sinks into some pleasant lair
    Of wavy grass, and reads a debonair
And gentle tale of love and languishment?
Returning home at evening, with an ear   9
    Catching the notes of Philomel,—an eye
    Watching the sailing cloudlet's bright career,
He mourns that day so soon has glided by:
    E'en like the passage of an angel's tear
    That falls through the clear ether silently.

Keats wrote this sonnet on a break from the city in June 1816, a few weeks after *To Solitude*. It is an on-site report, with the company of a book, fielding words for all city-pent souls. A "Simile brought it to my Mind," he will write to Reynolds, 22 November 1817 (*L* 1:189). In his mind this fine day is Milton's epic simile for escaped Hell-prisoner Satan, in awe at sunlit Eden:

As one who long in populous city pent,
Where houses thick and sewers annoy the air,
<u>Forth issuing on a summer's morn, to breathe</u>
<u>Among the pleasant villages and farms</u>
<u>Adjoin'd, from each thing met conceives delight;</u>   (*PL* 9.445–449)

Keats's underlining (*KPL* II:87). What a fine verbal fate Milton gives the *pent* of Ser*pent*: God's big plot in a word, soon with a nonce-rhymed, earned *fierce intent* (462). The only other "pent" in *Paradise Lost* was in the fall of Satan's legions, their armor crushed, *Into their substance pent* (6.657): God's arrest for the Big House, Hell. Keats casts Milton's epic simile for Satan's brief parole (the poetic grammar of his infinitive *to breathe* at the line's end) into an address "To" all post-lapsarian city-souls. Whether from Hell or from earth's hellish cities, such vacations are always time-stamped. *City pent* is modernism's meme, existential not theological hell. Coleridge sounded it to open *To* *the Nightingale:* "How many Bards in city garret pent" sigh from their lone windows. In *Frost at Midnight,* he recalls lonely school days in "the great city, pent 'mid cloisters dim" (52), *cloisters* literally pent in the chiasmus *mid/ dim.* He can hardly shake the phrase. Wordsworth's *Prelude* makes it epic.[1]

The grammar of Keats's invitation *To one who has been long in city pent* issues an open call. A simple present tense, *'Tis,* gathers the timeless infinitives, *to look . . . to breathe,* in lettered, figurative affinity to the dative "To." Not every poet can say *very sweet* without getting too sweet by half. Keats risks this for the antithesis to the city's narrow sky and hectic airs. Heaven is no afterlife; it has moments in this world. His reprieve from *city pent* greets the half-formed goddess in the sky, a full smile on an open face, with counterpointed rhymes: the open *firmament,* deep *hearts content,* reading of *languishment.* The ease of *breathe a prayer* finds figural air in the page-space at the line's end.[2] The chord of *fair/prayer* nicely rhymes its bed of ease, *lair* (on its way to *debonair*). On a caress of wavy grass, Keats replants the expected Satanism of *lair.* No plotting ground, this is a place to sink away for a day. Keats doubles the iambic adjective of "hearts con*tent*" into trochaic noun "*content.*" Favoring the adjective, Stillinger amends *hearts* to *heart's* (*Poems* 53, as in Tom Keats's copy) in logical alignment with the singular *he* (6).[3] I like the way Keats's own decision for *hearts* (*1817*) evokes the implied plural in the singular "To one."

The supplement for this happy cardio-community has a Keatsian skew: a post-lapsarian pastoral of pleasure reading. The urbane-toned "debonair" is just right in its literal sense, "of good air." It is the only *debonair* in Keats's poetry, risking a luxe excess for the value added: the *lair* for reading holding the reader and the lettering of the *air.* Such "good" country air is the opposite of a city's "bad-air" ("mal-aria") contagions, these leagued with the root sense of *languishment* (*languēre: to be faint, feeble, sick*). In good air, languishment is pleasure, the lettering of *anguish* the faintest of ghosts within the healthy antonym. Yet for all this word-alchemy, Keats's infinitives are not infinity, and his sonnet form is poised on this knowingness.

The volta at line 9 is a meta-formal figure, *Returning,* delivering the home mandate. This, along with the *Catching, Watching* (these words eye-rhymed), and a nongrammatical alliance with sounded *evening,* attach to *mourns.* The muse for this subsiding is *Philomel:* "lover of music," in Ovid's fanciful etymology (compare: *melody*). Keats could have written "the nightingale's singing," but he wanted *Philomel* in order to glance at, without investing in, the quite un-debonair, really sorrowful, violent tale in *Metamorphoses* (VI).[4] This is what Spenser summons into "*Philomele* her Song with Tears doth steep" ("November," *The Shepherd's Calendar; Works* 4:1110), and what Shakespeare gives to Lucrece's love and languishment in the horrific Philomel-twinned *Rape of Lucrece:*

> Come, Philomel, that sing'st of ravishment,
> Make thy sad grove in my dishevell'd hair:
> As the dank earth weeps at thy languishment,
> So I at each sad strain . . .   (*PW* p. 89)

Before the analogy *As/So* completes its sentence, *As* seems poised for a pathetic fallacy, a sympathetic sigh from the earth. Keats's sonnet works metamorphic arts with this painful Ovidian lore, leaving its origin so recessive and its after-song so sweet that the epithet *Philomel* seems just mellifluous, as in Coleridge's *Nightingale* (2). But the lore in the name is ore to mine, as is the godfathering of the simile that Keats's "city pent" grammatically transforms and de-Satanizes. Robert Frost, with his own characteristically light touch of mythology, will put it this way: *One had to be versed in country things/ Not to believe the phoebes wept* ("The need of being versed in country things"). Native bird, or pitying goddess? One has to be versed in country poetry to imagine a pathetic fallacy.

For Keats's evening-bound poet, mourning is a soft coda. No fall from Heaven, the sonnet's landing is as gentle as can be: *so soon has glided by.* Although the parolee *mourns,* he does not grieve. It is bitter-sweet. The tenor of the closing simile—

> E'en like the passage of an angel's tear
> That falls through the clear ether silently.

—is a scarcely perceptible passage from heaven, cadenced with the soft-stressed rhyme, *tear/clear,* and the dactyl *silently.* "Tears such as angels weep," writes Milton of Satan before his defeated comrades (*PL* 1.620). Keats underscored this and drew triple lines down the margin (1:20), and noted the tenderness in anguish, a "sublime pathetic" (2:44). As Adam and Eve exit Paradise, "Some natural tears they dropt" (12.645). Keats underlined the full passage (*KPL* 2:183), taking on board Wordsworth's human-poetic, as this vacation from city hell closes: "Poetry sheds no tears 'such as Angels weep' but natural and human tears," he said (1800 Preface, *Lyrical Ballads* I:xxvi). This is Keats's key. Satan's brief hiatus of <u>rapine sweet</u> on seeing Eve (9.461, Keats's underlining) is the sole instance of "rapine" in *Paradise Lost,* Satanic sweets soon incinerated in the "hot Hell that always in him burns, / Though in mid Heaven" (9.468–469). Keats negotiates the parole for humanity, and humanity's poets, across the lapses of time.

[*1817*, Sonnet X, 88]

[1] In *This Lime-tree Bower my Prison,* Coleridge images his friend Charles Lamb as one who "pined / And hunger'd after Nature, many a year, / In the great City pent." The 1805 *Prelude* opens with Wordsworth depicting himself as a "Captive" from "yon City's walls set free, / A prison where he hath been long immured." (Keats could not have read either poem at this time.)

[2] Here and elsewhere, I am grateful for Christopher Ricks's argument that one punctuation of which a verse line may avail itself is the page-space at the end, "an invisible boundary; an absence of a space which yet has significance . . . a pregnant silence" (*Essays in Criticism* 1–2).

[3] Woodhouse endorses Tom's manuscript (*SpW* 163), as do most editors.

[4] Briefly: when King Tereus and his wife Procne visit her sister Philomel, he is so smitten with Philomel that he rapes her, then cuts out her tongue to secure her silence. The sisters concoct a horrific revenge, and at its success flee for their lives, begging the gods for help. The gods change Procne into a swallow and Philomel into a nightingale, who sings perpetually in sorrow.

"How many bards gild the lapses of time!"

How many bards gild the lapses of time!
  A few of them have ever been the food
  Of my delighted fancy,—I could brood
Over their beauties, earthly, or sublime:
And often, when I sit me down to rhyme,
    These will in throngs before my mind intrude: 6
    But no confusion, no disturbance rude
Do they occasion; 'tis a pleasing chime.
So the unnumber'd sounds that evening store;
  The songs of birds—the whisp'ring of the leaves—
The voice of waters—the great bell that heaves
    With solemn sound,—and thousand others more,   12
That distance of recognizance bereaves,
    Make pleasing music, and not wild uproar.

"He devoured rather than read," recalled his mentor Charles Cowden Clarke (*KC* 2:148). "What Keats most valued in the English poets," adds Christopher Ricks, "was a sense of brotherhood with his peers" that declines "the dark melodrama of . . . *Anxiety of Influence*."[1] Keats exclaims at the feast. It was an appetite, a feeling, and a love, always generative. The riff on "How many Bards in city garret pent" (the opening words of Coleridge's *To the Nightingale*) leaves off before the allusion-laden "city pent." Not a quotation of Coleridge, Keats's phrase is a verbal muscle-memory.

    This sonnet was one of the poems that Clarke showed Hunt, prompting that invitation to visit in October 1816. Hunt was a bit jolted by the bold first line, its overriding "mere rhythmicality" by "jumping out the heroic measure": six stresses, four on the first five syllables. *How many bards gild the lapses of time!* While Hunt's musically tuned ear judged a fault rather than a beauty, he caught the drama.[2] Keats pretty much intuited Frost's axiom in poetry: "get cadences by skillfully breaking the sounds of sense with all their irregularity of accent across the regular beat of the metre."[3] This sonnet's *b*-chord—*time, sublime, rhyme, chime*—is more than a rhyme-run; it is a figure of poetry's way with sounds, accreting across time to make music. A midline sequenced *sound,—and thousand* (12) yields yet another rhyme-chime, and more: a thematic event in the way the letters of *sound and* replay in th*ousand*. Another rhyme in this mode takes *throngs* (6) into *songs* (10), not end-rhymed chimed, but audible in the

soundscape (legible, too). Keats underlined Milton's fine scene of the fallen an-
gels' solace in song (*KPL* I:44): <u>Their song was partial,</u> but the harmony . . .
Suspended Hell, and took with ravishment / The thronging audience," *thronging*
in the *song* (*PL* 2.552–555; *partial* means "self-interested").

Keats's sestet sends the analogy (*So . . .*) into an evening's soundscape,
brooded on for present poetry. *I could brood* is an idiom of mental mood that
also says "gestate." We'll see this again in *On the Sea.* Pun-ready Keats rustles
the trees' *leaves* into poetry's leaved books. A negative-prefixed *unnumber'd* bids
a poet's positive *numbers.* The evening store of musical cues is interspersed with
long dashes, rhetorical pauses for silent audition: birdsong, those whisp'ring
leaves, waters, church-bell; then *thousand others more, / That distance of recogni-
zance bereaves* (12–13). There is no grievance in *bereaves.*[4] Poet Horace Smith
(also at Hunt's party that day) so loved this phrase for its "well-condensed ex-
pression" that he "read out" the entire sestet, pausing to repeat this line (*CR*
133). Keats's intensity of imagination (as Smith attests) draws readers into the
life of words. A plenitude of sounds is poetry's resource for words: *music* is
muse-infused.

In Keats's pleasing music (14) even the antonym *wild uproar* can rhyme. One
poem he devours is *The Fairy-Queen,* with this description of Aeolus raging
over sea and firmament:

> And all the World confound with wide Uprore,
> As if in stead thereof, they *Chaos* would restore　　　　　　(IV.9.XXIII)

Milton heard this again, and filtered out the conjectured *As if* for immediate
events in *Paradise Lost.* Keats underlined one result (1:44): <u>Hell scarce holds</u>
<u>the wild uproar</u> of fallen angel-rage (2.541), Spenser's *wide* shifted to *wild*—a
roaring stress on six of these syllables. Is uproar held at all? The adverb *scarce*
can mean that it is, with difficulty; but it also suggests that the original pent
realm, Hell, is not fully up to the job of holding the rage, chaos in the offing.

Hell's *wild uproar* contrasts Milton's second instance in *Paradise Lost,* Arch-
angel Uriel's report of God's creation out of chaos:

> Confusion heard his voice, and wild Uproar
> Stood ruled　　　　　　　　　　　　　　　　　　　(3.710–711)

Keats margin-checked these lines (I:81), likely catching the drama of the line-cut.
This is a little drama in itself. As a discrete unit, line 710 makes it seem that
both Confusion and Uproar heard God's voice, perhaps in allied resistance.

Then the turn to a double-stressed *Stood ruled* settles *Uproar* as appositive to a *Confusion* arrested into rule. Keats's sonnet rules *uproar* in its own way. His sestet recasts Spenser's *restore* into a storehouse ever growing; *store* is always *more* ("store, supply, or furnish," Woodhouse notes; *SpW* 148). Keats then turns the Spenser-Milton positive to its antonym: *not wild uproar.*

What is not in his bard-store are the female poets he's been reading: Katherine Phillips, Charlotte Smith, Mary Tighe—an anxiety of influence that he is not able to, or ready to, address in the fraternity into which his early poetry rushes.

[*1817,* Sonnet IV, p. 82]

[1] Ricks, "Keats's Sources, Keats's Allusions," 154, alluding to Harold Bloom's *The Anxiety of Influence* (1973) and glancing at W. J. Bate's *The Burden of the Past and the English Poet* (1970).

[2] *Examiner* no. 497, 6 July 1817, p. 429. Robert Bridges (1894) quite liked the effect: "very musical and suitable to the exclamatory form" (lxxxix).

[3] Letter, 4 July 1913; Barry, ed., 60.

[4] For all its rhyme-readiness, *bereaves* appears only twice more in Keats's poetry, in strong sorrows. A moon-goddess aches for Endymion: "so long absence from thee doth bereave / My soul of any rest" (*Endymion* 2.777–778). A sick west wind "continually bereaves" the air of "gold tinge, and plays a roundelay / Of death among" (*Isabella* XXXII).

MUCH have I travel'd in the realms of Gold,
    And many goodly States and Kingdoms seen;
    Round many western Islands have I been,
Which Bards in fealty to Apollo hold;
But of one wide expanse had I been told,
    That deep-brow'd Homer ruled as his demesne;
    Yet could I never judge what men could mean,
Till I heard CHAPMAN speak out loud and bold.   8
Then felt I like some watcher of the skies,
    When a new planet swims into his ken;
Or like stout CORTEZ, when with eagle eyes
    He stared at the Pacific,—and all his men   12
Looked at each other with a wild surmise,—
    Silent, upon a peak in Darien.

Oct. 1816   JOHN KEATS.

October 1816 is the month Keats cast his vocation into a brotherhood of poets. This sonnet is his first really great poem, fired by reading Homer's epics in a translation that, for the first time, conveyed verbal vigor, energy in every line. *Looking into* nearly understates the excitement. Clarke had on loan a gorgeous 1616 folio edition of George Chapman's *Iliad* and *Odyssey,* and invited Keats over for an evening of reading that turned into an all-nighter. Clarke could recount the excitement half a century on (*CR* 128–130).

    The neoclassical gold standard was Pope's translation of Homer, which Clarke had on hand, book-marked for comparisons. Here is how Pope's *Odyssey* renders war veteran Odysseus, homeward bound for ever it seems, tempest-tossed, shipwrecked, staggering toward land:

>   fainting as he touch'd the shore,
> He dropp'd his sinewy arms; his knees no more
> Perform'd their office, or his weight upheld;
> His swoln heart heav'd; his bloated body swell'd;
> From mouth and nose the briny torrent ran;
> And lost in lassitude lay all the man,
> Deprived of voice, of motion, and of breath,
> The soul scarce waking in the arms of death.   (580–587)

Not bad! Pope poises *shore* at the line-edge, pauses the syntax on stressed rhymes, with a fine line-end pause on the rhyme-partner: "his knees no more / Perform'd their office." The pause lets the phrase *knees no more* seem a grammar that extinguishes the knees right there. As you can see, however, Pope's general preference is a synchrony of syntax and couplet, often with a midline caesura, either marked with punctuation or on a rhythmic stress. Compare (as Keats did) Chapman's version of the same event:

> Then forth he came, his both knees falt'ring, both
> His strong hands hanging down, and all with froth
> His cheeks and nostrils flowing, voice and breath
> Spent to all use, and down he sank to death.
> *The sea had soak'd his heart through;* all his veins
> His toils had rack'd t' a labouring woman's pains.
> Dead-weary was he.   (V. 608–614)

If you read this out loud (as they did), you can hear what blew Keats's mind. Chapman's rounds of enjambment, with a percussive drive against iambic pentameter—pulsed by a faltering *forth, both, froth,* failing *breath,* impending *death*—extend the syntax through four lines. Even when the sentence stops for *death* (611), it scarcely halts the agonized collapse down to *Dead* (614). Compare Pope's lilting "From *mouth* and *nose* the *bri*ny *tor*rent *ran*" to the pounding of "The *sea* had *soak'd* his *heart through*"—a line (said Clarke, with emphasis) that put Keats into "one of his delighted stares" (*CR* 130). This *heart* is not just the seat of feeling but the organ that must sustain life, about to drown. Sounding out Chapman, Keats comes to life as a poet.

Chapman was still beating in his head as he paced the miles back home. Too excited to sleep, he wrote a sonnet. As you can see from Figure 2 on the next page, Keats got it pretty much in one shot (such is genius), revising just *low brow'd* to *deep brow'd* to chime with the long-*e* sound of *demesne* (6). Note the quatrains marked out in steps of intensities: first, his wide reading, then hearing of Homer's world (to him uncharted), then a sensation of hearing Homer himself, loud and bold, in Chapman's poetry, with two similes for the sensation. Blotting the page, Keats messengered it over to Clarke, who found it on his breakfast-table. Best breakfast ever! Clarke showed it to Hunt, whose "admiration" was "unhesitating and prompt" (*CR* 132). He grabbed it for his essay "Young Poets" with this happy prologue: "we do not hesitate to pronounce [it] excellent, especially the last six lines. The word *swims* [10] is

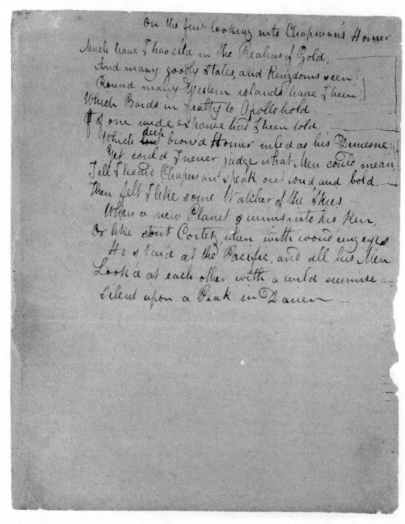

Figure 2: Keats's first draft of "On First Looking into Chapman's Homer" (1816), marking the octave's units. From *John Keats: Poetry Manuscripts at Harvard: A Facsimile Edition,* ed. Jack Stillinger (The Belknap Press of Harvard University Press, 1990), p. 13, from the original manuscript in the Houghton Library, Harvard University.

complete; and the conclusion is equally powerful and quiet:—," said Hunt, with his own mirroring dash at the end (*Examiner,* 1 December 1816). He really caught the dramatic force of Keats's pauses, suspensions, silences.

Quiet is not how the sonnet opens: *MUCH have I trav*el'd in the *realms of Gold*: arguably six stressed syllables. Then three stresses in *deep-brow'd Homer.* Keats risks some antiquey diction—*realms, goodly, fealty, kingdoms, demesne*—to convey the sense of a bookish encounter, Renaissance set. At the same time, getting into the spirit, he offers his own Homeric epithet: *deep-brow'd*. The metrical emphases hit a more plain-speaking, full-blown stress in *Till I heard* CHAPMAN *speak out loud and bold* (only *and* fails a stress-test). Hearing Chapman speak Homer, Keats senses the power of Homer's voice. The volta *Then felt I* (9) recasts the passive *had I been told* into energetically liberated similes. These both turn on stunned surprise: a planet discerned in the skies; an expanse beheld on this very earth. The first simile alludes to William Herschel (a sole watcher) seeing Uranus for the first time in 1781; the next one names Chapman's near contemporary, Cortez—Keats styles the name as "CORTEZ" to match "CHAPMAN"—seeing the Pacific for the first time, and not alone, but among fellow-wonderers.

Tuning up for his second-only publication, Keats sharpened Cortez's *wond'ring eyes* (in the draft) into far-scanning *eagle eyes* (11): the sonnet's second Homeric epithet, just right in its camelion poetics for the conquistador, his appetitive imperial gaze arrested in sublime awe. Setting vast *skies* at the end of line 9 and *eyes* at the end of 11, Keats draws the page-space into a figurative range. A fine, fleeting double-grammar comes in 12: *He stared at the Pacific, and all his men.* This line-unit nicely allows, for a moment of suspense, two objects for Cortez's stare: the Pacific and his wondering compeers. The rounding enjambment into line 13—*and all his men / Looked at each other*—transforms the gaze: all the men relay the wild surmise. With a comma at *surmise*, Keats then makes a dash for it into the mimesis of the blank page-space. This is a typographical rhyme for his second, final dash (breath-taken), after the falling rhyme of *Darien*, a sign of wonder for readers to take in.

Reviewing the sonnet for *Poems*, Keats decided a dash would work better in 12. So: *He star'd at the Pacific—and all his men.*[1] (He closed the sonnet with a period.) He also rethought his wording. Wincing at *Yet could I never judge what men could mean* as a bit "bald, and too simply wondering" (*CR* 130), he cast a new metaphor of high inspiration at line 6: *Yet did I never breathe its pure serene*—summoning an older sense of *serene,* an expanse of calm, clear sky. Pope used it this way (in *The Iliad,* even): "not a Breath disturbs the deep Serene" (VIII.689). So, too, Coleridge, in his *Hymn before Sunrise in the Vale of Chamouni* (1802), "the pure serene" (72), and Cary's Dante: "the pure serene / Of ne'er disturbed ether" (*Paradise* xix, 60–61), with nice sound-flow from *serene* to *ether.* Keats dovetails all these ethereal uses into Homer's inspiration, and into his reading of Chapman.

Homer did not rock Keats until Chapman opened the door. Keats's similes are about this sudden breathtaking sense: Herschel seeing Uranus, and Cortez seeing the Pacific. *CORTEZ* is often smirked at (or politely "corrected") as a mistake from Keats's impure education, beginning with Tennyson's cool advice (1861), "History requires here *Balbóa.*" But Keats means *CORTEZ: his* first look, not *the* first look. He has *Cortez* in all his drafts and publications; none of his learned friends thought it wrong.[2] The slaps at Keats's "error" began with Tennyson, and persist as routine callouts by critics who think they know better, and cluck at Keats's ignorance. Keats knew what he was doing. I think he also liked the echo of *Or* in *CORTEZ* (11). Herschel and Cortez are figurative company in surprise, and in remembered company from Keats's reading. One of his school-prizes was John Bonnycastle's *Introduction to Astronomy* (1787), with an account of Herschel, and he knew of the conquistadors in Panama from William Robertson's *History of America* (1777).

Keats's image of brotherhood extends from Cortez's company to Clarke and, more broadly, to a fraternity of modern poets, looking back to Chapman and forward into nineteenth-century promise. Hunt's introduction of Keats in *The Examiner* with this sonnet was prescient: its fame today was glimpsed as early as 1843, when it was featured as a epigraph to volume 2 of a new edition of Chapman's *Homer* (Keats, in effect, relaunching Chapman).[3] Noting that this young poet "has not yet published any thing except in a newspaper," Hunt mentions a sheaf of poems that "fairly surprised us with the truth of their ambition, and ardent grappling with Nature" (761): in effect, a kenning of Keats, with a hint of rhyming company in the way *surprised* echoes in Keats's all-absorbing *surmise.* Reading Chapman, Keats was reading himself, too, as a poet for whom looking is reading, and reading is looking—and here, ultimately, prospectively, in a sublime expanse: eagle eyes that stare; a silence of wild surmise.

Inspiration could also come in local gusts.

[*Examiner,* 1 December 1816, 761–762; compare *1817,* Sonnet XI, p. 89]

Portions of this commentary were previously published in Susan Wolfson, "On First Looking into Chapman's Homer," Cambridge University Press *fifteeneightyfour* blog, 26 October 2016.

[1] The only poem in *1817* that ends in a dash is the first: "My wand'ring spirit must no further soar.—" (p. 34), a diminuendo that also glances at prospects.

[2] As late as 1828, Hunt praised its specificity: "Cortez's 'eagle eyes' are a piece of historical painting, as the reader may see by Titian's portrait of him" (*Lord Byron &c* 1:412). This was done sometime in the mid-1500s; Chapman's Homer was published 1598–1616. For Tennyson's "correction," see *Golden Treasury* (333), Denise Gigante's *Keats Brothers* (2011), 40, and Erica McAlpine's smugly mistaken *The Poet's Mistake* (2020).

[3] Edited by W. Cooke Taylor, 2 vols. London: Charles Knight, 1843.

"Keen, fitful gusts"

KEEN, fitful gusts are whisp'ring here and there
    Among the bushes half leafless, and dry;
    The stars look very cold about the sky,
And I have many miles on foot to fare.
Yet feel I little of the cool bleak air,   5
    Or of the dead leaves rustling drearily,
    Or of those silver lamps that burn on high,
Or of the distance from home's pleasant lair:
For I am brimfull of the friendliness   9
    That in a little cottage I have found;
Of fair-hair'd Milton's eloquent distress,
    And all his love for gentle Lycid drown'd;
Of lovely Laura in her light green dress,
    And faithful Petrarch gloriously crown'd.

"Poetry plays the rhythms of dramatic speech on the grid of meter," writes Frost; "Footbeats for the meter and heartbeats for the rhythm."[1] With metric-wit, Keats's "And *I* have *many miles* on *foot* to *fare*" hums a poetic footing of alliterative iambic pentameter in a present-tense pacing from Hunt's cottage in the Vale of Health in Hampstead to the brothers' rooms in London. The sonnet starts with three blows, *Keen, fitful gusts,* wording a tactile aggression, in conspiracy with the monosyllabic percussions at the end of 5: *cool bleak air.* No "poetic diction" here; this is felt sensation. The present tense *whisp'ring* and the alliterative flutters of *half leafless* finely catch the season's *fitful* sound of dead dry leaves. Added to *rustling drearily,* the participles flirt into an onomatopoeia of eerie conspiracy. The *stars that look very cold about the sky* not only seem so to the poet's look, but seem gothic-animated to the star-seeing "I," as agents of a cold look.

All this hostility is negated, or made faint, by Keats's lively store of sociability and reading. The volta *Yet,* advanced to line 5, turns from outer weather to inner warming. Rehearsing the wintry hostility on an anaphora of *Or,* the echoing turn of "I am brim*full of*" undertones a *full love* force of friendliness. No usual spelling is this *brimfull* (Keats's only usage, too); it is a stressed etymology, figuring "I" as a vessel *full* to the very brim, the self's border on the "fit*ful*" world. Alliteratively, *Brimfull* allies with *faithful* company—not least poetry. The *half leafless* outside is a fading echo. The image of stars as silver lamps that burn on high may seem cliché; so, too, *home's pleasant lair,* a slack synonym to close off a rhyme chain, *there-fare-air*. Keats, however, measures the gamble. He wanted star-lamps to evoke the warm lamps of home; *lair*, as it is in the next, "city pent" sonnet (X), is cozied up for comfort.

In *Poems*, Keats sequenced these two sonnets on a through-line of comforts in an adverse world. And so the familiar home-names: "Lycid" for Milton's *Lycidas*, "Laura" for Petrarch's muse of faith through love, before he was "gloriously crown'd." Keats's words sing this world against the season. In October 1816, ready for a vocation in poetry, Keats's sonnet hovers over all these markers. Brimfull from Hunt's hospitality, he may wonder whether his path will be to Lycid drowned (Edward King, dead at twenty-five) or toward poetic fame. Even Petrarch's crown is sorrow-edged with Laura's death. Keats was reading *Canzoniere* (this story) in James Nott's translation (1808), and a picture of the lovers hung in Hunt's library, where he would spend a night in December and write *Sleep and Poetry*. "Keen fitful gusts" whispers the intimacy of poetry and death, conveying this in tender expression woven with subtle poetic craft.

[*1817*, Sonnet IX, p. 87]

---

[1] *Atlantic Monthly*, June 1951 (*Collected Poems* 809); "The Way There" (1958; *Collected Poems* 847).

SMALL, busy flames play through the fresh laid coals,
   And their faint cracklings o'er our silence creep
   Like whispers of the household gods that keep
A gentle empire o'er fraternal souls.
And while, for rhymes, I search around the poles,
   Your eyes are fix'd, as in poetic sleep,
   Upon the lore so voluble and deep,
That aye at fall of night our care condoles.   8
This is your birth-day Tom, and I rejoice
   That thus it passes smoothly, quietly.
Many such eves of gently whisp'ring noise
   May we together pass, and calmly try
What are this world's true joys,—ere the great voice,
   From its fair face, shall bid our spirits fly.
November 18, 1816.

This may be Keats's most intimate sonnet. The gentle stresses of his first line (all but two syllables) mime household gods whispering comfort, especially to Tom, as if joining Keats's birthday poem. The *wisp* sounding in *whispers,* echoing into *gently whisp'ring noise,* is a great tenderness to Tom, no longer able to work because of his health. In relief that this birthday is calm, Keats holds *noise* from a strong chime (as it is set to) with *rejoice* in order to gain a more audible internal rhyme with the *true joys* of the evening together. This comes as a midline sound, paused by a comma and a dash that knows another rhyme, the *great voice* that will summon all mortals sooner or later from the realm of household gods. The plural *our* is beyond poignant in this enduring fraternal affection: it means everyone, but also intimately *we* two.

The domestic *whispering* here contrasts the alien *whisp'ring* in "Keen fitful gusts." Keats tunes sonic through-lines in *1817*'s sonnet-unit for subtle differences. The brothers were now living at 76 Cheapside, in London's commercial district. The sonnet commemorates the real-time hominess of an evening at hearthside, Tom reading, Keats writing with affection as the bard of this little empire. His *search around the poles* for rhymes already reaches one here: *fraternal souls.* Tom's ease is graced with a Keatsian supplement, his calm eyes "fixed, as in poetic sleep, / Upon the lore so voluble and deep" (6–7). Books are audible company, *voluble:* "fluent of words" (*JnD*). Likely in Keats's thoughts, even as allusion, is one of Wordsworth's *Personal Talk* sonnets. Finding in books "personal themes . . . / Matter wherein right voluble I am," Wordsworth-the-reader is the voluble one (1815 *Poems* 2:141). In Keats's scene, the book is the voluble one, the communicator. The etymology of *voluble* is wound with "volume," the one a turning of the tongue, the other a scroll of writing, seemingly made for one another, word-fluency being the evolved meaning of *voluble.* It is also haunted by an older sense: "liable to change; inconstant, variable, mutable."

Keats feels this last turn, plangently: *our care condoles.* The verb is a searched-for last rhyme on the *a*-chord: "express[es] concern for the miseries of others" (*JnD*), and one of only two uses in Keats's poetry. "It is a most interesting paradox," comments Jack Stillinger, "that Keats the man of common-sense practicality" is also a "poet most concerned with dreams and visionary excursions into the un-real"; this is the "rich complexity" of the best poetry, which Stillinger locates in Keats's mature seasons of 1819 (*Complete Poems* xvi). I see it here, in reverse syntax: Keats knows that dreams and common-sense are intimately reflexive. The fair face of heaven will bid all *spirits fly*—a final greeting to, and of, the spirit, to them all: *our.* George's dimming prospects in England would send him to America in June 1818, as good as dead for intimate company. Tom's course toward death would end in December. Keen gusts were on the horizon in November 1816, Keats's poem of brotherly love taking the pulse of "this world's" fragile domestic bliss, as sweet for this as a day in the country away from urban grime and medical misery. When he left England for Italy in September 1820, sensing no return, he took this sonnet and *To My Brother George* with him (Motion 538), tokens of the fraternal empire of gentle souls. Now on earth, sojourning was not forever. On a blank leaf facing the sonnet, Woodhouse wrote, "John Keats, the author of it, died at Rome of a decline, on the 23. Feby 1821" (*SpW* 149).

But now on earth, spirits abound.

[*1817*, Sonnet VIII, p. 86]

"Great Spirits now on earth"

GREAT spirits now on earth are sojourning;
   He of the cloud, the cataract, the lake,
   Who on Helvellyn's summit, wide awake,
Catches his freshness from Archangel's wing:
He of the rose, the violet, the spring,
   The social smile, the chain for Freedom's sake:
   And lo! —whose stedfastness would never take   7
A meaner sound than Raphael's whispering.
And other spirits there are standing apart
   Upon the forehead of the age to come;
These, these will give the world another heart,
   And other pulses. Hear ye not the hum
Of mighty workings? ——————   13
   Listen awhile ye nations, and be dumb.

The "Great Spirit that reigns within them," declared that fierce champion of the Elgin Marbles, Benjamin Robert Haydon, to readers of *The Examiner*, 17 March 1816. He hailed a "Fame" whose "roaring will swell out as time advances; and nations now sunk in barbarism, and ages yet unborn, will in succession be roused by its thunder, and be refined by its harmony" (164). Writing this sonnet in November, Keats echoes Haydon's greeting in his tribute to the Great Spirits of this age in art.

    Epic painter, passionate advocate for the arts, defender of the Marbles' rough grandeur, ferocious critic of the Royal Academy's regime of polished refinement, Haydon was *Gusto* in spades. His rants about art and artists, his vision of epic purpose, swelled Keats with a sense of greatness at hand: in Hunt's Hampstead, in Wordsworth's Lakes, in Haydon's London. What Haydon wrote (later) of Shakespeare could be said of Haydon: "powers of expression and sublimity" with abounding beauties.[1] Poet by another name: "Poetry was to his mind the zenith of all his Aspirations," a fellow student at Guy's Hospital recalled of young Keats; "The greatest men in the world were the Poets, and to rank among them was the chief object of his ambition."[2] When Haydon met Keats in November 1816, the match was lit. He immediately decided to paint Keats into the crowd of his epic canvas, *Christ's Entry into Jerusalem*. He adored Keats, his artist's eye taken with his youth and beauty, his soul convinced of talent and promise.

Keats visited him on 19 November, and their talk fired through the night. (Hazlitt came by, too.) Keats may have paced the sonnet out on his way home— as he had after that blazing all-nighter with Chapman's Homer. Once again, too wired for sleep, he took up his pen. The next morning he messengered the sonnet over to Haydon, with this greeting.

> *Last Evening wrought me up, and I cannot forbear*
> *sending you the following –   Your's unfeignedly John Keats –*

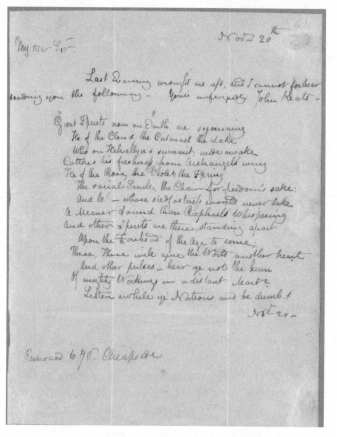

Figure 3: Keats's excited letter to Benjamin Robert Haydon, November 1816, including the first draft of "Great Spirits." MS Keats 1.3. Courtesy of Houghton Library, Harvard University.

How smart is Keats's verb *wrought,* mind and body coiled for action, ready to *write* (an etymologic sibling)—both senses perfectively, productively sonnet-inspiring.

"Great spirits now on earth are sojourning," Keats begins: two strong syllablesor really, three of the first four. Haydon responded by return messenger with a char-

acteristic mix of generosity and self-interest. Generously: he wanted to send Words-
worth the sonnet (Hunt would see it soon enough), and offered a great idea for
line 13. What if the penultimate question, *hear ye not the hum / Of mighty Workings
in a distant Mart?* stopped at *mighty Workings,* then open space? Keats loved the
drama, and with his poet's ear realized that a stop at *Workings* would also call in the
octave's *ing* rhymes for reverberation along the dash. He wrote quickly to Haydon
in deep appreciation and included a new fair copy for Wordsworth (MsK 1.4.13).

> *My dear Sir,*
> > *Your Letter has filled me with a proud pleasure*
> *and shall be kept by me as a stimulus to exertion – I begin to fix*
> *my eye upon one horizon – My feelings entirely fall in with*
> *yours' in regard to the Ellipsis and I glory in it the Idea of*
> *your sending it to Wordsworth put me out of breath – you know*
> *with what Reverence - I would send my Wellwishes to him[.]*

Haydon's great-spirited letter was an immediate, sustainable inspiration. As if
riding the propulsion of the newly dash-charged line, Keats set his eye on the
horizon of Wordsworth's reading it, and confessed his own reflex of inspiration:
out of breath . . . with what Reverence.

The sonnet sets up a Petrarchan plan, a form both Hunt and Wordsworth
favored. Keats plays with and against its protocols. He weaves the octave-rhymes
through all three honorees, with a relaxed trisyllable frame to enclose and offset
the single-syllable chimes: *sojourning / Lake / awake / wing / Spring / sake / take /
whispering.* The slight punctuation (no comma, even, until line 5) assists the
momentum of inspiration over prescription. Keats does shift the rhyme at 9,
but he's already advanced the volta to 7, with a triple-shot of old-school in-
terjection, exclamation point, and dash: *And lo!—.* This energizes the syntax,
enjambing it all the way to "Upon the Forehead of the Age to come;" (10). No
hard stop, the semicolon is just a pause to spring the final four lines into a nonce
quatrain, pulsed with the pleonasm *These, These* on two strong beats, then
that question ended midline, with a dash across the rest. The long-*e*'s of *These,
these* play into *hear ye . . . the.* The bottom line is Keats's own hum, the initial
exclamation canceled for a softer period, before the silent space.

First on the honor roll is Wordsworth, the eldest, not always loved by a
younger generation sorry for his Tory (reactionary) turn. Whatever the man
now, the poetry still rocked out the spiritual energy in everyday life and nature's
beauties, with seeming Archangelic inspiration. Lakeland is such legible code
that its poet needs no naming. Then come two lines for Hunt (also coded) that

weave his lovely poetry, his sociability, and his jailing *for Freedom's sake,* nicely undertoning the *Freedom's ache* of his courage. For Haydon, Keats saves that volta-interjection, *And lo!* Haydon's passion earns a double-Raphael: the Archangel and the namesake, the High Renaissance painter of Haydon's admiration. Pausing at *take* (7), Keats lets this transitive verb (*take/A . . . sound*) take up multiple senses, "draw from," "accept," "aspire to." It is a perfect catch in poetic form.

Keats's praise is also communally tuned, relayed through Hunt's sonnet the month before in the 20 October *Examiner* (no. 460, p. 663), "To Benjamin Robert Haydon, Painter":

> Painter indeed, gifted, laborious, true
> Fit to be numbered in succession due
> With Michael, whose idea austerely presses,
> And sweet-souled Raphael

Michel(angelo) is namesake of yet another Archangel. Hunt numbers Haydon with Haydon's heroes, "One of the spirits chosen by heaven" (13) to enlighten the age. Great spirits, Keats writes, inspire a new body, *another heart, / And other pulses.*

Keats's last two lines land with the force of a Shakespearean couplet, achieved with his own art. Ending a sentence in the middle of 12, he pivots the pause to a public "us": *Hear ye not . . . ?* We've "seen" it already, its letters drawn down from the end-word of 11, *heart,* this anagrammed from and hearkening back to *earth* (1), Keats's scene of celebration. The mighty *hum* summons another great spirit by echo, Milton catching "the busy hum of men" in his world (*L'Allegro*). Keats tunes his hum to the future.

Haydon must have been pleased to see his suggestion taken up in Keats's new fair copy. Keats meant it for Wordsworth, but Haydon jealously cadged it, sending a copy to Wordsworth—and not until the very last day of 1816! Even notoriously reluctant correspondent Wordsworth managed a reply in half the time, 20 January 1817. Jesting that Keats's praises allowed no impartial judgment, he still read with a poet's eye, recognizing energy and skill:

> Your account of young Keats interests me not a little; and the sonnet appears to be of good promise, of course neither you nor I being so highly complimented in the composition can be deemed judges altogether impartial – but it is assuredly vigorously conceived and well expressed; Leigh

Hunt's compliment is well deserved and the sonnet is very agreeably concluded. (*Letters, Middle Years* 2:360–361)

Hunt's compliment to Keats *is well deserved*, he means; and maybe Keats's to Hunt, at least in this aspect (Tory by now, Wordsworth rather detested the antimonarchal polemics).

If Haydon smiled at the remark on the sonnet's conclusion, Keats was over the moon. He had Wordsworth's 1815 *Poems* with him during his medical studies. He loved the passage in *The Excursion* (1814) about the old mythologies (4.846–882), one Hazlitt praised in *The Examiner* for its "expansive and animating principle" in comparison to the "cold . . . lifeless spirit" of science (556).[3] When Wordsworth was in town in December 1817, Haydon arranged for Keats to meet him. Wordsworth asked what he was up to, and Keats happily recited the choral hymn to Pan from *Endymion,* "walking up & down the room," pacing his meters. Wordsworth composed in this physical mode on the paths of Grasmere, a little crazed when the weather kept him indoors. His remark on Keats's performance (in perhaps less than great spirits), "a Very pretty piece of Paganism," struck Haydon as unfeeling, wounding even (*KC* 2:143–144); but Wordsworth may have appreciated the pagan vitality.[4]

Haydon brought them together again later that month for dinner at his studio, the event he later called an "immortal evening" (T. Taylor 1:387). He set the table beneath *Christ's Entry,* so that all (including Charles Lamb) could see themselves in it. Keats's profile (Figure 4, next page), ablaze in an intense gaze, was just above Wordsworth's reverentially bowed head—or as Hazlitt less kindly put it, "his drooping weight of thought and expression" ("My first Acquaintance" 40).[5]

Keats hailed his trio of Great Spirits in a letter to Haydon, 10 January 1818 (MsK 1.18.62):

> *every day older I get—the greater is my idea of your atchievements in Art:*
> *and I am convinced that there are three things to rejoice at in this Age—*
> *The Excursion Your Pictures, and Hazlitt's depth of Taste.*
> *Your's affectionately*
> *John Keats*

Haydon replied on the 11th, "allow me to add sincerely a fourth to be proud of—John Keats' genius!—and this I speak from my heart" (*L* 1:203). He had used Keats's epithet to reassure him in May 1817, in his low mood about *Endymion:* every "great Spirit . . . is at times thus tormented–"; "your own energy

Figure 4: Detail from Benjamin Robert Haydon's *Christ's Entry into Jerusalem* (1816–1819), with Keats and Wordsworth. The full epic painting is nearly thirteen by fifteen feet. Athenaeum of Ohio / Wikimedia Commons.

will give you strength" (1:135). Wordsworth kept his eye on Keats, asking after him when he wrote to Haydon on 16 January 1820 to congratulate him on the exhibition of *Christ's Entry.* "How is Keates, he is a youth of promise too great for the sorry company he keeps" (Hunt).[6] Doing Keats the honor of *great* promise for company among the spirits his sonnet had honored, Wordsworth, nearing fifty, could not know that young Keats was desperately ill, scarcely more than a year of sojourning on earth left to him.

Haydon added a posthumous endorsement, with a postscript to his portrait of Keats from November 1816: "Keats was a spirit that in passing over the earth came within its attraction and expired in fruitless struggles ~~to regain his former height~~ to make its dull inhabitants comprehend the beauty of his soarings."[7] In this narrative, mythologized by Shelley's *Adonais* (1821), Keats's great spirit was never of this earth in the first place.

[*1817*, Sonnet XIV: "Addressed to the Same," p. 92]

Portions of this commentary were previously published in Susan Wolfson, "Keats Wrought up to Writing," Cambridge University Press *fifteeneightyfour* blog, 19 November 2016.

[1] *Annals of the Fine Arts* IV (1820), 241.

[2] Henry Stephens to George Felton Matthew, March 1847 (*KC* 2:208).

[3] Haydon and Bailey also note Keats's love of this passage.

[4] Clarke thought so, citing "I'd rather be / A Pagan" from Wordsworth's sonnet "The world is too much with us," to the credit of both (*CR* 149). See also Hunt on Wordsworth's reception of Keats's Ode to Pan (*Lord Byron &c* 417).

[5] The tilted head next to Keats's may be Hazlitt's.

[6] *Letters, Middle Years,* 2:578.

[7] Sharp, 536 (Haydon's strike-though).

Written in disgust of vulgar superstition

round

The Church Bells ~~give~~ toll a melancholy sound,
   Calling the People to some other Prayers
Some other gloominess;   more dreadful
   ~~To fill their breasts with fear, and gloomy~~ Cares
More harkening to the Sermon's horrid sound.
Surely the Mind's of Man is closely bound   [5]
              seeing that
   In some black spell: ~~that now~~ each one tares
   Himself from fireside joys and Lydian airs
And converse high of those with glory crownd -
Still, still they toll, and I should feel a damp
   A Chill of   *Tomb*
   A Chill as from a ~~sepulche~~, did I not know   10
That they are ~~like last~~ going like an outburnt Lamp
    'tis their   *ere they go*
   That ~~they are~~ sighing, wailing, ~~in their woe~~
Into oblivion - that fresh flowers will grow
   And many glories of immortal stamp

JKeats

Written in 15 minutes

"Written in" is twice written in Tom Keats's clean copy, title and subscript (MsK 3.5.23), with pride at his brother's facility (the title may have been his, too, reflecting Keats's views). Writing sonnets, in inheritance and going forward, Keats turned to this form sometimes to chasten and contain his feelings. Disgust is his muse here. The sonnet is a bitter audit of horrid institution: a call from fireside joy, sociable converse, and music to the dead rituals, tolled in center-city Cheapside's Church of Saint Mary-le-Bow.[1] The opening tone, *The Church Bells toll a melancholy*... echoes the first line of Gray's famous churchyard *Elegy:* "The curfew tolls the knell of parting day." Keats weights the iambic pentameter with three thuds, *church bells toll,* a metrical code for *dreadful* (Tom copied a surplus *dreadfull*), *spell, Still, still* ("ever" as psychic arrest), *toll, chill.* He spells *tares* (6) to gain an eye-rhyme with *Cares* (3); it clearly means "tears: pulls away from." Keats tightens up his Petrarchan pattern to evoke the constriction he satirizes: *abba abba cdcddc*—just four rhymes, with four couplets (5–6, 11–12, 13–14), no opening for any break of enjambment. The *sound/bound* clasp (4–5) is rhymed arrest. With a sigh, Bailey recalled in the *Church of England Quarterly* (1949) that Keats

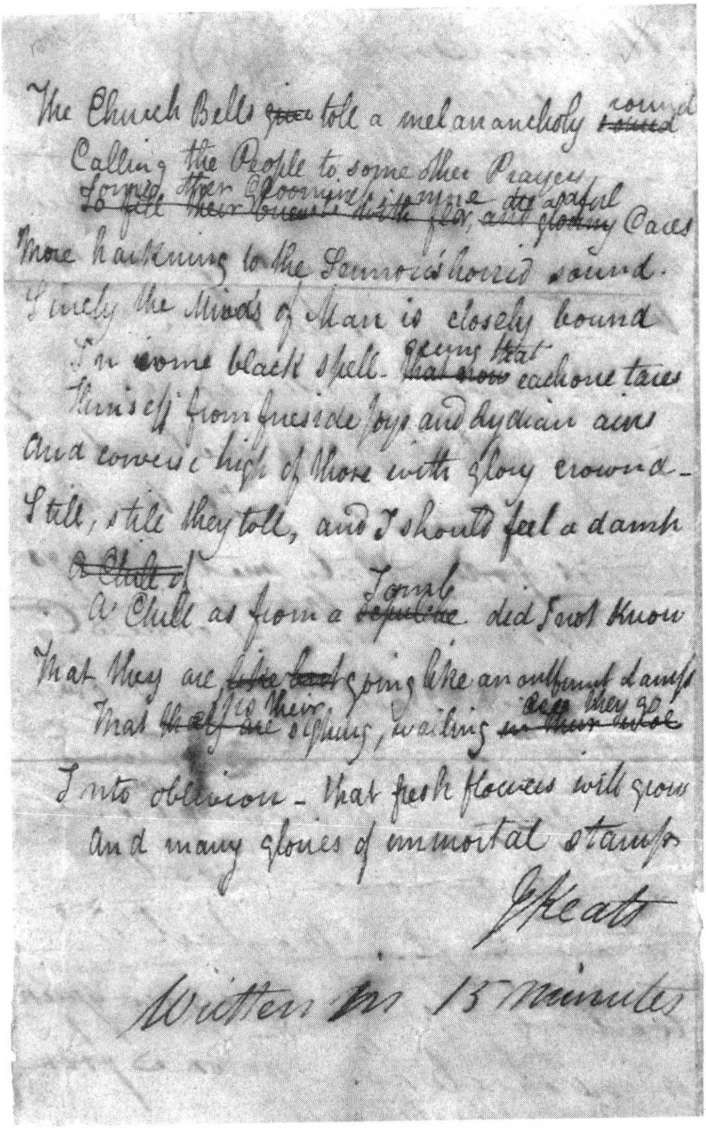

Figure 5: Keats's manuscript, "Written in disgust of vulgar superstition" (August 1816). From *John Keats: Poetry Manuscripts at Harvard: A Facsimile Edition*, ed. Jack Stillinger (The Belknap Press of Harvard University Press, 1990), p. 45, from the original manuscript in the Houghton Library, Harvard University.

"looked upon Church and King with much the same affection with which they were regarded by Milton" (140)—that is, no affection. Bailey knew this sonnet, which smears the Church of England with the "Superstition" that Anglicans liked to reserve for the Roman Church.

Keats's comforts are home-bodied. In the "converse high" with song and poetry, Miriam Allot nicely catches a reverse echo of James Thomson's "high Converse": home's warmth amid Winter's "cheerless Gloom," in the literary company of "the mighty Dead" who "humaniz'd a World."[2] Keats extends the converse to conjure Thomson himself (d. 1748). If the sonnet's last two lines sound a tad flat—promise without energy—this is to register religion's dampening even this counter-prospect. Superstition is an "outburnt lamp" (11), the only time Keats uses *outburnt* in poetry. It may be his coin (it is not in *JnD*); *OED* cites Keats's as the first usage in the sense of *burnt out*.

Keats was soon a silently amused audience at a dinner table (January 1817) where self-proclaimed "Atheist" Shelley, sitting across from ardent Christian Haydon, suddenly uttered, "as to that detestable religion, the Christian—." Haydon rose to the bait, and they went at it. The energies displayed in this quarrel were fine indeed. Hunt was sorry to have missed it, and wrote a sonnet-cheer *To Percy Shelley, On the Degrading Notions of Deity,* publishing it in 1818.[3] As Bailey's discomfort indicates, Keats's sonnet was not publishable for any aspiring poet in his day, or for later-day fame. Milnes kept it out of *1848,* although he tortured his "complete" Aldine edition of *Poetical Works* (1867) into hospitality, classing it with "early sonnets" under a pastoral title, *Written on a Summer Evening,* and tagging it as "a rare instance of any anti-religious feeling or expression, notwithstanding the poet's associations with the free thought of the time" (58–59). Two years later, Milnes, now "The Rt. Hon. Lord Houghton," purged it from his "new edition" (Moxon). No peer of the realm, especially one just elected to the Royal Society, could countenance this slur on the Church.

If the music of the Church is always dead in Keats's ear, the poetry of the earth never is.

[MsK 2.10.2, August 1816; Stillinger *Facsimile,* 45; title from MsK 3.5.23]

---

[1] Clarke recalled Keats writing it "one Sunday morning" (*KC* 2:154). An old definition of *Cockney,* circa 1600, is *born within the sound of Bow-bells* (*OED* 4a), hence "a Bowe-bell Cockney." Keats doesn't ring this chime, but the slur is the air, soon to hit him and Hunt.

[2] *Winter* (1812 edition; lines 432–435); Allott, 97n.

[3] *Foliage* cxxii. Keats owned this. For Haydon and Shelley atilt, see T. Taylor 1:362–364.

On the Grasshopper and Cricket

THE poetry of earth is never dead:
    When all the birds are faint with the hot sun,
    And hide in cooling trees, a voice will run
From hedge to hedge about the new-mown mead;
That is the Grasshopper's—he takes the lead
    In summer luxury,—he has never done
    With his delights; for when tired out with fun
He rests at ease beneath some pleasant weed.
The poetry of earth is ceasing never: 9
    On a lone winter evening, when the frost
        Has wrought a silence, from the stove there shrills   11
The Cricket's song, in warmth increasing ever,
    And seems to one in drowsiness half lost,
        The Grasshopper's among some grassy hills.

December 30, 1816

The subscripted date commemorates a Hunt-proposed contest to write a sonnet on the subject in fifteen minutes. "Keats won as to time," Clarke remembers, and Hunt generously cheered the result (*CR* 135). Keats begins with a summer lull, but his long game is winter pastoral. Spring songs, Summer rhythms, even Autumn music: that's easy. Where are the songs of Winter? Not dead to this poet's ear: even *frost . . . wrought* whispers a tune. In *1817*, this sonnet (XV) follows "Great spirits now on earth" on a facing page (92–93), a displayed diptych of life pulses and hums, *on earth, of earth.*

    The opening line is a headline. No rhyme for *dead*, the bid refused by the pattern's *mead / lead / weed* (*lead*, sounding "leed" against the rhyme-set sound of "led," is especially tart). As summer's birdsong faints in the hot sun, the undersong of the Grasshopper sounds forth. Keats's song-lines track this in a mimesis of run-ons—

          a voice will run
  From hedge to hedge,

           he has never done
  With his delights

—before completing the octave in the long-*e*–sounded languor of *He rests at ease beneath some pleasant weed.* Call it Grasshopper Poetics. A Petrarchan volta (9) repeats line 1 in a positive syntax that links *ease* to ce*asing never* and a pun for the well-tuned ear: catch the *sing* in ce*asing*, keyed to the rhyme "increa*sing ever.*" This is the quiet music of "a lone winter evening," and a cue to the sestet. Set at the end of 10, *frost* might figure into the white page-space. But Keats is not about to channel the grand last sentence of *The Dead*, the final tale in James Joyce's *Dubliners:* "the snow falling faintly through the universe and faintly falling, like the descent of their last end, upon all the living and the dead." Keats's last word is not *dead:* refused from the get-go.

As summer heat makes audible Grasshopper music, frost-silence makes audible Cricket song, not with an adjectival *shrill* but in onomatopoeic music, *shrills.* It's a fine verb, "indeed it images very happily" (*JnD*). Keats knows Johnson's example from Spenser's *Epithalamion* (Clarke had read to him; *CR* 125):

> Hark how the Minstrils 'gin to shrill aloud
> Their merry Musick that resounds from far   (5:1263)

Spenser's spelling abets, lettering Min*strils* to mirror *shrill.* Keats underlined <u>A shrilling Trumpet sounded from on high</u> in *The Fairy-Queen* (I.5.VI; 1:75). No need for *on high* in any homey hearth. Keats plays the very sound *shrills* before its minstrel-agent: *there shrills / The Cricket's song* (11–12). The blank page at the end of line 11 images a field for reverberation, increasing ever: *in warmth* not just in temperature but in intensity. An ear *in drowsiness half lost* might imagine *grass*hopper poetics among some *grassy* hills.

Keats's measured *half* concedes a fantasy, but only *half.* It may be a dream to hear a grasshopper instead of a cricket, or it may be that the *poetry of the earth* layers a harmony of present sense with remembered sense. As with all of these early sonnets in which Keats is testing the mettle of his verbal facility, you could say that hearing is believing, or the reverse, believing is hearing. Keats invites us into the relays. Hunt knew this when he republished the sonnet on 21 September 1817, on the cusp of summer's transition into autumn, for readers of *The Examiner.*

Seasons are portents for poetry-filled imaginations, but sometimes darkly edged for Keats's sense of prospects.

[1817, p. 93]

Sonnet ("After dark vapors")

AFTER dark vapors have oppress'd our plains
    For a long dreary season, comes a day
    Born of the gentle SOUTH, and clears away
From the sick heavens all unseemly stains.
The anxious Month, relieving of its pains,
    Takes as a long lost right the feel of MAY: 6
    The eyelids with the passing coolness play
Like Rose leaves with the drip of Summer rains.
The calmest thoughts come round us; as of leaves
    Budding—fruit ripening in stillness—Autumn Suns
Smiling at Eve upon the quiet sheaves—
    Sweet SAPPHO's Cheek—a sleeping infant's breath—   12
The gradual Sand that through an hour-glass runs—
    A woodland rivulet—a Poet's death.

                        J. K.

Keats wrote this sonnet on 31 January 1817, just as he sent the fair copy of *Poems* off to press. Hunt put it in *The Examiner*, 23 February, meaning to fan interest for the March debut. It is quite an artful sonnet: a Petrarchan pattern accruing a Shakespearean dramatic build, the volta coming at the last dash, and a final three-word shock. (I wonder what Hunt made of this sudden turn.)

To get there, Keats brimfully paces his imagery along promises naturalized into personified agents: Spring clearings, Summer ripenings, Autumn's harvest (even "Eve"). The first two lines slog the *p* sounds of *vapors, oppress'd, plains* into the mimetic pace of *a long dreary season,* as dramatic prelude (in the subordinate temporality of *After)* to rejuvenation from the gentle SOUTH (3). The typography evokes natural divinity, bringing health, light, and open air, *born of* and *born in:* how nicely Keats lets the first gentle couplet, *comes a day / and clears away,* prevail in sound and sense over *dreary* and ready a rhyme for the *feel of MAY* (6). The very sounding of "feel *of*" holds *love.* With two slight periods on the quatrains, the sonnet feels like a single flowing, flowering sentence. A categorical, intransitive verb, *relieving,* sighing a *re-living,* on the way to the re-leaving in actual *leaves* (8–9), mirrors the *feel* of May. It is not just *leaves* but *leaves / Budding:* a surreal fantasia of nature and a fine hope for the material leaves of *Poems.*[1] On this roll comes a sestet of calmest thoughts that need no syntax to gather a romance of sweetness, trust, and natural inevitability. Seven dashes hold the images in a luxury of slow time: of breath, of ripening (a process) in stillness (a stasis, a quiet peace). Line 10 is extravagantly languorous, with *Budding . . . ripening* extended by dashes along an already hypermetrical 12 syllables. Even 13 (also hexameter) takes a stock image of temporality, the hour-glass, to suspend it with a dash, then mirror its drift of sands in a "woodland rivulet": no dire portent at all.

But it is all a set-up. This last dash is a volta turn to *a Poet's death.* Dark vapors come again, in inner weather. Keats's cruelest inspiration is to sound-pair *infant's breath* with *Poet's death,* a startlingly short-circuited life span. Editors like to conjure Chatterton, but it seems more than this (and Chatterton ended his life in an August not a February), more even than the generic pathos of any poet's death in an awakening world. It is Keats's apprehension about the life of his *Poems.* He will reprise the delusory romance of the "the gentle SOUTH" in epic terms in his autobiography of poetic-testing and making, *The Fall of Hyperion:*

> When in mid-May the sickening east wind
> Shifts sudden to the south, the small warm rain
> Melts out the frozen incense from all flowers,
> And fills the air with so much pleasant health
> That even the dying man forgets his shroud.   (1.97–101)

Beautiful lines these, with *wind / Shifts* and *rain / Melts* finely turned across the lines; frozen flowers melting into fragrance; *sickening* yielding to *pleasant health; dying* so reversed in sensation as to seem altogether forgotten, canceled. What a gorgeously spread enjambment, *spread around / Forgetfulness,* that takes this incense (evoking the blessing of the goddess Maia) into a rhyming *bliss.* Yet here, on the arc of Keats's last nightmare of a poem, it's all treachery: what's at hand is near death.

This is the sonnet's dark dream of poetic vocation. And Keats published it. In one of those contingencies that redounds with semantic force, it got printed just below a report on the "efficacy" and "importance of Vaccination" against smallpox, and just above an article, featured in an all-capital headline, *MILI-TARY TORTURE,* on the "brutal and inefficient practice" of flogging. Keats's SONNET (its printed title) is a rather diminished story of ways to die, but placed on this page of *The Examiner,* it picks up the reverberations.

[*Examiner,* 23 February 1817 (124, column 2)]

---

[1] Poetry-leaves and tree-leaves converge when, a year on, Keats proposes that Poetry should come *as naturally as the Leaves to a tree* (to John Taylor, 27 February 1818; Morgan Library).

TO HAYDON,

WITH A SONNET WRITTEN ON SEEING THE ELGIN MARBLES.

HAYDON! Forgive me, that I cannot speak
   Definitively on these mighty things;
   Forgive me that I have not Eagle's wings—
That what I want I know not where to seek:
And think that I would not be overmeek   5
   In rolling out upfollow'd thunderings,
   Even to the steep of Heliconian springs,
Were I of ample strength for such a freak—
Think too, that all those numbers should be thine;
   Whose else? In this who touch thy vesture's hem?
For when men star'd at what was most divine   II
   With browless idiotism—o'erwise phlegm—
Thou hadst beheld the Hesperean shine
   Of their star in the East, and gone to worship them.

ON SEEING THE ELGIN MARBLES.

My Spirit is too weak—Mortality
   Weighs heavily on me like unwilling sleep,
   And each imagined pinnacle and steep
Of godlike hardship, tells me I must die
Like a sick Eagle looking at the sky.   5
   Yet 'tis a gentle Luxury to weep
   That I have not the cloudy winds to keep,
Fresh for the opening of the morning's eye.
Such dim-conceived glories of the brain   8
   Bring round the heart an undescribable feud;
So do these wonders a most dizzy pain,
   That mingles Grecian grandeur with the rude
Wasting of old time—with a billowy main—
   A sun—a shadow of a magnitude.   J. K

The acquisition of these sculptural fragments (today called the "Parthenon Marbles") from the Acropolis in Athens by the British government from the Earl of Elgin was controversial. As ambassador to Constantinople, 1799–1803, Elgin worried about ravages by the Ottoman occupiers of Greece, and possible theft by Napoleon. He ordered the sculptures pried off the buildings, packed them up for his private collection, then lost some at sea. In 1812, he offered to sell what he had to the government. Its purchase in 1816 was a notorious bone of contention, an extravagance amid postwar economic misery, and for works of dubious value. Some hailed a grandeur of art, with safety in England; others dismissed the mighty things as crude, and of questionable authenticity; others decried a theft of Greece's cultural heritage. This last was Byron's famous charge in *Childe Harold's Pilgrimage* Canto II (1812), even though, on different principles, he had satirized the "mutilated blocks of marble" as "Phidian freaks, / Mis-shapen monuments, and maimed antiques."[1]

Haydon, with no use for the Royal Academy's standard of polished grace, and no interest in the politics, championed the Marbles' historic and aesthetic power, not only enduring through centuries but promising a heroic foundation for modern (anti-neoclassical) British art. He took Keats for a private viewing on Sunday, 2 March 1817. Keats was astonished into two sonnets (or one poem in two sonnet-chapters). He gave copies to Haydon and Hunt, and wrote a copy for Reynolds into a prepublication copy of *Poems*. Reynolds got the brace into *The Champion*, just after his review of *Poems*.[2] Jack Stillinger thinks the second sonnet was written first (*P* 564): a confession of incapacity followed by apology and praise. This is plausible; but I think Keats wanted to honor Haydon first, then confess his acolyte humility.[3] Either way, it is an intimate pairing. For *The Examiner*, Hunt set a main title in bold capitals, TO HAYDON, then the secondary titles in small capitals, with Keats's signature (in initials) at the end.

Both sonnets speak of art in and as history, with a burning feud in Keats's heart and brain. It is the sublimity of ruin, almost beyond wording, that impresses him. Milton's sublime poetry was a help here, evoking what was, and is, waning. Keats underlined the description of Satan, Archangel no more, battle-beaten (*KPL* I:19):

> his form had not yet lost
> All her original brightness, nor appear'd
> Less than Arch-Angel ruin'd   (1.591–593)

It is this palimpsest of original and ruin that Keats feels in seeing the Marbles. As in *On first looking* (into Chapman's Homer), he concentrates on affect, here the gerund, *On Seeing*. Not objective ekphrasis, the sonnet is a record of subjective weight: *Forgive me, that I cannot speak; My Spirit is too weak . . . tells me I must die.* Setting out a Petrarchan pattern, Keats overwhelms it with a relentless roll of self-indicting meditation—or, to give him a credit he is about to claim, a poetics of inadequacy. Take the poised line-cut, *I cannot speak / Definitively.* First the halt, then the qualification, with a hint that definitive speaking would be the wrong mode. A reiteration pulses out in monosyllables: *That what I want I know not where to seek.* Keats's poet-seeking finds a fine phrase: *rolling out upfollow'd thunderings* (7). This is not just an optative "I would" (5) but an event in the line itself. Keats invented the word *upfollow'd* to echo *rolling,* and then deftly echoed *rolling* in *springs.* The second half of the sonnet, meant to honor Haydon, is flatter flattery, but not without the bouquet of an extravagant hexameter closing, comparing Christian Haydon to the magi honoring the birth of Christ, a world-historical pivot—and a notable stretch for skeptic satirist Keats.

The second sonnet is the one most intensely reckoning for "J. K" (K without a period). Sounded in three stresses, *Mortality / Weighs heavily* achieves a sensation of devastating *magnitude.* Suspending Mortality at the line-end (1), Keats gives it the weight (and wait) of a pause, then rounds to the two stressed syllables at the start of the next line. It is enjambment without a flow, a thud that sounds the vast distance between aspiration and accomplishment. This is history, conception to *shadow* (14). Keats's sonnet renders a mingled sensation of Grecian grandeur not ruined ("ruin," an expected noun, is absent) but in the slow, relentless temporality of *rude / Wasting.* Where TO HAYDON delivers sensation at the limits of expression, the pendant sonnet is all sensation. Keats's syntax draws a retrojected past sublimity into a hectic nightmare, *each imagined pinnacle and steep* of aspiration giving the same report, in a drumbeat of five stressed syllables: *tells me I must die.* The first sentence does not end until line 5, then with a diminuendo simile of failed glory: *Like a sick Eagle looking at the sky.* The first sonnet confesses a lack of "Eagle's wings—" with this yearning dash. The second is even more reduced. No Cortez eagle eyes.

Keats underlined an antithetical passage in *The Fairy-Queen,* double-scoring it in the left margin, writing "Milton" in a footnote to the X at the left of the third line (I:153). The "he" is a "holy Man" in a remote "Hermitage":

> Great grace that old Man to him given had;
> For <u>God he often saw from Heaven's height.</u>
> X   <u>All were his earthly Eyen both blunt and bad,</u>
>   <u>And through great Age had lost their kindly Sight,</u>
>   <u>Yet wondrous quick and pierceant was his Spright,</u>
>   <u>As Eagle's Eye, that can behold the Sun.</u>   (I.10.XLVII)

Milton is no ruin, but a spiritually able Eagle's Eye—and, for readers in 1817, a foil for fallen Napoleon, who had taken the Eagle as his icon, and who (argued the Elginists) had his sights on the Marbles for France's glory. All these vectors vibrate.

The soft volta at *Yet* (6) is Keats's sigh for relief from heroic endeavoring, but only in prelude to a stronger volta about what is left for modern poetry: *Such dim-conceived glories of the brain* (9). The sculptor's conceiving brain (dim, long gone) relays into the poet's heartfelt, brain-aching feud of art against time: *undescribable* (the word unique here in Keats's poetry) delivers a canny cardio-cerebral word power. Keats stretches the slow time of the line's pace to accommodate its five syllables, inscribing the event of the word against its sense. What a contrast to its close cousin, actor Edmund Kean's *indescribable gusto* (*K* 75). Kean is vibrantly present; the Marbles are slow-fading, their gran*deur* splayed into the lettering of *rude* wasting. Keats's copy for Reynolds gives "Time" the force of a personifying capital T.

In this sublime poetics of ruining, Keats grasps "the power implicit in the modern gesture of the fragment, the significance of the part that suggests the whole, the resonance released by the ruin" (in the elegant phrasing of Stanley Plumly, *Immortal* 65). It is synecdoche historicized—no better reader of this, especially in eerie relics, than T. S. Eliot:

> some of Donne's most successful and characteristic effects are secured by brief words and sudden contrasts:
> *A bracelet of bright hair about the bone,*
> where the most powerful effect is produced by the sudden contrast of associations of 'bright hair' and of 'bone.' This telescoping of images and multiplied associations is characteristic of the phrase of some of the dramatists of the period . . . one of the sources of the vitality of their language. (*Selected Essays* 269)

Donne's line, with its paused alliterations, is a vividly reversed memento mori.

About a year after viewing the Marbles (21 January 1818), Keats was stunned by such a synecdoche: "I was at Hunt's the other day, and he surprised me with a real authenticated Lock of <u>Milton's Hair</u>" (MsK 2.20.70–71).[4] Again a poetic event—*on seeing:*

> *On seeing a Lock of Milton's hair'* -

A sensation of apparitional presence unlocks

> *Even at the simplest vassal of thy Power;*
> *A Lock of thy bright hair!*
> *Sudden it came,*

And I was startled, when I caught thy name
Coupled so unaware -
Yet at the moment, temperate was my blood:
Methought I had beheld from the Flood

Such a reverse of Wordsworth's description of poetry in the Preface to *Lyrical Ballads* (1800) as "emotion recollected in tranquillity" (I:xxxii). Keats first wrote *temperate* as *unheated* (MsK 2.15.2). The (implied) heat in the moment of writing fuels the logic for *vassal*. Keats wanted this word: *vassal,* a servant to Power, instead of the expected fetish, *vessel*.[5] What do fragments, remnants, relics tell in this reverence? These may be fetishizing: desire's overinvestment in phantasmic magnitude, never sufficient in the return. Or they may be an uncanny claim against history, suddenly arcing from time past into present power.

With a strange poetic dignity, Keats closes his second sonnet to Haydon with a sentence of breathtaking dashes and fragmented phrasings that are suddenly, amazingly adequate to this double temporality: typography tasked with brain-weight. The word-minimalism is dizzy, baffled communication. Picking up his early heats of experiment, this is the sonnet's modernity. Sea and sun persist, the way the *voice mysterious* of Ocean does in *To My Brother George,* persist beyond human necessity, even as wonders anguish an undescribable feud. "J. K," receptor of epic magnitude, issues a most pained greeting of a *spirit . . . too weak,* echo-rhymed from the first sonnet's *I cannot speak* and *I know not where to seek* and a task that seems *such a freak.* Although editor Miriam Allott thinks he meant a more sensible "feat" and was stuck having to rhyme (106n), I think he chose "freak" to refute Byron's dismissal of the "Phidian freaks."

Expressed incapacity is proving a Keatsian muse with a difference, in the shadow-mode of magnitude. The sonnet's fragmented syntax and its muster of dashes yield dramatic power. If not yet a muscular negative capability, these are its elements, emanations of the *feud* that will flex Keats's coming poetic mode: division, quarrel, oscillation, irresolution. This is a poetic grammar, ever more describable.

[*Examiner,* 9 March 1817, 155]

---

[1] *English Bards and Scotch Reviewers* (3rd edition, 1810), 80.

[2] *The Examiner* sets this "Original Poetry" just above a "Fine Arts" notice of paintings at the British Institution. Haydon got the doublet republished in a Marbles-devoted issue of *Annals of the Fine Arts* (April 1818), this time signed with Keats's full signature (III.8:171–172).

³ This is the order in *Poems,* also *Examiner, Champion,* and *Annals.* Reynolds's *Poems* is held at the Houghton Library. In the *Champion* he introduced the sonnets both for "the grandeur of the subjects" and (with a boost for Keats) for "their own power and beauty."

⁴ Hunt was spurred to three sonnets on receiving this gift (*Foliage* cxxxi, cxxxii, cxxxiii).

⁵ When Keats fair-copied the ode, he kept "vassal" (*P* 224). I don't share Stillinger's conviction, on finding no usable sense of "vassal" in the *OED,* that Keats meant *vessel* (*Complete Poems* 436).

On the Sea

From want of regular rest, I have been rather <u>narvus</u> - and the passage in
Lear - "Do you not hear the sea?" - has haunted me intensely.

On the Sea.

<s>*O Sea*</s> *It keeps eternal Whisperings around*
  Desolate shores, and with its mighty swell
  Gluts twice ten thousand Caverns; till the spell
Of Hecate leaves them their old shadowy sound.
often 'tis in such gentle temper found
  That scarcely will the very smallest shell
  Be moved for days from whence it sometime fell
When last the winds of Heaven were unbound.
O ye who have your eyeballs vext and tir'd   9
  Feast them upon the wideness of the Sea
O ye whose Ears are dinned with uproar rude
  Or fed too much with cloying melody —
Sit ye near some old Cavern's Mouth and brood   13
  Until ye start as if the Sea Nymphs quired—

From a lock of bright hair to a haunting line in *King Lear:* for Keats, reading
can be apparitional, words conjured and reverbed along strata of memory, per-
sonal and literary. At a borderland for imagination, sometimes, by sudden
mental chemistry, this turns into writing. The alpha-haunter is Shakespeare,
deliverer of an uncanny "Passage . . . that may have come rather new" (Keats
says to Reynolds the day after writing out the sonnet for him), striking "for-
cibly . . . at present" (*L* 1:133). He was pulled into the sonnet on 17 April 1817,
"all in a Tremble from not having written any thing of late" (133), especially
for *Endymion.* His cockney-colloquial <u>narvus</u> is self-mockery, naming a plight
and making light of it. "In diseases Medical Men guess, if they cannot ascer-
tain a disease they call it nervous," wrote medical student Keats (*Note book,*
ed. Forman 57).

What's the cure? Scanning the blank slate of the sea, Keats tried a lyric in-
vocation, *O Sea,* with the sounded pun-mot "see." He wanted more: O hear a
greeting to his spirit. Shakespeare's words coming new to him, Keats canceled
the vocative, and began a meditation on the variable moods, oceanic-nerved,
of the Sea. He had turned seaward in *Sleep and Poetry* (1817) for a descriptive
assist, but got carried away by this inadvertent imagination:

as when ocean

Heaves calmly its broad swelling smoothiness o'er
Its rocky marge, and balances once more
The patient weeds; that now unshent by foam
Feel all about their undulating home.   (*Poems*, p. 119)

A front-stressed *Heaves* propels a six-beat line. Keats confected *smoothiness* to carry its swelling to the last beat, *o'er,* hung over the line's end, before the verse bends this preposition to the destined *marge.* From this caesural pause, Keats takes the line to a balancing *more,* then turns the syntax to its object, *patient* weeds, giving the sound-cue to *unshent* (the only instance of this archaism in Keats's poetry), then a flow into *undulating.* This "un-" is no negative, but a rhythm in the sea that gives a rhythm to the line, in a camelion feel for the weeds' *Feel* of release and return.

This is a great small case of how simile can become a generative occasion. Staring at the sea, Keats reads his shifting moods as a generative rhythm, variously agitated, calm, excited, still. *Sea* is found sound:

> Those of us who may have been thinking of the path of poetry, those who understand that words are thoughts and not only our own thoughts . . . must be conscious of this: that, above everything else, poetry is words; and that words, above everything else, are, in poetry, sounds.

This is Wallace Stevens, on "the Sound of Words" (32). From his title, *On the Sea,* Keats finds a path to his first rhyme: "keep*s* *e*ternal" soundscapes *sea;* "Whispering*s around*" releases *surround* to greet *twice ten thousand Caverns.* A synonym for 10,000 is *myriad* (Latinist Keats knows), a trope for countless. He will use it this way in *Endymion:* "myriads of bees" (2.999); "myriads of lingering leaves" (4.943). In the sonnet, vast imagination is relief for nerves, for *eyeballs vext and tir'd* (versus, say, metaphor-ready *eyes*). Whose eyeballs?—a student's, a surgeon's dresser's, any pent soul's. This turn (9) is where the vocative O makes better sense, an invitation to the readerly *ye* to see the rhyme-*Sea* (10), poised at the end of the line, for the figural sea of page-space. The line-end dashes at 12 and 14 extend the invitation.

Keats sees the sea with a poet's spirit. This is Edgar's challenge in *King Lear,* conjuring a scene for his father, his eyeballs gone, longing to leap to death from the cliffs of Dover, into the same sea at which Keats is staring. "Hark, do you hear the sea?" is Edgar's prompt for the grim farce he would stage (4.6; *DW* 7:76). Edgar lets *sea* delicately avert a pun for Gloucester's unseeing eyes, in order to activate a hearing imagination. The cue doesn't catch, Gloucester finishing the metrical line, "No, truly." Keats skews Edgar's cue into "Do you *not* hear the sea?"—a gently coercive greeting of a spirit. It is a train of communicating imaginations: Edgar to Gloucester, Shakespeare to Keats, Keats to us.

Eliciting and replenishing Shakespeare's scene, Keats broods on sounds and silences as proto-poetry: whispering, shadowy sound, winds of Heaven, and then a sudden *start,* a verb double-loaded to convey *startle* and pun-ready *start* for work. Keats's *as if* self-consciously reads the Sea formed into a Sea-Nymph chorus of greeting to him. The verb he wanted is not *choired* but *quired* (the only time he uses this word in poetry), synonym in sound, and in this antique-spelling evoking an oracular *old Cavern's mouth.* It also hosts another sounded pun, a *quire* (sheaf) of literary success.[1] Philosopher Hans Vaihinger is a great help on the canny two-ply of *as if* modalities: a simile-prone *as* gains an *if* that, while conceding "something unreal or impossible" (91–93), advances an "apperceptive construct"; an "impossible case" may be "posited for the moment as possible or real" (258–259). He might as well have said *as if possible or real.* Rereading, Keats smartly pared his syntax to *as:* this allows *as if,* while bringing on board the conjunctive *as* to coordinate sea-brooding with a mythic temporality, the answering cheering deities. And so his wonderful verb, *brood,* with a light glance at blind Milton's muse: "<u>Dove-like sat'st brooding on the vast abyss, / And madest it pregnant</u>" (*PL* 1.19–23; *KPL* I:3).

"The sonnet overleaf did me some good," he tells Reynolds the next morning (*L* 1:133). Reynolds got it into *The Champion* on 17 August, Keats's only new publication in the fourteen months between mid-March 1817 (just after *Poems*) and mid-May 1818, when *Endymion* came out. Sonnet-writing was no little *good.* Everywhere from here on out, Keats's precisions and felicities of phrase come forth in longer forms, with no loss of intensity or lively pressure.

[Woodhouse's copy of a lost letter to Reynolds, 17 April 1817; *L* 1:132]

---

[1] Woodhouse summons the phrase when, in September 1819, he tells Taylor that as Keats read *Lamia* to him, a sensation of its promise "made me 'start, as tho' a Sea Nymph quired" (ALS Morgan Library, p. 3), nicely noted by Christopher Miller (*Surprise* 206–207). Keats used *quire* once more in book-sense (with a sea-muse, no less), writing that Naples harbor had enough material *to fill a quire of Paper* (*L* 2:349).

Poems and a "Long Poem"

March 1817–March 1818

from *Poems*

DEDICATION.

———

=====

TO LEIGH HUNT, ESQ.

GLORY and loveliness have passed away;
    For if we wander out in early morn,
    No wreathed incense do we see upborne
Into the east, to meet the smiling day:
No crowd of nymphs soft voic'd and young, and gay,
    In woven baskets bringing ears of corn,
    Roses, and pinks, and violets, to adorn
The shrine of Flora in her early May.
But there are left delights as high as these,
    And I shall ever bless my destiny,
That in a time, when under pleasant trees
    Pan is no longer sought, I feel a free
A leafy luxury, seeing I could please
    With these poor offerings, a man like thee.

8

Poems debuted in March 1817, heralded by four sonnets in the *Examiner* and Hunt's "Young Poets" (December 1816). Keats was excited, apprehensive, full of plans. He wrote this sonnet extempore in late February 1817 as he was proof-reading and inserted it at the front of the sheaf (*CR* 137–138). It is a beautiful turn on the Petrarchan form Hunt loved, and so in this way a bouquet, in addition to the earnest tribute.

We might miss its political angle. The celebration of ancient religion was legibly counter–Christian institution. The "Grecian religion gave animation and life to all existence," declared Edward Baldwin (William Godwin), in a Wordsworthian spirit (5). This religion was not other-worldly but in the world. Commenting on Byron's *Childe Harold's Pilgrimage* (1812), the orthodox *British Review* could worry that his Lordship's warm "reverence" for the "divinities" of yore affronted Christian Truth; the word "God" is "a little too scriptural for our squeamish ears" (294). Keats's sonnet romances a pantheon of the ancient everyday, the familiars Flora and old Pan, to lament disenchanted modernity, with an echo of Wordsworth's *Ode: Intimations of Immortality from Recollections of Early Childhood* (1815): "There hath past away a glory from the earth" (18). For nostalgic Wordsworth, this is the absolute, differential *past* of childhood consciousness in a spiritually diminished adulthood.

Keats begs to differ: his volta (*But there are . . .*) hails the immediate delights of Hunt's poetry (and poetry in this spirit). Keats nicely tunes all the sestet's long-*e* end-rhymes to *Leigh*. You can even read an anagram in "d*eligh*ts," and hear the name sounded in *leafy* (and in reverse, in *feel*). Keats's very words issue a *wreathed* and *woven* tribute to his sponsor and mentor. The tacit hope is that the *leafy luxury* of Hunt's poetry will be joined by the leaves of *Poems*. But Hunt was more than this pastoral champion; and the dedication to him was a lightning rod for urban politics.

[*1817*, front]

from *Sleep and Poetry*: the ten-year plan

Sleep is a flagrant misnomer. In October 1816, Keats spent a "sleepless night" in Hunt's library, musing on poetry—as imagination, as his life, as epic aspiration. He began this poem the next day, completing it late December. Set as the closer of *Poems,* commanding 25 of its 121 pages, it was his longest work so far. In 404 lines of experimental, extravagant couplets, Keats performs as well as explains his principles and ideals, pausing for a critique of neoclassical poetics and modern movements, and boldly arraying a ten-year career-plan.

a lovely tale of human life we'll read

> Life is the rose's hope while yet unblown;
> The reading of an ever-changing tale;
> The light uplifting of a maiden's veil;
> A pigeon tumbling in clear summer air;
> A laughing school-boy, without grief or care,
> Riding the springy branches of an elm.   95
>
> O for ten years, that I may overwhelm
> Myself in poesy; so I may do the deed
> That my own soul has to itself decreed.
> Then will I pass the countries that I see
> In long perspective, and continually   100
> Taste their pure fountains. First the realm I'll pass
> Of Flora, and old Pan: sleep in the grass,
> Feed upon apples red, and strawberries,
> And choose each pleasure that my fancy sees;
> Catch the white-handed nymphs in shady places,
> To woo sweet kisses from averted faces,—
> Play with their fingers, touch their shoulders white
> Into a pretty shrinking with a bite
> As hard as lips can make it: till agreed,
> A lovely tale of human life we'll read.   110
> And one will teach a tame dove how it best
> May fan the cool air gently o'er my rest;
> Another, bending o'er her nimble tread,

Will set a green robe floating round her head,
And still will dance with ever varied ease,
Smiling upon the flowers and the trees:
Another will entice me on, and on
Through almond blossoms and rich cinnamon;
Till in the bosom of a leafy world
We rest in silence, like two gems upcurl'd   120
In the recesses of a pearly shell.

Keats lovingly depicts his "first" chapter of laughing, sensuous school-boy delights. At every turn, his words produce events of poetic forming, imagination, irony, and doubt. He had just sighed, with exuberance and a little circumspection, "life is but a day . . ." (85), *without grief or care.* These words know what is coming (as does *springy,* with its lexical glances at a limited season); but Keats holds off. Even as he turns to a new verse paragraph to project the long plan, he carries the last word of the play-world paragraph, *elm,* over to the new paragraph for its rhyme partnering with *overwhelm,* housing the very syllable there to headline twenty-six lines of boy-world indulgence. If this is licensed preparation for the deed of man-poetry—the doing and the contract—the wording is otherwise. Holding on, *elm* resounds in a *realm* of pastoral playmates (102) for a juvenile syllabus: *A lovely tale of human life we'll read* (110)—an end-rhyme that echoes, to deplete, the prospective *deed/decreed* (97–98), promising in the first word both an act and contract to honor. Off to nymph-wooing, the path to poetic manhood is fast fading, covered up in leaves: the coming eye-rhyme for *read* is an uptake in nymph-t*read* and a lovely garbed *head* (113–114). Byron could only mock Keats's "faun and satyr machinery."[1] Keats would risk spelling his adhesive school-boy ardors of pursuit (without even Byronic satyring), giving rein to the enchanted sounding of *entice me on, and on . . . almond blossoms and rich cinnamon . . . in the bosom* to a dead-end (both verse paragraph and existential) in *the recesses of a pearly shell,* echo-chamber for a self *upcurl'd* (117–121).

Alert reader Keats knows, however, that a poet in love with this *rest in silence* (120) is not on the same page as Hamlet-tragedy, ending life and voice together with "The rest is silence" (5.2). This is the only time Keats uses *upcurl'd* in his poetry. In a flux of dramatic thinking that will become the mastery of his later odes, he hears himself and catches his breath, summoning (again) to a new verse paragraph.

[1] Medwin, *Conversations,* 239.

O that I might know

In the recesses of a pearly shell.

And can I ever bid these joys farewell?   122
Yes, I must pass them for a nobler life,
Where I may find the agonies, the strife
Of human hearts: for lo! I see afar,
O'er sailing the blue cragginess, a car
And steeds with streamy manes—the charioteer
Looks out upon the winds with glorious fear:
And now the numerous tramplings quiver lightly
Along a huge cloud's ridge; and now with sprightly   130
Wheel downward come they into fresher skies,
Tipt round with silver from the sun's bright eyes.
Still downward with capacious whirl they glide,
And now I see them on a green-hill's side
In breezy rest among the nodding stalks.
The charioteer with wond'rous gesture talks
To the trees and mountains; and there soon appear
Shapes of delight, of mystery, and fear,
Passing along before a dusky space
Made by some mighty oaks: as they would chase   140
Some ever-fleeting music on they sweep.
Lo! how they murmur, laugh, and smile, and weep:
Some with upholden hand and mouth severe;
Some with their faces muffled to the ear
Between their arms; some, clear in youthful bloom,
Go glad and smilingly athwart the gloom;
Some looking back, and some with upward gaze;
Yes, thousands in a thousand different ways
Flit onward—now a lovely wreath of girls
Dancing their sleek hair into tangled curls;   150
And now broad wings. Most awfully intent
The driver of those steeds is forward bent,
And seems to listen: O that I might know
All that he writes with such a hurrying glow.

The visions all are fled—the car is fled
Into the light of heaven, and in their stead
A sense of real things comes doubly strong,
And, like a muddy stream, would bear along
My soul to nothingness: but I will strive
Against all doubts, and will keep alive   160
The thought of that same chariot, and the strange
Journey it went.

For all the rhetorical sobering up, the *And* at this paragraph's top lingers as a conjunction (no volta) to a line whose rhyme-word *farewell* is coupled in sound no less than site (and readerly sight) to the regressive *recesses of a pearly shell*. If the social tradition is that *farewell* is bid to one departing, Keats's words stay.[1] Even the *these* keeps the joys present. It was no stretch for critic Ernest de Selincourt to read a "love of luxuriating . . . in no way connected with his essential poetic development" (*Poems*, 407).

Keats's rhetorical reflex is the upbeat *Yes, I must* on a new line, a stance accidentally reinforced in the material book of *Poems* by its placement at the top of a new page (106). The prospect literally turns a page, on a march of seven syllables in a line of disciplined determination: *Yes, I must pass them* for a *nobler life* (123). Nymphs no more, we think, especially in the new cast: a heroic charioteer come from afar, portent of mysterious vision and high promise. These are Apollo-tropes: light, poetry, medicine, adequate to the agonies, the strife of human hearts.[2] Keats greets this spirit in real-time repetitions: *And now . . . and now . . . downward . . . Still downward . . . And now* I see. "As the *charioteer* with wond'rous gesture talks," the "Shapes" that "soon appear" (137–138) figure a proto-language for post-nymph poetics: "delight" in company with "mystery and fear"—a vision of apostrophic power.[3]

For all this, however, the vision is pretty hazy. Notwithstanding the line-end stress on *appear* and the front-stressed *Shapes* at the new line (137–138), the content is notional only. No help are the trailing clouds of nymph-land: *now a wreath of girls / Dancing their sleek hair into tangled curls* (149–150), *curls* conjuring the up*curl*'d gems of boyish recess. Alpha-Keatsian Amy Lowell could only blush at this "mere vision" of poetic "manhood": "Was ever a more unsatisfactory statement of intention put into words?" (1:222–223). Yet Keats so loved these words that he couldn't cancel them. The *now* of poetic intention, poetic possibility, and poetic confidence is all over the visionary place. The place-marker *now* lingers, atonally, in the rhyme-words at the vision's close: *O that I might know / All that he writes with such a hurrying glow* (153–154). From a sighed

"O" (not even an apostrophe) to *know* to *glow,* Keats lets this *with* clause apply to what he would know and to its object, divinely inspired writing.

Yet this is no sooner said than a new verse paragraph drops the curtain, with no back-looking rhyme, except to itself: *The visions all are fled—the car is fled* (155). This *might know* and its collapse into *nothingness* with resistance to *all doubtings* (159–160) are not yet negative capability, just a fleeting greeting of the spirit. Glory and loveliness have passed away. For now.

Five weeks after the debut of *Poems,* Keats writes to Hunt in a spirited wit of wry luxury:

> *Does Shelly go on telling strange Stories of the Death of Kings? Tell him there are strange Stories of the death of Poets – some have died before they were conceived "how do you make that out Master Vellum"*
> (10 May 1817, British Library Ashley MS 4869.f3; *K 51*)

Such a lively riff, from Richard II's self-dramatizing melancholy (*RII,* 3.2), to Shelley's blaze-out with anti-monarchal poetry (*Queen Mab*), to Sir George Vellum in Joseph Addison's comedy *The Drummer,* all woven with puns on death and conception, and gleefully ringing (Cockney) chimes on *Shelley/telling/Tell him/Vellum.* This fun with language, this haunting by vocation and the contingencies of fame, this intertextual relay: *Endymion* will field them all.

[*1817,* 104–107]

[1] Christopher Miller nicely remarks the social ritual, *Invention,* 158.

[2] Woodhouse glossed: "Personification of the Epic poet, when the enthusiasm of inspiration is upon him–" (*SpW* 154).

[3] Jonathan Culler reads the gestures of the charioteer as performing this trope ("Apostrophe" 62).

from *Endymion: A Poetic Romance*

Endymion had been in Keats's head since 1816. The first piece in *Poems* ("I stood tip-toe") was initially titled "Endymion," reflecting its summary episode on this shepherd's romance with a moon goddess, an allegory for poetic inspiration. On their nuptial night, the "languid sick" are miraculously cured (Keats's medical sublime) and all mortal tongues are "loos'd in poesy." "Was there a Poet born?" this poet asks of the lovers' issue, then leaves off: "—but now no more, / My wand'ring spirit must no further soar.—" (p. 14). Sort of: this long dash is both a temporal modesty and a typography of prospect: *more* is materially at hand in the next hundred-plus pages of *Poems,* and soon, in the very season of the volume's debut, the gestation of epic *Endymion.* Could a poet, maybe Poet, be born in this myth, and from its telling?

Endymion was materially born from Keats's compact with Shelley to finish a long poem by the end of 1817. All "great Poets," by long tradition, produce a long poem. It will be "a test a trial of my Powers of Imagination and chiefly of my invention," Keats writes in the spring to George: "I must make 4000 Lines of one bare circumstance and fill them with Poetry."[1] This qualifying exam proved far more difficult than the apothecary exam he aced in summer 1816. By 10 May, he was confessing to Haydon, *truth is I have been in such a state of Mind as to read over my Lines and hate them. I am "one that gathers Samphire dreadful trade" the Cliff of poesy Towers above me* (MsK 1.7.21)—another riff on Edgar's scene-spinning, with a fatally prone risk-taker on the "Horrible steep" cliffs below (4.6).

The "bare circumstance" that Keats defined—a mortal's dream of divine love, made real after a long trial—is a stage he sets for poetic self-realization. *Invention* was his test, but for what filling? Shelley thought *Endymion* over-invented, "treasures poured forth with indistinct profusion" (*K* 425). Bridges agrees: the effect is to "fatigue the reader, who feels like a sightseer in a gallery overcrowded with pictures" (xcv–xcvi). Critic John Jones blames the mandate of Invention itself (noting that it comes and goes with *Endymion*), just "a rambling store-house of pleasures" with a ludicrous claim to "gravity" in Keats's doting, "narcissistic exercise" of poetic "self-caressing" (127–129)—in sum, a genre-farce. "Summoning goodwill towards *Endymion* is like trying to get interested in a monstrously overblown and diluted ode," he growls (63). *Encyclopædia Britannica* had already tolled this tale, with emphatic authority: only "single lines" have charm, while the story gets "lost in ornament," and "full of . . . barbarous and dissonant diction, . . . lax and nerveless versification."[2] Keats's wordplay

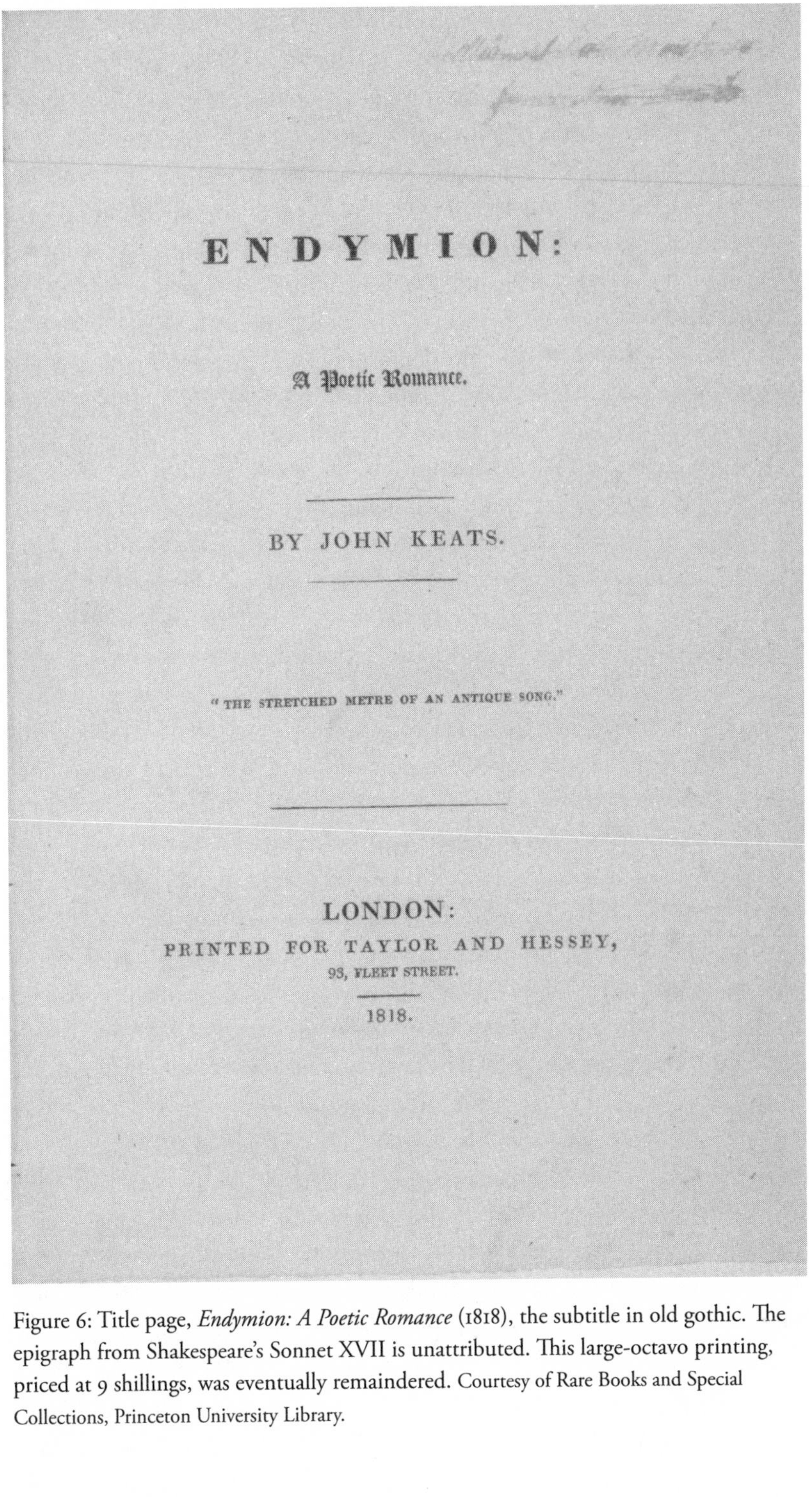

ENDYMION:

A Poetic Romance.

BY JOHN KEATS.

"THE STRETCHED METRE OF AN ANTIQUE SONG."

LONDON:
PRINTED FOR TAYLOR AND HESSEY,
93, FLEET STREET.

1818.

Figure 6: Title page, *Endymion: A Poetic Romance* (1818), the subtitle in old gothic. The epigraph from Shakespeare's Sonnet XVII is unattributed. This large-octavo printing, priced at 9 shillings, was eventually remaindered. Courtesy of Rare Books and Special Collections, Princeton University Library.

proved a peculiar trial, even for Keats-ready Hunt. He was not alone in balking at "the wilfulness of its rhymes" (*Lord Byron,* 1:418).

To re-angle these measures, however, is to find Keats proactively experimenting in a new form of "poetic capital" (Christopher Rovee's wording, 995). The *Edinburgh*'s editor and major critic Francis Jeffrey revised his opinion within two years, writing in 1820 that *Endymion* is "as full of genius as absurdity" (205). Even as Arnold described the poem's macrostructure as "utterly incoherent," he, too, felt a "breath of genius" in the particulars (1853 *Poems* xxii). If J. R. Lowell in 1876 had to invent the word *overlanguaged* to complain of a "superabundance" in Keats's way with words (322), he, too, saw the kinship of "lavish indiscrimination" and "genius": an "instinct for . . . words" in combined powers of expression and conception (325).

Over the course of Keats's composition, the master-plot of *Endymion* becomes increasingly ironic about its generating principles, but from the get-go the poetry is full of verbal flash and invention. As in *Sleep and Poetry,* the form is flexible couplets, with wild turns of conception and outrageous rhymes (*turtles–myrtles; fish–purplish; umbrageous–forest-house; camel-draughts–barbed shafts; mountain tarn–squirrel's barn*), cannily tuned ones (*breeze–teaze; muse–Morpheus; folly–melancholy; feel of bliss–drear abyss;* then *abyss–hiss*), and hilarious satires of its cherished themes. *Endymion* is epic wordplay, making words strange and strange words familiar, spun with canny forms of conception, whirlpools of imagination—all far more productive of Keats's poetic self-actualization than any quantifying of lines on "one bare circumstance."[3]

A brief tour of the golden-threaded bare plot, then. A proem declares the ideal of "Beauty," then a calendar for this flourishing, spring start to fall harvest. The fable opens in pastoral Latmos, a festival day celebrating its woodland god Pan. Shepherd-Prince Endymion could care less, sitting like a frozen man among the elders, conversing about bliss in the hereafter. His sister Peona, irked by this delinquent torpor, draws him away for interrogation. He explains a dream of mad lovemaking in the night sky with the Moon-goddess, so enchanting that the return to "human neighbourhood" seems positively envenomed (622). He would rather "sleep in love's elysium" (824), his sleepy syllables already there. Peona's effort at reproof is an epic fail.

Book II has the "Brain-sick shepherd-prince" (43), on the mere prompt of a butterfly, off to the underworld to search for his goddess. He comes across an embarrassing double, Adonis sleeping in a bower, thrall to his lover Venus, the goddess of love herself. Dismayed by his fatal wounding during a hunt, she bargained for a limited immortality, an annual return to the upper world after six month's of sleep underground. Witnessing her arrival for Adonis's parole, Endymion is struck afresh by his own lovelornness. Venus assures him of eventual bliss; he swoons to sleep, dreaming again of his Moon goddess. No Adonis, he awakes forlorn and deranged.

Book III brings him to a macabre double, superannuated Glaucus. In his youth Glaucus was smitten with elusive sea-nymph Scylla. Seeking aid from enchantress Circe, he winds up seduced by her. One morning, he discovers Circe in a dark glade, taunting a horde of groveling beasts, her former suitors transformed. She thrusts the corpse of Scylla at him with a gloat, and curses him to gothic immortality: for ever old and never to be enjoyed. A millennium on, he found a scroll washed up from a shipwreck, promising restoration to him and all the drowned lovers, when a certain youth appears to decipher it. "Thou art the man!" he now hails Endymion (256). He is indeed, and everyone, including Glaucus and Scylla, gets reunited, then heads to Neptune's palace to celebrate. Left alone, Endymion falls into a dream, and hears his moon-goddess promise, with enchanting sibilance, their *Immortal bliss* in *endless heaven* (1034–1037). But not before more trials in Book IV.

Endymion comes upon a forlorn Maid singing love-melancholy to the breezes. Down on his moon-goddess, he has a sky-fling with her. But even she vanishes! When she beams down in Latmos, Endymion decides to love the one he's with—only to hear her say, "I am forbidden" (757), and pledges herself to goddess Diana's chaste sorority. What's a brain-sick Shepherd-Prince to do? Best option: find some "mossy cave" and live out life as a hermit. In one last sigh, Endymion wishes he had "command . . . on our sad fate" (984–985). Who knew? This is all it takes for Indian Maid to morph into "Cynthia bright" (1005; right: she's the moon-goddess) and to inform Endymion that he's to be *spiritualiz'd* (1002) so they can range the forests together, evermore. "They vanish'd far away!—Peona went / Home through the gloomy wood in wonderment" (1011–1012), the frisson of wonder fizzled into a dull rhyme on a flat finale.

My slightly parodic retelling means no disrespect to Keats. Even as he knocked himself out for "4000 Lines," he was tiring of his moonstruck hero. In January 1818, he was rereading *King Lear,* a devastation of all romance imaginings. The Preface he drafted for *Endymion* in March was so self-castigating that his publisher rejected it. Although Keats dialed it back, it left enough for hostile reviewers to feast on. No less than his hero, the Preface-poet presented himself as a fevered adolescent: "the soul is in a ferment, the character undecided, the way of life uncertain" (*1818* ix). Yet in retrospect of what we know Keats will become, we can reangle this affirmatively. *Undecided, uncertain:* this is the grammar, if not yet a proactive project, of *negative capability*—that aesthetic resource formulated late in December 1817.

Keats's best description of *Endymion* presents no allegory. It was "a little Region" for "Lovers of Poetry" (rather than lovers of a moon-goddess) to "wander in where they may pick and choose, and which the images are so numerous that many are forgotten and found new in a second Reading" (*K* 61). No need for an epic master-map of wandering, headed for a shrine or a home, in this greeting of the spirit. To Oscar Wilde, Keats's verbal inspirations were as consequential as the epics of Wordsworth or Byron.

[1] Keats copied this lost letter for Bailey, 8 October 1817 (*K* 61).
[2] XIII:56 (by poet Alexander Smith).
[3] For this long-formation, see my "Accidental Anthologies of 1818."

from Book I "with full happiness . . . I / will trace the story of Endymion"

A THING of beauty is a joy for ever:
Its loveliness increases; it will never
Pass into nothingness; but still will keep
A bower quiet for us, and a sleep
Full of sweet dreams, and health, and quiet breathing.
Therefore, on every morrow, are we wreathing
A flowery band to bind us to the earth,
Spite of despondence, of the inhuman dearth
Of noble natures, of the gloomy days,
Of all the unhealthy and o'er-darkened ways   10
Made for our searching: yes, in spite of all,
Some shape of beauty moves away the pall
From our dark spirits. Such the sun, the moon,
Trees old, and young, sprouting a shady boon
For simple sheep; and such are daffodils
With the green world they live in; and clear rills
That for themselves a cooling covert make
'Gainst the hot season; the mid forest brake,
Rich with a sprinkling of fair musk-rose blooms:
And such too is the grandeur of the dooms   20
We have imagined for the mighty dead;
All lovely tales that we have heard or read:
An endless fountain of immortal drink,
Pouring unto us from the heaven's brink.

Nor do we merely feel these essences
For one short hour; no, even as the trees
That whisper round a temple become soon
Dear as the temple's self, so does the moon,
The passion poesy, glories infinite,
Haunt us till they become a cheering light
Unto our souls, and bound to us so fast,
That, whether there be shine, or gloom o'ercast,
They alway must be with us, or we die.

$\qquad$ Therefore, 'tis with full happiness that I
Will trace the story of Endymion.
The very music of the name has gone
Into my being . . .

A thing of beauty is a joy for ever is Keats's most famous opening line; most famous, period.[1] It "has passed into a proverb, and become a motto to Exhibition catalogues of Fine Art," Clarke could say in 1878 (*CR* 131). A few years on, the opening twenty-four lines got Keats into *The Golden Treasury*.[2] This was the spirit of the age, echoed from Wordsworth's Prospectus to his longest poem yet, *The Excursion* (1814): "Beauty — a living Presence of the earth" (xii). Keats would make poetry itself such an epic presence. *A thing of beauty* is not the partitive but the equative genitive, the thing that is beauty more immediately than just partaking of it. Yet for all this phrase's renown, Keats presses it into a question, not only over the course of this *Romance* but in every Romance-tuned adventure after. His gorgeous *Ode on Melancholy* declares that "Beauty . . . must die."

His first phrasing was *A thing of beauty is a constant joy* in lambent iambic pentameter.[3] He revised to get the epic claim, *for ever.* He wanted these two words, *ever* marked for uptake into its rhyme, and the antonym, *never.* These rhymes weave around the soft caesura-chords of *increases—nothingness—for us* (2–4), the syntax run all the way to 5. With some medial stops, the first two paragraphs compose only four full sentences (periods at 5, 13, 24, and 33), evoking the blank verse of *Paradise Lost:* "sense variously drawn out from one verse into another" (*KPL* 1:xxiii). To draw blank verse this way had Miltonic license. But to do this with couplets could bother even the poetic liberal Wordsworth, who muttered to a fellow poet, in the summer following the publication of *Endymion* (though not about this in particular), of his "detestation of couplets running into each other. . . . The Couplet promises rest at agreeable intervals," and a reader ought not to be "mocked and disappointed from paragraph to paragraph" (*Letters, Middle Years* 2:547). Keats interplays couplet-patterning and blank-verse effects, musically tuned with rhythm-stresses, diminuendo rhymes, slant rhymes, enjambments, and percussive line-starts: *Full, There*fore, *Spite* of, *Made, Rich, All, Pou*ring, *Some*—this last even front-rhyming *From* (12–13). There are trochee-rhymes (*ever–never*) and frills of rhyme: *daffodils—and clear rills* (15–16).

Keats splits one trochee-rhyme across a couplet: "Full of sweet dreams, and health, and quiet breathing. / Therefore, on every morrow, are we wreathing" (5–6). The new sentence breathes into the next line, *wreathing / A flowery band to bind us* (7). Evoking the root of *anthology* (a binding of literary flowers) and writing itself as *wreathing*, Keats figures poetry in poetry. This is a through-line, poetry telling a tale of itself in recurrent plays on weaving, twining, wreathing. Word-love is a plenitude, *full of* sounding *full love*—a music Keats often plays. No abstract prologue on poetry's beauty, his words are vividly real. As much as episode-plots, words have careers in *Endymion,* turning this way or that, gathering and accumulating.

A *thing* of beauty is a keyword for the poet who nuanced things real, things semireal, and nothings. *Endymion* is poetry about poetry as a real thing, a bid to be among *All lovely tales that we have heard or read* (22). But what is a "thing of beauty"? As the lower-case *beauty* may suggest, Keats does not mean a Platonic Ideal but a material reality, for anyone's greeting. It is *a joy for ever* in being ever discoverable in reading's animation. Keats's joy is always in words, but also inflected by the world in which one reads. *Spite of* frames *despondence, inhuman dearth . . . gloomy days, unhealthy and o'er-darkened ways* (these, too, are punctuated rhymes). As a flowery band binds "us" to *earth,* Keats's band of rhyme binds *earth* to *dearth,* puts it into the very lettering (8–10). The wish for *sweet dreams, and health, and quiet breathing* is dialectical with this knowing, especially with *unhealthy* (10) Tom so near—the only time Keats uses this diagnosis-pained word in his poetry.

After the remedy of beauty that *moves away the pall / From our dark spirits,* Keats tried *and before us dances / Like the glitter on the points of Arthur's Lances.* He knew better right away, crossing it out. If things of beauty *bind us to the earth* and so are fast-bound to us (31), these matter dialectically. This logic comes in three hard-stressed syllables at the end of this one-sentence stanza, also the end of the prologue: *They alway must be with us, or we die* (33). Keats wants this literary torque of the more normal word, *always,* to display the root (*all* + *way*), refresh the archaism, and gain a front-line rhyme-chime with *They.*[4] Then, in a practice he was honing, he completes the end-rhyme in a new verse paragraph, with his first self-inscription, "I." Set at the line-end (34), "I" is rhyme-bound to *die* (33), even as its new verse paragraph drives over the line to living purpose: *I / Will trace the story of Endymion* (34–35).

On this syntax Keats retraces his earlier word-work, with reperception. The first couplet of the new paragraph sounds in reverse his rhymes for the pre-view poem ("I stood tip-toe"):

> Into some won'drous region he had gone,
> To search for thee, divine Endymion!   (*1817*, p. 11)

This was a fantasy about the fable's first poet. In the new rhyme-order, Keats makes *gone* the verb for his inspiration: "Endymion. / The very music of the name has gone / Into my being" (35–37). Not just a name, word music itself will become Keats's poetic being.

[*1818*, pp. 3–5]

[1] Line numbers are *1818*'s, not *P*'s.

[2] Ed. Francis F. Browne (Thompson, 1883), 662.

[3] Henry Stephen (fellow student at Guy's), in B. W. Richardson, *The Aesculapiad* (April 1884), 148–149.

[4] This is a rare word in Keats's poetry (only three times), rare even in the nineteenth century. *OED* tags it obsolete and archaic, citing Coleridge's retro-antique *Rime of the Ancient Mariner*.

from Book I   "fellowship divine"

> Wherein lies happiness? In that which becks
> Our ready minds to fellowship divine,
> A fellowship with essence; till we shine,   780
> Full alchemiz'd, and free of space. Behold
> The clear religion of heaven! Fold
> A rose leaf round thy finger's taperness,
> And soothe thy lips: hist, when the airy stress
> Of music's kiss impregnates the free winds,
> And with a sympathetic touch unbinds
> Eolian magic from their lucid wombs:
> Then old songs waken from enclouded tombs;
> Old ditties sigh above their father's grave;
> Ghosts of melodious prophecyings rave   790

Round every spot were trod Apollo's foot;
Bronze clarions awake, and faintly bruit,
Where long ago a giant battle was;
And, from the turf, a lullaby doth pass
In every place where infant Orpheus slept.
Feel we these things?——that moment have we stept
Into a sort of oneness, and our state
Is like a floating spirit's. But there are
Richer entanglements, enthralments far
More self-destroying, leading, by degrees,   800
To the chief intensity: the crown of these
Is made of love and friendship, and sits high
Upon the forehead of humanity.
All its more ponderous and bulky worth
Is friendship, whence there ever issues forth
A steady splendour; but at the tip-top,
There hangs by unseen film, an orbed drop
Of light, and that is love: its influence,
Thrown in our eyes, genders a novel sense,
At which we start and fret; till in the end,   810
Melting into its radiance, we blend,
Mingle, and so become a part of it,—
Nor with aught else can our souls interknit
So wingedly: when we combine therewith,
Life's self is nourish'd by its proper pith,
We are nurtured like a pelican brood.
Aye, so delicious is the unsating food,
That men, who might have tower'd in the van
Of all the congregated world, to fan
And winnow from the coming step of time   820
All chaff of custom, wipe away all slime
Left by men-slugs and human serpentry,
Have been content to let occasion die,
Whilst they did sleep in love's elysium.
And, truly, I would rather be struck dumb,
Than speak against this ardent listlessness:
For I have ever thought that it might bless
The world with benefits unknowingly;
As does the nightingale, upperched high,

And cloister'd among cool and bunched leaves— 830
She sings but to her love, nor e'er conceives
How tiptoe Night holds back her dark-grey hood.
Just so may love, although 'tis understood
The mere commingling of passionate breath,
Produce more than our searching witnesseth:
What I know not: but who, of men, can tell
That flowers would bloom, or that green fruit would swell
To melting pulp, that fish would have bright mail,
The earth its dower of river, wood, and vale,
The meadows runnels, runnels pebble-stones, 840
The seed its harvest, or the lute its tones,
Tones ravishment, or ravishment its sweet,
If human souls did never kiss and greet?

Now, if this earthly love has power to make
Men's being mortal, immortal; to shake
Ambition from their memories, and brim
Their measure of content; what merest whim,
Seems all this poor endeavor after fame,
To one, who keeps within his stedfast aim
A love immortal, an immortal too. 850

I unfurl this famous passage at one stretch because its momentum is its vi-
tality, enacting what it describes with accumulating verbal drama. Keats
calls it *lifeful* (779). A self-generating alchemy from passionate love to a ra-
diant spiritual ecstasy, Endymion's defense is an inset-piece of performance
art, a *clear religion of heaven* even for those not in the congregation. On 30
January 1818, Keats wrote to Taylor (who was reading the poem and offering
advice):

These Lines, as they now stand, about Happiness have rung
in my ears like a 'chime a mending'. see here,
            Behold
        Wherein Lies happiness Pœona? fold—
This appears to me the very contrary of blessed. I hope this will
appear to you more elegible.
            Wherein lies Happiness? In that which becks
            Our ready Minds to fellowship divine;

A fellowship with essence, till we shine
Full alchymized and free of space. Behold
The clear Religion of heaven - fold &c—
You must indulge me by putting this in . . . such a preface is
necessary to the Subject. The whole thing must I think have appeared
to you, who are a consequitive Man, as a thing almost of mere words -
but I assure you that when I wrote it, it was a regular stepping of the
Imagination towards a Truth. My having written that ~~Passage~~
Argument will perhaps be of the greatest Service to me of any thing I
ever did. It set before me at once the gradations of Happiness even like
a Kind of Pleasure Thermometer - and is my first Step towards the
chief Attempt in the Drama - the playing of different Natures with Joy
and Sorrow-

      Do me this favor and believe Me, Your sincere friend

                John Keats

            (Morgan Library ALS; *L* 1:218)

This is nearly the whole letter, about theme, argument, and a care for poetry as no *thing . . . of mere words.* Words make the *Argument.*[1] Keats's first draft (ms. f31ʳ) reads:

> *Wherein lies happiness? In that which becks*
> *Our ready minds to blending pleasurable:*
> *And that delight is the most treasurable*
> *That makes the richest Alchymy.*   (*Facsimile,* p. 71)

It is winning of Keats to wince at the bubbly *pleasurable / treasurable* rhyme and go for the sturdier sonics of *divine shine,* framed by "*fellow*ship," echo-ready for "*full* alchemized." Remembering Shakespeare's fine image of the sun's "heavenly alchemy" (Sonnet XXXIII; *KS* 40), he channels this into human happiness, revising *Alchymy* to *alchemized,* an energized past participle of radiant perfection: a "poetic chemistry of the imagination," says Stuart Sperry.[2]

Poets as well as scientists delighted in scientist and poet Humphry Davy's dynamic lectures on chemistry as the new master-art of material transformation. Keats's medical wit imagines *the gradations of Happiness even like a kind of Pleasure Thermometer,* with a poet's bonus of *meter.* It is characteristic of Keats to ironize as he alchemizes. His simile, *like a 'chime a mending'* (needing a tune-up), riffs on Ulysses's report to Agamemnon about their delinquent alpha-warrior

Achilles's mimicry of his general's voice (*Troilus and Cressida* 1.3.159). Not (yet) in a mood to parody his full-felt alchemical passion, Keats knows its trial for any *consequitive* reader, an inventive portmanteau packing of "consequent" and "consecutive." He hopes his revision clarifies a regular stepping (in conception and its metering) *towards a Truth*. The preposition is deft. It is a process, not an apocalypse: a capital T hints high value; the indefinite article shades contingency. In November 1817, he and Bailey were weighing poetry against philosophy. As Keats worked on *Endymion*, he had given this theology student a *momentary start* with a brief for *the authenticity of the Imagination*. Keats reargues his case with a clear religion of energy (MsK 1.16.54; *K* 69):

> *What the imagination seizes as Beauty must be truth – whether it existed*
> *before or not – for I have the same Idea of all our Passions as of Love they are*
> *all in their sublime, creative of essential Beauty . . . I am the more zealous in*
> *this affair, because I have never yet been able to perceive how any thing can be*
> *known for truth by consequitive reasoning.*

That word again: *consequitive*, not Keats's path to a poet's "truth."

Endymion's defense gains a plural *we*, inviting not only Peona (her name drawn, uselessly, from Paeon, physician to the gods) but all readers to follow—not least along Keats's creative verbal pulsations. If you read these lines, you can hear him rapping out the degrees of rapture.[3] The pleasure thermometer rises from erotic sense to erotic essence on degrees of syncopated improvisation, repetitions of key words, unfolding sensation. The feel of a rose leaf wrapped around a finger's *taperness* (the only event of this strange word in Keats's poetry) is then imagined as a feel on the lips. The sound of *kiss,* already forming, breathes into *hist . . . airy stress* (784). This kiss impregnates the *free winds,* unbound from the sound of *unbinds* (785–786), a rhyme seen but not heard. Then *unbinds* (mimetically) blows over the line to its object, *Eolian magic from . . . lucid wombs* (787), releasing the sound of its action, *loosed,* in *lucid.* And so it goes, with the flex of *Apollo's foot* against clarions' *bruit* (791–792).

Such is the mobility of Keats's experimental "Cockney" poetics. If you can follow his steps, you have *stept/Into a sort of oneness* with him. The poetic reward—*our state/Is like a floating spirit's* (796–798)—involves a *state* that is singularly unbound to any rhyme. No wonder Keats re-marked this whole passage in his copy of *Endymion* for his re-reading pleasure, drawing two lines down the margin and underscoring (*KS* 12n3). "A melodious passage in poetry is full of pleasures both sensual and spiritual," he said on hearing Shakespeare's words in Kean's voice (*K* 74). So we can voice and hear *Endymion*'s music. "Proximity breeds immersion," advises Garrett Stewart; "Like his verse, reading operates from the inside out, silent music rippling with inference" (*CCJK* 135). Feel we these things? If so, you're on board.

Keats marks *Endymion*'s next gradation at a midline volta: *. . . floating spirit's. But there are* (798–799). The path of sound flows from the line-end *there are* to *Richer . . . far.* The full phrasing is *entanglements, enthralments far / More self-destroying* (799–800), this then swelling to *issues forth* (805), this last word beautifully poised at the line-end, to issue into the page's figural potential, with a pregnant echo of *far.* To read these lines is to experience their steppings toward the tip-top orb of *love* (808). This is not a transformed self but a self divinely unformed.[4] The first sensation is a surprise, even a distress: *we start and fret,* with *start* nicely double-played from surprise to genesis, and *fret* from consternation to potential music. Then a better *end,* the word melting its letters into its rhyme, *blend* (810–811). Here is the micro-stylistics of loss becoming a finding. It could be religion, but Keats calls it *love*—and not without a disturbance, legible and audible in his key words. The rhyme-paired *entanglements / enthralments* stretches around *tangle* and *thral* (*thrall:* slave). If a better event impends with *melting, Mingle, become a part, interknit, combine* (810–814), it is not without depletions. A pelican brood feeds from its parents' mouths (in some fables, their lifeblood) to their exhaustion and sometimes death, hence *unsating* (816–817)—the only time Keats uses this word in his poetry. He underlined King Lear's curse of his "pelican daughters" (*KL* 3.4; *RS* 50) and he derided "Pelican duns" (for payments due) as he was writing *Endymion* (10 June 1817, *L* 1:148).

Such entanglements are no one-off for Endymion. So unsating is a dream of divinity that he is sure that the world's very heroes would rather *sleep in love's Elysium:* letter-ready for *Endymion* (a near rhyme, too) on its way to the dire enough assigned rhyme, *struck dumb* (824–825). Against the plodding steps of *time* and *slime* of human endeavor (821–822) and a subhuman reverse alchemy into *serpentry,* Endymion issues a high ideal of *ardent listlessness* (826). Keats's poetry keeps us mindful that the passport to Elysium is the radical, self-destroying listlessness of death. For all the gorgeousness of this set piece, Keats's larger narrative exposes its gradations as an abstraction imposed upon frustration. A dream can be a fragile fantasy or a high idea, an escape or an ambition, a refusal of things as they are, a reach to what may be, or complete delusion.

In another worded one-off (and not in *JnD* or *OED*), Keats confects the intensified participle *upperched* (829), exploiting the bonus syllabic rung in *upper* to station a nightingale's singing blessings unknowable (blueprint for *Ode to a Nightingale*). This is Endymion's love-logic: "who, of men, can tell / That flowers would bloom, or that green fruit would swell / To melting pulp . . ." (836–838). Who can tell, even in counting? The wording of *would swell* needs this eleventh syllable, then swells over the line to its own melting. As an extravagance of "beauties," Endymion's defense is matchless, a great gradation. Each line from 840 to 843 is a love-pulsed stepping-stone: *pebble-stones* steps into a lettered rhyme with "its *tones*" and a reflexive sounding of *pebbles' tones*. On such lovely stepping-stone poetics, Keats marks his vocation, a poetical character of delight in the what words can do.

The library at Latmos seems to have held Davy's *Elements of Chemical Philosophy* (1812), with this fetching account, *Of Radiant or Ethereal Matter,* as agents in "the phænomena of chemistry" whose "principal effects" seem to work by "communicating motion to the particles of common matter, or modifying their attractions" (193). Physical chemistry is alchemized in Endymion-metaphysics, the power of love *to make / Men's being mortal, immortal* (844–845), a great oxymoron charged across the comma. Implied is any mortal's qualifications (from Latmos to London) for such fellowship. Not everyone stepped up, stept in. Byron thought the poetry ludicrously "sentimental."[5] To Keats's theology-friend Bailey, the offense was sensual: that "abominable" Shelley theme "that *Sensual Love* is the principle of *things*" (his disgusted emphasis). He hoped that it was an "unconscious" intensity of imagination that drew Keats to this "false, delusive, & dangerous conclusion" (*KC*1:35). He wasn't wrong about the perils; but to conscious Keats, these were existential (dreamland) and erotic (unmanning) conclusions, not heretical. What do you think? "With what sensation do you read?"[6]

A passage Keats marked and underscored in Shakespeare's *Troilus and Cressida* (*KS* 152) is Agamemnon's branding of the Greek soldiers' frustrated success as a test of mettle, <u>rich in Vertue, and vnmingled</u> (1.3). *Endymion* will test Endymion's mettle with a mingle of ironies in the fire of his radiance. One site—gorgeous and outrageous—is the Bower of Adonis.

[*1818*, pp. 39–43]

[1] John Jones's radar is perfect: "The word 'argument', which always sounds right when we hear it (as we often do) on Wordsworth's lips, has a sudden denaturing effect when Keats uses it (as he never does in his verse)" in this letter (89).

[2] *Keats the Poet* 49; his pioneering discussion of Keats and chemistry, 36–42. Keats took two courses in chemistry at Guy's Hospital.

[3] For this great metaphor, I owe Stuart Mitchener ("Rackett Roars Out of the Garage Into the Studio," *Town Topics*, April 12, Princeton, NJ, 2006).

[4] Keats ventures a "cockney" flourish at the apex of his "Argument." De Selincourt identifies *tip-top* as a "colloquial" usage, with no precedent in poetry (*Poems*, 623); not even in *JnD*, it is unique here in Keats's poetry.

[5] Medwin, *Conversations*, 239.

[6] To George and Georgiana; *L* 2:18.

from Book II   the Bower of Adonis

> For as the sunset peeps into a wood
> So saw he panting light, and towards it went
> Through winding alleys; and lo, wonderment!
> Upon soft verdure saw, one here, one there,
> Cupids a slumbering on their pinions fair.
>
> After a thousand mazes overgone,
> At last, with sudden step, he came upon
> A chamber, myrtle wall'd, embowered high,   390
> Full of light, incense, tender minstrelsy,
> And more of beautiful and strange beside:
> For on a silken couch of rosy pride,
> In midst of all, there lay a sleeping youth
> Of fondest beauty; fonder, in fair sooth,
> Than sighs could fathom, or contentment reach:
> And coverlids gold-tinted like the peach,
> Or ripe October's faded marigolds,
> Fell sleek about him in a thousand folds—
> Not hiding up an Apollonian curve   400
> Of neck and shoulder, nor the tenting swerve
> Of knee from knee, nor ankles pointing light;
> But rather, giving them to the filled sight
> Officiously. Sideway his face repos'd
> On one white arm, and tenderly unclos'd,
> By tenderest pressure, a faint damask mouth
> To slumbery pout; just as the morning south
> Disparts a dew-lipp'd rose. Above his head,
> Four lily stalks did their white honours wed
> To make a coronal; and round him grew   410

All tendrils green, of every bloom and hue,
Together intertwin'd and trammel'd fresh:
The vine of glossy sprout; the ivy mesh,
Shading its Ethiop berries; and woodbine,
Of velvet leaves and bugle-blooms divine;
Convolvulus in streaked vases flush;
The creeper, mellowing for an autumn blush;
And virgin's bower, trailing airily;
With others of the sisterhood. Hard by,
Stood serene Cupids watching silently.   420
One, kneeling to a lyre, touch'd the strings,
Muffling to death the pathos with his wings;
And, ever and anon, uprose to look
At the youth's slumber; while another took
A willow-bough, distilling odorous dew,
And shook it on his hair; another flew
In through the woven roof, and fluttering-wise
Rain'd violets upon his sleeping eyes.

　　At these enchantments, and yet many more,
The breathless Latmian wonder'd o'er and o'er;   430
Until, impatient in embarrassment,
He forthright pass'd

Endymion comes upon this bower in a pace of palpable erotics. Only Keats
could image a flicker as *panting,* then swell *went* into a rhymed *wonderment*
that brings the *w* along (384–385). The sightline (for Endymion and us) is an
erotic unveiling: sleepy cupids, *one here, one there,* teasingly toward sleeping
Adonis, the chief intensity. Keats moves the poetry, line by line, through a suc-
cession of frames. A rim of thick myrtle branches (379) opens onto those cu-
pids (386–387), then a myrtle-wall'd chamber (390), then a silken couch, a coverlid,
a lightly open mouth, then a zoom-out to a coronal of lilies, a wreath of green
tendrils (*tender* in collusion), vines, the mesh, the rain of flowers, a circle of
cupids (393–428). Rhymes sighing in repetitions and the sonic currents of
lines 404–408—*face reposed–tenderly unclos'd–tenderest pressure–faint damask
mouth–slumbery pout*—invite readers to die a death of luxury. Max Reinhart
could not have done better with the luxe legato cinematography of *A Mid-
summer Night's Dream* (1935).

As we get to that *vine of glossy sprout* (413), we hear a delayed rhyme for the dreamer's *slumbery pout* (407), one of those *havens of intenseness* that Keats would describe, with lilting hendiadys, a few months on to Haydon: a *trembling delicate and snail-horn perception of Beauty* (8 April 1818; MsK 1.26.94). More than hendiadys, Keats's syntax gives *delicate* nominative substance. For *The creeper, mellowing for an autumn blush; / And virgin's bower, trailing airily* (417–418), it scarcely takes a greeting of the spirit to sense a figure for lovers meeting. Keats took care with the delicacy. He first wrote a rime-riche, *The creeper, blushing deep at Autumn's blush* (*P* 145n), then let the double-take, along with the echoing *deep,* go, and dialed back to one blush. Line by line, element by element, the poetry draws us in to this infant chamber, each luxury *intertwin'd and trammel'd: the ivy mesh, the creeper,* cupid-wings *Muffling to death* the pathos of music. Keats palpates poetry's pleasure thermometer into a physiology of language, a pulse and flow, a momentum of breathings and breathless suspensions, word-wit and music.

At the core slumbers an indolent, infant man: too luxurious by half, sated, gratified, adorned, perfected, protected. If Keats's blazon of *filled sight* (403) was low-hanging fruit for sniping reviews, it put even his friends to the test, and has sent recent criticism into toils of theory to queer it up as an aggressive superficiality, a deliberate outrage. So richly entangled, how can we tell satire from saturation, stylizing from style? The limbs "have a luxurious softness and delicacy, which appears conscious of the pleasure of the beholder," wrote Hazlitt about Italian Renaissance painter Titian's "female figures" (Gusto 332). Keats's Adonis (not yet named) is a virtual "female figure" this way, zoned out, but with none of the coy vamping of Hazlitt's sceptic imagination. Keats's blazon is a *woven* thing of beauty (427), a textual pun (*textus: woven*) which he revised from a mere *branched* (*P* 145n). Endymion's scan of Adonis doubles into our reading of Keats's words. With our gaze paused at *coverlids gold-tinted like the peach, / Or ripe October's faded marigolds* (397–398), we might think that *coverlids* (an odd word, not in *JnD*) are eyelids, smooth reflectors of the luminous couch-silk. They're actually sheets (Keats first wrote *draperies; P* 144n), teasing at the body underneath.[1]

It is a signature Keats-move, to be perfected in Madeline's *warmed jewels* (*Eve of St. Agnes*) and already tested in *1817* as a pleasure-plucking poet flaunts this titillation:

> sweet buds which with a modest pride
> Pull droopingly, in slanting curve aside,
> Their scantly leaved, and finely tapering stems   (p. 1)

Peer we must. "In Keats's erotic poetry," remarks Christopher Ricks, "the sense not just that something is happening but that something is being watched is an important giver of depth" (*Embarrassment* 9). As with Adonis, depth yields a recession of surfaces, the stems similized to "starry diadems," then this vehicle turned upward to the sky. Tricky master of seductive ceremonies: this, too, is a Keatsian Poetical character.

Mute, opaque, self-enclosed, unconscious, Adonis cannot but solicit prurient fascination. From the tenting coverlet, Keats brings the curve of his neck and shoulder swelling into reality; then with suspense at the line-end, *the tenting swerve / Of knee from knee* and those delicate ankles meet *the filled sight / Officiously* (401–404). As with the coverlids, the surface is so readable that the reveal is a joking redundancy: *Lo! this is he, / That same Adonis* (479–480). Adonis the Oblivious in the *still region of all his winter-sleep* (481) is another love-wrapped youth, his curator the very goddess of love in that clear religion of heaven. The moral (a virtuous philosophy even) given by such a spectacle is impossible to know, in no small part because of Keats's overproduced signs.

While offering no decoding-ring, the legible grammar is Spenser's Bower of Adonis:

> There wont fair *Venus* often to enjoy
> Her dear *Adonis'* joyous company,
> And reap sweet Pleasure of the wanton Boy;
> There yet some say in secret he doth lie,
> Lapped in Flowers and precious Spicery,
> By her hid from the World, and from the Skill
> Of *Stygian* Gods, which do her Love envy:
> But she her self, when ever that she will,
> Possesseth him, and of his Sweetness takes her Fill.   (*FQ* III.6.XLVI)

Such a Boy is there for Venus's delectation, *sweet Pleasure* to the very essence, *Sweetness*. If the near rhyming of *enjoy-company-Boy-lie-Spicery* is a shorthand menu for her, it is a dicey scrim for any modern poet auditioning for professional manhood. Keats marked this stanza, then distilled it into *Endymion's* Adonis, putting us in Venus's place.[2] The poetry feels like ekphrasis, but it isn't: it's so palpably immediate that any recessive reference was off the table long ago. To Karen Swann, the difficulty is distinguishing "between an embarrassingly sentimental effect and demystifying allegorical one."[3] I'll say that such effect *is* the allegory, an allegory not in, but of, words as poetic event. This is becoming Keats's poetic pulse.

Poor Bailey could still be intoxicated, thirty years on (in that *Church of England Review,* no less), by Keats's skill "in building up scenes of magic, through which the wanderer travels in amazement" (158), or evidently, any reader seduced away from moral pressure. "The whole poem abounds in pictures like these," he sighed, quite in love with the porn of Cynthia and Endymion as *They trembled to each other* (2.718), thoroughly enchanted by "the power with which Keats paints pictures on the canvass of the mind with nought but empty words" (159), or fills the mind with words in *empty* readiness for our filling in, filling out. We feel such invitation in the visual scan of this *sleeping youth / Of fondest beauty* (394–395), the suspended animation in a bliss-reposed face, the one white arm, the soft syntactic suspense of *tenderly unclos'd, / By tenderest pressure* (405–406): pressure on what? (we may wonder). In a heartbeat, in a line-beat, we follow the telescoped intimacy to *a faint damask mouth* to *slumbery pout*—a lover's mouth, likened to the way a kiss of the warm *south* in the morning *Disparts a dew-lipp'd rose* (406–408). Tenor and vehicle are one: dewy rose-petals look like, sound like, *dual lips,* and lips look like rose-petals. The *just as* comparison brings further fusion, as the simile summons a simultaneity: the lips dispart in the same moment that a soft wind disparts a rose's petals. *Dispart* usually means "rive" (*JnD*); for Keats's sleeper, it reports *quiet breathing,* on view for weird word-wonder. Sound-puffed by *mouth* and *south* (406–407), *pout* is Keats's word-risk, worth taking. Were Adonis conscious, it would be a sexy, sensual moue, then as now.[4] Unconscious, it is artless infant satiety. While Hazlitt reviled the Tory-bashing of Keats's diction, he choked on *slumbery pout* as a slut-worthy "vile phrase" (riffing Polonius on Hamlet's bad poetry).[5] Feel we these things? And if so, how: in astonishment? with queasy unease?

It's not too long before Keats has Adonis's internal witness, Endymion himself, at first *breathless* at these *enchantments,* wax *impatient in embarrassment,* a triple rhyme chord in ten syllables, woven around the tripping triplet, *wonder'd o'er and o'er* (429–431). It is the first time Keats puts *impatient* in his poetry (only once again, later in Book II). Here, too (surprisingly), is the sole site of the word *embarrassment* in his poetry. Embarrassment is more than wincing discomfort; the eighteenth-century sense is "perplexity," literally entanglement.[6] This recalls the love-thermometer's *richer entanglements* of self-loss (1.799–800), now in synonymy with embarrassment to the beholder. Keats uses *entangle* in his poetry as sparingly as he does *embarrass.* The next time is for the *Dolt* Lycius in *Lamia* (so Keats calls him; *L* 2:158), as he would *entangle, trammel up, and snare* elusive Lamia's soul (2.52). As if! No lad in Keats's poetry ever does this.

In reperception, Keats spoke of a social embarrassment, just as *Endymion* was published. He had neglected his ailing friend Reynolds: "the most unhappy hours in our lives are those in which we recollect times past to our own blushing—if we are immortal that must be the Hell" (April 1818, *L* 1:273). This is a human (and humane) confession. "I see you well," Keats wrote in the sentence just prior, a relief to mitigate its coming rhyme with his self-seeing *Hell*. Milton's Satan, forever in the Hell of his mind, never blushes. *Hours, times:* Keats knows that the twinge of embarrassment is a halt, not a hard reform. And so a Cupid can baffle Endymion with new delicacies, which Keats's poetry produces, unembarrassed.

> Here is wine,
> Alive with sparkles—never, I aver,
> Since Ariadne was a vintager,
> So cool a purple: taste these juicy pears,
>
> . . . here is cream,
> Deepening to richness from a snowy gleam;
> Sweeter than that nurse Amalthea skimm'd
> For the boy Jupiter: and here, undimm'd
> By any touch, a bunch of blooming plums
> Ready to melt between an infant's gums:
> And here is manna pick'd from Syrian trees,
> In starlight, by the three Hesperides.
> Feast on . . .   (442–455)

If Pope insisted "the sound must seem an echo of the sense" (*Essay on Criticism*), Keats makes sound the sense, right *here* on the page: *never, I aver; plums/Ready* evoke *reddy*; *wine* is *Alive*; *cream* has a *gleam*; *undimm'd* blooms into *blooming plums* ready for *gums*. Even the adjective *blooming* feels verby with surreal agency. High stakes. Victorian Alexander Smith, who otherwise celebrated Keats, was revolted by this "babyish effeminacy" (56). Yet even as G. B. Shaw deemed these Keats's "worst lines," he liked the gambit: "nothing minor about them . . . they are brazenly infamous" (173). *Feast on* (enjoy, and enjoy again) is our invitation to the poetry no less than a banquet for Endymion. If you can't plot epic quest with such infamies, you sure can serve up a brief feast. Keats puts the lovers on the same page. He'll reprise this pleasure when Porphyro sets the love-feast in *The Eve of St. Agnes*. Even more infamous than the hospitable cupidity to Endymion are the "slippery blisses" confected by his "power to dream deliciously" of his lover, as he wraps his arms around her "naked waist" (715).

[*1818*, pp. 71–73]

[1] The only other time Keats uses the word is a "cold coverlid" of clouds over Ailsa Rock.

[2] Greg Kucich notes the markup (*KSR* 3, 12).

[3] "Tracing Keats," 43. This essay and the one in *CCJK* are wonderful critical meditations.

[4] *OED* n2.1, among the citations for *pout* is one from 1700, on the female arts of "the Winning Air, the Bewitching Glance, the Amorous Smirk, and the Sullen Pout." No better discussion of Keats's swerve-effect than Ricks, *Embarrassment*, 12–13.

[5] *London Magazine* (December 1820), 686n.

[6] A metaphor from the original sense of leashing, *embarrass: em + baraço* (restraining cord).

from Book II   "slippery blisses"

                              there ran
Two bubbling springs of talk from their sweet lips.   740
"O known Unknown! from whom my being sips
Such darling essence, wherefore may I not
Be ever in these arms? in this sweet spot
Pillow my chin for ever? ever press
These toying hands and kiss their smooth excess?
Why not for ever and for ever feel
That breath about my eyes?

                              ⁓ ⁓

Let me entwine thee surer, surer—now
How can we part? Elysium! who art thou?
Who, that thou canst not be for ever here,
Or lift me with thee to some starry sphere?
Enchantress! Tell me by this soft embrace,
By the most soft completion of thy face,
Those lips, O slippery blisses, twinkling eyes,   760
And by these tenderest, milky sovereignties—
These tenderest, and by the nectar-wine,
The passion" ———

The whisperings of *darling essence, ever press, smooth excess,* and *Enchantress* are a fevered pleasure thermometer, sheer addiction on course to the fatal bargain of sonorous *Elysium* (755). From *sweet lips* to full *sips* (740–741) to the slush of *Those lips, O slippery blisses* (760)—"*Those lips*" slipping into *O slip*—Keats's very words are lovemaking (Ricks 104–106). The *British Critic* could only sputter (in one of the first notices) its contempt of this "gross slang of voluptuousness . . . not all the flimsy veil of words in which he would involve immoral images, can atone for their impurity" and "vicious refinement" (652). It is not even that words veil flimsily; these words are the erotic film (a voluptuousness that the *Critic's* censure managed to advertise). This is about as voluptuous as Keats's wordings get, a lexical pornography on the way to the opening of Nabokov's *Lolita.*

Infancy, ecstasy, and sexuality in one infusion: "O he had swoon'd / Drunken from pleasure's nipple" (871–872). Keats swoons *swoon'd* right into the phonics of *Drunken. Drunken* is doubled, as a participle appositive to swooned, and as the adjective to name the effect. So rapt (and wrapped) is Keats's poetry in verbal sensation that the hero recedes into a mere vehicle for a poetics of intoxication. *JnD* gives both "drank" and "drunk" as past tenses of "drink," but only *drunken* (with a resounded *drunk in*) will satisfy Keats, and cue the brutal parody awaiting in Circe's bower.

[*1818*, 88–89]

from Book III   Circe and Glaucus

"Who could resist? Who in this universe?
She did so breathe ambrosia; so immerse
My fine existence in a golden clime.
She took me like a child of suckling time,
And cradled me in roses. Thus condemn'd,
The current of my former life was stemm'd,   460
And to this arbitrary queen of sense
I bow'd a tranced vassal: nor would thence
Have mov'd, even though Amphiron's harp had woo'd
Me back to Scylla o'er the billows rude.
For as Apollo each eve doth devise
A new appareling for western skies;
So every eve, nay every spendthrift hour
Shed balmy consciousness within that bower.
And I was free of haunts umbrageous;

Could wander in the mazy forest-house 470
Of squirrels, foxes shy, and antler'd deer,
And birds from coverts innermost and drear
Warbling for very joy mellifluous sorrow—
To me new born delights!
                                    Now let me borrow,
For moments few, a temperament as stern
As Pluto's sceptre, that my words not burn
These uttering lips, while I in calm speech tell
How specious heaven was changed to real hell.

One morn she left me sleeping: half awake 480
I sought for her smooth arms and lips, to slake
My greedy thirst with nectarous camel-draughts;
But she was gone. Whereat the barbed shafts
Of disappointment stuck in me so sore,
That out I ran and search'd the forest o'er.
Wandering about in pine and cedar gloom
Damp awe assail'd me; for there 'gan to boom
A sound of moan, an agony of sound,
Sepulchral from the distance all around.
Then came a conquering earth-thunder, and rumbled 490
That fierce complain to silence: while I stumbled
Down a precipitous path, as if impell'd.
I came to a dark valley.—Groanings swell'd
Poisonous about my ears, and louder grew,
The nearer I approach'd a flame's gaunt blue,
That glar'd before me through a thorny brake.
This fire, like the eye of gordian snake,
Bewitch'd me towards; and I soon was near
A sight too fearful for the feel of fear:
In thicket hid I curs'd the haggard scene— 500
The banquet of my arms, my arbour queen,
Seated upon an uptorn forest root;
And all around her shapes, wizard and brute,
Laughing, and wailing, groveling, serpenting,
Shewing tooth, tusk, and venom-bag, and sting!
O such deformities! Old Charon's self,
Should he give up awhile his penny pelf,

And take a dream 'mong rushes Stygian,
It could not be so phantasied. Fierce, wan,
And tyrannizing was the lady's look,   510
As over them a gnarled staff she shook.
Oft-times upon the sudden she laugh'd out,
And from a basket emptied to the rout
Clusters of grapes, the which they raven'd quick
And roar'd for more; with many a hungry lick
About their shaggy jaws."

From the disturbing mirror of she-enthralled, paradise-infantilized Adonis,
Endymion finds a burlesque pathos in passion-duped, lovelorn, witch-torn
Glaucus. By now, it is a comic redundancy for Glaucus to tell Endymion they
are "twin brothers in . . . destiny" (3.717). His own story, from long ago, has
two chapters: a youthful passion for sea-nymph Scylla, then his snaring by en-
chantress Circe's "arbitrary" arts of sensual love (461)—the pleasure thermom-
eter's intensities splayed into opposite genres. Such splitting, Keats knows from
The Fairy-Queen, is typical "romance" narratology, the negative version as foil
to, and credit for, the positive form. Glaucus's story is not so much this counter-
point as a parody with common signatures.

The meaning of *arbitrary* (unique here in Keats's poetry) in this satire is not
"random" but "despotic," absolute power. The grammar of the Bower of Adonis
(1000 lines ago) returns with a Circean warp in the weave of enthrallment:

With tears, and smiles, and honey-words she wove
A net whose thraldom was more bliss than all
The range of flower'd Elysium . . .   (428–430)

The attribute *flower'd* recalls both the anthology woven for *Endymion* itself (1.7)
and the hero's ode to *love's elysium* (1.824). What fuels Circe's arts of love is a
thra*l*dom of words, surpassing *all* other bliss. Keats was enthralled by Enobar-
bus's notoriously lush report of Cleopatra's barging, with full captivating flair,
into Antony's court (*A&C,* 2.2), underlining away (*DW* 6:127):

Purple the sails, and so perfum'd that
The winds were love-sick with them: the oars were silver;
Which to the tune of flutes kept stroke, and made
The water, which they beat, to follow faster,
As amorous of their strokes.

On alliteration and assonance, accelerating repetitions, and hypermetrics, Shakespeare pulses out a phonic erotics. Following ever faster, Keats double-underlines with a "double relish" of gusto.

He brings these sound-effects into Glaucus's account of Circe's seductive voice:

> she link'd
> Her charming syllables, till indistinct
> Their music came to my o'er-sweeten'd soul.   (3.445–447)

A treacherous meta-rhyme if ever there was one is *link'd / indistinct.* The question Glaucus imagines for his auditor, *How then, was Scylla quite forgot?* (454), answers in its very words, *Scylla* charmed away by Circe's *syll*ables. Glaucus's Circe-sweetening comes with *nectarous camel-draughts* (482). *OED* gives *Paradise Lost* the nod on *nectarous:* the *nectarous draughts* Eve prepares for Adam from Eden's bounty (5.306); Keats underlined it (*KPL* I:125). Circe seems as literate in Eve's confection as she is in *Endymion Book I*, which Keats rewrites here in a wryer tone. There was already some burlesque in Endymion's musing on his *greedy* love-madness, drawing *draughts of life from the gold fount* (1.656–660). Glaucus brings it home. His *camel* thirst is halfway to Circean metamorphosis. For this farce, Keats infuses another joke: Glaucus's stumble *about in pine* (486) is Cockney-sounded *pain.* This is a frill on Ovid's primer of transformation, *Metamorphoses.* In a hart-beat, Glaucus produces himself as a poor beast stuck with barbed shafts—such a love-poetry cliché that it can be only parodic, for Glaucus in retrospect and for any well-versed reader.

Keats writes his satire into a surreal soundscape, a grating rather than a greeting of the spirit. The agony of *sound . . . all around* has us hearing in *ear*th-*thunder* the rumble of an *under*world of abjection (488–490). *Complain* (491) is a substantive, no sooner fiercely produced than silenced. The *sound of moan* (488) swells to *Groanings* (493). At the epicenter is a fire *like the eye of gordian snake* (497). No coincidence that bright *gordian'd* is a Keats-coined fancy for Cynthia's braided locks (1.614). *Gordian* will return to shape Lamia, and before then, Keats's confession to Bailey of his "Gordian complication" of feelings about women (18 July 1818; *K* 191–192). Here the trope crazily metamorphoses into Circe's enthralling eye, in a swirl of words that swell about the *ears* in syllables of shuddering repetition at the bourn of conception: "too *fearful for* the *feel of fear*" (499). This "feel of fear" is a "feel of <u>ear</u>" in the sublime of *fearful.* Quite an earful.

All this replays Endymion's ode to love in Book I in a mordant key. Recall those *men-slugs and human serpentry* in his contempt of those of no heroic capacity (1.822). One slug of Circe's love and men become beasts. Consider the *wizard* (503). The noun denotes a professional conjurer, presumably Circe's match, but now only the shape of the word. In accord, Keats's syntax also situates *wizard* as an adjective for the shapes of Circe's enchantments; as thin, it can no longer denote command (*OED, adj* 1) but instead its antonym, *bewitched* (*adj* 2). This is Keats's word-wizardry, a lexical metamorphosis on the way to *wizened.* The templates are transparently Ovidian and, deeper back, Circean (*Odyssey* Book 10), both progenitrices of Acrasia's Bower of Blisse in *The Fairy-Queen* (II.12). All tell stories of men passioned into beasts—and not alpha-animals either, just abject supplicants to scornful enchantresses, magnets for comic turns by Spenser and Keats. When Guyon and the Palmer work some magic to turn Acrasia's herd back into men, one named "Grille protests," rather fancying his hoghood. The Palmer sighs, "Let *Grill* be *Grill,* and have his hoggish Mind"—paring the Frenchy "e" from his name (Grille) to get to the Greek etymology of *grill* (pig) for this happiness. Keats renders the abjection. An elephant-man, agonized by his degradation, pleads politely to Circe (in terms so courtly that Spenserian moralizers might approve) to "be deliver'd from this cumbrous flesh,/From this gross detestable, filthy mesh" (554–555), the sorry body given in a synonym for the nets of passion that bought him to this pass.

Glaucus calls the collective a *serpenting* herd (504), a verb-form not in *JnD,* and here, Keats's sole, extraordinary use in his poetry (not even *Lamia* summons it). More than the metaphor that Endymion's scorn of *human serpentry* was (1.822), this *serpenting* is a verbal metamorphosis for "How specious heaven was changed to real hell" (479). Keats writes the *deformities* into a clamor of *Laughing, and wailing, groveling, serpenting,/Shewing tooth, tusk, and venom-bag, and sting!* (504–505), a crescendo sounded in the casing letters of "*s*(erpen)*ting.*" From this brilliant *tyrannizing* in song and sense, he spells the transformations of *they raven'd quick/And roar'd for more* (514–515). The line cut *quick/And* sounds *quicken'd,* on the way to sounding *roar'd for more* as its own onomatopoeia, as *raven* morphs from bird to verb.

While the etymologies of *raven*-verb and *raven*-bird are distinct, Keats convincingly dovetails them. "It is astonishing how they raven down scenery like children do sweetmeats," he satirizes tourists with the double edge in their "hunting after the picturesque" (15 July 1819, *L* 2:130). In his mind's eye is Claudio, death-sentenced for lechery (*Measure for Measure* I.3), lamenting how, in lines that Keats underlined (*DW* I:9; *RS* 106):

<u>our natures do pursue</u>
<u>(Like rats that ravin down their proper bane,)</u>
<u>A thirsty evil; and when we drink, we die.</u>

Men become rats, and rats get verbed into ravin. In a whirl of transformative effects, Milton picked up the phrase *ravin down* (as Keats knew) for the "inchanting ravishment" of the Lady's song in *Comus:* "At every fall smoothing the Raven doune / Of darkness till it smil'd" (251–252). Enchanter Comus compares it to the singing (no less) of his mother Circe, with power over Glaucus's nymph of desire: "*Scylla* wept" (257).

The month after Keats fair-copied Book III, he resounded verb-*raven* in a dark mood of his own mind, imaging a "gentle Robin, like a pard or ounce, / Ravening a worm" (*Dear Reynolds*). Across the paired feline similes, *Robin* metamorphoses, as sound and bird, to *raven*. This line and Circe's den are unique sites of the verb *raven* in Keats's poetry. Circe is his most caustic figure of unmanning female treachery, crueler than her sorority sisters, La belle dame sans merci and Lamia, who bear a mysterious pathos. When Glaucus beholds Scylla murdered, Keats wields his syllable-poetics for the vengeance: *'twas Scylla! Cursed, cursed Circe!* (622)—a double *curse* in the chord from *Scylla* to *Circe.*

> Love's madness he had known:
> Often with more than tortured lion's groan
> Moanings had burst from him.

This moaning might have issued from one of Circe's dupes. But it's Endymion, back in Book II (863–865), seduced, abandoned—and not done, by a long shot.

[*1818*, pp. 128–130]

from Book IV   "this Cave of Quietude"

>   There lies a den,
> Beyond the seeming confines of the space
> Made for the soul to wander in and trace
> Its own existence, of remotest glooms.
> Dark regions are around it, where the tombs
> Of buried griefs the spirit sees, but scarce
> One hour doth linger weeping, for the pierce
> Of new-born woe it feels more inly smart:
> And in these regions many a venom'd dart

520

At random flies; they are the proper home
Of every ill: the man is yet to come
Who hath not journeyed in this native hell.
But few have ever felt how calm and well
Sleep may be had in that deep den of all.
There anguish does not sting; nor pleasure pall:
Woe-hurricanes beat ever at the gate,   530
Yet all is still within and desolate.
Beset with plainful gusts, within ye hear
No sound so loud as when on curtain'd bier
The death-watch tick is stifled. Enter none
Who strive therefore: on the sudden it is won.
Just when the sufferer begins to burn,
Then it is free to him; and from an urn,
Still fed by melting ice, he takes a draught—
Young Semele such richness never quaft
In her maternal longing! Happy gloom!   540
Dark Paradise! where pale becomes the bloom
Of health by due; where silence dreariest
Is most articulate; where hopes infest;
Where those eyes are the brightest far that keep
Their lids shut longest in a dreamless sleep.
O happy spirit-home! O wondrous soul!
Pregnant with such a den to save the whole
In thine own depth. Hail, gentle Carian!
For, never since thy griefs and woes began,
Hast thou felt so content: a grievous feud   550
Hath let thee to this Cave of Quietude.
Aye, his lull'd soul was there, although upborne
With dangerous speed: and so he did not mourn
Because he knew not whither he was going.
So happy was he, not the aerial blowing
Of trumpets at clear parley from the east
Could rouse from that fine relish, that high feast.

In *The Fairy-Queen,* Spenser writes of "a Cave ywrought by wondrous Art, /
Deep, dark, uneasy, doleful, comfortless" (I.5.XXXVI). This drew Keats's
underlining (I:83), not least because this is where Aesculapius, Apollo's son and

renowned medical healer, fails. Keats wonders about the wondrous arts of dark places, with no penalty of pain. The Cave of Quietude is his first sustained place-poetics as a figure for the mind. It comes into *Endymion* as a virtual inset Ode to Apathy. It seems "the real stuff of experience," standing out "with a strange vividness from its vague and somewhat fantastic surroundings" (writes de Selincourt, *Poems* 449). *There lies* is a present-tense field report from Keatsian psyche, and a psyche-scene for a reader to enter on his words.

This Cave is the last bower and darkest art in *Endymion,* a mind's own hell (*hell:* slang for *dungeon*). Waking in the first Hell, Satan declares,

> The mind is its own place, and in it self
> Can make a Heav'n of Hell, a Hell of Heav'n. (*PL* 1.254–255)

Milton's devastating irony is the boaster's deafness to the sound of *its hell* in "*it self*" (and "in it"). The zinger is that the Heavenizing of Hell harbors a chiasmus: every heavenly delight will be hellified by Satan's mind, in his mind. So audible is Keats's *a den* as a phonic phantom of long-lost *Eden,* that the present tense and the ambiguously locative, the self-echoing *a den, / Beyond* (515–516), flow into a poem-scape of spirit-seeing. *Dark . . . are around* (519) feeds its gloom of sound and sense into *inly smart* and *venom'd dart* (522–523). *Venom'd art* in spades! The hellifying repeats in the spell of intimate, unschemed sounds: *every ill / native hell* (525–526). The intensity of working out conceits involves exquisite verbal density, in sound, sense, and enigmatic formations.

The volta at *But* (527) pivots to an unexpected claim. This is no Miltonic Hell, but native hell, with dividends: *how calm and well / Sleep may be had* (527–528). Keats images an existential reprieve, undertoning *commonweal,* echoing to supersede *hell* into a new chord of sound and sense: *well, all, pall, all it still,* and then an arresting *plainful* (528–532). This is a *still* that is silent, unmoving, and durable. On this new path of hell-softened sound, *deep den of all* flirts in sound with, only to refuse, a sounding of *fall.* Who but Keats could summon, for this occasion only, the archaic *plainful,* refreshing it for a darkly brilliant blend of *painful* with poetry's *plaint?* It is a great word, sadly emended (without comment) by many editors to *painful,* at the expense of Keats's pathological muse.[1]

After the sensual riot in Circe's bower, this Cave-bower quiets all sensation, all desire, in a cool modernism that, were it prose rendered 150 years on, could have been Samuel Beckett's. Such a refuge can be conceived only by a mind that knows its opposite. It takes anguish to imagine an anguish that does not sting; it takes an agony of pall to imagine pleasures that do not go this way; it takes a sufferer's *burn* (536) to imagine its relief of melting ice from an *urn.* It is knowing the assault of woe at hurricane-strength to be half in love with a stillness in which *desolate* is positive comfort; *No sound so loud* (533) knows the loud sounds. This is a complexly unquiet quietude. Keats's "I stood tip-toe" had briefly figured this paradox, without pain, as "noiseless noise . . . / Born of the very sigh that silence heaves" (11–12), a counter-phonics in *noiseless noise* and *sigh . . . silence.* The poet of *Endymion* ventures the more intensely informed oxymorons *Happy gloom! / Dark Paradise!* (540–541), leading to and hosting another kind of metamorphosis, not Circean hot but self-willed cool, *where pale becomes the bloom / Of health,* where *silence dreariest* gets a sounded poetics (540–543), where the guiding, greeted spirit of a *wondrous soul* can sound, briefly, what a love-epic wants: *wondrous whole* (546).

In an old translingual riff, *Cave* is Latin for "beware," word-ready for the perils usually lurking in such recesses, not least in *The Fairy-Queen. Enter none* (534) seems just such a signpost—and such a twist on Dante's doorway to Hell: "All hope abandon, ye who enter here" (Canto III.9; Carey's *Hell,* p. 21). Keats turns the entrance bar into a qualified pass for admission: you can't get what you want if you pursue what you want, *strive* for it. *On the sudden it is won* (535) is the tempo of victory. Keats has in mind, for reversal, the most dramatic pivot in *Paradise Lost,* when, in an irreparable mortal differentiation, Adam beholds Eve, apple in hand,

> how on a sudden lost,
> Defaced, deflower'd, and now to death devote! (9.900–901)

Milton hits all the sounds of death across these lines, every *de-* keynoted by the sud*den* sensation. Keats underlined the verse just above these lines (890–895): Adam, astonished, vein-chilled and pale, all but dead (*KPL* II:100). Recasting Adam's sudden loss for Endymion's sudden gain, Keats risks any logic for living in the world.

His palimpsest holds Spenser's Cave of Despair (*Fairy-Queen* I.9), site of moral trial *in extremis,* hell on earth, life without hope. Keats underlined the grave-lull of <u>lays the soul to sleep in quiet</u> (XL, p. 138). Despair coos a poetry of seduction (XLIV; I:139):

> Then do no further go, no further stray,
> But here lie down, and to thy Rest betake,
> Th' ill to prevent, that Life ensuen may:
> For, what hath Life, that may it loved make,
> And gives nor rather cause it to forsake?

Fear, Sickness, Age, Loss, Labour, Sorrow, Strife,
Pain, Hunger, Cold, that makes the Heart to quake;
And ever fickle Fortune rageth rife,
All which, and thousands more, do make a loathsom Life.

Not heart-ache, but heart-quake: such a "fine moral declamation . . . on the evils of life, almost makes one in love with death," said Hazlitt of this word-power (*Lectures* 82). For a Christian knight, this is a test of faith (Despair is a sin of Pride). Keats shifts theology to psychology: Quietude. This verge on easeful death vexes some readers into arguments of beneficent therapy. Sperry reads a peace in renunciation of quest; Dickstein (among the emenders of *plainful* to *painful*) maps a bottoming-out on the way to "regeneration."[2] Keats must have known Dr. John Abernethy's prescription of "perfect quietude" for healing (cited in *OED*). But right here, in conceiving his Cave, he indulges a Spenserian wording that takes Hazlitt's *almost makes one in love with death* to full degree, sounding *quietude* not only from *grievous feud* but also against a waiting rhyme with *multitude* (561), the hum of the world all around this permeable retreat.

"In Endymion," Keats reflected to Taylor's publishing partner James Hessey, "I leaped headlong into the Sea." He spoke a little better than even he knew when he said he had "become better acquainted with the Soundings" (8 October 1818, *L* 1:374). By *Soundings* Keats means *depths,* but he also voices (if not fully audits) the phonic tunings ever, and increasingly, in his poetic adventures. This is a resource for working words through sensations unruly but not ruled out. Paradoxically, in the poetry of quietude, Keats was coming to realize, further, and above all, the nuances of emotion that the push-pull of verbal explicitness might waveringly elicit.

[*1818,* pp. 184–186]

[1] The culprits include Murry, 41, into the 5th edition (1955), 175; Bush, 120; Dickstein, *Keats,* 122–123. Keats knew what he wanted, having chimed *paining* into *plaining* when bereft Endymion, with a "Sweet paining on his ear" (2.859), responds with *plainings* (draft 865; *P* 158n).

[2] Sperry, *Keats,* 110; Dickstein, 122–123; Bush, 120.

Training, Retraining, "New Romance"

December 1817–May 1818

RELIEVED AT FINISHING *ENDYMION*, Keats was less relieved about what he had accomplished. While the workout was generative, the result seemed adolescent, feverish. He kept writing, not for publication, but to exercise imagination. Here is some of the poetry from the weeks when he was proofreading *Endymion* (December 1817) up to spring 1818, after it was published. Keats plays around with and flexes various modes: sonnets again, from playful to meditative to melancholy; bawdy songs to share with his poetry bros; a strange verse-epistle to a sick friend; a new manner of "romance," *Isabella; or, The Pot of Basil.* This last was meant for publication (it is in *1820*). He writes to train and retrain himself, indulging pleasures and purposes, private thinking and sociable communication.

Song ("In drear nighted December")

In drear nighted December
     happy
   Too happy, ^ Tree;
Thy branches ne'er remember
    Their green felicity,
   The North cannot undo them
   With a sleety whistle through them
   Nor frozen thawings glew them
      From budding at the Prime.   8

In drear nighted December
   Too happy happy brook
Thy bubblings ne'er remember
   Apollo's summer look:
   But with a sweet forgetting
   They stay their crystal fretting;—
   Never, never petting
     About the frozen time.   16

Ah! Would 'twere so with many,
     gentle
A ~~happy~~ ^ girl & boy!
   But were there ever any,
    Writh'd not at passed Joy? —
   The feel of not to feel it,
   When there is none to heal it
   Nor numbed sense to steel it,
     Was never said in Rhyme.   24

J Keats

Keats wrote this song a few weeks after wrapping *Endymion*, December 1817, the same month he formulated *negative capability*. It wasn't intended for publication but rather as an exercise of thinking about what rhyme can do in a world of temporal depletions. Each stanza delivers a quatrain (*abab*), a triplet of fastened meanings (*ccc*), and a close on *d*, with accumulating intensity.

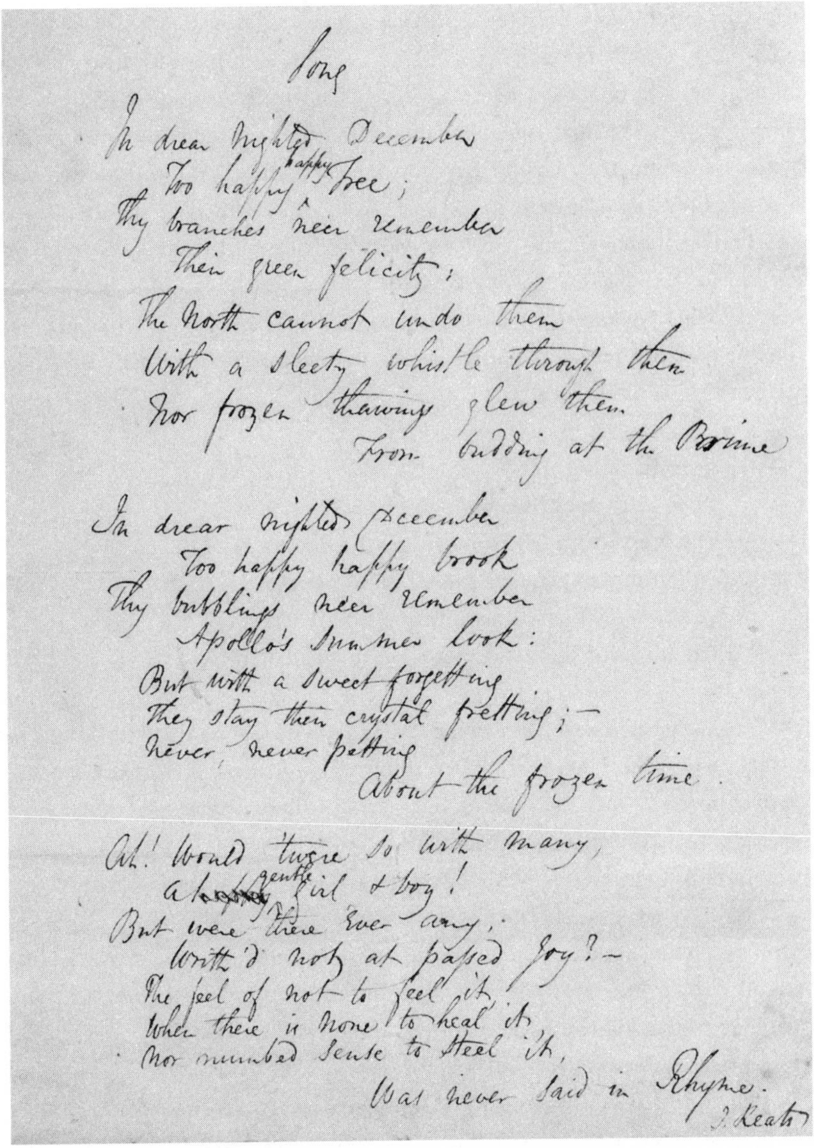

Song

In drear nighted December
    Too happy, happy tree;
Thy branches ne'er remember
    Their green felicity;
The north cannot undo them
With a sleety whistle through them
Nor frozen thawings glew them
        From budding at the Prime

In drear nighted December
    Too happy happy brook
Thy bubblings ne'er remember
    Apollo's Summer look:
But with a sweet forgetting
They stay their crystal fretting; —
Never, never petting
        About the frozen time.

Ah! would 'twere so with many,
    A gentle girl & boy!
But were there ever any,
    Writh'd not at passed Joy? —
The feel of not to feel it,
When there is none to heal it,
Nor numbed Sense to steel it,
        Was never said in Rhyme.
                    J. Keats

Figure 7: Keats's draft, "In drear nighted December" (December 1817). Courtesy of Keats-Shelley House, Rome.

In the last lines of *Endymion,* when the Indian Maid tells Endymion, "Drear, drear / Has been our delaying" (4.997–998), the double-dosed *drear* serves as foreplay to blessings, blisses and kisses mere lines on (1005–1010). In this *Song,* Keats sets *drear* as sonic native to a *December brr,* a chill of thinking by <u>human mortals</u> (his double-scoring in *Midsummer Night's Dream* 2.2; DW 2:16). The tree immunized from *drear* (even by the antiphone, *ne'er*) is not just *happy;* it is *Too happy* (Keats inserted an extra *happy*) in ignorant bliss. In spring 1819, a human poet will imagine a nightingale *too happy* in its happiness, with no capacity for *envy.* This isn't culpable excess; this happiness is mindlessness by the fortune of genetics (*hap:* chance). In the *Song* of December 1817, the tree weathers a season of *sleety whistle* (more than a keen, fitful gust in this alliterative onomatopoeia) on an annual guarantee of new *green felicity,* even delivering the sound of *sleet* into *felicity.* The painful sequence for mortal human knowing is the compressed *frozen thawings,* the relief of *thaw* caught in a fresh *glew* of a freeze.

Keats read this temporal consciousness in Shakespeare's Sonnet XII in November 1817, summer long past:

> Is this to be borne? Hark ye!
>> When lofty trees I see barren of leaves
>> Which erst from heat did canopy the herd,
>> And Summer's green all girded up in sheaves,
>> Borne on the bier with white and bristly beard.
> He has left nothing to say about nothing or any thing   (*K* 72)

Keats's faux-question keys *borne* to the sonnet-lines he is about to write out: *borne* as *endured* (he jokes); as *conveyed* to reading; as *appreciated.* Shakespeare's words "seem to be full of fine things said unintentionally—in the intensity of working out conceits" (72), un*intention*ally nicely allied to imagination *in . . . intensity.* It takes a readerly spirit to grasp this. What Keats *harks* (hears and notes) in Shakespeare's conceit is more than the chord of [lof]*ty-tree-see-leaves.* Embedded is a palindromic "*trees I see,*" with *I* at the center, the presence that conjures the leaves that a summer ago canopied an entire *herd,* reverberating into the summer field *girded up.*[1] And then the line that kills Keats: all that *green borne on* a *bier.* This is *to be borne.* Had he known the Quarto text of Shakespeare's sonnet, he would have harked to see *bier* pun-spelled *beare.* The wrench of verse elicits *born* and *bear* (words of life-giving) only to refuse the sense: it is all *barren, borne, bier, beard. Borne* as generative is a poignant "anti-pun": though logically averted, unintentionally present.[2]

Keats's December *Song* partners tree-felicity to an insensate brook. The triple repetition of the first stanza's single *ne'er* into *ne'er, Never, never* is the greeting of bitter mortal consciousness. Even the brook's *fretting* is unpained fretwork: its bubblings *stay* (abide in, halt for now) in crystal state with no complaint. It is a *crystal* lacework to the eye and, to the ear, the sound of music: "fretting: that stop of the musical instrument which causes or regulates the vibrations of the string" (*JnD*). Keats underlined Milton's phrasing of <u>All sounds on fret by String or Golden Wire</u>

and a roof of <u>fretted gold</u>: the only two *frets* in *Paradise Lost,* both in charms for pained minds.[3] Keats's *Song* takes all this in, in tacit relay with human fretting.

Ah! (17) sounds this feeling, even for the Wordsworthian idyll of childhood: the happiest *gentle girl & boy* can't help but writhe at *passed Joy.* Keats margin-marked a virtual intertext, a song in *Cymbeline* (4.2; *DW* 6:71) with grim avatars:

> *Fear no more the heat o'the sun,*
> *Nor the furious winter's rages;*
> *Thou thy worldly task hast done,*
> *Home art gone, and ta'en thy wages:*
> *Golden lads and girls all must,*
> *As chimney-sweepers, come to dust.*

Shakespeare's song sends everything human into dust.

Keats's last move is not this but a payoff for poetry, with a twist on *never.* Nonimmunity to feeling is unveiled as a positive resource of *Rhyme. The feel of not to feel it* is poetry's grammar.[4] With a medical pressure on the verbal pulse of *not to feel,* Keats wanted *feel* as a noun, too: visceral sense, conscious sensation. He had used it this way in *Endymion,* in close company, for the hero—with *drear* and *deadly* and *fear,* no less:

> such a breathless honey-feel of bliss
> Alone preserved me from the drear abyss
> Of death . . .   (1.904–906)

> 'tis the thought,
> The deadly feel of solitude . . .   (2.284–285)

> A sight too fearful for the feel of fear . . .   (3.499)

In each case, *feel* is a substantive noun. Even the adjective *fearful* feels substantive in dominating the syllable-reversed *feel of fear.* In his *Song,* Keats condenses a seemingly antithetical *feel of not to feel* into a logical sensation. His ready advocate (his publisher's adviser) Woodhouse saw the experiment, but winced, confiding to Taylor, 23 November 1818, his "utter abhorrence of the word 'feel' for feeling (substantively)"; but he concedes Keats's fondness for it, with a guess that his verse would "ingraft it 'in aeternum' on our language" (*KC* 1:64). Nicely witty is Woodhouse's *ingraft* for Keats's substantive and its lexical infusion; the noun *feel,* comments John Jones, "is Keats's word" (4). I admire Woodhouse's ability to "conquer [his] dislike" on this one, especially in light of the corruption applied to the song's first publication: "To know the change and feel it."[5]

Woodhouse had no feeling, however, for the next three, last lines (22–24): an "excrescence" with no "connection" to the stanza's first four lines, which at least seemed "an application of or rather antithesis to the 1 & 2 Stanzas" (1:64). Meaning *outgrowth* (especially abnormal), *excrescence* is Woodhouse's lexically inventive wrench on *ingraft*, with a warp into a new *essence* that ought to be extirpated. As with the noun *feel*, he grasped Keats's venture. In these last lines, Keats's verbal excrescence swells into a twist that he set for, saved for, the punchline close: *Was never said in Rhyme.* Overturning the bitter weather report on unconscious nature that seemed a 23-line romance, this volta re-verses everything. Keats needed the negative *never* to make his claim of *Rhyme.* This is both a punning difference from the *rime* of crystal fretting and the excrescence, even essence, undertoned in the way *versèd* says the sound of "ne*ver said.*"[6]

In a springtime letter, Keats will fantasize (an experiment in thinking) a natural thing with human consciousness:

> suppose a rose to have sensation, it blooms on a beautiful morning it enjoys itself - but there comes a cold wind, a hot sun - it cannot escape it, it cannot destroy its annoyances [he could have said fretting]; they are as native to the world as itself: no more can man be happy in spite, the worldly elements will prey up his nature   (21 April 1819; MsK 1.53.260)

Feline sensation is another thing.

[holograph fair copy; Keats Museum, Rome. See *KSR* 32.1, 23]

---

[1] Woodhouse's clerk heard it as *heard* and copied it this way (*Letter-Book* 51; *L* 1:188).

[2] This is Christopher Ricks's term for this dynamic, *Force*, 100.

[3] *PL* 7.597; 1.717; *KPL* II:47–48; I:25.

[4] *Not to feel* is dialectic: "no longer to feel." It "does not . . . could not, mean never to have felt" (Jones 176).

[5] First in *Literary Gazette*, 19 September 1829, 618. Forman's *Poetical Works &c* (1883) reported, but did not privilege, *the feel of change* in Keats's holograph (2:245n). The corruption, *to know the change,* is still in the 1937 edition (Oxford UP, 338), even after Colvin ridiculed the urge to get "rid of the vulgar substantive form of 'feel' for feeling" (160), noting that it was good enough for eighteenth-century writers Horace Walpole, Frances Burney, and everyday usage (as today). Murry agreed, with emphasis: "the feel" is "the true and authentic meaning" (65); but Garrod kept *to know the change* right up to the second edition of *Poetical Works* (1958). Bush's classroom edition (131) pretty much settled the score on behalf of *feel*.

[6] This audit is Garrett Stewart's fine catch.

To Mrs. Reynolds's Cat

Cat! who hast past thy grand climacteric,
   How many mice and rats hast in thy days
   Destroy'd? – How many tit bits stolen? Gaze
With those bright languid segments green and prick
Those velvet ears – but prythee do not stick   5
   Thy latent talons in me – and upraise
   Thy gentle mew – and tell me all thy frays
Of fish and mice, and rats and tender chick.
Nay, look not down, nor lick thy dainty wrists –
   For all thy wheezy asthma – and for all
Thy tail's tip is nicked off – and though the fists
   Of many a maid have given thee many a maul,
Still is that fur as soft as when the lists   13
   In youth thou enter'dst on glass bottled wall.

Mrs. Reynolds is the mother of Keats's friend J. H. Reynolds. Taking a break from fair-copying *Endymion*, Keats dashed off this sonnet on 16 January 1818. It's an affectionately tuned, mock-heroic call to an old warrior, past her prime but still with a glint of youthful adventure. The *grand climacteric* for humans is usually pegged to age sixty-three, when (back then, anyway) active life is deemed pretty much done, with only time to serve out. A woman's first climacteric is menopause.

Keats invites this she-cat to retail past glories and victories, as if she were a voluble veteran. "The old sailor's tongue was as active by the fire-side as his arm had been busy where blows were plentiful; and, from his tales of excitement, the young listeners drew that sort of sustenance which feels imagination." This was Keats's memory of his uncle (Bailey 144.) Mrs. Reynolds's cat is completely indifferent, just gazing, languidly and enigmatically, with those green eyes and a feline instinct to keep ears pricked. Halfway into line 5, Keats turns a soft volta: *– but prythee*. The usual spelling is *prithee*, slanging *pray thee*. Keats's wry *prythee* slant-concedes the defeat of prying out any tale, the cat's only reaction a reflex warrior-swipe at the annoyance. For this, Keats nicely figures the lettering of *latent talons*, the first syllable *lat*ent ready for reversing into *tal*ons.

Keats's Petrarchan sonnet mimes a courtly tribute, with the rhyme scheme relaxed by enjambments to coax the cat with line-leaps: *prick / Thy velvet ears; stick / Thy talons; upraise / Thy gentle mew.* All futile: no tale of conquest "Of fish and mice, and rats and tender chick"; no feline epic catalogue. The hoped-for *frays* redound into a supplicative *Nay* against the cat's absorbed self-grooming. Keats's wit is this Petrarchan failure, the courtship venture of *gentle* and *tender* of no avail with this old girl. The counter-move is to read the tell-tale body: breathing is harder; the tail is embattled; she's lost a few rounds. Keats turns a couplet-worthy close to the unavailing interview. The nearly metaphysical wonder of this veteran is fur unravaged, as soft as in its first combats (*lists* are rosters for contests of young knights). Her old field of combat, that glass-bottled wall, still shines in the "bright languid segments green" of her eyes.

When Thomas Hood printed this sonnet in his *Comic Annual* (1830, p. 14), he used a less conclusive *pass'd* in line 1, instead of a hard *past*. A year or so after writing the sonnet, Keats was still musing on an unanswering female cat, this one in his own household, passing freely from the attached house next door. His prose report reads like poetic latency:

> *Mrs. Dilke has two Cats – a Mother and a Daughter – now the Mother is a tabby . . . they may one and several of them come into my room ad libitum. But no – the Tabby only comes . . . The Cat is not an old Maid herself – her daughter is a proof of it – I have questioned her – I have look'd at the lines of her paw – I have felt her pulse – to no purpose – Why should the <u>old</u> Cat come to me? I ask myself – and myself has not a word to answer.*
>
> (3 January 1819; MsK 1.45.187)

Self-asking, no answering: the grammar of Keats's poetry. A week later he'll raise the stakes, as a (re-)reader of *King Lear*.

[holograph fair copy; P 222–223]

On Sitting Down to Read King Lear Once Again

My dear Brothers,

    I was thinking what hindered me from writing so long, for I have so many things to say to you & know not where to begin. It shall be upon a thing most interesting to you my Poem. Well! I have given the Ist Book to Taylor; he seemed more than satisfied with it, & to my surprise proposed publishing it in Quarto if Haydon would make a drawing of some event therein, for a Frontispiece. I called on Haydon, he said he would do anything I liked, but said he would rather paint a finished picture, from it, which he seems eager to do; this in a year or two will be a glorious thing for us; & it will be, for Haydon is struck with the Ist Book. I left Haydon & the next day received a letter from him, proposing to make, as he says, with all his might, a finished chalk sketch of my head, to be engraved in the first style & put at the head of my Poem, saying at the same time he had never done the thing for any human being, & that it must have considerable effect as he will put the name to it—I begin to day to copy my 2nd Book "thus far into the bowels of the Land"—You shall hear whether it will be Quarto or non Quarto, picture or non Picture. Leigh Hunt I showed my Ist Book to, he allows it not much merit as a whole; says it is unnatural & made ten objections to it in the mere skimming over. He says the conversation is unnatural and too high-flown for Brother & Sister. Says it should be simple forgetting do ye mind, that they are both overshadowed by a Supernatural Power, & of force could not speak like Franchesca in the Rimini. He must first prove that Caliban's poetry is unnatural,—This with me completely overturns his objections—the fact is he & Shelley are hurt & perhaps justly, at my not having showed them the affair officiously & from several hints I have had they appear much disposed to dissect & anatomize any trip or slip I may have made.— But whose afraid? [. . .] Rice has been ill, but has been mending much lately—I think a little change has taken place in my intellect lately–I cannot bear to be uninterested or unemployed [. . .] Nothing is finer for the purposes of great productions, than a very gradual ripening of the intellectual powers—As an instance of this—observe—I sat down yesterday to read King Lear once again the thing appeared to demand the prologue of a Sonnet, I wrote it & began to read—(I know you would like to see it)[1]

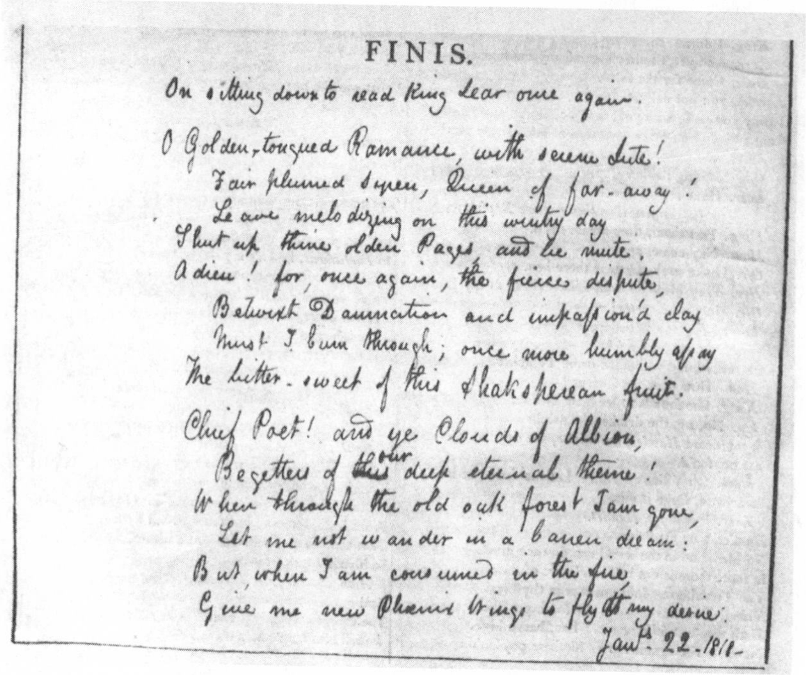

FINIS.

On sitting down to read King Lear once again.

O Golden-tongued Romance, with serene Lute!
  Fair plumed Syren, Queen of far-away!
  Leave melodizing on this wintry day
Shut up thine olden Pages and be mute.
Adieu! for, once again, the fierce dispute,
  Betwixt Damnation and impassion'd clay
  Must I burn through; once more humbly assay
The bitter-sweet of this Shaksperean fruit.
Chief Poet! and ye Clouds of Albion,
  Begetters of our deep eternal theme!
When through the old oak forest I am gone,
  Let me not wander in a barren dream:
But when I am consumed in the fire
Give me new Phœnix wings to fly at my desire.
                                  Jan.ᵗ 22. 1818.

Figure 8: Keats's draft, "On sitting down to read King Lear once again" (January 1818), written in his copy of Shakespeare's tragedies. The printed word FINIS indicates the end of *Hamlet*. This verso page faces the recto on which *King Lear* begins. Reproduced from Caroline Spurgeon, *Keats's Shakespeare*. Oxford University Press, 1928, plate 20.

On sitting down to read King Lear once again.

O Golden-tongued Romance, with serene Lute!
  Fair plumed Syren! Queen of far-away!
  Leave melodizing on this wintry day
Shut up thine olden Pages, and be mute.
Adieu! for, once again, the fierce dispute,
  Betwixt Damnation and impassion'd clay
  Must I burn through; once more humbly assay
The bitter-sweet of this Shaksperean fruit.
Chief Poet! and ye Clouds of Albion,
  Begetters of this our deep eternal theme!
When through the old oak forest I am gone,
  Let me not wander in a barren dream:

But, when I am consumed in the fire,
Give me new Phœnix Wings to fly at my desire.
                                                        Jany. 22.1818 -

Keats copied his sonnet into this letter to his brothers, 23 January 1818, just after fair-copying Book I of *Endymion: A Poetic Romance*. His publisher John Taylor was so keen on it that he proposed an upscale quarto, and asked Haydon for a frontispiece.[2] Haydon not only promptly agreed but also proposed some sequel illustrations to accompany the likely fame. Getting ready to fair-copy Book II (the one with the Bower of Adonis), Keats arms up with a riff from Shakespeare: *thus far into the bowels of the Land,* Richmond's rally to his troops as they head into battle against Richard III, the rest of the line implied: "Have we march'd on without impediment" (5.2.1–4). Keats's impediment is (surprisingly) Hunt, who winced at the too arty diction and idiom. He would reform Caliban into a suburban conversationalist for his Francesca (the heroine of his *Story of Rimini*, 1816), Keats jests.

Keats's affair with *Romance* was less easy to deal with. He takes physic with Shakespeare's severest tragedy, *King Lear*. Instead of John Jeffrey's (variant) transcript of the sonnet in the letter above, I interpolate the text Keats wrote out on a page in his 1808 edition of Shakespeare's first folio, using a blank space at the end of *Hamlet,* across from the opening of *King Lear.* Tragedy is on his mind this winter. His brief comment about their dear friend Jemmy Rice's mending is over-determined. On the same day he wrote to Bailey: *Tom is getting stronger but his Spitting of blood continues. I sat down to read King Lear yesterday, and felt the greatness of the thing.* He then adds: *There were some miserable reports of Rice's health – I went and lo! Master Jemmy had been to [a] play the night before and was out at the time* (MsK 1.20.72). What is the calculus?—is Tom *getting stronger?* is Jemmy's recovery a pattern, or a counterpart?[3]

Keats writes his sonnet in these measures and as a self-measuring. His title, one of his longest ever, has the look of a journal entry. It is about more than rereading *King Lear;* it is the drill of sitting down to it, reading *once again,* knowing the story in store in this severe tragedy. It is not the first time he has read it; no Chapman's Homer revelation. *To read* this play, moreover, is crucial, because the stage was held by Nahum Tate's *The History of King Lear,* a "Romance" rewriting (1681) applauded by no less an authority than Dr. Johnson, who found Shakespeare's fierce ending unendurable.[4] Tate keeps Lear alive to regain the throne and then happily abdicate to newly married Edgar and

Cordelia (she survives, too). Shakespeare's tragedy is piercingly fringed with "Romance," especially the (futile) hope of rescue. To read Shakespeare's play is to experience Johnson's shock, and then on rereading, to feel it again.

"Romance" was Keats's first poetic love, but its "golden" ring was coming to feel hollow. *Hellens* golden tongue is a phrase he underlines when he sits down to read *Troilus and Cressida* (*KS* 151), Paris's abducted lover a too-merry palace-wit amid the Trojan war. The sonnet's *Queen* Romance is allied, in sense and sound, with a too *serene* seduction. *Serene:* the metaphor for Homer's poetry so differently situated here. Romance's *far away* is alluring and delusional, counterpointed in rhyme with the *wintry day* of mortal miseries. It takes just four syllables to get to *Syren,* music hard to resist, fatal to indulge. The sonnet is less a settled argument, however, than a dramatic oscillation. This poet still hears the *lute* he would *mute,* and issues his indictment with terms of endearment: *golden, melody, fair, far away.* If *olden* depletes the value of its sounded twin *golden,* such pages, apparently, are still open to Keats's eye. The poet set to reread *Lear* doesn't *leave* "Romance" (the leaves of *Endymion* are on his desk). He can only bid the pages be *shut up.* This imperative means *close up,* and was acquiring our sense of *be silent.*

And so the lingering *Adieu!*—a word of tender leave-taking, its exclamation point both an elegiac sigh and a forward-thrust determination. Keats fortifies the pledge in prospect (*Must I . . .*) with a formal decisiveness, shifting from his Petrarchan octave to a Shakespearean sestet. This undergirds a point-by-point genre-turn from Romance to *King Lear,* expressed with vigorous verbs and worthy objects: *fierce dispute / burn through / assay / bitter-sweet fruit.* This chiasmus of *object-verb-verb-object,* comments Helen Vendler, is "a figure of forethought" ("Perfecting" 64). At the same time, Keats's temporal markers, *once again* and *once more,* know about regression. Breaking up is hard to do. The enduring *fierce dispute* Keats reads in *Lear* is also his own agon, of mortal fate and the *impassion'd clay* of mortal life.

The hazard of the word *assay* is just right: it means *analyze the content of*—specifically, gold content. Keats plays this against *golden Romance.* The fruit of his reading twists *bitter-sweet:* not pure *melodizing*—literally, making sweet song (*mel:* Greek for *honey*)—but compounded with its antonym. As the poet who will write *Ode on Melancholy* in spring 1819 knows, the syllable *mel* evokes the black bile *melano.* The etymologies are different, but the echo is potent: one syllable cuts both ways. This is the only time in his poetry that Keats uses the word *melodizing.* Not even an adjective, it is a substantive and degraded. It plays this status against *bitter-sweet,* a severe detox after a binge on about eighty forms of *sweet* in *Endymion* alone. Keats will soon be rhyming *melodize* to *floridize,* his coinage to satirize Hunt's spinning for the poetry market (*L* 2:14).

These turns coincide with Keats's replacing the exotic she-seducer with a noble he, a tribal chief begetter in the native clouds of Albion. A *Poet of Romance,* he writes in June 1819 (still thinking cloudwise), *is not a miserable and mighty Poet of the human Heart;* Shakespeare's days were *all c[l]ouded over; . . . not more happy than Hamlet's* (*L* 2:115–116). This is *human* cardiology. Keats knows the *Lear*-pulsation: "then shall the realm of Albion / Come to great confusion," murmurs the Fool, in the play's sole instance of *Albion* (3.2).[5] A sonnet that Keats sends to Reynolds on 19 February 1818 images *Snow clouds hung in Mist* ("the Thrush said"). Keats will darken the skies of *Hyperion* with *clouds of evil days* and a *dismal rack of clouds* (1.39, 302).

Yet at its very pitch of commitment to *Lear*-burning, this sonnet stalls in prospect and petition. Even as the syntax of *When through the old oak forest I am gone* points beyond Romance, Romance lingers in metaphor and word-sounding: *old* reverberating *golden* and *olden.* Every sense of the forward-charged preposition *through* is loaded: *working through, aiming beyond,* even *by a methodical practice.* Yet as often as I have reread the full phrase, the tenor of *old oak forest* eludes me. Editors' glosses are (tellingly) all over the place. Paul de Man is sure it means romance; Miriam Allot says the "sombre nature" of *Lear.* Douglas Bush is plum flummoxed: "Logic suggests" that the forest is the rereading of *Lear,* although the "image" seems drawn from *Endymion* and elsewhere "symbolizes *The Faerie Queene.*"[6] Does Keats himself know? Burning through *Lear* promises to burn down the forests of old Romance, incinerate the poet of Romance, and release him, reborn into *our deep eternal theme—our,* the badge of the new company. That's one outcome. The other is a barren dream, a flaming out into futile wandering, the very trope of romance proven on its Latin pulses (*errare: to wander*). *Let me not wander* is Keats's penultimate plea: *allow me not to, don't doom me to, protect me from.* The flight path for *Give me new Phoenix Wings* is just a prospect, an infinitive, and a vague destination: *to fly at my desire.* Keats first wrote *fly to my . . .* , then *at my . . . :* appetitive, and less certain of success. And so the medial lingering, the medial uncertainty, and a wince that this is likely not the last time he will be sitting down to *King Lear.* Reading it once again on 4 October 1818, he underlines <u>poore Tom</u> (*KS* 43), with a pang.

Blame the Phoenix: rising from the ashes of its progenitor, it is not evolutionary but cyclical, reduplicative. The poetry of Keats's last line recycles in accord, a hexameter evoking the Spenserian stanza of "Romance." Rekindling this stanza, Byron blazed out *Childe Harold's Pilgrimage, A Romaunt* (1812), Canto III a sensation in 1816 (Canto IV in the wings for spring 1818, to rival *Endymion*). Keats was not yet ready for such a venture, even in form. Two weeks on, he writes another (also unpublished) sonnet in Shakespearean form, with apologies to Spenser:[7]

> But Elfin-Poet 'tis impossible
>> For an inhabitant of wintry Earth
> To rise like Phœbus with a golden quell,
>> Fire - wing'd, and make a morning in his Mirth

Keats wants human models, not this impossible Apollo (nor Elfin Spenser). *Fire-wing'd* is Phœnix-Plus, *impossible* for a poet of wintry days and wintry earth. Keats's *quell* teases *quill* (Apollo's golden pen) with an olden-book sense of the noun: murder.[8] What is possible, he wonders, for a romance-addict in winter? "So you see I am getting at it, with a sort of determination & strength, though verily I do not feel it at this moment . . . my head rather swimming," he writes to his brothers, after copying out his *Lear* sonnet (*L* 1:215). Two jots of *at: at it* in strong desire; *at this* moment of writing, less so. He needed some refreshment before this regimen of bitter-sweet: maybe "Eve's sweet Pipin."

[sonnet: *KS* plate 20; *L* 1:213–215]

[1] The letter is from John Jeffrey's transcript (the only source); the sonnet is Keats's own hand.

[2] A quarto assembles sheets of four pages printed on each side (an octavo, such as *1817*, is more economical, eight pages printed on each side). Taylor and Hessey decided, after all, to print *Endymion* in octavo, and to forgo a frontispiece.

[3] Endearing for his wit and fun, struggling for health the rest of his life, Jemmy survived Tom by nearly fourteen years and outlived Keats by more than a decade.

[4] *The Plays of William Shakespeare* (1765; 10 vols., London, 1778), 9:566.

[5] I thank Tommy Dayzie, Princeton University class of '22, for this alert report.

[6] De Man, 258n. So, too, de Selincourt, "Warton Lecture," 7; Allott, *Poems*, 296n11; Bush, 325n.

[7] Morgan Library holograph (MA 213.4), dated "Feb 5."

[8] *JnD* cites the Macbeths' "great quell" of King Duncan (3.7; *DW* 3:17), a passage Keats read with care. Reynolds's sister transcribed Keats's *quell* as *quill* (*P* 596n).

"O blush not so"

My Dear Reynolds

    I have parcelld out this day for Letter Writing - more resolved thereon because your Letter will come as a refreshment and will have (sic parvis &c) the same effect as a Kiss in certain situations where people become over-generous. I have read this first sentence over, and think it savours rather; however an inward innocence is like a nested dove; or as the old song says.

I

O blush not so, O blush not so
    or I shall think ye knowing;
And if ye smile, the blushing while,
    Then Maidenheads are going.

2

There's a blush for want, and a blush for shan't
    And a blush for having done it,
There's a blush for thought, and a blush for naught
    And a blush for just begun it.

3

O sigh not so, O sigh not so
    For it sounds of Eve's sweet Pipin
By those loosen'd hips, you have tasted the pips
    And fought in an amorous nipping.

4

Will ye play once more, at nice cut core
    For it only will last our youth out,
And we have the prime, of the Kissing time
    We have not one sweet tooth out.

There's a sigh for yes, and a sigh for no,
    And a sigh for "I can't bear it"—
O what can be done, shall we stay or run
    O cut the sweet apple and share it?

Keats's greeting to Reynolds jests about "innocence" in the various manifestations of the female "blush," fun conveyed with a sort of "Kiss" to his correspondent. Part of the amusement is the parody of a schoolroom exercise, the training signaled by the shorthand schoolboy-Latin from Virgil's *Eclogue I: sic parvis componere magna solebam* (23: thus I used to compare great things with small). Studying Latin is he-gendered, not for misses, especially the erotic archive.

In *Endymion* a small blush could be a great thing; here it is a great word in a blazon (nine times) about how to interpret Maidenhead's blushes. What do maidens (virgins) know when they blush, and what do lads make of this body (of) language? The adjective/verb *knowing* is not just cognitive awareness; it is also a term of sexual experience (in line with *want, having done it,* and *naught—* this last, a bawdy Shakespearean bit of slang for a receptive vagina). A rare word is *blush* in *Paradise Lost*. Milton has Eve "blushing like morn" as Adam leads her to the "nuptial bower" (8.510–511; Keats underlined this, *KPL* I:67). The only other blush is a bitter parody, a "short blush of morn" as the world goes to Hell (11.184). C. S. Lewis, a critic more ready than Milton himself to justify the ways of God to Man, is disturbed by Eve's blush. Milton "has dared to represent Paradisal sexuality," he says, noting the nuptial anticipation, but worrying about its "incentive to male desire" (118–120). More delicate was Dr. John Gregory's advice to his daughters (1793): "When a girl ceases to blush, she has lost the most powerful charm of beauty . . . it is particularly engaging . . . and has forced us to love you because you do so." Even so, this father has to keep insisting that a blush conveys no consciousness of "crime" or "attendant on guilt" (27). Reverend Richard Polwhele hailed the "blush of modesty" as he fulminated against its absence in the brazen women named in the title of his tirade, *The Unsex'd Females* (1798). He appended a footnote to remind his readers "that at several of our boarding-schools for young ladies, a blush incurs a penalty" (p. 13n), as if a blush could betray the consciousness that Dr. Gregory would fend off.

Keats's song volleys female blush into erotic slang between men, with an affected worldly knowingness about it all. A blush incentivizes the course of

Maidenheads . . . going by blending in one exhibition the prospect of conquest, seduction, and knowingness about women. The fun is fantasizing a female code, an innocent flush, or a flush that symptomizes sexual excitement, all the better if "innocent." Keats was learning the language of sexual commerce and bandying it around with his correspondents. He wrote to his brothers earlier this month, retailing some tensile town-slang about "getting initiated into a little Cant—they call . . . good Wine a pretty tipple, and call getting a Child knocking out an apple" (*L* 1:197)—or a pippin. *Tipple* is strong drink. With a hint of *cunt* in *cant* (Byron does this), *tipple* tips sexually, into Eve's apple-fed fallen knowledge. The controlled play of language is the superstructure of Keats's complicated feelings about women, descended from the *pure Goddess of Boyish imagination* (he tells his friend Bailey in July 1819) to logical *reality* (*K* 191).

The song's tease, *Oh sigh not so,* sighs for both innocence and experience, with some cute, musical-hall, cockney punning *sigh* as *say* (Woodhouse thought it should be *say; P* 226n). Keats's song, in quatrains of alternating tetrameter and trimeter, is peppered with bawdy boy-talk that is cockney-current and literate in the (generally, male) *carpe diem* ploys of *it will only last our youth out* (4). Playing along, Woodhouse decided that stanza 5's first line should tighten up its phonics to "There's *a sigh for aye,* and a sigh for nay," *aye* prone to the surrender of "*a sigh for I* can't bear it!" (with no thought, on Keats's part, of what else might be born in consequence).

Keats's wordplay involves *Pipin. Eve's sweet Pipin* is her piping, come-hither song (Keats's Cockney would not pronounce the *g* in *ing*). *Pipin* is also a sweet apple with red-flushed skin, a fruit seed (pip), and from these, a term of endearment, a darling. And foundationally, it is what knowing Eve, having eaten, offers Adam. As a verb, *pip* is what chicks do to break out of a shell, or their chamber of innocence. Keats's worldly friend Charles Brown would be writing a story about a year on, on Valentine's Day, that uses *pip* in Eve's several keys. The Devil in disguise visits an old woman; "On going he leaves her three pips of eve's apple – and some how – she, having liv'd a virgin all her life, begins to repent of it and wishes herself beautiful enough to make all the world and even the other world fall in love with her . . . The devil himself falls in love with her" (*L* 2:61). These *pips* are sexually pregnant seeds. In Keats's song, the rose's *hips* are seed-pods, the female body in shape and suggestion. His phrasing had more than a few men of letters considering the "bawdy song . . . unfit for publication," including sensuous poet Swinburne (*L* 1:219n, his words). Even Keats's later editor R. M. Milnes, collector of erotica and pornography, couldn't bring himself to put it in *1848.*

Having read a transcript, Dante Gabriel Rossetti (no prude about sensuous poetry) wrote to a later editor, H. B. Forman, on 9 May 1881, urging him not to print the poem:

> I don't on reflection like it at all. It would certainly do Keats's fame no credit. You said yourself that it is 'rather vulgar,' and ought Keats to seem so through that being printed which he never meant except as a private pleasantry? (15)

Forman seemed swayed, and on 19 May, Rossetti wrote to congratulate him, adding, "Of course I do not consider that sexual passion, if nobly expressed, should be excluded from poetry for any reason except that of not restricting its circulation." Noble is one thing, vulgar another. Even by 1881, Keats was not scrubbed of class-slurs. Rossetti's objection was less philosophical than strategic on behalf of Keats's innate nobility of mind (if not class): "here we have a poet, conspicuously noble in essential tone of mind, yielding by some freak of the moment in private to a triviality which gives no idea of his true nature" (16–17). He thought he had prevailed with Forman on this firm ground. But this song was also a true, if not public, nature.

What is a conscientious, embarrassed Victorian man of letters, editing Keats, to do? "Notwithstanding the brilliant qualities of some of the stanzas, I should have hesitated to be instrumental in adding it to the poet's published works, had it not been handed about in manuscript and more than once copied"—so Forman sighed in footnote (2:280), treating the song as a promiscuous woman with whom one is forced to acknowledge commerce. In his edition of 1883, he gives it the title *Sharing Eve's Apple,* as if it were a primer of sexual history and sexual knowing. Yet *hips* overtaxed his largesse. Relieved for Woodhouse's authority (*P* 590), he changed it to *lips*—still salacious, but losing the loose hips that could sink the Keats-ship. For all this tact, Forman's emendation achieved little more than an upward displacement of knowing foreplay (*play once more*). He kept *lips,* anyway, in editions right up to 1926. De Selincourt refused notice to the song at all.

Keats has other moods to share with Reynolds on this late January day.

[letter, 31 January 1818, *K* 94–95]

"When I have fears that I may cease to be"

When I have fears that I may cease to be
　　Before my pen has glean'd my teeming brain,
Before high piled Books in charactery
　　Hold like rich garners the full ripen'd grain—
When I behold upon the night's starr'd face,
　　Huge cloudy symbols of a high romance,
And think that I may never live to trace
　　Their shadows with the magic hand of Chance:
And when I feel, fair creature of an hour,
　　That I shall never look upon thee more
Never have relish in the fairy power
　　Of unreflecting Love: then on the Shore　　　　　　12
Of the wide world I stand alone and think
Till Love and Fame to Nothingness do sink.—

Written 31 January, this sonnet renders Keats's lowest mood as he was fair-copying *Endymion,* a depression-twin to "After dark vapors," written just before the debut of *Poems.* "I cannot write sense this Morning," he confesses to Reynolds before copying out this sonnet (*K* 97). It is another diary-piece, not for publication.[1] Keats thinks as poet, writing poetry, in sonnet-writing, through sonnet-writing. The dignified formal pacing, on the pattern of a Shakespearean sonnet (three stages and a summation), strains against an anxiety that knows from its first syllable where it is going. The quiet latency of *cease to be* is poised to plummet into this totalized nullity. No Phoenix-poetics here. In this winter mood, Keats spins a pre-posthumous epitaph, writing a life of writing undone, no immortality after the death of the author. The opening of *Endymion* declares that *a thing of beauty* (poetry included) will *never pass into nothingness.* This sonnet delivers ontological *Nothingness.*

The glossary for *DW* lists for *Cease:* decease, die (sq. 3332). In Keats's sonnet, this verb precedes *to be,* and forecloses everything after the bitter syllable-repetition, "*Be*fore." Keats's syntax is paced to build pressure, with a climax in self-annihilation. A formal-literacy feeds this temporal gloom, his syntax echoing Shakespeare's Sonnet XII (*When I do count the clock that tells the time*), marked in his copy (*KS* 40), and Milton's Sonnet XVI (*When I consider how my light is spent*) about his failing eyesight. Both sonnets pivot on a reckoning volta. Shakespeare turns the accounting outward to his addressee, *Then of thy beauty do I question make,* in order to urge *him* to act against wasting time by

having a child, a second self. Milton's considering advances its volta to line 8—
But Patience to prevent / That murmur (hardly prevented, having claimed more
than half the sonnet)—then calibrates what steadfast faith requires, and doesn't
require, of someone who is losing powers of sight.

Keats's opening words *When I* initiate an anaphora that picks up the mirror
rhyme *my pen* as it builds to an expected, and rhyming, *then,* the temporal sense
contending with the argument-sense: *in consequence, therefore.* Keats capital-
izes on his Shakespearean pattern to delay this release until the middle of line
12 (this is the volta), where it springs it open to no saving clause at all: *then on
the Shore / Of the wide world I stand alone. Shore* meets blank page space, fig-
uring the *Nothingness* into which Keats's astonishing single-sentence pile-up of
thinkings sinks. The initial words *cease to be* are haunted by his anxious hopes
for *Endymion,* begun in assurance that a "thing of beauty" (itself implied) "will
never / Pass into nothingness." The sonnet's metaphor of the harvest not to be
is both surreal and real: a brain, not even a mind, with harvest potential. The
poet of "To one who has been long in city pent" greeted "the fair / And open
face of heaven" and "the smile of the blue firmament." The poet of this sonnet
looks at a night sky's "Huge cloudy symbols of a high romance" with a shiver
of impossibility. *I may cease to be* relays into *I may never live.* Even were this
poet to *live,* the great gamble is the chance of a magic moment, nebulous
shadows, tenuous tracing.

The shadow of regret is not just about vocation and but also "Love." It is an
ideal, so categorical and abstract as to be "poetry," too: a fair creature of no
name, a muse of passion, imagined with Keats's signature intensity of gusto,
relish. How paradoxical that he calls Love *unreflecting:* this might denote
"without self-consciousness" or "without any required response." Its stronger
force is as antonym of *reflecting,* in the sense of "throwing back the thoughts
upon the past or on themselves" (*JnD*), or in Keats's sonnet, *thinking* and
thinking upon: the mental action that sends Love and Fame together into Noth-
ingness. This final substantive of insubstantiality is not equivalent to those
Nothings that are, Keats writes less than two months on, *made Great and dig-
nified by an ardent pursuit* (*K* 114). It is existential.

The conjunction *then* (14) jolts into this nullity with its double-grammar:
then pulsed into a temporality with *when* on redoubled thinking. It is *conse-
quitive:* as consequence, as the very result of thinking. The seascape again: this
will hellify at the end of Keats's verse-letter to Reynolds, soon to come in March.
The poet on the shore of this sonnet is no Cortez, staring at the wide sea in
sublime wonder and imperial satisfaction. It is a place of self-cancellation; *think*
is intransitive, no object, just collateral damage from *Love and Fame.* This son-

net's final dash is no punctuation of prospect but a blank typographus of nothingness.

If the sea is Time itself, is there any possibility of arrest?

[letter to J. H. Reynolds, 31 January 1818; *K* 97]

---

[1] First published in *1848*, a lifetime after Keats ceased to be.

To—— ("Time's sea")

Time's sea hath been five years at its slow ebb;
  Long hours have to and fro let creep the sand,
Since I was tangled in thy beauty's web,
  And snared by the ungloving of thine hand:
And yet I never look on midnight sky,
  But I behold thine eyes' well-memoried light;
I cannot look upon the rose's dye,
  But to thy cheek my soul doth take its flight:
I cannot look on any budding flower,
  But my fond ear, in fancy at thy lips,
And hearkening for a love-sound, doth devour
  Its sweets in the wrong sense:—Thou dost eclipse
Every delight with sweet remembering,
And grief unto my darling joys dost bring.

8

With *Endymion* Book II just off his desk, Keats pauses on 4 February 1818 for a time-piece sonnet of obsession. Were Wordsworth writing such a memory, he would call it a consequential *spot of time*. Keats's story, addressed with a blank *To——*, lodges no psycho-autobiography. For all its swoon of passion, the moment of entanglement by Beauty's web feels like a motivated pretext for a stylized critical knowingness about such a dynamic, even a reverse-engineered "cause." The dash's blank typography is purely arbitrary. "A lady whom he saw for some few moments at Vauxhall," Milnes heard from Wood-house (*1848* 2:297). This south-bank entertainment park, famed for alley-ways of amorous intrigue, is Keats's fabricated web-map, the lady its fabri-cated webmistress. Who is the object of *To——* scarcely matters; it is the captivating strip-tease (in an elegant ungloving) that counts, a spell woven in a moment. This is all it takes for a "poet" who is pre-wired, conventionally prepped, to write up enchantment, with default blame (also conventional) on beauty's web.

Keats's words are just as ready. The *slow ebb* leaves a *slow web*, a phonic un-dertow of *low ebb* in the slowed meter that letters *web* in advance of the rhyme at line 3. No better style for an ungloved hand's unwitting snare of attention: for all the drama of chance, Keats's artistic hand is evident. Two arts, then: the slight art of beauty in the ungloving of a hand; the art of the poetic hand in this sonnet of erotic capture. The poetry is perverse eros, or normative male love-verse, Keatsian issue, the warp of which we (and he) know by now: beauty's snare, a gaze at the midnight sky, budding flowers, the fond, devouring ear, the calendrics of memory, a joy and grief never to be forgotten.

Post hoc, ergo propter hoc (after this, therefore because of this) is the argument. The poetry's figural logic is reverse: the desire to spin a love-complaint produces its cause. Decades ahead of Freud, here is Keats forming (if not theoretically formulating) fetishism, the confecting of an arbitrary queen of sense to install as the muse of this poet's affair with a love-sonnet. The power of a fetish, Freud argues, is no intrinsic quality but the irrational effect, an overproduced, overdetermined metonymic substitution. When it is not a religion of beauty, call it "Vulgar Superstition." This is the sliding scale of Keatsian epistemology for greetings of the spirit, to things absolutely *real* to those *nothings* given to *ardent* minds able to <u>consecrate whate'er they look upon</u> (*K* 114). The consecration Keats stages in "Time's sea" so compresses this scale that it becomes a fetish of fetishism. He is wry about the consecrations: *As Tradesmen say every thing is worth what it will fetch, so probably every mental pursuit takes its reality and worth from the ardour of the pursuer* (*K* 114). Nicely packed is this word *takes: draws and derives, catches and claims, sets as foundation.* Set in a foreign, primitive culture, such derivatives of fascinated desire get credited to supernatural power. The arbitrary thing is a *fetish,* a French-Portuguese coinage (*fétiche, feitiço*), another culture's belief-work. But the binary is bogus. The word-draw is European: Italian *fattizio,* Old French *faitis,* Latin *factīcius,* made, made up. Keats's wit gives fetish-logic (superstition to religion) a local habitation, Vauxhall, and a name, *To——*. His sonnet knows this involute, the effect generating a factitious cause.

At the same time, this poem is a fabulous work of art, a counter-formation to its tangle in beauty's web. The Shakespearean weave of Keats's sonnet flaunts a formal mastery. "In rhythm, in the peculiar effect gained by the repetition of phrase, in emotional structure and the management of its crescendo it is probably the most Shakespearean sonnet that Keats ever wrote." This is de Selincourt, following the happy upgrade of Poet Laureate Robert Bridges: "it might have been written by Shakespeare" (*Poems* 544). You can see such skill in the way Keats paces the end-paused lines of the first quatrains toward a volta quite in advance of the pattern, at line 5's *And yet,* then unfurls everything further from this. If *Time's sea* seems to measure objective slow time, this volta draws it to a poet's calendar, on the same page as "Five years have passed, five years with the length / Of five long winters" (so begins *Tintern Abbey,* a poem Keats knew on his pulses). Against personified Time, the person "I" emerges in the ebb and flow of anaphora: *And yet I never look . . . / But; I cannot look . . . / But; I cannot look . . . / But.* Then the finely tuned, punctuated stop and start of *in the wrong sense: —Thou dost eclipse* distills the intensely styled paradox of sweet grief.

Such a brilliant poetic expansion on the grammar of fetishized *wrong sense!* In the poet's sober reflection, it gets called this; but it is the right sense for the events of fascination. Keats displays a logic of fetish that also looks like a poet's logic: the way "my fon*d ear*" sounds into "my fond *dear.*" Deftly tuned to the libidinal foreplay in the poetics of the unconsummated, Keats's sensuous investment has paid off with a palpable distillation of sonnet "logic" and process, the latent *son*[song, sound]*net* ready in the word *net,* the erotic captivation webbed into art. This sonnet's poetic franchise is large indeed, a logic for metaphor, for metonymy, and their figural license: a *flower* looks like *lips; lips* are hearkened to for sound; sound becomes a taste (*flower* to *devour* is the shorthand rhyme). Remembering's *eclipse* draws the entire phenomenological world into a poet's blazon, lettered and spellbound in the very words: *lips* to "ec*lips*e," every *delight* remembering the rhymes, *midnight, light, flight.* With *my . . . dear* curled into *my darling* (an echo and derivative of *dear*), with *its sweets* arrested by *sweet remembering,* Keats invests this gerund for the final delivery, *bring,* this word already in contraction by *rememb'ring.* The word *devour,* John Jones remarks, "elevates the 'wrong sense' of honest commentary into the right sense of poetic intensification" (199).

In this intensity, what is Keats's investment? Is the sonnet too evidently a sequel-fetish of exquisite artistry?[1] Keats (yet again) did not write for publication. What he did publish stars a gothic twin, an alpha fetishist in female form: Isabella. The glove that she exhumes from her lover's grave, to be embroidered with her purple phantasies (*Isabella* XLVII), is the least of her treasured fetchings, her pathological webwork. While male entanglement by a female web is cliché, Keats could feel on his pulses what animates it in breathing male life. This is what he describes in a letter to George and Georgiana in October 1818 about an enchanting exotic visitor, Jane Cox (a Reynolds-cousin), a beauty so self-possessed as to make all observers epiphenomena (*K* 209–210). Just weeks before, Keats had assured his publisher James Hessey that he was ready to write with judgment (*K* 207). In this mode, he writes about the Cox-effect as if he were giving Jane Austen cool copy for *Emma.*

> *She is an east indian and ought to be her Grandfather's Heir [. . .] the young Ladies were warm in her praises down stairs calling her genteel, interesting and a thousand other pretty things to which I gave no heed, not being partial to 9 days wonders - Now all is completely changed— they hate her; [. . .] women of inferior charms hate her.*

A wry bystander's report, delivered with a male smirk about vacillations on the female social thermometer. Keats then gives his own measure, drawing himself into the dynamic:

> She is not a Cleopatra; but she is at least a Charmian. She has a rich eastern look; she has fine eyes and fine manners. When she comes into a room she makes an impression the same as the Beauty of a Leopardess. She is too fine and too concious of her Self to repulse any Man who may address her - from habit she thinks that nothing <u>particular</u>.

The reciprocal of this habit, Keats realizes, is his release from his habitually awkward self-consciousness, able to enjoy her spectacle as camelion Poet, annihilating self to *live in her:*

> I always find myself more at ease with such a woman; the picture before me always gives me a life and animation which I cannot possibly feel with any thing inferiour — I am at such times too much occupied in admiring to be awkward or on a tremble. I forget myself entirely because I live in her.

This is not love, Keats insists, but an aesthetic contract, on both sides, *at ease,* played, maybe overplayed, against *a tease:*

> she kept me awake one Night as a tune of Mozart's might do - I speak of the thing as a passtime and an amuzement than which I can feel none deeper than a conversation with an imperial woman the very 'yes' and 'no' of whose Lips is to me a Banquet. I dont cry to take the moon home with me in my Pocket not do I fret to leave her behind me. I like her and her like because one has no <u>sensations</u> - what we both are is taken for granted – . . . she walks across a room in such a manner that Man is drawn towards her with a magnetic Power

The draw of *her manner* on *Man*-Keats *towards her* maps *To*———, but with a critical difference: it is not pained, not plained, not pathological. It is a *pastime,* on no tidal wave of Time.

> she is a fine thing speaking in a worldly way: for there are two distinct tempers of mind in which we judge of things — the worldly, theatrical and pantomimical; and the unearthly, spiritual and ethereal — in the former Buonaparte, Lord Byron and this Charmian hold the first place in our Minds

In the second temper, enroll the addressee of *To——*, or any woman of terrific charm, of which *Charmian* (Cleopatra's servant) is the verbal emanation—with the Keatsian twist that its scene is worldly, theatrical, and pantomimical. Or so Keats protests at length, perhaps too much, overplaying his hand. The sonnet entertains the character of a poet as a perverse devourer of sweets, *unearthly, spiritual and ethereal,* with Keats the poet behind the scenes as a worldly, theatrical, and pantomimical manager of the display.

From Charmian in Alexandria to the exotic Nile, *I'the east my pleasure lies,* Keats could say in sincere imagination (he marked this line in *Antony and Cleopatra* 2.3; *DW* 6:29).

[Woodhouse's ms.; *P* 232–233]

---

[1]In a fine discussion of fetish and Keats's early poetry, Marjorie Levinson remarks that "the sexual fetishism which Freud treats as a pathological state is, in effect, a parody of the historically normative . . . fetishism which characterizes the nineteenth-century (male) gaze" (*Keats's Life* 229).

Sonnet / To the Nile

Son of the old moon-mountains African!
  Chief of the pyramid and crocodile!
  We call thee fruitful, and, that very while,
A desert fills our seeing's inward span;
Nurse of swart nations since the world began,
  Art thou so fruitful? or dost thou beguile
  Such men to honor thee, who, worn with toil,
Rest for a space 'twixt Cairo and Decan?
O may dark fancies err! they surely do;   9
  'Tis ignorance that makes a barren waste
Of all beyond itself: thou dost bedew
  Green rushes like our rivers, and dost taste
The pleasant sun-rise; green isles hast thou too,
  And to the sea as happily dost haste.

On the same day he wrote "Time's sea," Keats tells his brothers, "Shelley, Hunt & I wrote each a Sonnet on the River Nile" (*L* 1:227–228). This was another of Hunt's contests, timed to fifteen minutes (there was some suspicion that Hunt had pre-composed). Hunt promptly published his effort. Keats did not, soon or late.[1]

In 1818, the Nile was still a river of mystery, the romance of its source magnetic. A famous passage in James Bruce's *Travels to Discover the Source of the Nile, in the Years 1768, 1769, 1770, 1771, 1772, and 1773* (1790) recounts his long arc of aspiration, triumph, disappointment, and despondency. At last "in possession of what had, for many years, been the principal object of my ambition and wishes," Bruce records a diminished thing:

The marsh, and the fountains, upon comparison with the rise of many of our rivers, became now a trifling object in my sight. I remembered that magnificent scene in my own native country, where the Tweed, Clyde, and Annan, rise in one hill; three rivers, as I now thought, not inferior to the Nile in beauty . . . I had seen the rise of the Rhine and the Rhone, and the more magnificent sources of the Seine. I began, in my sorrow, to treat the inquiry about the source of the Nile as a violent effort of a distempered fancy . . . Grief or despondency now rolling upon me like a torrent . . . the Nile indeed as no more than rising from springs, as all other rivers do, but widely different in this, that it was the palm for three thousand years held out to all the nations in the world as a *detur dignissimo,* which, in my cool hours, I had thought was worth the attempting at the risk of my life. (1791 edition, 4:328–330)

Keats may have read this passage at school, or heard it paraphrased. *To the Nile* is his volley of *tribute to* exotic wonder and a *comparison to* home measures.

His sonnet begins in a camelion imagining of a Nile-traveler's greeting of a spirit. It is a perfect first Petrarch step, prelude to a dispiriting. Keats's terrain is not geography but the "inward span" of imagination. He does not name the Nile except in the title, deciding to evoke it along the sounded rhyme-chain of *crocodile* (the exotic), *while* (the time of imagination), and *beguile* (the lure to imagination). The octave rehearses the myths; the sestet reflects on the myth-making, including the "fancies" of this very sonnet. Scotsman Bruce's story turns from fantasy to reality; Keats takes on the fancies. How sure-footed he is in making the game of writing about the Nile into a sonnet on the game. He begins with the wordings of Egyptian mythology, moon-mountains, pyramid, crocodile, using the *of* grammar to blend "mythic-genealogical and partitive-description."[2] Line 3 frames the invocations as discourse, what *we call* this river, imagining it as a fertile corridor in the desert or *Nurse of swart nations.* This is not geography but the discourse of Euro-*we.* The second quatrain, seemingly primed to reprise the mythology of a fruitful river, instead questions the mythology: *Art thou so fruitful?* The Nile beguiles India-bound travelers into thinking of fruitfulness, when, on the toil south from the Mediterranean port Alexandria to Cairo, they face an eastern desert spanning to the Red Sea, thence to Decan (India). Keats cared enough to write lines 6–8 on the copy Charles Brown was making.

Keats's sestet plays along, satirizing any *dark fancies* (9). This is a sonnet about romance as a projection of desire: given the desert ground, a perilous romance. Such are Keats's musings, pained and playful, in these post-*Endymion* winter months. Bruce deems the sources of his native rivers and those in Europe equal to or superior to the Nile's; it was only a fancy distempered by hype that made the Nile beckon as an extraordinary sublimity. Keats addresses the Nile as just one more of the world's rivers, *like, too, as happily.* The Nile is more real for being unsublimed. If Morris Dickstein deems Keats's sonnet "very bad," it still prompts this critic to three very good pages on it (146–149). I think it is a success of real-time meditation in poetic form—pretty remarkable, too: Keatsian, to its core.

[Charles Brown's ms., marked by Keats]

[1] First published in a weekly journal in 1838, then in *1848,* with Hunt's and Shelley's *Ozymandias.* Hunt wrongly gave Keats's sonnet to Milnes as Shelley's (which was not published until 1876). All three are in *K* 103–104.

[2] So Geoffrey Hartman reads *To Autumn*'s "Season of mists and mellow fruitfulness" ("Poem and Ideology" 142). The Mountains of the Moon are in Abyssinia, fabled fount of the Nile.

Answer to a Sonnet Ending Thus ("BLUE!")

Answer to a Sonnet Ending Thus:—

"Dark eyes are dearer far
Than those that mock the hyacinthine bell;"

By J. H. Reynolds.

Feb. 1818.

BLUE! 'tis the life of heaven,—the domain
   Of Cynthia,—the wide palace of the sun,—
The tent of Hesperus, and all his train,—
   The bosomer of clouds, gold, grey and dun.
Blue! 'tis the life of waters—ocean
   And all its vassal streams: pools numberless   6
May rage, and foam, and fret, but never can
   Subside, if not to dark-blue nativeness.
Blue! Gentle cousin of the forest-green,
   Married to green in all the sweetest flowers—
Forget-me-not,—the blue bell,—and, that queen
   Of secrecy, the violet: what strange powers
Hast thou, as a mere shadow! But how great,
When in an Eye thou art, alive with fate!

Keats wrote this sonnet on 8 February 1818, on another break from *Endymion*. Its chiming *Blue!* is part of a volley with Reynolds, stimulated by a sonnet that he had sent to Keats (and later published in *The Garden of Florence*, 1821):

Sweet poets of the gentle antique line,
   That made the hue of beauty all eterne,
   And gave earth's melodies a silver turn,—
Where did you steal your art so right divine?—
Sweetly ye memoried every golden twine
   Of your ladies' tresses:—teach me how to spurn
   Death's lone decaying and oblivion stern
From the sweet forehead of a lady mine.

The golden clusters of enamouring hair

Glow'd in poetic pictures sweetly well;—
Why should not tresses dusk, that are so fair
　On the live brow, have an eternal spell
In poesy?—dark eyes are dearer far
　Than orbs that mock the hyacinthine-bell.　　　　　(pp. 128–129)

Reynolds's Petrarchan sonnet alludes to the convention of blazon, the item-izing of a beloved's beauties. It is gently satiric, the word *antique* naming a long tradition (*line*) with a modern tinge of triteness, inflected by the English pro-nunciation of *antique* as *antic*. With poem-punning in the full phrase, *gentle antique line,* Reynolds protests the draw of blazons on impossibilities: pure gold for tresses, eyes that surpass a hyacinth's luxuriant blue (*mock: to mimic in con-tempt*). Shakespeare's Sonnet 130 ("My mistress's eyes are nothing like the sun") is the primer of such counter-blazons, marked by Keats in his copy (*KS* 40). Reynolds's sonnet is not contrary, just arguing for dark hair and dark eyes against the esteem of gold and blue.

Keats makes a point of itemizing *blue* in the lucidity of the ordinary world: the sky (recall *the blue firmament* of *1817*'s Sonnet X); the ocean (recall the *blue green* ocean in Sonnet I); the humble flowers forget-me-not, blue bell, violet, all sprinkled through Keats's poetry (about fifty times so far). Its most potent site is a lively beloved's eye. That's the basic argument, but how remarkable is the facility of the sonnet that unfolds it. Not only does Keats meet Reynolds's Petrarchan-form plea with a Shakespearean-form riposte, but on the light challenge of praising *blue* he matches the rhyme pattern with a front-line *Blue!* at each quatrain's start, with chimes in *dark blue* and a *blue bell* that ring against Reynolds's *hyacinthine-bell.* Poetic conceiving and poetic conceit seem simultaneous. Keats's "BLUE!" summons poetic figures (Cynthia and Hesperus; the anthology of flowers) for a modern ironizing of "sweet poets of the antique line." Keats argues a Keatsian case, calling on the dactyls *numberless* and *nativeness:* native Keatsian numbers.

Fun with *blue* marks a playful letter to Fanny Brawne two years on. Keats had accidentally *disfigured* Brown's prized edition of Ben Jonson with a *smear of black currant jelly.* The smear could not be *lick'd* off, he sighs about the defeat of his strenuous tongue; but the residue yielded a new portmanteau of blue:

> *it remains very purple~~ue~~ – I did not know whether to say purple or blue so in the mixture of the thought wrote purple which may be an excellent name for a colour made up of those two.*　　　(MsK 1.75.357; compare *L* 2:262)

Here is Keats's verbal inventiveness on record, coining a word and rhyming in lexical pastiches from *purpleue*, to *purple or blue*, to *purplue*, to meta-chromatic rhyme with *those two*. He also invented the word *interassimulate* (*K* 274) to describe the dynamics of mutual influencing between contiguities.

Oscar Wilde may have known this letter from Forman's edition *Letters of John Keats to Fanny Brawne* (XVI). He quoted "BLUE!" with warm admiration for its chromo-aesthetics in a lecture during his American tour, 21 February 1882. In the audience at the Masonic Grand Lodge in Louisville, Kentucky, was Keats's niece, Emma Keats Speed (now almost sixty). She introduced herself to Wilde afterwards, inviting him to visit her home, where she showed him a wealth of Keats's letters and poems in Keats's hand, including "BLUE!" Wilde read the page with his fine sense of beauty, noting how Keats had written *Lakes* in line 6, then wrote *pools*, for the assonance with *blue*. In the same line, he saw Keats trying out *Pools and seas*, then canceling this for a trisyllable *Waterfalls*, then revising this to the gently falling numbers of *numberless*.[1]

Touched by such careful, rapt attention, Emma Speed sent the sonnet to Wilde on 12 March. He replied on the 21st from Omaha, Nebraska, in astounded gratitude for the gift of Keats's living hand:

> more golden than gold, more precious than any treasure this great country could yield me . . . It is a sonnet I have loved always, and indeed who but the supreme and perfect artist could have got from a mere colour a motive so full of marvel: and now I am half enamoured of the paper that touched his hand, and the ink that did his bidding, grown fond of the sweet comeliness of his charactery, for since my boyhood I have loved none better than your marvellous kinsman . . . (*Letters* 198)

The word *charactery* is a tacit tribute to Keats's phrasing of fears that he may cease to be, before his pen can give *charactry—impression, mark, distinction* (*JnD*)—to the ideas in his teeming brain. Wilde puts a charactery of sound in *love* in "ful*l* *of* marvel" at this gift, beyond any mere fetish. He had the manuscript framed, which (alas!) disappeared after the forced auction of his effects on 24 April 1895, in a lot at a "knocked-down" price of 38 shillings.[2] Before this catastrophe, Wilde had published a sonnet, *The Grave of Keats*, with chromo-honors: "RID of the world's injustice, and his pain, / He rests at last beneath God's veil of blue" (1–2).[3]

[first publication, *1848* 2:295]

[1]A facsimile of the lost original, minus its first line, is in Wilde's essay, "Keats' Sonnet on Blue," recounting his meeting Emma Speed, his day with Keats's manuscripts, and acutely comparing the manuscript with *1848*'s "BLUE!".

[2]After losing a suit of slander against Lord Queensberry, Wilde was tried and convicted of indecency and sentenced to two years of hard labor. To recover legal expenses, Queensberry secured a lien on Wilde's property and ransacked his home for a devastating, soul-crushing forced auction of everything, from exquisite books and artwork to minor housewares.

[3]*Poems*, 20.

"the Thrush said"

(from Keats's letter to J. H. Reynolds, 19 February 1818)

- a strain of musick conducts to 'an odd angle of the Isle' and when the leaves whisper it puts 'a girdle round the earth[']. Nor will this sparing touch of noble Books be any irreverance to their Writers - for perhaps the honors paid by Man to Man are trifles in comparison to the Benefit done by great Works to the 'Spirit and pulse of good' by their mere passive existence.

Memory should not be called Knowledge . . . Now it appears to me that almost any Man may like the Spider spin from his own [in]wards his own airy Citadel - the points of leaves and twigs on which the spider begins her work are few and she fills the Air with a beautiful circuiting: man should be content with as few points to tip with the fine Webb of his Soul and weave a tapestry empyrean - full of Symbols for his spiritual eye, of softness for his spiritual touch, of space for his wandering of distinctness for his Luxury –

[. . .]

It has been an old Comparison for our urging on - the Bee hive - however it seems to me that we should rather be the flower than the Bee - for it is a false notion that more is gained by receiving than giving - no the receiver and the giver are equal in their benefits - The f[l]ower I doubt not receives a fair guerdon from the Bee - its leaves blush deeper in the next spring - and who shall say between Man and Woman which is the most delighted? Now it is more noble to sit like Jove tha[n] to fly like Mercury - let us not therefore go hurrying about and collecting honey bee-like, buzzing here and there impatiently from a Knowledge of what is to be arrived at: but let us open our leaves like a flower and be passive and receptive - budding patiently under the eye of Apollo and taking hints from every noble insect that favours us with a visit - sap will be given us for Meat and dew for drink – I was led into these thoughts, my dear Reynolds, by the beauty of the morning operating on a sense of Idleness - I have not read any Books - the Morning said I was right - I had no Idea but of the Morning, and the Thrush said I was right - seeming to say -

> *'O thou whose face hath felt the Winter's wind;*
> *Whose eye has seen the Snow clouds hung in Mist*
> *And the black elm tops 'mong the freezing Stars*
> *To thee the Spring will be a harvest-time -*

3

O thou whose only book has been the light
  supreme
Of ^ darkness which thou feddest on
Night after night, when Phœbus was away
To thee the Spring shall be a t[r]ipple morn -   8
O fret not after Knowledge - I have none
And yet my song comes native with the warmth
O fret not after Knowledge - I have none
And yet the Evening listens. He who saddens
At thought of Idleness cannot be idle,
And he's awake who thinks himself asleep.'

Now I am sensible all this is a mere sophistication, however it may neighbour
to any truths, to excuse my own indolence - so I will not deceive myself that
Man should be equal with Jove - but think himself very well off as a sort of
scullion-Mercury or even a hum ble Bee - It is not matter whether I am right
or wrong either one way or another, if there is sufficient to lift a little time from
your Shoulders. Your affectionate friend
  John Keats —

In my excerpt from a longer letter, Keats tenders a brief for "indolence," a mood he indulged during work on *Endymion,* not as relapse but for refueling. The etymology is apt: *in + dolens, not feeling pain*—but not inactive. In the full, conspicuously un-indolent, four-and-a-half-page letter, Keats issues a seriocomic treatise on busyness and indolence. His witty, mellifluous oxymoron, *delicious diligent indolence,* upgrades Endymion's best shot, *ardent listlessness* (1.826).

Keats diligently, indolently, volleys his case with phrases from his reading, soundings for Reynolds's recognition. The quotations in the first paragraph above draw on wordings he underlined in *The Tempest* (1.2; *DW* 1:12) and *A Midsummer Night's Dream* (Act 2, *DW* 2:18). The third phrase is from Wordsworth's *Old Cumberland Beggar* (*Lyrical Ballads*). Keats also tips in another text. He knew how to spell *web. Webb* winks at the first "Cockney School" barb in *Blackwood's,* its epigraph-verse attributed to "Cornelius Webb" and signaling Keats's coming abuse.[1] Keats retunes the slur for his own webwork of tapestry empyrean. His sequel trope is the bee-hive, analogous to a web as a site for nature's workings. What sort of model is the busy instinct of hive-working bees?

Keats cartoons indolence as a love-affair, a patient nurture of intellect at odds with any buzzing and hurrying, and refuting the "old comparison" in Isaac Watt's famous didactic hymn, *Against Idleness and Mischief:*

How doth the little busy Bee
Improve each shining Hour,
And gather Honey all the day
From every opening Flower!   (1715)

To Keats, a flower rather than a Bee as thing to be. Like Jove, like a flower: the blend is an oxymoron of what it is to be productively *passive and receptive*—for poets especially, who may approve of indolence as a *budding patiently under the eye of Apollo,* the poets' god.

Keats cues the sonnet with the prose-prelude's lilting *sense of idleness.* A triple-sounded *morning* muse contests Watts's busy bee: *the Thrush said I was right.* Wordsworth's defense of sonnet-writing argues *fret not:* this scanty plot is ground for better things. Keats's Thrush makes it categorical: *fret not after Knowledge.* This is no "pathetic fallacy" (nature's sympathy with us), nor is it camelion poetics (oh, to be a thrush!). This thrush is a *Keatsian* singer. In his sole experiment with a stand-alone, blank-verse quatorzain, Keats's sonic punctuations are repetitions in imitation of thrush-song—*O thou whose . . . to thee/O thou whose . . . /To thee;* then *O fret not/O fret not* (the line repeated)—chimed with alliterations (*Winter's wind; seen the snow*) and internal rhymes (*light/Night after night,* literally). Keats still has a feel for Petrarchan sonnet-form. *O thou . . . to thee* is an octave; *O fret not/O fret not/And yet* mark out a sestet. The octave jests about February's mental calendar. To a wintered mind, *freezing Stars* work overtime. The stars on that night of "Keen, fitful gusts" *look very cold* (an irrational hint of active agency). The participle *freezing* here (3) delivers a similar sensation. In such assault, any spring-time would feel like a harvest bounty. So, too, in a surreal darkness as the only light, spring shines like a *tripple* morn (8), a measure super-lettered. Keats seems to have started writing *third,* then *Triple* (the usual emendation); he left the doubly enriched *thipple* uncorrected.[2] It was right for the moment.

The business of the sestet is advice: *fret not after (reach for, be querulous about)* anything—springtime, knowledge, light—but trust potential, reserves, and natural rhythms. A quasi-Shakespearean close distills a paradox. A *thought of Idleness* is not idle; only a waking mind can *think* itself asleep: not out of it, but in the metaphor. This isn't a fret of song but a witty irony about having to hear this lesson. Typically, Keats parodies its pulse.

Still sensible (thinking, theorizing), Keats post-scripts himself as the writer of letter and sonnet: he's been rationalizing his idleness this winter morn. He knows that a case for godlike indolence can look like self-flattery: a godling servant or a humble worker bee, however busy, is no Jove of power. His affec-tion for Reynolds's lassitude, however, is sincere. Reynolds is unwell, and Keats means to cheer him with a generous morning's work, and play. The sonnet wasn't for publication; it was a gift, friendship's greeting of the spirit. The next month, high-spirited Rice got an even more spirited letter.

[Robert H. Taylor collection, Princeton University Library; see also *K* 105–112]

[1] That was summer 1817 (*Blackwood's* p. 38). In 1822, Webb honored Keats with a sonnet, *To John Keats, on his first Poems*. A proofreader for *The Quarterly*, Webb would have known the abuse coming in fall 1818.

[2] *JnD* does not list it, even as a variant. *Tripple* is a retro-antique spelling from the Renaissance, revived in Nahum Tate and William Stonestreet's translation of *Metamorphoses* (1717). In the first printing of Keats's letter (and sonnet), Milnes emended to *triple* (*1848* 1:90), generally followed. Rare exceptions are *tripple* in Stillinger (*P* 235) and Cook (175). My *John Keats* (sigh) overproduced, misreading a faint *r* as a compressed *hr* to get *thripple* (112). I did include a photograph of the Princeton ms. (p. 5), which, in my reperception, does show *thipple* (110).

"Rantipole Betty, a dawlish fair"

Teignmouth Tuesday [24 March 1818]

My dear Rice,

   Being in the midst of your favorite Devon, I should not by rights, pen one word but it should contain a vast portion of Wit, Wisdom, and learning – for I have heard that Milton ere he wrote his answer to Salmasius came into these parts, and for on whole Month, rolled himself, for three whole hours in a certain meadow hard by us – where the mark of his nose at equidistances is still shown. The exhibitor of said Meadow further saith that after these rollings, not a nettle sprang up in all the seven acres for seven years and that from said time a new sort of plant was made from the white thorn, of a thornless nature very much used by the Bucks of the present day to rap their Boots withal [. . .] I was very peedisposed to a Country I had heard you speak so highly of, I took particular notice of every thing during my journey and have bought some folio asses skin for Memorandums – I have seen every thing but the wind– [. . .] Some of the Barmaids look'd at me as if I knew Jem Rice – but when I took [lost text] Brandy they were quite convinced. One asked whether [lost text]ed a secret she gave you on the nail— [. . .] I hope you are showing poor Reynolds the way to get well – send me a good account of him and if I can I'll send you one of Tom – Oh! for a day and all well!

I went yesterday to a dawlish fair –
  Over the hill and over the dale,
  And over the bourn to Dawlish -
  Where Gingerbread Wives have a scanty sale
  And gingerbread nuts are smallish.

  Rantipole Betty she ran downa hill
  And kick'd up her petticats fairly
  Says I I'll be Jack if you will be Gill -
  So she sat on the Grass debonnairly -

  Here's somebody coming, here's somebody coming!
   Says I 'tis the wind at a parley
  So without any fuss any hawing and humming
   She lay on the grass debonairly -

Here's somebody here and here's somebody <u>there</u>!
  Say's I hold your tongue you young Gipsey.
So she held her tongue and lay plump and fair
  And dead as a venus tipsy -

O who would'nt hie to Dawlish fair
  O who would'nt stop in a Meadow
O would not rumple the daisies there
  And make the wild fern for a bed do –
    Tom's Remembrances
    and mine to all –
      your sincere friend
        John Keats

Keats is with Tom, who is spending the winter (first with George) on the south coast, in Teignmouth. Tom seemed to be improving, Keats told Bailey on 13 March; but by the time he closed this very letter, Tom, "poor fellow," was coughing up blood (*L* 1:241, 244). Keats was fair-copying *Endymion Book IV* and planning a preface. He had fallen out of love with *Endymion,* the rain was relentless, and he needed a day off. The Monday after Easter, he walked three miles over to Dawlish Fair, and had, or fantasized having, a sexcapade, perhaps with prostitute (*venus* in slang). *Wherein lies happiness?* Fellowship divine, says Endymion; fellowship on the grass, says Keats. His letter to Rice is full of the bawdy banter he enjoys with the guys: Reynolds on blushing; now with Rice who had his own fun in the region; always with ribald Brown; and Haydon too, to whom he just sent a *rhyming fit,* in rhyme, *a bit of B_hrell,* the blanks for him to fill in. Keats having just written *doggerel,* the pun-pairing was cued (MsK 1.24.86).

I give some of Keats's letter to Rice as stage-setting for "Rantipole Betty." It opens, comically and outrageously (sq. 89), with a fantasy of Milton, rolling down the same hills, his head picking up nettles and getting battered by acorns. Keats imagines this as a material preparation for his *Defensio pro Populo Anglicano* (1651), a fierce attack on Salmasius's royalist tract on Charles I. Anti-royalist Milton's fearsome head so scorched the ground, Keats jests, that not even nettles could grow thereafter. A minor bounty: the thornless stumps proved useful for polishing up the boots of city-swells (Bucks) on the make at the local fair. These dandy heirs supply Keats's *theory of Nettles* (sq. 90) and his fraternity brothers at (and with) the *dawlish fair.* No anxiety of influence, just cheerful succession.

Rollins does transcribe *peedisposed*, but hopes it was a pen-slip, "*For* predisposed" (*L* 1:255n4). In his dreams! Keats delivers a proactively penile coinage, ready for *on the nail*, the coming Hamlet-punning on *Country* matters and his own medium, *asses skin*.[1] He doesn't stop here: the paragraph spools a full portion of wit for Jemmy Rice's amusement. Warming to his song (extempore or from some discarded draft), Keats tunes up his prose with rhythmic three- and four-beats, on the rhythm of Milton's downhill roll: *Oh for a day and all well/ /I went yesterday to a dawlish fair –* . A term for young woman (adjective nominalized), *fair* swings into the verbal erotics. *Rantipole* is a word in *JnD: wild, roving, rakish; a low word*—for men as well as women. "Junkets," Hunt's affectionate nickname for him, is also a rantipole.

Keats raises *Rantipole* to a sexual pun, for them both. *Rantipole Betty* (Betty: generic servant) marks a willing partner, worth her name as she *ran* down a hill, then settling, as maid and word, into the chimes of *rumple the daisies*, as debonair a euphemism as any Buck could sublimate. It is as if Keats had confected her name as a foundational grammar. He nicely supersedes sublime Milton in the air of shared fun. *Jack* is his responsive randy-pole, she his *Gill*, the verse progressing from *ran* to *sat* to *lay*, double-punctuated by this singular use of *debonairly* in Keats's poetry, in a burlesque of urbane *debonair*. Where Milton rolled down in solitary self-sufficiency, Keats finds a happy partner. *Rantipole Betty* is a type, not a person, and may not even have been a real lass. Keats writes as if she were, in Regency-Buck styling. The city boys may bond over this circulated fun with country girls from lower ranks.

Milnes, that collector of erotica, pulled back, putting only the folk-songy first stanza in *1848* (1:19). Victorian editors followed. Even urbane Ernest de Selincourt (not shy about outing Wordsworth's French affair and daughter thereby) kept the decorum for his 1905 edition (*Poems* 357, all the way into the 1926 reprinting). It was up to Amy Lowell to do Rantipole Keats right, with a smirk at her predecessors' "squeamishness," and a modest boast that her pages provide "All but the first stanza published for the first time" (*John Keats* 1:610–611, 2:533).

Keats's fun is a holiday. He knows darker weather and darker moods—all back in force the next day.

> [MsK 1.25.89–92; Keats folded the page on which he had written, wrote the poem on the back (92), then folded it again, so that the verses would be inside]

---

[1]Gittings (*John Keats* 651) doesn't gloss these two words, but does *secret, nail, kit, puddle, pepper, drops, affair* (MsK 1.25.91; *L* 1:256).

"Dear Reynolds"

Dear Reynolds, as last night I lay in bed

> Dear Reynolds, as last night I lay in bed,
> There came before my eyes that wonted thread
> Of Shapes, and Shadows and Remembrances,
> That every other minute vex and please:
> Things all disjointed come from North and south,
> Two witch's eyes above a cherub's mouth,
> Voltaire with casque and shield and Habergeon,
> And Alexander with his night-cap on—
> Old Socrates a tying his cravat;
> And Hazlitt playing with Miss Edgworth's cat;   10
> And Junius Brutus pretty well so, so,
> Making the best of 's way towards Soho.
>
>   Few are there who escape these visitings—
> P'erhaps one or two, whose lives have patent wings;
> And through whose curtains peeps no hellish nose,
> No wild boar tushes, and no Mermaid's toes:
> But flowers bursting out with lusty pride;
> And young Æolian harps personified,
> Some, Titian colours touch'd into real life. —
> The sacrifice goes on; the pontif knife   20
> Gloams in the sun, the milk-white heifer lows,
> The pipes go shrilly, the libation flows:
> A white sail shews above the green-head cliff
> Moves round the point, and throws her anchor stiff.
> The Mariners join hymn with those on land. —
> You know the Enchanted Castle it doth stand
> Upon a Rock on the Border of a Lake
> Nested in Trees, which all do seem to shake
>
>   Urganda's
> From some old Magic like ~~the witch's~~ sword.
> O Phœbus that I had thy sacred word   30
> To shew this Castle in fair dreaming wise
> Unto my friend, while sick and ill he lies.
>
>   You know it well enough, where it doth seem
> A mossy place, a Merlin's Hall, a dream.

You know the clear Lake, and the little Isles,
The Mountains blue, and cold near neighbour rills—
All which elsewhere are but half animate
Here do they look alive to love and hate;
To smiles and frowns; they seem a lifted mound
Above some giant, pulsing underground.   40
    Part of the building was a chosen See
Built by a banish'd santon of Chaldee:
The other part two thousand years from him
~~Poor Man he left the Terrace Walls of Ur.~~
Was built by Cuthbert de Saint Aldebrim;
Then there's a little wing, far from the sun,
Built by a Lapland Witch turn'd maudlin nun—
And many other juts of aged stone
Founded with many a mason-devil's groan.
    The doors all look as if they oped themselves,
The windows as if latch'd by fays & elves—   50
And from them comes a silver flash of light
As from the Westward of a summer's night;
Or like a beauteous woman's large blue eyes
Gone mad through olden songs and Poesies—
    See what is coming from the distance dim!
A golden galley all in silken trim!
Three rows of oars are lightening moment-whiles
Into the verdurous bosoms of those Isles.
Towards the shade under the Castle Wall
It comes in silence—now tis hidden all.   60
The clarion sounds; and from a postern grate
An echo of sweet music doth create
A fear in the poor herdsman who doth bring
His beasts to trouble the enchanted spring:
He tells of the sweet music and the spot
To all his friends, and they believe him not.
    O that our dreamings all of sleep or wake
Would all their colours from the sunset take:
From something of material sublime,
Rather than shadow our own Soul's daytime   70
In the dark void of Night. For in the world
We jostle—but my flag is not unfurl'd

On the Admiral staff—and to philosophize
I dare not yet!—Oh never will the prize,
High reason, and the lore of good and ill,
Be my award. Things cannot to the will
Be settled, but they tease us out of thought.
Or is it that Imagination brought
Beyond its proper bound, yet still confined,—
Lost in a sort of Purgatory blind,   80
Cannot refer to any standard law
Of either earth or heaven?—It is a flaw
In happiness to see beyond our bourn—
It forces us in Summer skies to mourn:
It spoils the singing of the Nightingale.

Confined: metaphysical and physical. "I am confined to my room, with a heavy cold & fever, leading a life of pain, sleeplessness & bleeding," Keats's friend Reynolds wrote to James Hessey (Taylor's publishing partner), asking for Hazlitt's *Lectures* and the proofs of *Endymion* to "beguile the time."[1] Still with Tom in Teignmouth, Keats sent Reynolds a long verse letter to help out.[2] I present this in the two stages of Keats's pulse of composition: an effort to amuse winding to a severely dark passage (line 85); then a start, to begin again.

Greeting Reynolds in a sympathetic spirit of sleeplessness, Keats weaves a tapestry of amusements from his *wonted* threads of thought, *disjointed* and re-joined in a surreal fancies. As with *Sleep and Poetry*, which produced poetry instead of sleep, this is another such night. Rather than go all pedantic on its whirl of names (for which, see Wikipedia), let's accept that we are overhearing Keats's playful volleying for a close friend, bandying references for him to enjoy, *while sick and ill he lies.* Keats conjures a comical array: Voltaire off to war, Alexander the Great off to bed, Socrates as Regency dandy, Hazlitt enjoying Maria Edgeworth's cat (he didn't much like her writing), Kean's rival, famous American actor Junius Brutus Booth (father of later infamous John Wilkes Booth) off the stage and weaving tipsily to the shady district Soho. Soon in the mix are romance characters: Merlin, Urganda, witches, and a totally Keats-confected Cuthbert de Saint Aldebrim. Fun also comes in Keats's visitings of rhymes: *cat/cravat; Soho/so, so; hellish nose/Mermaid's toes.*

Varying the mood, Keats joins images of higher aesthetic gloss and dire events: Titian's *Europa* (the goddess captured by a bull) mashed up with or fused into Claude Lorrain's *Landscape with the Father of Psyche Sacrificing at the Milesian Temple of Apollo,* both exhibited in London in 1816. For this last,

Keats represents an idyll of ancient communal life, full of light, color, music, wine—but assembled for the ritual sacrifice of a clueless heifer (also to appear in stanza 4 of *Ode on a Grecian Urn*). The painting that draws his fullest description, and draws into one of his darkest turns of meditation is Claude's celebrated *Enchanted Castle* (the usual short title of *Landscape with Psyche outside the Palace of Cupid*), widely known from engravings and from Hazlitt's praises. Keats conducts a tour of the canvas (26–66), playing master of ekphrastic ceremonies. This is another mash-up, a confection of various architectural styles and purposes: ancient Roman, medieval, later Palladian.[3] Longing for Apollo's inspiration (that's *Phœbus*) to render this surreal fantasy, Keats compensates with his poet's skillset: phonic orchestration. A *golden galley all* (56) sends its sounds to Castle W*all* and hidden *all* (59–60), picking up "tho*se Isle*s" (58) for a fine, paradoxical sounding board for the ship coming in *sile*nce (60). Scene and sound converge punningly on a *herd*sman, camelion-imagined by Keats (in an unheard melody), as one who *tells* his thrilling, fearful enchantments to *all* (nicely echoing) his friends.

It is here that Keats seems to have forgotten his addressee, as the verse spirals into his own waking nightmare. Below the pastoral surface is a "giant, pulsing underground." It is a grammatical crash-pad: *giant* and *pulsing* describe the underground; *giant, pulsing* also evoke a pulsing substantive underground deity, a persona of the subconscious well before Freud got there. The proto-poetic pulse of enchanted music recoils into an unresponsive audience, even of friends. From a dead stop at *believe him not* (66), Keats starts talking to himself, to produce "one of the more disconcerting 'get well' poems in the unwritten history of the genre," quips David Luke ("Notes" 661). Disconcerting to an already depressed Reynolds, it is in tune with what Keats has been keeping underground in his effort to entertain this friend.

The "O" at a new paragraph (67) is Keats's self-sighing, pulling the enchanted thread of *all* (56, 60, 66) into a depleted mood of his own mind, weaving a frail wish into impossibility. He has to speak this out, write it out. Notwithstanding the plurals—*our, we, us*—Keats means himself. He overloads *would . . . take* (68) for dreaming's nervous grasp at the material world: *derive, draw, grab, and claim*. The object clause, *From some material sublime* (69), loads every rift with phonics (the hum of *m*) and a grammatical double-fold on *material sublime* that plays as both adjective-noun and noun-adjective. A personified *Night* involves the noun *shadow* as a conspiratorial verb against Soul-sanity (70–71). Keats longs for the epitome of material sublime, the sunset. It is surprising how rare the word *sunset* is in his poetry.[4] He knows it from *Manfred*. Manfred, Byron's most tormented dreamer, deathward progressing to known death, hails as his "material God" the "Glorious Orb" of the last sunset he'll ever see (3.2.3–14).

If Keats's *jostle* is too slight for this world-despiser's metaphysical agons, it is just the word, the only word, for what Keats wants to say about why *material sublime* matters (72). This is the only time, even, that *jostle* comes into his poetry. You might expect the passive, *are jostled*. Keats writes himself (even *we*) as active agents of this buffeting. He is enough of a knight-junkie to know its rooting in *joust*, those dangerously heroic, sometimes fatal clashes of court entertainments. The heroism that Keats flaunts is his individual refusal *to philosophize* (73; this, too, single use). He makes a provisional deferral (*dare not* yet) into a principle, in disdain of a thematically rhymed *prize* (74): *High reason, and the lore of good and ill* (74–75). This is the lore soon cartooned for Reynolds (in another letter, on 3 May) at Milton's expense, as religion's sure point and resting place in reasoning, from which the theologian wielded a *ballance of good and evil* (*K* 130). Keats's verse-letter parodies such *lore* as a dubious *award*, sheer willfulness: *Things cannot to the will / Be settled but they tease us out of thought* (76–77). Yet how Keatsian is the full swing of thinking. No sooner does he write out this principle than he teases it with reperception. The famous reprise, in May 1819, is in the last stanza of *Ode on a Grecian Urn*: "Thou, silent form, dost tease us out of thought." What *tease* is not is *ease*, its rime-riche antonym. The sense of *tease* as *play mischievously*, not yet in the dictionary, is clearly in Keats's thoughts.

Voicing a disdain of easy settlements, Keats needs no formal volta to spring *Or* (78) from the soundscape of *lore/award*. Its pause sends the couplet past the triumphant period at line 77 (*out of thought.*) into a question, *Or is that imagination brought . . .* (78) which takes five lines to unfold. Is hesitation *to philosophize* a negatively capable strength, or confessed inadequacy? Keats thinks the question through in poetic formations: the negative landing places, *Be my award* and *Be settled* (76–77), tilt into a new phono-prefix, *(Be)yond its proper bound* (79) on the way to *Purgatory blind* (80), the adjective *blind* nominalized as a purgatorial state of non-seeing. Keats's casually prefacing *a sort of* (80) does not get sorted out. The question opened at *Or is it . . . ?* (78) crash-lands on three stark judgments of disease: *it is a flaw . . . It forces us . . . it spoils* (82–85). More than any fissure, *flaw* bears the old sense, a fierce storm. The very word absorbs *law* into its superseding rhyme (81–82), and invades the material world: *brought / Beyond our bourn* (83), summer skies roil into sites for mourning; a nightingale's song is spoiled into a metaphysical *Night* (71).

Keats's initial intent to vex and please has teased itself, by rhyme and reason, into this vexing dead end. Better to be a friend-stymied herdsman than such a friend to Reynolds. Still, the letter is genuine Keats. "Your tearing, my dear friend, a spiritless and gloomy Letter up ~~and~~ to rewrite to me is what I shall never forget—it was to me a real thing," he chided Bailey in January (MsK 1.20.69). The *real thing* is both the torn-up letter and a mindfulness of the mood that made it. *Real* for Keats are both things: the spiritless start and the fresh greeting of the spirit. Tearing nothing up in his verse-letter to Reynolds, Keats makes a show of restarting, and writes another 28 lines of verse in attempted self-correction for Reynolds's benefit.

[1] Reynolds, *Letters*, 11–12. Bleeding, a standard medical "treatment" (well into the nineteenth century), drained "bad" blood. Keats performed such procedures at Guy's, and would be subjected to it in 1820.

[2] Unlike the verse-*Epistles* in *1817*, this wasn't for publication. It first appeared, truncated to the poetry, even this curtailed, in *1848* (1:113–116). Even Stillinger truncates the prose coda (*P* 244).

[3] Colvin, *John Keats*, 264. Although Sperry reads a failure of associative process (*Keats* 124–125), I think this is a success in a different register, a new architecture of fancy.

[4] Keats's only other *sunsets* are for two fantastic similes in *Endymion* (2.383; 3.883) and a weather-report, in the *Eve of St. Mark*, with the adjective *chilly* (7).

"Dear Reynolds, I have a mysterious tale . . ."

> Dear Reynolds, I have a mysterious tale
> And cannot speak it. The first page I read
> Upon a Lampit Rock of green sea weed
> Among the breakers—'Twas a quiet Eve;
> The rocks were silent—the wide sea did weave   90
> An untumultuous fringe of silver foam
> Along the flat brown sand. I was at home,
> And should have been most happy—but I saw
> Too far into the sea; where every maw
> The greater on the less feeds evermore:—
> But I saw too distinct into the core
> Of an eternal fierce destruction,
> And so from Happiness I far was gone.
> Still am I sick of it: and though to day
> I've gathered young spring-leaves, and flowers gay   100
> Of Periwinkle and wild strawberry,
> Still do I that most fierce destruction see,

The shark at savage prey—the hawk at pounce,
The gentle Robin, like a pard or ounce,
Ravening a worm —Away ye horrid moods,   105
Moods of one's mind! You know I hate them well,
You know I'd sooner be a clapping bell
To some Kamschatkan missionary church,
Than with these horrid moods be left in lurch—
Do you get health—and Tom the same—I'll dance,
And from detested moods in new Romance
Take refuge—Of bad lines a Centaine dose   112
Is sure enough—and so "here follows prose."—

My Dear Reynolds,

In hopes of cheering you through a Minute or two I was determined nill he will he to send you some lines so you will excuse the unconnected subject, and careless verse—You know, I am sure, Claude's Enchanted Castle and I wish you may be pleased with my remembrance of it—The Rain is Come on again—I think with me Devonshire stands a very poor chance, I shall damn it up hill and down dale, if it keeps up to the average of 6 fine days in three weeks. Let me have better news of you.

Your affectionate friend
John Keats

Toms Rememb^s to you. Rem^r
us to all—

A new paragraph, a new greeting, complete the couplet rhyme for the spoiled song *Nightingale* (85), with Keats inhabiting the philomel legend, unable to speak his *tale* (86). What he can do is read the shoreline: a pastoral of quiet eve, lovely silver-foam fringe patterning, with the sole use of *untumultuous* (91) in all his writing. This negative prefix elicits its antonym, on the axis of *should have been most happy—but* (93). Fortified by a dash, *but* is a volta, swerving from pastoral surface-reading to hectic deep-reading, in imagination's scan.

Spoiling the singing of a nightingale is the least of it. The sightline of *but I saw / Too far into the sea* (93–94) brings a tumultuous crash of words over the pastoral: *straw*berry (101) gets claimed in the soundscape of *every maw* and its near rhyme, *evermore* (94–95); *flowers gay* (100) cannot survive an internal phrase baited to rhyme *savage prey* (103). Flower-gathering turns into an "anthology" swallowed up by a Keatsian supplement to the gothic bloodbath in Canto IV of poet-scientist Erasmus Darwin's *Temple of Nature* (1803):

In ocean's pearly haunts, the waves beneath
Sits the grim monarch of insatiate Death;
The shark rapacious with descending blow
Darts on the scaly brood, that swims below;
The crawling crocodiles, beneath that move,
Arrest with rising jaw the tribes above;
With monstrous gape sepulchral whales devour
Shoals at a gulp, a million in an hour.
—Air, earth, and ocean, to astonish'd day
One scene of blood, one mighty tomb display!
From Hunger's arm the shafts of Death are hurl'd,
And one great Slaughter-house the warring world!   (55–66)

Darwin's tidy couplets string rhymes as relentless as Keats's verbal ricochets and
perverse chimes. From such precedents, Tennyson's memorable "Nature, red
in tooth and claw / With ravine" (*In Memoriam*) seems merely belated. Keats's
vision of perpetual rapacity, savagery, and destruction is not even the divinely
amped malevolence of Darwin's poetry. It is just quotidian nature. A gentle
robin turns raven, *Ravening a worm* (105), not in fierce sea savagery but in door-
yard life.

Keats plays this quotidian metamorphosis against the old mythology: the
raven as the prophet of ill, a character he could ironize in his own moods of
mind. "I am a little given to bode ill like the raven," he will tell Fanny Brawne
as he is writing away for his third volume of poetry, then apologizes for raving:
"I will no more trouble either you or myself with sad Prophecies. . . . I can be
a raven no more" (July 1819; *L* 2:129). Reminding himself in March that he is
writing to cheer Reynolds, he will stop ravening. He takes a beat with a dash:
—*Away ye horrid moods . . . !* (105). Exclamation is one thing, writing another,
however; Keats keeps writing the phrase he would banish. Wordsworth's *Moods
of my own Mind* (a section of his 1807 *Poems*) is no credential for Keats's mind;
it is a foil. Wordsworth is famously moody, but the poems in *Moods* are mostly
on nature's delights: butterflies, nightingales, sparrows and stockdoves, celan-
dines, rainbows, and stars, a few shadows but no nightmares. Keats's patho-
poetics won't even rhyme *moods* except with itself, in drumbeat spasms:
moods, / Moods . . . these horrid moods (106, 109). This is a spoken tale for sure:
my spirit is fevered . . . I have a horrid Morbidity of Temperament, he had con-
fessed, seaside, to Haydon ten months before (*K* 53), a mood his brothers knew
so well as to worry about his mental health.

Back then, he was vexed by getting *Endymion* off the ground. In March 1818, he is trying to draft a preface, seeing no vocational health. *Still am I sick of it,* he sighs in this latest seaside horror (99), "*of it*" lettering into *fit*—and this spasm-word summoning, sounding, poetry's old *fytte*. The only cure is a radical reduction into "not to feel it": a clanging bell, tolling vulgar religion in the north-Pacific regions of Russia (Kamschatka). To lurch back from the depths of the seas and the ravening in his own backyard, seeking reprieve from Arctic self-sentencing, Keats recalls the initial motive for this correspondence. His own cure insecure, he will send best wishes to others: *Do you get health,* he writes, but not without one more inscription of *detested moods* (110–111). The dashes that punctuate 108–113 are a hectic pulsing of an effort to write back into sociability.

Only a change of genre, uncoupled from the connective tissue of couplets, will save both himself and Reynolds. *Let me have better news of you.* Better news implies Tom, too. Keats frequently adds Tom's remembrances in postscript, to keep him in everyone's mind.[5] It's not just that Keats's March *moods* are *horrid;* it is the mortal suffering that no better mood can save. Keats cannot say it, but everyone knew Tom was failing (Reynolds would get better by the summer). Not tearing up his mixed-mood letter, Keats treats it as a pharmacological unit, a *Centaine dose.* Set to rhyme with *prose* (112–113), *dose* cutely sounds *doze,* a waking-dream. It also cues a modal shift to actual prose. Poet Keats keeps the rhyming thread: *dear* Reynolds into *cheer*ing, then this sound into *nill he* to *will he* (and *you will* and *up hill*), with a replay of *you know* from the poetry (106–107). His full phrase, *here follows prose,* is a witty riff on Shakespeare's Malvolio (the name means *bad will*) puzzling over a letter he's received: "Soft! here follows prose" (*Twelfth Night* 2.5). Malvolio thinks he is being encouraged to a courtship. Keats uses the line to ask for Reynolds's understanding of his moody friend.

Twelfth Night is still in the air in Keats's letter: "For the rain it raineth every day" is the refrain of Feste's song (at the end) about existential weather. It pours into Keats's daily news, *The Rain is Come on again.* Feste makes a song of the circumstance, to dance and play, and "strive to please you every day" mid life's guaranteed ills. Keats sports a vigorous pun, a rally against the rain to *damn it up hill and down dale.* With *damn* doing double-time as a curse and a resistance, Keats renders an ad hoc tune for a determination to *dance, / And from detested moods in new Romance / Take refuge* (110–112). As he knows, Shakespeare's other sounding of *the rain it raineth every day* is no festive comedy. It is the Fool's report, material and existential, of life on the bleak and barren, crazy-making heath in *King Lear* (3.2).

A promising rhyme seems sounded in Keats's *dance–Romance*, on the way to a determined *take refuge*. Keats knows what the word *refuge* loads: a flight from, not to (etymologically: *a place to flee back*). Satan, in his mind's hell, has no "refuge" (*PL* 9.119). Keats is only in Purgatory blind. *Romance* is now a mode to ironize, parody, complicate. His "new Romance" is *Isabella; or The Pot of Basil, A Tale from Boccaccio,* already begun. It is also a "new" mode of romance, with no refuge from horrid imaginings and material circumstances.

[*L* 1:259–263; based on Woodhouse's copies of a lost original]

[5] For the effect of Tom's sick body on Keats's letter-writing in 1818, see Annabel Barry's essay, which protests the distortion that editors of Keats's poems effect in deleting this prose sequel.

from *Isabella; or, The Poet of Basil. A Story from Boccaccio*

Having heard Hazlitt mention in his lecture on 3 February 1818 that "a modern translation" of *Isabella*, a tale in Giovanni Boccaccio's *Decameron*, "could not fail to succeed in the present day" (*Lectures* 162), Keats began *Isabella; or The Pot of Basil* the very month.[1] By May, he had it in fair copy. The frame for *Decameron* is a set of young aristocrats who have taken refuge from plague-ridden Florence in a country estate, and amuse themselves with story-telling. Boccaccio was no escape artist. Three-quarters of Florence's population fell to the Black Death of 1348, including his father, stepmother, and many friends. Written in this wake, the *Decameron* is rife with disease, pathology, and death. Its *Isabella* is set in Messina, a Sicilian port infected in 1347, with quick export to the mainland. Keats resets the tale in Florence, the city that Boccaccio's aristocrats escape (and at the time Europe's economic center), and renders a genre-bender of old "tale," "modern rhyme" (XX), and "venturing syllables" into meta-narrative patter.

Keats opens with the love-aching of Isabella and Lorenzo, a clerk in her brothers' mercantile firm. They plan to marry her to "some high noble and his olive-trees" (XXI), a coup of class and commodity, so the lovers must tryst in secret. Doping this out, the brothers invite Lorenzo for a day of hunting. He's their prey. They bury him in the forest, telling Isabella that he went abroad on sudden business. In Keats's most gothic greeting of the spirit ever, Lorenzo's shade appears to her in a dream, to report his fate and gravesite. She digs up his corpse, cuts off the head, takes the head home, dolls it up, and hides it in a pot of sweet basil. Wondering at her doting on this pot, the brothers steal it, uncover its secret, and flee Florence. Isabella suffers the double bereavement and dies forlorn, survived by, memorialized by, her sad ditty of woe.

Keats's *Isabella* is "new Romance" with a vengeance. Writing for the market, he teases any "fair reader" about the genre-contract of finding pleasure in a tale, and retail, of woe: not just lovers' but more severely (and in a supplement to Boccaccio) the brutalities of the mercantile world. Rereading *King Lear*, he bade adieu to "golden-tongued Romance" and its "far-away." *Isabella* has gold aplenty, wrung from regions of labor far away from Florence, a city named for its gold coin, the florin. The Boccaccio-brothers are class snobs. The Keatsian avatars are ruthless ledger-men. Marriage-plot novels of Keats's day were rife with matches maneuvered for financial boon, usually enlisting readers to cheer for true love. Keats unsettles such readers by aligning the lovers with economies that wring gold from misery. Isabella is more than her brothers' pawn; she's a naïve beneficiary of their dark business. My selections present the stanzas in which the complexity of Keats's new venture with "Romance" (the genre and the love-plot) draws our critical attention, both to the artifice of the satisfactions and to the economic base-work of this particular tale. Not least is Keats's skill in weaving the keywords *fair, gold, rich* from romance to rapacity. He knows how to deliver "a poem in a word," said Lamb (494). Reader, get ready.

Isabella's Lover; Isabella's Brothers

I.

FAIR Isabel, poor simple Isabel!
   Lorenzo, a young palmer in Love's eye!
They could not in the self-same mansion dwell
   Without some stir of heart, some malady;
They could not sit at meals but feel how well
   It soothed each to be the other by;
They could not, sure, beneath the same roof sleep
But to each other dream, and nightly weep.

II.

With every morn their love grew tenderer,
   With every eve deeper and tenderer still;
He might not in house, field, or garden stir,
   But her full shape would all his seeing fill;
And his continual voice was pleasanter
   To her, than noise of trees or hidden rill;
Her lute-string gave an echo of his name,
She spoilt her half-done broidery with the same.

~ ~ ~ ~

XI.

All close they met again, before the dusk
   Had taken from the stars its pleasant veil,
All close they met, all eves, before the dusk
   Had taken from the stars its pleasant veil,

Close in a bower of hyacinth and musk,
  Unknown of any, free from whispering tale.
Ah! better had it been for ever so,
Than idle ears should pleasure in their woe.

XII.

Were they unhappy then?—It cannot be—
  Too many tears for lovers have been shed,
Too many sighs give we to them in fee,
  Too much of pity after they are dead,
Too many doleful stories do we see,
  Whose matter in bright gold were best be read;
Except in such a page where Theseus' spouse
Over the pathless waves towards him bows.

XIII.

But, for the general award of love,
  The little sweet doth kill much bitterness;
Though Dido silent is in under-grove,
  And Isabella's was a great distress,
Though young Lorenzo in warm Indian clove
  Was not embalm'd, this truth is not the less—
Even bees, the little almsmen of spring-bowers,
Know there is richest juice in poison-flowers.

XIV.

With her two brothers this fair lady dwelt,
  Enriched from ancestral merchandize,
And for them many a weary hand did swelt
  In torched mines and noisy factories,
And many once proud-quiver'd loins did melt
  In blood from stinging whip;—with hollow eyes
Many all day in dazzling river stood,
To take the rich-ored driftings of the flood.

XV.

For them the Ceylon diver held his breath,
    And went all naked to the hungry shark;
For them his ears gush'd blood; for them in death
    The seal on the cold ice with piteous bark
Lay full of darts; for them alone did seethe
    A thousand men in troubles wide and dark:
Half-ignorant, they turn'd an easy wheel,
That set sharp racks at work, to pinch and peel.

~ ~ ~ ~

XXVII.

So the two brothers and their murder'd man
    Rode past fair Florence, to where Arno's stream
Gurgles through straiten'd banks, and still doth fan
    Itself with dancing bulrush, and the bream
Keeps head against the freshets. Sick and wan
    The brothers' faces in the ford did seem,
Lorenzo's flush with love.——They pass'd the water
Into a forest quiet for the slaughter.

XXVIII.

There was Lorenzo slain and buried in,
    There in that forest did his great love cease;
Ah! when a soul doth thus its freedom win,
    It aches in loneliness—is ill at peace
As the break-covert blood-hounds of such sin:
    They dipp'd their swords in the water, and did tease
Their horses homeward, with convulsed spur,
Each richer by his being a murderer.

Keats's stanza is the Italian *ottava rima, abababcc,* refreshed by Byron for his comic Italian romance, *Beppo,* just published in February. Its rhymes can be paced out or accelerated, its lines end-stopped or enjambed; its couplet concentrating or twisting a development. Keats's first stanzas render a love idyll, too sweet by half, indulging a Byron-style jesting rhyme in the closing couplet of II. Yet *fair* and *simple* vibrate a bit problematically, especially with *weep* and *malady* limited to lovers' heart-ache. After ten exquisitely sweet stanzas on this heart-misery, XI slants the sightline to a peril. In a secrecy not immune to detection, Keats positions us as the first spies: ahead of, and in our knowledge, aligned with the malevolent brothers. Scanning the lovers' secret bower, the *ottava rima* builds the serenade, punctuating with breathless commas and phrasal repetitions, then turns the couplet to us, on a campy, theatrical *Ah!* Boccaccio-literates know the temporal score of *better had it been;* if you don't, you can't help but glean it. The shift to *woe* speaks the fatal consequence of a *whispering tale.* The undertone of *idle leers* in *idle ears* teases a reader's ethically dicey voyeurism.

Keats turns XII to converse with us about genre protocols of this kind of tale. With theatrical dashes, *Were they unhappy then?—It cannot be—,* the narrator affects a fair reader's protest. The love-ledger of tears and sighs is given *in fee* (a *feudal* economy) for a tale of woe. But here it looks like an overcharge on the genre-contract of Romance, where tears *shed,* pity for the *dead,* ought to be alchemized into matter to be *read* in gold (*gold* and *golden* may "be read" about forty times in *Endymion, A Romance*). Yet the high affectation of this turn to us is a cue that this rhyme-chain is going to whip around on us. The couplet retracts the gold-standard for the dark tale of *Theseus' spouse.* Named only by this epithet, it implies the doleful story. She secretly assisted this prince's escape from her father's death sentence to the labyrinth, believing his pledge of love and marriage, only to find herself, after their escape, quickly ditched by him on the isle of Naxos. The present tense of her longing gaze, *bows,* speaks the enduring pathos in *pathless,* no following possible. Keats selected XII–XIII to send to still-ailing Reynolds, to encourage him to try a tale. When he is feeling better, Keats says, "put your passion to it,— and I shall be bound up with you," no Theseus of broken vows (*L* 1:274).

XIII is a pretty bitter dose, giving the literary consuming of golden riches a venomous turn, with a stinging twist on bee-fables (recall Watt's instructive "How doth the busy bee"—). By this point, we sense *Isabella* as a double-track poem: an old tale coursing with meta-narrative conversation. The poet who summoned the *bitter-sweet* fruit of *King Lear* and whose *Ode on Melancholy* (1819) will imagine Pleasure "Turning to poison while the bee-mouth sips" is a complex chemist. XIII's *b*-rhymes, busy subordinating *much bitterness* and *distress,* build to land on *this truth is not the less—.* The dash heralds the couplet-epigram. *Even bees . . .* is not, of course, about bees. The old lore is that bees are wonderful little factories, drawing nectar into a bio-alchemy of wax, honey, and poison, all for the greater, corporate hive. Keats's bees are not these communists but knowing venture capitalists out to find *richest juice* in poison resources, the way savvy *almsmen* get the most return from the richest sinners. Or the way Romance-junkies lap up distress for richest pleasure. This is the stanza that spoils the embroidery with the news that Lorenzo is soon to be a corpse, chiming *not embalm'd*.

Tweaking his commercial muse, Keats writes a ledger with words that expose the base of golden superstructures. The bees of XIII preview the alignment in XIV of literary riches with brutal mercantilism. Isabella is not exempt. Her love-bower "of hyacinth and musk" (XI) is planted with very expensive horticulture. Musk is an exotic import from India, and hyacinth was quite costly. A story in Madame de Genlis's *Les Veillées du Château* (1784) reports a payment of "Three hundred guineas" for a root, with this endnote: "A famous florist in Holland, told me that he had given 6,800 livres (£263) . . . adding, that he had seen others far dearer."[2]

If Isabella is "innocent" of all this economy, she is also, on this very plane, a proxy for a naïve reader. *With her two brothers this fair lady dwelt, / Enriched from ancestral merchandize.* Keats's surprise by syntax is the placement of *Enriched* for all three. If her love-affair can't have her brothers knowing about it, the reciprocal is her not knowing about their unlovely affairs. Lorenzo, a clerk in their machinery, is not exactly unwitting. And the anaphora *for them* across XIV–XV emphasizes them all as beneficiaries of the miserable labor that produces new riches. Keats presents the oppressed laborers as bodies deformed, unformed, reduced to weary hands and the horrifically abbreviated *swelt* in a hell-on-earth of mines and factories: *burn'd, consum'd with heat* says the Glossary in his *Spenser* (I:cxxxvi). This is the only *swelt* in Keats's poetry, close to the analogous *melt,* and just a letter off from the romance antidote, *sweet* (XIII). For thighs melted into blood, Keats's adjective *proud-quiver'd* is a masterpiece poem-in-a-word: present suffering evoking the prehistory of proud hunters (quivers of arrows on their loins), now quivering slaves.

The metonymy of the brethren as *ledger-men* and *money-bags* (in XVIII) had Bernard Shaw admiring Keats's Marx-moxy voice of "a very fullblooded modern revolutionist," scanning a world where every thing and every one is a commodity, the merchants named only by this self-identity. XIV–XVII render virtual "Factory Commission Reports," an "immense indictment of the profiteers and exploiters with which Marx has shaken capitalistic civilization to its foundations." If Karl Marx can be imagined "writing a poem instead of a treatise on Capital," it would have been *Isabella,* Shaw quipped, with this codicil: "Marx is more euphuistic in calling the profiteers *bourgeoisie*" (175–176). A

Keats-friendly review of *1820* tried to put a spin on this "political" poetry as "schoolboy vituperation" and "idle hostilities against the realities of life."[3] Shaw knew better.

Shavian Keats hones the couplet of XIV to set that hallmark term of Romance, bright gold, against human suffering. Sunlight *dazzling* a river would be a rich-ored picturesque for a far-off connoisseur, like the "dazzling sun-rise" in a picture in Hunt's library (*Sleep and Poetry* 367). For *hollow eyes,* rhymed through the enforcements of *factories* and *merchandize,* such dazzle is agony. "Their eyes were so fatigued with the eternal dazzle and whiteness that they lay down on their backs upon the deck to relieve their sight on the blue Sky," Keats recalled a report of "the vast mountains and crags of ice" that assailed some polar explorers on a commercial enterprise, to find a northwest passage for trade (16 December 1818; *L* 2:6–7).[4]

The anaphora of *for them* that pulses from XIV into XV does not excuse Isabella. While no agent of misery, her bower of hyacinth and musk, her life of leisure, is a product of this family plural. If the poem's opening line "FAIR Isabel, poor simple Isabel" plays *poor* in a sentimental, not material register, what is *simple* is her ignorance. Her only misery is "some stir of heart, some malady" (I) and desire's "sick longing" (III): not happy, but not slavery either. These are just "Honeyless" days of longing (IV), senseless of the brutal economy underwriting her *fair* world. No less than Isabella, readers imbibing the "honey-feel" of romance may forget this, too. Keats's term for Isabella at the top of XIV, *this fair lady,* braids the poem's opening line into the *Fair reader* of *old Romance* (XLIX). In *Robin Hood,* written the same winter and also published in *1820,* Keats quips, "honey / Can't be got without hard money!" (p. 135).

Hard money is the story of XV, a report, in brutal spondees, on the engines and effects of misery: *gushed blood, cold ice, sharp racks.* The seal sprawled on the ice *full of darts* is a grim counterpart to the *honey'd dart* in Isabella's ditty of love (X), and for a reader's increasingly uneasy delectation of literary sweets, *honey'd art.* Although it is a marine *hungry shark* that sups on the Ceylon diver, Keats slants the wording into an epithet for the brethren's ventures and, on this axis, even excuses the shark for just doing its sharky thing, like a ravening robin. The simile of "like the shark at savage prey" in *Dear Reynolds* drops a line here to the rapacious creditor.[5] From Ceylon to the arctic, resounding the British trochee pronunciation of *Ceylon* in *seal on,* this is a violent global economy. Unlike Isabella, her brothers are only *Half-ignorant* (XV) in turning their *easy wheel.* The machinery elicits the penal wheel of torture, both wheels spinning the global economy. *Half,* David Bromwich nicely observes, tells us that they were "legally equipped to claim ignorance."[6] Keats does not so equip his readers. Take that anomalous rhyme-word *seethe*. It doesn't even qualify as an eye-rhyme, let alone a phonic one for *breath and death*. Yet it's an eyeful: the letters spell out, invite us to *see the* wide, dark world from which wealth is drawn *for them* all. Charles Lamb admired the proleptic epithet as the brothers ride off with Lorenzo, "their *murder'd* man" (XXVII).[7] Keats rhyme-chimes the audit: "Each richer by his being a murderer" (XXVIII). Reading for Romance's bright gold finds hard accounting here.

Keats's sightline poetics spell the finale for woefully "simple" Isabella: "How was it these same ledger-men could spy / Fair Isabella in her downy nest?" (XVIII). We have espied this already, and Keats knows the thrill from his compatible spy-self. Just a few months after finishing *Isabella,* he elaborates to Bailey that "Schoolboy" ideal of "fair Woman": *my mind was a soft nest in which some one of them slept, though she knew it not* (*K* 191). Lorenzo appears to Isabella in a dream to report his gothic nest of a gravesite. Her adventure there produces the grimmest nest of all: a Pot of Basil, composted with the deadhead fetish of a gone romance, Marx's treatise on "capital" distilled into a mordant, literal "head."

Isabella's Pot of Basil

XLIV.

See, as they creep along the river side,
　　How she doth whisper to that aged Dame,
And, after looking round the champaign wide,
　　Shows her a knife.—"What feverous hectic flame
Burns in thee, child?—What good can thee betide,
　　That thou should'st smile again?"—The evening came,
And they had found Lorenzo's earthy bed;
The flint was there, the berries at his head.

XLV.

Who hath not loiter'd in a green church-yard,
　　And let his spirit, like a demon-mole,
Work through the clayey soil and gravel hard,
　　To see scull, coffin'd bones, and funeral stole;
Pitying each form that hungry Death hath marr'd,
　　And filling it once more with human soul?

Ah! this is holiday to what was felt
When Isabella by Lorenzo knelt.

XLVI.

She gaz'd into the fresh-thrown mould, as though
   One glance did fully all its secrets tell;
Clearly she saw, as other eyes would know
   Pale limbs at bottom of a crystal well;
Upon the murderous spot she seem'd to grow,
   Like to a native lily of the dell:
Then with her knife, all sudden, she began
To dig more fervently than misers can.

~ ~ ~ ~

XLIX.

Ah! wherefore all this wormy circumstance?
   Why linger at the yawning tomb so long?
O for the gentleness of old Romance,
   The simple plaining of a minstrel's song!
Fair reader, at the old tale take a glance,
   For here, in truth, it doth not well belong
To speak:—O turn thee to the very tale,
And taste the music of that vision pale.

L.

With duller steel than the Perséan sword
   They cut away no formless monster's head,
But one, whose gentleness did well accord
   With death, as life. The ancient harps have said,
Love never dies, but lives, immortal Lord:
   If Love impersonate was ever dead,
Pale Isabella kiss'd it, and low moan'd.
'Twas love; cold,—dead indeed, but not dethroned.

LI.

In anxious secrecy they took it home,
    And then the prize was all for Isabel:
She calm'd its wild hair with a golden comb,
    And all around each eye's sepulchral cell
Pointed each fringed lash; the smeared loam
    With tears, as chilly as a dripping well,
She drench'd away:—and still she comb'd, and kept
Sighing all day—and still she kiss'd, and wept.

LII.

Then in a silken scarf,—sweet with the dews
    Of precious flowers pluck'd in Araby,
And divine liquids come with odorous ooze
    Through the cold serpent pipe refreshfully,—
She wrapp'd it up; and for its tomb did choose
    A garden-pot, wherein she laid it by,
And cover'd it with mould, and o'er it set
Sweet Basil, which her tears kept ever wet.

~~~~

LIV.

And so she ever fed it with thin tears,
    Whence thick, and green, and beautiful it grew,
So that it smelt more balmy than its peers
    Of Basil-tufts in Florence; for it drew
Nurture besides, and life, from human fears,
    From the fast mouldering head there shut from view:
So that the jewel, safely casketed,
Came forth, and in perfumed leafits spread.

~~~~

LVI.

Moan hither, all ye syllables of woe,
    From the deep throat of sad Melpomene!
Through bronzed lyre in tragic order go,
    And touch the strings into a mystery;
Sound mournfully upon the winds and low;
    For simple Isabel is soon to be
Among the dead: She withers, like a palm
Cut by an Indian for its juicy balm.

~ ~ ~ ~

LXI.

O Melancholy, turn thine eyes away!
    O Music, Music, breathe despondingly!
O Echo, Echo, on some other day,
    From isles Lethean, sigh to us—O sigh!
Spirits of grief, sing not your "Well-a-way!"
    For Isabel, sweet Isabel, will die;
Will die a death too lone and incomplete,
      Now they have ta'en away her Basil sweet.

~ ~ ~ ~

LXIII.

And so she pined, and so she died forlorn,
    Imploring for her Basil to the last.
No heart was there in Florence but did mourn
    In pity of her love, so overcast.
And a sad ditty of this story born
    From mouth to mouth through all the country pass'd
Still is the burthen sung—"O cruelty,
To steal my Basil-pot away from me!"

Isabella enters the world of "dismal labouring" (XLVIII) with three hours of
exhumation. Keats takes us there through stanzas that might well have served

a gothic novel. Those pale limbs at the bottom of a crystal well (such dispatch another method of murder) are a queasy enough drain of romance (XLVI). Hitting this change of genre, the narrator flaunts, in rhymed antithesis, our dismay at this usurpation of *the gentleness of old Romance* by *all this wormy circumstance* (XLIX), and implies our appetite for this gothic-menu graveyard romp.

Gentleness gets perverted into Isabella's fetishy doting. And so Keats's auto-mimetic figure of romance's sentimental superstructure and gruesome base: bowery green fed by fever-tears and invisible love-rot, "vile with green and livid spot" (LX). What a reversal of the throb of one his early (unpublished) songs: *in thy heart inurn me—/O love me truly!* (P 98). LIV exfoliates a one-sentence new Romance into a radical retraction of his whole dossier of blissful bowers. For *smelt more balmy*, Keats first wrote *flourish'd sweet above* (P 260n); *smelt* is better for delivering this sensation with a surplus echo of *swelt*, the slave labor. *Florence* evokes flora, drawing a dividend from its economic base, *florin*. When Woodhouse scanned *From the fast mouldering head there shut from view*, he advised smoothing out the meter by deleting *fast*, but Keats wanted the hypermetrical spondee and its alliterations with *From/from*. He also wanted *leafits*, an obsolete *leaflets* not even in *JnD*. It means *little leaf*; Coleridge liked the romance-riff of "moonlight bushes, / Whose dewy leafits are but half disclosed" (*The Nightingale*). *OED* says the sense of *leaf* as a sheet of paper was not current then, but it does cite *Isabella* here for the botanical sense. Yet in a poem that satirizes old romance, the biblio-punning seems ready: the jewel that is rotting to feed perfumed pages.

And so a horrible history feeds a popular song (LVI), with Keats's finely harmonic, half-anagramming of *syllables* and *Isabel is*. If, in this mode, enchanting *Mystery* averts its phono-twin *misery*, Keats has tuned his sentimental key for a couplet-volta zing at any remaining fair readers. Isabel withers in grief *like a palm / Cut by an Indian for its juicy balm*. A palm might wither softly, but *Cut* is a hard turn—on the spondee, the line-cut, and in the action itself, a macabre edge and reverberation. Isabella has (moreover) *cut away* the head of *palmer* Lorenzo (I). The religious devotee is named for the palm leaves stripped for his talisman; an Indian cuts into the trunk for sweet juice. Keats's simile *like a palm* writes Isabella's sorrow as pathological plunder, for Love and for juice. She has cut her palmer for a fetish. By the time *sweet* is reprised in LXI, it is sicklied o'er with the pale cast of thought. John Florio's translation of *Basil* as *Basile* too aptly letters the fetish-plant as an anagram of *Isabel*. Keats intensifies this lexical luxe with a spectral chiasmus of *sweet Isabel* and *Basil sweet*. This is word-work bitter-sweet.

Keats ends his "Story from Boccaccio" with its afterlife, the familiar song now delightfully informed by its story, the stolen Basil-pot surviving as a literary property, not past, but *pass'd* along (LXIII). This was the tenor of Boccaccio's close, too: when the story "came to be publikely knowne, an excellent ditty was composed thereof." Sad theme, sentimental pleasure. Boccaccio's brief prologue to the next day's stories even reports that the "Novell" of Isabella "was highly pleasing" to the fair "Ladies; because they had oftentimes heard the Song, without knowing who made it, or uppon what occasion it was composed." In this framing, the back-story supplies one more pleasure. Boccaccio's *Induction* took pains, on its first paragraph, to assure "Gracious Ladies" that the origin of these entertainments in the Florentine plague ("the last Pestilence") will not cost you "sighes and teares" on every page, and for those paid, he offers the measure of this simile:

> so fearfull a beginning should seeme but as an high and steepy hil appeares to them, that attempt to travell farre on foote, and ascending the same with some difficulty, come afterward to walk upon a goodly even plaine, which causeth the more contentment in them, because the attayning thereto was hard and painfull. For, even as pleasures are cut off by griefe and anguish; so sorrowes cease by joyes most sweete and happie arriving.

A nice chiasmus in the aesthetic contract. Keats, the poet who satirized this economy as an overcharge *in fee* (XII), must have caught *pleasures are cut off*, sounding it twice: Lorenzo's head, *cut* from his corpse (L), and literary pleasure likened to a palm *Cut . . . for its juicy balm* (LVI). The final stanza (LXIII) gives the pleasure-principle a twist with the inner rhymed *pity / ditty* and a double-toned *burthen sung*. In song, *burthen* means refrain; in *this story born,* it comes with a weight of cruelty carried in each transmission. A tale passed from mouth to mouth is literary consumption: richest juice, juicy balm in the materials of sorrow.

In October 1818, Reynolds generously urged Keats to get *Isabella* into print without waiting for a partnered tale from him, so as to answer the *Quarterly's* blow (*L* 1:376–377).[8] Even so, Keats would wonder to Woodhouse, as he was assembling his poems for *1820*, if this new-Romance of *amusing sober-sadness* was still too *mawkish,* therefore *smokeable:* open to ridicule, prone to "be laugh'd at." Keats would differentiate between the self composing the poetry and the self who, reviewing it, *should be apt to quiz it* (22 September 1819).[9] Neither *smokeable* nor *quiz* is in *JnD. OED* gives Keats the sole entry on this "rare" sense of *smokeable* (adj. 2). The verb *quiz* was fairly new slang for *tease, mock, ridicule*. New vistas, not poisoned by self-criticism, might be the cure. Keats returns to Homer, blind but not in purgatory blind, and far from disabled.

[*1820, 47–80*]

[1] Keats read a 1684 edition of the first English translation of *Decameron,* by John Florio (1620); Isabella's story is in "The Fourth Day, The Fift Novell" (see *K* 333–337).

[2] *Tales of the Castle,* translated by Thomas Holcroft, 2 vols. (2nd ed.; London, 1785); "Leontine and Eugenia, or, the Masquerade Habit" (2:42; endnote, 241).

[3] *London Magazine,* September 1820, 316–317.

[4] Here is an uncanny coincidence: the source may have been John Ross's *A Voyage of Discovery* (1819), commanded by a ship named *Isabella*.

[5] *OED* 2a: "with allusion to the predatory habits and voracity of the shark[,] one who enriches himself by taking advantage of the necessities of others," a sense in Keats's day.

[6] "Keats's Radicalism," 203.

[7] *Examiner,* 494. It is more than prolepsis; it is the language of unjust execution. In a grim Newgate Prison report just after Lamb's review, "murder'd man" is what one unjustly condemned man calls himself (495). For this register, see Rejack and Wolfson.

[8] Taylor and Hessey decided to keep *Isabella* for Keats's next volume.

[9] MsK, 1.64.315; *K,* 267–268. Woodhouse thought Keats's calling it (in conversation) *mawkish* the reflux of a "sobered & unpassionate" mood, wincing "where any thing of great tenderness & excessive simplicity is met with when we are not in a sufficiently tender & simple frame of mind to bear it: when we experience a sort of revulsion, or resiliency (if there be such a word) from the sentiment or expression" (to Taylor, 19 September 1819; ALS Morgan Library, MA 215.14, p. 2). It *was* a word, meaning "leaping back" (*JnD*); it would take Christopher Ricks's *Embarrassment* to enlist Woodhouse's review of *mawkish* into Keats's "truest imaginings" (146).

Sonnet / To Homer. 1818

Standing aloof in giant ignorance,
Of thee I hear and of the Cyclades,
As one who sits ashore and longs perchance
To visit dolphin-coral in deep seas,
So wast thou blind;– but then the veil was rent,   5
For Jove uncurtain'd Heaven to let thee live,
And Neptune made for thee a spumy tent,
And Pan made sing for thee his forest-hive.
Aye on the shores of darkness there is light,   9
And precipices show untrodden green,
There is a budding morrow in midnight,
There is a triple sight in blindness keen;
Such seeing hadst thou, as it once befel
To Dian, Queen of Earth, and Heaven, and Hell.

Keats wanted to hear Homer in the gusto of Greek; "shall learn Greek," he pledges to Reynolds in late April 1818, the same letter that reports his finishing *Isabella.* "I long to feast upon old Homer" (*L* 1:274): again, reading as devouring. He asks Reynolds to mediate some passages for him, to which his *ignorance* would otherwise leave him blind, without Homer's visionary imagination as a resource. Homer's Greek and the Greek world are so exotic to Keats as to seem dolphin-coral in deep seas. His hope is for access to the recompense of Homer's sight-blindness, pregnant with revelations to come, as vast as creation's skies, oceans, forest.

Present blindness to blindness keen, paced in the drama of a Shakespearean sonnet. Like the sonnet on rereading *King Lear,* this wasn't for publishing; it was a diagnostic self-reading, in a form that Keats now summons almost instinctively, with a feel for its prismatic compression. The first quatrain recalls the intellectual grammar of the first quatrain of "On First Looking into Chapman's Homer": a confession of ignorance. The second quatrain stages a little drama, a volta (*but then*) midline in line 5. Keats puts a stress on each word of *So wast thou blind,* before a semicolon stop and a dramatic dash of a hypermetrical beat: *blind;—but then the veil was rent.* Homer's blindness, he conceives, was met by Heaven-light, the ocular veil rent and metaphysically *uncurtain'd* (the only time Keats uses this verb in poetry) to vivify imagination, from the depth of Neptune's realm (in the super-exotic phrasing of *spumy tent*), or Pan's music of the hive-lively forests, or Dian's visionary gift.

The strong volta (Petrarchan-wise) is line 9's intensifying *Aye,* loaded with personal ore: it echoes "*I* hear" (2), and winks at *eye*—the reading eye that sighted Keats would bring to blind Homer's Greek, and sigh for *light* in the language that is dark to him at this moment. The poet longing *ashore* for this access is now on *shores of darkness* charged with light, a *midnight* that buds with and rhymes with *light.* These rhymes conjure light in all its valences, interweaving with the triple sight and aural chord of Keats's insistent imagination: *There is* (9, 11, 12). In analogy to *So wast thou blind,* Keats embraces *such seeing* as abundant recompense, one that his present *Standing* might join. The sonnet is more than a program; it is an initiating event, with powers of self-transformation. Keats produces this with the last word, *Hell,* no Christian Hell (nor is Heaven Christian), but a mythic elsewhere, a new world from long ago.

He was reading *Paradise Lost* around this time, and thinking of *Milton's Blindness* and *the magnitude of his conceptions* (I:5). He wanted access to Homer's conceptions, still blind to his language but with a glimmer in the promise of literacy—what "may" be in the offing.

[MsK 3.6, p. 40; Charles Brown's transcription of a lost original]

ode to Maia

With respect to the affections and Poetry you must know by a sympathy
my thoughts that way; and I dare say these few lines will be but a ratifi-
cation: I wrote this on May-day - and intend to finish the ode all in good
time. —

Mother of Hermes! and still youthful Maia!
　　　May I sing to thee
As thou wast hymned on the shores of Baiæ?
　　　Or may I woo thee
In earlier Sicilian? Or thy smiles
Seek, as they once were sought, in Grecian Isles,
By Bards who died content in pleasant sward,
Leaving great verse unto a little clan? 　　　　　　　　　　　　8
O, give me their old vigour, and unheard,
Save of the quiet Primrose, and the span 　　　　　　　　　　　10
　　　Of Heaven, and few ears rounded by thee
My Song should die away content as theirs 　　　　　　　　　　12
Rich in the simple worship of a day——.

In this May-day petition to *Maia*, the young goddess-mother of boy-god mes-
senger Hermes, Keats sings as an honorary (or virtual) Greek Bard. He sets
short lines at 2 and 4 to feature the petitioning phrase *May I / may I* in phonic
harmony with its addressee, *Maia*. This felt to him like the first installment of
an "ode," to "finish" in the confidence of good time.

　　It is close enough in this present form to Keats's home-court, the sonnet,
that editors have liked Woodhouse's redrafting of it into 14 lines.[1] Reviewing
his clerk's transcription of Keats's now lost letter of 3 May 1818 to Reynolds (*L*
1:278), Woodhouse wrote in the right margin, *Perhaps the lines sho^d be divided*
as shown in red Ink. His proposed division reworked lines 11–12 into three lines
(italicized below), producing a fourteen-line sonnet in a new form: four short
lines amid the pentameter field, with Woodhouse's two newly crafted short lines
nicely matching Keats's (2 and 4).

　　　Of heaven, and few ears
Rounded by thee, my song should die away,
　　　Content as theirs
Rich in the simple worship of a day.

Milnes took this design for the first publication (*1848* 1:135), and it became canonical (even for judicious Stillinger, *P* 264). You can see the merits: a quatrain *fgfg*, with near rhyme of *ears / theirs,* that also releases *away* from the middle of Keats's line 12, to end-rhyme the last word, *day.* This is an alert, thoughtful collaboration—but not Keats's experiment after all.

Keats surely could have written a sonnet, if he had wanted to. With the turn at line 9 from question to invocation, he had a volta in hand and surely knew how to spring 14 lines. But he wanted 13 lines, to imagine an ode forming in a gentle, visible relay with sonnet forms. His first quatrain (*abab*) turns to a couplet (*cc*) wooing with the music of *smiles / Seek and sought in Grecian isles.* Keats then gives the thematic link of *Bards* and *sward* a stronger chime than the pattern-set diminuendo *unheard.* The carefully suspended *span* (10) recruits the page space for figural extension, and subtly echoes, with pregnant *clan*-phonics, *Sicilian* and *Grecian.* On his gesture of petition, Keats places a triple *thee* in the place of rhyme (2, 4, 11).

He did not publish this ode-start, but he did share it with Reynolds, in that long letter of 3 May 1818. He quietly leaves his song *unheard,* content to let the ephemeron *die away,* in a limit-case of Milton's petition to his muse, "fit audience find, though few" (*PL* 7.31). In lines that Woodhouse let ride, Keats casts two splendid, beautifully simple mottos about poets' devotions: *Leaving great verse unto a little clan,* and *the simple worship of a day,* each varying the iambic currency with lilts of trochee (*Leaving*) and spondee (*great verse; worship*). His initial petitions, *May I sing* and *May I woo,* don't need Woodhouse's featuring of *away* for a chord. Keats has tuned up the rhyme that matters to this occasion, and sums the whole: *the simple worship of a day.* Not leaving the pun of page-leaves to the winds, Keats catches the drift here, coming to these great simplicities as he audits the tradition of May-oding, from the music of Tasso on the shores of Baiæ (Bay of Naples, Tasso's birthplace) and Sicilian poet Theocritus, to Wordsworth's modern devotion to "A simple produce of the common day" (*Excursion* xii). Sounding these poet-clan allusions and echoes, Keats sings his May-day ode in fine company.

The thought of *leaving great verses unto a little clan*—Keats's uncrabby version of Milton's demographic—would find fulfillment through this very line. It spoke to Yeats in 1903 as the "happiest fate that could come to a poet," a measure he "constantly tested" as his "own ambition."[2] Editor Milnes italicized the line in his 1854 memoir for *The Poetical Works of John Keats* (xix), maybe the text that Yeats read, had in mind, in memory, in ambition.

The other clan-bard on Keats's mind is Robert Burns. "One song of Burns's is of more worth . . . than all I could think of for a whole year in his native country" (*L* 1:325). Keats will be in this country two months on, in strange moods. He needed to get away, from bracing for the reviews to come and the daily sorrows of caring for Tom, and to freshen himself for his next big project, *Hyperion*. An invitation to join vigorous, reliably amusing, worldly Charles Brown on a walking tour of northern England, Scotland, and Ireland was an irresistible romance.

[Woodhouse's Commonplace book, MsK 3.3.69–70]

[1] On this basis, Bate reads this "fourteen-line fragment" as a bridge to the May 1819 odes, which shape sonnet elements into new stanza-forms (*John Keats* 336).

[2] *Collected Letters*, 406; *The Trembling of the Veil*, 10.

To the North, to the North

Summer 1818

ON 22 JUNE 1818 at Liverpool harbor, Keats saw off George, just twenty-one, and his seventeen-year-old bride, to interior America. He then headed north with a brother-proxy, energetic, literate, good-humored, happy traveler Charles Brown, for a walking tour in regions exotic to a London lad. It was the first fine summer of temperate blue skies since the eruption of Mount Tambora in Indonesia in April 1815 (the largest in recorded history) ignited a global nightmare that rendered 1816, even in Europe, "The Year Without a Summer."

Looking into the fair and open face of the heavenly North, Keats called the tour "a sort of Prologue to the Life I intend to pursue—that is to write, to study and to see all" (*L* 1:264). If no Grand Tour, the North was an invigorating prospect. Keats's nominated Prologue is more than a metaphor; it was a promise for writing, inspired by various occasions, and a medium of thinking things out. Vacation fuels vocation. From the Lake District of Wordsworth's inspiration, he reports to Tom:

> I shall learn poetry here and shall henceforth write more than ever, for the abstract endeavor of being able to add a mite to that mass of beauty which is harvested from these grand materials, by the finest spirits, and put into etherial existence for the relish of one's fellows. (*L* 1:301)

Only Keats could put it this way, inspiration, with *relish*. He wasn't writing for publication (though Hunt grabbed one sonnet). The summer is ready-resting, limbering up, especially with words, no matter where his body takes him. Always thinking of Tom, left behind and not well, Keats includes him, virtually, in his adventures, knowing, too, that his letters would be "news" that would draw their friends to him. No less than twenty-five days of this tour had him writing for Tom. Also conscious of their sister Fanny, Keats writes a playful poem for her, a silly bit of autobiographical self-satirizing.

On the itinerary were two shrines of literary respect, Wordsworth's home, Rydal Mount (himself absent when they arrived), and Burns's cottage. The Scots poet was long gone, dead at thirty-six, in 1796 (one year after Keats was born). His fame gathered to his manly art and native strength. "He held the plough or the pen with the same firm, manly grasp," said Hazlitt in a lecture that Keats attended, 24 February 1818 (*Lectures* 254). An antidote for Keats's dark moods, the character of Burns was "gusto, humor and independence, and above all . . . courage and determination to succeed against the obstacles humble birth or a hostile society could place in his way" (Sperry, *Keats* 139)—no Chatterton, that is. Even so, in Keats's psychic imaginary, the two poets gone were specters of fate in a hostile world. Wordsworth's bluesy stanza in *Resolution and Independence* on "marvellous Boy" Chatterton conjures this shade and extends it to Burns, the man "who walked in glory and in joy / Behind his plough, upon the mountain-side," yet on a path of dark passages destined for "despondency and madness." The poetry that Keats writes in Burns country inhabits this psychic topography, coming in a dreamscape of light and shade, pulsing on obscure syntax, fevered repetition, peculiar punctuation, weird evocations, canny and uncanny wording.

—On visiting the Tomb of Burns—

> The Town, the churchyard, & the setting sun,
> The Clouds, the trees, the rounded hills all seem
> Though beautiful, Cold—strange—as in a dream,
> I dreamed long ago, now new begun
> The shortlived, paly summer is but won
> From winters ague, for one hours gleam;
> Through saphire-warm, their stars do never beam,   7
> All is cold Beauty; pain is never done.
> For who has mind to relish, Minos-wise,
> The real of Beauty, free from that dead hue
> Fickly imagination & sick pride
>   * wan upon it! Burns! with honor due   12
> I have oft honoured thee. Great shadow; hide
> Thy face, I sin against thy native skies.

[. . .] This Sonnet I have written in a strange mood, half asleep. I know not how it is, the Clouds, the sky, the Houses, all seem anti Grecian & anti Charlemagnish . . .

So Keats wrote to Tom on 1 July 1818. Writing again on 7 July, he pities Burns as a victim of cultural dissonance and constrained imagination:

> *Poor unfortunate fellow - his disposition was southern - how sad it is when a luxurious imagination is obliged in selfdefence to deaden its delicacy in vulgarity, and riot in things attainable that it may not have leisure to go mad after* [things] *which are not.*   (MsK 1.33.120)

Things real: the poet's greeting of the spirit left to the riot of drink-spirits. As he neared Burns's cottage, Keats could hope that his preoccupation with Burns's material misfortunes might yield to a sanctified pleasure of imagination. He writes in this mood to Reynolds on 11 July:

> One of the pleasantest means of annulling self is approaching such a shrine as the Cottage of Burns—we need not think of his misery—that is all gone—bad luck to it—I shall look upon it hereafter with unmixed pleasure. (*L* 1:323)

His melancholy self annulled, or anesthetized, Keats is richly rewarded on the 13th:

> We were talking on different and indifferent things, when on a sudden
> we turned a corner upon the immediate County of Air—the Sight was as
> rich as possible—I had no Conception that the native place of Burns was
> so beautiful—the Idea I had was more desolate, his rigs of Barley seemed
> always to me but a few strips of Green on a cold hill—O prejudice! it
> was rich as Devon—I endeavour'd to drink in the Prospect. (323)

No better cue for a sonnet volta than *on a sudden we turned.* The prejudice is
the "Burns" in his mind and the Country in his mind. The prejudice is coun-
tered but not canceled. Keats so feels Burns's misery that he can barely write,
let alone write a poem.

> His Misery is a dead weight upon the nimbleness of one's quill—I tried to
> forget it—to drink Toddy without any Care—to write a merry Sonnet—
> it wont do— . . . he was miserable—We can see horribly clear in the works
> of such a man his whole life, as if we were God's spies. (325)

The *as if* alludes to Lear's attempt to cheer Cordelia in their imprisonment (5.3,
p. 91). As a spy into Burns, Keats is unable to alchemize Burns's material misery
into the beauty of the native place. Even his liquid greeting of spirits (that
Toddy) is futile. Writing *Tomb*, Keats felt himself writing *Tom*.

On visiting the tomb, Keats can't help but measure his own highest aspira-
tion, great verses unto a little clan, along the vector of his deepest fear, a poet
dead too soon from poverty, sickness, and depression. These contraries, re-
pressed beyond even scarce expression, stir the strange temporality of the son-
net's mood, seeming something *dreamed long ago,* yet queerly feeling *now new
begun.* Keats's gerund-title, *On visiting,* joins the titles of *On first looking, On
seeing, On Sitting Down, On Receiving. On visiting* comes with a strain of neg-
ative *in*capability: *I know not how it is.* Its occasion—not Burns himself but
the "Burns" of Keatsian self-accounting—distills a half-conscious Petrarchan
sonnet. Rhyme-patterned from mental muscle-memory, an octave (*abbaabba*)
slides into a sestet with a Shakespearean quatrain (*dede*) that refuses any couplet-
climax, instead distributing a *c*-rhyme into a frame around a second quatrain:
cdedec, but with an assonance in *hide/skies* that whispers rhyme-like.

The punctuation that survives (Keats's original is lost) is beyond dreamlike:
dashes, ampersand links, syntax-crashing compressions. The octave opens by
itemizing the scene in surreal alienation of the aesthetics of *visiting:* beautiful

and cold (like a Grecian Urn's *Cold Pastoral*). Keats wrestles with the clash of *beautiful, Cold*. Earning a capital letter, *Cold* drains *beautiful*, thins its fullness. By line 8, it is *cold Beauty*, with *cold* subordinate to an elevated *Beauty*. It is on this shifting dreamscape, not to be measured by any pleasure thermometer, that the sonnet's first grammatical phantasmagoria shimmers. In the first long clause (1–6), Keats seems to have meant to pause at *now new begun* (4), allowing *new begun* to modify both *dream* and *summer*. Mindful of the bitter calendar of short northern summers, Miriam Allott plops a period after *ago* (midline 4) and signals, with a capital N, a new sentence at *Now new begun*. This temporality, she insists, "refers to the late starting Scottish summer and not to K.'s 'dream'" (357n). Why settle it one way or another? Keats's syntax sustains a psychology that blends one into another, *one* on track to a rhyme-chord to *won*, then, homophonically, to just *one* hour.

Allott's fiddling takes a cue from *1848* (1:156–157), and Milnes's text was pretty much accepted. I appreciate the restraint, then, of Stillinger's "it is not clear" (*P* 611)—no clearer than Keats's fluctuation. Another crux is *Through saphire warm* (7), which editors like to emend to *though sapphire-warm* to achieve the sense "*though* seeming this way, northern stars are not so." I get the logic and the bonus of a syntactic and semantic parallel to line 3's *Though beautiful, Cold*. Yet to smooth this out is to efface the surreal imagination that shapes Keats's poetic sequence: first, the thought of a gleaming *through saphire warm* (even warming the jewel-like medium), then a stark subtraction: no material sublime at all.

Keats pauses at the octave to underscore this subtraction with two blunt sentences (it seems): *beautiful, Cold* gets marched into *All is cold Beauty*. And the pleasureless thermometer is *pain is never done* (8). The antithesis is Minos (9), an impossibly deified, self-exculpating standard: one who may judge *The real of Beauty* (10) unfiltered by the self-involvement that Keats confesses. And so that Keatsian word, *relish*, is no sensation at hand but an unattainable "real" for one overwhelmed by cold and pain in a scene of beauty. Minos's "real of Beauty" is apprehension uninfected by *Fickly imagination and sick pride*. But is this brain-sick King of Crete, proud arbiter of life and death, managed by his (eponym) Minotaur hungering in the Labyrinth, any model for mortal appetite? Keats's unpunctuated question, more an exclamation, subtracts the ideal in projecting it.

And here's another crux. The naming of, the calling to, *Burns!* (12) is a charged syntactic ambiguity. Does the emphatic exclamation reiterate the one just before (*wan upon it!*), as a double-shot? Or is *Burns!* a volta turn against Minos? Exploiting the contingency of the name, Keats may even be calling for something that *Burns!* against a too cold beauty—not impossible for the poet determined to *burn through King Lear,* and who could imagine "Meadows sweet where flames burn under" ("Welcome Joy" 8; *P* 231); and not impossible for the poet who heard Hazlitt flirt a name-pun: "if you had shaken hands with him, his hand would have burnt yours" (*Lectures* 254).

The ambiguous grammar of *Burns!* matters to the poet whose dispirit sighed of *that dead hue / Fickly imagination.* Part of the honor Keats brings to Burns is a strange lexicon. First, *paly* ("used only in poetry," says *JnD,* with three examples from Shakespeare), which is a shade that Keats sets on a temporality of fragile light; then the much-disputed adjective *Fickly,* which many editors emend to *Sickly* (in alignment with *sick pride*). Keats despised such meddlings, fuming in a note in his folio Shakespeare about those who "have hocus pocus'd" his words as they have "contrived to twist many beautiful passages into common places" (*KS* 149). Keats's seeming-strange word *Fickly* is deliberately no commonplace for the uncommon place of Burns's tomb; it is anti-Charlemagnish. In some editions of Spenser's Cave of Despair, "fickle Fortune" is written as *fickly.* I think Keats means *fickly,* in honour due to Burns.[1] He would have liked Joyce Carol Oates's appreciation of the "weird lexicon as the so-brilliant mind turns upon itself to produce *fickly, paly.*"[2] It is a credit to not always scrupulous transcriber John Jeffrey (the only source for this sonnet) that he both allowed *Fickly* and admitted that he couldn't figure out the first word (and foot) of 12, so left it blank, with a * keyed to "*Note. An illegible word occurs here—." Milnes thought *Cast* a good enough guess (1:157), in tune with Hamlet's "sicklied o'er with the pale cast of thought" (*Hamlet* 3.1). This has become the standard reading (even in Stillinger), summoning all manner of Hamlet-angles for Keats's mood.[3]

Whatever your cast of thought, what is legible, audible, in Keats's words, is his chord *begun—won—one—wan—upon—hon*(oured). Vocative, evocative, invocative, Burns looms in the summer sunset as a Great shadow, there and not there. The midline period after *thee* (13) may first have been a comma (with lower-cased *great*), and so an epithet for Burns. To one who has been long in city pent, a blue firmament is the fair and open face of heaven. To Keats at the Tomb of Burns, the cold pain of these native skies is anything but. It is a great shadow face, imaged by Keats, who is then unable to hide from this imagination. And so *hide / Thy face, I sin.* It doesn't get more direct, more soul-baring, than this.

Living in the body, Keats can camelionize himself into another creature, no sinner, but an exuberant naughty boy.

[1 July to Tom Keats, *L* 1:308–309, John Jeffrey's transcript of a lost original]

[1] Jeffrey's ms. has *Fickly. JnD* gives *Fickly* as the adverb form of *fickle,* citing Southerne in 1721; *OED* provides four more citations. The fix to *Sickly* in *1848* (1:157) is accepted by Allott (358), Ward (198), Sperry (140), Dickstein (171), Bush (158), and Stillinger (*P* 266, with explanation, 611).

[2] Personal correspondence, 2 July 2019.

[3] A stellar exception, and a valuable labor for me, is J. C. Maxwell's essay on the sonnet.

a song about mys elf
("There was a naughty Boy")

> *My dear Fanny,*
>   *. . . we have*
> *walked through a beautiful*
> *— Country to Kirkudbright —*
> *at which place I will write*
> *you a song about mys elf -*
>   *There was a naughty Boy*
>   *A naughty boy was he,*
> *He would not stop at home*
>   *He could not quiet be -*
>   *He took*
>   *In his Knapsack*
>   *A Book*
>   *Full of vowels*
>   *And a shirt*
>   *With some towels -*
>   *A slight cap*
>   *For night cap —*
>   *A hair brush,*
>   *Comb ditto,*
>   *New Stockings*
>   *For old ones*
>   *Would split O!*
>   *This Knapsack*
>   *Tight at 's back*
>   *He rivetted close*
>   *And followéd his Nose*
>   *To the North,*
>   *To the North,*
> *And follow'd his nose*
>   *To the North –*

From oppression to fun, so swing Keats's moods. In early July 1818, he writes to his sister, spinning this verse extempore. He used one sheet, folded in half for four pages. On the middle pages, he writes short lines of poetry in long columns. His prose prologue, also in short lines, seems already humming poetry in a nonce couplet—*Country to Kirkudbright—/ at which place I will write.* Keats, the *naughty Boy,* divides the pronoun *myself* into *mys elf,* to play along with his alter-ego elf-self: *a poor witless elf,* he'll call himself in another of the tour-sonnets ("on top of Ben Nevis"), where the *s* of *witless* cutely slides to *(s)elf.* Here, *a naughty Boy* mischievously flouts social and lexical decorum. Shifting from monometer to dimeter to trimeter, Keats paces a nursery-rhyming jaunt for Fanny to play along, as the happy muse for *a song about mys elf.*

The twin in paronomasia is *noughty:* the poet of "no self" greeting the spirited fun of words. Who but Boy-John would pack a book full of ready vowels? The sense of *naughty* as "mischievous, disobedient" sounds the root sense, *nothing (nought).* Naughty Boy is father to the man who in a few months will be describing his "poetical Character" (wittily) as one of "no character," "no Identity" (*K* 214). This *song about mys elf* is a parody of epic adventuring, the columns unfurling a comic catalogue. Elfin Keats entertains no elevated or convoluted syntax. There is scarcely any grammatical subordination: everything is present, simultaneous, stressed, metonymic. The only limit is the material page.

Conscious of his short stature, Keats imaged himself (in a letter to Bailey, late July) in the minimizing regard of *Womankind* in general, *Mister John Keats five feet hight* (*K* 192). Free of London's womankind, and out in regions of astonishing natural magnitude, he forgets it all: "I cannot think with Hazlitt that these scenes make man appear little," he writes to Tom; "I never forgot my stature so completely—I live in the eye; and my imagination, surpassed, is at rest" (*L* 1:301). Farther north, writing to Fanny, he cartoons his height. Inkstand in one hand and a mock-heroic *pen/ Big as ten* in the other, he mimes landscape romping with scriptive romping, scribbling and scampering in one rhythm. Haydon relates a back-story about boy-Keats: "When he could just speak, instead of answering questions put to him he would always make a rhyme to the last word people said, and then laugh" (T. Taylor 1:361). This fun must have stayed with him, at least in mind if not behavior; and it winks at Fanny's inner naughty-girl.

The scribble (so Keats calls it) fills two columns on page 2, and these three columns on page 3. This is my typographical transcription of Keats's letter:

There was a naughty boy
  And a naughty boy was
      he,
For nothing would he do
    But scribble poetry—
      He took
      An ink stand
      In his hand
      And a Pen
      Big as ten
      In the other,
        And away
      In a Pother
        He ran
      To the mountains
    And fountains
    And ghostes
    And Postes
    And witches
    And ditches
    And wrote
    In his coat
    When the wather
    Was ~~warm~~ cool -
        Fear of gout,
    And without
    When the weather
        warm
      Was ~~cool~~ -
    Och the charm
    When we choose
    To follow ones
        nose
        To the north,
        To the north,
    To follow one's nose
    to the north!

There was a naughty boy
  And a naughty boy we
      he,
He kept little fishes
  In washing tubs three
  In spite
  Of the might
  Of the Maid

Nor affraid
Of his Granny-good -

  He often would
  Hurly burly
  Get up early
    And go
  By hook or crook
To the brook
  And bring home
  Miller's thumb
  Tittlebat
  Not over fat
  Minnows small
  As the stall
  Of a glove
  Not above
  The size
  Of a nice
  Little Baby's
  Little fingers —
  O he made
  'Twas his trade
  Of Fish a pretty
    Kettle
  A Kettle - A Kettle
  Of Fish a pretty
    Kettle
  A Kettle!

There was a naughty Boy
  And a naughty Boy was
      he
He ran away to Scotland
  The people for to see —
    Then he found
    That the ground
    Was as hard,
    That a yard
    Was as long,
    That a song
    Was as merry,
    That a cherry
    Was as red -
    That lead
    Was as weighty,

That fourscore
Was as eighty

That a door
Was as wooden
As in england -
So he stood in
His shoes
And he wonderd
He wonderd
He stood in his
Shoes and he
wonder'd -

My dear Fanny I
am ashamed of
writing you such
stuff, nor would
I if it were not
for being tired after
my days walking,
and ready to

tumble into bed
so fatigued that
when I am asleep
you might sew
my nose to my
great toe and
trundle me round
the town like a
Hoop without wa-
king me - Then
I get so hungry
- a Ham goes but
a very little way
and fowls are
like Larks to me -
A Batch of Bread
I make no more
ado with than a
sheet of parliament;
and I can eat a
Bull's head as easily

This song is a greeting of the spirit to homebound Fanny. *She is very much prisoned from me. I am affraid it will be some time before I can take her to many places I wish,* Keats tells Bailey (MsK 1.34.125). He ends with a silly self-correction: the thirst for new sensations meets flat familiarities. The Boy who *ran away to Scotland* winds up stalled: *he stood in his / Shoes and he / wonder'd—* no material sublime, just material exhaustion, in a parody of an ode's epode (stand). The self-parody is a generous sibling wink. Out of step with wonder, Keats's rhymes step into Fanny's world. He liked this mode, this mood. So, too, his jesting to Georgiana's mother, from Inverness: "But I must leave joking & seriously aver, that I have been <u>werry</u> romantic indeed, among these Mountains & Lakes" (*L* 1:359–360).

Even as the third column of the song shifts into prose a quarter of the way down the page (at *My dear Fanny*), its short lines and silly self-cartooning hybridize a poetic pulse into the prose. The rest of the letter, margin to margin, is on the obverse (overpage), with fresh self-cartooning:

[from: *eat a Bull's head as easily*]

as I used to do Bull's eyes—I take a whole string of Pork Sausages down as easily as a Penorth of Lady's fingers - Oh dear I must soon be contented with an acre or two of oaten cake a hogshead of Milk and a Cloaths basket of Eggs morning noon and night when I get among the Highlanders –
[. . .] *God bless you—*
         Your affectionate Brother John-

Shifting to letter-lines, Keats keeps up the fun, burlesquing himself as a Giant of appetite, a giant of walking. *And a pen, big as ten:* no match for what comes next, a Giant size.

       [ALS, 2–3 July 1818, Pierpont Morgan Library]

To Ailsa Rock—

Hearken thou craggy ocean pyramid,
　　Give answer by thy voice the Sea fowls screams!
　　When were thy shoulders mantled in huge Streams?
When from the Sun was thy broad forehead hid?
How long ist since the mighty Power bid
　　Thee heave to airy sleep from fathom dreams—
　　Sleep in the Lap of Thunder or Sunbeams,
Or when grey clouds are thy cold Coverlid—
Thou answerst not for thou art dead asleep
　　Thy life ~~has been will be~~ is but two dead eternities
The last in Air, the former in the deep—
　　First with the Whales, last with the eglle skies—
Drown'd wast thou till an Earthquake made thee steep—
　　Another cannot wake thy giant Size!

8

Facing massive Ailsa Rock, rising 1,100 feet from the sea and seeming "close upon" even at fifteen miles distant, it "struck me very suddenly—really I was a little alarmed," Keats writes to Tom. Collecting himself, he strikes back with sonnet that campily blandishes serial interrogatives, addressing Ailsa Rock as a primitive (and perhaps primed) oracle of earth-history, communicating, as oracles may, through the augury (divination) of its regent birds. What augury? As solid and insentient a dreamer as Keats ever figured, this Rock shimmers into an oxymoron of airy sleep and fathom dreams—the only time in his poetry that Keats uses *fathom* as an adjective to figure the deepest delve of an origin story: some intention, some latency to emerge.

Mystery, duration, immensity, primitive formation: Keats lets this go. In forgoing an expected question-mark at line 8, the grammar of *Sleep in the Lap of Thunder* (7) gets double-angled. On one slant, as a repetition of line 6's *sleep* and ready for a repetition in line 9's *dead asleep*, this *Sleep* sits syntactically as the object of, and under, some *mighty Power*. On another slant, with the thrust of the new line (7), *Sleep* floats a brief imperative mode, slyly turning the ready idiom, *clap of thunder*, into another ready idiom, *Lap of Slumber*, in which Endymion might have dreamt away. This imperative verve lasts only as long as lines 7–8, however.

At line 9 Keats retracts poetic power with three thuds: *Thou answerst not.* The ninth line is the pattern-place for a Petrarchan volta. The turn Keats takes on this ground is to recast the Rock's intractable silence into a poetic value: a scene for pondering unknowable deep geological time. The double-sounded *dead—dead asleep/dead eternities*—plays a parody of a lullaby, epic-tuned, sheerly redundant to an entity that cannot but sleep. No thought of unheard melodies sweeter still! The unmelodious, still Rock is a counter-inspiration for a poetics of non-correspondence. The very sound of *dead asleep* undertones *dead as sleep*. The Earthquake is the sublime creator: *made thee steep* (13) plays a triple grammar of adjective-*steep* (vertical), noun-*steep* (precipice), and imperative-*steep* (immerse in the sea).

"This is the only Sonnet of any worth I have of late written," Keats post-scripts. If Ailsa Rock is no "material sublime" on the scale of Mont Blanc (no Grand Tour stop), Keats works the down-scaled occasion, with self-ironizing flair. The commentary in *Blackwood's* missed this wry theatrical tone when it merely ridiculed, with its ready class put-downs, "Mister John Keates standing on the sea-shore at Dunbar, without a neckcloth, according to custom of Cockaigne, and cross-questioning the Crag of Ailsa!"[1] He was actually on the "tops of the Mountains" when he looked down, vertiginously, on the rock-ruptured seascape.

[*L* 1:329–330]

---

[1] Review of Hunt's *Literary-Pocket Book,* also printing Keats's sonnet (239). Why a mountain hiker would sport a neckcloth it does not say; *Cockaigne,* the site of Thomson's *Castle of Indolence* (1748), bends the allusion into a slur on Cockney poets.

Sonnet ("This mortal body")

This mortal body of a thousand days
    Now fills, O Burns, a space in thine own room,
Where thou didst dream alone on budded bays,
    Happy and thoughtless of thy day of doom!
My pulse is warm with thine own Barley-bree,
    My head is light with pledging a great soul,
My eyes are wandering, and I cannot see,
    Fancy is dead and drunken at its goal;
Yet can I stamp my foot upon the floor,
    Yet can I ope thy window-sash to find
The meadow thou hast tramped o'er and o'er,—
    Yet can I think of thee till thought is blind,—
Yet can I gulp a bumper to thy name,—
O smile among the shades, for this is fame!

"I intend to pass a whole year with George if I live to the completion of the three next," Keats writes to his friend Bailey, 22 July 1818 (*L* 1:343): three months more than a thousand days. He was dead two years and seven months on, almost to the very day. Feeling the weight of mortality, with near-dead certainty, could have him pairing to dead Burns. Tombs have a way of oppressing this dead sense. Keats's sonnet is filled with this, in the arrest of what Milton felt in writing his first poem in English, at Shakespeare's tomb: it "Dost make us Marble with too much conceiving"—*Marble* ghosting the likely affect, *marvel.* In a surplus of conceiving, Milton renders a sonnet-plus, eight couplets of extravagant honor.

Keats averts marmoreal Milton to insist on embodied mortal life. Doubling Burns alive, he conjures him into felt presence (*O Burns*), imagining what it was like for him to be looking forward to *budded bays, | Happy and thoughtless of thy day of doom!* Keats's consciousness of his own *mortal* body is no lodge of *thoughtless,* however, and Burns's *room* (stanza, too) reaches in phonetic memory back to the Burns-site from ten days ago, *the Tomb.* Keats's pronoun for addressing Burns, *thy,* may echo his first-person pronouns: the triple anaphora, *My| My| My* (5–7). The possessives interplay with the indicative, *I cannot see* (7), followed by four single-stress spondees, *Yet can I stamp, Yet can I ope, Yet can I think, Yet can I gulp.* These chimes are insistent, contrapunto declarations of physical life, in meter-wise poetic presence: *I can stamp my foot.* This vigor, ending with a pledge to Burns, claims the first line of the Shakespearean plotted couplet, *Yet can I gulp a bumper to thy name*—. The three long dashes at the end are for living breath, before the super-ready rhyme to *fame!* the very one on which Milton mocked formal tomb-sculpture:

> Dear son of memory, great heir of Fame,
> What need'st thou such weak witnes of thy name?
> Thou in our wonder and astonishment
> Hast built thyself a live-long Monument.   (On *Shakespear* 5–8)

Keats's monument, a moment's monument, is his sonnet. It is about more than Burns. *O smile among the shades* conjures *Burns* to cheer his shade in the shades of live-long fame. It is also self-addressed: Keats, burning among the shades, thirsting for and ironizing the thirst for fame. The irony does not dispel the genesis of foreboding. "I had determined to write a Sonnet in the Cottage. I did but lauk it was so wretched I destroyed it—," he told Bailey (*L* 1:343). But not before Brown could copy it out.

[*1848*, 1:159, based on Charles Brown's now lost transcript]

Lines written in the highlands after a visit to Burns's Country –

There is a joy in footing slow across a silent plain
Where Patriot Battle has been fought when Glory had the gain;
There is a pleasure on the heath where Druids old have been,
Where Mantles grey have rustled by and swept the nettles green:
There is a joy in every spot, made known by times of old,
New to the feet, although the tale a hundred times be told:
There is a deeper joy than all, more solemn in the heart,
More parching to the tongue than all, of more divine a smart,
When weary feet forget themselves upon a pleasant turf,
Upon hot sand, or flinty road, or Sea shore iron scurf,   10
Toward the Castle or the Cot, where long ago was born
One who was great through mortal days and died of fame unshorn.
Light Hether bells may tremble then, but they are far away;
Woodlark may sing from sandy fern,—the Sun may hear his Lay;
Runnels may kiss the grass on shelves and shallows clear
But their low voices are not heard though come on travels drear;
Bloodred the sun may set b{e}hind black mountain peaks;
Blue tides may sluice and drench their time in Caves and weedy creeks;
Eagles may seem to sleep wing wide upon the Air;
Ring doves may fly convuls'd across to some high cedar'd lair;
But the forgotten eye is still fast wedded to the ground—
As Palmer's that with weariness mid desert shrine hath found.
At such a time the Soul's a Child, in Childhood is the brain   23
Forgotten is the worldly heart—alone, it beats in vain—
Aye if a Madman could have leave to pass a healthful day,
To tell his forehead's swoon and faint when first began decay,
He might make tremble many a Man whose Spirit had gone forth
To find a Bard's low Cradle place about the silent north.
Scanty the hour and few the steps, beyond the Bourn of Care,
Beyond the sweet and bitter world—beyond it unaware;   30
Scanty the hour and few the steps because a longer stay
Would bar return, and make a Man forget his mortal way.
O horrible! to lose the sight of well remember'd face,
Of Brother's eyes, Of Sister's Brow, constant to every place;
Filling the Air as on we move with Portraiture intense;
More warm than those heroic tints that fill a Painter's sense—

When Shapes of old come striding by, and visages of old,
Locks shining black, hair scanty grey and passions manifold.
No, No that horror cannot be—for at the Cable's length
Man feels the gentle Anchor pull and gladdens in its strength—
One hour half ideot, he stands by mossy waterfall, 41
But in the very next he reads his Soul's memorial:
He reads it on the Mountain's height where chance he may sit down
Upon rough marble diadem, that Hills eternal crown.
Yet be the Anchor e'er so fast, room is there for a prayer
That Man may never lose his Mind {on} Mountains bleak and bare;
That he may stray league after League some great Berthplace to find,
And keep his vision clear from speck, his inward sight unblind— 48

Even in open northern skies, Keats's sonnets in Burns-country throb with psy-
chic constriction: oppressed, self-oppressed, succumbing, or too urgently re-
sisting. Writing these lines after visiting the Burns-shrines, Keats exhales into
the rhythmic pleasures of long lines. This is dream-poetry, not as an event but
as a reflection on the way obsession can eclipse all other sensations. He drafted
these lines on two sheets of paper, then copied them, cross-wise (to save postage,
but a real trial to read!), into a letter to Bailey, 22 July 1818. Keats experiments
on a roll of propulsive, extravagant fourteener couplets (a unique form here).
Chapman's *Homer* had excited him with this kind of line. Paced with the me-
dial pauses (dashes, commas, or stays in rhythm), Keats's *Lines* mimes his *joy
in footing slow.* Read it out loud: you can feel the rhythm of iambic stepping
and *footing slow,* with the music of rhymes and rhyming repetitions. Fourteeners
are amenable to ballad prosody (four feet, three feet), singing to the beat of
walking. When Brown copied this poem, then published some eight quatrains
in *New Monthly Magazine* (4 March 1822), he actually set the lines in balladry
(p. 252).

Keats paces this joy in stages, moment to moment, strength to strength. The
first stage is the feel of his feet on historic land, the lodge of Scot and Druid.
He conjures these denizens in imagination, the present-tense anaphora of *There
is* in relay with and layered with *times of old.* Then, with a comparison accu-
mulated on a Miltonic escalation, *There is a deeper joy than all,* Keats scans the
present world in beautiful particularity, with a strong greeting of the spirit about
the personal drive of this footing, invested in the shrines that await. It is Keats's
Nile-mode sonnet done in his own steps, extravagantly, and with a latent tug
about the immersion of his mind, even brain, in *One who was great through
mortal days and died of fame unshorn.* The poetry rides over a vividly imaged

material highland: hot sand, flinty road, sea shore iron scurf, heather bells, woodlark singing from sandy ferns, runnels in the grass and, more melodramatically, bloodred sun behind black mountain peaks, tide waters sluicing into caves and creeks, eagles in the air, anxious doves seeking cover. Keats's outward eye catches all this with his inner eye's obsession. The auxiliaries of *may* both itemize and suspend the phenomenal world: *may tremble, may sing, may kiss, may set, may sluice, may seem, may fly.* This is the *forgotten eye wedded to ground,* so that the footing won't fall, in contest with the inner eye fixated on its far-off reward.

In rapid succession, Keats casts psychological alter egos for the disparate facets of his devotion. First is a Palmer enduring the trek to a desert shrine (22). The vertical line left of line 23 marks a turn: a reflection on what obsession may be sacrificing, without knowing it at the time. This summons two more doubles: a Soul-Child / Childhood brain, innocent of adversity and heart-knowledge of the world; then a Madman-brain in *decay.* A Child-Soul has no presence in Keats's identity-forging Vale of Soul-Making. A Madman cannot know otherwise. Keats, however, can take the pulse. *Aye if a Madman* floats a shadow-syntax: *I, if a Madman*—a specter beyond the reprieve for those long in city pent. Another relay of sound plays from the obsessive goal, the *Bard's* cradle-place: once achieved, this may *bar* return. This is the entailed peril, Keats writing it out and hearing the self-lessoning. However alluring a world with nothing *bitter* (including the *bitter-sweet* of Shakespearean fruit), or any tug *beyond the Bourn of Care,* the vacation is the time-stamp, *Scanty the hour.* The percussive of *beyond-Beyond-beyond* is drawn to *unaware* (29–31), counter-rhymed to *Care.* This is dialectical: suspended, not erased.

Keats's *after*-writing shifts to writing in the moment. And so the volta, with a bolt of exclamation: *O horrible!* (33). If the way is *mortal* for his *mortal body,* this mind in this body holds the bonds of present affections. *Brother's eyes, Sister's Brow;* Tom and Fanny, George and Georgiana: inner-sight portraiture more intense and warm than any cold beauty of art. A Cable's length and Anchor are needful tugs against the call *beyond.* The Madman's lease for Keats is *One hour half ideot* (41). Keats uses this strange Anglo-Norman spelling (*ideot* is not in *JnD,* or *OED* otherwise) for this brief spell of identification. In sub-limities of mountain heights and gleaming hilltops, Keats the poet-reader finds his soul bleak and bare without human affections.

The obsession with a "birthplace" shrine (so editors emend) is a word that Keats cares to write as *Berthplace* (47), a place for a traveler to *stray* for a while, but not forget to *keep his vision clear from speck, his inward sight unblind—* (48).[1] Keats might have said, in heroic terms, *strive;* but he wanted the sense of errancy in *stray.* On this score, he gives this final line a fine double grammar. The object of *keep* might be *inward sight,* with *unblind* as its adjective (*OED* gives Keats unique listing for this). Or, after the comma, the grammar might shift into verb and object: (might) *unblind his inward sight,* as if not yet completely rehabilitated.

When these *Lines* were published in Hunt's *Examiner,* Bastille Day (14 July) 1822, they could conjure the sight of their "lamented Author" (who died in February 1821, in Rome, thousands of miles away). In spring 1821, Brown, who was as intimate with Keats's fluctuation of moods as he was with the poetry, provided this prologue to his balladized excerpt:

> Keats walked in the Highlands . . . in that hallowed pleasure of the soul, which, in its fulness, is a-kin to pain . . . intensity of feeling to the dread of madness. It was written . . . not for the gaze of the world, but as a record for himself of the temper of his mind at the time . . . his melancholy, as he thinks upon so young a poet dying of a broken heart.
>
> (252, excepted)

Soon ascending Ben Nevis with burly Brown, Keats may well have lost his life on this dubiously undertaken venture. He at least expected a big reward at the summit, as most avid scalers do.

> [letter text, MsK 1.34 and *L* 1:344–345;
> with reference to K's first draft, MsK 2.19,
> which subscripts the title]

¹The spelling *birthplace* debuted in *The Examiner* (14 July 1822, p. 445), accepted by Allott (372), Stillinger (*P* 277), Norton Critical (263).

Writing Ben Nevis

from a letter to Tom Keats, 3–6 August 1818

While the *Sonnet* in this wonderful (long) letter for Tom is always printed independently, context matters. My excerpt supplies context. I begin with Keats's wonderfully detailed account of his and Brown's ascent of Ben Nevis on 2 August. This pauses for Keats's fantasia of a "conversation" (in comic couplets) between a legendary Lady and a personified Ben Nevis, grumbling of being roused from sleep by mountaineer "Mrs Cameron of 50 years of age and the fattest woman in all of inverness shire who got up this Mountain some few years ago." Then Keats renders his own conversation, on the top of Ben Nevis.

> I have nothing of conseqence to tell you till yesterday when we went up Ben Nevis, the highest Mountain in Great Britain — On that account I will never ascend another in this empire — Skiddaw is no thing to it either in height or in difficulty. It is above 4300 feet from the Sea level . . . we took it completely from that level.[1] I am heartily glad it is done—it is almost like a fly crawling up a wainscoat — Imagine the task of mounting 10 Saint Pauls without the convenience of Stair cases. We set out about five in the morning with a Guide in the Tartan and Cap and soon arrived at the foot of the first ascent which we immediately began upon — after much fag and tug and a rest and a glass of whiskey apiece we gained the top of the first rise and saw then a tremendous chap above us which the guide said was still far from the top — After the first Rise our way lay along a heath valley in which there was a Loch — after about a Mile in this Valley we began upon the next ascent more formidable by far than the last and kept mounting with short intervals of rest untill we got above all vegetation, among nothing but loose Stones which lasted us to the very top — the Guide said we had three Miles of a stony ascent — we gained the first tolerable level after the valley to the height of what in the Valley we had thought the top and saw still above us another huge crag which still the Guide said was not the top — to that we made with an obstinate fag and having gained it there came on a Mist, so that from that part to the verry top we walked in a Mist.

Keats's in-the-moment account of heroic adventure, material struggle (including a sore throat), nothing like hiking boots, formidable challenges, dismay, and reward of Mist, seems already to be composing the sonnet.

The spirit for this mist-girt band is a quite materially liquid greeting: whiskey. Among the unforgiving, relentless stones come a series of sublime astonishments:

The whole immense head of the Mountain is composed of large loose stones —thousands of acres — Before we had got halfway up we passed large patches of snow and near the top there is a chasm some hundred feet deep completely glutted with it —Talking of chasms they are the finest wonder of the whole—the[y] appear great rents in very heart of the mountain though they are not, being at the side of it, but other huge crags arising round it give the appearance to Nevis of a shattered heart or Core in itself- —These Chasms are 1500 feet in depth are the most tremendous places I have ever seen — they turn one giddy if you choose to give way to it — We tumbled in large stones and set the echoes at work in fine style. Sometimes these chasms are tolerably clear, sometimes there is a misty cloud which seems to steam up and sometimes they are entirely smothered with clouds —

The sublime heights and chasms (*the finest wonder of the whole*) inspire giddy echoes in fine style, in Keats's writing, too. He pauses his report here, to reread and review its pace, miming their stopping to rest, then resumes writing on a new line, a newly emerging clime:

After a little time the Mist cleared away but still there were large Clouds about attracted by old Ben to a certain distance so as to form as it appeared large dome curtains which kept sailing about, opening and shutting at intervals here and there and everrywhere; so that although we did not see one vast wide extent of prospect all round we saw something perhaps finer — these cloud-veils opening with a dissolving motion and showing us the mountainous region beneath as through a loop hole — these [C]loudy loop holes ever varrying and discovering fresh prospect east, west north and South —Then it was misty and again it was fair —then puff came a cold breeze of wind and bared a craggy chap we had not yet seen though in close neighbourhood — Every now and then we had overhead blue Sky clear and the sun pretty warm.

Keats amuses Tom with real-time fluctuations: now *fair,* now *bare;* now *cold,* now *warm;* now *clear,* now *cloudy.* He plays at picturesque aesthetics, loopholes framing various views, the erotic fun of veiling and unveiling, the surprise of perpetual change. Tom, in imagination (*you*), can share the ascent with him:

> I do not know whether I can give you an Idea of the prospect from a large Mountain top— You are on stony plain which of course makes you forget you are on any but low ground—the horison or rather edges of this plain being above 4000 feet above the Sea hide all the Country immediately beneath you, so that the next objects you see all round next to the edges of the flat top are the Summits of Mountains of some distance off—as you move about on all sides you see more or less of the near neighbour country according as the Mountain you stand upon is in different parts steep or rounded — but the new thing of all is the sudden leap of the eye from the extremity of what appears a plain into so vast a distance On one part of the top there is a handsome pile of stones done pointedly by some soldiers of artillery, I climed onto them and so got a little higher than old Ben himself. It was not so cold as I expected — yet cold enough for glass of Wiskey now and then — There is not a more fickle thing than the top of a Mountain— [. . .] I have said nothing yet of out [our] getting on among the loose stones large and small sometimes on two sometimes on three, sometimes four legs — sometimes two and stick, sometimes three and stick, then four again, then two then a jump, so that we kept on ringing changes on foot, hand, Stick, jump boggl sumble, foot, hand, foot, (very gingerly) stick again, and then again a game at all fours . . .

In succession, Keats renders a mountain-top prospect too sublime for words, a comic rivalry of human piling higher than the mountain top (*boggl sumble*), and his own burlesque conquest, a thrill in the transformations, then a funny reduction of the human body to an incompetent mountain animal, Keats naughty-boying his efforts of getting on with getting off.

[1] Ben Nevis is actually 4,500 feet. Lakeland's Skiddaw is about 3,500; St Paul's Cathedral, 365 (in Keats's day and for the next 150 years, London's tallest building). Nevis is a long, formidable, and dangerous ascent/descent, especially for nontechnical climbers. The weather can be terrible, and parts are snow-covered all year.

"a little conversation . . . between the mountain and the Lady, . . . M^rs C—."

This mock-agon leads to the story of M^rs C, that fat lady who managed the ascent. I excerpt from the 80 couplets Keats spun for her summit conversation with the spirit of the place, "Sir Nevis" (*L* 1:354–357):

> 'Tis said a little conversation took place between the mountain and the Lady — After taking a glass of Wiskey as she was tolerably seated at ease she thus begun
>
> M^rs C—
>
> Upon my Life Sir Nevis I am pique'd
> That I have so far panted tugg'd and reek'd
> To do an honor to your old bald pate
> And now am sitting on you just to bate,
> Without your paying me one compliment. [. . .]
> Still dumb ungrateful Nevis—still so cold!

Always ready to work the word *still*, Keats imbues it with stark silence, sublime immobility, sheer endurance. Sir Nevis, irked at being roused from a "Slumber of a thousand years" (Keats reprises Ailsa Rock), responds with a vengeance, tongue-lashing with a promise of an amorous earthquake: "Dear Madam I must kiss you, faith I must! / I must Embrace you with my dearest gust!" Keats ends his fantasy with a narrative of its sequel, and his own postscript.

> O Muses weep the rest —
>
> The Lady fainted and he thought her dead
> So pulled the clouds again about his head
> And went to sleep again — soon she was rous'd
> By her affrighed Servants — next day hous'd
> Safe on the lowly ground she bless'd her fate
> That fainting fit was not delayed too late

But what surprises me above all is how this Lady got down again —I felt it horribly — 'T was the most vile descent— shook me all to pieces— Over leaf you will find a Sonnet I wrote on the top of Ben Nevis

From *fainted* to *affrighed* (*affrighted* written as if *a-fried*) to *fate*, to *fainting fit*, Keats's muse issues a verbal burlesque for the Lady that his own vile descent can't manage. Only later could he joke about it to Georgiana's mother: "went up Ben Nevis, & N.B. came down again" (*L* 1:360), inverting the mountain's initials into a scholarly abbreviation for Nota Bene.

At the time, such wit was scarce: Keats's "shaken . . . all to pieces" retracts the composition that he managed at the summit. "He sat on the stones, a few feet from the edge of that fearfull precipice, fifteen hundred feet perpendicular from the valley below, and wrote this sonnet" (Brown; *KC* 2:63):

"a Sonnet I wrote on the top of Ben Nevis"

> Read me a Lesson, muse, and speak it loud
>   Upon the top of Nevis, blind in Mist!
> I look into the Chasms and a Shroud
>   Vaprous doth hide them; just so much I wist
> Mankind do know of Hell: I look o'erhead,
>   And there is sullen Mist; even so much
>   Mankind can tell of Heaven: Mist is spread
>   Before the Earth beneath me— even such
> Even so vague is Man's sight of himself.
> Here are the craggy stones beneath my feet;
>   Thus much I know, that a poor witless elf
>   I tread on them; that all my eye doth meet
>   Is mist and Crag — not only on this height,
>   But in the World of thought and mental might –
> Good bye till tomorrow
>   *your most affectionate brother*
>   *John*

Nominally addressing some muse with Shakespearean organization, Keats's hectic pulse issues from a self-accounting, arrayed in the close lettering of *me* and *muse*. His invocation can be only self-answered, on the advantage of the double grammar of *Read me*: *me* the indirect object of his call (read a lesson to me); *me* the direct object (read me as a textbook case of aspiration and disappointment). Men go to mountain-tops for divine colloquy: Moses on Mount Sinai, Petrarch on Mount Ventoux, Wordsworth on Mount Snowden. Keats's mountain-top Muse refuses the bid. *Nevis, blind in Mist,* figures an allegory for what anyone can *know of Hell,* and in chime, *tell of Heaven* and ultimately *of him<u>self</u>.* The lexical division Keats played into *a song about mys elf* resounds here: *himself* as *witless elf,* rhymed and lettered into *witless self.* Keats's tone is wry, not cynical, disenchanted, or despairing. He can still play with words.

And so it goes. Against the sobering up with *inward sight unblind* at the end of *Lines written in the highlands,* this sonnet sets *blind in Mist* to rhyme into and modify the summit of *Nevis. Nevis* and poet are in such close syntactical proximity as to produce allegory from phonics. In Keats's fine audit, *Nevis* whispers into *Mist, wist, is . . . Mist; Mist is, Is mist,* the sound itself a *spread of Mist.*[1] The map of Keats's prepositions, *Upon, in, into, o'er, Before, beneath, on, on,* and the final *in the World of,* is such a failure of orientation as to whirl into sheer synonymy (rhymes and near-rhymes collaborating). Mental *might* is nothing at *this height,* where *Mist* is the existential reckoning. The midline rhyme at 9, *Man's sight,* is a recessive chime at best. Mists had been in Keats's mental sight all that spring, from his verse letter to Reynolds about the mind in *Purgatory blind,* without a "law / Of either earth or heaven" (80–82), to life's dark Passages where "We are in a Mist" (*K* 130). On the anti-sublime summit of Nevis, laws of Hell, Heaven, and Earth are no better than a phantasmatic Mist. Visible Mist is the real thing, and Keats, in his craft and sullen art, gives it his best greeting of the spirit.

Then he signs off as if to deny the whole mood, in cheery affection. Poor Tom died on 1 December 1818 (two years to the day after Keats's debut in "Young Poets"). It wasn't until the next spring that Keats felt able to go over to the lodgings they shared to collect his papers (*L* 2:82). He mentions this errand to George and Georgiana, folding in this August 1818 letter about the adventure he shared with Tom this way—and now, is sharing it with them, hollowed by the loss of Tom. He had known what awaited his return that summer: Tom dying while he wrestled with the challenge of writing with conviction about the victory of Apollo, the god of medicine and poetry, over Hyperion, who is sensing his mortality from the fall of his brothers. What law of earth or heaven could rule this siege of contraries?

The failed mountain-muse of Ben Nevis will haunt *Hyperion.* Classical mythology and its vision of humanlike gods toppled like stone carvings rather than looming in natural rocky preeminence: Keats is ready to bend and blend Miltonic mythography into Shakespearean tragedy.

[MsK 1.36.131–134 (sonnet at 132). Variants, *L* 1:352–358]

---

[1] I think the compositor of the first publication, *Plymouth and Devonport Weekly Journal,* September 1838, had the sound of *is* in his ear in setting the title and line 2 with *Nivis* (240).

Wide Venturing

Fall 1818–April 1819

AN EPIC FRAGMENT, A ROAMING, A ROMANCE, A BALLAD

SPANNING FROM FALL 1818 to spring 1819, *Hyperion, Fancy, The Eve of St. Agnes,* and *La belle dame sans merci* show Keats finding and firming up his talents on multiple fronts: a spectacular blank-verse Miltonic epic; a rondeau rounded in sprightly tetrameters; a dark-bright-dark romance in skillful Spenserian stanzas; and a fevered lyrical ballad.

from *Hyperion. A Fragment*

This incomplete work so impressed Woodhouse that he urged it into the 1820 volume, "contrary to the wish of the author."[1] *Contrary* is understatement. Keats was livid, both at the failure conceded by a "Fragment" and at the publishers' excuse in an Advertisement at the front of the volume, which attributed this state to a discouragement by the reception of *Endymion.*

Keats left it a fragment because the masterplan was making less and less sense to him as his brother was dying in the next room. Apollo, *a fore-seeing God will shape his actions like one,* Keats told epic-man Haydon (*K* 88), meant to symbolize an advance over the mere Titan sun-driver Hyperion, as a new light of medicine, philosophy, music, and poetry. Keats felt the spirit in his own age: as civilization becomes "gradually more enlighten'd," he wrote in September 1818 to George and Georgiana, there will be "a continual change for the better" (*L* 2:193), on which a poet's vision might shine a light. Yet right after characterizing Apollo to Haydon, he adds, with circumspection about success, *But I am counting &c.* The deepest throb of *Hyperion* turned out to be not this Apollonian logic but the pathos of the Titan god Hyperion, sensing his doom from, and in, the fall of his brothers into a hellish mortal world. In September 1818, hell was in Keats's heart, in his art. Writing "Poetry," he says to Reynolds, let him "feel escaped from a new strange and threatening sorrow"; but the escape artist cannot shrug off the propellant: I'll be Tom. Even the turn to "Poetry" was feeling like a "feverous relief" and something of a "crime" to indulge (*K* 201).

Tom's proximity presses him into self-division: desperate for relief, criminal in self-concentration. The day before, Keats had written to another friend, Charles Dilke,

> *I wish I could say Tom was any better. His identity presses upon me so all day that I am obliged to go out – and although I intended to have given some time to study alone I am obliged to write, and plunge into abstract images to ease myself of his countenance his voice and feebleness – so that I live now in a continual fever. . . . Imagine 'the hateful siege of contraries' – if I think of fame of poetry it seems a crime to me, and yet I must do so or suffer - -I am sorry to give you pain – I am almost resolv'd to burn this – (K 200)[2]*

Much confessed in a winningly honest *almost:* agony and desperation. Epics privilege the prepositional launch *Of: Of arms and the man; Of man's first*

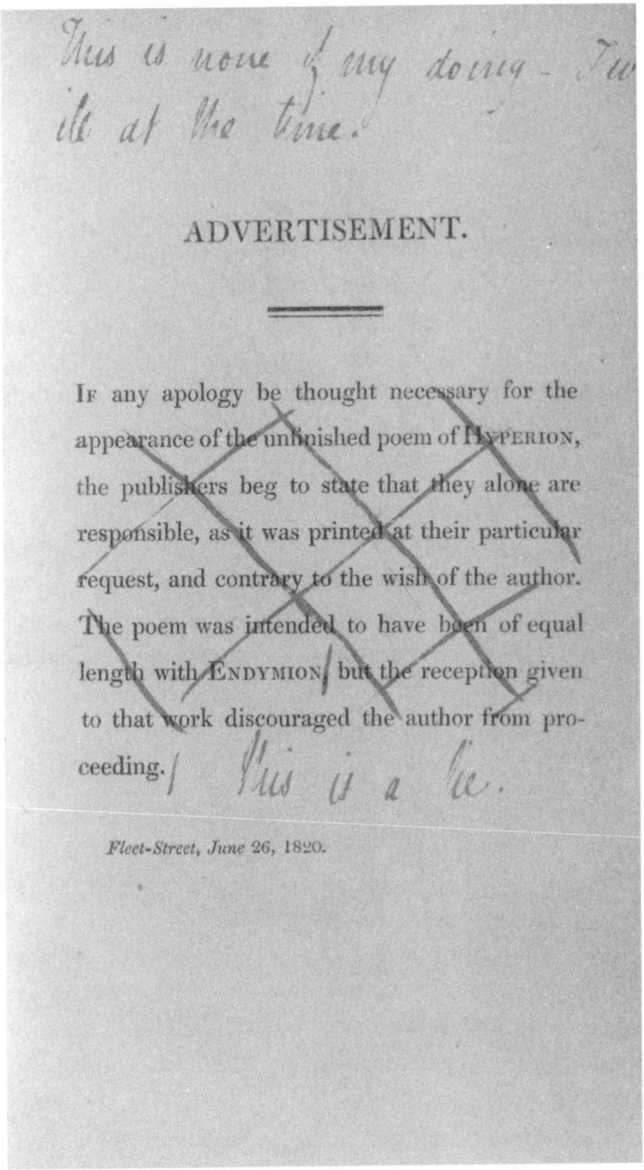

This is none of my doing — I was ill at the time.

ADVERTISEMENT.

IF any apology be thought necessary for the appearance of the unfinished poem of HYPERION, the publishers beg to state that they alone are responsible, as it was printed at their particular request, and contrary to the wish of the author. The poem was intended to have been of equal length with ENDYMION, but the reception given to that work discouraged the author from proceeding. *This is a lie.*

Fleet-Street, June 26, 1820.

Figure 9: Not having seen this advertisement added to the volume prior to publication, Keats angrily marked the page in his presentation copy for Burridge Davenport, a Hampstead banker who had been kind to him and his brother Tom. Keats EC8.K2262.820ℓ (G). Courtesy of Houghton Library, Harvard University.

disobedience. Keats's string of repetitions—*of* his countenance, *of* contraries, *of* fame, *of* poetry—is so agonized as to summon an allusion to Satan's complex sensations amid Eden's pleasures, rendered by Milton in lines that Keats underscored and margin-checked (*KPL* II:78):

> the more I see
> Pleasures about me, so much more I feel
> Torment within me, <u>as from the hateful siege</u>
> ||| <u>Of contraries</u>   (9.119–122)

Suffering either way (writing or not), Keats apologizes to Dilke for communicating pain: *but I really have not self possession and magnanimity enough to manage the thing otherwise* – (*K* 200). No Apollo, he.

When, in December 1816, the aspiring poet had set his sights on "the agonies, the strife / Of human hearts" (*Sleep and Poetry* 124–125), he imagined this in epic abstractions, not visceral sympathy. Reading an earlier passage in *Paradise Lost*, Keats took notice of the old myths, the war of generations. This arrayed a repeating, abstract destiny for all generations. Heaven and Earth, the first gods, fell to their first-born, Saturn, who with his "enormous brood," seized rule, then, in turn,

> <u>from mightier Jove</u>
> <u>His own and Rhea's son like measure found;</u>
> <u>So Jove usurping reign'd</u> . . .   (1.510–514; *KPL* I:17)

The generational change in *Hyperion* has no such symmetry to score. Keats sets its temporality at the end of one usurpation, in a slow aftermath of stunned realizations. What magnetizes *Paradise Lost* for Keats is not cosmology but the way theological Milton can write epic feeling, *godlike in the sublime pathetic* in scenes of the defeated angels, in *delicacies of passion, living in and from their immortality* (*KPL* I:44). A "mingled pathos and sublimity," Hazlitt called such poetry in a lecture that Keats attended in winter 1818 (*Lectures* 130).

Keats's mingling has a different distillation, however. Where Milton's downcast angels are still alive in spirit, Keats's fallen gods are sick, dispirited, almost dead. In scene after scene, Keats delivers a human-nerved sublime pathetic, traced in subtleties of wording wrought from revision and rewriting.[3] Who isn't glad for Woodhouse's insistence on having this *Fragment* published? The "sustained grandeur and quiet power," he said, made him "regret that such an attempt should have been abandoned" (Finney

2:536). It is a thrill to follow his rescue of Keats's stunning experiment in epic psychology and verbal phenomenology.

[1] He drafted the Advertisement in June 1820. Taylor approved it (*KC* 1:115–116) without consulting Keats, who'd been coughing blood all week.

[2] ALS, in Williamson, *The Keats Letters, Papers & c.,* plate xx.

[3] British Library Add. MS 37000, cited by folio, *Manuscripts of the Younger Romantics,* vol. 5, ed. Jack Stillinger (Garland, 1988).

Book I: "the shady sadness of a vale"

DEEP in the shady sadness of a vale
Far sunken from the healthy breath of morn,
Far from the fiery noon, and eve's one star,
Sat gray-hair'd Saturn, quiet as a stone,   4
Still as the silence round about his lair;
Forest on forest hung about his head
Like cloud on cloud. No stir of air was there,
Not so much life as on a summer's day
Robs not one light seed from the feather'd grass,   9
But where the dead leaf fell, there did it rest.
A stream went voiceless by, still deadened more
By reason of his fallen divinity
Spreading a shade: the Naiad 'mid her reeds
Press'd her cold finger closer to her lips.

Along the margin-sand large foot-marks went,   15
No further than to where his feet had stray'd,
And slept there since. Upon the sodden ground
His old right hand lay nerveless, listless, dead,
Unsceptred; and his realmless eyes were closed;
While his bow'd head seem'd list'ning to the Earth,
His ancient mother, for some comfort yet.

No surprise is Keats's keen attention on Milton's technical management (*PL* 1.56; *KPL* I:3):

the first step must be heroic and full of power; and nothing can be more impressive and shaded than the commencement of the action here— <u>*'round he throws his baleful eyes'*</u>

Sorrowful, unfortunate, full of harm weigh in the meaning of *baleful* (Spenser, Glossary I:cxvii). How wrenching is this sympathy with hellishly blind Milton conceiving the Hell that Satan sees this way. Keats underlines Satan's survey, in awe of Milton's power of "imagining" such sensation (*KPL* I:4–5):

> At once, as far as Angels' ken he views
> The dismal situation waste and wild: [1.59–60]

>   sights of woe,
> Regions of sorrow, doleful shades, where peace
> And rest can never dwell, hope never comes
> That comes to all   [1.64–67]

Milton builds word by word—*views, waste, wild, woe, sorrow*—pained by the vanished antonyms: *never dwell / never comes* completes its syntax with the benefit open to mere mortals, *comes to all*. Milton's paces of negation give Keats his first epic step.

No call to a muse, no moral argument opens *Hyperion*. The verse unfurls a tableau of paralyzed divinity on earth, one vast region of sorrow. Keats rises to this fall, opening with a spectacular sonnet-stanza (1–14) of implacably intensifying arrest, layer by layer, line by line, word by word, syllable by syllable. Setting *vale*—given a capital emphasis, *Vale*, in the manuscript (f.1ʳ)—at the end of his first line, Keats remembered its force in *Paradise Lost*:

> *There is a cool pleasure in the very sound of vale—The english word is of the happiest chance. Milton has put vales in heaven and hell with the very utter affection and yearning of a great Poet.*   (*KPL* I:12)

In the Titans' hellish vale, Keats's ear could also catch the Spenserian verb *avale* (*lower, bring down, descend*), and the antithetical homophone *avail*, a Spenserian noun for *equivalent* (*Works*, Glossary I:cxvii). From *Hyperion's* first downbeat *Deep*, the stressed sound-path engraves the score. You have to wait until line 7 for any frontline lilt of iambics ("Like *cloud* on *cloud*"). The positional extension, *Deep in* (1), resounds as *deepen*, with *sunken* (2) reflexively undertoning *sunk in*. *Far from* is the soundscape but not the heaven-scape of one *star* (3); its closer tune is *Forest on forest* (6).[1]

On this sunken soundscape, Keats sets *Sat . . . Saturn* (4): *nomen est omen*. Bailey admired the "perfect" way "the sameness of the sound increases the melancholy & monotony of the situation," Bailey's own *melancholy & monotony* supplying a nice mimesis (*KC* 2:277). Keats's phonic allusion, with import, is Milton's *Satan exalted sat* (*PL* 2.5). How apt that Bailey recalled Keats's Saturn as "dethroned Satan in his melancholy solitude."[2] They are intimate twins in displacement. Hazlitt loved the mixture of "regal splendor and fallen power" in Milton's figure (*Lectures* 104). Keats had heard this lecture, and measured the skill in Milton's <u>Stationing</u> (*KPL* II:43), not only for Satan:

> He is not content with simple description, he must station—*Thus here, we not only see how the Birds* '<u>with clang despised</u> *the* <u>ground</u>' *but we see them* '<u>under a cloud in prospect</u>' *So we see Adam* '<u>Fair indeed and tall—under a plantane</u> *and so we see Satan,* '<u>disfigured — on the Assyrian Mount</u>'[3]

Keats writes *we see* four times: imagination's visual field of prepositions.

Saturn is no Satan of self-possession. The magnificent opening paragraph of *Hyperion* spells and spills its clauses to station all that has been lost: healthy breath of morn, living leaves, summer, air stirring, Naiad's singing, and not least, Saturn's vital pulse. The word *air* is literally caught in *lair,* the place of paralysis that possesses every *where* and *there.*

> One's very breath while leaning over these Pages is held for fear of blowing this line away—as easily as the gentlest breeze ~~despoils~~ Robs dandelions of their fleecy Crowns,

Keats wrote this about a line in *Troilus and Cressida* (*KS* 157). He tries out this breathless measure for line 9 here, *Robs not at all the dandelion's fleece* (f.1ʳ). He then stripped it down to *Robs not one light seed from the feather'd grass.* Keeping the tenor of *light* as weightless, *light seed* also elicits the merest visual light amid the darkness visible.

Keats uses *voiceless* in his poetry only here, an adjective choked from *voicelessly.* Wordsworth used the adjective to describe a retreat amid "Rocks and Stones" where "no breeze" can enter, "no trace / Of motion" can be seen. Even a waterfall descends "like a breath of air": "—Voiceless the Stream descends into the gulph / With timid lapse," under a "chasm of sky above" (*Excursion,* pp. 96–98). So opens Book 3, *Despondency* (literally: *lost promise*). Even so, Wordsworth's material scene holds "shadowy intimations" of divinity, "Of purposes akin to those of Man" (pp. 91–94). Keats makes divinity itself fallen, deadened by shadowy intimations of human mortality. His very rhythm delivers materially, metaphorically: *where the dead leaf fell, there did it rest* (every syllable a thud), then *still deadened more* (10–11), reverberating as *dead-end,* and echoing from *Still as the silence* (6).

The next paragraph zooms in on dethroned Saturn as the embodied logic of this dead world. *Along the margin-sand large foot-marks went* (15) gets seven thuds, five on the monosyllabic words, Keats's poetic feet in the pace. He first wrote *feet had stay'd* (f.1ʳ), then an aimless *stray'd* (16), ending in *slept* (17), the negative echo of *stept.* Line 18 imposes three (medically informed) negatives: *His old right hand lay nerveless, listless, dead.* Keats rewrote the line to get the last two adjectives in place, working the phonics from *nerveless* and *voiceless* (11), ready for an inserted *realmless* in line 19 (f.1ʳ). These words are history-packed negations, formings by remnant identity; *realmless* is unique in his poetry, *nerveless* almost so.[4] This is new grammar for the old god. Saturn can hardly move "his tongue with the full weight of utterless thought" (2:120). Keats draws out a hypermetric line to accommodate *utterless.* He may have coined this negative (here, too, only in his poetry).[5] He surely coined a phonic twin, those seeming foes of *untremendous* might that riddle Saturn's reasoning (2.155).

How bitter the relay into the aftermath, *Unsceptred* (1.19): literal for Saturn's hand, figural for *realmless.* Around *Unsceptred* is the layered, crowned (closely sounded) rhyme, *dead/bow'd head.* Having tried *broad head* (f.1ʳ), Keats went for a stationed intensity of defeat, life at its lowest ebb: <u>statury</u> (*KPL* II:43), Keats-coined synonym for <u>stationing</u> with a faint pulse.

[*1820,* 145–146]

[1] Jack Stillinger nicely reads these accumulating effects, *Complete Poems,* xxv.

[2] H.E. Rollins, ever careful to write *sic* (even here), leaves the *Satan*-error unmarked. Bailey's transcriber (his daughter) may have misheard him, but he didn't correct it (nor a surreally mistaken *fiery moon,* Nabokov-ready, for Keats's *fiery noon*).

[3] Keats underlined these phrases in the verse-text: 7.424 (II:43); 4.477–478 (I:98); 4.126–127, with triple lines in the left margin next to Satan's station (I:88).

[4] It is as if Keats were speaking back to Z's contempt of the "loose, nerveless versification" of his early poetry ("Cockney School IV" 522).

[5] *OED* lists only one *utterless* before Keats; Google Books turns up just one more. Weighted with the sense of *utter* as *complete, extreme,* the subtraction is severe: "*Utterance,* the extremity of defiance" (*DW* Glossary, sq. 3350).

Saturn and Thea ("tender spouse of gold Hyperion")

> As when, upon a tranced summer-night,
> Those green-rob'd senators of mighty woods,
> Tall oaks, branch-charmed by the earnest stars,
> Dream, and so dream all night without a stir,
> Save from one gradual solitary gust
> Which comes upon the silence, and dies off,
> As if the ebbing air had but one wave;   78
> So came these words and went; the while in tears
> She touch'd her fair large forehead to the ground,
> Just where her falling hair might be outspread
> A soft and silken mat for Saturn's feet.
> One moon, with alteration slow, had shed
> Her silver seasons four upon the night,
> And still these two were postured motionless,
> Like natural sculpture in cathedral cavern;
> The frozen God still couchant on the earth,
> And the sad Goddess weeping at his feet:
> Until at length old Saturn lifted up
> His faded eyes, and saw his kingdom gone,   90
> And all the gloom and sorrow of the place,
> And that fair kneeling Goddess . . .

If the Elgin marbles had been a tableau mort, this would be it, in the poem's first epic simile. By convention, an epic simile imports the wording of another situation (the vehicle), to dovetail into its tenor. Keats involves vehicle and tenor in one scene, to double-fold a deathscape. The haunting compound (his coinage), *branch-charmed* (74; f.3ʳ), shimmers strangely in the ambiguous rule of its preposition *by*. This seems a stationing marker: branches *by* a starry night sky. But a weirdly adjectival, intimately lettered *earnest stars* hints an astral agency (*charmed by, by force of*). The stars / Look'd down on him with pity, Keats writes of Hyperion (1.305–306), as if these distant lights were acutely, feelingly attentive. The trees, too, *dream* in seeming sentience, ruffled by a gust of ebbing air. Keats first wrote *sudden momentary gust* (76; f.3r), then paced the agon of slow time (with new alliteration) to *one gradual solitary gust*. If *gust* is part of the simile-vehicle, by the time it hits the tenor, *So came these words and went,* Keats has concentrated simile into synonym.

The centerpiece is *The frozen God still couchant on the earth* (87), depotentiated into a static heraldic emblem. The only end-rhyme in this marmoreal blank verse is *outspread–shed* (81, 83), action degree-zero. In a repetition with a sounded rhyme-punctuation on the blank-verse field, Keats finely halts Saturn's *feet* at the line-ends (82, 88) for meta-poetic stress. Time itself seems paused in the Miltonic inversion *alteration slow* (83). On such verbal tracks, Keats stages an epic poetics of inaction. He downfurls the epic simile, *As when . . .* (72) into a merely notional *as if . . .* (78). Slow-motion moon-phases, the faintest of shifts in a world so *still* (85, 87), usurp natural seasons. Saturn's faded eyes are sunken, too deep for tears. Keats refines a futile *lifted up* at the end of line 89, then turns the verse line to the sightline of *saw his kingdom gone*, and *all the gloom and sorrow of the place* (90–91), a devastating hendiadys of simultaneity.

The cosmography of Saturn's new *place* is literally beneath the realm *still* held by his yet unfallen brother-god Hyperion. Keats has been drawing an accumulating *Still* as a master-chord, soon to sound into a precarious temporality for Hyperion.

[*1820*, 149–150]

"Blazing Hyperion . . . yet unsecure"

> But one of the whole mammoth-brood still kept
> His sov'reignty, and rule, and majesty; —
> Blazing Hyperion on his orbed fire
> Still sat, still snuff'd the incense, teeming up
> From man to the sun's God; yet unsecure:
> For as among us mortals omens drear
> Fright and perplex, so also shuddered he—   170
> Not at dog's howl, or gloom-bird's hated screech,
> Or the familiar visiting of one
> Upon the first toll of his passing-bell,
> Or prophesyings of the midnight lamp;
> But horrors, portion'd to a giant nerve,
> Oft made Hyperion ache. His palace bright
> Bastion'd with pyramids of glowing gold,
> And touch'd with shade of bronzed obelisks,
> Glar'd a blood-red through all its thousand courts,
> Arches, and domes, and fiery galleries;   180

And all its curtains of Aurorian clouds
Flush'd angerly: while sometimes eagle's wings,
Unseen before by Gods or wondering men,
Darken'd the place; and neighing steeds were heard,
Not heard before by Gods or wondering men.
Also, when he would taste the spicy wreaths
Of incense, breath'd aloft from sacred hills,
Instead of sweets, his ample palate took
Savour of poisonous brass and metal sick: 189
And so, when harbour'd in the sleepy west,
After the full completion of fair day,—
For rest divine upon exalted couch
And slumber in the arms of melody,
He pac'd away the pleasant hours of ease
With stride colossal, on from hall to hall;
While far within each aisle and deep recess,
His winged minions in close clusters stood,
Amaz'd and full of fear; like anxious men
Who on wide plains gather in panting troops,
When earthquakes jar their battlements and towers.   200
Even now, while Saturn, rous'd from icy trance,
Went step for step with Thea through the woods,
Hyperion, leaving twilight in the rear,
Came slope upon the threshold of the west;
Then, as was wont, his palace-door flew open
In smoothest silence, save what solemn tubes,
Blown by the serious Zephyrs, gave of sweet
And wandering sounds, slow-breathed melodies;
And like a rose in vermeil tint and shape,
In fragrance soft, and coolness to the eye,
That inlet to severe magnificence
Stood full blown, for the God to enter in.   212

   He enter'd, but he enter'd full of wrath;
His flaming robes stream'd out beyond his heels,
And gave a roar, as if of earthly fire,
That scar'd away the meek ethereal Hours
And made their dove-wings tremble. On he flared,
From stately nave to nave, from vault to vault,

Through bowers of fragrant and enwreathed light,
And diamond-paved lustrous long arcades, 220
Until he reach'd the great main cupola;
There standing fierce beneath, he stampt his foot,
And from the basements deep to the high towers
Jarr'd his own golden region; and before
The quavering thunder thereupon had ceas'd,
His voice leapt out, despite of godlike curb,
To this result: "O dreams of day and night!
    O monstrous forms! O effigies of pain!
    O spectres busy in a cold, cold gloom!
    O lank-ear'd Phantoms of black-weeded pools! 230
    Why do I know ye? why have I seen ye? why
    Is my eternal essence thus distraught
    To see and to behold these horrors new?
    Saturn is fallen, am I too to fall?
    Am I to leave this haven of my rest,
    This cradle of my glory, this soft clime,
    This calm luxuriance of blissful light,
    These crystalline pavilions, and pure fanes,
    Of all my lucent empire? It is left
    Deserted, void, nor any haunt of mine. 240
    The blaze, the splendor, and the symmetry,
    I cannot see—but darkness, death and darkness.
    Even here, into my centre of repose,
    The shady visions come to domineer,
    Insult, and blind, and stifle up my pomp.—
    Fall!—No, by Tellus and her briny robes!
    Over the fiery frontier of my realms
    I will advance a terrible right arm
    Shall scare that infant thunderer, rebel Jove,
    And bid old Saturn take his throne again."—
He spake, and ceas'd, the while a heavier threat
Held struggle with his throat but came not forth; 252
For as in theatres of crowded men
Hubbub increases more they call out "Hush!"
So at Hyperion's words the Phantoms pale
Bestirr'd themselves, thrice horrible and cold;
And from the mirror'd level where he stood

A mist arose, as from a scummy marsh.
At this, through all his bulk an agony
Crept gradual, from the feet unto the crown,   260
Like a lithe serpent vast and muscular
Making slow way, with head and neck convuls'd
From over-strained might. Releas'd, he fled
To the eastern gates, and full six dewy hours
Before the dawn in season due should blush,
He breath'd fierce breath against the sleepy portals,
Clear'd them of heavy vapours, burst them wide
Suddenly on the ocean's chilly streams.
The planet orb of fire, whereon he rode
Each day from east to west the heavens through,   270
Spun round in sable curtaining of clouds;
Not therefore veiled quite, blindfold, and hid,
But ever and anon the glancing spheres,
Circles, and arcs, and broad-belting colure,
Glow'd through, and wrought upon the muffling dark
Sweet-shaped lightnings from the nadir deep
Up to the zenith,—hieroglyphics old,
Which sages and keen-eyed astrologers
Then living on the earth, with labouring thought
Won from the gaze of many centuries: 280
Now lost, save what we find on remnants huge
Of stone, or marble swart; their import gone,
Their wisdom long since fled.—Two wings this orb
Possess'd for glory, two fair argent wings,
Ever exalted at the God's approach:
And now, from forth the gloom their plumes immense
Rose, one by one, till all outspreaded were;
While still the dazzling globe maintain'd eclipse,
Awaiting for Hyperion's command.   289
Fain would he have commanded, fain took throne
And bid the day begin, if but for change.
He might not:—No, though a primeval God:
The sacred seasons might not be disturb'd.
Therefore the operations of the dawn
Stay'd in their birth, even as here 'tis told.
Those silver wings expanded sisterly,

Eager to sail their orb; the porches wide
Open'd upon the dusk demesnes of night;
And the bright Titan, phrenzied with new woes,
Unus'd to bend, by hard compulsion bent   300
His spirit to the sorrow of the time;
And all along a dismal rack of clouds,
Upon the boundaries of day and night,
He stretch'd himself in grief and radiance faint.
There as he lay, the Heaven with its stars   305
Look'd down on him with pity . . .

Midway in Book I, an epic volta pans over to Hyperion, in his palace *still,* a situation with a timed-out reign. In the crescendo of these magnificent 142 lines Keats shows a sublime god-fall in the mind: dawning unsecurity, to anxious wrath, to despairing collapse in grief and radiance faint.

The onset, line 163's *But one . . .* , rolls its sentence on to 176, *Oft made Hyperion ache.* Its first throb is *But . . . yet unsecure* (163, 168). These qualifiers frame *Still sat, still* (167) with a situational unease that is also time-cast. Keats counts on our recognizing these syllables before: *Sat . . . Saturn . . . /Still* (4–5), a palimpsest that underwrites and shades into Hyperion. In *unsecure,* Keats sounds the fraternity of *unsceptred* Saturn (19), both words unique in his poetry, the latter distinctly obsolete (not even in *JnD*). The relay of "*sun's* God; yet *unsecure*" (168) issues a lettered microplot (*un's* to *uns*), subtler and more sinister.[1] Setting *yet unsecure* between a semicolon and a colon is finely punctuated mid-stationing.

The prefix *un-* corrodes the absence of *secure* (*sine cura:* without care) to set the stage for Keats's next great epic simile (in *1820* at the top of a new page, 155): *For as among us mortals . . .* (169). The analogy aligns Hyperion's ominous sensation of regime change with the ungodly lives of human history. Keats's mordantly worded figures condense God-agon into God's agony, in the new fragilities of *oft* and *Also when he would.* No little force is drawn from Milton's omen-poetics: how a lunar eclipse "with fear of change / Perplexes monarchs" (1.598–599; *KPL* I:19–20). This is Keats's underlining, with a cheer for republican Milton in his margin:

How noble and collected an indignation against Kings . . . His very wishing should have had power to pull that feeble animal Charles from his bloody throne.

His import to *Hyperion* comes with a different slant of affect. Milton's jab at the "sun king" was blocked by Charles II's Licenser for the Press. Keats catches it for sympathy with Hyperion's human-like agitation, unsecure of everything he knows, has ever known. On a cascade of verse, he propels this sensation along analogies to dire human apprehensions, all named and marked, in a poetics of Miltonic sublime wired into a Titanic nervous system (171–174).

The privilege and force of poetry, Wordsworth argued in 1815 (with emphases), is "to treat of things not as they exist in themselves, but as they *seem* to exist to the *senses* and to the *passions*."[2] To the senses, to the passions: Keats radiates God-ache into Hyperion's fevered palace, glaring blood-red all over its flushed body, fiery with the crazed light of a sun god's agitation, the figure's tenor and vehicle drawn from the same material.[3] Keats's stressed front-line words *Glar'd* and *Flush'd* (179, 182) pulse beyond high-color, into surreal action. *Glared: gazed upon, looked fiercely* (*DW* Glossary, sq. 3338). So, too, the *pyramids of glowing gold* (177). Keats first wrote of pyramids *with chequer black* by the shadows of obelisks (f.6ʳ). Then he hit the richer wording of *glowing:* a frisson of internal power, beyond reflection, in relay with *touch'd with shade* (178), the visual *shade* with a shudder of spectral presence. All these wordings throb into mortalized equivalences of new orders of apprehension, with a sublime *Un-* prefixing: *Unseen before by Gods or wondering men* (Keats revised to get this; f.6ʳ) //*Not heard before by Gods or wondering men* (184, 186). Even taste mutates. It is not that the air has turned toxic; it is that a capacity for any other savor is gone. Apollo was the theory; Hyperion is the experience.

At *metal sick* (189), Keats plants a colon for a dramatic halt that pivots symptom into consequence. The 23 lines to 212 come forth on just two sentences (with marked pauses), to set the god's new stage of sensation. To achieve this epic trauma, Keats reworked and fine-tuned this poetry more than any other passage in *Hyperion* (f.6r). There are only three events, the last two more staging than action: *He pac'd* (194); *minions . . . stood* (197); *palace-door flew ope* (205). Everything else is conjunctive (*And, when, while, Then*), prepositional (*with, on from, far within, on*), splayed into gerunds and participles, to map a Titanic tectonic shift. Across this tableau, Keats pulses the iambic pentameter into Hyperion's aching heartbeat for the old luxurious hours. There is no slumber in the arms of melody (no Adonis, he)—not even a sensation of force in abeyance, like *might half slumb'ring on its own right arm* (*Sleep and Poetry* 237). Just a frantic *pac'd away* during habitual hours of ease, this prepositional phrase marks time and erosion.

More than a measure comes on Keats's next preposition, *with stride colossal* (195). The adjective is tremendously allusive. Of the huge statues erected by mortal men to gods, the most famous is the 100-foot Colossus of Rhodes (Hyperion's son, no less: sun-god Helios). One of the wonders of the ancient world, it was felled by an earthquake. Keats imprints this known history *among us mortals* into Hyperion's agitated pacing. In the theogony, Apollo preempts Hyperion's heir Helios. In human history, all Colossi fall to ruin. He "doth bestride the narrow world / Like a Colossus" (mutters a regime-changer in Shakespeare's *Julius Caesar,* 1.2). To give Hyperion a *stride colossal* is to mark a Caesar-fate. Shelley's sonnet *Ozymandias* (published in the *Examiner,* January 1818) ironizes a trumpeting king reduced to a *Colossal Wreck* of a vainglorious statue. Hunt must have had this in mind when, in 1820, he described *Hyperion* as "a fragment,—a gigantic one, like a ruin in the desart," then redeemed Keats's regret about its publication: "truly of a piece with it subject, . . . the downfall of the elder gods" (*Indicator* 347).

A Keatsian figure ready for ruining is the bower. Bowery *Endymion* goes dark in the Cave of Quietude; goes gothic in Isabella's demented pot of basil. Hyperion's still "palace bright" teeters on superlative decadence: *smoothest silence, sweet . . . sounds, slow-breathed melodies, rose vermeil* (206–209). Keats ends the blazon in *Hyperion* abruptly at *Stood full blown, for the God to enter in* (212), blasting away the sweet melodies "Blown by the serious Zephyrs" for the god's pleasure (207). He sets line 212's *blown,* in the last line of this verse-paragraph, at the crux of two syntaxes. It arrives on a simile for how the doors of Hyperion's hall have swung open (full blown) for his entrance. Then *full blown* arcs across the syntax, across the page, into a new verse paragraph, to station the "severe magnificence" of Hyperion himself: *Stood full blown . . . full of wrath* (211–213). With a superb run to line 250, Keats takes Hyperion from this taut entrance, into restless pacing, then into dark passages of thought, then agonized outburst. Every element of this poetry detonates from *full of wrath,* with the devastating futurism measured out in the analogy, *as if of earthly fire* (215)—a fire all but struck as the word *if* sounds into *of* then *fire.* Onto this syntax, Keats double-loads *scar'd* (216): the ethereal hours that wrath has scared away, and a slant sound and lettering into fire-*scarred.* From preposition to preposition, right into a devastating rhyme-echo in *Jarr'd,* Hyperion produces a heaven-quake in his golden region. As the god stampt his foot, the poet stamps his meters, the resonance of a body in anger, protest, refusal.

Ever the visceral poet, Keats knows by now how to render a voice in a crisis of restraint, wringing this through 23 lines (my excerpt stops a bit short). Coleridge was impressed by Shakespeare's "intimately conscious" genius about "the flux and reflux of the mind in all its subtlest thoughts and feelings, . . . placing the whole before our view."[4] Keats shows how *shady visions come to domineer* (244) not as external forces but as latencies in a mind *come to* horrid viewing: *dreams, monstrous forms, effigies, spectres,* and *Phantoms* (227–230). This tortured psychology is gothic grammar in such dark passages of thought that the realized events are redundant. The barrage of *why . . . ?* on the sound-stream of *eternal essence thus distraught* (231–233) is interrogative syntax as double agent, turned upon itself with its devastating premises, most severely in the climax: *Saturn is fallen, am I too to fall?* (234). "The moment the Gods speak," wrote Hunt about this, with alert sensation, "they feel like ourselves . . . and what is sympathy with a God, but turning him into a man?" (*Indicator* 351). How great is this reciprocal twist of the phrase, *they feel like ourselves:* they feel as we do; they seem images of us. Keats's deadened Titans deliver figures of mortal humanity.

For this effect, Keats inserted new lines to place after the loaded question at the bottom of page 7 of his manuscript, *am I too to fall?* (234). He turned over the page and wrote the lines on page 8, just after *this cradle of my Glory* (236–239). What a fine addition! Keats's unerring ear sets Hyperion's mortally darkening knowledge into an echo-chamber of literary history in recognitions of unappeasable loss. Keats's lines for Hyperion evoke Shakespeare's John of Gaunt's dying hymn to an England lost and gone in regime change and impending civil war:

> This royal throne of kings, this sceptred isle,
> This earth of majesty, this seat of Mars,
> This other Eden, demi-paradise . . .   (*Richard II* 2.1)

In this gaunt nightmare, even Olympian Mars is set for unseating. Milton echoed this elegy (and Keats could hear it, having marked it) in ruined Satan's measure of Hell (*KPL* I:10):

> Is this the region, this the soil, the clime,
> Said then the lost Archangel, this the seat
> That we must change for Heaven, this mournful gloom
> For that celestial light?
>   [. . .]
>   <u>Farewell happy fields,</u>
> <u>Where joy for ever dwells: Hail horrors, hail</u>
> <u>Infernal world, and thou profoundest Hell</u>   (*PL* 1.242–245, 249–252)

Farewell is said to what is departing—in Satan's case, all happy fields. How surprising that a poem titled *Paradise Lost* has *farewell* only once more, in Book II, for a simile on the flash of virtue in the fallen angels as they honor Satan's bravery (Keats's underlining): <u>If chance the radiant sun with farewell sweet / Extend his evening beam</u>, then all nature revives into a brief daytime (492–493; *KPL* I:43). This is acutely poignant nostalgia. *Farewell* is Satan's devastated elegy, nuanced in modulations of *fields, dwells, Hail, hail,* in a crescendo to *Hell.*

Keats gives this elegiac grammar to Hyperion, in a strangulation of horror. In intimate, visceral medical sympathy, he delivers a convulsion of iambic pentameter at Hyperion's *Held struggle* (252). The *mirror'd* level (floor) from which a mist rises (257–278) is no mere polish (revised from a flat *glossy; f.8ʳ*), but a reflector of mind-mist scum, rhyme-reflecting the mind *Bestirr'd* (256). A homophone in "mist a*rose*" (258) sounds the death-knell of the divine bower's "*rose* in vermeil" (210).

> the rapid, irregular starts of imagination, suddenly wrenched from all its accustomed holds and resting-places in the soul . . . We see the ebb and flow of the feeling, its pauses and feverish starts, its impatience of opposition, its accumulating force when it has time to recollect itself, the manner in which it avails itself of every passing word or gesture, its haste to repel insinuation, the alternate contraction and dilation of the soul.

This is Hazlitt's passion for the passion of *King Lear.* Keats margin-marked and underlined these sentences in *Characters of Shakespear's Plays* (1817).[5] We can see why.

What a canny terminus is Keats's word *crown* (260): no longer emblem of rule, just a cranium for an agonized brain. Hyperion's agony climaxes and halts at 263's mid-line period: *From over-strained might.* Completing the line *Released he fled,* Keats suspends the motion, then turns its course to a site of desperate action: the sun's nighttime lodge. In an overcharged power-test, Hyperion tries to command the sun before its hour—a sublime pathetic that wrenches the time out of joint, rupturing the symphony of *dewy dawn due* with a fiercely literal *carpe diem* (seize the day). Those "horrors, *portion'd* to a giant nerve" (175) burst in sound and sense upon these "sleepy *portals*" (264). Shelley's *Ode to the West Wind* describes a "heavy weight of hours" that sounds a temporal *wait.* Keats charges a divine impatience so crazed that it radiates into human historiography. Merely to open the gates is catastrophic, electrocuting the darkness with such intensity as to provoke mortal scribes into hieroglyphics (a rare noun in Keats's poetry)—now unreadable, then a cosmic ekphrasis of *Sweet-shaped lightnings* (276). Keats wanted the weird spin of *broad-belting colure* (274).[6] He took it into *"wrought* upon the muffling dark" (275), to catch an end-rhyme with laboring human *thought* (279) on this sky-writing.

Keats's present-tense epic voice, *as here 'tis told* (295), does not lighten this darkness but spells it into durably fabulous lore, rhymed on an arc back to *hieroglyphics old* (277). These markings are *Now lost, save what we find on remnants huge / Of stone, or marble swart; their import gone* (281–282), Keats adeptly mirroring the remnant medium, *stone,* into an eye-rhyme with *gone:* his severest ditty of no tone. With hallucinatory power, the temporality of this *Now* reverberates into the *now* of the narrative progressive: *And now, from forth the gloom their plumes immense / Rose* (286–287). Peter Brooks calls such a *now* "paralogical" narrative, a tracking with "double logic": the *now* of the poet's script claims its legitimacy from the *now* in the narrative of inscription (29–30).[7] Keats's verb of solar greeting, *Rose,* brings a triple logic, even, working overtime from Hyperion's vanishing bower *rose* (209) into *A mist arose* (258).

This passage has to a great degree the hieroglyphic visioning

—so wrote Keats about Hazlitt's rendition of Lear's agony (p. 157, sq. 185). Hazlitt had given him the words he needed back in May to speak his dissatisfaction with Milton's *certain points and resting places in reasoning* (*K* 130). Not in any alignment with this kind of reasoning, Keats's poetry becomes most acutely Miltonic in the way he orchestrates, sounds, and resounds words as dramatic agents in his own hieroglyphs of visioning.

The turn of suspense, *awaiting for Hyperion's command* (289), conflates grammar into a conflict of present participle against the cosmic stasis of *maintain'd eclipse* (288), this last word straight from *Paradise Lost* as that omen to perplex kings. Echo relays into mordant allusion, to thwart Hyperion's test of power. The arc of sound from *maintain'd* to the desperate *Fain . . . fain* (290) is already foregone in time and tone, foreknown by the historically later, far later, narrator whose syllable *No* (292) is redundant rhetorical punctuation. The chord that Keats sounds along *night . . . bright Titan* (298–299) to *day and night* (303) thrusts the drama of syntax into meta-enjambment: *Unus'd to bend, by hard compulsion bent / His spirit* (300–301). Keats bends the god's spirit in uncanny poetic perfection. Hyperion's collapse *in grief and radiance faint* (304) devastates *in* with affective placement and divine displacement. So knocked out was Hunt by this "core and inner diamond of the poem" that he quoted the full run from "His palace bright" (176) to Hyperion's collapse "in grief and radiance faint" (304).[8]

Keats's own agon shades this epic collapse. Recall his desperate "plunge" into poetry to "ease" himself of Tom's mortal sentence (*K* 200). At the close of Book I, his poetry plunges nearly beyond words in Hyperion's course downward to darkness, on no extended wings. The Titan has been listening to the solemn whisper of his father, sky-god Cœlus, telling him of catastrophic change. At this report,

> Hyperion arose, and on the stars
> Lifted his curved lids, and kept them wide
> Until it ceas'd; and still he kept them wide:
> And still they were the same bright, patient stars.
> Then with a slow incline of his broad breast,
> Like to a diver in the pearly seas,
> Forward he stoop'd over the airy shore,
> And plung'd all noiseless into the deep night.   (350–357)

Hyperion's final station in his world is star-witnessed: unchanging, ever patient. Keats intensifies this witnessing with a *still*-woven chiasmus, *stars/. . . kept them wide/. . . still kept them wide:/. . . still . . . stars.*[9] Star-*bright* arcs by terrible rhyming into Book I's last word, *night.* The soundwave from *Forward* to *shore* halts at *all noiseless:* a sound beyond any sounding. Book I closes here: grand, dark, radically silent—a total negation where we might have expected epic thunder.

What kind of sublimity awaits golden Apollo? What poet's words could carry the day?

[*1820*, 154–162, 165]

---

[1] For lexical microplots, see Garrett Stewart, *The Value of Style*, 132.

[2] "Essay," *Poems*, 1815, 1:343.

[3] See W.K. Wimsatt on such structuring of Romantic-era imagery, especially 109–110.

[4] *BL*, chapter 15 (2:15–16).

[5] Houghton Library, Harvard: Keats *EC8.K2262.Z17h, p. 154, sq. 182.

[6] Keats underlines Satan's casing of Earth, "traversing each Colure" (the two great circles intersecting at right angles at the poles; 9.66; *KPL* II:77). With no allusion, he gives Hyperion the same sightline.

[7] See also Culler on present discursive *now* versus narrative *now* ("Apostrophe" 66).

[8] *Indicator*, 348–350.

[9] I am grateful to Peter McDonald (134) for noting this celestial chiasmus.

Book III: "Apollo, the Father of all verse"

—"Yes," said the supreme shape,
"Thou hast dream'd of me; and awaking up
Didst find a lyre all golden by thy side,
Whose strings touch'd by thy fingers, all the vast
Unwearied ear of the whole universe   65
Listen'd in pain and pleasure at the birth
Of such new tuneful wonder."

~ ~ ~

"I can read
A wondrous lesson in thy silent face:
Knowledge enormous makes a God of me.
Names, deeds, gray legends, dire events, rebellions,
Majesties, sovran voices, agonies,   115
Creations and destroyings all at once
Pour into the wide hollows of my brain,
And deify me, as if some blithe wine
Or bright elixir peerless I had drunk,
And so become immortal,"—Thus the God,
While his enkindled eyes, with level glance
Beneath his white soft temples, stedfast kept
Trembling with light upon Mnemosyne.
Soon wild commotions shook him, and made flush   124
All the immortal fairness of his limbs;
Most like the struggle at the gate of death;
Or liker still to one who should take leave
Of pale immortal death, and with a pang
As hot as death's is chill, with fierce convulse
Die into life: so young Apollo anguish'd:
His very hair, his golden tresses famed
Kept undulation round his eager neck.
During the pain Mnemosyne upheld
Her arms as one who prophesied.—At length
Apollo shriek'd; —and lo! from all his limbs   135
Celestial *   *   *   *   *   *
*   *   *   *   *   *   *   *

THE END.

At the opening of Book III, the epic poet (at last) hails the advent of Apollo, recharging the resources of negative suffixes in anticipation. Two words Keats coined and spent only here have Apollo's *gloomless* eyes (80) scanning a *liegeless* air ready for his domain (92). "Apollonian" is the word Keats summoned for Milton's "management" of scene-settings (*KPL* I:62). In this mode, he gorgeously plays the syllables of Apollo's attribute, "go*ld*en me*lod*y" (2.280), in advance of the melody of the name itself. Here is his sound-stage for young Clymene's news to the Titan assembly, in anguish and rapture:

> A voice came sweeter, sweeter than all tune,
> And still it cried, "Apollo! young Apollo!
> The morning-bright Apollo! young Apollo!"
> I fled, it follow'd me, and cried "Apollo!"   (2.292–295)

The reverberated *Apollo!* is this crescendo, sounded from *all* tune to *follow*'d ravishment. The name is soon in the poet's voice, with a hailing *lo!* (3.13) for the very name: "Apo*lo* is once more the golden theme!" (28).

Once more? It is as if, after his fabulous Hyperion-poetry, Keats had to remind himself of this mandate, the epic narrative turning around into a dramatic monologue on the big plan. It is clear that *once more* he needed to wean his poetry from romance confections, to draw Apollo into heroism, and he was conscious of a structural weight that this progress might not be able to bear, at least at the outset. So he begins (once again) in a romance world, debuting the new god in the realm of Flora, "Full ankle-deep in lilies" (35). The upgrade that Keats intends impends as a goddess arrives "over the unfooted sea" with "purport in her looks" (46–50). The word *unfooted* is surreally prophetic. Keats first tried out *pathless,* an adjective he had used for the poignant seascape in *Isabella* (XII); he then revised to *unfooted* (f.24ʳ), a coinage (*OED* gives him the nod) in the sense of "untrodden." The new adjective is more than this synonymy; it is poetic potential: the footing of epic verse. The first words from this "supreme shape" are in this key.

Keats loved the mytho-genetics in Book IV of Wordsworth's *Excursion.* In a passage he knew by heart, a lonely herdsman, "in some fit of weariness," hears a "distant strain," and imagines Apollo:

> Fancy fetched,
> Even from the blazing Chariot of the Sun,
> A beardless Youth, who touched a golden lute,
> And filled the illumined groves with ravishment.   (p. 179)

This is the only time the distinctly un-Wordsworthy word *ravishment* inhabits *The Excursion*. Keats regretted it: Wordsworth should "have left it to the imagination to complete" the effect, he thought, be willing to trust a reader's activated greeting of the spirit (*KC* 2:276). When Keats writes about Apollo's first music (63–67), he initiates our cooperation. With metrical stress on *strings touch'd*, he solicits audience in the universal ear, *unwearied* in its pain and pleasure, the two responses more simultaneous than successive. Keats's word-poetry is in the very chord: the *ear* in *unwearied*, the *verse* in *universe*. *Hyperion* has begun anew.

That "supreme shape" is deified memory, mother of the muses in the new order, instantly hailed: "Mnemosyne! / Thy name is on my tongue," Apollo cries out (82–83), Keats making her name synonymous in sound and sense with *no mystery* (86). The god-aborning moans, "dark, dark, / And painful vile oblivion seals my eyes" (86–87), on track to awakening, while our eyes are opened to *vile* mirrored in ob*liv*ion. Yet for all this deft tracking, Keats seems unsure what mode of poem to write here. "I am so sad," the natant god murmurs; "a melancholy numbs my limbs, / And then upon the grass I sit, and moan" (88–90). Even Hunt, Poet Laureate of Luxury, thought this languor too much: "too effeminate and human," Apollo "weeps and wonders somewhat too fondly."[1] If his "aching ignorance" (105–107), catching an "alarum in the elements" (that "pain"), intuits "other regions" (86–96), Keats's feet get stuck in retro-*Endymion* measures. A hot romance with some "particular beauteous star" is the finest craving he can project for Apollo: "I will flit into it with my lyre, / And make its silvery splendour pant with bliss" (100–102): *Sleep and Poetry* redux.

For the scene of transformation (111–118), Keats invests in an asyndeton of abstractions. Talk is cheap. This superflux of nouns—*names, deeds*, etc.—is no great poetry. It is another *flit*: a declarative end-run around the vale of Soul-making, for an express pass on a wash of categories of no "momentous depth of speculation" (this is the language of Keats's grumble about a painting of *King Lear*; *K* 77). What Keats's plan was panting for is an epiphany, with an explosion that would launch god and poet into epic magnificence. Here, too, he had to begin, again, in lush romance:

> made flush
> All ~~his white~~ the immortal fairness of his limbs,
> ~~Roseate and pained as any ravish'd nymph~~
> Into a hue more roseate than sweet pain
> Gives to a / ^{ravish'd} Nymph ~~new~~ when her / ^{warm} tears
> Gush luscious with no sob -   (f.27ʳ)

From *flush* to *ravish'd* to *Gush luscious,* Keats seem to have needed to write his way through this. In reperception, he tried again. Worth saving was *made flush,* with its doubled grammatical force: a rich verb (made to flush) and an effect realized by the adjective.

Keats was ready for the climax, writing a near pornography of anguish and agony. Operating with medical experience, he rocks the verse, pulls out all the stops for word-magic, in force and compression (121–136). The progressive similes—*Most like* and *liker still*—give the sublime gradations of struggle that is a heartbeat from death, then a pang from *pale immortal death* (a hell if ever there was one) into hot godlife, framed by the famed golden tresses. *JnD* has no noun *convulse* (only *convulsion*). Keats does. He compacts verb-energy into noun-intensity (*OED* cites this as the first instance of this noun). At the climax, Keats writes as poet-herald, and delivers the deity from his birth pangs: *Apollo shriek'd;— and lo!* He wrote, then crossed out ~~he was the God!/And godlike~~ (f.27ʳ). Maybe some *sparks of the divinity* in mortal men (MsK 1.53.261)? The coda splatter of asterisks on page 199 of *1820* is printer-typography, but it looks like semantic typology.[2]

Yet hitting the confirmation of *Celestial,* Keats couldn't go on, not with Tom's mortality such a weight. In the year after Tom died, he took up the project intermittently, then handed it off to Woodhouse, sighing to Reynolds (at the end of summer 1819) that he could no longer tell a true voice of feeling from a false beauty proceeding from art (*K* 267). No one else, it seems, felt this way. Although this *Fragment* was placed at the back of *1820,* it was the first poem that Shelley (who never warmed to *Endymion*) wanted to read—read it out loud, even, telling a friend that it "destined" Keats "to become one of the first writers of the age."[3] "I consider the fragment of *Hyperion* as second to nothing that was ever produced by a writer of the same years," he declared in his *Preface* to *Adonais* (1821). Even Byron told the publisher of the savage *Quarterly,* John Murray (30 July 1821), "Hyperion is a fine monument & will keep his name" (*LJ* 8:163). Reviewer John Scott gave it a long extract in *London Magazine,* hailing it as "one of the most extraordinary creations of any modern imagination" (319). By December 1829, H. C. Robinson, a memoirist who read everything and knew everybody, saw "a force, wildness, and originality" that promised Keats's place "at the head of the next generation of poets" (*Life,* 150).

This was all to come. At the end of 1818, Keats was exhausted: Tom dead; two hopefully launched books ridiculed by the main reviews; a high-investment epic fissured in its foundation. While he was laboring on *Hyperion,* he let himself be Fancy-fetched for relief.

[*1820,* 192–199]

[1] *Indicator,* 350. In *Lord Byron &c,* Hunt comments further on the "tendency to poetical effeminacy": though on track to "a Divus Major," Apollo "suffers a little too exquisitely among his lilies" (419).

[2] THE END marks the finale of both the fragment and volume. Keats's ms (f.27^r) has no stars.

[3] 17 October 1820; *The Journals of Mary Shelley,* 335; *Letters of Percy Bysshe Shelley,* 2:239.

Fancy

Ever let the Fancy roam,
Pleasure never is at home:
At a touch sweet Pleasure melteth,
Like to bubbles when rain pelteth;
Then let winged Fancy wander
Through the thought still spread beyond her:
Open wide the mind's cage-door,
She'll dart forth, and cloudward soar.
O sweet Fancy! let her loose;
Summer's joys are spoilt by use,   10
And the enjoying of the Spring
Fades as does its blossoming;
Autumn's red-lipp'd fruitage too,
Blushing through the mist and dew,
Cloys with tasting: What do then?
Sit thee by the ingle, when
The sear faggot blazes bright,
Spirit of a winter's night;
When the soundless earth is muffled,
And the caked snow is shuffled   20
From the ploughboy's heavy shoon;
When the Night doth meet the Noon
In a dark conspiracy
To banish Even from her sky.
Sit thee there, and send abroad,
With a mind self-overaw'd,
Fancy, high-commission'd:—send her!
She has vassals to attend her:
She will bring, in spite of frost,
Beauties that the earth hath lost;   30
She will bring thee, all together,
All delights of summer weather;
All the buds and bells of May,
From dewy sward or thorny spray;
All the heaped Autumn's wealth,
With a still, mysterious stealth:
She will mix these pleasures up

Like three fit wines in a cup,
And thou shalt quaff it:—thou shalt hear
Distant harvest-carols clear;   40
Rustle of the reaped corn;
Sweet birds antheming the morn:
And, in the same moment—hark!
'Tis the early April lark,
Or the rooks, with busy caw,
Foraging for sticks and straw.
Thou shalt, at one glance, behold
The daisy and the marigold;
White-plum'd lilies, and the first
Hedge-grown primrose that hath burst;   50
Shaded hyacinth, alway
Sapphire queen of the mid-May;
And every leaf, and every flower
Pearled with the self-same shower.
Thou shalt see the field-mouse peep
Meagre from its celled sleep;
And the snake all winter-thin
Cast on sunny bank its skin;
Freckled nest-eggs thou shalt see
Hatching in the hawthorn-tree,   60
When the hen-bird's wing doth rest
Quiet on her mossy nest;
Then the hurry and alarm
When the bee-hive casts its swarm;
Acorns ripe down-pattering,
While the autumn breezes sing.

Oh, sweet Fancy! let her loose;
Every thing is spoilt by use:
Where's the cheek that doth not fade,   70
Too much gaz'd at? Where's the maid
Whose lip mature is ever new?
Where's the eye, however blue,
Doth not weary? Where's the face
One would meet in every place?
Where's the voice, however soft,

One would hear so very oft?
At a touch sweet Pleasure melteth
Like to bubbles when rain pelteth.
Let, then, winged Fancy find
Thee a mistress to thy mind: 80
Dulcet-eyed as Ceres' daughter,
Ere the God of Torment taught her
How to frown and how to chide;
With a waist and with a side
White as Hebe's, when her zone
Slipt its golden clasp, and down
Fell her kirtle to her feet,
While she held the goblet sweet,
And Jove grew languid.—Break the mesh
Of the Fancy's silken leash;   90
Quickly break her prison-string
And such joys as these she'll bring.-
Let the winged Fancy roam,
Pleasure never is at home.

Kean full-gusto as Richard III may seem remote from a Keatsian poetics of Fancy, but when Keats saw the play (late 1817), he was struck by the constraint imposed on Shakespeare's imagination by "the prison house of history" (he said in a review), the poetry "ironed and manacled with a chain of facts" when it should be

> generally free as is the wind—a perfect thing of the elements, winged and sweetly coloured. Poetry must be free! It is of the air, not of the earth; and the higher it soars the nearer it gets to its home. (Forman, *CW* 3:234–235)

A true home away from home: Keats winged *Fancy* late in 1818, ready to breathe again after agonizing months of caring for Tom.

Joseph Addison's essay *The Pleasures of the Imagination* (1712) gave a virtual diagnostic and cure: "the Pleasures of the Fancy are . . . conducive to Health . . . able to disperse Grief and Melancholy, and to set the Animal Spirits in pleasing and agreeable Motions" (93–94). Doyen of the Vale of Health (on Hampstead Heath), Hunt hailed fancy as "a lighter play of imagination," a "feeling of analogy coming short of seriousness, in order that it may laugh with what it loves, and show how it can decorate it with fairy ornament" (*Imagination and Fancy* 2). Even so, such terms (as you may sense) turn a damning feint of praise: no serious muse, no true imagination, just decorative arts with fairy ornament, or worse.

Keats knew the value-scale in *Paradise Lost*. He underlined the God-given dreams in Eden that Adam recounts to Archangel Raphael. One gently moved / My fancy (8.293–294) to true belief (*KPL* II:61). Another, as he slept, "open left the cell / Of fancy" to "internal sight" of newly created Eve (8.460–461), a fancy continuous with vital "Imagination," the faculty Keats compared to "Adam's dream —he awoke and found it truth."[1] Adam awake can worry about mimic Fancy (when nature rests, 5.110), operating on Eve's dreams. Keats underlines this (*KPL* I:120):

> Oft in her absence mimic Fancy wakes
> To imitate her; but misjoining shapes,
> Wild work produces oft, and most in dreams;
> Ill matching words and deeds long past or late. (5.111–514)

To Milton-proxy Adam, this "lesser" faculty (5.101) is a dissembler and anarchist, especially in the patriarchal order. Keats, however, could discern the very grammar of poetry (and with better matching, the fancies of rhyme):

A sense of independence, of power from the fancy's creating a world of its own by the sense of probabilities.

—so he comments on Milton's freedom to envision worlds other than his own (*KPL* I:23).

To read Keats's brisk 94 lines of *fancy's creating* is to be swept up in mobility and momentum, in meters and rhymes. There "are few Words in the *English* Language which are employed in more loose and uncircumscribed Sense than those of the *Fancy* and the *Imagination*," remarks Addison (91), as if Fancy had co-opted the very dictionary. When in 1802 Wordsworth differentiated "emanations of reality and truth" from "fancy or imagination," this *or* hinged a partnership: Imagination "produces impressive effects out of simple elements"; Fancy is a "surprize" of wordings "excited by sudden varieties of situation and by accumulated imagery."[2] Addison gave to both faculties an answer to address how "quickly tired" we become "where every thing continues fixt and . . . settled"; the cure is "entertaining the Sight every Moment with something that is new" (97–98). In 1815, Wordsworth granted this entertainment less to imagination than to fancy: "as capricious as the accidents of things," fancy (now she-gendered) is "playful, ludicrous, amusing, tender, or pathetic, as the objects happen to be appositely produced or fortunately combined" (Preface I:xxxiv). It was such good company that Coleridge was provoked to "desynonymize," citing the Greek *Phantasia* in distinction from the Latin *Imaginatio*. *Imagination* is totalized sensation: Lear's cry at Poor Tom, "What, have his daughters brought him to this pass?—" (*King Lear* 3.4). No "varieties" of data (that's fancy) are needed to convey this traumatized, absolute phenomenology: in unfancy words, this daughter-tormented, king-no-more cannot imagine otherwise.[3] What may be "contra-distinguished as *fancy*" is a kaleidoscope like *Lutes, lobsters, seas of milk, and ships of amber:* random sense-data, the "fixities and definites" of memory "emancipated from the order of time and space" and rematched by whim.[4]

Imagination is the higher faculty, but Coleridge lets slip a keyword, *emancipated:* foot-loose and fancy-free. For his turn with *Fancy,* Keats trips the light fantastic of Milton's *L'Allegro.* In a liberated love-play with fast-paced tetrameters in careening rhymes, he finds "a sort of rondeau which I think I shall become partial to – because you have one idea amplified with greater ease and more delight and freedom than in the sonnet." Why not a volume of such "minor poems" (he wonders), which "people will realish who cannot bear the burthen of a long poem" (*L* 2:26)? Feeling his own deferred burden, Keats fancies a new word, a confection of *real-ish* and *relish.* If Wordsworth will not demote *she* Fancy, Keats's *Fancy* turns Adam's worry about ill-matching to a proactive pleasure of wild rhymes that could go on for ever, go anywhere. His opening rhyme says it all, in absolutes: a liberal *ever roam* pairs with *never home.* Speaking "promiscuously" of such license, Addison went extreme: home as prison, fancy as supernatural talent; "by this Faculty a Man in a Dungeon is capable of entertaining himself with Scenes and Landskips more beautiful than any" in merely material "Nature" (90).

Under auto-compression from pulsating repetition, Keats's rhymes take off: *cage-door* to *cloudward soar* (7–8; his sole use of *cloudward*), *use* against *loose* (9–10), *wander* in Fancy's range, *through the thought still spread beyond her* (5–6), to the cued horizon *yonder,* extending the word *through* from the sense of *by means of* into ever-expanding possibility. Fancy is self-replicating, her license to *wander* going ever *beyond her* in rhyming guarantee. If Keats's *Ode on Melancholy* (to come in 1819) accepts transience as the sad bargain of joy, pleasure, and delight, the poet of *Fancy* gives change a positive lease. It is not just that transience gives pleasure its intensity; transience itself is the pleasure:

> At a touch sweet Pleasure melteth
> Like to bubbles when rain pelteth   (77–78)

This rondeau repetition of lines 3–4 melts away even a comma-halt at the line's turn.

A cajoling *What do then?* (15) vibrates a double-rhetoric: a poet thinking out loud, and a question for us. *Fancy* addresses not just winter's quarantine but any season's. No prison, *home* gets a cozy recast as a stage for fancy's entertainment amid, and against, a material *dark conspiracy* (23). Keats's self-coined compound, *self-overaw'd*, is a double-intensifier, a partner in capacity and a rhyme for *send abroad* (25–26). "Fancy is given to quicken and to beguile the temporal part of our Nature," Wordsworth says (1815 Preface xxxv), with a fine double sense in *given to:* a gift and an instinct. If Winter's early Night can *banish Even,* Fancy evens the score with a rhyming refutation, conjuring *all delights* of summer (32). Refusing elegy (the *ubi sunt* of irremediable loss), Fancy comes *high-commission'd* (27) to transcend time and space, mixing the seasons (37), recovering summer amid frost, bringing May flowers, gathering Autumn's copia, harvest-carols, birds and creatures of all seasons. "The food of the imagination is supplied by the senses . . . and formed into new combinations by fancy," lectured Humphry Davy, speaking chemistry in the language of poetry (*Discourse Introductory* 324–325).

Even Keats's formal ode-call (O) echoes with a difference:

> O sweet Fancy! let her loose;
> Summer's joys are spoiled by use, (9–10)

> Oh, sweet Fancy! let her loose;
> Every thing is spoilt by use: (67–68)

In *1820,* lines 67–68 even arrive on a new page (126), with a new paragraph, a fresh start. Keats's two-worded *Every thing* does more than spell out dull fixities. It releases *thing* for poetry's play on multiple chimes: an oversated *spring/blossoming* (11–12), to Fancy's power to *bring* a world of delights (31), to the new music of acorns *down-pattering/ While the autumn breezes sing* (65–66)—and not least, a ride with *winged* Fancy herself (5, 79). The last chime of this rhyme chord (and cord), *bring,* ends on a dash, a scriptive figure for the rondeau, open to as much as fancy can bring on board:

> Quickly break her prison-string
> And such joys as these she'll bring.—
> Let the winged Fancy roam.
> Pleasure never is at home. (91–94)

In poetry's paradise, she-Fancy is a poet's Eve, better than any mortal *maid* (70). The poet who sings, *Let, then, winged Fancy find / Thee a mistress to thy mind* (79–80) finds his perfect mistress-rhyme. Keats twice canceled a slightly more bondage-imprinted capital-M *Mistress* (*P* 292–293n) to gain a looser *maid* (71), its sound fancifully poem-punned (*poēma:* Greek for *made thing*). This is the ultimate romance, an epithalamion of poetic self-marrying.

For this marriage, Keats courts Fancy with two similes that reverse fables of female falling. The star of the first is *Ceres' daughter* (81) before her capture by Pluto, God of Torment, to be his underworld mistress. The second simile is a scene of liberation. Young goddess Hebe was honored in her station as cup-bearer to the gods. One day, her golden belt-clasp slipped, the garment's fall exposing her (86–87). Jove, already in his cups and scowling at this lapse, gives Keats the cue to remake the belt-slip into a prison-break (89–91). Keats surely knew a verse, in the same meters, in Chatterton's imagination of Juno's endorsement:

> When a woman's ty'd down
> To a spiritless log;
> Let her fondle or frown,
> Yet still he's a clog.
>
> Let her please her own mind,
> Abroad let her roam;
> Abroad she may find,
> What she can't find at home.[5]

The second stanza's rhymes come into Keats's *Fancy* as she-gendered freedom-*find* for a male poet's *mind* (79–80), along with the frame-rhymes of antithesis, *roam / home*.

She-gendered and eroticized for caprice, freedom and mobility, Keats-Fancy figures "the other woman," a liberator from patriarchy and institution. "If she can win you over to her purpose, and impart to you her feelings, she cares not how unstable or transitory may be her influence, knowing that it will not be out of her power to resume it upon an apt occasion." This is Wordsworth, a few sentences on, in his hospitality to Fancy (1815 Preface xxxv). Keats's refrain, *pleasure never is at home,* is not just a poetic framing. It is also his frame for life. Just two months before *Fancy,* he wrote in disdain of domesticity—in a letter (24 October 1818) to newlyweds George and Georgiana Keats, no less:

*The mighty abstract Idea I have of Beauty in all things stifles the more divided
and minute domestic happiness [. . .] I am content to be alone. These things
combined with the opinion I have of the generallity of women – who appear
to me as children to whom I would rather give a Sugar Plum than my time,
form a barrier against Matrimony which I rejoice in.* (MsK 1.39.156–157)

"*Fancy*, often used for *love*," is a glossary entry in *Shakespeare's Dramatic Works*
(sq. 3337). As a *maid . . . ever new* (72), Keats-Fancy has no matrimonial bars.
Wings of independence is a phrase that mattered to him (MsK 1.60.294). His
mental "barrier" is overdetermined to say the least, and, to say the most, a nearly
genetic impediment. Fancy is just one letter away from Fanny, the name of his
erratic mother and (poor girl) his new love, Fanny Brawne.

Fancy is Keats's last free fling with Fancy. In his next romance, begun a month
on in this winter season, *fancy* reappears as a faery hoodwinker. A lover's faith-
fully promised matrimony to his fancy-duped maid may be a ruse—so, too
the fancy he spins of a home awaiting them both "o'er the southern moors,"
through and beyond a raging sleet-storm.

[*1820*, 122–127]

[1] To Bailey, 22 November 1817 (MsK 1.16.54; *K* 69).

[2] *Lyrical Ballads*, 1802, Preface, I:xxxi, "Note" to *The Thorn* (1:202).

[3] "What a wrench of the imagination, that cannot be brought to conceive of any other
cause of misery than that which has bowed it down, and absorbs all other sorrow in its
own!" exclaimed Hazlitt (*Lectures* 9). Keats heard the lecture in January 1818.

[4] Coleridge discusses "desynonymize" in *BL*, chapter 4, applying this operation to these
key faculties (1:86–89), and again at the end of chapter 13 (1:296). His example of *fancy* is
from Thomas Otway's Restoration tragedy, *Venice Preserved*, with Coleridge's fanciful
import of *lobsters* from Samuel Butler's seventeenth-century satire, *Hudibras* (Bate and
Engell edition, 1:84–85n2).

[5] *The Revenge, A Burletta*, performed 1770, printed 1795, then in 1803 *Works* (I:227–272).
This song is from I.III (239). I owe this reference to Penelope Dineley (63).

The Eve of St. Agnes

Romance again: relish or *realish*? (*L* 2:26). Lord Byron blazed out an ironized, retro-modern *Romaunt* in 1812, *Childe Harold's Pilgrimage*, two sensational cantos in nearly 200 Spenserian stanzas. Canto III refired the franchise in December 1816, the month that Leigh Hunt featured Keats (with a nod to Byron) in "Young Poets." Canto IV, published 28 April 1818, filled the bookstores, overwhelming *Endymion, A Romance*. The stanza is an art form in itself. Rhyming *ababbcbcc*, in eight lines of iambic pentameter, it holds a mid-stanza couplet opportunity, and another at the close, with the last line an alexandrine (six feet).

Having bid "golden-tongued Romance" *Adieu!* in winter 1818, Keats comes back with a winter-genre Romance and a complex palette, gold only one of its glowing tinges. Its core of hot love (and Keats's hottest poetry ever) is set amid a chill world, with a storm brewing. He wanted *The Eve of St. Agnes* to open *1820* (*L* 2:276); his publishers thought the "Author of *Endymion*," his title-page identifier, should lead with edgier *Lamia. Isabella* brutalizes "old Romance"; *Lamia* corrodes it. *The Eve of St. Agnes* slants it into a new mode that exposes its weaves, foregrounds its artifice, and indulges its ephemeral magic. The poem is by turns campy, satirical, ironic, and reality-minded; the poetry is artful, gorgeous, artificial, and for stretches almost anesthetizes consciousness of the winter world. Almost: troubling signs, signals, and allusions hover about.

Not least is the eponymous fourth-century martyr. Young, wealthy Agnes of Rome, a devoted virgin age twelve or thirteen, refused so many noble suitors that in revenge she was reported to the emperor as a likely Christian. In exquisite symmetry, she was condemned and sent to the brothels the night before her execution. Saved from this serial rape by a miracle, her consecration spun into a legend for all virgins: a dream of true love "Upon the honey'd middle of the night," if certain rituals are done aright on her sacred Eve (20 January). Keats's *Eve* leaves unresolved whether the name-date is merely a midwinter calendric or a loaded allusion, whether its chill world is foil or foe to the legend's promise of true love. It is a shimmer, but not a ruler.

Everything pulses with puzzles for reading, enigmas in the heart of its luminous arts—not least the lovers. Madeline is by rapid turns a fairy-tale heroine, a restless virgin, a self-enchanted dupe. Dreamboat Porphyro is a complex piece of work: a hero braving wintery moors and bloodthirsty "foemen" in Madeline's castle, a pilgrim of true love, a comic spectacle "brushing the cobwebs with his lofty plume" (XIII), a lad of Keatsian gusto, a deceiver with a stratagem on Madeline's "faery fancy." The narrator is quite shifty, too: now stagey, campy, performative, then with stylized affectation, then immersive story-telling, coy allusioning, brutal realism. No wonder critical interpretations are all over the place: an existential synthesis of sense and spirit; erotic liberty; sexist dynamics; the corruptions of feudalism; true love entangled with salacious allure and dream-enabled rape; a playground of narrative arts and rhetoric; a poetics of irony and indeterminacy. (Stuart Sperry's chapter is a diplomatic reading of both skepticism and wish-fulfillment.) What always shines is the intensity of Keats's romance with words. Leigh Hunt printed the poem in full on the opening pages of his *London Journal* on St. Agnes Eve, 21 January (so Hunt said) 1835, interspersed with a "commentary" that issues the first sustained close attention to Keats's verbal art, and says, in effect, that this poem is worth such attention.

"Ah! bitter chill it was!"

I.

St. Agnes' Eve—Ah, bitter chill it was!
The owl, for all his feathers, was a-cold;
The hare limp'd trembling through the frozen grass,
And silent was the flock in woolly fold:
Numb were the Beadsman's fingers, while he told
His rosary, and while his frosted breath,
Like pious incense from a censer old,
Seem'd taking flight for heaven, without a death,
Past the sweet Virgin's picture, while his prayer he saith.

II.

His prayer he saith, this patient, holy man;
Then takes his lamp, and riseth from his knees,
And back returneth, meagre, barefoot, wan,
Along the chapel aisle by slow degrees:
The sculptur'd dead, on each side, seem to freeze,
Emprison'd in black, purgatorial rails:
Knights, ladies, praying in dumb orat'ries,
He passeth by; and his weak spirit fails
To think how they may ache in icy hoods and mails.

III.

Northward he turneth through a little door,
  And scarce three steps, ere Music's golden tongue
Flatter'd to tears this aged man and poor;
  But no—already had his deathbell rung;
  The joys of all his life were said and sung:
His was harsh penance on St. Agnes' Eve:
  Another way he went, and soon among
  Rough ashes sat he for his soul's reprieve,
And all night kept awake, for sinners' sake to grieve.

IV.

That ancient Beadsman heard the prelude soft;
  And so it chanc'd, for many a door was wide,
From hurry to and fro. Soon, up aloft,
  The silver, snarling trumpets 'gan to chide:
  The level chambers, ready with their pride,
Were glowing to receive a thousand guests:
  The carved angels, ever eager-eyed,
  Star'd, where upon their heads the cornice rests,
With hair blown back, and wings put cross-wise on their breasts.

Right away, narrative as performance: not five syllables into the first stanza, *Ah* delivers sensation and exclamation. By convention, "Romance" is a spring-time genre. This stanza paces through a single sentence of winter weather-reporting so remorseless as to spin a genre-joke on the theme, *how chill was it?* So chill that ice lames a hare (*limp'd trembling* limps the very meter), a woolly fold is no coziness, breath turns to frost, owl-feathers are useless. Keats revised *chill* from *cold* "to avoid the echo cold in the next line," he said to Taylor; better, too, for the feel of temperature.[1] Hunt italicized the *owl* line, to admire an "image so warm and comfortable in itself, and, therefore, better contradicted by the season," camelion-reading Keats's camelion poetics:

> We feel the plump, feathery bird in his nook, shivering in spite of his natural household warmth, and staring out at the strange weather. The hare cringing through the chill grass is very piteous, and the "silent flock" very patient. (17)

Also piteous is the Beadsman, saying prayers on behalf of his patrons partying indoors. The numbed fingers that *told his rosary*—*told* as *spoke* and as *tallied*—are past even trembling. If his frosted breath *Seem'd* off to heaven *without a death,* actual death seems not far behind. Andrew Bennett brings nice attention (102) to the sightline of *Seem'd: seem'd* to the Beadsman, *seem'd* to any witness (i.e., us). This is the first installment of our recruitment into the narrative dynamics. One seed for our reading is the syllable *rose* in *rosary,* a lettering that will recur, sometimes as a flower and sometimes as verbal action, sometimes both.

Here it is planted in cold soil: the beadsman more than half-dead (meagre, barefoot, wan). A camelion imaginer himself, this Beadsman grimly-whimsically fancies the sculptures of the dead aching in their *icy hoods and mails* (II). Loving this *ache,* Hunt italicized the whole line: "Most wintery as well as penitential" is the sensation, and "most felicitous" is *black* for the "Catholic idea in the word 'purgatorial'" (17). This hard gloom serves as foil to the narrator's camelion casting of the castle-statues, *carved angels, ever eager-eyed,* gazing on the thousand guests (IV), as if issued from "old Romance" central-casting to join the party. The Beadsman's already sounding *deathbell* (III) contrasts *Music's golden tongue* in the castle party.

[1] Mid-June 1820; MsK, 1.80.377–378. Woodhouse had mistranscribed *cold* (Gittings, *John Keats,* 572–573). Still alertly reviewing and revising, Keats messengered a correction to Taylor's offices. *1820* was set to publish on June 24.

her "faery fancy"; his "heart on fire"

V.

> At length burst in the argent revelry,
> With plume, tiara, and all rich array,
> Numerous as shadows haunting fairily
> The brain, new stuff'd, in youth, with triumphs gay
> Of old romance. These let us wish away,
> And turn, sole-thoughted, to one Lady there,
> Whose heart had brooded, all that wintry day,
> On love, and wing'd St. Agnes' saintly care,
> As she had heard old dames full many times declare.

VI.

They told her how, upon St. Agnes' Eve,
Young virgins might have visions of delight,
And soft adorings from their loves receive
Upon the honey'd middle of the night,
If ceremonies due they did aright;
As, supperless to bed they must retire,
And couch supine their beauties, lily white;
Nor look behind, nor sideways, but require
Of Heaven with upward eyes for all that they desire.

VII.

Full of this whim was thoughtful Madeline:
The music, yearning like a God in pain,
She scarcely heard: her maiden eyes divine,
Fix'd on the floor, saw many a sweeping train
Pass by—she heeded not at all: in vain
Came many a tiptoe, amorous cavalier,
And back retir'd; not cool'd by high disdain,
But she saw not: her heart was otherwhere:
She sigh'd for Agnes' dreams, the sweetest of the year.

VIII.

She danc'd along with vague, regardless eyes,
Anxious her lips, her breathing quick and short:
The hallow'd hour was near at hand: she sighs
Amid the timbrels, and the throng'd resort
Of whisperers in anger, or in sport;
'Mid looks of love, defiance, hate, and scorn,
Hoodwink'd with faery fancy; all amort,
Save to St. Agnes and her lambs unshorn,
And all the bliss to be before to-morrow morn.

IX.

So, purposing each moment to retire,
She linger'd still. Meantime, across the moors,

Had come young Porphyro, with heart on fire
For Madeline. Beside the portal doors,
Buttress'd from moonlight, stands he, and implores
All saints to give him sight of Madeline,
But for one moment in the tedious hours,
That he might gaze and worship all unseen;
Perchance speak, kneel, touch, kiss—in sooth such things have been.

X.

He ventures in: let no buzz'd whisper tell:
All eyes be muffled, or a hundred swords
Will storm his heart, Love's fev'rous citadel:
For him, those chambers held barbarian hordes,
Hyena foemen, and hot-blooded lords,
Whose very dogs would execrations howl
Against his lineage: not one breast affords
Him any mercy, in that mansion foul,
Save one old beldame, weak in body and in soul.

XI.

Ah, happy chance! the aged creature came,
Shuffling along with ivory-headed wand,
To where he stood, hid from the torch's flame,
Behind a broad hall-pillar, far beyond
The sound of merriment and chorus bland:
He startled her; but soon she knew his face,
And grasp'd his fingers in her palsied hand,
Saying, "Mercy, Porphyro! hie thee from this place;
They are all here to-night, the whole blood-thirsty race!

XII.

Get hence! get hence! there's dwarfish Hildebrand;
He had a fever late, and in the fit
He cursed thee and thine, both house and land:
Then there's that old Lord Maurice, not a whit
More tame for his grey hairs—Alas me! flit!

Flit like a ghost away." — "Ah, Gossip dear,
We're safe enough; here in this arm-chair sit,
And tell me how"—"Good Saints! not here, not here;
Follow me, child, or else these stones will be thy bier."

XIII.

He follow'd through a lowly arched way,
Brushing the cobwebs with his lofty plume,
And as she mutter'd "Well-a—well-a-day!"
He found him in a little moonlight room,
Pale, lattic'd, chill, and silent as a tomb.
"Now tell me where is Madeline," said he,
"O tell me, Angela, by the holy loom
Which none but secret sisterhood may see,
When they St. Agnes' wool are weaving piously."

XIV.

"St. Agnes! Ah! it is St. Agnes' Eve—
Yet men will murder upon holy days:
Thou must hold water in a witch's sieve,
And be liege-lord of all the Elves and Fays,
To venture so: it fills me with amaze
To see thee, Porphyro!—St. Agnes' Eve!
God's help! my lady fair the conjuror plays
This very night: good angels her deceive!
But let me laugh awhile, I've mickle time to grieve."

XV.

Feebly she laugheth in the languid moon,
While Porphyro upon her face doth look,
Like puzzled urchin on an aged crone
Who keepeth clos'd a wond'rous riddle-book,
As spectacled she sits in chimney nook.
But soon his eyes grew brilliant, when she told
His lady's purpose; and he scarce could brook

Tears, at the thought of those enchantments cold,
And Madeline asleep in lap of legends old.

XVI.

Sudden a thought came like a full-blown rose,
Flushing his brow, and in his pained heart
Made purple riot: then doth he propose
A stratagem, that makes the beldame start:
"A cruel man and impious thou art:
Sweet lady, let her pray, and sleep, and dream
Alone with her good angels, far apart
From wicked men like thee. Go, go! —I deem
Thou canst not surely be the same that thou didst seem."

XVII.

"I will not harm her, by all saints I swear,"
Quoth Porphyro: "O may I ne'er find grace
When my weak voice shall whisper its last prayer,
If one of her soft ringlets I displace,
Or look with ruffian passion in her face:
Good Angela, believe me by these tears;
Or I will, even in a moment's space,
Awake, with horrid shout, my foemen's ears,
And beard them, though they be more fang'd than wolves and bears."

XVIII.

"Ah! why wilt thou affright a feeble soul?
A poor, weak, palsy-stricken, churchyard thing,
Whose passing-bell may ere the midnight toll;
Whose prayers for thee, each morn and evening,
Were never miss'd." —Thus plaining, doth she bring
A gentler speech from burning Porphyro;
So woful, and of such deep sorrowing,
That Angela gives promise she will do
Whatever he shall wish, betide her weal or woe.

XIX.

Which was, to lead him, in close secrecy,
Even to Madeline's chamber, and there hide
Him in a closet, of such privacy
That he might see her beauty unespied,
And win perhaps that night a peerless bride,
While legion'd fairies pac'd the coverlet,
And pale enchantment held her sleepy-eyed.
Never on such a night have lovers met,
Since Merlin paid his Demon all the monstrous debt.

XX.

"It shall be as thou wishest," said the Dame:
"All cates and dainties shall be stored there
Quickly on this feast-night: by the tambour frame
Her own lute thou wilt see: no time to spare,
For I am slow and feeble, and scarce dare
On such a catering trust my dizzy head.
Wait here, my child, with patience; kneel in prayer
The while: Ah! thou must needs the lady wed,
Or may I never leave my grave among the dead."

XXI.

So saying, she hobbled off with busy fear.
The lover's endless minutes slowly pass'd;
The dame return'd, and whisper'd in his ear
To follow her; with aged eyes aghast
From fright of dim espial. Safe at last,
Through many a dusky gallery, they gain
The maiden's chamber, silken, hush'd, and chaste;
Where Porphyro took covert, pleas'd amain.
His poor guide hurried back with agues in her brain.

An ironic shade on "shadows haunting *fairily* / The brain, new stuff'd, in youth," with "old romance" comes early on (V). The only other time Keats uses the overstuffed adverb *fairily* (*OED* gives him this credit) is in the poem that precedes *The Eve* in *1820,* and so shades the sequel: Lamia's pose to snare Lycius in *Lamia* (1.200). Guiding our sight-line, the narrator turns us to one brain filled with a romance of a different stripe.

The sole-thoughted Lady seems the anomaly in the numerous party-flares of old romance. Keats's soft joke is that she isn't. She is brooding on the legend of St. Agnes' Eve, pledging herself to the sorority of "young virgins" who "require / Of Heaven with upward eyes for all that they desire" in rhyming synonyms. There is a light, slight danger in the tunnel-vision focus of her "look" (VI). *Full of* her *whim,* thought*ful* of nothing else (VII), this Lady is a shadow at the festival, already a sensuous devotee of a ripe and *honey'd* dreamland (VI). Even the *music, yearning like a God in pain—yearning:* a Keats-coined soundache (*OED*) that Hunt scored for admiration (18)—slips its syntax across the lines for a wry joke. First seeming a presence in Madeline's thoughtfulness, this *music* turns the corner of the line to reveal a sound *scarcely heard.* A jest about the tune-out completes this line: *her maiden eyes divine.* Set in rhyme to *Madeline* (this is her first naming), *divine* nets a double-play: her eyes look *divine* in a futile suitor's gaze, while in a divine upward focus on the promise of Heaven. Proofreading, Keats noticed some hand had rewritten this to *her maiden eyes incline / Still on the floor.* Forget the semantic gain in *Still* (*unmoving, quietly, ever*); Keats thought it "very much for the worse, . . . my meaning quite destroyed." He wanted the focus *Fix'd on the floor,* seeing only *many a sweeping train.* "I do not use train for concourse of passers by but for S̶k̶i̶t̶s̶ Skirts sweeping along the floor—" (he wrote to Taylor, MsK 1.80.377). This is all Madeline sees because her *heart was otherwhere.* The long medial dash at "Pass by—" is no script of suspense; it's a dividing line. Those cavaliers haven't a prayer. The sequel, *she heeded not,* wryly graphs *she* to *he:* what is *not* in the cards for these lads. As Madeline spins her dream, Keats has us reading the dreamer who *saw not* anything outside her chamber of maiden thought.

Keats turns stanza VIII from her dreamy distraction to her dream-primed arousal: *Anxious her lips, her breathing quick and short.*[1] The syllables reverberate from her erotic panting for "the h*allo*w'd hour" with "*all* amort," both notes tuned to "*all* the bliss to be." The symptom *regardless* (Keats revised *uneager* to this) condenses to *Hoodwink'd with faery fancy;* he inserted *faery* for alliterative stress (sq. 5). The deft *with* (instead of *by*) not only hums with *wink'd;* it also winks at Madeline's self-dosing. This unique *Hoodwink'd* in Keats's poetry drew Hunt's italics (18) and would theme Jack Stillinger's landmark essay on dream delusion.[2]

The measure on Madeline's fixation shifts at the start of stanza IX, her intuition of the erotic boon of holding off: *She linger'd still,* paused at a period. Then with a wonderful midline caesura that tropes itself, Keats writes *Mean-*

time. How canny of him to complete this line with the debut of loverboy Porphyro in the narrative, charging across the moors (the very ground that lames that poor hare), *with heart on fire / For Madeline,* the cardio-fuel and its destination, his very name hitting the *fire* in *phyr.* Whatever Madeline's pledge of desire for Heaven's boon, Porphyro is no bearer of this brand. His desire to *gaze and worship all unseen* is more practical than pious. As loaded as the name *Madeline* (*Magdalene,* the iconic fallen woman, was Keats's first thought) is *Porphyro.* Drawing on old Greek for purple (πορφύρα), *Porphyro* has a name-fraternity: the purple serpent porphyre (also hissing the sound of *fire*); and Porphyrius, a famous third-century Roman antagonist of Christianity. Porphyro at the portal is a high parody of religious adoration. (*Love, love, love . . . comes in like a flood and seems like religion,* sing the Eurhythmics.) With its medial dash, the final alexandrine of IX gets an extra syllable's worth of breath.

Keats has campy fun with the gothic repertoire of stanzas X–XV: imminent peril from castle foes with "fine mother Radcliff names" (*L* 2:62; the spectacularly successful gothic novelist); old beldame Angela's nervous assistance; Porphyro's heat frustrated by the *thought of those enchantments cold, / And Madeline asleep in lap of legends old* (XV). These are Hunt's italics, admiring Keats's tact and taste in "fusing together the tangible and the spiritual, the real and the fanciful, the remote and the near. Madeline is asleep in her bed; but she is also asleep in accordance with the legends of the season; and therefore the bed becomes *their* lap as well as sleep's" (18). How finely Hunt grasps Keats's staging of Porphyro's work cut out for him, and how finely he positions his advantage in keeping himself *all unseen* (X).

The turning point for the lad is stanza XVI's volta-signaling *Sudden,* coming "like a full-blown rose, / Flushing his brow, and in his pained heart / Made purple riot"—as if literally *Made* for *Made*line. Hunt loved the simile, setting it in italics (18). Before Keats purpled this (heated beyond mere *purplue*), he wrote *riot fierce* (sq. 9). Its issue is a *stratagem:* "an artifice in war; a trick by which an enemy is deceived" (*JnD*). The lodge of "love's fev'rous citadel" (X), flushed Porphyro warms to *burning Porphyro* (XVIII), spinning the kaleidoscope of our regard. Is he a Satanic predator? impassioned lover? a soulful suitor? capable seducer? Angela's practical misgivings and soul-quaking fears are not exactly reducible to comic fluster. She extracts a pledge of marriage from him (she's read *Romeo and Juliet* and *Sleeping Beauty*). But what's up with the narrator's cryptic calendar, *Since Merlin paid his Demon all that Monstrous debt* (XIX)? Critics have never settled Hunt's perplexity: "What he means . . . we cannot say," notwithstanding that "Merlin, the famous enchanter" is "the son of a devil, and conversant with the race, we are aware of no debt that he owed them" (18). Keats's frisson is a tease: sounds ominous, but what's the omen? And for whom? What debts, monstrous perhaps, will there be?

Stanza IX's casually dropped, deftly invested *all unseen* (Porphyro's first hope of approach) now pays practical dividends. A secret seeing, far from sad fetishizing, is imagination's foreplay. He hides *in a closet* (small room) "to see her beauty unespied, / And win perhaps that night a peerless bride" (XIX). Keats's *perhaps* jests about a plan of positive capability. By XXI, *closet* has become a place to take pleasing *covert:* a hunter's blind, inflected by the adjective-iamb *covert*, in alliance with *stratagem*. Keats first wrote *panting covert* (sq. 11), then decided on calculated advantage: *unseen*, upgraded to *unespied*. The rhyme-paired *peerless bride*, meaning "without peer," pun-winks at those *regardless eyes* (back in VIII), and anticipates iteration in XXII, *unaware*. Erotic spectacle is at hand.

[1] Keats first wrote juicily of lips *full pulped with rosy thoughts* (MsK 2.21.5).

[2] "The Hoodwinking of Madeline" (1961), with much outrage from "metaphysical" Keatsians.

she prays; he peers

XXII.

> Her falt'ring hand upon the balustrade,
> Old Angela was feeling for the stair,
> When Madeline, St. Agnes' charmed maid,
> Rose, like a mission'd spirit, unaware:
> With silver taper's light, and pious care,
> She turn'd, and down the aged gossip led
> To a safe level matting. Now prepare,
> Young Porphyro, for gazing on that bed;
> She comes, she comes again, like ring-dove fray'd and fled.

XXIII.

> Out went the taper as she hurried in;
> Its little smoke, in pallid moonshine, died:
> She clos'd the door, she panted, all akin

To spirits of the air, and visions wide:
No uttered syllable, or, woe betide!
But to her heart, her heart was voluble,
Paining with eloquence her balmy side;
As though a tongueless nightingale should swell
Her throat in vain, and die, heart-stifled, in her dell.

XXIV.

A casement high and triple-arch'd there was,
All garlanded with carven imag'ries
Of fruits, and flowers, and bunches of knot-grass,
And diamonded with panes of quaint device,
Innumerable of stains and splendid dyes,
As are the tiger-moth's deep-damask'd wings;
And in the midst, 'mong thousand heraldries,
And twilight saints, and dim emblazonings,
A shielded scutcheon blush'd with blood of queens and kings.

XXV.

Full on this casement shone the wintry moon,
And threw warm gules on Madeline's fair breast,
As down she knelt for heaven's grace and boon;
Rose-bloom fell on her hands, together prest,
And on her silver cross soft amethyst,
And on her hair a glory, like a saint:
She seem'd a splendid angel, newly drest,
Save wings, for heaven:—Porphyro grew faint:
She knelt, so pure a thing, so free from mortal taint.

XXVI.

Anon his heart revives: her vespers done,
Of all its wreathed pearls her hair she frees;
Unclasps her warmed jewels one by one;
Loosens her fragrant bodice; by degrees
Her rich attire creeps rustling to her knees:
Half-hidden, like a mermaid in sea-weed,

Pensive awhile she dreams awake, and sees,
    In fancy, fair St. Agnes in her bed,
But dares not look behind, or all the charm is fled.

XXVII.

Soon, trembling in her soft and chilly nest,
    In sort of wakeful swoon, perplex'd she lay,
    Until the poppied warmth of sleep oppress'd
    Her soothed limbs, and soul fatigued away;
    Flown, like a thought, until the morrow-day;
    Blissfully haven'd both from joy and pain;
    Clasp'd like a missal where swart Paynims pray;
    Blinded alike from sunshine and from rain,
As though a rose should shut, and be a bud again.

XXVIII.

Stol'n to this paradise, and so entranced,
    Porphyro gazed upon her empty dress,
    And listen'd to her breathing, if it chanced
    To wake into a slumberous tenderness;
    Which when he heard, that minute did he bless,
    And breath'd himself: then from the closet crept,
    Noiseless as fear in a wide wilderness,
    And over the hush'd carpet, silent, stept,
And 'tween the curtains peep'd, where, lo!—how fast she slept.

It is not just Porphyro who peers. Keats enlists us as spectators of the predation that stanza XXII unveils. *Now prepare* is a rhetorical as well as fictive address: to him and, in its present tense, to voyeur-readers. The supererogatory *She comes, she comes again* is no narrative necessity; it is a pant for our reading, with a simile-slid alliteration, *fray'd and fled,* for excitement (*ringdove* is ready prey). This is a gendered sightline: male savoring a *Hoodwink'd* she. While no gender theorist, Keats knows the vector: a maid of fairy fancy caught in a voluptuary gaze. The word *fray'd* layers the modern sense of *afraid* on the archaic one, *disturbed, or startled* (*OED*, citing *The Eve* twice on this, the second to come in XXXIII). The surplus semantics deliver pangs of lexical reperception.

Eager to dream, Madeline practices the rules, but it is the narrator who is master of ceremonies and sensations. The first line of stanza XXIII is a little comedy, not least for its verbal rush of *Out* to *in:* Madeline's hurry letting in a draft, or producing one, that snuffs out her candle. In the pallid moonshine, the only sound is *she panted.* Otherwise, *No uttered syllable, or, woe betide!* the narrator camps in free indirect style for her difficult discipline of passion. "To be moved . . . by a passion," writes Wordsworth, is "to be excited often to external, and always to internal, effort; whether for the continuance and strengthening of the passion, or for its suppression, accordingly as the course which it takes may be painful or pleasurable" ("Essay" 370–371). Physician Keats words Madeline's utterly audible "internal" effort: *to her heart, her heart was voluble.* With dexterous double-grammar, the throb in *her heart* plays *to her heart,* a cardiophonics (meter-stressed, repeated just for the sensation, with a beat on the comma) that presses her body into eloquence, yearning like a god in pain. Hunt thrilled at the body language (18). *Paining/ in vain* is a sound of suppression. Keats's *heart*-words spell it silently to the eye: *hear* in *heart, ear* doubly within. He had been there before, with a stethoscope on Lorenzo's heartbeats for Isabella:

> His heart beat awfully against his side;
> And to his heart he inwardly did pray
>   For power to speak; but still the ruddy tide
> Stifled his voice, and puls'd revolve away—
>   Fever'd his high conceit   (VI)

Yet even with this template, it is hard to measure Keats's analogy of Madeline's panting heart into the agony of a *tongueless nightingale.* The tenor solicits a myth-allusion to the nightingale that was tongueless Philomel, mutilated to prevent her reporting a rape. The fable is impossible to avert, but difficult to apply, both over-productive (is Philomel Madeline's avatar?) and underproductive (are we overthinking?). As with other allusion-teases, Keats dangles a thread without weaving a design. *The Eve,* we're coming to realize, is a rhetoric about how we read, and we are never fully certain about what is before us, let alone how to interpret it. Perplexing effects are accumulating into a Keatsian poetics of perplexity.

The most famous site for reading is the next stanza, XXIV: Madeline's chamber-window, a stand-alone of gorgeous art within Keats's artful stanzas. Dante Gabriel Rossetti had it nearly by heart, and spread it into his own poetry.[1] Hunt just gave up selecting, and italicized the whole damn thing (19); "It throws a light upon one's book," he said in 1828 (*Lord Byron* 1:428). This jewel-scape is not quite a stand-alone, however. Like Isabella's tear-watered, head-fed Pot of Basil, the casement is a meta-romance figure about aesthetic production and transformations. Keats's lines build images into a tableau and words into figures, *emblazonings* punned into the genre of *blazon* and the *zonings* of a reader's eye. Primed by this paronomasia, *mid*st mirrors in *dim,* a verbal gem in itself. The anagram of *stains* and *saints* is a fine lexical aesthetics of stylistic equivalence. This is the same planning that makes *A shielded scutcheon blush'd with blood* suggest, then deflect, bloodshed: it is the design of Madeline's bloodline.[2] So, too, *tiger-moth,* named for its toxic defensive bodily fluids, is a displayed simile of gorgeous coloring. Everything is teased then disarmed into *quaint device.* Keats underlined this very phrase in *The Tempest,* a stage-direction for fairy Ariel's magic arts (*KS* 78).

How nicely, too, *blush'd* vibrates from past-participle adjective to active verb. The casement is also the device, beyond quaint, of a surreal optical illusion: winter moonlight prismed to bathe Madeline in a glow of colors as sexual as saintly. The window, divider of a hard winter and a chamber of love, not only makes color of pale light but also keeps the winter at bay—in effect, the melodizing of "olden Romance." Keats's draft (sq. 13) shows him working the chromo-magic in stanza XXIV, before separating this out into XXV. Cast through stained glass *gules,* moonlight gets body-warmed, even sifts into a springtime bath of *Rose-bloom.* Hunt felt the thrill of a tableau vivant, loving the very sound as well as sense of *warm gules.* "*Red* would not have been a fiftieth part so good."[3] He italicized *gules,* then, in a rush, everything in XXV from *Rose-bloom* to *heaven* (19). If Hunt seems ready to faint with Porphyro, we can hardly blame him. Keats's blazon unfurls a lettered design of *on:* mo*on* to its bo*on; on* her breast; *on* her hands, *on* her silver cross, *on* her hair. Not a metamorphosis, the prepositions array a spectacle of a body transformed by art. Even a silver-cool *cross* glows amethyst-toned for purple-Porphyro, and pun-echoing his dash *across* the moors to her. Keats gives us Madeline full-body, canceling *fair face* for *fair breast* (sq. 14).

That long midline dash in *Save wings, for heaven:—Porphyro grew faint* (XXV) is heartbeat punctuation. It is a question "whether most to admire the magical delicacy of the hazardous picture, or its consummate irresistible attraction," said reviewer John Scott. Italicizing the last four lines, he extended his swoon to the next three stanzas, quoting these entire.[4] In stanza XXVI, Keats revives fainting Porphyro to a capable seeing of this angel *newly drest* undressing into a woman, and he paces the poetry syllable by syllable, punctuation by punctuation, so that we share his pleasure thermometer. The first line pivots from one last chime of *on* in the arc from its first word *Anon* to its last, *done*. Before the syntax of the ablative absolute absorbs *her vespers done*, Keats's line-unit parallels it with "his heart revives:"—the colon is a curtain-raising punctuation. Porphyro repassionates into physical life. The next five lines proceed through the spectacle of her undressing, Porhyro's steps pacing our reading. We have to let the iambic pentameter pant out two syllables for *wreath-ed*, *warm-ed*, and *je-wels*.[5] Temperature and fragrance index the warm body even more immediately than Adonis's languorous limbs did under his coverlid. Keats slow-pulses *one by one* in the scene and in the poetics.

Meter-marked, punctuation delayed, this fabulous one-sentence stanza lingers in the sensuous suspense of erotic temporality: *Unclasps . . . Loosens . . . by degrees . . . /creeps rustling*. At the climax of *mermaid*-porn, Scott was already italicizing everything from *by degrees* to *sea-weed*. The "rustling downward attire," Hunt chorused, "the mixture of dress and undress, and dishevelled hair," show a gift for "rendering . . . words almost as tangible as the objects they speak of" (19). Keats labored for this effect, shaping and reshaping the strip-teasing on two of his most worked-over pages (sq. 14–15):

> ~~She lays aside her necl~~
>   ~~strips her hair of all its~~ ^{pearled} ~~wreathes pearl~~
> ~~Unclasps her bosom jewels~~
> *~~Unclasps her warmed jewels one by one~~*
>   *~~her bursting~~*
>   *~~Loosens the bodice from her~~*
>   *~~her Bodice lace string~~*
>   *~~her Boddice; and her bosom bar~~*
>   *~~her~~*
> *Loosens ~~her fragrant bodice and doth bare~~*
> *~~Her~~*
>
>   *[. . .]*
>
>   *frees*
>   *Of all her wreathed pearl her hair she* ~~strips~~
>   *Unclasps her warmed jewels one by one*
>   *by degrees*
>   ~~*to her knees*~~
>   *Loosens her fragrant bodice;* ~~*and down slips*~~
>   *Her sweet attire* ~~*falls light creeps down by*~~
>   *creeps rusteling to her knees*
>   *Mermaid   in sea weed*
>   *Half hidden like a* ~~*Syren of the Sea*~~

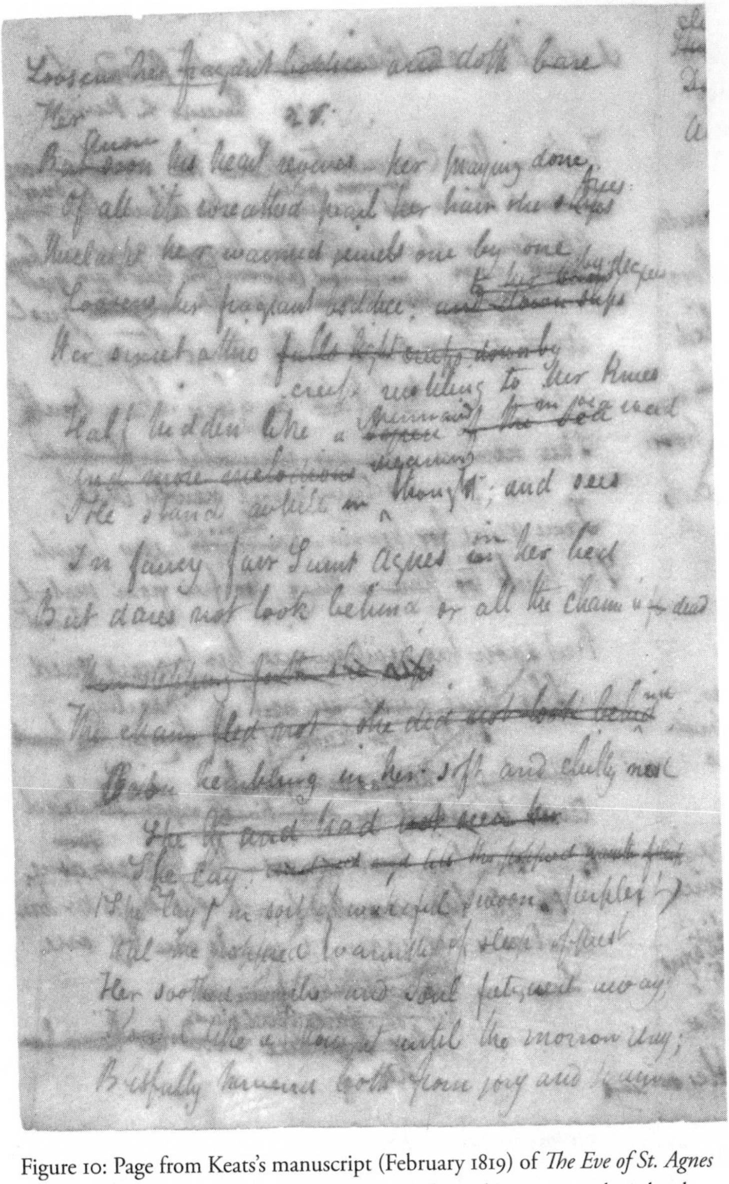

Figure 10: Page from Keats's manuscript (February 1819) of *The Eve of St. Agnes* XXVI. Although revisions and bleed-through from the reverse make it hard to decipher (see transcription in text), this page shows how much labor Keats expended on the spectacle of Madeline's slow, innocently erotic undressing. From *John Keats: Poetry Manuscripts at Harvard: A Facsimile Edition,* ed. Jack Stillinger (The Belknap Press of Harvard University Press, 1990), p. 115, from the original manuscript in the Houghton Library, Harvard University.

A sensationalism of bursting bodice, bare bosom, and Syren-vamping was too easy. Keats's more refined wording rouses us to supply what's half-hidden, from *creeps* to *knees* by *degrees*. Satan's sightline has a blueprint, as he <u>half spied</u> Eve alone in Eden (9.426; *KPL* I:94).

Madeline, Keats's latest nested maid, is innocent of all gazing: she's drugged on the "poppied warmth" of her fantasy, bereft of consciousness and "soul." Her dream state is a regressive Chamber of Infant Thought, *Blissfully haven'd from joy and pain/. . . Blinded alike from sunshine and from rain,* with apt-rhymed rose-work: *As though a rose should shut, and be a bud again* (XXVII). If this is the charm of bliss, it is also a peril in a world with operators like Porphyro. The participle-clause that opens stanza XXVIII, *Stol'n to this paradise, and so entranced,* is Satan's brand. While Keats is not writing Satanic code, his wording is tuned to it. As an iambic pun, en*tranced* is both an adjective (the lad, too, is charmed by now) and a participle-adjective that aligns with *Stol'n* for a nonce-verb pun, trochee-sounded *en*tranced: the lad *having gained entrance,* on track with Satan's stratagem for Eve-ravishing. If Porphyro lacks "hellish rancour" (9.409)—a phrase Keats notes (*KPL* II:86)—he's up to speed in Satan-scoptics as he gazes on the empty dress and audits her breathings asleep, with that splendid calculus of her waking *into a slumberous tenderness.* How much more expectant is this than the expected grammar, "tender slumber." Tender would be this night for her; but *tenderness* is for him.

Keats's verse mimes Porphyro's careful steps with the swells and halts of meter and hisses of sound: *crept, / Noiseless, hush'd carpet, silent, stept, fast she slept.* The master-chord is the surreal simile, *Noiseless as fear in a wide wilderness,* the first and last words sounding a falling rhyme, with *wilderness* stretching *wide* to a limit of communicative capacity. Hunt's unerring ear featured this line in italics (19). In the next turn, *And over the hush'd carpet, silent, stept,* meter and triple reverberation force *silent* from potential adverb (*silently*) into an adjective— no less for *Porphyro* than for *the hush'd carpet*—in line with *noiseless*. In the surplus sound-play on the very subject of silence, words act as characters in the dramatic suspense. The climax at *lo!—how fast she slept,* with a beat at the dash, is a bed-check prologue for the stratagem's next move.

The last lines of stanza XXVI put undressed Madeline to bed with her waking dream: *she dreams awake, and sees, / In fancy, fair St. Agnes in her bed.* Keats's syntax cutely aligns the *in* clauses. She sees in a state of fancy, and in this state sees what she fancies: *fair St. Agnes* as her bedmate. Keats lets us hear in the lexical sequence of *fancy, fair* an echo of *faery fancy,* Madeline's fore-seeing fore-play (VIII). Another chord comes on *fair . . . dares.* The full predicate, *dares not look behind,* and its penalty, *or all the charm is fled,* is another of those Keats-tease conjurings. The wording elicits the old myth of Orpheus's fateful glance back at beloved Eurydice. While Madeline does not give in to Orpheus's gaze and fate, her not looking is not without peril. It is a perfect serve to foreseeing Porphyro. It takes less than half of XXVII to put her into oblivious sleep.

[1] For this impact, see Ford, 128–131.

[2] *OED* drops the ball, citing this line only for *blush'd* as *made red* (defn. 6). Keats revives a more expansive, obsolete sense (defn. 1): *shining forth.* Pettet (19–20) is reminded of Walter Scott's popular *Lay of the Last Minstrel* II:XI, where moonlight on a window-pane irradiates a militant "Cross of Red" that "threw on the pavement a bloody stain." Keats's *blood* is more ambiguous.

[3] "*Red* is redundant," pun-quips Ridley (152).

[4] *London Magazine,* 318–319. Colvin, liking the illusion, felt compelled to note "that moonlight has not the power to transmit the separate hues of painted glass" (*John Keats* [1887], 160). Pettet issued an "error" card to both Scott and Keats (19n).

[5] That Keats uses the one-syllable *wreath'd* in *Ode to Psyche* suggests his deliberation here.

blazoning the love feast

XXIX.

Then by the bed-side, where the faded moon
Made a dim, silver twilight, soft he set
A table, and, half anguish'd, threw thereon
A cloth of woven crimson, gold, and jet:—
O for some drowsy Morphean amulet!
The boisterous, midnight, festive clarion,
The kettle-drum, and far-heard clarionet,
Affray his ears, though but in dying tone:—
The hall door shuts again, and all the noise is gone.

XXX.

And still she slept an azure-lidded sleep,
In blanched linen, smooth, and lavender'd
While he from forth the closet brought a heap
Of candied apple, quince, and plum, and gourd;

With jellies soother than the creamy curd,
And lucent syrops, tinct with cinnamon;
Manna and dates, in argosy transferr'd
From Fez; and spiced dainties, every one,
From silken Samarcand to cedar'd Lebanon.

XXXI.

These delicates he heap'd with glowing hand
On golden dishes and in baskets bright
Of wreathed silver: sumptuous they stand
In the retired quiet of the night,
Filling the chilly room with perfume light. —
"And now, my love, my seraph fair, awake!
Thou art my heaven, and I thine eremite:
Open thine eyes, for meek St. Agnes' sake,
Or I shall drowse beside thee, so my soul doth ache."

XXXII.

Thus whispering, his warm, unnerved arm
Sank in her pillow. Shaded was her dream
By the dusk curtains:—'twas a midnight charm
Impossible to melt as iced stream:
The lustrous salvers in the moonlight gleam;
Broad golden fringe upon the carpet lies:
It seem'd he never, never could redeem
From such a stedfast spell his lady's eyes;
So mus'd awhile, entoil'd in woofed phantasies.

The closet Porphyro hides in is conveniently a pantry for the party's "cates and dainties" (XX), which he ably raids. Said Hunt of XXX, this is a stanza "for which Persian kings would fill a poet's mouth with gold." He recalled Keats reading it "with great relish and particularity, conscious of what he had set forth. The melody is as sweet as the subject" (*Lord Byron* 1:430). "So delicious is the unsating food," sighs Endymion of the menu in *love's Elysium,* in a deliciousness of sounding. Keats's wording doubles Porphyro in the catering, happily importing *spiced dainties* from *The Fairy-Queen,* Sarazin's feasting on <u>dainty</u>

Spices fetch'd from furthest Ind (V.4); Keats's underlining (Lowell 2:559). To wonder if this feast is for the eating is to miss the mark: it is a fabulously worded fetish, an extravagant Keats-blazon, full of fresh coinages. From Madeline's sound-zone *azure-lidded* in *linen, smooth, and lavender'd*, Keats exports *smooth* into the dainties, blending *soothe* into a tactile jelly-essence, *soother*.[1] On the luxe sound of *lucent syrops, tinct with cinnamon*, Hunt exclaimed at the "delicate modulation, and super-refined epicurean nicety!" that "make us read the line delicately, and at the tip-end, as it were, of one's tongue" (*Indicator* 19). Arcing from *lucent* to *cinnamon*, Keats plumbs *tinct* (the sole time in his poetry) for all its worth: *tinct* as colored; *tinct* as tip-end taste.[2]

Hunt's tangible imagination catches the fine double-grammar of *every one*, itemizing *spiced dainties*, then drawing in their exotic sources, given in soundings that rival sense: *silken Samarcand to cedar'd Lebanon.* Lebanon we know, but *Samarcand?* A sonic wave more than any referent. The exotic delicacies are words to charm the tongue, no more extravagantly than, with a mimetic verse turn, *in argosy transferred/From Fez.* The pun on *metaphor* ("transfer") rivals the import, Keats sourcing words in their etymologies as much as delicacies in their terroir.[3] Whether or not Porphyro's spread is love's labors lost, we've won a seat at this great feast of language. For the sheer cuisine-erotics, Keats drafted a stanza for the legend:

> 'Twas said her future lord would there appear
> Offering, as sacrifice—all in the dream—
> Delicious food, even to her lips brought near,
> viands, and wine, and fruit, and sugar'd cream,
> To touch her palate with the fine extreme
> Of relish   (*P* 301n)

How finely set is *fine extreme* at the line's extreme. While Keats didn't use this draft after all, *Delicious* distills into the *delicates* that he did array (XXXI): not the same root, but you have to believe it must be so. Porphyro's art seems, briefly, even to alchemize its impresario in this stanza. Although we realize his hand is *glowing* by *golden* reflection, it seems to do so wondrously on its own. Even the waft of *perfume light* from his delicates seems a new kind of synesthetic radiance. Of course Hunt italicized it (19).

Everything set, Porphyro tries to rouse Madeline from her dream into his world of silver and gold. But her enchantments are more than cold; they're iced in: crisis with no volta at hand. To revive her, Porphyro revives a song Keats himself would revive a few months on, "La belle dame sans mercy" (XXXIII).

There may be *mercy* in Madeline's hearing the *melody*—or so Keats's rhyme in this stanza hopes, along with a "tumultuous" throb. Satan's stratagem <u>boils in his tumultuous breast</u> (*PL* 4.16), Keats's underlining (*KPL* 1:85). Porphyro is not this heartless, but the fuel is kin. The only other *tumultuous* in Milton's epic is also for Satan (2.936).

---

[1] *OED* credits *soother* to Keats. De Selincourt says *lavender'd* was not used before this, "but much since" Keats's indulgence, noting Thomas Hood and Alfred Tennyson (617).

[2] *JnD* has the second sense; *OED* cites Keats here for this rare "poetic" usage.

[3] Keats might even loop this back to that *ardent pursuit—which by the by stamps the burgundy mark on the bottles of our Minds* (to Bailey, 13 March 1818; MsK 1.23.81 and *L* 1:243).

Awakening, dreamland, solution sweet, frost-wind, happy speed, ashes cold

XXXIII.

Awakening up, he took her hollow lute, —
Tumultuous,—and, in chords that tenderest be,
He play'd an ancient ditty, long since mute,
In Provence call'd, "La belle dame sans mercy":
Close to her ear touching the melody; —
Wherewith disturb'd, she utter'd a soft moan:
He ceased—she panted quick—and suddenly
Her blue affrayed eyes wide open shone:
Upon his knees he sank, pale as smooth-sculptured stone.

XXXIV.

Her eyes were open, but she still beheld,
Now wide awake, the vision of her sleep:
There was a painful change, that nigh expell'd
The blisses of her dream so pure and deep
At which fair Madeline began to weep,
And moan forth witless words with many a sigh;
While still her gaze on Porphyro would keep;
Who knelt, with joined hands and piteous eye,
Fearing to move or speak, she look'd so dreamingly.

XXXV.

"Ah, Porphyro!" said she, "but even now
Thy voice was at sweet tremble in mine ear,
Made tuneable with every sweetest vow;
And those sad eyes were spiritual and clear:
How chang'd thou art! how pallid, chill, and drear!
Give me that voice again, my Porphyro,
Those looks immortal, those complainings dear!
Oh leave me not in this eternal woe,
For if thou diest, my Love, I know not where to go."

XXXVI.

Beyond a mortal man impassion'd far
At these voluptuous accents, he arose,
Ethereal, flush'd, and like a throbbing star
Seen mid the sapphire heaven's deep repose;
Into her dream he melted, as the rose
Blendeth its odour with the violet,—
Solution sweet: meantime the frost-wind blows
Like Love's alarum pattering the sharp sleet
Against the window-panes; St. Agnes' moon hath set.

XXXVII.

'Tis dark; quick pattereth the flaw-blown sleet:
"This is no dream, my bride, my Madeline!"
'Tis dark: the iced gust will rave and beat:
"No dream, alas! alas! and woe is mine!
Porphyro will leave me here to fade and pine.—
Cruel! what traitor could thee hither bring?
I curse not, for my heart is lost in thine,
Though thou forsakest a deceived thing;—
A dove forlorn and lost with sick unpruned wing."

XXXVIII.

"My Madeline! sweet dreamer! lovely bride!
Say, may I be for aye thy vassal blest?

Thy beauty's shield, heart-shaped and vermeil dyed?
Ah, silver shrine, here will I take my rest
After so many hours of toil and quest,
A famish'd pilgrim,—saved by miracle.
Though I have found, I will not rob thy nest
Saving of thy sweet self; if thou think'st well
To trust, fair Madeline, to no rude infidel.

XXXIX.

Hark! 'tis an elfin-storm from faery land,
Of haggard seeming, but a boon indeed:
Arise—arise! the morning is at hand;—
The bloated wassaillers will never heed:—
Let us away, my love, with happy speed;
There are no ears to hear, or eyes to see,—
Drown'd all in Rhenish and the sleepy mead:
Awake! arise! my love, and fearless be,
For o'er the southern moors I have a home for thee."

XL.

She hurried at his words, beset with fears,
For there were sleeping dragons all around,
At glaring watch, perhaps, with ready spears—
Down the wide stairs a darkling way they found.—
In all the house was heard no human sound.
A chain-droop'd lamp was flickering by each door;
The arras, rich with horseman, hawk, and hound,
Flutter'd in the besieging wind's uproar;
And the long carpets rose along the gusty floor.

XLI.

They glide, like phantoms, into the wide hall;
Like phantoms, to the iron porch, they glide;
Where lay the Porter, in uneasy sprawl,
With a huge empty flaggon by his side:
The wakeful bloodhound rose, and shook his hide,

But his sagacious eye an inmate owns:
By one, and one, the bolts full easy slide:—
The chains lie silent on the footworn stones;—
The key turns, and the door upon its hinges groans.

XLII.

And they are gone: ay, ages long ago
These lovers fled away into the storm.
That night the Baron dreamt of many a woe,
And all his warrior-guests, with shade and form
Of witch, and demon, and large coffin-worm,
Were long be-nightmar'd. Angela the old
Died palsy-twitch'd, with meagre face deform;
The Beadsman, after thousand aves told,
For aye unsought for slept among his ashes cold.

For all his arts, Porphyro can hardly savor success. Slipped in next to dreaming Madeline, his arm is surprisingly *unnerved,* incapacity sadly anagrammed, *never, never* (XXXII) (recall Saturn's *nerveless* hand). When she at last opens her eyes to Keats's resounded *affrayed,* her would-be lover is beyond disarmed. The stanza that Keats punctuated with five dramatically pregnant dashes subsides into sudden arrest: "Upon his knees he sank, pale as smooth-sculptured stone" (XXXIII), the tumultuous lover now looking like one of the outer-chapel's "sculptured dead" (II). Keats beautifully double-syntaxes Madeline's visual aspect: *she look'd so dreamingly* (XXIV). In Porphyro's dream-sights she is so, mercifully for him; in her sightline, she may be still in "the vision of her sleep." Then, seeing her hot dream-lover actually by her side so "pallid, chill, and drear" (XXXV), she cries to dream again, in fully "voluptuous accents."

This phrase is in the second line of stanza XXXVI, site of the long anticipated, desired, suspense-delayed climax of lovemaking. Porphyro is born again, rising to Madeline's call—in a phenomenal appeal to our negative capability—by entering into her dream. Keats's melting rhyme of *arose* to *rose* is an outrageous erotic pun, drawing in the *full-blown rose* of Porphyro's stratagem (XVI) to activate a much-loved anagram of old Romance, *rose/eros,* which Keats inscribes right into "the *rose.*" The first line speaks elevation into immortal love; the next makes it voluptuous, and the next, a synthesis, *Ethereal, flush'd.* Milton's fantasy of angel-sex hardly comes close. Keats underlined Raphael's getting into this, "with a smile that glow'd / Celestial rosy red,

Loves proper hue" and then his coy demur, "I can now no more" (8:618–620, 630; *KPL* II:70). Keats could, first with a draft rather more voluptuous than celestial in glow.[1]

> *So, while she speaks his arms encroaching slow*
> *Have zoned her, heart to heart, loud, loud the dark winds blow!*

> *For on the midnight came a tempest fell;*
> *More sooth, for that his close rejoinder flows*
> *Into her burning ear: and still the spell*
> *Unbroken guards her in serene repose.*
> *With her wild dream he mingled, as a rose*
> *Marrieth its odour to a violet.*
> *Still, still she dreams . . .*

Keats's *heart to heart* surpasses Raphael's "union of pure with pure / Desiring" (8.627–628), with a dash of Satan whispering into Eve's ready ear as she sleeps (*PL* 5.36).

Madeline's spell saved her virtue, Keats thought. Not Woodhouse. He was so rattled after hearing Keats read this scene that he alerted Taylor of a shock to "<u>we</u> innocent ones (ladies & myself)" on seeing Porphyro in "all the acts of a bonâ fide husband" upon the dreamer. He hoped that "all is left to inference," but the post-innocent man in him conceded otherwise: "the Interest on the reader's imagination is greatly heightened" in a spirit that could render the poem "unfit for ladies & indeed scarcely to be mentioned to them."[2] In friendly helpfulness and hopefulness, he said as much to Keats. Keats blew his stack (Woodhouse continues to Taylor): "He says he does not want ladies to read his poetry: that he writes for men—& that if . . . there was an opening for doubt what took place, it was his fault for not writing clearly & comprehensively . . . &c &c &c—and all this sort of Keats-like rhodomontade" (2). Taylor was ready to say that if Keats persisted in "flying in the face of all Decency & Discretion," he would have to find another "Imprimatur" (*L* 2:182–183). So Keats retailored, doing sex with stars and color-coded flowers. This was beyond coy. Porphyro *flush'd and like a throbbing star* is patent surrogacy: stars don't throb; they twinkle.[3] So, too, the proxy palette of *sapphire heaven,* and *rose* and *violet.* The virtuous men's objections, ironically, generated poetry that was even sexier for soliciting a reader's complicity in decoding the patent stand-ins.

At this erotic climax, the romance pivots suddenly to the world outside. This could have commanded a new-stanza volta. Keats does it in line 7 of stanza

XXXVI, with an abrupt, colon-stressed caesura at *Solution sweet: meantime the frost-wind blows*. This is the poem's second *meantime;* the first was the sudden turn to Porphyro at the portal doors (IX) on track to this solution sweet. The repetition here is a dire time-stamp. Keats ends the lovemaking at *sweet,* its *rose* brutally rhymed to "frost-wind *blows.*" The thrust into *pattering the sharp sleet/Against the window panes* comes on an extremely rare transitive verb-use of *pattering,* with *sleet* as its direct object, sent against that casement window. By slant-rhyming the couplet *sleet/set,* Keats can release *sleet* to swallow *sweet,* and to key up the first rhyme of stanza XXXVII: "flaw-blown *sleet/* rave and *beat,*" a beat in the very meters, propelled by the repeated weather report and a now moonless night. The arc from XXXVI to XXXVII is this gone light: *St Agnes' moon hath set. / / 'Tis dark* (chimed twice). What a compound for hell, now on earth, is *flaw-blown!*—not only the sole use of this compound in Keats's poetry but also the *OED*'s only citation. Keats underscored Milton's Hellscape (*KPL* I:45):

a frozen continent

<u>Lies dark and wild, beat with perpetual storms</u>

<u>Of whirlwind and dire hail</u>   (2.587–589)

He also underscored the forecast of fallen earth's winters, <u>arm'd with ice, / And snow, and hail, and stormy gust and flaw</u> (10.697–698; *KPL* II:130). In such a climate, Madeline's dream succumbs to her worst nightmare: real *woe,* a cruel treachery, a ring-dove undone (XXXVII).

Porphyro answers with a tale made for maiden thought: chiming his pledge, *My . . . bride . . . I . . . aye* (XXVIII), he presents himself as famish'd pilgrim, saved by the miracle of her mercy, and now her vassal in eternal devotion. Is this a faery fancy, on the same page as his transposing the sleet-storm into an *elfin-storm from faery land?* Looks bad, but actually a boon (he says), a cover for their eloping (XXXIX). Keats puts four dashes into this stanza to dramatize emergency, and no wonder, given the signs of a dire storm: a heavy arras "Flutter'd in the besieging wind's uproar; / And the long carpets rose along the gusty floor" (XL). Keats drives his words into the siege, drawing the alexandrine into a mimetic *long . . . along*. This is almost the poem's last *rose,* the bloom long gone in the verb of wind-force. The last *rose* is a past-tense verb for bloodhound's unalarmed sentry-check (XLI). Is this a boon indeed?

At this point, Keats turns a last bit of magic: the foemen, who might also be military *dragoons,* are seen in fairy-tale idiom as *sleeping dragons;* the egress is an enchanted-sounding *darkling way* (XL). And the physically panting, throbbing lovers fade into the present tense of another temporal order, sealed off by a chiasmus: *They glide, like phantoms . . . Like phantoms . . . they glide* (XLI), not even imprinting *footworn stones* (the only event of this adjective in Keats's poetry).[4] Keats's grammar, comments Earl Wasserman, takes them "outside time and activity" (125), a metamorphosis on the slide of simile.

By another of those accidents of book-printing that bears semantic force, Keats's last stanza sits solo on a new verso page (104), with the impact of a volta-pivot into a stark epitaph. He begins this finale in the fictive present of the lovers' vanishing, *they are* gone, then shifts to deep time, interjection-stressed: *ay, ages long ago.* The rest of the stanza returns the world from which the lovers have *fled* and depletes it of any fairy-landing. It is *long be-nightmar'd,* a Keats-coined participle drawn out from *benighted.* A postscript tells of two grim avatars of the lovers: old Angela for angel Madeline; the holy Beadsman for pilgrim Porphyro. For Angela, *palsy-twitch'd* rings *witch'd,* the nominative already in a nightmare *form/Of witch.* Keats wanted this cruel, contracted adjective for her *meager face deform.* Especially in this syntactic inversion, *deform* elicits Milton's only two usages in *Paradise Lost,* Death "dreadful and deform" (2.706), and Archangel Michael unveiling to Adam a foresight of mortal suffering, "so deform what heart of rock could long/Dry-eyed behold? Adam could not, but wept" (11.494–495). This perverse Orpheus makes the rocks weep at the pathos of human deformation, uncreation. The Beadsman freezes into a hellish sentence, *after a thousand aves told,/For aye unsought for* (8). The numbering of *a thousand aves* also sums a numbed life, and *aye* draws bitter sequel. The poor man was not *ever* missed by his patrons.

Keats's chord *storm–form–worm–deform* mirrors an early stanza (Spenserian, too) in Thomson's *Castle of Indolence* to reflect an impossibly fairy counterpoint. Wizard Indolence coos of "a pure ethereal calm that knows no storm," abiding "above those passions that this world deform,/And torture man, a proud malignant worm," offering "a place to form/A quicker sense of joy" (I.16). No such luck for Keats's readers: *ashes cold* are his cold last words. Woodhouse was as upset by this dead thud as he was by the hot love, lamenting to Taylor that Keats "altered the last 3 lines to leave on the reader a sense of pettish disgust." Even worse, Keats "says he likes that the poem should leave off with this Change of Sentiment – it was what he aimed at, & was glad to find from my objections to it that he had succeeded." Woodhouse saw him affecting a (Byronic) "'Don Juan' style of mingling up sentiment & sneering," with "a fancy for trying his hand at an attempt to play with his reader, & fling him off at last" (2), like a double-dealing lover. It's now clear that Keats wants a fully greeted reader to feel the end of romance.

Porphyro's hope to rouse Madeline by playing "La belle dame sans mercy" (XXXIII) summons a tune where mercy is in the Lady's grant. In Porphyro's peril in the castle, it was the old *beldame* Angela who gave him his first "mercy" (X). The epithet is loaded. What of belle dames and mercy? *Beldame* is a medieval "appellation of respect to women of ordinary rank" (Spenser, Glossary, I:cxviii); its cousin *beldam* is a synonym for *hag*—as in *Macbeth* (3.5; *DW* 5:40). *La belle dame sans merci* divides and frenchifies the epithet. But the ballad is no woman's song. It is a categorical male grievance, about broken expectations, even deception. With no mercy.

[*1820*, 81–104]

[1] Woodhouse's transcript of Keats's (now lost) draft, MsK, 3.2.226.

[2] ALS, 19–20 September 1819; Morgan Library, p. 2. See also *L* 2:163.

[3] "Twinkle, twinkle, little star," begins Jane Taylor's *The Star* (*Poems for the Nursery*, 1806, with 100 editions). She was on Taylor and Hessey's list. Keats gave her *Essays in Rhyme* to his sister, September 1817 (*L* 1:155).

[4] Keats may have recalled Wordsworth's image of a church-floor's "foot-worn epitaphs." *The Excursion* (1814), *Book the Fifth*, p. 209.

La belle dame sans merci and La Belle Dame sans Mercy

La belle dame sans merci --
O what can ail thee Knight at arms
  Alone and palely loitering?
The sedge has wither'd from the Lake
  and no birds sing!   4

O what can ail thee knight at arms
  So haggard, and so woe begone?
The squirrel's granary is full
  and the harvest's done.   8

            a
I see ~~death's~~ lilly on thy brow
  With anguish moist and fever dew,

                    a
and on thy cheeks ~~death's~~ fading rose
Fast Withereth too -   12

  I met a Lady in the ~~Wilds~~ Meads
    Full beautiful, a faery's child,
  Her hair was long, her foot was light
      And her eyes were wild -   16
  I made a Garland for her head,
  And bracelets too, and fragrant Zones
    She look'd at me as she did love
      And made sweet moan —   20

I set her on my pacing steed
  and nothing else saw all day long
For sidelong would she bend, and sing
  a faerys song -   24
She found me roots of relish sweet,

              manna
  And honey wild, and ~~honey~~ dew
And sure in language strange she said
    I love thee true-   28
  She took me to her elfin grot,

and sigh'd full sore
And there she wept ~~and there she sighed fill sore~~
And there I shut her wild wild eyes
With kisses four.   32
And there she Lulled me asleep,
And there I dream'd Ah woe betide!
The latest dream I ever dreamt
On the cold hill side   36

I saw pale Kings and Princes too
Pale warriors death pale were they all
They cried - La belle dame sans merci
Thee hath in thrall -   40
I saw their starv'd lips in the gloam
~~All tremble~~   *gaped*
With horrid warning wide ~~agape~~
And I awoke and found me here,
On the cold hill's side.   44

And this is why I ~~wither~~ sojourn here,
Alone and palely loitering;
Though the sedge is wither'd from the lake,
and no birds sing – –   48
Why four Kisses - you will say — why four because I wish to
restrain the headlong impetuousity of my Muse - she would have
fain said 's core' without hurting the rhyme— but we must temper
the Imagination - as the Critics say with Judgment. I was obliged to
choose an even number that both eyes might have fair play: and to
speak truly I think two a piece quite sufficient - Suppose I had said
seven; there would have been three and a half a piece - a very
awkward affair - and well got out of on my side —

La belle dame may be thematically duplicitous. It is certainly textually so, rendered by Keats in two versions, each with a distinct readership. One is in a letter to George and Georgiana (late April 1819). Milnes tidied this text up into the ballad he printed in *1848* (2:268–270), and until the 1980s, this was the canonical text. The other, published in Keats's lifetime, is in Leigh Hunt's literary weekly *The Indicator* (1820), prefaced by a two-page essay by Hunt on the lore.[1]

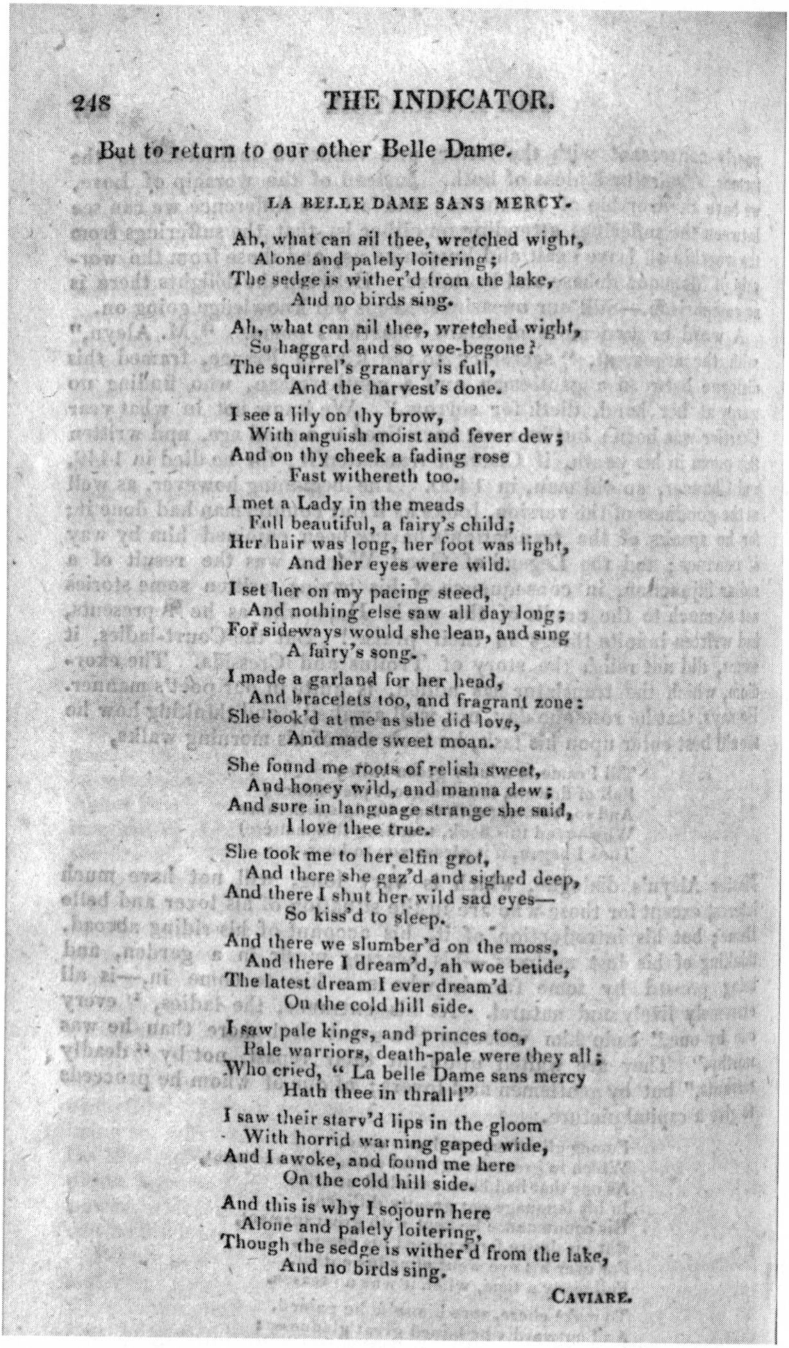

But to return to our other Belle Dame.

LA BELLE DAME SANS MERCY.

Ah, what can ail thee, wretched wight,
    Alone and palely loitering;
The sedge is wither'd from the lake,
    And no birds sing.

Ah, what can ail thee, wretched wight,
    So haggard and so woe-begone?
The squirrel's granary is full,
    And the harvest's done.

I see a lily on thy brow,
    With anguish moist and fever dew;
And on thy cheek a fading rose
    Fast withereth too.

I met a Lady in the meads
    Full beautiful, a fairy's child;
Her hair was long, her foot was light,
    And her eyes were wild.

I set her on my pacing steed,
    And nothing else saw all day long;
For sideways would she lean, and sing
    A fairy's song.

I made a garland for her head,
    And bracelets too, and fragrant zone:
She look'd at me as she did love,
    And made sweet moan.

She found me roots of relish sweet,
    And honey wild, and manna dew;
And sure in language strange she said,
    I love thee true.

She took me to her elfin grot,
    And there she gaz'd and sighed deep,
And there I shut her wild sad eyes—
    So kiss'd to sleep.

And there we slumber'd on the moss,
    And there I dream'd, ah woe betide,
The latest dream I ever dream'd
    On the cold hill side.

I saw pale kings, and princes too,
    Pale warriors, death-pale were they all;
Who cried, " La belle Dame sans mercy
    Hath thee in thrall!"

I saw their starv'd lips in the gloom
    With horrid warning gaped wide,
And I awoke, and found me here
    On the cold hill side.

And this is why I sojourn here
    Alone and palely loitering,
Though the sedge is wither'd from the lake,
    And no birds sing.

                                CAVIARE.

Figure 11: "La Belle Dame sans Mercy," *Indicator,* 10 May 1820. In its
first publication, it is nicely featured on its own page with Keats's *nom
de plume,* following a brief essay by Leigh Hunt on the legend. Keats
EC8 H9135 LIn25. Courtesy of Houghton Library, Harvard University.

The chief differences are a generic *wretched wight* instead of truant *Knight at arms*, and *mercy* instead of *merci*. Both words derive from *merces:* price or wages (here, sexual contract). *Merci* is the language of courtly love; *mercy* lodges a more bitter, visceral complaint. These tonal inflections notwithstanding, in both registers Keats's folk-ballad stanza implies an old story, with the common denominator of a *femme fatale*, a trope that Hunt's essay details, satirizes, and critiques. I'll say more later about this supplement. I turn first to the letter-text so you can follow Keats's careful revising and enjoy his postscript.

The postscript seems a bit perverse, overdetermined even, in its self-possessed wit. From the dashes and ellipses that trail away from the Knight's tale about his disastrous self-dispossession by a faithless lady comes Keats's sure-footed patter of he-mastery about his tangle with a she-muse. In October 1818, he had pledged to his publishers to "write <u>with judgment</u>" after having "leaped head-long into the Sea" with *Endymion* (*K* 207). His joking in the postscript about one judgment, *Why four Kisses*, nicely puns *whyfore* in *why four.* If Dante Gabriel Rossetti preferred the *Indicator* text's *With kisses four* to this one's *So kissed to sleep*—finding in the number-naming "suggestiveness of undermeaning which is no gain" (Letter III, pp. 14–15)—Keats wryly wrings poetic meaning from erotic undermeaning. His she-Muse *would have fain said 's core':* in a heart's *core*, Keats's pun-script implies, with a bonus of *keeping score.* The wish to *restrain—rein back, re-strain, re-chord—*to *four* takes a sidelong glance at the balladry: four-line stanzas, the last line often four beats, sometimes four words, this another ring on *score* as musical script. This is crafty judgment.

The Knight's tale is something else. Addison's description (1712) of the dissolve of "pleasing Delusion" offers a virtual blueprint for this bluesy ballad: "the inchanted Hero in a Romance . . . upon the finishing of some secret Spell, the fantastick Scene breaks up, and the disconsolate Knight finds himself on a barren Heath" ("Pleasures of Imagination" 105). For his Knight-tale of sad self-finding, Keats aligns the balladry with the distinction in Wordsworth's Preface to *Lyrical Ballads* (1800): "the feeling therein developed gives importance to the action and situation and not the action and situation to the feeling" (1:xvii). Keats takes this to a radical extreme. There is no action at all, just a conversation full of strange feeling. The action is in the past; the present scene is one bare, withering circumstance for a diagnostic questioner and a song to die for. The loaded dash that Keats puts after the title hovers as an implied pre-logic for the spectacle of a *Knight at arms* disturbingly disarmed. "That then, hence this now," is the invited surmise (the fallacy *post hoc ergo propter hoc*).

Keats's verbal repetitions beckon as planted clues. The poem opens *in medias res* as an unoriginated voice addresses some Knight, situated under the sign of a title.

> *La belle dame sans merci* —
> *O what can ail thee Knight at arms*
> *Alone and palely loitering?*

Keats's first rhyme draws *sans merci* to a chime with *ail thee:* a micro-tale, soon adding *palely,* on the way to *Lady,* all trochaic beats. This is the only *palely* in Keats's poetry. He underlined apt verse in Burton's *Anatomy of Melancholy* (Part 2, 1364–1366), set therein in historically textured black-letter, about lovelorn Arcite (from Chaucer's *Knights Tale*).[2] The symptoms would have caught his medically trained attention:

> His hew pale and ashen to unfold,
> And solitary he was and ever alone,
> And waking all the night, making mone.

Such words tinct love-sad Paulo in Hunt's *Story of Rimini*: *pale, pallid, moist anguish, woe, wan, wretchedness, pain, suffering* (p. 85). The lexicon spools back to Chatterton's *Excelente Balade of Charitie* (1777), his Rowleie confection ("1464") about a "hapless pilgrim": "his glommed face, his sprighte there scanne; / Howe woe-be-gone, howe withered, forwynd, deade!"[3]

Well versed in the anatomy of melancholy, Keats's questioner reads the sad-sack Knight with the data of his depleted environment: *the sedge has wither'd* and, on three stresses, *no birds sing!* (3–4). Cautions about improvidence abound in this late season:

> *The squirrel's granary is full*
> *and the harvest's done*

So ends a stanza already bearing forensic pressure in *So haggard, and so woe begone*—a shaming rhyme for *harvest's done. So* and *woe* chime in, *So* as a front-line word harkening back to the hailing *O* of the first two stanzas. This is the sound-track for *woe begone,* a story of *woe begun,* then *gone in woe* (*JnD*) to near degree-zero. *So haggard* hints a backstory. *Haggard* means *wild and irreclaimable,* with etiology in etymology: *hag, a wild or intractable person* (usually she) with a *"wild" expression of the eyes* (*JnD, OED*). Glaucus witnesses a *hag-*

gard scene in Circe's bower (*Endymion* 3.500). Porphyro assures Madeline that the storm is one of *haggard seeming* (XXXIX). When the ballad comes to a *Lady* of *wild* eyes (16), *wild wild eyes* (31), we have already been greeted by the symbolic symptomology of *haggard* commerce:

>   *a*
> I see ~~death's~~ lilly on thy brow
>   With anguish moist and fever dew,
>
>   *a*
> and on thy cheeks ~~death's~~ fading rose
> Fast Withereth too -
>   (9–12)

By the book, *lilly* is fatal pallor; *fading rose* is love no more (everyone knows Burns's "My love is like a red, red rose"), wither'd like that sedge. Keats improved his poetry as he wrote it out. Having cast *death's*-sentences, he decided that flowers could say so, and added *Fast* for the emergency (the capital W and indented *Withereth* suggest that this was originally line 12's first word). At the same time, there is a strange over-drive in this scene of reading. The syntax is so surreally condensed that for all the charge to read, it proves hard to read. Line 10 seems to set both *anguish moist* and *fever dew* as parallel noun-adjective detailings of a hallucinated *lilly on* the *brow*. But *anguish* and *fever* may be distinct, rather than appositive, reports: a symbolic *lilly*, *moist* from metaphoric *anguish*, then materially confirmed by dew-beads of fever.[4] If this seems a distinction without much of difference, the blur of seeing and projecting that Keats writes into the syntax is honed toward prediction.

    Without missing a beat, with no punctuation of a second speaker, a story begins, in parallel syntax and metrical symmetry, with *I see a lily on thy brow, I met a Lady in the ~~Wilds~~ Meads* (12–13). Deciding to hold *wild* in reserve, Keats sets a phonic conspiracy of encounter and site, *met*/*Meads*. The Knight's report holds multiple signs for our recognition, so legible as to seem diagnostic: a double-full *Full beautiful* (13) betrayed into the depletions itemized in the opening stanzas; a *manna dew* (26) diseased into *fever dew* (10); *woe-betide* (32, a campy warning in *The Eve of St. Agnes* XXII) confirmed by *woe-begone*; *starv'd lips* in the dream-chorus (41) prefigured in *haggard*—and, not least, *pale* played into repetition (37–38), in line with the remnant spectacle of ailing *palely* (2).

    At the core of the Knight's report is that *Lady*. Her introduction as a surreal *faery* (14) evokes the archaic idiom of *I met*, a portal to dreamland. A slant of delusion throbs in the ambiguities of some keynote syntax for our apprehension, and perhaps, in retrospect, the Knight's too. The temporality of *She look'd at me as she did love* (19) oscillates with a compressed *as if* that prompts a second look at *look'd*. Was this a con? The question also stirs in *And made sweet moan* (20) in kinship with artifice: recall poēma, a *made thing*. For Keats-readers, the lover's report, *I . . . nothing else saw all day long* (21–22), has to ring a bell: Madeline, *sole-thoughted*, with *regardless eyes*. To hear the Knight's report, *And sure in language strange she said / I love thee true –* (27–28), is to hear a too-invested *sure*, strained by uncertainty, haunted by doubt about her *language strange*.

Strange, too, is her menu of *relish sweet, / And honey wild, and manna dew* (24–25): the first two may be natural, *honey wild* even in kinship with *mead*: a *honey-water. JnD*, moreover, lists *mead* just above and with etymological kinship to *Meads: meadows* (wetland), the site of the Knight's encounter with his maid—a wonderful bit of word-conjuring on Keats's part. The third item, however, *manna dew*, is sheer miracle (manna is on Porphyro's table); in a subtle omen, it holds the poem's only sounding of *man*, seduced into *manna*. Keats underlined this word, about wording itself, in *Paradise Lost:* "all was false and hollow; though his tongue / Dropt manna . . ." we hear of Belial's counsel in Hell (2.112–113; *KPL* 1:32). Milton (and Keats, underlining) knew the fatal cooings of Despair in Spenser's *Fairy-Queen* (I.9.XXXI):

> His subtle Tongue, like dropping Honey, melt'th
> Into the Heart, and searcheth every Vein,
> That ere one be aware, by secret Stealth
> His Power is reft, and Weakness doth remain.

Words usurp lifeblood to become a new sinister circulation in the body. Such a fine stealthy rhyme, *ere* to *aware*. Keats has the lover lap it up, with fairy's songs and sighs, and trusting sleep (intimate and infantine), spelled into her mastery.

The recognition-scene comes as in the language of nightmare-revelation: *Ah woe betide!*

> *I saw pale Kings and Princes too*
> *Pale warriors death pale were they all*
> *They cried - La belle dame sans merci*
> *Thee hath in thrall -*

(37–40)

But for all the exclamation, Keats lets us wonder what, exactly, is being reported: an epiphanic name, or the story of this naming? With *pale* played across an entire masculine power-grid, the dream tells what men cry, not what they know. As with *man* in *manna*, Keats spells their plight with figural rhyme: *all* is literally inside *thrall*, the full phrasing *in thrall* (moreover) under-sounding *enthrall*, its etymology in bondage. *JnD* lists examples for *thrall* that Keats would know so intimately as to seem allusions: the moan of a "captive quite forlorn" in Spenser's Sonnet XXIX, "Let her accept me as her faithful *thrall*"; "Fallen" Belial's tremble at the thought of being one of the *thralls* to the Almighty (*PL* 1.149–150). The chorus of thralls in *La Belle Dame—with horrid warning gaping wide* (42)—could well whirl in one of Dante's sad circles of hell.

Another name for this verbal action is "projection," a psychoanalytic that Leon Waldoff calls up to read a dreamer displacing what he most fears in himself onto these alter egos (97). I would put it this way: the act of projection is the origin-story of the headline-name, *La belle dame sans merci.* This is the lore that male culture assembles to blame a disarming she for men's ambivalence about the eros-depleted vocational mandates of their professional missions. The transition from the erotic dream is an awakening to professional hell on earth, in severely alienated, punitive self-division: *And I awoke and found me here* (43). Not the idiomatic *found myself,* Keats places his pronouns in a fully grammatical disjunction. *I* and *me* divide a *here* in both the scene and state of mind, a liminal site (no-man's land) where the temporality of the lover's story (from *I met* to *here*) and the temporality of its telling (from *here* to *I met*) overlap. Keats's last revision was to revise *I wither here* to *I sojourn here* (45), a tarrying in both temporalities that saves *wither* for a return call in the present tense. The final stanza echoes the prequel with a different conjunction, "*Though* the sedge *is wither'd* . . . ," to register a sadly alert, helplessly awakened consciousness, and a final convergence, with oblique realization, with that chord of *no–O–woe–So.*

That's one arrest. Another, beyond this, is the opaque logic of *And this is why.* "The poem is not only uncertain but a poem about uncertainty," is David Perkins's wit (*Quest* 263). Metrically weighted, the declarative *this,* writes Waldoff, "is one of the most overdetermined words in all of Keats's poetry, suddenly bearing the burden of meaning for the entire poem and at the same time frustrating efforts to interpret it" (86). This distancing gesture is not *that,* but *this,* coterminous with its ongoing blight and inertia, and host to everything: cold hillside, the dream's snare, the enthralling seduction, and its very telling from the lilt of *I met a Lady* to the diminishing thuds of the finale, *And no birds sing.*

That strain again. Not a *why,* this is a rueful echo of the initiating questions, a frame as refrain, in arrested repetition. They "cannot tell what ails them; you . . . cannot well tell what to make of their sayings," says Burton's *Anatomy* of melancholy women; "they think themselves bewitched; they are in despair"

(1:302). What of men who think themselves bewitched? Keats's title floats a categorical, critical gendering: *ail thee* is rhyme-answered by *sans merci*. While the Knight's story issues this "answer" (the diagnosis), his story is readable as a veiling effect.[5] Male truancy, in fatal alienation from vocational identity, summons a darkly gendered fable to take the rap. As a story about a story, *And this is why* is conjured by present embarrassment. Signposted for warning, *La belle dame sans merci* is men's forensic with a vengeance.

The old beldame in *The Eve of St. Agnes* "keepeth clos'd a wondrous riddle-book" (XV). *La belle dame sans merci* is a little book of riddles. The latest one is the *Indicator* author, CAVIARE. What's in this name? Performing a masking task, this signature compacts with Hamlet's contempt of good verse wasted on dull ears as "caviare to the general."[6] Hunt's preface models a better reception for Keats's verse: "The union of the imaginative and the real is very striking throughout, particularly in the dream." This is the riddle of "love," he argues: "the kindest looks . . . haunt us with a spell-like power, which makes us shudder to guess at the sufferings of those who can be fascinated by unkind ones" (246). His advocacy is not just for Keats's (now) *wretched wight*; it is for all male love-sufferers, a corporate *us* against *unkind* them. Hunt leverages this into a critique of modern love: "either a grossness or a formality," this because "the modern systems of morals would ostensibly divide women into two classes, those who have no charity, and those who have no restraint," leaving a man with "bad ideas of both." Hunt's bigger story is the travesty of commerce: "Instead of the worship of Love, we have the worship of Mammon . . . the sufferings from the worship of Love exalt and humanize us, and those from the worship of Mammon debase and brutalize" (246–247). *La Belle Dame sans Mercy* is cast on the forge of Mammon, *mercy* and *merchant* wrung from the same root. If, three months on, Keats will be advising Shelley that "an <u>artist</u> must serve Mammon" (*K* 426), this *wretched wight* is no aesthetic hero, just a sucker hailed in pity and derision.

Common to both versions of the ballad is an absence of punctuation at stanza 4 to mark a new voice at *I met a Lady*. The usual readings mark out two voices: the questioner and the respondent. Without distinguishing punctuation, however, the entire ballad is readable as voiced by the Knight (no longer at-arms) questioning himself in an alienated third-person address, then sighing out the benighted backstory that enlists all men for confirmation. Or, it might be entirely the questioner's voice, loitering on the withering hillside, greeting a Knight in knowing fraternal solidarity, then telling his own story to him: *I met a lady . . . this is why I* sojourn here (the Knight ever silent).[7] The rhyming slide of *I / thy* (9) may figure mirrored experience. Two voices or one? If one, whose? This is a poetics of—and for—radical negative capability. Keats leaves everything darkly, brilliantly, double-bound: fairy's child / merciless enchanter; sweet meat / fatal meeting; enchantment / enthrallment; awakening / addiction; vocation / truancy.

And in the framing around all this: question and answer / answer for questioning. Keats has discovered in a form more compressed than ever a deep grammar for what he wanted to do with lyric.

[letter, April 1819; MsK 1.53.253–255; *K* 247–249]

[1] Jack Stillinger concedes that his basis in *P,* Brown's copy of the letter-text without Keats's postscript, is "purely arbitrary" (*P* 644). Jerome McGann took this concession as grounds to argue for the priority of the text Keats actually published in *The Indicator.*

[2] *Love-Melancholy* ("Knights Tale," Burton's antique-font). Miriam Allott notes Keats's underlining (501n) and details a copia of literary analogues throughout the ballad (500–506).

[3] *Works* (1803) 2:362. This glossary lists GLOMMED: *clouded, dejected.* FORWYND: *dry, sapless.* Keats makes *gloam* the atmosphere of the Knight's nightmare (41), which the *Indicator* text normalizes to *gloom.*

[4] Andrew Bennett nicely lingers over the strange diagnosis in this stanza (120).

[5] Peter Brooks explains "double logic": "prior events, causes, are so only retrospectively, in a reading back from the end"; the "need to plot meanings" produces "narrative" (29–30).

[6] *Hamlet,* 2.2. Keats may have read a defense of *Endymion* in the *Chester Guardian* that wielded Hamlet's phrase of contempt against the *Quarterly's* cut-up (Hewlett 186).

[7] For the effect of the Knight's third-person self-reading and then rehearsal, see my *Questioning Presence,* 296–300, and *Reading John Keats,* 83–86. Bennet reads the entire poem as the first questioner's monologue: concerned notice, then a sympathetic recounting of the questioner's own misadventure (121).

Garlands of their Own

Spring–Summer 1819

"Why did I laugh to-night?"

*I am ever affraid that your anxiety for me will lead you to fear for the
violence of my temperament continually smothered down: for that reason I
did not intend to have sent you the following sonnet - but look over the two
last pages and ask yourselves whether I have not that in me which will well
bear the buffets of the world. It will be the best comment on my sonnet; it will
show you that it was written with no Agony but that of ignorance; with no
thirst of any thing but Knowledge when pushed to the point though the first
steps to it were through my human passions - they went away, and I wrote
with my Mind - and perhaps I must confess a little bit of my heart -*

> P   *Why did I laugh tonight? No voice will tell:*
>   *No God no Deamon of severe response*
> *Deigns to reply from heaven or from Hell —*
>   *Then to my human heart I turn at once —*
> *Heart! thou and I are here sad and alone;*
>   *Say, wherefore did I laugh? O mortal pain!*
> *O Darkness! Darkness! ever must I moan*
>   *To question Heaven and Hell and Heart in vain!*
> *Why did I laugh? I know this being's lease*
>   *My fancy to its utmost blisses spreads:*
> *Yet could I on this very midnight cease*
>   *and the world's gaudy ensigns see in shreds.*
> *Verse, fame and Beauty are intense indeed*
>   *But Death intenser – Deaths is Life's high mead."*

*I went to ~~bead~~ bed, and enjoyed an uninterrupted Sleep - Sane I went to bed
and sane I ~~rose~~ arose.*

Keats knows George and Georgiana's concern about his mood-swings. As these
newlyweds were readying to leave England, he didn't tell them how deep he
had plunged. *I cannot write . . . my hand feels like lead,* he did tell Bailey in late
May 1818; *I am troubling you with Moods of my own Mind,* again slanting into
the Wordsworthian genre riffed in *Dear Reynolds*. He goes Wordsworth one
better: *or rather body – for Mind there is none. I am in that temper that if were
under Water I would scarcely Kick to come to the top.* Hitting bottom, Keats
kicks himself in the next sentence: *I know very well 't is all nonsense* (MsK
1.28.100).

There is always complex sense in Keats's wordings, including laughter. "A laughing school-boy, without grief or care" is a life-stage that the poet of *Sleep and Poetry* knows will shear off the suffix "-out." Adult laughter comes on such currents. "But let me laugh awhile, I've mickle time to grieve," sighs castle crone Angela at Porphyro's antics in *The Eve of St. Agnes* (XIV). Keats wrote his sonnet-report about night-laughing on 19 March 1819, having just commented

> *While we are laughing the seed of some trouble is put into the wide arable land*
> *of events - while we are laughing it sprouts i[t] grows and suddenly bears a*
> *poison fruit which we must pluck —*   (MsK 1.53.231)

This is the ecology for *Ode to Melancholy,* soon to come. The sonnet compresses *while* into a simultaneity of laughter and darkness. Such high-reckoning indulges some high-camp stylizing, a defense against being laughed at. *I intend to use more finesse with the Public,* Keats will assure Woodhouse after a round of reviewer-ridiculing. Pledging to write *fine things which cannot be laugh'd at in any way,* he tests himself as a self-reviewer (22 September 1819). One self-cartoon, just the page before, is a neologism of self-negation, *unpoeted I write.*[1]

Self-review can split Keats in two, the twin close to the bone: *A Man in love I do think cuts the sorryest figure in the world – Even when I know a poor fool to be really in pain about it, I could burst out laughing in his face – His pathetic visage becomes irrisistable,* he had just written to George and Georgiana about his dear friend Haslam, a new-born "Lover" (17 September 1819; *L* 2:187–188), risible in his very visage, *rediculous* in his full-flush adoring. Only one who knows himself such a *figure* (Keats in love with Fanny Brawne) could laugh this way, the spectator intimate with the spectacle, lover or poet.[2] Writing in a blue mood to Haydon on 8 March 1819, Keats was ready to swear off the minor *toil of sonneteering* and all affectations of poetic self-capitalizing: *I will not spoil my love of gloom by writing an ode to darkness* (*L* 2:43). Yet here is the gloom-lover reflexively rhyming from *toil* to *spoil.*

What he could write by 19 March is the sonnet "Why did I laugh?" in stringent parody, in no toil at all, with big stakes for laughs: *God, Deamon, Heaven and Hell, bliss* and *pain, Life and Death.* Its sure-footed Shakespearean pattern is a masterpiece of self-possessed, gothic laughter, epic matter in short form. Grand terms squeeze into a word-list, intensity is camp, inspiration manic, horror risible. "Why did I laugh?" is not a self-interrogatory; it is rhetorical stand-up, a prompt and refrain for performance, a moment's monument in demystified amusement at Death's dominion. This is ultimately a poetics of sanity. After assigning all cares to the spoils of Death, Keats's postscript adds a last slant-rhyme for *Life's high mead: I went to ~~bead~~ bed.*

Here is no religion of laughter that, Troilus-like, surrenders to fate. Keats's campy *O Darkness! darkness! ever must I moan!* is literacy felt on the pulses, with a self-poeted immune system. The exclamations and staccato punctuation index a little heart of darkness: questions moaned *in vain* know the Latin "vanus": empty. In his late winter mood, Keats tests a soft sonnet-stop, *on this very midnight cease.* The next month, he will write *Ode to a Nightingale,* half-wishing to *cease upon the midnight with no pain* (stanza 6). The sonnet's couplet goes all in:

> Verse, fame and Beauty are intense indeed
> But Death intenser – Deaths is Life's high mead.

Deaths is may be oversupply for "Death is Life's high mead." This is how Still-inger emends it, all lower-case (*P* 323n). Maybe. Or maybe Keats was on the way to the intensest of plurals (awaiting a plural verb): a consciousness of Death as *Deaths,* serial sensations and events spelling a Life-sentence on mortal terms. The grammatical foldbacks are compressed sensations at this zero-degree on the intensity thermometer, where full blown vertigo awaits. That is a circle of sad hell. Or maybe just venting, to produce a new form of lullaby.

[19 March 1819, end of a long letter to George and Georgiana Keats; MsK 1.53.234–235]

---

[1] MsK 1.64.315, 314. Keats puts quotations around the last phrase, implying a citation, or knowing riff. That both *OED* and Literature Online (LION) have no listing confirms Keats's patent on *unpoeted.*

[2] I am indebted to Christopher Ricks's attention to this lexical play (*Embarrassment* 59).

A dream, after reading Dante's Episode of Paolo and Francesca

The fifth canto of Dante pleases me more and
more - it is that one in which he meets with
Paulo and Franchesca - I had passed many
days in rather a low state of mind, and in the
midst of them I dreamt of being in that region
of Hell. The dream was one of the most delight-
ful enjoyments I ever had in my life - I floated
about the whirling atmosphere as it is described
with a beautiful figure to whose lips mine
were joined at it seem'd for an age - and in
the midst of all this cold and darkness I was
warm - even flowery tree tops sprung up
and we rested on them sometimes with the
lightness of a cloud till the wind blew us
away again-- I tried a Sonnet upon it—
there are fourteen lines but nothing of what
I felt in it- O that I could dream it every
night

as Hermes once took to his feathers light
When lulled Argus, baffled, swoon'd and slept
So on a delphic reed my idle spright
So play'd, so charm'd so conquer'd, so bereft
The dragon world of all its hundred eyes
And seeing it asleep so fled away
Not to pure Ida with its snowclad cold skies,
Nor unto Tempe where Jove grieved that day,
But to that second circle of sad hell,
Where in the gust, the whirlwind and the flaw   [10]
Of Rain and hailstones lovers need not tell
Their sorrows - Pale were the sweet lips I saw ≈

*≈ Pale were the lips I kiss'd and fair the form
I floated with about that melancholy storm—[1]*

I take my title from the poem published in *The Indicator.* Keats's letter-draft
(Figure 12) has none, just a prologue, transcribed here with his line-endings. The
letter-text (Figure 12, next page) reads like a prose-poetry warm-up. The last
single-word prose-line, *night,* hovers over the sonnet to gather a nonce-rhyme
at "feathers *light.*" Keats then unfurls an impressive one-sentence sonnet, a

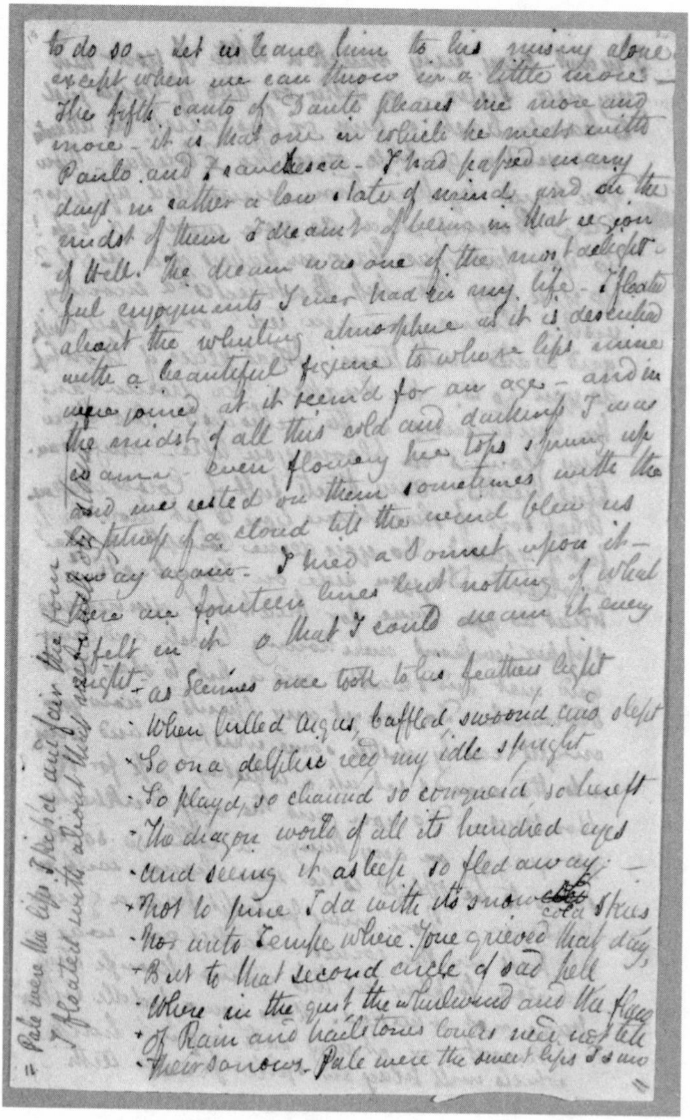

Figure 12: Keats's letter-text prologue and sonnet on his dream of Dante's Paolo and Francesca in Hell (April 1819). Lacking sufficient space on the page, he wrote the last two lines up the left margin. MS Keats 1.53. Courtesy of Houghton Library, Harvard University.

rehearsal of reading so absorbing that he dreams and redreams it into poetry. He wrote this the same week as *La belle dame*.

La belle dame vanished (or never was). Dante's lovers are for ever in each other's sights, in tormented separation. Keats and his "Frances" (Fanny Brawne) had been reading Canto V of Cary's *Hell* (*Inferno*), where Francesca tells Dante of her and Paolo reading of Launcelot and Guinevere (in *Lancelot of the Lake*) with throbbing sympathy for their forbidden love (in a political détente, she was married to Paolo's brother, who, on a really bad idea, allowed Paolo to be her tutor). In a famous swoon over the adulterous lovers, "that day / We read no more," she says (134–135; Cary, p. 18). Erotic biblio-genetics. On the front fly-leaf of *Hell*, Fanny Brawne had copied Keats's first version of "Bright star." Keats began writing the dream-sonnet across it at right angles, then, sensing an impending cross-hatch mess, wrote it clean at the back of the volume.[2] Thus set, the two sonnets literally bookend this shared *Hell*, inscribing extremes of infernal separation and blissful union.

Keats becomes what he reads. The dream-sonnet's opening on *As* anchors a twinship of artful dragon-slayer Hermes (tagged for a call-back in *Lamia*) and the poet who *bereft / The dragon world of all its hundred eyes*. In Ovid's fable, Hera has sent hundred-eyed Argus (Argus Panoptes, hence "panopticon") to guard nymph Io (whom Zeus disguised as a heifer) from her husband's amorous access. Zeus dispatches Hermes to lull and slay this dragon: quite a challenge. D. G. Rossetti, who thought this sonnet one of Keats's two "finest," objected only to *bereft* as a "singular defect of a misrhyme" for *slept*, thinking it "all the more curious when we consider the sort of echo it gives of a line in *Endymion:—So sad, so melancholy, so bereft*."[3] Keats wanted heroic action, *bereft / The dragon world*, for the sonnet's adventure into dreamland. He underlined Milton's oppositional panopticon of severely "watchful cherubim" over the gates of Eden as Adam and Eve are evicted, with an allusion to the Hermes venture (*KPL* II:149):

> Spangled with eyes more numerous than those
> Of Argus, and more wakeful than to drowse,
> Charm'd with Arcadian pipe, the pastoral reed
> Of Hermes, or his opiate rod.   (11.130–133)

Keats's analogy to Hermes's charm is set for antithesis. The reader's dreamer goes to reading-hell, *in for—and filling* (camelion-wise) Paolo's place in his *circle of sad hell* (9).

Having refused to damn Dante's adulterers in *The Story of Rimini* (1816), and taking a lot of heat for making their passion into a tragic romance, Hunt published Keats's sympathetic sonnet in *The Indicator*, again pointedly signed CAVIARE.[4] Tuned to Regency culture-wars as much as to Renaissance political machinations, Keats's dream-report cannot dream the world away. For his letter-text's *whirlwind* (10), the word he uses here is *world-wind*. The letter-text word echoes the *whirling atmosphere* in the prose prologue. *The Indicator's world-wind* is tuned to *whirl'd* in Cary's *Hell*:

> The stormy blast of hell
> With restless fury drives the spirits on
> Whirl'd round and dash'd amain with sore annoy. (V.32–34)

Keats images a "dragon *world*" of surveillance (5). In his evocative coinage *world-wind*, he spells the hell of Dante's lovers, not there by sin but in existential sympathy.[5] Keats's prose prologue writes the dream out of hell into flowery tree tops. The sonnet rolls to *sad hell* and its eternal echo chamber of *hail, tell, Pale, Pale,* the last evoking *Paulo*. There is no lullaby in the lull of *fair the form / I floated with*. Keats gives the sonic stream a hexameter to end in *melancholy storm*.[6] How remote, in sense and rhyme, from the dream-report's *I was warm*. And how eerie, in the metric trace of a Spenserian stanza, is the revenance of Madeline and Porphyro, *fled away into the storm*.

Reading Hazlitt's great essay on *King Lear*, Keats wrote in the margins and underscored his own annotated praise of this severest play: the greatest strength of genius is shewn in describing the strongest passions. He imagines that Shakespeare must have drawn from his own world-winds, to *paint from memory of gone selfstorms*—another brilliant Keats-coinage from the forge of his reading (*Characters* 177; sq. 205). Such selfstorms whirl even around what, for Keats, might weather them: fame.

[MsK 1.53.247, journal letter, 16 April 1819]

---

[1] The script-marks at the end of line 12 and the start of 13 are Keats's. See Figure 12.

[2] For the text-situations, see *P,* 635–636. For the medium of Cary's *Hell,* see Gittings, *John Keats,* 438.

[3] 10 February 1880, to H. B. Forman (Rossetti 6–7; see *Endymion* 2.686–687).

[4] 28 June 1820 (p. 304), a publication Keats read in health-hell. On the 22nd, he had started vomiting blood. The bout went on for days, necessitating the end of his living independently (*L* 2:300).

[5] *OED* does not list *world-wind,* a confection Jerome McGann appreciates for capturing the plight of lovers who "suffer not in the misery of their sinful love, but in the cruel assaults of an indifferent and hostile world": "not in a 'whirlwind' but in a 'world-wind'" (1005). McGann's essay brought the *Indicator* text back from neglect to fresh attention.

[6] The letter-text inscribes this couplet as a visual volta. Reaching the page's bottom (sq. 247), Keats turned it sideways and wrote the couplet vertically up the margin to the left of lines 1–12, then "crossed" the prose prelude (with curious force) at *the midst of all this cold and darkness I was* (the line's end), with *warm* starting the next line, intersected by the sonnet's last word, *storm.* For a canny reading of this scriptive circling, see Jeffrey Robinson, *Reception and Poetics,* 9–10.

On Fame and *Another on Fame*

I have just written one on Fame which Brown is transcribing . . . I must employ
myself perhaps in a sonnet on the same subject -

On Fame

<u>You cannot eat your Cake and have it too</u>

Proverb.

How ᴸ^{feverd} is that Man ~~misled~~ who cannot look
   Upon his mortal days with temperate blood
Who vexes all the leaves of his Life's book
    And robs his fair name of its maidenhood   [4]
It is as if the rose should pluck herself
   Or the ripe plumb finger its ᴸ^{misty} bloom
As if a clear Lake meddling with itself
    Should ~~fill~~ cloud its pureness with a muddy gloom
But the rose leaves herself upon the Briar
   For winds to kiss and grateful Bees to ~~taste~~ feed
And the ripe plumb ~~still will~~ still wears its dim attire
    The undisturbed Lake has crystal space
                 teasing the world for grace
Why then should Man ~~his own bright name deface~~   [13]
~~And spoil burn our pleasure in his selfish fire.~~
Spoil his salvation by a fierce miscreed

Another on Fame

Fame like a wayward girl will still be coy
   To those who woo her with too slavish knees
   But makes surrender to some thoughtless boy
And dotes the more upon a heart at ease
She is a Gipsey will not speak to those
   Who have not learnt to be content without her
A Jilt whose ear was never whisper'd close
   Who think they scandal her who talk about her
A very Gipsey is she Nilus born,
Sister in law to jealous Potiphar:
Ye lovesick Bards, repay her scorn for scorn -
Ye lovelorn Artists madmen that ye are,
Make your best bow to her and bid adieu
Then if she likes it she will follow you.

"Do you get Fame," Reynolds urged Keats in October 1818 (*L* 1:377). Leaguing with ever fired-up Haydon, Keats could hope that fame would crown their endeavors. A letter to him that harkens to, despairs of, and despises the "Trumpet of Fame" (*L* 1:140–141) opens with the opening lines of *Love's Labor's Lost*, which Keats vigorously underlined in his copy (*DW* 2, sq. 612), and now summons as an anthem for him and Haydon:

> Let Fame, which all hunt after in their Lives,
> Live register'd upon our brazen tombs,
> And so grace us in the disgrace of death:
> When spite of cormorant devouring time
> The endeavour of this present breath may buy
> That Honour which shall bate this Scythe's keen edge
> And make us heirs of all eternity.

So the king issues the code of honor to men determined not to let love corrupt this hunt.

Keats's sonnets conflate such distinction, making Fame the ultimate, ungettable love-object. The cautionary, or counter-, primer (which everyone knew) is Milton's famously conflicted meditation in *Lycidas* (1645):

> *Fame* is the spur that the clear spirit doth raise
> (That last infirmity of Noble mind)
> To scorn delights, and live laborious dayes.   (70–72)

In the frame of these lines, *Fame* is a greeting to the heroic spirit; in the parentheses, it is an unheroic pathology. And in the lore of men's grievances, Fame (like Fortune) is a fickle woman. The next lines growl that "the fair Guerdon when we hope to find, / And think to burst out into sudden blaze," is ruined by the shears of another she, "blind Fury" (73–76). *Tell her to procure some fatal Scissars and cut the thread of Life of all to be disappointed Poets,* Keats jests to Hunt about Mary Shelley (soon the famous "Author of *Frankenstein*"), just weeks after the debut of his *Poems* (*L* 1:140). Milton trusts to vindication by he-divinity: Phoebus / Apollo assures fame in the grant of the "perfet witnes of all judging *Jove*" (82). Time will tell.

Keats thirsted for fame with the best of them—and with no little irony. Toward the end of *Sleep and Poetry,* its poet surveys Hunt's library with a sigh:

> Round about were hung
> The glorious features of the bards who sung

In other ages—cold and sacred busts
Smiled at each other. Happy he who trusts
To clear Futurity his darling fame! (*1817*, p. 118)

Cold comfort in these famed bards reduced to a generic pantheon of interior
decor, self-fingering, smiling plumishly at each other, unaware of their fame
in the market of wax-stamp "heads of great Men such as Shakspeare, Milton
&c" (*L* 2:46). This satire of *darling fame* could well rival Byron's, two years on
(1819):

What is the end of fame? 'tis but to fill
    A certain portion of uncertain paper:
Some liken it to climbing up a hill,
    Whose summit, like all hills, is lost in vapour;
For this men write speak, preach, and heroes kill,
    And bards burn what they call their "midnight taper,"
To have, when the original is dust,
A name, a wretched picture, and worse bust.

(*Don Juan* I.CCXVIII, p. 112)

The trustee of Keats's inheritance, Richard Abbey, enjoyed needling him with
this stanza (*L* 2:192n9).

Milton's addiction is telling. Keats's irony is keen, but sufficiently unstable
that it has to be refueled. The overall reception of his first two volumes had
been inauspicious. These sonnets are disciplinary exercises, copied in sequence,
in his April 1819 letter to George and Georgiana. Deeming *On Fame* written
while Brown copied *Another on Fame*, Milnes put *Another* first (2:299–300); so
do Stillinger (*P* 366–367) and Allott (512–514). Yet the letter-sequence tells a
story, too. Read it both ways: Keats presenting a prescription and relapse (per-
haps the sequence of composition); Keats giving a wry diagnosis with a pre-
scription (the letter-sequence). I offer the latter, provisionally. Either way de-
livers a Keats-relay, in his anticipation of a third attempt on the marketplace
of fame.

On Fame casts a *fever'd . . . Man* as Keatsian alter ego, a self-form that he
sets out, in a tortured Shakespearean sonnet, as a case-study in self-pollution.
Keats turns the gender tables (a bit) by calling a Man's *fair name* a *maidenhood*
unspoiled by fame-questing. Two tidy diagnostic quatrains avert the rhyme-
allure of *Fame* for this midline *fair name* (4). Then the form goes haywire (*efe
ggf*), burying the rhyme-couplet for a two-line sentence, *Why then . . .* (13),

which, with no terminal punctuation, hangs between an outraged exclamation and an aggravated question about self-spoiling. Keats summons an alternative model from nature, a self free of fame-fever and vexing the leaves of Life's book into a demented biographia literaria and a *fierce miscreed*. This last noun, only here in Keats's poetry, is not in *JnD;* "obsolete" says *OED,* giving Keats the invention. The *s*-hiss of *fierce* sounds *creed* into *screed,* Keats's present rhetoric. He will dose the religion of Fame with a secularized *salvation* of self-possession, self-respect. Health is how *the rose leaves herself.* Not the leaves of book-bidding, but flourishing self-distributed, coming as naturally as leaves to a tree. Left to the breezes, communication is accomplished by chance and relaxation.

Diagnosis is one thing; cure another. Writing sober prescription, Keats cannot help but voice the ailments. This double-bind warps his underscored motto, Keats switching the familiar form of fetishizing ("you cannot have your cake and eat it, too") to emphasize the hunger: "you cannot eat . . ." *I vow that I have been down in the Mouth lately,* he had written two years before, in rhyming mood (*vow–down–Mouth*) as he was working on *Endymion.* He bucked up then at the thought of another mouth: *What a thing to be in the mouth of Fame,* he sighed to Hunt in a letter written the same day as the one to Haydon, 10 May 1817 (*K* 50). This trope is overloaded: Fame's mouth may chew up as well as trumpet praise. The motto of the 1819 sonnet pretty much refuses orality, either in appetite or cloying satisfaction.

Sonia Hofkosh tells a story about Byron (celebrity and aristocrat, no less) that holds a pattern for Keats. If the marketplace defeats "the fantasy of autonomous creativity," a he-writer may retaliate by casting a degraded she-arbiter. By August 1819, Keats will be sighing in this very grammar to his publisher of his disdain of one form of fame, *popular writer:*

> *I equally dislike the favour of the public with the love of a woman – they are both a cloying treacle to the wings of independence . . . I have of late been indulging my spleen by composing a preface <u>at</u> them: after all resolving never to write a preface at all* (MsK 1.60.294)

The psychic imaginary of readership, "them," is as low in "favour" as a woman's nod. *Another on Fame* switches the erotics from sick self-stimulation to a disdain of worthless courtship.

Reynolds had written in this key to refute the *Quarterly*'s trashing of *Endymion:* "There is not one poet of the present day, that enjoys any popularity that will live; each writes for his booksellers and the ladies of fashion." Yet for all this, "Poetry is the coyest creature that ever was wooed by man: she has something of the coquet in her; for she flirts with many, and seldom loves one" (*Examiner* 648–649). And so Keats issues *Another on Fame*. Its first quatrain stages a farce of investing in a fickle lass, *wayward, coy*, perversely more responsive to indifference than to suits of woe: to woo is pathetic; to scorn reaps success. Keats nicely letters *heart at ease* to slide-spell what is refused: *a tease* to the *heart* and the *art* of wooing. The second quatrain turns from the Fame-simile (*like a wayward girl*) to a defamed character: Gipsey. No mere tarty miss, this is a professional (con) artist of refusal, attracting Keats's sole uses of *jilt* and *scandal* (8)—this last, moreover, no noun but a transitive verb for the futility of even disparaging Fame.[1]

Keats's sonnet is counter-aggression: although he knows the immunity of Fame to a scandal take-down, he spouts his best shot *Gipsey* twice. In phonic folk etymology, gipsies were thought to be Egyptian (*Nilus borne*). Keats summons one Egyptian from Genesis 39, Potiphar, to make his case. Smitten with her husband's slave David (future king of Israel) and cross at his refusals of her advances, she frames him for attempted rape, sending him to prison. *Gipsey*, jealous, *Jilt:* no true bard should hazard the games of Fame or the spins of the book-market. Keats works his turn through the paces of a Shakespearean sonnet, aiming at the couplet's snap, the closing move: to bid *adieu* will release *you* (the very sound in *ieu*) from the slavery of abjection, madness, lovesickness, into the cure of self-mastery.

Another liberation comes in Keats's thinking about, and gendering, sonnetforming itself. Here, the poet is master of a female-figured challenge.

[30 April 1819; MsK 1.53.265–266 (*K* 252–253)]

---

[1] *OED* tags this verb rare, obsolete after 1700, last used in a poem that Keats knew, Dryden's *The Flower & Leaf:* "ill Tongues that scandal Innocence" (*Fables, Ancient and Modern* [1774], 232).

Incipit Altera Sonneta ("If by dull rhymes our english must be chaind")

Incipit Altera Sonneta

—

I have been endeavouring to discover a better Sonnet Stanza than we have.
The legitimate does not suit the language over-well from the pouncing
rhymes - the other kind appears too elegiac—and the couplet at the end of it
has seldom a pleasing effect - I do not pretend to have succeeded - it will
explain itself—

If by dull rhymes our english must be chaind
And, like Andromeda, the Sonnet sweet
Fetterd in spite of pained Loveliness . .
Let us find out, if we must be constrain'd,   4
Sandals more interwoven and complete
To fit the naked foot of Poesy -   6
Let us inspect the Lyre, and weigh the stress
Of every chord, and see what may be gain'd
By ear industrious, and attention meet.   9
Misers of sound and syllable, no less
Than Midas of his coinage, let us be   11
Jealous of dead leaves in the bay wreath crown;   12
So, if we may not let the muse be free,
She will be bound with Garlands of her own.

Here endeth the other Sonnet —

By now, supremely skilled in sonnet-forming, its traditions, its resources, its pleasurable workouts, Keats was ready to review and reconceive the whole business. Having copied several sonnets in his 1819 winter-spring letter to George and Georgiana, he set a headline for this last one, *Incipit Altera Sonneta,* with a Latin jest.[1] (See Figure 13, next page.) It means *Here begins another sonnet,* with a twist on *altera:* not only the next one but also *an other* way of doing it.[2] While every sonnet is implicitly about the form, there is a notable subgenre of "sonnets about sonnets." Not written for publication, this "other" sonnet is Keats's communication to his circle, in the voice of a public-minded *we* issuing a manifesto for a reform movement already afoot in his working.

Wordsworth published his brief for sonnets with "Nun's fret not at their convent's narrow room" (that *Prefatory Sonnet* to the unit of his 1807 *Poems*).

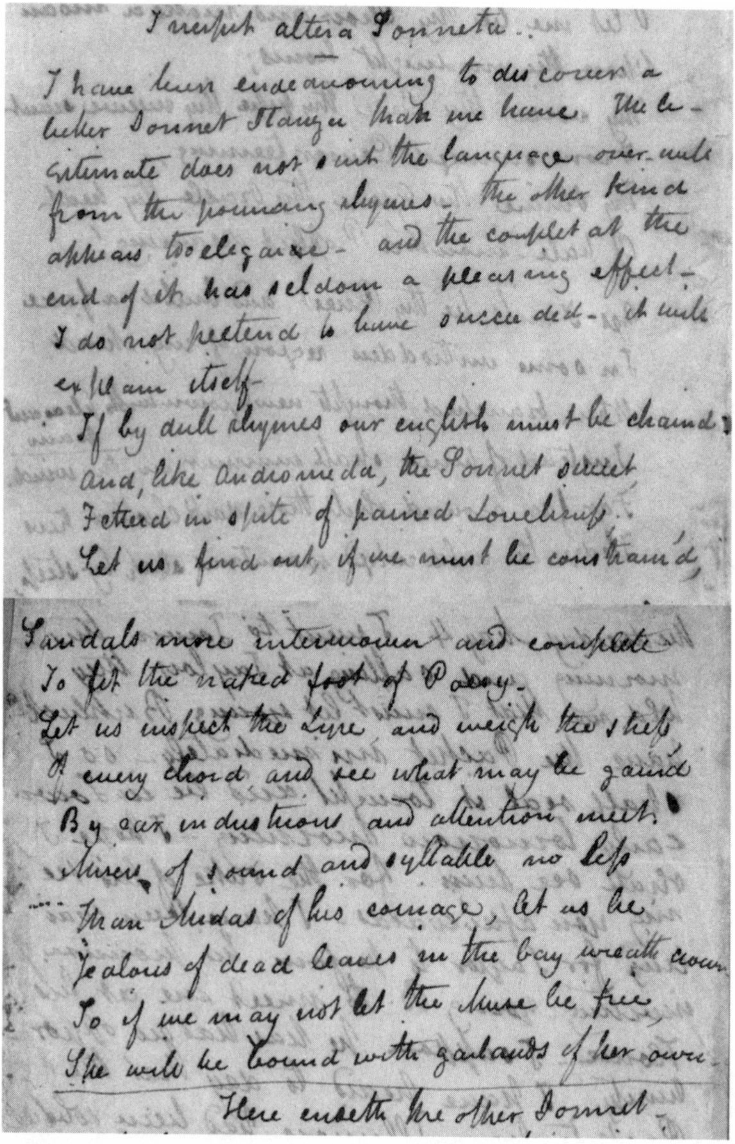

Incipit altera Sonneta.

I have been endeavouring to discover a
better Sonnet Stanza than we have. The le-
gitimate does not suit the language over-well
from the pouncing rhymes — the other kind
appears too elegant — and the couplet at the
end of it has seldom a pleasing effect —
I do not pretend to have succeeded — it will
explain itself

If by dull rhymes our english must be chaind,
And, like Andromeda, the Sonnet sweet
Fetterd in spite of pained Loveliness;
Let us find out, if we must be constraind,
Sandals more interwoven and complete
To fit the naked foot of Poesy.
Let us inspect the Lyre and weigh the stress
Of every chord and see what may be gaind
By ear industrious and attention meet;
Misers of sound and syllable no less
Than Midas of his coinage, let us be
Jealous of dead leaves in the bay wreath crown;
So if we may not let the Muse be free,
She will be bound with garlands of her own.

Here endeth the other Sonnet —

Figure 13: "Incipit Altera Sonneta," assembled from two pages, written in late April to early May 1819, of a long letter from Keats to his brother and sister-in-law, George and Georgiana. This meta-sonnet is also known by its first line, "If by dull rhymes . . ." MS Keats 1.53. Courtesy of Houghton Library, Harvard University.

"Though I have written so many, I have scarcely made up my own mind upon the subject," he said in 1833 to Alexander Dyce, who was assembling *Specimens of English Sonnets.*[3] He did appreciate Shakespeare's pacing: "the Sonnet . . . ought have a beginning, a middle, and an end . . . like the three propositions of a syllogism." But he didn't like fixed "architecture"; even the "Italian model" has too "strict" a "division of the sense into two parts." So he also appreciated how Milton's "sense . . . overflows" from octave to sestet, not "merely to gratify the ear by variety and freedom of sound, but also to aid in giving that pervading sense of intense Unity," like "an orbicular body,—a sphere—or a dew-drop" (*Later Years* 2:604–605). The mimetic echoings of *aid/pervading* and *sense of intense* are nice supplements. Even if the orb is a narrow room, one need not fret in mood or music.

The "legitimate" means the Italian model, with a tightly rhymed octave, *abbaabba,* that Keats finds irritating. The "other kind" is "our english." While its quatrains are looser (*abab, cdcd, efef*) and more various, it is still too formulaic.[4] And the closing couplet (*gg*) is another unpleasant pounce. Keats has no quarrel with meter or rhyme, just the mechanized mandates. He's no free-verser. "What's the good of rhythm unless it is on something that trips it—that it ruffles? . . . it's got to ruffle the meter." This is Robert Frost, ruffling the meter of this very sentence with the stress of *trips it.* Frost is just as loyal to rhyme: "I'd as soon write free verse as play tennis with the net down. I want something there—the other thing—something to hold and something for me to put a strain on; and I'd be lost in the air with just cutting loose."[5] Keats's strain is to test new schemes on a leveraged *If.* The fun of reading this sonnet is tracking the fabulous artistry of three sentences of interwoven rhymes. Try marking this out and you'll see the rhymes wreathing through the punctuated pauses of syntax: *abc* ellipsis / *abd* dash / *cab* period / *cde* semicolon / *de* period. If you mark the meter you'll be scoring its feet along the rhythms of trochees, spondees, and elided stresses. Only the last two lines issue iambic pentameter without torture.

This unchained melody is footed by the trochee-percussions at the front of lines 3 and 4, *Fettered/Let us,* and the infinitive *To fit* (6). *Fettered* is set for a new fitting (fit) more apt (fit) to Keatsian poetics—or meta-poetics: *To fit the naked foot of Poesy.* Energized by gendering this adventure, Keats masters his maid: *naked* means unshod with rhyme, with a bit of boyish glee; *foot* puns on the steps of meter; *fit* is also an old term for poetry, *fytte.* Keats's wordplay stages his argument. As soon as the first rhyme, *chaind/constrain'd,* he is turning his puns to make his points. The original meaning of "fetters" is "chains on feet." Setting out two past participles figuratively and formally fit (with a link to *pained*) for a Petrarchan quatrain, Keats refuses this potential and instead re-charges his inaugural *If* at line 4, to propel the syntax all the way to the worded genre, *Poesy* (6). *Poesy*, aptly, is the poem's softest rhyme—arguably no rhyme at all: asymmetrical, atonal, casting off the iambic (*iamb:* literally, *to put forth*) scheme. Both fit and refit, then.

Well met is the call for *attention meet* (9), the sense of *meet* as "due" pun-ning meter into the meetings. Keats's formative actions dislodge prescription, threading his anchor-rhetoric *If* into a proposal, *Let us,* as both a call and a subject for demonstration. *Let us* gathers its own sound-chord, repeating in 7 and 11, evoked at 13's *let,* with phonic alliances on the roster, from *stress, no less, jealous.* Keats's chords are no cords. And with such tact! A sonnet about rhyming with ear industrious might have taken a cue from *bound* (rhyme's very principle) to scheme with *sound* (rhyme itself), but Keats makes a display of positioning then shunning the bait. While he sets *free* to rhyme with *be* (11), it is with no-table freedom: swept into enjambment, *be* vibrates across line 13, from *we* to *be free.*

Midas, that miserly king of Ovid's *Metamorphoses,* got his wish for a golden touch—only to realize that it dooms him to starvation. "How Keats restamps his borrowed coin!"[6] Let poets be canny misers of their resources, he argues. Even as the final lines mime a Shakespearean couplet, no rhyme pounces. Keats's *crown-own* is not just atonal but a graphic reverb on this effect: (garlands of) "her *own*" takes four letters from *crown,* but refuses the reign of its sound. If Poets crave *the bay wreath crown* (bay-laurel, laureate badge), Keats elides the word "laurel" because it indexes more than he wants from *Metamorphoses,* where, in another chapter, the nymph Daphne begs the gods to help her es-cape rapacious Apollo, god of poetry. They transform her into a laurel tree. Not to be undone, Apollo strips its leaves for his attribute. Keats negotiates the wreathing.

Keats's master-trope for tyranny is fettered Andromeda, the sonnet's first im-port from *Metamorphosis.* The cue of the name ("men's ruler") has led to a re-venge against her beauty. She gets chained to a rock for sea-monster ravaging. Her liberator is the alpha-male of poetic potency: Perseus on his winged steed Pegasus, emblem of soaring imagination. Perseus earned his spurs as the de-capitator of Medusa, the Gorgon whose gaze turns men to stone. Taking her head as a trophy, he assumed its power, while Pegasus rose from her corpse. Keats takes all this gendering on board in the spare, compacted metonymy of "Andromeda," and puts his own male poetic power to the rescue of a too tightly bound feminine form. Fetter-free, the she-sonnet is rebound, or rewoven (you decide) with Keats's garlands of poetic form. No coincidence that "garland" is a term for a collection of poetry (*OED* 4). Even the *english* shrub *andromeda* might contribute to the garlands.

Sonnet-writing once again, Keats is refining resources for a last great burst of genius. By spring 1819, he had written about sixty sonnets, and would write only a few more thereafter. He didn't put any in *1820*. Even so, sonnet-training served his brilliant innovations with the ode—*the* Keatsian innovation—in a career that was hitting a radiant, consequential, pace. The irregular *Ode to Psyche* shapes a sonnet-stanza to bridge the poetry from "too late antique vows" to modern prospects. The stanzas of *Ode to a Nightingale, Ode on a Grecian Urn,* and *To Autumn* join Shakespearean quatrains (*abab*) to Petrarchan sestets (*cde cde*), with sonnet-like voltas.[7] Intimate with this adventure is Keats's word-work, weighing the stress of every chord, no ear more industrious, no attention more meet than his.

[MsK 1.5.270–271; *K* 254–255]

---

[1] The others are "Why did I laugh?"; "As Hermes once"; the two on Fame; *To Sleep;* and, arguably, a stanza in *Ode to Psyche.*

[2] For the loosening of "rhyming's chains without actually breaking them or having them slip off," see John Hollander's subtle accounting, 93–96.

[3] Dyce dedicated *Specimens* (1833) to Wordsworth, whose fifteen sonnets he ranked with Milton's and Shakespeare's (205). Keats got in with *Chapman's Homer.*

[4] The stanza got termed "elegiac" after its use in Thomas Gray's widely admired *Elegy Written in A Country Churchyard* (1751).

[5] Barry, ed., 156, 159.

[6] Christopher Caldwell on another Keats-event (83), worth echoing here.

[7] In 1926, Garrod noted the sonnet imprints on the odes (*Keats* 87–90). Paul Fry argues that Keats was "the first poet to evolve an ode stanza from experimentation with the sonnet," describing the arc of the 1819's "Great Odes" as "an extended sonnet or sonnet sequence" (*Poet's Calling* 219).

Re: generating the Ode, Spring 1819

Keats wrote odes early and late, from *Ode to Apollo* (1814) to *Ode to Fanny* (1820). The shortest ode of the 1819 spring season is *Ode on Melancholy*, a taut three-part argument in 30 lines; the longest, *Ode to Psyche*, is an 80-line prolegomena for (and enactment of) modern poetry. Given the fame of these nowcalled Great Odes, it is stunning to see them so unheralded in the title of the 1820 volume: *Lamia, Isabella, The Eve of St. Agnes, and Other Poems* (the last words in smaller font). They were not even grouped together.

In the nineteenth century, these Odes were admired, and often culled, for phrasal beauties.[1] By 1865 J. R. Lowell was seeing something else: an extraordinary sense of "form and proportion" ("Keats" 325) in what Keats long admired in Shakespeare's sonnets, "the intensity of working out conceits" (*K* 72). Keats also wanted to follow Shakespeare by making a great "revolution in modern dramatic writing" (*L* 2:139). While he didn't live to do so, he sort of did with the work-out of these Odes. Mid-twentieth-century New Criticism, the first dedicated school of close-reading, focused on their structuring as dramas of mind, figured in developing conceits, shaped into paradoxes, complexities, and contradictions. Critical conversation soon became interested in the way the poetry's intelligent ironies (word-ricochets, double-plays, reperceptions) leaned into indeterminacies (undecidable oscillations), conceptual and even grammatical and syntactical. My fascination is Keats's activations of words as virtual characters, with a spirited greeting to active reading that often runs ahead of, as well as alongside, the dramatic action in the speaker's consciousness. A "perpetual activity of attention required on the part of the reader," engaged with "the rapid flow, the quick change, and the playful nature of thoughts and images"; not just *required* but "forced into . . . action . . . roused and awakened": so Coleridge speaks of Shakespeare's poetry (*BL* chapter 15; 2:16–17)—perfect for Keats's greeted readers, too. By now, Keats is Shakespeare-skilled at making a primary action of words and word-careers:

> every line tells and adds something. He does not expatiate, but moves forward: if he repeats, it is because the repetition has a real force of expression; if he accumulates, each new word or phrase represents a new development, a substantive addition to what he is saying. He assimilates his material and advances by means of it.

Again, not about these Odes, but it could have been.[2] This is their pulse along arcs of development that take zigzag turns of desire, draw shades of qualification, produce sudden recognitions, and subside in irresolutions of purposeful negative capability.

A Question is the best beacon towards a little Speculation, Keats once said, always ready for *question and answer – a little pro and con.*[3]

> "Surely I dreamt to-day, or did I see
> The winged Psyche with awaken'd eyes?"

> "Was it a deep-disguised plot . . . ?"

> "Was it a vision, or a waking dream?"
>> "Do I wake or sleep?"

> "What leaf-fring'd legend haunts about thy shape . . . ?"

> "Where are the songs of Spring? Ay, where are they?"

Even seeming answers, such as "Beauty is truth, truth beauty," or the advice, "No, no, go not to Lethe," linger in pro and con. Final answers are fixed knowings. Words are the life of imagination: what they tell, what they do.

---

[1] Hunt is a qualified exception, printing all of *Ode to a Nightingale* at the front of his *Indicator* review (345–347).

[2] F. E. Brightman, introduction to Lancelot Andrewes's *Preces Privatae* (1903), a comment admired by Eliot, *Selected Essays,* 293.

[3] *L* 1:175 (to Bailey, 30 October 1817); 1:153 (to his sister).

Ode on Indolence

I.

ONE morn before me were three figures seen,
  With bowed necks, and joined hands, side-faced;
And one behind the other stepp'd serene,
  In placid sandals, and in white robes graced;
    They pass'd, like figures on a marble urn,
  When shifted round to see the other side;
They came again; as when the urn once more
    Is shifted round, the first seen shades return;
  And they were strange to me, as may betide
With vases, to one deep in Phidian lore.   10

II.

How is it, Shadows! that I knew ye not?
  How came ye muffled in so hush a mask?
Was it a silent deep-disguised plot
  To steal away, and leave without a task
    My idle days? Ripe was the drowsy hour;
  The blissful cloud of summer-indolence
Benumb'd my eyes; my pulse grew less and less;
    Pain had no sting, and pleasure's wreath no flower:
  O, why did ye not melt, and leave my sense
Unhaunted quite of all but—nothingness?   20

III.

A third time pass'd they by, and, passing, turn'd
  Each one the face a moment whiles to me;
Then faded, and to follow them I burn'd
  And ached for wings, because I knew the three;
    The first was a fair Maid, and Love her name;
  The second was Ambition, pale of cheek,

And ever watchful with fatigued eye;
> The last, whom I love more, the more of blame
> Is heap'd upon her, Maiden most unmeek, —
I knew to be my demon Poesy.   30

IV.

They faded, and, forsooth! I wanted wings:
> O folly! What is Love? and where is it?
And for that poor Ambition! it springs
> From a man's little heart's short fever-fit;
> For Poesy!—no,—she has not a joy,—
> At least for me,—so sweet as drowsy noons,
And evenings steep'd in honied indolence;
> O, for an age so shelter'd from annoy,
> That I may never know how change the moons,
Or hear the voice of busy common-sense!   40

V.

And once more came they by;—alas! wherefore?
> My sleep had been embroider'd with dim dreams;
My soul had been a lawn besprinkled o'er
> With flowers, and stirring shades, and baffled beams:
> The morn was clouded, but no shower fell,
> Tho' in her lids hung the sweet tears of May;
The open casement press'd a new-leaved vine,
> Let in the budding warmth and throstle's lay;
> O Shadows! 'twas a time to bid farewell!
Upon your skirts had fallen no tears of mine.   50

VI.

So, ye three Ghosts, adieu! Ye cannot raise
> My head cool-bedded in the flowery grass;
For I would not be dieted with praise,
> A pet-lamb in a sentimental farce!
> Fade softly from my eyes, and be once more
> In masque-like figures on the dreamy urn;

Farewell! I yet have visions for the night,
    And for the day faint visions there is store;
Vanish, ye Phantoms! from my idle spright,
    Into the clouds, and never more return!   [60]

Indolence is protected Keatsian terrain, but not without wry regard. *Endymion* is his only other poetic site for the word, in a gorgeous simile for unfolding flowers:

                        as when heav'd anew
    Old ocean rolls a lengthened wave to the shore,
    Down whose green back the short-liv'd foam, all hoar,
    Bursts gradual, with a wayward indolence.   (2.348–351)

Wayward, too, are the hypermetrical lines 349 and 351, mimetically "length-ened" when Keats could have easily done without "the" in 349 or "a" in 351. He wanted the languor. The modifying *a wayward* is nicely inflected, leaving *a way* suspended in the leisure burst of foam. No surprise that Keats rhymes *indolence* to *pleasant sense* (352).

When, however, it is a poet and not an ocean wave, when it is a mood of mind and body rather than a simile for flowers, the stakes shift. Endymion's dream-forlorn *indolent arms* (714) are impotent, unmanned. In the wake of *Endymion,* a romance with "Indolence" would call up the cops—or call down social censure. Consider Wordsworth, taking pains in the Preface to his first consequential volume, *Lyrical Ballads,* to explain his principles to his readers: "the most dishonorable accusation which can be brought against an Author" is "an indolence which prevents him from endeavouring" (I:x). Here is Keats, writing wryly to his friend Bailey, after tramping around all day in the North with Brown, ready to plop on a *couple of Chairs.* Not so Brown:

> *he affronts my indolence and Luxury by pulling out of his knapsack 1st his paper – 2ndy his pens and last his ink - Now I would not cure if he would change about a little –*   (Ms K 1.34.126)

Editor Rollins says Keats meant *not care* for *not cure* (*L* 1:344n4), but Keats's script is clear: even if Brown (who was sending Bailey reams on their adven-tures) could be a little less busy, Keats would *not cure* his own indolence, a mood that knows and suspends *dolor* in its counter-construction. Such a carefully witty self-reflection on Keats's part.

Such care and cure are the double-effects of the iconic eighteenth-century mini-epic, that redoubt of useless industry and enervation, James Thomson's *Castle of Indolence* (1748). Its 158 Spenserian stanzas are a luxury on this score alone, but they also display notable industry with a "structure of verse . . . almost insurmountably difficult"—so Wordsworth advised an aspirant to the form. Lord Byron "spoiled" it (he said in envy of the spectacularly popular *Childe Harold's Pilgrimage,* all four cantos with nearly 500 of these stanzas) but Thomson made it "exquisitely harmonious" (1829; *Later Years* 2:58). Labor or leisure? Depending on mood, or need, one may visit the *Castle* for satire or satiation, reveling or reform. Thomson has "poured out the whole soul of indolence, diffuse, relaxed, supine, dissolved into a voluptuous dream; and surrounded himself with a set of objects and companions, in entire unison with the listlessness of his own temper," said Hazlitt in a lecture that Keats attended. If this wasn't Thomson's "best" poem, it was a great date for dissolution.[1] Hazlitt certainly enjoyed this temper, for reading, writing, and lecturing.

No one was more tuned to this doubleness than the Poet Laureate of Luxury, ever-industrious Hunt. His Preface to his selections from *The Castle* sits under a title of alliteratively balanced *Enchantments of . . . Indolence/Exploits of . . . Industry,* as if these were equivalent variables rather than a sequenced correction. "Everybody delights in occasionally being indolent . . . hence the enjoyment of poems such as this," advises Hunt. It is occasional, not vocational. Who could not, therefore, "resent the termination of our pleasures" and despise Thomson's designated terminator, "the reforming knight": a "dull and meddling fellow. Why should he wake us from such a pleasant dream?" Hunt concedes the reform-schooling, but he won't allow woke moralism to overrule, let alone outlaw, pleasure. We may, "on reflection," realize "that we should wake up in a far worse manner, if Sir Industry did not rouse us." But Hunt is sure that Thomson knew better, having planted "beautiful poetry in the second part" (when the Knight arrives), "even exquisite *indolent* bits, or places at least in which we *might* be indolent" (9, Hunt's italics). When Hunt says, "in fine, we congratulate ourselves on our virtue, and begin like the knight to abuse the old rascally wizard" who governs the Castle and would "make us his victims" too (9), it is on a fine swerve: "the tone of Spenser is charmingly imitated, with an arch but delighted reverence"—Hunt's final words (11). Rascally recasting Milton's "sage and serious poet Spenser" (*Areopagitica*) as a charmer, Hunt reads Thomson's reverence for Spenser as a performance of style. What really intrigues him is the paradox of Thomson himself, "both very indolent and very industrious, for his mind was always at work on his enjoyments" (10).

Keats's *Ode* is deeply tuned to this doubleness, with twinned sproutings: a recollection of indolence interrupted, and a poetics of interruption. Amid a long journal letter to George and Georgiana, he moans on 17 March 1819 about a stretch of *uneasy indolence:* boredom, void of *speculations.* It is the epitome of vacuity: *nothing - nothing - nothing -* (MsK 1.53.228; *K* 240–241). In May, he'll call it *dunderheaded* (1.54.274). Not yet there on 19 March, he is surprised by a morning of "easy" indolence—and more:

> I am in a sort of temper indolent and supremely careless . . . and to such a
> happy degree that pleasure has no show of enticement and pain no unbearable
> frown. Neither Poetry, nor Ambition, nor Love have any alertness of counte-
> nance as they pass by me: they seem rather like figures on a greek vase . . . This
> is the only happiness; and is a rare instance of advantage in the body overpow-
> ering the Mind. (1.53.230–231)

No escape, this temper is an interval, a rare instance: *careless* has a subtractable suffix; *indolent,* a subtractable prefix. As Keats's next sentence shows, the morning is not immune to mourning:

> I have this moment received a note from Haslam in which he expects the death
> of his Father who has been for some time in a state of insensibility . . . This is
> the world - thus we cannot expect to give way many hours to pleasure - Circum-
> stances are like Clouds continually gathering and bursting. While we are laughing
> the seed of some trouble is put into the wide arable land of events - while we are
> laughing it sprouts it grows and suddenly bears a poison fruit which we must
> pluck — (231)

While we are laughing: this is the temporality of "Why did I laugh tonight?" Here, Keats's words ring the changes from *no unbearable,* to *bears* up, to *trouble,* to *arable* (pun-lettered into *unbearable*) to *suddenly bears.* Temporal modulations pluck poetic fruit.

Keats takes care / cure to mark a manly line into his overpowered Mind. He is nursing a black eye from a cricket game with the guys the day before (noting this twice). Describing the sequel *state of effeminacy,* he camps it up with *teeth of pearl and the breath of lillies,* longing *after a stanza or two of Thomson's Castle of indolence* (1.53.230–231). That the Castle's site is the land of Cockaigne winks at *Blackwood's* slur on the effeminacy of Cockney-Cockaigned poets. "Resolve! resolve! and to be Men aspire!" is the buzz-kill from Sir Industry's clarion at the Castle doors (Canto II.LXII). Keats's self-immunizing theatrical "temper" takes a morning's pass on the manhood vexations of Poetry, Ambition, and Love. In his wide arable imagination, however, these personifications haunt about to seed a formal ode. And for this, it is not Thomson whom Keats summons for an epigraph.

Ode on Indolence is the only one of this season's Odes to get an epigraph. It alludes to Jesus's lesson on trusting providence: "Consider the lilies of the field, how they grow; they toil not, neither do they spin" (Matthew 6:26–29). Keats calls on this verse seemingly to cull the wording after the semicolon. So culled, however, the designated *They* strains against the "I" who speaks this *Ode*. Indolent Keats is no lily. His *breath of lillies* is drollery; men mime lillies at peril. The poet of indolence is not in the "state of insensibility" that has Haslam's father on a course to death. This poet is post-indolent, nothing if not active, heeding the call to "consider," and spinning six finely crafted dexains, by turns indulgent, critical, satirical, addictive. Keats's mind "goes round . . . in its speculations and its dreams," Reynolds said; "It does not set itself a task" (*Examiner*, p. 648). Keats's poetry of mind can't help but find a task, first in rounding a shadow-play.

The placid anecdote that opens stanza I, *One morn . . .* , came with a poetic pulse that imaged *figures* on a poetic footing: *And one behind the other stepp'd serene.* There was (implicitly) a hand spinning the optical illusion of *They pass'd, like figures on a marble urn.* And it is a working poet who rhymes and letters *urn* into *return*, who knows that *turn* is what "verse" does. Even then, indolence attenuated. Indolent no more, stanza II recalls promoting hazy *shades* (8) to substantive *Shadows,* to interrogate for purpose, intention, information, self-knowing (11–13). In this casting, *mask* was double-tasked: it hints at a *deep-disguised plot;* it puns into *masque,* the artform of stanza VI's *masque-like figures.*[2] When the watchword *indolence* lands, it is already, tellingly, past tense (15–18).

The present tense is active questioning: *How is it . . . ?* (11). Far from a rhetorical affectation, the syntax toils into ambiguous punctuating about a hidden design:

> Was it a silent deep-disguised plot
> To steal away, and leave without a task
> My idle days?   (13–15)

The midline comma at *To steal away* (14) anchors two antithetical plots. One has the Shadows intent to sneak off (intransitive) and let the days stay idle.[3] The other sets *To steal away* as a transitive verb to a direct object, *My idle days.*

No scene of indolence in this last plot. The syntactic doubling is a vibrant micro-drama in the Shadow-caster's ambivalent recalling.[4]

If puzzling over all this is no task for indolence, it is one for a Keatsian Ode on Indolence. *O why did ye not melt, and leave my sense/Unhaunted quite of all but—nothingness?* (19–20) is no question. Too late. Even the trademark, *without a task* (15), is rhymed to a working *mask*. "Idleness denied" is stanza II's virtual, advance ruling. Ruled out is any romance of *sense* at degree zero, *less and less: no sting, no flower. Unhaunted quite of all but—nothingness* (17–20): the finely tuned sibilance of this long phrase takes work! Keats is writing, in effect, an "Elegy for an Ode on Indolence." Stacey McDowell (30) nicely notes the slide of the adverb *quite* from *Unhaunted* (completely so) to *of all but* (exquisitely this exception). This is the feel of not to feel it, with a vengeance. Especially after the breath-weighted dash, *nothingness* is not nothing, but a substantive drag on *indolence*.

On this drag, stanza I's *They pass'd . . . They came again . . . once more . . . return* returns its wording to cue stanza III: *A third time pass'd they by, and, passing turn'd.* The inverted syntax (*pass'd they*) that sets the predicate before the subject nicely aligns with the hand-spun urn-turning that produced the optical illusion. It's a poet's game. The word *turn'd* is triple-worked: it is a term of recursive syntax; it is the turn of enjambment; and it is a rhyme for the incinerated indolence of *I burn'd.* A Keatsian ardor of pursuit—*I . . . ached for wings*—distills Shadows into names he knows: *Love* (the spark), *Ambition* (burn'd out), and the always hot demon *Poesy,* fuel of this very poetry.

In Keats's letter, these keynote figures stepp'd in reverse (and syntactically inverse) order, gender-blurred:

> *Poetry . . . Ambition . . . Love . . . a Man and two women whom no one but myself could distinguish in their disguisement*
>
> (1.53.231; *K* 241–242)

No idle word, this *disguisement.* It sits in *The Fairy-Queen* (Book III, Canto 7) in a scene with a she-witch, a she-ghost, and a loutish lad beyond the pale of a morning's indolence, "A lazy Loord, for nothing good to done, / But stretched forth in Idleness always" (XII). One day, he finds a fair-masked apparition in his home, and not in idleness, wonders

> whence deriv'd,
> That in so strange Disguizement there did mask,
> And by what Accident she there arriv'd   (XIV)

Lazybones will soon be roused by this masked maid into a futile passion. Without taking on this large plot (she's Florimel), Keats draws down the ready words—*Idleness, strange, Disguizement, mask*—for stanza III's trio. The maids in the Ode are *Love* and *Poesy*. Ambition must be the "Man," but hardly (even parodically): pale and pooped, ever on a waning watch. And the letter's shade "Poetry" comes back as *my demon Poesy*, winning the trio's only possessive, and only thrill: *most unmeek* (the sole *unmeek* in Keats's poesy), her heaps of blame firing up the poet's *I love more*, against which even that fancy maid *Love* pales.

If, however, *Ode on Indolence* seems about to tilt into an "Ode to Poesy Most Unmeek," a dramatically minded Keats turns a counterplot in stanza IV. Repeating *faded* from stanza III, a now unindolent poet burned to follow, but futilely: *I wanted wings*. The recoil to lame satire is a squeeze of sour grapes. Love is dismissed as a delusion; Ambition is an infirmity of mind and a chugging clog on the poetic line, *man's little heart's short fever-fit*. How different from Keats's fascination at how eagles may "move about without the least motion of Wings when in an indolent fit" (*L* 1:338), with a nice poetic lilt in *move about without*, and with *fit* no spasm but easy accommodation. It is only a semicolon after *fit* that halts the odist's hectic-punning *fever fytte* for Poesy. By the time he utters a dismissal, *Poesy!—no,—she has not a joy,–/At least for me,—*, this poet doth protest too much. He has already spun 34 lines and is not about to stop. Notwithstanding the anti-odic plea at 38—*O, for an age so shelter'd from annoy* (Keats liked this last noun, noting it in Spenser[5]), so as *never* to *hear the voice of busy common-sense*—the Ode stays busy, rhyming *sense* back to *honied indolence*: refusal in argument, poetically in tune. All petitions to the Muse of Annoy by now are performatively parodic ode-calling.

With one more return, Keats spins stanza V as a decadent nine-line inset "Ode to Indolence" that might have been (42–50). Reading no parody here, Helen Vendler deems this the Ode's "most successful 'writing'": a "powerful and sensual recreation of the drowsy hour."[6] Although she doesn't wring it, I would say parodic *recreation* is the right word in her audit. Keats's ironic gesture is the prefix: a reanimation in poetic magic (Vendler) tuned to *relief* from business and common sense. Yet this lost recreation is conspicuously decadent, artificial: *embroider'd with dim dreams, . . . besprinkled o'er / With flowers, and stirring shades, and baffled beams . . . a new-leaved vine . . . budding warmth and throstle's lay*. These opulences and euphonies (*embroider'd dim dreams* is quite good!) are Keats-issue luxuries, tinted for critical review. Even the birdsong *throstle's lay* manages a discreet Keats puncast on the spinning machine called "throstle," the very antithesis of the epigraph's exemplum against *toil* and *spin*.[7]

The closing vocative—*O Shadows! 'twas a time to bid farewell!* (49)—about a past time keeps them present in melodious utterance.

For *1848*, Milnes changed the first words of the manuscript's stanza V, *A third time*, to *And once more*, apparently tripping on a time-warp of repetition from the top of stanza III and wanting to sequence the turns, straighten out a confusion.[8] But confusion is the order of the day. Shadows are not gone, and as the present-tense final stanza (VI) shows, *farewell* is not done, either: first *adieu!*, then *Farewell!*, then an exasperated *Vanish, ye Phantoms!* Fat chance. Recall the rhetorical difference: *adieu* is bid by a departer; *farewell* to a departer. This poet says both, ambivalently. The first gesture satirizes what ambition may produce, the poet as *A pet-lamb in a sentimental farce*—*farce* frou-frou pronounced to rhyme with *grass*. "I have been very idle lately," Keats tells a female friend in June 1819, "very averse to writing; both from the overpowering idea of our dead poets and from abatement of my love of fame," *averse* undertoning "*a versifying Pet-lamb*" (*K* 257). That's one endpoint, a Pet that's no Poet, but ever a poet word-playing.

The other key is in the Ode's lingering farewell: *be once more / In masque-like figures on the dreamy urn.* Sounding into "dreamy yearn," the very words defeat a fade-out. It is the kind of nominalized gerund Keats would have coined if he had thought of it—which here it seems he almost did. Indolence sends words into wordplay. When Keats ends this stanza, and Ode, *never more return!*, the last word is like a bell, returning *return*, then refusing *never more*, harboring *turn*, and within, *urn*, the figure that had spun it all into play. No wonder (Keats wrote to a friend, 9 June 1819), "the thing I have most enjoyed this year has been writing an ode to Indolence" (*K* 257): not the indolence but the writing.

A slight, but not to be slighted, slip tells the tale: Ode *on* Indolence, not *to* (a meditation, not a petition). By 22 September 1819, Keats says he is "determined to spin" for a living, turning out, toiling out, the business of writing. Still, there is time for luxury: "Talking of Pleasure, this moment I was writing with one hand, and with the other holding to my Mouth a Nectarine – good god how fine – It went down soft pulpy, slushy, oozy" (*K* 268–269). Keats, a two-handed engine. With such a busy *Ode on Indolence*, we can see why he tells George and Georgiana, *I am affraid more from indolence of mind than any thing else* (15 April 1819; MsK 1.53.236). Not wanting to yield to the mood, let alone be tagged its advocate (the poet of *Endymion* had repair-work to do), he would still indulge it. You would not be afraid if you did not feel the lure. "I would rather conquer my indolence and strain my nerves at some grand Poem," he writes to a friend on 31 May (MsK.1.54.274).

Nineteenth-century editors contorted themselves into a professional hospitality to this Ode, and critical tradition mostly cordons it off: a failed exercise, at best, fertile ground for better flourishings. Keats himself shelters indolence, in temper and in writing. It is a magnetic field across which the zigzags of contradiction were clarifying the grammar that was becoming the energy, the fuel, of his poetic imagination. The enjoyment of its composition, the pleasure taken, unlocks one of the secrets of his verbal and emotional dispositions, alternately convergent and conflicted. It is the psychic labor of writing *Ode on Indolence* that he needed.

Let's recall one image of luxury lost: *The open casement press'd a new-leaved vine* (47), with a little sound-sprout of *new/ly* to bring it forth. A *casement ope at night* is invitation of another ode in this season, one that took *moderate pains* (1.53.267). This is *Ode to Psyche*, where a working brain, imagining a wreath'd trellis of answerable words, branches into thoughts *new grown with pleasant pain*. Psyche is taken up and into an internalized personification, worth direct addressing, not just musing upon. It will be with further inference and inward turning that Keats's odes get shaped.

[*1848*, 2:276–278, the first publication, and long standard]

---

[1] *On Thomson and Cowper,* 10 February 1818 (*Lectures* 173).

[2] Charles Brown's copy even has *masque* in line 12 (*P* 375).

[3] Keats teases Brown about bad weather, "let it . . . steal out of your company," riffing on Shakespeare's *Much Ado* (III.3): an apprehended thief, advises Dogberry, will "steal out of your company" (June 1820, *L* 2:299).

[4] Stacey McDowell finely reads this ambiguous syntax (29).

[5] Keats underlined it (1:92) for a poor wight who "pin'd away in . . . self-will'd Annoy" (*FQ* I.VI.XVIII). Editor de Selincourt (611) notes the plural noun in Chapman's *Odyssey* XV (598): "tales of our annoyes."

[6] Vendler's scare-quotes tag a comparatively "limited" accomplishment (*Odes* 30).

[7] *OED:* "spinning-machine . . . having a continuous action, the processes of drawing, twisting, and winding being carried on simultaneously"; the earliest listing is 1825, close enough for Keats to have picked up in his reading about displaced weaver-politics.

[8] *1848*, 2:278; Milnes relied on Brown's transcript (*Brown*, p. 24). Milnes's fiddling "to avoid a second third time," is nicely noted by McDowell: "It is never made clear whether the repeated third time is the same time seen from two different perspectives, or whether it represents 'a counter-shift or return,' as Stillinter suggests" (32, citing *Hoodwinking* 178). All these variant temporalities reflect a conceptual indeterminacy in Keats's waverings of resolution and enchantment.

Ode to Psyche

O Goddess! hear these tuneless numbers, wrung
   By sweet enforcement and remembrance dear,
And pardon that thy secrets should be sung
   Even into thine own soft-conchèd ear:
Surely I dreamt to-day, or did I see
   The wingèd Psyche with awaken'd eyes?
I wander'd in a forest thoughtlessly,
   And, on the sudden, fainting with surprise,
Saw two fair creatures, couchèd side by side   9
   In deepest grass, beneath the whisp'ring roof
   Of leaves and trembled blossoms, where there ran
      A brooklet, scarce espied:
'Mid hush'd, cool-rooted flowers, fragrant-eyed,
   Blue, silver-white, and budded Tyrian,
They lay calm-breathing on the bedded grass;
   Their arms embraced, and their pinions too;
   Their lips touch'd not, but had not bade adieu
As if disjoined by soft-handed slumber,
And ready still past kisses to outnumber   19
   At tender eye-dawn of aurorean love:
      The wingèd boy I knew;
   But who wast thou, O happy, happy dove?
      His Psyche true!

O latest born and loveliest vision far
   Of all Olympus' faded hierarchy!   25
Fairer than Phœbe's sapphire-region'd star,
   Or Vesper, amorous glow-worm of the sky;
Fairer than these, though temple thou hast none,
     Nor altar heap'd with flowers;
Nor virgin-choir to make delicious moan
     Upon the midnight hours;
No voice, no lute, no pipe, no incense sweet
   From chain-swung censer teeming;
No shrine, no grove, no oracle, no heat
   Of pale-mouth'd prophet dreaming.   35

O brightest! though too late for antique vows,
    Too, too late for the fond believing lyre,
When holy were the haunted forest boughs,
    Holy the air, the water, and the fire;
Yet even in these days so far retir'd   40
    From happy pieties, thy lucent fans,
    Fluttering among the faint Olympians,
I see, and sing, by my own eyes inspired.
So let me be thy choir, and make a moan
        Upon the midnight hours;
Thy voice, thy lute, thy pipe, thy incense sweet
    From swinged censer teeming;
Thy shrine, thy grove, thy oracle, thy heat
    Of pale-mouth'd prophet dreaming.

Yes, I will be thy priest, and build a fane   50
    In some untrodden region of my mind,
Where branched thoughts, new grown with pleasant pain,
    Instead of pines shall murmur in the wind:
Far, far around shall those dark-cluster'd trees
    Fledge the wild-ridged mountains steep by steep;
And there by zephyrs, streams, and birds, and bees,
    The moss-lain Dryads shall be lull'd to sleep;
And in the midst of this wide quietness
A rosy sanctuary will I dress
With the wreath'd trellis of a working brain,   60
    With buds, and bells, and stars without a name,
With all the gardener Fancy e'er could feign,
    Who breeding flowers, will never breed the same:
And there shall be for thee all soft delight
    That shadowy thought can win,
A bright torch, and a casement ope at night,
    To let the warm Love in!

In the 30 April 1819 letter (to George and Georgiana) Keats supplies this pro-
logue, a poetic origin-story (MsK 1.53.267):

You must recollect that Psyche was not embodied as a goddess before the time
of Apulieus the Platonist who lived afteir Agustan age, and consequently the

*Goddess was never worshipped or sacrificed to with any of the ancient fervour
– and perhaps never thought of in the old religion . . . I am more orthodox that
[sic] to let a hethen Goddess be so neglected –*

Such faux pedantry (*You must recollect . . .*) is as tonally disparate from the
formal ode as was the jocular postscript to the joyless *La belle dame.* Here, in-
stead of a satirical review, is a master-of-ceremonies preview, on a self-constituting
logic from what history *neglected: ne-legere* (not respected, not noticed, not *read*).
What was *never thought of in the old religion* supplies a project for modern *thought*
poetry.[1] This is Keats's historical moment. He is ironically orthodox, ready to
perform with, and against, classical ode tradition.

Post-antiquity and post-Enlightenment positivism at once, Keats's new
grammar is *psychology*, the soul's word-system, eponym-bequest of *Psyche*.[2] *OED*
says *psychology* first denoted soul-science (1654), then cognitive science: "Psy-
chology, or the Theory of the human Mind" is a unit in David Hartley's *Ob-
servations on Man* (1749).[3] Just a few pages back in his letter, Keats was de-
scribing existential life as *Soul-making*. For explanation, he called on *hethen
mythology* as no mere "old religion" but a proto-poetic archive of *Mediators in
abstractions . . . personified* (1.53.216, 263). *Ode to Psyche* stages a poet discov-
ering this language—in effect, an "Ode to *Ode to Psyche*." The rhetoric is court-
ship: a poet petitioning as a worthy lover, offering worthy poetry, this a temple
in his very mind, delivered with a *delicious moan*. As in much love-poetry, the
love-object is a pretext, here especially "Psyche," less a figure than a figure for
thinking. Autogenesis is the master-script, its actors a wordplay that reverses
never thought of into modern poetry's *branched thoughts, new grown* (52).

On this twist, the opening vocative is archly decadent:

> O GODDESS! hear these tuneless numbers, wrung
>   By sweet enforcement and remembrance dear,
> And pardon that thy secrets should be sung
>   Even into thine own soft-conched ear: (1–4)

The poet's *tuneless numbers* are new-tuned to close-listening and close-reading.
On the soundwave of the vocative *hear* into the poet's self-placement, *here,*
Keats's quatrain sets *rung* in *wrung*: what the very words have done, in wry
contradiction to *tuneless* (the sole instance in his poetry). His first rhyme, aptly,
is *hear/dear.* Set at the end of line 2, *dear* is posed for rhyme-repetition in "soft-
conch*ed ear*" (4), ringing back to *hear*.[4] *Poetry . . . should strike the Reader as a
wording of his own highest thoughts, and appear almost a Remembrance,* Keats

thought back in February 1818 (*K* 113). *Ode to Psyche* flaunts a poetics of self-hearing (ev*en in*to th*ine*), wording for thoughts already in formation. The Goddess is there as a redundant, nearly contingent occasion. Self-singing is both figured and prefigured, and modern to the core: words "juxtaposed in new and sudden combinations" with the charge to poets "to force, to dislocate . . . language into . . . meaning." This is T. S. Eliot's modernist appreciation.[5]

But why (*even*) sing at all? The redundant self-singing turns out to be grounded in a self-questioning, reported with stagey flair and its own grammatical tease:

> Surely I dreamt to-day, or did I see
> The winged Psyche with awaken'd eyes?   (5–6)

Ode to a Nightingale will murmur this question at its close and leave it hanging: *Was it a vision, or a waking dream?* Knowing by remembrance dear Spenser's *Was it a Dream, or did I see it plain?* (*Sonnet* LXVII), Keats overrides such balanced syntax with dramatic action: first, the coy comma-pause at *Surely I dreamt to-day,* then the alternative *see,* paused and poised at the line's end, before a turn to its object. It is not just that dreaming seems like seeing, but that seeing is the drama. Surprised by syntax, both *I see* and *Psyche* have a grammatical (and phonic) claim on *awaken'd eyes.* "I" and object are so made for one another that the question is pointless. It is a romance of poetry with its own grammar. *Psyche* is the muse of this amusement.

Keats's Psyche-poetics begin with wordings which, were they Dante's or Spenser's, would signpost epic errancy: *I wander'd in a forest thoughtlessly* (7). For Keats, it is a pun-prologue to reparative thought-work, sparked *on the sudden* (8). It is metaphor-plus, "a sudden perception of an objective relation."[6] Here, a question about the epistemology of *awaken'd eyes* comes (back) in play: is this an awakening from sleep? or from ordinary vision into a supercharged visionary realm, on a sudden, by surprise?[7] Post-surprise, the poet presents the origin scene: two fair creatures couched (9–20), evoking the stationing of the "loveliest pair" espied in Satan's casing of Eden, Under a tuft of shade that on a green / Stood whispering soft (*PL* 4.325–326).[8] And then (even better), Eve separate he spies (9.424). Keats underlined all of 424–435 for remembrance dear (*KPL* I:94, II:87), but with no Satanic predation.

The poet of *Ode to Psyche* is not writing Miltonic code. He is staging a delicate "hethen" romance: *scarce espied, whisp'ring,* and *trembled.* This last word is finely chosen: aligned with *couched,* it seems a past-tense verb; with *whisp'ring,* an adjective for present reverberation. No surprise (by now) that *trembled* gets

OED's unique citation for the sense "made to tremble." Keats gives the scene a delicate stationing: *side by side/ In . . . beneath . . . where there.* It's juvenile scopophilia, not Freudian trauma. The last item, that *brooklet, scarce espied* (12), is a tableau vivant in itself: *see* sounds across "scar*ce e*spied," as a microplot for close hearing.

Lines 1–12, by force of being set alone on page 117 in *1820*, shape a plausible stanza, ending in this *espied* suspense.[9] With the turn to page 118, the curiosity stimulates a surmise: *As if disjoined by soft-handed slumber* (18). The *calm-breathing*, the full embrace, the temporal uncertainty of *lips touch'd not, but had not bade adieu* (15–17): all tremble into interpretive foreplay.[10] The poised *ready still past kisses to outnumber* (19) fuels *ready still* with a double-grammar: for the adjective, the lovers are freeze-framed in this anticipation, forever *still* in readiness; for an adverb, *still* leans temporally into potential re-enacting. No wonder Keats wanted an infinitive, *to outnumber* (this verb only here in his poetry), to elicit the origin of poetic *numbers* (1), just caught and ready for ongoing. For this double logic (narrative and odic), the two-timing of this scene at *tender eye-dawn of* (20)—dawn of day and of seeing—is just right, taking the "I" sounded in *awaken'd eyes* into a fine reciprocal: *tender-eyed dawn*, which itself reverbs *tender eye-dawn*. Keats revised to fine-tune these phonics (in his draft, it was *dawning of*). On this soundstage, the odist sets *The winged boy I knew* (21) so that the object-subject-verb syntax also yields a lexically sequenced *winged boy I:* the successor boy is the poet-I. This knowing is the prehistory of *Ode to Psyche.*

To ask *But who wast thou, O happy, happy dove?* (22), then, is disingenuous, no more than a rhetorical cue answered in two shakes of an iamb's tail, and already by the presence of the *Ode.* The usual Odic apostrophe, *O Thou* underwrites this in-the-moment *thou, O.* In Keats's letter-draft, the next words, the next line, are *His Psyche true?* (sq. 268). Why the faux suspense? *His Psyche true!* (23, also the draft). Such exclamation might end a traditional ode's strophe. But instead of turning an antistrophe, Keats suspends this discovery-story for a swerve into an ode within the *Ode:* its theme, his modern poetry of mind. The poet's accolades, *loveliest vision far . . . /Fairer than . . . Fairer than* (24–28), are a sound-stream that is more about this poetry than its referent. Psyche is no longer named, just hailed *O latest born . . . !* (24); *O brightest!* (36). It is her situation as remainder of *all Olympus' faded Hierarchy* (25) that is the provocative (literally vocational) matter: *temple thou hast none, Nor altar . . . Nor virgin-choir . . . No voice, no lute, no pipe, no incense . . . No shrine, no grove, no oracle, no . . . prophet* (28–35). The repair-job summoned to these negative notations is conspicuously post-Miltonic. Having de-Satanized Satan's sightline in Eden,

Keats now summons Milton's ode *On the Morning of Christ's Nativity* (1629) for outright reversal. Milton gloated at this morning's expulsion of the heathen gods and the ruining of the Temple at Delphi: *No nightly trance, or breathèd spell, / Inspires the pale-ey'd Priest from the prophetic cell* (*The Hymn* XIX). Keats redeems the words for modern *thought* poetry, launching its letters in *though/thou* (28), and even recalling *thou* from 22 (*who wast thou?*). Post-antique poetry is the event of this ode, now: the mind's medium of words.

The belatedness of Psyche's being even *too late for antique vows, / Too, too late for the fond believing lyre* (36–37) is no abjection for this modern poet but words to play with. Keats's meter sounds *antic* in *antique* (the old ring), and his lexical irony shades *fond* with thoughtful irony (affectionate and foolish). Keats signals his own poetic history here, turning a sonnet-stanza at *O brightest!* (36–49) to get from the scene of hethen worship to the poetry of mind.[11] You can see an octave-ending at *I see, and sing, by my own eyes inspired* (43) then pivoting, volta-wise, to *So let me be thy choir* (44). Keats tunes his sounds for this success. The previously paired *I* and *Psyche* is now *I . . . my . . . eyes*. Who needs her? The lead-up grammar is a dramatic event in itself:

> Yet even in these days so far retir'd
>> From happy pieties, thy lucent fans,
>> Fluttering among the faint Olympians,
> I see, and sing, by my own eyes inspired.   (40–43)

A tricky syntactical shift of *far retir'd / From* is part of the grammar-drama. On a first reading, the phrase seems prepositional for both the old happy *pieties* and their object, *lucent fans* (her wings), with a par-odic modern punning of *fans* as devotees (abbreviated *fanatics, fane*-worshippers). By line 43, we realize that the caesura comma at *pieties* (41) was a sorting-out: *thy lucent fans* is the direct object of *I see, and sing*. Not even an allonym, Psyche thins to a spectral-effect, *lucent . . . Fluttering*. This is a poet who has read and metamorphosed the material of Lemprière: "Psyche is generally represented with the wings of a butterfly, to intimate the lightness of the soul, of which the butterfly is a symbol." From symbol to intimation to representation to self-authorizing poetic language, "Psyche" becomes modern.

Capitalizing on all the "I" puns, this poet declares himself *by my own eyes inspired* (43). *So let me be* (44–49) delivers a symmetrical reparation, item by item, of Olympian neglect. Amid his rehearsal for *these days* (40), Keats slyly torques one repetition. The lovely sound-swing of *no incense sweet / From chain-swung censer* (32–33) becomes lovelier yet with *swinged censer* (47): *swinged* is the modern, unchained victory in its verbal capture of *winged* Psyche (6) and *winged* boy (21). Keats's letter-text shows *s winged Censer* (sq. 269). He means "swinged," of course, but the discrete *s* releases *winged*.[12] The graphemics feel like scripted punning. On such a key, "fainting with surprise" (8) in the embodied origin story comes back, first in the wordplay of *fans* among the *faint* Olympians (41–42), then into modern poetry's *fane* of mind (50) and all that "*Fancy* e'er could *feign*" (62). Such layering of meanings—antique, modern, full of etymology—is Keats's developing lexical game.

The modern poet who is set to *build a fane / In some untrodden region of my mind*, knows his fictions. Keats tested *frame* for *feign* (sq. 270) and cut back an initial vaunting capital-M Mind (sq. 269). His clear foils are Spenser's love-struck Britomart, prone to "feigning Fancy" (*Fairy-Queen* III.IV.5), and the poet of Spenser's Sonnet XXII:

> Her Temple fair is built within my Mind,
>   In which her glorious Image placed is,
> On which my Thoughts do day and night attend,
>   Like sacred Priests that never think amiss.   (5–8)

The old Priests could never think a miss. Keats's retro-interior décor for his miss is flagrantly psychedelic: *flowers, fragrant-eyed* (13), a weird enough preview for *branched thoughts* (52) on a *wreath'd trellis of a working brain* (60), Keats's rhyme for *fane*. Not just a poet's promise, *Ode to Psyche* itself delivers a radical brain poetics, successor of wandering in a *forest thoughtlessly* (7). The old constellation of *Phœbe's sapphire-region'd star* and *Vesper* (26–27) are now a prospect of *stars without a name* (61).[13] All the old gods, Keats says (and virtually does with his sibilance), *shall be lull'd to sleep* (57)—lull'd in a sounding that his first thought, *charm'd,* didn't yield (sq. 270). Their sleep opens into a brainscape of *wide quietness* (58) in *some untrodden region of my mind* (51). The only other *untrodden* in Keats's poetry is an *untrodden* precipice in blind Homer's ken (*To Homer*).

Back in May 1818, Keats had written out a master-simile for a mind's emergence: *thoughtless Chamber* to *the Chamber of Maiden Thought,* then all *dark Passages* (*K* 130). If *Ode to Psyche* sets the last figuring only in far prospect, its wordings are already there. Keats's cast of *Shadowy thought* (65) is mindful of Wordsworth's modern-minded pledge in his Prospectus to *The Excursion* to "tread on shadowy ground," in a venture to make "the Mind" the "haunt, and the main region of my Song" (xi–xii). Keats ups the ante to brainful physiology: *branched thoughts, new grown with pleasant pain, / Instead of pines shall murmur in the wind* (52–53). In a phonic ambush, a soft *groan* vibrates along the central nervous system of his verbal imagination from *grown*. Keats might have made *wind* a long-i verb (say, *shall murmur as they wind*), but he lets the short-i slant-rhyme float, refusing to go baroque. What is in the wings is a surreal verb for branched thoughts:

> Far, far around shall those dark-cluster'd trees
>> Fledge the wild-ridged mountains steep by steep.　　　　(54–55)

I shall come to *Fledge.* First, note the echo of Wordsworth's wild mountains of the mind:

>> steep and lofty cliffs,
> Which on a wild secluded scene impress
> Thoughts of more deep seclusion.　　　　(*Tintern Abbey* 5–7)

Wordsworth is master of double syntax when it comes to such correspondences. A secluded scene impresses thoughts even more secluded than the scene: these thoughts are "not only *about* deep seclusion, they are themselves deep and secluded."[14] Keats's *steep by steep* evokes and echoes this *deep,* a branching into Wordsworth's poetic territory: words for thoughts; and by the strange agency of *impress,* the mind's projection on the scene of the scene's impress on the mind.

The Keatsian imprint is a figurally transformed Psyche. As *dark-cluster'd* reverberates *dark-luster'd,* her "lucent fans" metamorphose into a verb, *Fledge:* "feather, furnish with wings." It's not a far-fetched pun. Keats soon tells Fanny Brawne of his half-thought "to let the verses of an half-fledged brain tumble into the reading-rooms and drawing room windows" (July 1819; *L* 2:130). Out of the drawing rooms and reading-rooms, and onto the mind's mountain-steeps, Keats casts a poet on the wing. John Ruskin was inspired to bring his own mind to the scene: so taken was this art critic by Keats's "figurative pines" that he added his own rhyme-tuned visual supplement, "the pine in exquisite fineness" (*pine/fine*), nerve-ended by branches "in fringes." He printed the final stanza entire, with emphasis on *fledge the wild-ridged mountains.*[15] Keats's exponential linguistic intricacy has this strange epiphenomenal force.

Keats's ode concludes with a modern poet in readiness for his modern muse, provisionally syntaxed in the infinitive:

> A bright torch, and a casement ope at night
>> To let the warm Love in!

The arc of *Ode to Psyche,* comments Stuart Sperry, "is given a kind of circularity by its opening lines, which both prefigure and complete the irony of its conclusion." Reversing this smart spin, we could also say that the conclusion is knowingly ironized. As Christopher Miller puts it, *Ode to Psyche* produces "a frame of mind . . . rather than an *object* of thought."[16] Instead of "rather than," though, I would say the object of thought *is* this frame of mind.

In the letter of 30 April 1819, it is not even Keats's last word. Camping "antique vows," his letter postscripts with a quaintly feigned verb (not in *OED*):

Here endethe ye Ode to Psyche   (1.53.270)

Endethe, but still open: darkling, Keats keeps listening to what his words can sound, can tell.

[*1820,* 117–121]

---

[1] Keats read Apuleius (ch. xxi) in William Adlington's translation (1566); Colvin (1917) 412n1.

[2] Keats had handy Lemprière's *Classical Dictionary* (*CR* 124); PSYCHE: "The word signifies *the soul.*" While *JnD* has neither *psyche* nor *psychology, OED* cites contemporaneous treatises in which *psychology* indicates a science of mind or soul.

[3] Part I, Section II, p. 354.

[4] The word is *chonched* in both Keats's letter-text (1.53.267) and the Morgan Library draft (hereafter *D*). As a unique instance in his poetry (and not in any dictionary), I think *chonched* may be deliberate. The preparers of *1820* opted for shell-form *conched.* I like the lexical mystery.

[5] The first in *The Sacred Wood* (1920), 117; the second is a famous comment on the metaphysical poets (1921; *Selected Essays,* 248).

[6] Herbert Read (not writing about Keats), 25.

[7] See David Perkins on this ambiguity, *Quest,* 223–224.

[8] Keats prefers this curiosity to Milton's more explicit repetition many lines on: "two fair Creatures" making love in their blissful bower, then "asleep secure of harme" (*PL* 4.790–791).

[9] The letter-text (sq. 268) and ms. *D* have a continuous stanza, no colon-pause, all the way to *His Psyche true?* (23). Stillinger's edition follows this, for a 4-stanza irregular ode, the first dramatically expansive (the next are 12, 14, and 18 lines). Every other Ode in *1820* has stanzas of equal length, at most, 11 lines. The accident of *1820*'s p. 117 makes it plausible that Keats's latest thought was to craft five, more proportionate, stanzas.

[10] Ms. *D* has *adieu;* sq. 268 has *adiew,* as if Keats were rhyming ahead to what he *knew,* affecting a bit of retro-Middle-English: the last words of Burton's Argument to the Frontispiece of *The Anatomy of Melancholy* (which Keats was reading) are "Reader, adiew" (ix).

[11] Gittings convincingly proposes that Keats began a sonnet, *To Psyche*. Fiddling with lines 13–14, he kept going, adding *Ode* to his title (*Odes* 71, 73). Garrod notes sonnet-pattern rhymes throughout, variously Petrarchan and Shakespearean (*Keats* 87–88).

[12] Not so widely, *s winged* is also separated in ms. *D* (as *sweet* is not).

[13] In the letter-text (sq. 270), Keats wrote *mane*. He meant *name* (ms. *D*) but the anagram came to his ear on the rhyme from *brain* (60) to *feign* (62).

[14] Clarke, *Romantic Paradox*, 45.

[15] *Modern Painters*, v. 5 (1860), Part VI, chapter IX, 88.

[16] Sperry, *Keats the Poet*, 249. Miller, 216.

Ode to a Nightingale

I.

My heart aches, and a drowsy numbness pains
    My sense, as though of hemlock I had drunk,
Or emptied some dull opiate to the drains
    One minute past, and Lethe-wards had sunk:
'Tis not through envy of thy happy lot,
    But being too happy in thine happiness,—
        That thou, light-winged Dryad of the trees,
            In some melodious plot
    Of beechen green, and shadows numberless,
        Singest of summer in full-throated ease.   10

2.

O, for a draught of vintage! that hath been
    Cool'd a long age in the deep-delved earth,
Tasting of Flora and the country green,
    Dance, and Provençal song, and sunburnt mirth!
O for a beaker full of the warm South,
    Full of the true, the blushful Hippocrene,
        With beaded bubbles winking at the brim,
            And purple-stained mouth;
    That I might drink, and leave the world unseen,
        And with thee fade away into the forest dim: 20

3.

Fade far away, dissolve, and quite forget
    What thou among the leaves hast never known,
The weariness, the fever, and the fret
    Here, where men sit and hear each other groan;
Where palsy shakes a few, sad, last gray hairs,
    Where youth grows pale, and spectre-thin, and dies;
        Where but to think is to be full of sorrow

And leaden-eyed despairs,
    Where Beauty cannot keep her lustrous eyes,
        Or new Love pine at them beyond to-morrow. 30

4.

Away! away! for I will fly to thee,
    Not charioted by Bacchus and his pards,
But on the viewless wings of Poesy,
    Though the dull brain perplexes and retards:
Already with thee! tender is the night,
    And haply the Queen-Moon is on her throne,
        Cluster'd around by all her starry Fays;
            But here there is no light,
    Save what from heaven is with the breezes blown
        Through verdurous glooms and winding mossy ways. 40

5.

I cannot see what flowers are at my feet,
    Nor what soft incense hangs upon the boughs,
But, in embalmed darkness, guess each sweet
    Wherewith the seasonable month endows
The grass, the thicket, and the fruit-tree wild;
    White hawthorn, and the pastoral eglantine;
        Fast fading violets cover'd up in leaves;
            And mid-May's eldest child,
    The coming musk-rose, full of dewy wine,
        The murmurous haunt of flies on summer eves. 50

6.

Darkling I listen; and, for many a time
    I have been half in love with easeful Death,
Call'd him soft names in many a mused rhyme,
    To take into the air my quiet breath;
Now more than ever seems it rich to die,
    To cease upon the midnight with no pain,
        While thou art pouring forth thy soul abroad

In such an ecstasy!
    Still wouldst thou sing, and I have ears in vain—
        To thy high requiem become a sod.   60

7.

Thou wast not born for death, immortal Bird!
    No hungry generations tread thee down;
The voice I hear this passing night was heard
    In ancient days by emperor and clown:
Perhaps the self-same song that found a path
    Through the sad heart of Ruth, when, sick for home,
        She stood in tears amid the alien corn;
            The same that oft-times hath
Charm'd magic casements, opening on the foam
    Of perilous seas, in faery lands forlorn.   70

8.

Forlorn! the very word is like a bell
    To toll me back from thee to my sole self!
Adieu! the fancy cannot cheat so well
    As she is fam'd to do, deceiving elf.
Adieu! adieu! thy plaintive anthem fades
    Past the near meadows, over the still stream,
        Up the hill-side; and now 'tis buried deep
            In the next valley-glades:
    Was it a vision, or a waking dream?
        Fled is that music:—Do I wake or sleep?   80

This ode is the first of *1820*'s mid-volume "Poems" unit. Having experimented with varying stanza lengths in *Ode to Psyche,* Keats refines a new form of sonnet-resourceful symmetrical stanzas (*ababcdecde*). As these stanzas sequence a drama of thinking about and thinking through, the poetry delivers a verbal ecology of keywords and wordings. Keats turns and returns words, often on loaded syllables, to track alongside and through a poet's yearning for nightingale-happiness, with complicating reflections and unresolved questions.

Not least is of these is "Nightingale." More than a word, it is a poetic language. Keats summons the implied lore in *The Eve of St. Agnes* to compare excited

Madeline to a heart-swelled, tongueless nightingale (XXIII). Shorn of the Phil-omel affiliations, the poet of "To one who has been long in city pent" still likes this name. In the season of this ode, Keats discussed "Nightingales, Poetry" with Coleridge, on Hampstead Heath in April 1819 (*L* 2:88). It is a copious genre.[1] Milton's Sonnet I begins, "O nightingale." In his *Nightingale: A Conversa-tion Poem,* Coleridge hails a "'Most musical, most melancholy' bird!"—then, in the turn of a line, retracts "most melancholy" as an overdetermined projection by one who

> fill'd all things with himself
> And made all gentle sounds tell back the tale
> Of his own sorrow[:] he, and such as he,
> First named these notes a melancholy strain:
> And many a poet echoes the conceit.

With footnote-apologies to Milton ("most melancholy" is from *Il Penseroso*), Coleridge explains a "dramatic propriety" in speaking in "the character of the melancholy Man."[2] John Ruskin's famous term for such relay is "pathetic fal-lacy," the external world in sympathy with the moods of one's mind.[3] Coleridge corrects *melancholy* with a "different lore . . . of love / And joyance." Words-worth loved the intervention: "What false notions have prevailed from gener-ation to generation as to the true character of the nightingale."[4] This themed his own contribution to the genre (*1815* 1:312). Keats knew Wordsworth's poem, too, which begins, in bardic alliance, with the opening words of Milton's Sonnet I.[5]

> O NIGHTINGALE! thou surely art
> A Creature of ebullient heart:—
> These notes of thine—they pierce and pierce;
> Tumultuous harmony and fierce!
> Thou sing'st as if the God of wine
> Had helped thee to a Valentine;
> A song in mockery and despite
> Of shades, and dews, and silent Night;
> And steady bliss, and all the loves
> Now sleeping in these peaceful Groves.

The argument of *surely* and *as if* transforms the Philomel-myth's *pierce and pierce* into the song of an ebullient heart ("a fiery heart" in Wordsworth's 1807 version).

Wordsworth does his phonic best with a poetry keyed to the nightingale *notes* of *steady bliss.*

Ode to a Nightingale is tuned to Coleridge's paradigm of "dramatic propriety" in the subjective filters of song-listening. Having started with an un-melancholy epithet (*Small, winged Dryad*), Keats began again, by foregrounding a human listener.[6] The ode opens *in medias res* with three human-felt throbs of cardio-existentialism, *My heart aches,* and stays on this sensation for four lines before its contrast cause, *thy happy lot,* even gets noted (5). Keats first tried a substantive *Heart aches,* to echo Hamlet's theme, "the heart-ache . . . / That flesh is heir to" (*Hamlet* 3.1), a line he had rehearsed to Reynolds (with Tom close by) about the general "ill 'that flesh is heir to'" (3 May 1818, *K* 127–128). He then decided to make the condition a dramatically present sensation. A speaker (*My*) gets a subject and a predicate, *Heart aches.*[7]

On this throb, the ode heads toward verbal decadence: how close to degree-zero sensation can poetry get and still have words? Only the paradox, *pains / My sense* (1–2) will do. Keats took his own pains here, testing *a fearful numbness* [*fills / falls / fells*] */My sense,* then declining the lull of alliteration for a stab at *pains* as a verb-action against numbness, tormented into sensation. He spends 32 words to work through analogies: hemlock; opiate; Lethe. Hemlock is suicide. Lethe is its sequel. *Opiate* is a material fact of life. *Confessions of an English Opium-Eater* would soon appear in two autumn 1821 issues of *London Magazine.* Coining the compound *Opium-Eater,* the Confessor outed a national diet, a painkiller and sedative that often became an addiction.[8] Opium was typically taken in a tincture of alcohol called *laudanum* ("to be praised").[9] Keats would beg for this draught in his dying days, not only for pain-relief but also suicide.

The colon at the end of line 4 (*had sunk:*) pivots from opiate to its cause, hearing a nightingale's song. Keats produces a devious drama of poetic grammar here, from sympathetic identification to radical difference. The generous syntax of *'Tis not through envy of thy happy lot* (5) looks packed for a sequel, such as *That I* (listen to your song . . .). When it continues, however, into the clause *But being too happy in thine happiness,* — */ That thou . . . Singest* (6–10), the wording turns out to be exclusive nightingale-song.[10] Bird-*being* is so distinct from human-being as to seem out of ancient myth: a *light-winged Dryad* at one with *some melodious plot.* In this world, *shadows* are no portent of dark passages, just pleasing variety; *numberless* is no *numbness;* spring (48) can be sung into *summer*—and, not least, song is *full-throated ease.* Who wouldn't envy? The poet's claim *not through envy of* is double-voiced, evoking what it denies. Throat-strangled Hyperion, throat-stifled Madeline, Keats's nagging sore throat (since summer 1818): all haunt the romance of *full-throated*. Keep *full* and *ease* in your reading-mind. Keats sets them for resoundings into reperception. In this drama of mind, words are not supporting actors but key actors, repeating with a difference, coming into review, telling against their previous senses.

Milton's sonnet and Wordsworth's lyric began with the poet-signal "O nightingale," a tribute to and a call to. Keats defers the odic gesture to stanza 2, and here it is not a call to a nightingale but a petition for transit to its melodious plot.[11] Stanza 2 is this inset ode: *O, for draught of vintage!* The only *draught* in *Paradise Lost* (recall) is the one Keats underlined: the <u>nectarous draughts</u> Eve prepares from Eden's bounty (5.306; *KPL* I:125). *Draft* is a more usual spelling; *draught* (pronounced "drawt," from "draw") is closer in letters and sound to what it would slake: drought. *Cool'd a long age in the deep-delved earth* (12) coos six stressed syllables to give in sensation what is longed for in imagination. It is a drunk-drawn sentence. As Keats knows, a draught is both a gulp and a medical dose. The poem's draught of vintage is a draw of pastoral mythology so potent that *sunburnt* is no pain, just a chime for *mirth* (14). Here *full* returns trebly: *full* of the warm South, / *Full* of the true, the blush*ful* Hippocrene (15–16). The very fountain blushes in color and in sympathy. Keats juices words into sensation, imagining *beaded bubbles winking at the brim* / *And purple-stained mouth* (17–18). Mouth is a beaker's rim; Keats doubles it for the drinker, pur*ple* joining an already vibrating *full* chord. It is over the top—then, in the turn of the line, strangely muted and thinned.

For all the eager petitioning, Keats leaves the stanza at a diminuendo, with a Shakespearean-sonnet-like volta on the last two lines:

> That I might drink, and leave the world unseen,
> And with thee fade away into the forest dim: (19–20)

Not just a diminuendo, this is double-loaded: *I might drink* that draft (inverted syntax), in order *that I might drink* away the world, pauses in colon-suspense. By stanza 6, the impulse to *leave the world* will be equated with *easeful Death* (52). You can sense it here. More than a fade-away, the modifying *unseen*—set at the end of 19 so that it can apply both to *world* and the *I* who would fade from it—speaks erasure. If this were Dantean epic, *forest dim* would be an antechamber to the underworld. Keats knows this as early as the call for a vintage from deep-delved earth (12), the words eliciting the haunt of Merlin, a "deep Delve, far from the view of Day, / That no living Wight he mote be found" (*FQ* III.III.vii). Line 20, the ode's sole hexameter, is a Spenserian signature.

Keats's "thinking goes on through the images and receives its precise definition and qualification from the images," writes Cleanth Brooks, this *through* naming both a mapping and a means.[12] Even Keats's punctuation is such an "image." The colon after *dim* raises the curtain on stanza 3, which opens repeating the last line of 2 in hyperbole: *Fade far away, dissolve, and quite forget* (21). This fuller wording echoes Hamlet-heartache, which Keats underlined: "O, that this too too solid flesh would melt, / Thaw, and resolve itself into a dew" (1.2; *DW* 7:12). Keats revs up the desire, a fade-away *with thee,* then snaps it into categorical difference and bitter recognition: *What thou among the leaves hast never known* (22). *Never!* Line by remorseless line, stanza 3, far from fading, delivers human-knowing, *quite forget* pitilessly emptied into the first rhyme, *fret: The weariness, the fever, and the fret / Here, where men sit and hear each other groan* (23–24). *Here* ricochets a rhyme-sound from *wear*iness, then sends the echoing song into what the poet cannot help but *hear:* an amplifying anaphora of *where* (five times, 23–29), *here* in its very lettering. A conspirator is *fret,* usually a verb. Keats makes it a noun for life in the world. Not only is it no petulance, it is also a part of a human-played musical instrument.

In this chord (in Keats's well-tuned ear) is Wordsworth's "fretful stir / Unprofitable, and the fever of the world" (*Tintern Abbey* 53–54). Both poets have Hamlet's first soliloquy by heart, "How weary . . . seem to me all the uses the world!" (1.2), as well as Macbeth's envy of Duncan, sent to peace . . . in his grave; / After life's fitful fever (3.2), Keats's underlining again (*DW* 3:34, 7:12). Nightingale-song cannot know this; human song cannot forget it. Hamlet's Must I remember? (1.2) also drew his underlining. On Wordsworth's calendar, "man grows old, and dwindles, and decays" (*Excursion* IV, p. 175). Keats's *Where youth grows pale, and spectre-thin, and dies* (26) contracts a lifespan to *youth:* Tom; likely himself.[13] The phrasing of *Where but to think is to be full of sorrow* (27) at once contrasts a nightingale's *full-throated ease* and ruthlessly satirizes the triple-*full* anodynes of stanza 2 (15–16). The infinitive *to think* is foundational for *leaden-eyed despairs.* No deader line for a poet to sing. The plural is a killer: no mood of mind, but unending experience.

Keats begins stanza 4 on a double-volta. A thinking poet's cry, *Away! away!* (31) swings against stanza 3's *Fade far away* and toward the new agenda: *I will fly to thee, / Not charioted by Bacchus* (that draught of vintage), *But on the viewless wings of Poesy* (31–33). The poet verbs himself, birdlike: *I will fly to thee.* Never mind the *dull brain* (34) and its muse, that *dull opiate* (3). Keats first wrote "I will fly *with* thee" (ms. *C* 39), then made it a goal, *to thee,* then an arrival: *Already with thee! tender is the night* (35). The exclamation conveys both success and surprise, *with thee into the forest dim* (20) opening into tender night and fabulous light, where *haply the Queen-Moon is on her throne, / Cluster'd around by all her starry Fays* (36–37). No dark-cluster'd images here: it scarcely matters whether *haply* means *perhaps* or (recalling the key of the song in stanza 1) *happily*.

What does matter is Keats's ironizing, critical literacy. Such a vision of *Poesy* is tinsel-artificial, antique. *Poesy:* "the art of writing poems" says *JnD. Fay* is *fairy* with a whiff of faery fancy. "Spenser's poetry is all fairy-land," wrote Hazlitt.[14] As stanza 4 develops, the exclamation-pointed *with thee!* (35) reverses into a devastating reperception. The punctuation turns out to have been a stress-mark on *thee* in exclusion of *I*, heading into a brutally antithetical rhyme for the tender *night: But here there is no light* (38), except for faint siftings of that litany of *here* in stanza 2.[15] For his last, tragic novel, *Tender is the Night* (1933), F. Scott Fitzgerald compressed Keats's reperception into his title-page epigraph:

> *Already with thee! tender is the night . . .*
> *. . . But here there is no light,*
> *Save what from heaven is with the breezes blown*
> *Through verdurous glooms and winding mossy ways.*

> —ODE TO A NIGHTINGALE

Writing *But here there is no light* (38), Keats redraws his melodious plot onto a new stage across the oddness of the idiomatic contrast *here there*.

I cannot see . . . opens stanza 5; yet quite surprisingly, it is no poverty. Keats delivers a poetry of the earth, never dead, even at night, and with no bird-song at all. The poet ready to *leave the world unseen* (stanza 2) returns with new imagination to a scene unseen: *darkness, guess* (43) is a micro-rhyme for a new ecology, reverberated into *guess each sweet*. The gorgeous venture of this stanza is Keats's conflation, in a single-sentence immersion, of poet-report and reader-phenomenology. His words shape our guesses. On this license, sweet air can be a substantive: *what soft incense hangs upon the boughs*. No set-piece still life, this darkness pulses fadings and emergences: *Fast fading violets cover'd up in leaves* mingle with *coming musk-rose*, so *full* of scent that its dew may as well be *wine* (47–49). Who needs Bacchus, or a remote draft of vintage? Every thing is intensely present in this temporality—not least, Keats's grammar: participles, tenses, even past participles rounding into a fullness, *embalm'd, cover'd*.

Keats fills out in verbal sensation what Fairy-Queen Titania (in a fit, no less) calls "the middle Summers spring," a phrase he marked in his folio *Midsummer Night's Dream* (2.2), underlined in *DW* (2:15), and in his quarto, with this note (*RS* 52):

> There is something exquisitely rich and luxurious in Titania's saying "since the middle summer's spring" as if Bowers were not exuberant and covert enough for fairy sports until their second sprouting—which is surely the most bounteous overwhelming of all of Nature's goodnesses.

In Keats's bower-borrowing is Fairy-King Oberon's poetry, shortly on, in the same scene (2.2):

> I know a bank whereon the wild thyme blows,
> Where ox-lips and the nodding violet grows;
> Quite over-canopied with lush woodbine,
> With sweet musk-roses, and with eglantine.

Oberon speaks from memory. Keats underlines it for memory (*DW* 2:20).[16] These are plantings for the anthology (flower gathering) of stanza 5, so much richer than the tinsel-Poesy of stanza 4. Shakespeare rhymes *blows* and *glows*, echoing into *roses*. Keats replenishes the sound into *flowers, boughs,* and the month's gift, *endows*. Shakespeare's sweet *musk-rose* feeds Keats's *musk rose, full of dewy-wine* (and rhyme for *eglantine*). In such sproutings, mortal markers transform. A mortuary-seeming *embalmed* becomes a cover-term for each living sweet. The *murmurous haunt of flies on summer eves* (50) is no gothic graveyard; it is a melodious plot, humming *murmurous . . . summer,* with a verbal jest at the delusory *fly* away (31). *Guess each sweet* speaks its own worded sweetness.

Keats's nocturne has darker haunts, however, and the deflected funereal senses I just mentioned return with force on a volta-turn to stanza 6, *Darkling I listen.* What an adjective!—"a participle it seems, from *darkle,* which yet I have never found," said Dr. Johnson (*JnD*). Keats found it, for reperception. As it situates what "I cannot see," *Darkling* attaches to a very dark passage in his reading memory:

> Then feed on thoughts, that voluntary move
> Harmonious numbers; as the wakeful bird
> Sings darkling, and in shadiest covert hid
> Tunes her nocturnal note.   (3.38–40; *KPL* I:62)

This is the poignancy of blind Milton's song, where *Sings darkling* pivots on a double-loaded *as:* it is a companionable comparative, and it is a temporal simultaneity of a blind poet hearing a bird-song as he struggles to make positive sense of his darkness invisible. Matthew Arnold, mindful of Keats's Ode, takes this word to a universal, existential "darkling plain" of ignorant armies clashing by night (*Dover Beach*). At the century's end Thomas Hardy listens to a "Darkling Thrush" who, old and wrecked as it is, can still "fling his soul / Upon the growing gloom" with an inspiration that the listener can conjecture but not know.

Keats's full chord, soon tuned to a recognition that he has *been half in love with easeful Death* (51–52), holds the echo of soul-brother Hamlet:

> To die,—to sleep,—
> No more;—and, by a sleep, to say we end
> The heart-ache, and the thousand natural shocks
> That flesh is heir to . . .   (3.1)

Hamlet thinks to end *heart-ache* in the Big Sleep. Keats writes this as *To die, / To cease* (55–56). Hamlet halts at the "conscience" (consciousness) that death may be an eternity of bad dreams (he has seen a tormented ghost). For skeptic Keats, the halt at *half* is the love, however pained, of conscious life. It infuses the pun-ready poet who could hear "amused" for the odist who has romanced Death with *many a mused rhyme* (53). This is related to the half-infinitive, half-petitioning *To take into the air my quiet breath* (52, 54). As Latin-literate Keats knows, this spells the reverse of *in-spire,* a taking in of transformative breath. The success of *no pain* is rebuked in rhyme itself: *ears in vain.*

The bottom line is a *high requiem* for a poet who would *become a sod* (60), a deeply unmelodious plot.[17] At this dead end, the odist declares his divorce: *Thou wast not born for death, immortal Bird!* begins stanza 7 (61). No ornithology, this is bitter mythology. Keats's capital "B" is symbolic. A bird can have no mortal, existential knowing of death. It is "immortal" by antithesis to human heartache from ancient days to 1819, from highest to lowest, *emperor and clown* (64). Keats piercingly concentrates this in biblical Ruth, the migrant gleaner whose very name means "sorrow."

> Perhaps the self-same song found a path
> Through the sad heart of Ruth, when, sick for home,
> She stood in tears amid the alien corn.   (65–68)

"The story of Ruth," said Hazlitt in a lecture that Keats attended on 13 January 1818, "is as if all the depth of natural affection in the human race was involved in her breast" (*Lectures* 33). Keats's grammar is a story in itself. It's not just that Ruth hears the song, but that it invades her heart *through* (sounding *rue*, the etymology of *Ruth*). In the diagnosis, *sick for home: in tears amid the alien corn*, Keats images an entire sociology of migrant labor. The material condition *amid alien corn* gets a prepositional equivalence with the stationing of the gleaner *in tears*.[18] One reviewer was blown away by the brilliance of *alien*, "hitching the faculty of imagination on a single word."[19] "Home-sickness is a wasting pang," wrote Coleridge in Germany, for his *Home-Sick* poem (*Sibylline Leaves*, p. 153). Medical student, Coleridge-reader, poet, Keats evokes Ruth as a staged etymology.

To all such sorrowful listeners, nightingale-song is a charm, an enchantment that is delusion, no harbinger of *ease* but, in words already laden, a call to *perilous seas in faery lands forlorn*. Keats refined the sound of *perilous seas* for this recoil on the romance of *ease*. He first wrote *ruthless seas* (*C* 41), lexical antonym of *Ruth*. He then decided that the name-pun was overkill. A better tune was a final sounding of *ease* in the undercurrent of "perilous *seas*," once heard, the knell of fantasy. *Charm'd magic casements* is a Keatsian self-listening to the genre of "old romance," his phrasing for naïve wishing in *The Eve of St. Agnes* (V), the poem, earlier in *1820*, with that fabulous art-worked casement that divides Madeline's chamber from winter and magically refracts cold moonlight into warm splendor (XXIV–XXV). Even if you didn't know this sibling scene, the words that end stanza 7 tell the illusion: *faery lands forlorn* (69–70). Here there is no light. Keats first wrote *fairy* (ms. *C* 41), then called up antiqued *faery*. The final word *forlorn* is a stressful spondee, to answer, with the same alliterated stress, *faery lands*.[20]

Then comes the most eventful self-listening in the ode, in all of Keats: a punctuated echo *Forlorn!* as the volta into the final stanza. (In *1820*, a turn of the page sets the stanza alone on page 112 to give it the effect of a coda or epitaph.) In an ode where six of its eight stanzas are strung on one sentence (with medial pauses), this last is a stark variant, striking four (maybe five) emphatic declarations, with medial punctuations weighted like periods.[21] The *toll* of *Forlorn!* into *sole self* frames the words *back from thee*. This sounds like a firm recall (echo and revocation) of stanza 4's way too hopeful *Already with thee!* The near couplet of stanza 8's first two lines (*bell*/*self*) might have rung the case closed. But Keats is writing drama, not argument, and in this pulse of candor, the poet's divorce is no sooner stated than attenuated. The ambiguously toned judgment, *the fancy cannot cheat so well / As she is famed to do, deceiving elf* (73–

74), is symptomatic. Is this sigh bitter? bittersweet? accepting, or sorrowful? Keats first wrote *deceitful* (ms. *C* 43), a fine coda to the *full/ful* chain, not least *easeful*. The present-participle *deceiving* delivers a still active allure, with an ambiguity worthy of William Empson's attention: either she-fancy cheats categorically, or has proven sadly inept on this night, not up to her *fam'd* standard. All it takes is a pause on *forlorn* to break the charm.

The self-listening, in Keats's reckoning, goes back to a scene of elf-cheating in *Endymion*.[22]

> thoughts of self came on, how crude and sore
> The journey homeward to habitual self!
> A mad-pursuing of the fog-born elf,
> Whose flitting lantern, through rude nettle-briar,
> Cheats us into a swamp . . .   (2.276–280)

This self is a fatally cheated *fog-born elf* in genesis, destination, and delivery. The fated rhyme of the doubly sounded *self* is *elf*. Fancy-mad. In *Nightingale's* last stanza, Keats issues a bill of separation, a bit bitter, but promisingly unfogged. How finely painful is the way the tripled *Adieu! . . . Adieu! adieu!* (73, 75) revokes *away . . . Away! away!* (10, 31).

Yet even as this verbal symmetry shapes this argument, the echoing *Adieu!* is the sound-track of the drama (as it was in *Ode on Indolence*). The word is a tender sigh, and not likely a final break. The listener lingers on its sound:

> Adieu! adieu! thy plaintive anthem fades
>   Past the near meadows, over the still stream,
>   Up the hill-side; and now 'tis buried deep
>   In the next valley-glades: (75–78)

Adieu, adieu, adieu! remember me, says a ghost to Hamlet (1.5), and it will return. Keats check-marked this line (*DW* 7:24). Having longed to *fade away,* having sensed *fast-fading violets,* this *fades/Past* is a last fade, and it is no firm fade-out. The poetry follows the song, line by line, phrase by phrase, chime by chime (*still . . . hill*), tender-tautened preposition by preposition: *Past, near, over, Up,* then *In the next,* still near, a dream-scape ready for recall.

Wordsworth's poetry, said Hazlitt, infuses sense-data with "the shadowy brightness of a waking dream," actual objects "lost . . . as sound in the multiplication of echoes."[23] Spenser's *all-fairyland* is the more extreme lure: he "was the poet of our waking dreams" who "invented not only a language, but a music of his own for them . . . lulling the senses in a deep oblivion of the jarring noises of the world, from which we have no wish ever to be recalled" (*Lectures* 85). Keats's next, and last, lines hover between Wordsworth and Spenser:

> Was it a vision, or a waking dream?
> Fled is that music:—Do I wake or sleep? (79–80)

When the poet of *Ode to Psyche* coyly mused, *Surely I dreamt to-day, or did I see?* as prologue to an origin-story, *or* scarcely mattered. The twice-tolled *or* in the epilogue to *Ode to a Nightingale* is critical. No better test of Negative Capability for a reader, too. Such questions, about modes of musing and doubting, are active interrogative poetics, evocative, open, unsettled. Even the *it* of *Was it* is involved: the enchantment or the disenchantment? *Do I wake or sleep?* is the finale of elusive grammar. Does *wake* mean "smarten up," or "am dream-forlorn"? Is *sleep* a metaphor for life "here," on track for awakening beyond (Wordsworth's and Shelley's metaphysics), or does it come from a lingering, longing enchantment?

To Coleridge, such effects are the very energy of "imagination":

> an effort in the mind when it would describe what it cannot satisfy itself with the description of . . . when it is hovering between . . . as soon as it ~~becomes~~ is fixed ~~on one~~ it becomes understanding and when it is waving between them attaching itself to neither it is imagination. (*Lectures* 1:311)

Not just the questions of Keats's *Ode* but even the finale of its inspiration, *Fled is that music,* hover this way. What is not *fled* is the presence of this most musical ode. Which "I" governs *Do I wake or sleep?* The poet *in* the ode, or the poet *of* the ode? In a dissolve rather than resolve, Keats hands it all to us.

In a new turn of Keats's thinking-through, *Ode on a Grecian Urn* begins with questions, bearing several namings, each poised for irony: dramatic, conceptual, foundational.

> [*1820*, 107–112. Lines 59–60 are apparently mis-set in *1820*. I follow the other stanzas' pattern, as do Stillinger (*P* 371) and Allott (529)]

[1] Helen Vendler advertises her chapter (*Odes* 73) with the title-page of *The Nightingale. Containing a Collection of Four Hundred and Ninety Two of the most Celebrated English Songs* (1742). Additions to the lore include Charlotte Smith's popular *Elegiac Sonnets* (1784 on).

[2] First published in 1800; I quote the text Keats would know, *Sibylline Leaves* (1817), 204–209. In *Il Penseroso,* Philomel sings "her sweetest, saddest plight, / . . . Most musical, most melancholy" (56–57, 62).

[3] *Modern Painters,* vol. 3, chapter XII (London: Smith, Elder, 1856).

[4] Coleridge's poem "will contribute greatly to rectify these" (7 June 1802; *EY* 355–356). Among the culprits is Coleridge's earlier *To the Nightingale,* immersed in Philomel lore and resounding of Milton's phrase (1796 *Poems,* pp. 71–72).

[5] The parallels with Wordsworth are carefully explicated by Peter Manning (*ELN*).

[6] The manuscript shows a first start on a page that Keats set aside, to start afresh on a new page; Gittings, *Odes,* 39; Stillinger, *P,* 652–653.

[7] Gittings, *Odes,* 36–37. Suzanne Reynolds finely pauses over the revision of the first words (146); I think Keats gets double mileage, undertoning *my heartaches.* Ms. *C* refers to the Cambridge manuscript (*Odes* 37–43).

[8] Thomas De Quincey is the pseudonym-confessor, instantly famous.

[9] In the first publication of *Kubla Khan,* 1816 (the one Keats knew), Coleridge images the inspired poet as one who *drank the milk of Paradise.* His first wording was *drunk* (1798 ms.; *Poems,* ed. E. H. Coleridge, 298), inebriation over nurture. For *drank,* see *Christabel &c,* p. 58.

[10] This misprision is so forecast that it captures sharp reader John Jones ("the poet . . . finds himself, momentarily, 'too happy'"; 219). So, too (among others), Wasserman, 180, 186; Dickstein, 206; Ende, 132.

[11] I thank Beatrix Bondor, Princeton University class of 2023, for this smart catch.

[12] "Artistry," 251. Brooks is atoning for his earlier dismissal (in *Understanding Poetry,* 1938) of Keats's imagery as superficial, confused, lax.

[13] *London Magazine*'s obituary on Keats (April 1822) quoted line 26, in italics (3:426).

[14] Keats missed this lecture, 20 January 1818, but heard about it, and read it (*Lectures* 68).

[15] I follow Wasserman's fine attention to this drama of syntax, 198–199.

[16] For a supple reading of this allusion as a poetics of allusion, see Ricks, *CCJK,* 160–161.

[17] Keats underlined Claudio's terror of his <u>sensible warm motion</u> becoming a dead <u>clod</u> (*Measure for Measure* 3.1). *DW*'s printer mis-set the word as *cold* (1:38), perhaps by force of <u>cold obstruction</u> two lines above, but Keats read it aright. A poet is anyone *whose soul is not a clod,* he'll write in the opening of *The Fall of Hyperion* (MsK 3.2.311).

[18] Gleaning is abject stoop-labor, gathering harvest remnants (*corn* is all grains).

[19] *London Magazine* (Gold's), December 1820, 559.

[20] David Bromwich notes the double alliteration, limiting it to intuitive phonic association ("Keats" 387).

[21] Even the colons in the previous stanzas are mostly not terminally weighted, but pulse comma-like pauses, or hinges between syntactic units, and in the case of stanza 2's aperture to stanza 3.

[22] Kingsley Amis caught the parallel, with no favor.

[23] Review of *The Excursion, Examiner* (21 August 1814), 541.

Ode on a Grecian Urn

I.

Thou still unravish'd bride of quietness,
    Thou foster-child of silence and slow time,
Sylvan historian, who canst thus express
    A flowery tale more sweetly than our rhyme:
What leaf-fring'd legend haunts about thy shape
    Of deities or mortals, or of both,
        In Tempe or the dales of Arcady?
What men or gods are these? What maidens loth?
    What mad pursuit? What struggle to escape?
        What pipes and timbrels? What wild ecstasy?   10

2.

Heard melodies are sweet, but those unheard
    Are sweeter; therefore, ye soft pipes, play on;
Not to the sensual ear, but, more endear'd,
    Pipe to the spirit ditties of no tone:
Fair youth, beneath the trees, thou canst not leave
    Thy song, nor ever can those trees be bare;
        Bold Lover, never, never canst thou kiss,
Though winning near the goal—yet, do not grieve;
    She cannot fade, though thou hast not thy bliss,
        For ever wilt thou love, and she be fair!   20

3.

Ah, happy, happy boughs! that cannot shed
    Your leaves, nor ever bid the Spring adieu;
And, happy melodist, unwearied,
    For ever piping songs for ever new;
More happy love! more happy, happy love!
    For ever warm and still to be enjoy'd,
        For ever panting, and for ever young;
All breathing human passion far above,

That leaves a heart high-sorrowful and cloy'd,
    A burning forehead, and a parching tongue.   30

4.

Who are these coming to the sacrifice?
    To what green altar, O mysterious priest,
Lead'st thou that heifer lowing at the skies,
    And all her silken flanks with garlands drest?
What little town by river or sea shore,
    Or mountain-built with peaceful citadel,
        Is emptied of this folk, this pious morn?
And, little town, thy streets for evermore
    Will silent be; and not a soul to tell
        Why thou art desolate, can e'er return.   40

5.

O Attic shape! Fair attitude! with brede
    Of marble men and maidens overwrought,
With forest branches and the trodden weed;
    Thou, silent form, dost tease us out of thought
As doth eternity: Cold Pastoral!
    When old age shall this generation waste,
        Thou shalt remain, in midst of other woe
Than ours, a friend to man, to whom thou say'st,
    "Beauty is truth, truth beauty,"—that is all
        Ye know on earth, and all ye need to know.   50

Ode to a Nightingale and *Ode on a Grecian Urn* are Keats's most famous odes, arguably his two most famous poems. *On a Grecian Urn* was the title of its first publication, in *Annals of the Fine Arts* (January 1820, p. 638). The genre-tag added in *1820* is *Ode on . . .* , with the effect of marking a sequel to *Ode to a Nightingale* (which it follows), now treating an illusion for the eye rather than the ear. *Ode on a Grecian Urn* "invents a whole new category of lyric," argues Stanley Plumly; this is "the ekphrastic experience as a poem in response to a work of art" (*Immortal Evening* 109). It is also a conversation with the reader about ekphrasis, the encounter of words and object.

This is Keats's brainiest, most intellectual ode, a taut, witty experiment with short-form interrogative poetics. The speaker is not a dramatized discoverer (as in *Psyche, Indolence,* and *Nightingale*) but a game-master of meta-ekphrasis. The difficulties "are built into the poem from the start," says Morris Dickstein (221). Deconstructive critique is redundant, quips Jack Stillinger, because "Keats himself had already written into his text those very incongruities and discordances" that such critique means to "expose" ("Fifty-nine Ways" 205). The most important contest is between the static spatial array of the visual object and the temporal arc of the poet's language. This contest bears on the gendering of *Thou still unravish'd bride*, a blazon that conflates, in Peter Manning's memorable phrase, "reading and ravishing." Keats plays these actions through four stanzas: a mad pursuit of maidens by men or he-gods (1), a bold Lover in courtship of a fair she (2–4), a procession to sacrifice a garlanded she-calf (4). Then a last act (5) ditches the whole affair of ravishing, with a sarcastic pun on the alluring *bride* as merely an overwrought *brede* (intertwining), immune to address, impenetrable to reading.

Reading is Keats's master-trope. As the poet reads the Urn's shapes and figures, we read *Urn*, the ode's verbal shapes and figuring. If Keats's greetings of the spirit solicit engaged reading, this ode insists on it. *Ode to a Nightingale* has us following word careers and reversals of syntax into a conclusion on unsettled questions. *Ode on a Grecian Urn* opens with questions—of a particular kind. These are begged, premised: there is a legend; figures can be determined; actions can be explained. A *still unravish'd bride* may reside in *quietness* (one meaning of *still*), but this also leans into a temporal *still:* an "as yet," poised for the right approach.[1] Words, even syllables, are what John Jones calls "Keats's iceberg statements," a "visible tip" of larger matter (219). We sense a game afoot.

Keats teases the *still unravish'd bride of quietness* with epithets of origin: *Thou foster-child* (the artisanal creators long gone) and a sequel parentage *of silence and slow time.* This phrase doubles into what it is to read with care, too. Haydon liked to insist on the superior immediacy of visual "imitation" and "representation" over poetry's "artificial assemblage of words." Even so, his own evocative ekphrastic writing about visual arts may have us thinking that his distinction rather fungible.[2] While Keats seems to agree with the argument that the Urn's imagery delivers *A flowery tale more sweetly than our rhyme* (4), he also winks that it takes rhyme to present the case, with no little wit in rhyming *rhyme* to endurance in *time.*

Sylvan historian is a nicely rhymed melody itself. This epithet is also about reading. A historian is a professional double for what the poet is doing: the root of *historia* is a Greek word for "learning or knowing by inquiry" (*OED*). With a barrage of questions, the odist stages history in poetry. *What leaf-fring'd legend haunts about thy shape . . . ?* further figures reading (*legend:* Latin, "to be read"). If Keats wittily letters *ring* into *fring'd,* the verb *haunts* makes it spectral, not even present for interpretation. And so a coolly mused *What* heats up, peppered seven times, and in such fast time to *What maidens loth?/What mad pursuit?* that the questions could just as well be about the poet's mad pursuit. *What* nouns or verbs are these?

In another of those fortunate book-events, stanza 1 stands alone on *1820's* page 113, poised for answering. Turn the page and you get no answers from stanza 2, but find a new gambit, a game reset: frustrating silence issuing a counter-greeting to the spirit of imagination. *What creates the intense pleasure of not Knowing?* Keats wrote in the margins of *Paradise Lost* and stayed to answer: *A sense of independence, of power from the fancy's creating a world of its own by the sense of probabilities* (I:23). That was the fun of *Fancy.* The theme for stanza 2, with visual word-work on its behalf, canny-cagey, is how *our rhyme* may greet the spirit:

> Heard melodies are sweet, but those unheard
>   Are sweeter; therefore, ye soft pipes, play on;
> Not to the sensual ear, but, more endear'd,
>   Pipe to the spirit ditties of no tone: (11–14)

We get it: the pleasure of possibility. Yet see how Keats's conducting of this score plays visibly with shapes of words read in silence and slow time. A few weeks before hearing Hazlitt praise Shakespeare's "hieroglyphical" language for how it "translates thoughts into visible images," Keats wrote about a "hieroglyphics of beauty" in "the very points and letters of charactered language." Hazlitt's *hieroglyphical* means metaphor (literally, "translate"). Keats's nominalized *hieroglyphics* treats language itself as charactered image.[3] He sets *ear* (tentatively anticipated) inside the span from "H*ear*d" to "un*hear*d." Then he spells it and sounds it in a hieroglyph for spiritual reception, "more end*ear*'d": the *ear* within, beyond the *end* of the sensual receptor. If the rhyme-sounded *unheard/endear'd* is faint at best, and there is hardly a rhyme in *play on/no tone,* it is to yield a lovely visual conceit: the call of *on* reversed in *no* and spelled to the eye in t*one.* The quatrain ends on this word, with a colon cue (*no tone:*).

This is answered with a full-toned double-exposure of *still* that translates the romance of immortality into the agony of frustrated arrest. What is the tone: celebratory? sarcastic? campy? The wordings elude negotiation, even clear syntax. Keats wryly opens *for ever* into irony, on zigzags between transfixing promise and satirical reperception. The ecstasy: a fair youth beneath the trees will never *leave* his song; leaved trees will never bare (15–16). The agony: the breathless run of lines 17–20 to the flagrant exclamation *For ever wilt thou love, and she be fair!* cannot extinguish all the preceding qualifications (*never, never though thou has not*). Earl Wasserman does his best: "the negation of these verbs . . . creates an infinity of mutable or chronological time, an absolute extension" (34). But it is a question whether the ideal frieze can survive rhyme's grammatical freeze. In January 1818, Keats heard Hazlitt lecture that poetry has just such advantage over painting, progress rather than stasis. Even stasis is dramatic:

> in the interval of expectation and suspense, while our hopes and fears are strained to the highest pitch of breathless agony, that the pinch of the interest lies . . . But by the time that the picture is painted, all is over. (*Lectures* 20–21)

Keats remembered this, I think, in his poetry of arrested narrative and unmoving design, more pinch than pitch.

For all this controlled wit, the tone of stanza 3 has long troubled readers.[4] The six cries of *happy,* two amped to *more happy,* make exclamation itself the main event. Keats also brings his close double, the melodist, to sing the endear'd *ear* of stanza 2 into an "unwea*ried*" inspiration. Is it wild ecstasy, or stylized excess? With *nor ever* (22) braided with five iterations of *for ever* (24, 26–27), the phrase *still to be enjoy'd* (26) is ambiguously twinned to *still unravish'd:* promise, possibility, impossibility. Turning this arrest in paradox around to a poet's credit, Keats shows us that the urn we cannot really "see" is being constituted by poetry's words, and spun with his tones.

The cresting tide of *happy* washes into a last iteration of *for ever* with an enigmatic punctuation at the end of the line.

> For ever panting, and for ever young;
> All breathing human passion far above,
> That leaves a heart high-sorrowful and cloy'd,
> A burning forehead, and a parching tongue.   (27–30)

From the end of line 27, Keats springs another one of his surprises by syntax. *All breathing human passion far above* (28) is ready made for William Empson's catch at "any verbal nuance, however slight, which gives room for alternative reactions to the same piece of language" (*Seven Types* 1). Line 27 is grammatically closed by a semicolon. But even a punctuation-mark in Keats's hands can double-deal. This one reads less like a firm stop than a pause of breath, a comma-like summing up of the condition of forever *piping* and *panting,* for a collective noun-phrase that comes in the next line: *All breathing human passion far above* our human world.[5] This *far above* could image the highest passion, rinsed of Hazlitt's sensation of "breathless agony." Wasserman is on board: "a human passion, and at the same time it is far above all mutable human passion"; the "syntactical oxymoron" serves a "mystic oxymoron" of "mortal and immortal" (39–40). Yet at this very pitch, Wasserman wonders if Keats has been forced into unexpected "bewilderment" (41).

Bewildering is Keats's game. If the flow into line 28 courts the illusion, line 29 takes it all back. Human passion has no pass to urn-illusion: *far above* turns out to be no prepositional extension but an impossible comparison. The participle kin for *breathing* is not (after all) the twins *piping* and *panting* but mortal sequels of a pathetic *burning* and *parching.* What a letdown! An *Urn* can know nothing of *burning.* Yet in the midst of the course-correction, Keats slips the words *breathing human* out of the temporality of frozen *forever.*

The notion of a human world haunts about the shape of stanza 4, as Keats turns to a new scene: *Who are these coming to the sacrifice?* It is a poet's imagination, not an unknown Sylvan historian, who maps origins and destinations: *green* altar and *little town.* Actual history is impossible, desolated.

> And, little town, thy streets for evermore
> > Will silent be; and not a soul to tell
> > > Why thou art desolate, can e'er return.   (38–40)

Mindful of Haydon's evocative ekphrasis on Raphael's *Sacrifice,* Keats borrows some of its lush description for this stanza.[6] While it is all notional, Keats renders it so vividly that no less a poet than W. B. Yeats could think this an actual description.[7] The ode-reader turns out to be the historian he has been calling for. It is "our rhyme" that sounds *not a soul* into *desolate,* that tolls *evermore . . . silent* against the surmise of *more sweetly* (4) and *more endear'd* (13), that hyper-tunes *not . . . e'er* as the last note of eleven forms of *ever.* The *for ever* of art's endurance fades into a vacated *for evermore . . . silent.*

Like the last stanza of *Ode to a Nightingale,* this ode's last stanza issues a divorce from illusion: *Thou, silent form* (44). The rhyme pattern of stanza 4 subtly collaborates. Its final word *return* (40) is pattern-linked to *pious morn* (37), a pretty weak sound, and no eye rhyme at all. What Keats gains (by ear industrious and attention meet) is a stress on *urn* in the iamb *return:* a verbal figure in potent rhyme to the title-word *Urn.* Empson discerns a "crisis" in "the sudden exertion of muscle by which Keats skids round the corner from selfpity to an imaginative view of the world." He means the town without pity in stanza 4, and a recognition that "Beauty is both a cause and escape from suffering, and either way suffering is deeply involved in its production."[8] I don't think *selfpity* is Keats's groove. Where Empson impatiently sees skid, I see a counter-turn to a new Urning, an artifact hailed in parody of an ode-calling. Disillusioned of correspondent humanity (bride, foster-child, historian), this urn-reader names a shape, a design, a form, an artifactual endurance, a riddle instead of an oracle.

The muse now is what rhyme *can* express: *O Attic shape! Fair attitude!* (41) and *Thou, silent form* are all vocatives of conspicuously decadent punning, all pointed in disgust at *Cold Pastoral!*[9] Hazlitt described Greek statues as "ideal, spiritual . . . beauty . . . raised above the frailties of pain or passion."[10] He elaborated this (in a lecture Keats attended, 13 January 1818) with a slant on marble form that clearly helped Keats into stanza 5:

> It is for want of some such resting-place for the imagination that the Greek statues are little else than specious forms. They are marble to the touch and to the heart . . . In their faultless excellence they appear sufficient to themselves. (*Lectures* 21–22)[11]

Mindful of this marble finish, Keats recasts a seeming legend-laden scene into a *brede / Of marble men and maidens overwrought* (41–42). The forms that his poetry breeds are lively word-plays: puns, visual figures, cues, quips, and parodies, for evermore Keats's brand. From the skid of *Attic* (Greek dialect) into *attitude* (a pose, a mental state), Keats has fun with *overwrought*.[12] It denotes figures wrought over (upon) a surface, in a Spenser-sense: "a Fountain . . . with pure Imagery / Was over-wrought" (*FQ* II.II.LX). At the same time, it glances, with ironic sympathy, at figures frozen in agonized passion.[13]

The rhyme Keats has waiting for *overwrought* is no pun, but an earned reaction to a plot against *thought*:

> Thou, silent form, dost tease us out of thought
>   As doth eternity: Cold Pastoral!
>
> (44–45)

No *ease* in this *tease*. *Thou* will not yield to *thought*, however lettered into it the word is. While the analogy to eternity is a formal service, it is no conceptual help: the no-time of "eternity" is beyond thought. Here the tease and the courtship end, on a last exclamation point.

Keats's final turn is not this dismissal, however, but a reflection on what it took to get there. The Urn-art setting of *this pious morn* (37) is not the same temporal present as *this generation* (46). The second *this* is a really haunting one, because it speaks to the immediate time of reading (then and now), by readers who know what mortal woe and mortal wasting are:

> When old age shall this generation waste,
>   Thou shalt remain, in midst of other woe
> Than ours, a friend to man, to whom thou say'st,
>   "Beauty is truth, truth beauty,"—that is all
>   Ye know on earth, and all ye need to know.   (46–50)

Back in late 1817, Keats was sure that *What the imagination seizes as Beauty must be truth* (*K* 69), and that truth would purge "all disagreeables" (*K* 77). Keats being Keats, this is not his last word, but another round in a life-long quarrel. In his latest turn, the Urn's hallucinated *say'st* not only withholds Platonizing capitals but also issues an unravishable tautology. The penultimate aphorism has been exported to epigraphs, library walls, coffee cups, T-shirts, pins, and "beauty" salons, but its enigmatic ring won't tell for the Ode's scenes.[14]

This is the final parody of Keats's ode. For all its big-ticket wording, *Beauty is truth, truth beauty* is self-enclosed circular syntax, a legend "about" the shape of the urn that might as well be fringed leaves. In a landmark essay, "Keats's Sylvan Historian," Cleanth Brooks calls it a "consciously riddling paradox" modified by the dramatic context of the questioner's wanting to gain some saying out of this intractable silence (141–142).[15] The only thing to *know* is that old age wastes all generations. Like the tread of *hungry generations* about which a Nightingale knows nothing, the temporal marker here, *When old age shall this generation waste,* layers bitterness and stoicism. Keats's last rhyme is keyed by the existential guarantee, *midst of other woe.* This *woe* is a sound-back from the ironized vocative "O" that launched this stanza, and forward-cast to its last word, a double-said *know*—as opaque a verb as can be for an Ode that began in full-throated inquiry. Achingly human Ruth "amid the alien corn" in *Ode to a Nightingale* is a chapter of this woe. The Urn's art is sheer non-humanity: a *brede / Of marble men and maidens.* No more ironic rhyme, then, for the exclamation-pointed *Cold Pastoral!* than Keats's asymmetric, line-end stressed *—that is all.*

How uncanny that the puzzle of these last lines has generated a textual puzzle: what to read? Keats's holograph is lost, not a soul to tell, except in competing forms. The first publication, in *Annals of the Fine Arts* (IV:639), sets the last lines to have the Urn seeming to say,

> Beauty is Truth, Truth Beauty.—That is all
> Ye know on Earth, and all ye need to know.

Brown's manuscript has it this way, too. But *1820* (p. 116) not only lacks the Platonizing capitals but also quotes the tautology in quotation marks, an Urn-saying that the poet hands off to us (*ye*).

> "Beauty is truth, truth beauty,"—That is all
> Ye know on earth, and all ye need to know.

All versions keep the meter-paused, midline weighted dash. But for *all* this drama, the poet's adieu is a final ditty of no tone: a grand flair of plenitude, or a flippant kiss-off? In a memorably meticulous forensic, "Who Says What to Whom at the End of *Ode on a Grecian Urn?*," Jack Stillinger concludes that "no single explanation can satisfy the demands of text, grammar, dramatic consistency, and common sense" (*Hoodwinking* 171). The epiphenomenon is a perfect Keatsian irony: all we can know is that we cannot know, the know of not to know it. Seeming to promise a "hieroglyphics of beauty," *Ode on a Grecian Urn* produces a Keats-witted "-<u>rogue</u>glyphics."[16]

What would it be to have a roguish premise and craftily overwrought rhyme? This is *Ode on Melancholy,* no question, no "I", but a subject that Keats could feel on his pulses, and charge his words into its existential actions.

[*1820*, 113–116; mis-setting lines 8–9, which I pattern on the other stanzas]

---

[1] For the double-sense play of *still* (static and temporal), see John Barnard, *John Keats,* 105.

[2] *The Sacrifice at Lystra,* 238–239, in the same number of *Annals* (IV.13) as the first publication of *Ode to the Nightingale* (354–356, the title therein). Notwithstanding his argument for the superiority of visual art, Haydon's generous ekphrasis (227–236) of Raphael's cartoon (for a tapestry in the Sistine Chapel) is quite gripping!

[3] Keats heard Hazlitt lecture on this on 20 January 1818 (*Lectures* 107). His wording is in his review of Kean in *The Champion,* 21 December 1817 (*K* 74). Hazlitt was reading and writing for *The Champion* at the time (Wu 1:xxxix–xl), and would notice an article on Shakespeare and Kean.

[4] I assemble some of the notable ones (up to 1986) in *Questioning Presence,* 321n23.

[5] Three manuscripts even have a comma at the end of 27 (Keats's original is lost): George Keats's (Gittings, *Odes,* 47), Brown's (p. 28), and Woodhouse's ("from C.B."; MsK 3.2.359).

Moreover, lines 22 (*nor ever bid the Spring adieu*) and 24 (*songs for ever new*) end on semicolons weighted like strong commas, pauses for breath in the ardor of syntactic pursuit.

[6] Paul Magnuson makes this connection (207–208). The next number of *Annals of the Fine Arts* (IV.14) hosted the first publication of *On a Grecian Urn* (638–639, the title, sans *Ode*).

[7] "This is an indescribably lovely place – some little Greek town one imagines – there is a passage in Keats describing just such a town," Yeats wrote from Rapallo, 24 February 1928 (*Letters* 738).

[8] Empson, "Thy Darling," 694.

[9] Bridges's wince at the first two puns as "stumbling" (*Poems*, ed. Drury 1:lxvi) cued a train of detractors, including Empson, who thought this the ode's worst line ("Thy Darling" 694–695).

[10] *On Gusto*, 549; then in *The Round Table* (1817), then the same issue of *Annals* (IV.15, 543–549) as Keats's *Ode*. Magnuson argues (168–170) that the *Annals'* opposition to Royal Academy classical aesthetics amplifies Keats's rejected idealism, in accord with his praises of Haydon and the Elgin Marbles (his two sonnets republished in *Annals* 3, April 1818, 171–172). We need not agree with Magnuson that the meaning of *Ode on a Grecian Urn* is governed by this paratext (180) to appreciate the context. Haydon got all these poems into *Annals* (*KC* 2:142).

[11] Some echoes are noted by Allott (535n) and discussed by Bromwich, 391.

[12] *JnD* on the static pose defines *attitude*; *OED* indicates eighteenth-century usages for implied mental state. Empson is not alone in groaning at *attitude/Attic*; Brooks, too ("Postscript" 697–698).

[13] In *Childe Harold III* (1816) Byron cites his "o'erwrought" brain (7); so Keats, frustrated with *Endymion: my Brain so overwrought that I had neither Rhyme nor reason in it*, he writes in a theatrically abject letter to his publishers that opens in flourish of puns and parodies (MsK 1.8.26). Rollins's transcription, *over-wrought,* unhappily stabilizes the pun-play (*L* 1:146).

[14] Forman uses the last two lines (in the *1820* form) as an epigraph for vol. II (1883).

[15] I. A. Richards is the pioneer theoretical ironist: "Urns induce states of mind in their beholders; they do not enunciate philosophical positions—not in this kind of poetry—and 'say'st' is here used by a metaphor." He took T. S. Eliot's objection to the aphorism—so "grammatically meaningless" as to be a "serious blemish"—to expose his weak training in interpretation, "an arresting confession of linguistic disability to come from such a source." (Eliot says, disingenuously, either that he has failed "to understand it, or that it is a statement which is untrue.") To Richards, it is Keats's "superfluity of meanings, not any lack of meaning" that is "the difficulty" (*Mencius* 116–117).

[16] The page is torn at the left edge, losing some lettering before <u>rogue</u> (Beinecke Library, Yale; object 2013952). Rollins reads "{hie}*rogue*glyphics" (*L* 2:247), generally accepted. Given Keats's verbal hijinks and his characteristic underlining of puns, I can (negatively capable) imagine rogue-punning, perhaps even "high <u>rogue</u>glyphics." Keats enjoyed, underlined, and margin-marked *The Rogue,* given to him by his merry friend Jemme Rice (Amy Lowell 2:578–587).

Ode on Melancholy

1.

No, no, go not to Lethe, neither twist
    Wolf's-bane, tight-rooted, for its poisonous wine;
Nor suffer thy pale forehead to be kiss'd
    By nightshade, ruby grape of Proserpine;
Make not your rosary of yew-berries,
    Nor let the beetle, nor the death-moth be
        Your mournful Psyche, nor the downy owl
A partner in your sorrow's mysteries;
    For shade to shade will come too drowsily,
        And drown the wakeful anguish of the soul.   10

2.

But when the melancholy fit shall fall
    Sudden from heaven like a weeping cloud,
That fosters the droop-headed flowers all,
    And hides the green hill in an April shroud;
Then glut thy sorrow on a morning rose,
    Or on the rainbow of the salt sand-wave,
        Or on the wealth of globed peonies;
Or if thy mistress some rich anger shows,
    Emprison her soft hand, and let her rave,
        And feed deep, deep upon her peerless eyes.   20

3.

She dwells with Beauty—Beauty that must die;
    And Joy, whose hand is ever at his lips
Bidding adieu; and aching Pleasure nigh,
    Turning to poison while the bee-mouth sips:
Ay, in the very temple of Delight
    Veil'd Melancholy has her sovran shrine,
        Though seen of none save him whose strenuous tongue
Can burst Joy's grape against his palate fine;

His soul shall taste the sadness of her might,
    And be among her cloudy trophies hung.   30

This, too, was first titled *On Melancholy*, without *Ode*.[1] The closer of the section of *1820* titled "Poems," *Ode on Melancholy* seemed poised for a theatrical finale, as lush, wry, and tricky as they come. Keats may have imagined it as the close to *1820* itself (given his surprise at *Hyperion*). In late May 1819, he invoked for his fading dream of vocational success these lines in Wordsworth's "Great Ode" (*Intimations of Immortality*):

> 'Nothing can bring back the hour
> Of splendour in the grass and glory in the flower'
> I once thought this a Melancholist's dream ——   (*K* 256)

Wordsworth took care to put this elegy in subordinate syntax ("Though nothing can . . ."), set for main-clause mastery: "We will grieve not, rather find / Strength in what remains behind" (*1815* 2:354). Keats hears the double-voicing: a discipline that exposes the wording that needs it, summons it.

Ode to a Nightingale leaves no lesson; *Ode on a Grecian Urn* ironizes its lesson. *Ode on Melancholy* is a lesson with a vengeance: a thesis on temporality, not only in words, but also in the very phenomenology of reading them. This is no petitioning "Ode to." It is existential: "on" as a condition. Wordsworth's time-figure for lost beauty is *hour* (a metonym for early childhood). Keatsian temporality may be a nano-second, or even simultaneously *while*. *This is the world*, he writes on 19 March 1819; *we cannot expect to give way many hours to pleasure – Circumstances are like Clouds continually gathering and bursting* (*K* 242; MsK 1.5.231).

Propped and propelled by Robert Burton's *Anatomy of Melancholy* (1621), "Melancholy" flourished into an eighteenth-century cult, and cultivation, of sorrows so exquisite as to be death-ready, with just a pause for some suicidal poetry. Its dark star was "Melancholy Dane" Hamlet, with no little poetic flair (all those world-weary soliloquies). The root is *Melano*, the black bile (*khole*) that feeds black moods, and so the muse of pathological poetics. In Keats's copy of *Anatomy*, the section on Love-Melancholy (vol. 2) is more heavily underlined and marked than any other. Back in 1818, Keats had young Apollo moan that "a melancholy numbs my limbs . . . Like one who once had wings" (3.89–91), an inexplicable sensation of lost power. Keats now sets *Melancholy*, as he had *Nightingale*, against this ready default. He could have written an *Ode on Mutability* (say) but he wanted the flair of rebranding the prestigious mode.

This flair has Keatsian "melancholy" spinning aesthetical capital from inevitable transience, with a draught of another root: *mel,* the Greek syllable that gives *melody* (*sweet ode*). One syllable packs both sweet and bile. No pathology, no fleshing out of Burton's *Anatomy,* Keats-*Melancholy* is a laboratory of existential philosophy and answerable style, wakeful and intense, campy and unavoidably costly. In three polished stanzas, set out on the classical pattern of thesis (strophe: don't), antithesis (antistrophe: do), and condensation (epode: why), *Ode on Melancholy* not only theorizes transience but stages it, transmuting old lore into new poetic ore, and transmuting the poet into collateral effect of nothing in himself. Each stanza is one sentence, paused by punctuation, twisting around this pole of argument.

Keats's first draft had four stanzas, the first one a parody of the cult.[2] Spooled out in one sentence, it cartoons a futile (male) romance-quest for the haunt of she-Melancholy:

> *Tho' you should build a bark of dead men's bones,*
> *And rear a phantom gibbet for a mast,*
>
>   *shrouds*
> *Stitch <u>creeds</u> together for a sail, with groans*
> *To fill it out, bloodstained and aghast;*
> *Altho' your rudder be a Dragon's tail,*
> *Long sever'd, yet still hard with agony,*
>   *Your cordage large uprootings from the skull*
> *Of bald Medusa; certes you would fail*
> *To find the Melancholy, whether she*
>   *Dreameth in any isle of Lethe dull.*

The protagonist *you* might gather remnants of agons to craft a passage, on a pumped-up quest, for lasting rest. Lethe, the river of forgetfulness, seems an obvious goal. But *dull* is the bottom line, sheer insensate stupidity. The story of *fail* is latent with an alternative grammar.

Keats decided to start again with the sound of *Tho'/Altho'* for an *in medias res* admonition: *No, no, go not to Lethe.* In this sounding, the first words also get to the "Ode" signal "O." The addressee is not Melancholy but those bummed out by life in a transient, mortal world. The built-in risk of spelling out negative advice, however, is advertising what it would deny: "somebody, or some force in the poet's mind, must have wanted to go to Lethe very much, if it took four negatives in the first line to stop them," remarks ambiguity-alert William Empson. The "disorder in the action of the negative . . . being too easily passed over or too much insisted upon" is a dramatic effect, registered in a "contrariety of the pathological splendours."[3] Following up, Helen Vendler sees a "homilist subversively attracted by what he reproves" (*Odes* 172). Back in December 1817, Keats insisted that excellent art was "intensity, capable of making all disagreeables evaporate, from their being in close relationship with Beauty and Truth" (*K* 77). He would struggle with this alchemical ideal, and be haunted by the entailment "evaporate."

Empson congratulates the mature poet of *Ode on a Grecian Urn* for "trying to work the 'disagreeables' into the theory" ("Thy Darling" 696). By the time Keats was theorizing Melancholy, disagreeables *were* the theory, a theory of art. Even that *downy owl,* rejected mascot for *sorrow's miseries* (7–8), comes in tones half in love with the sound of *drowsily* (9). Keats gives the adverb pride of place for the luxe flow from *owl* into *drown* (10), after having auditioned *heavily,* then *sleepily* (*T* ms.). Who remembers *No, no, go not* by this point? Keats's romance with words across the stanza has us ready to hear a suppressed love of *languish* in the lexical sliding of the higher ideal, "wakeful *anguish."*

In such romance, the rhetoric of advice takes an inward turn. Keats invites a mournful Psyche (evolved from hethen goddess to mental trope) into a wakeful soul, alive to the complex compounds of fleeting beauty. Stanza 2 rejects the traditional dosing of "melancholy fits," the fever-feeding in Burton's *Anatomy.* Keats takes a *melancholy fit* into modern poetry, transmuted from the archaic *fytte* of poetry. Such a soothing cascade, with musical alliteration, falls across the phrase *when the melancholy fit shall fall,* with a fine line-pause at *fall* (11), to linger in this fit. The line-turn to *Sudden* distills two figural comparisons in rapid alternation: weeping sorrow turned to nurture for thirsty flowers and green hills; then a shroud, a covering both funereal and protective. Keats has us thinking both ways (his poetic principle) about the complexities of April weather and its meteorological metaphors (12–14). So too, the gusto of *glut* (15). This is a rare word for Keats, in this form only here. Aggressive, appetitive, immersive, nearly parodic in its intensity, *glut* distills the large argument. The *morning* rose (15), evoking to refuse *mournful* (7), cannot forbid the sound of *mourning,* nor keep *rose* from sounding an illogical antonym, the *fall* to melancholy, and the *rosary* refused in the pharmacopeia of stanza 1 (5).

These relays are complexities rather than sad subtractions. The briefest luxury of all is the *rainbow of the salt sand-wave* (16), a sheen no sooner seen than gone, lingered over with five stresses on seven syllables that take longer to sound out than the iridescence could last. Keats knows Wordsworth's poetics of glory in the *Intimations* Ode: "The Rainbow comes and goes, / And lovely is the Rose" (*1815* 2:347), the capital lettering no stay against mortal dissolution. Keats's aesthetic is the transience, in acceleration. The third object for *glut* in his melancholy litany, *globed peonies* (17), is pure Keats: *globed* for world in a peony, a flower famed, in old, for medicinal power, but here an intensely brief indulgence.[4] Though it looks like one syllable, the iambic lilt stretches the sounding into a luxurious *glo-bed*. On a roll of riches, the didact of Melancholy moves on to an extravagant (unwoke) lesson on erotic splendor:

> Or if thy mistress some rich anger shows,
>   Emprison her soft hand, and let her rave,
>   And feed deep, deep upon her peerless eyes.   (18–20)

The poetry feeds on the phonics of the last line as much as anything else. It is no little economy that *peerless,* "without equal," involves a secondary sense of "not peering": objects rather than agents of aesthetic delectation. Stuart Sperry had to pause his professional analysis for a parenthesis of personal embarrassment: "(Viewed in purely human terms, the situation is the perfect one for a poet having his face slapped)."[5] We know the cliché, "you're so beautiful when you're angry." Keats's clinch is theatrically hyperbolic, a set-up for a severe reversal.

This is delivered with Keats's skill at grammatical whiplash. The first line of stanza 3, *She dwells with Beauty—Beauty that must die* (21), seems to refer to the mistress of stanza 2: her beauty, like her anger, will pass. So there! But the referent turns out to be sovran Melancholy, a potent *She* who (like Fame) has no particular interest in any one devotee. This ironic revelation may have been planted by the capital M on *Mistress* in manuscript T. But we hardly need this preview. For all his macho aesthetic swagger, the connoisseur of Melancholy is headed for a death of luxury at her shrine. Giving those peerless *eyes* (20) such a weak rhyme with *peonies* (17), Keats can save *eyes* to sound with *die* at the start of stanza 3 (21).

Stated in abstractions, the present-event verbs in stanza 3 are no Urn-forevering, but actors of change right before our reading eyes. This is a new form of personification, says John Barnard: "gestural rather than static, the emotion felt and experienced rather than intellectual and abstract" (*John Keats* 115). *Joy* is ever *Bidding adieu;* Pleasure is *turning* to poison in the pitch of aching sweetness (22–24). The iconic capital letters have no metaphysics; they are sheer power. Keats's rhyme-echoes are co-conspirators in this treachery: the ruby grape of *Proserpine* (4)—the meter is dactylic—returns as Joy's grape bursting against a palate *fine* (28), both grapes, figurally and phonically, sacrifices to the sovran *shrine* of Melancholy (26). Oscar Wilde will give Keats's burst maximum intensity: "What an exquisite life you have had!" Lord Henry exclaims to Dorian Gray; "You have drunk deeply of everything. You have crushed the grapes against your palate fine."[6] Like Hunt at Porphyro's feast, he savors Keats's very words.

While Keats solicits this luxury, it is with a twist that escapes the irony-clad Lord. Wilde rings the indulgence; Keats wrings the existential economy, the dues paid in fee to this aesthetic fraternity. This is the mighty sadness of trophy-status—and no special trophy either, just one *among* many *hung* out, cruelly rhymed. Hence the pathos, the rueful wit of it all. In this fraternity is Keats's avatar of love-melancholy, Shakespeare's Troilus (*Troilus and Cressida*, 3.2; *RS* 164):

<blockquote>

what will it be

When that the watry pallats taste indeede

Loues thrice reputed Nectar? Death I feare me

   woon

Sounding distruction, or some ioy too fine,

Too subtile, potent, and too sharpe in sweetnesse . . .

</blockquote>

Keats's hand corrected the misprint in his 1808 reprint of the 1623 folio of *sound* to *swoon* (he gave Endymion such a *swoon*, also to a lover's bliss at the close of "Bright star!"). What *Ode on Melancholy* saves from destruction is an exquisite poetry. Next to a phrase in Shakespeare's sonnet XXXI, *Hung with the trophies of my lovers gone*, Keats wrote "conceit," shorthand for what he loved: *the intensity of working out conceits* (*K* 72). He recalls Shakespeare's words to tune his "trophie*s hung*" with an undertoned *sung*.[7]

On amplifying rhyme, the word *sung* sounds this way in Melancholy's primer, Milton's *Il Penseroso*: great Bards "In sage and solemn tunes have *sung*, / Of Turneys and of Trophie*s hung*" (117–118, my emphases). The transferred sound comes again in *Samson Agonistes*: Samson's melancholy father means to build a monument for his son "With all his Trophie*s hung*," and to inspire a lore of "sweet Lyric song" (1736–1737). Keats echoes "Trophie*s hung*" in a diminuendo of ecstasy, mutability, and spiritual apocalypse all at once. With the aesthetic time-stamp that is, on principle, self-surrendering, self-annihilating, how absent from Keats's ode is the lyric "I." This sounds only in a theatrical *Ay* (25), rhyme-schemed, moreover, with *die*: the self sighed into melancholy ecstasy. The temple of delight is *seen of none save him* (27) but the acolyte of dissolution. The wording has a fine-tuned double grammar. Keats first wrote *none but him* (Berg manuscript), nicely tuning *but* to a willing *burst*. The revision is better for punning the sense of *save* as "except" into a double-grammar, "beyond saving."

Ode on Melancholy is Keats's Mortality Ode. The true Melancholist, good for his words, succeeds at his own expense. It is a severe aesthetic, but not (Wilde knows this) without heroic fun. Keats hits a master-nerve about how and why we read, finding pleasure in a luxury of words, even if the theme is unappeasable transience. The transformations of *Lamia* and Lamia wait in the wings. In this coming game, everyone gets burned, including the foreknowing reader—but not without an extraordinary aesthetic cash-out in unrivalled words.

[*1820*, 140–412]

[1] R. H. Taylor Collection, Princeton University Library, ms. RTC01; hereafter *T* (see *K* 369).

[2] *Brown*, p. 9 (crossed out), first published *1848* (1:287).

[3] Empson, *Seven Types*, 205, 215.

[4] Up to 2007, *OED* credited Keats with the first use of *globed* in the sense of *globe-like*. Two new listings of earlier cases are visual only, with no Keatsian feel for the intensely palpable feeling of roundedness, let alone a brain packed with word-history.

[5] Sperry, *Keats the Poet*, 282–283. Keats puns similarly for Porphyro's hope of winning a *peerless bride* (*Eve of St. Agnes* XIX).

[6] Wilde, *The Picture of Dorian Gray*, chapter XIII (96).

[7] Miriam Allott reports Keats's marking of this sonnet (541). The undertoning is in Garrett Stewart's ear (*CCJK* 145).

All I Live For

Last Poems, August 1819–Winter 1820

from *Lamia*

First in the title and order of Keats's last lifetime volume (see Figure 14, next page), *Lamia* commands 46 of its 200 pages.

Although Keats hoped that *The Eve of St. Agnes* would lead off, Keats's publishers and advisers saw *Lamia* as a stronger broadcast of "new Keats." *Endymion* (Keats admitted) was done "without Judgment" (*L* 1:374); *Lamia* (he confided to Reynolds) gave him "great hopes of success, because I make use of my Judgment more deliberately than I yet have done" (11 July 1819; *L* 2:128). "I am certain there is that sort of fire in it which must take hold of people in some way – give them either pleasant or unpleasant sensation," he could assure George and Georgiana (18 September; *K* 272). One firing is style. *Endymion* luxuriates in romance couplets. *Lamia*'s are Dryden-crisped, "with many triplets, & many alexandrines," Woodhouse reported to Taylor, "quite in character with the langage [*sic*] & sentiment."[1] Keats flexes his meters with superb weight and balance, tricks of grammar, syntax, and enjambment. Woodhouse loved hearing it read (even "badly" by Keats), and loved previewing it to publisher Taylor.

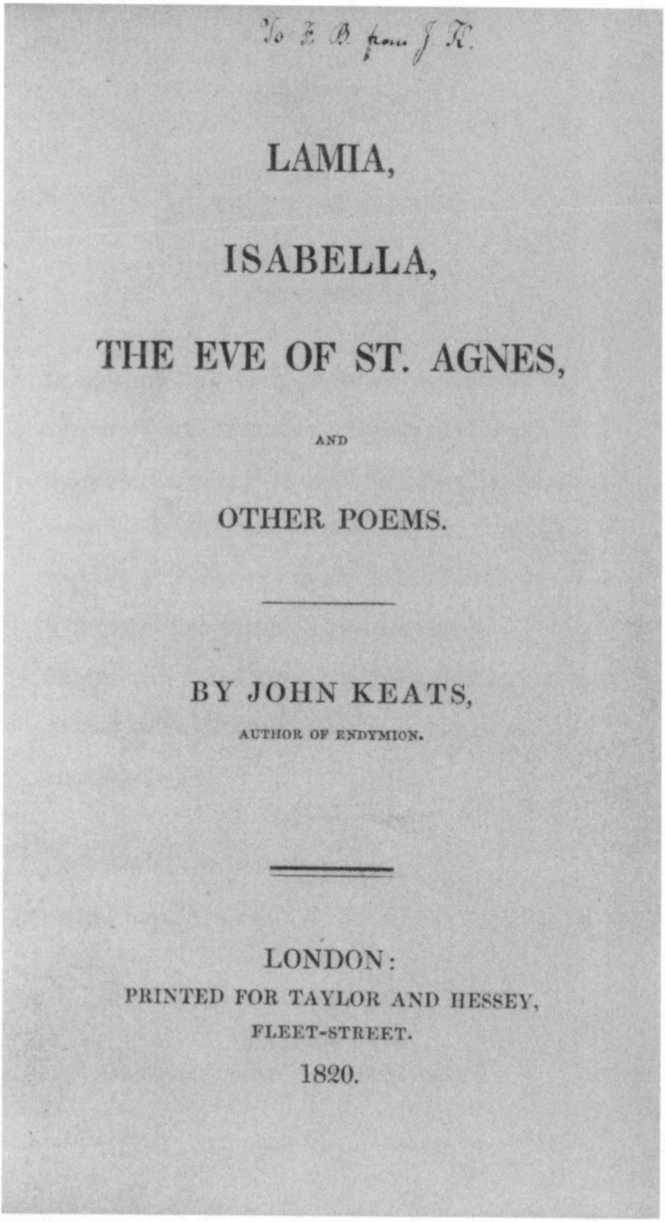

To F. B. from J. K.

LAMIA,

ISABELLA,

THE EVE OF ST. AGNES,

AND

OTHER POEMS.

BY JOHN KEATS,

AUTHOR OF ENDYMION.

LONDON:

PRINTED FOR TAYLOR AND HESSEY,

FLEET-STREET.

1820.

Figure 14: Title page, 1820 volume, inscribed to F. B. (Fanny Brawne). Keats was quite ill at the time. Even with a print run of only five hundred copies (also the runs of *Poems* and *Endymion*), this volume, priced at 7 shillings 6 pence, was also remaindered, though it sold enough to cover expenses. Keats EC8.K2262.820ℓ (F). Courtesy of Houghton Library, Harvard University.

Lamia begins in a seaside forest on Crete, then moves to the outskirts of Corinth, then into this decadent Greek city, its rich economy serviced by slaves. Corinth was as famed for its temple of Venus as for its school of Platonic philosophy. The star couple in this last romance is a dreamy philosophy student, Lycius (about Keats's age) and a mysterious woman, Lamia, skilled in the arts of love. She wasn't always a woman; we see her first as a dazzling serpent. A locus of kinetic fine arts, phenomenological flux, and conceptual instability, she magnetizes Keats's complex feelings about women: enchanting, loving, suspect. Her antagonist is Lycius's "trusted guide / And good instructor," Apollonius, whose "quick eyes" sense something off in this sudden girlfriend (1.374–376). Keats's title, *Lamia,* is itself a slippery sign, the first of several. Here is Lemprière's *Classical Dictionary:*

> LAMIÆ. Certain monsters of Africa, who had the face and breast of a woman, and the rest of the body like that of a serpent. They allured strangers to come to them, that they might devour them, and though they were not endowed with the faculty of speech, yet their hissings were pleasing and agreeable.

Keats's Lamia is no tight match, however. Her origins are not known: she may be African but this is never said; we meet her in Crete. We don't know if she is originally a lamia or a woman. Keats doesn't use the name "Lamia" until she materializes as woman. She's alluring, artfully flirtatious, but no predator (except in metaphors); her aching agenda is to love in a woman's body. Not limited to sibilant hissings, her cool skill with words is one any politician, or poet, might envy. The only certainty is that she is a shapeshifter, shimmering as Keats's latest, most extravagant greeting of the spirit to poetry. No coincidence that Pegasus, icon of soaring poetic imagination, is the emblem of Corinth, where Lamia works her arts, and site of king Minos's labyrinth.

Keats's paths are "always labyrinthian," comments John Jones (215, of a different context). Labyrinth is *Lamia*'s master-trope. Keats coins the word into a transitive verb (2.53) and everywhere figures it in mazes, wreathes, coils, and snares, across a plot of twists and turns. Nothing is straightforward, even when (especially when) it seems so. Take the fairy-tale cue, evoking and slanting the full cliché, "Once upon a time . . ."

[1] 19–20 September 1819; ALS Morgan Library, p. 3.

Part I   "Upon a Time"

UPON a time, before the faery broods
Drove Nymph and Satyr from the prosperous woods,
Before King Oberon's bright diadem,
Sceptre, and mantle, clasp'd with dewy gem,
Frighted away the Dryads and the Fauns
From rushes green, and brakes, and cowslip'd lawns,
The ever-smitten Hermes empty left
His golden throne, bent warm on amorous theft:
From high Olympus had he stolen light,
On this side of Jove's clouds, to escape the sight   10
Of his great summoner, and made retreat
Into a forest on the shores of Crete.
For somewhere in that sacred island dwelt
A nymph, to whom all hoofed Satyrs knelt;
At whose white feet the languid Tritons poured
Pearls, while on land they wither'd and adored.
Fast by the springs where she to bathe was wont,
And in those meads where sometime she might haunt,
Were strewn rich gifts, unknown to any Muse,
Though Fancy's casket were unlock'd to choose.   20
Ah, what a world of love was at her feet!
So Hermes thought, and a celestial heat
Burnt from his winged heels to either ear,
That from a whiteness, as the lily clear,
Blush'd into roses 'mid his golden hair,
Fallen in jealous curls about his shoulders bare.
From vale to vale, from wood to wood, he flew,
Breathing upon the flowers his passion new,
And wound with many a river to its head,
To find where this sweet nymph prepar'd her secret bed: 30
In vain; the sweet nymph might nowhere be found,
And so he rested, on the lonely ground,
Pensive, and full of painful jealousies
Of the Wood-Gods, and even the very trees.
There as he stood, he heard a mournful voice,
Such as once heard, in gentle heart, destroys

All pain but pity: thus the lone voice spake:
"When from this wreathed tomb shall I awake!
When move in a sweet body fit for life,
And love, and pleasure, and the ruddy strife   40
Of hearts and lips! Ah, miserable me!"
The God, dove-footed, glided silently
Round bush and tree, soft-brushing, in his speed,
The taller grasses and full-flowering weed,
Until he found a palpitating snake,
Bright, and cirque-couchant in a dusky brake.

The poem begins as a parodic fairytale. The scene is wonderfully worldly, a panorama of erotic anguishing in ante-bellum sylvan history, before the invasion of tyrant Oberon and his fairy broods (a militant population Keats knew from Shakespeare's *Midsummer Night's Dream*). Triton mermen are dying on land while they *poured/Pearls* (nice enjambment!) to woo some elusive nymph: they *wither'd and adored* (15–16).

The most aggressive suitor is *ever-smitten Hermes,* a foreseeing god if ever there was one, *bent warm on amorous theft*—so throbbingly overheated as to issue an impatient anagram of *amor* out of *warm on* before the theft actually receives its epithet. Keats's words are exquisitely witty. He introduces Hermes with a seeming adjective, *empty,* then turns it to his delinquency: *empty left/His gold throne* (7–8). "From high Olympus had he stolen light, / On this side of Jove's clouds" (9–10) parodies, with punning (illogical) grammar, Prometheus the light-stealer.[1] Hermes is no benefactor to humanity. For this juvenile delinquent, *light* means artful method. Keats has his own fun with the nymph-news that drives the boy, *Ah, what a world of love was at her feet!* (21). On the turn of a line, a seeming omniscient report gets bent into hermetic psychosis: *So Hermes thought* (22). Keats's own nymph-mad boy-glee in *Sleep and Poetry* is the godfather of this burning boy, passioned from winged heels to ear-tips, his golden hair a blazon of lily and rose, blushing sentimental tropes into patent lust: *Fallen in jealous curls about his shoulder bare* (26). Count the syllables: a hexameter "quite in character" (Woodhouse felt it) with passion's excess and its propulsion *To find where this sweet nymph prepar'd her secret bed* (30). Hexameter-Hermes is so *full of painful jealousies* that only a double *full / ful* will do for his appetitive scoping of Wood-Gods and the very trees. Not yet jealous of Fanny Brawne this way, Keats could, in imagination, camelionize this avatar.

The other character in this fairyland is the (presumed) eponym in a bright snake-form (she will not be named "Lamia" until she gets woman-formed). Her *mournful* voice (35) has Hermes's number, with a plan to enlist his magic for her agenda: to gain a

> sweet body fit for life,
> And love, and pleasure, and the ruddy strife
> Of hearts and lips! (39–41)

—about as soft-porn as Keats's (published) poetry gets after *Endymion*'s notorious slippery blisses. Her naming of her state as a *wreathed tomb* is the first of *Lamia*'s wreathings. This one is a phallic throb in female form: *a palpitating snake, / Bright and cirque-couchant* (45–46). Bearer of a *serpent rod* (89), Hermes is symbolic kin. Keats invented the faux-heraldic *cirque-couchant* just for this greeting, an artful she-stylizing worth any god's attention, with a snaky hiss in the wording. The spectacle whirls Keats's poetry into a kaleidoscope of signals and seeming signs: a text-case for reading.

---

[1] Garrett Stewart owns this reading ("Language of Metamorphosis" 9), and inspires much of my attention to how verbal slippages, cross-lexical matches, puns, and syntactic slides in *Lamia* press wordplay into metamorphoses of epistemic consequence (40).

"a gordian shape"

> She was a gordian shape of dazzling hue,
> Vermilion-spotted, golden, green, and blue;
> Striped like a zebra, freckled like a pard,
> Eyed like a peacock, and all crimson barr'd;
> And full of silver moons, that, as she breathed,
> Dissolv'd, or brighter shone, or interwreathed
> Their lustres with the gloomier tapestries—
> So rainbow-sided, touch'd with miseries,
> She seem'd, at once, some penanced lady elf,
> Some demon's mistress, or the demon's self.
> Upon her crest she wore a wannish fire
> Sprinkled with stars, like Ariadne's tiar:
> Her head was serpent, but ah, bitter-sweet!

50

She had a woman's mouth with all its pearls complete: 60
And for her eyes: what could such eyes do there
But weep, and weep, that they were born so fair?
As Proserpine still weeps for her Sicilian air.
Her throat was serpent, but the words she spake
Came, as through bubbling honey, for Love's sake,
And thus; while Hermes on his pinions lay,
Like a stoop'd falcon ere he takes his prey.

   "Fair Hermes, crown'd with feathers, fluttering light,
I had a splendid dream of thee last night:
I saw thee sitting, on a throne of gold,   70
Among the Gods, upon Olympus old,
The only sad one; for thou didst not hear
The soft, lute-finger'd Muses chaunting clear,
Nor even Apollo when he sang alone,
Deaf to his throbbing throat's long, long melodious moan.

The snake is as skilled as Keats in word-magic. Hermes may have been deaf to Apollo's song, but the poetry sounds it out into the wonderfully mimetic alexandrine+ of line 75. From "the first word," Hunt reacted "with shuddering and compassion": "The admiration, pity, and horror, to be excited by humanity in a brute shape, were never perhaps called upon by a greater mixture of beauty and deformity" (*Indicator* 338). Satan, mere archangel in brute shape, pales in comparison. *Mixture* is the right word, not only for sensation but in Keats's very words. This is his most vivid blazon ever, a palpitating, paratactic tour-de-force.

   Gordian! the very word is like a bell.[1] Keats gave it to Moon-Goddess Cynthia's *gordian'd up* "locks" (tresses, hinting chains), coining the participle just for her (*Endymion* 1.614). Circe's fire bewitches like "the eye of a gordian snake" (3.497). Patron of this sorority is Satan: <u>the serpent sly, / Insinuating, wove with Gordian twine / His braided train</u>, the very sounds woven along the train of words (4.347–349; Keats's underlining, *KPL* I:95). Readers of *1848* would find the smoking gun in Keats's letter to Bailey in summer *1818* (1:175–176):

I am certain I have not a right feeling towards women—at this moment
I am striving to be just to them, but I cannot. Is it because they fall so far
beneath my boyish imagination? When I was a schoolboy I thought a fair

woman a pure goddess; my mind was a soft nest in which some one of them slept, though she knew it not. I have no right to expect more than their reality. I thought them ethereal, above men. I find them perhaps equal—great by comparison is very small.

Keats is winningly astute about the stain of his schoolboy, book-soaked idealizing upon his later encounters with actual women: not only disappointed, but so hostile that thy might as well be aliens, or latent lamiae. He confesses this with another coil from Milton:

> When I am among women I have evil thoughts, malice spleen . . . I am full of suspicions . . . You must be charitable, and put all this perversity to my being disappointed since my boyhood. . . . I must absolutely get over this—but how? the only way is to find the root of evil, and so cure it, "with backward mutters of dissevering power." That is a difficult thing; for an obstinate prejudice can seldom be produced but from a gordian complication of feelings, which must take time to unravel, and care to keep unravelled. I could say a good deal about this

The quotation knots Keats's perversity into the Lady imprisoned by enchanter Comus: no release for her "without his rod revers't, / And backwards mutters of dissevering power" (*Comus* 816–817). Bad enough for a lad to be feminine-fettered this way. The allusion to Alexander the Great in *gordian* is double-damning. Instead of unraveling the Gordian Knot, he whips out his terrible swift sword, gives it a chop, and gains a continent in return.

"The principle of the imagination resembles the emblem of the serpent," writes Hazlitt, "undulating folds, for ever varying and for ever flowing into itself,—circular, and without beginning or end": this is the "spirit of genuine poetry."[2] Hazlitt's lambent prose, *resembles the emblem*, plays along, one word undulating into the next. Rife with erotic heat, the hottest love affair in *Lamia* is Keats's with poetic language. His palette for the snake-blazon is a ravishing ravel: the cold casement window in *Eve of St. Agnes* hasn't a prayer against this blazing, breathing art. Lamia defeats stable reading, flashing *all at once* the seemings of a *penanced lady elf*, a *demon's mistress, or the demon's self*, with a shimmer of *demon's elf* (55–56). We may hear *penance* in ser*pent* (59) in line with the back-story, *I was a woman* (117).

The present shape is more than snake. It is a magical menagerie, simile-shifted into zebra, leopard, peacock; then a lunar system, a rainbow, a volatile constellation, *Sprinkled with stars, like Ariadne's tiar* (58). This last simile seems thematic, but is also lexically tricky. Ariadne*'s tiar* nicely echoes *star*, to evoke a Cretan sisterhood of betrayed, lovelorn maids. But the colon after *tiar* is tricky. If you expect more about that faint fire on her crest, what you get is a queasy chimera: *Her head was serpent, but ah, bitter-sweet!/She had a woman's mouth with all its pearls complete* (59–60). By this point you can't tell whether this is a jewelry, rich and strange (those are pearls that were her teeth), or a hyperbolic cliché (with another flair of hexameter) from a handbook for doters. The question hovers over weeping eyes *so fair* (61–62): real pathos, or suspect *Tragedy-tears*—to use Keats's term (*K* 71)? Line 63, *As Proserpine still weeps for her Sicilian air*, sits alone as an enigmatic sentence-fragment. It could be comparative syntax: Proserpine, another imprisoned maid, pining for her former life. Or it could be a temporal *As*, conjunction to a world of still weeping demons' mistresses. The verb of mourning, *pine* (meter-stressed) is one way to go with Pros-er*pine*. Another is to see the lettering of *serpenting* forming in Pro*serpine*.

If this feels like manic reading, blame Keats's snake-script. The words he writes are a flux of teases: *the words she spake/Came, as through bubbling honey, for Love's sake* (64–65). Is this sweet-talking in the rhyme-field of *snake* (45)? Recall Circe's snare of *honey-words* (*Endymion* 3.428). Or, with large sympathy, is Keats sounding *Love's ache* in the motive *Love's sake*? He used *ache* for Satan's temporary hideout: *Whose spirit does not ache at the smothering and confinement . . . in this serpent prison?* (*KPL* II:80). Lamia's ache is her *serpent prison-house* (1.203). With no sinister weave, Keats plaits her plight with psychological and aesthetic surfeits. The turbulence is not only in its narrative but in its language. The "very emblems that characterize" her, writes Sperry, are "bewilderingly varied and contradictory . . . not clearly separated or distinguishable" but given to "striking mobility and fluctuation" (*Keats* 296–297). We don't yet know whether *She* is a lamia, or a creature prejudiced by cultural slander.

What we do see is that she is a savvy negotiator, capably tuned to Hermes-heat with a sure-fire pickup line, "I had a splendid dream of thee last night," this about his melancholy frustration in the nymph-hunt. The nymph's safety is her invisibility. It is also Lamia's bargaining-chip. Hermes, god of deal-making as well as magic, is ready to give Lamia the shape she desires in exchange for an unveiling.

[1] W. T. Arnold may have been the first to note Keats's "fondness for the word 'Gordian'" (xxxiii).

[2] *London Magazine* (December 1820), 688.

Hermes and the nymph; She-serpent to woman's form

        . . . the God fostering her chilled hand,   140
She felt the warmth, her eyelids open'd bland,
And, like new flowers at morning song of bees,
Bloom'd, and gave up her honey to the lees.
Into the green-recessed woods they flew;
Nor grew they pale, as mortal lovers do.

   Left to herself, the serpent now began
To change; her elfin blood in madness ran,
Her mouth foam'd, and the grass, therewith besprent,
Wither'd at dew so sweet and virulent;
Her eyes in torture fix'd, and anguish drear,   150
Hot, glaz'd, and wide, with lid-lashes all sear,
Flash'd phosphor and sharp sparks, without one cooling tear.
The colours all inflam'd throughout her train,
She writh'd about, convuls'd with scarlet pain:
A deep volcanian yellow took the place
Of all her milder-mooned body's grace;
And, as the lava ravishes the mead,
Spoilt all her silver mail, and golden brede;
Made gloom of all her frecklings, streaks and bars,
Eclips'd her crescents, and lick'd up her stars: 160
So that, in moments few, she was undrest
Of all her sapphires, greens, and amethyst,
And rubious-argent: of all these bereft,
Nothing but pain and ugliness were left.
Still shone her crown; that vanish'd, also she
Melted and disappear'd as suddenly;
And in the air, her new voice luting soft,
Cried, "Lycius! gentle Lycius!"—Borne aloft
With the bright mists about the mountains hoar
These words dissolv'd: Crete's forests heard no more.   170

   Whither fled Lamia, now a lady bright,
A full-blown beauty new and exquisite?
She fled into that valley they pass o'er
Who go to Corinth from Cenchreas' shore;

And rested at the foot of those wild hills,
The rugged founts of the Peræan rills,
And of that other ridge whose barren back
Stretches, with all its mist and cloudy rack,
South-westward to Cleone. There she stood
About a young bird's flutter from a wood,   180
Fair, on a sloping green of mossy tread,
By a clear pool, wherein she passioned
To see herself escap'd from so sore ills,
While her robes flaunted with the daffodils.

Hermes's hot amorous bent softens into a healthy heat that metamorphoses *chilled* nymph into happy partner. For the poet who produced Porphyro and Madeline's "solution sweet" with throbbing star and melting flowers, *gave up her honey to the lees* is a breeze. Hermes's aggression is at once naturalized (*Bloom'd*), meliorized, immortalized. Lamia breathes upon his eyes, and both see

> the guarded nymph near-smiling on the green.
> It was no dream; or say a dream it was,
> Real are the dreams of Gods, and smoothly pass
> Their pleasures in a long immortal dream.   (125–128)

Real are the dreams of Gods arrives on finely tuned grammar, *of* both possessive and objective: Gods' dreams realized are what mortals dream of Gods. The pause at *pass* is a cruel trick on the reader. Gods' dreams do not *pass*. The turn of the line gives these passages to immortality. A tale is told in the antonymic prefix. Keats could have wrapped this episode at *Into the green-recessed woods they flew* (144). But he wanted to rhyme it to an aggrieved reprise of *mortal* difference. The couplet, the verse paragraph, and the vignette end on this key: *Nor grew they pale, as mortal lovers do* (145). This is the sentencing in all of Keats's books of human love.

Next up is she-snake's metamorphosis into human (perhaps perishable) form. No natural nymph-blooming, it is a violent explosion. In *The Odyssey*, Hermes releases men from their Circe-cursed beast forms with a rod of intertwined snakes, a caduceus that symbolizes the reciprocity of rivals in the commercial world of which Hermes is patron. Keats has this *lythe Caducean charm* (133) satisfy the bargain with Lamia, and release thereby the second great blazon in *Lamia*, a blazing spectacle, *writh'd about* and *convuls'd* in word-flexing no less than in agon. The first mercurial change deforms *serpent* into *besprent*, then rhyme-wrings this into *virulent* (this and *besprent* only here in Keats's poetry). The snake-eyes become *fix't*, not with agency but paralyzed in a torture (in the wrenched meter as well) that *Flash'd phosphor and sharp sparks, without one cooling tear* (152). "Epic sublimed," declared a review in Gold's *London Magazine* (163). Like *fix't*, *Flash'd* is no act of vision; it is a hellish spectacle, alliterated and meter-ruptured into *phosphor sharp sparks*. So, too, *glaz'd* (151) and *inflam'd* (153): no transitive verbs, just spewed alchemy. No surprise (by now) that *inflam'd* is also unique here in Keats's poetry, torqued from an adjective to a livid verb.

Agony-*anguish* (150) we'll soon encounter metamorphosed into the woman's aura of *idle languishment* (199), the double *l* lulling the very sound of *anguish*. In the undress-rehearsal, *convuls'd* wrenches serpent-splendor into the anagrammatic disarray, *volcanian* (155), this word yet another one-off in the Keatsian lexicon. Keats's fair copy had a vowel-linked (to *convuls'd*) *vulcanian* (MsK 2.26.14), a draw from Roman fire-god *Vulcan*. He switched to the etymonic derivative, *volcanian*. *JnD* has neither word; *OED* gives Keats the coin on this metaphor-metamorphosis. *London Magazine* exclaimed (again) at a "grandeur . . . heroically described" (163). On a lexical rush, Keats magnetizes the anagram-torqued simile, *as the lava ravishes* (157), a dramatic word-ravishing, soon metamorphosed into *vanish'd* (165).

"To compare the fiery pangs of Lamia's etherealization with the 'fierce convulse' and 'wild commotion' of Apollo's dying into life" is to confront a "deliberate travesty" of a "serious conception," comments Sperry (*Keats* 303). Nice catch, but may I query the contrast? For one, Keats's poetry for Apollo verges on travesty; for another, there is serious poetic work in his poetry for Lamia. For readers of *1820*, moreover, *Lamia* precedes *Hyperion*, with the effect of allowing Apollo's somewhat twee convulse to look like an exalted, reverse mimicry of hers. In both scenes, Keats's transformational grammars spawn a symbolic grammar of transformation. The she-snake's finale is his severest strip-tease: *she was undrest*, a line-end halt before the turn *Of all her sapphires, greens, and amethyst, / And rubious-argent* (161–163), the gems blazoned in their vanishing, leaving no *bereft* body behind.[1] The tease is a double-play: *Still shone her crown; that vanish'd, also she* (165), both gone together, but in Keats's line-sequencing, the crown lingering just a bit. *Vanish'd* then gets modified to *disappear'd* (166), set to lose its *dis-* to a new appearance. A *new voice luting soft, / Cried "Lycius! gentle Lycius"—Borne aloft* (167–168). The luting of *d'licious* in "Cried'*Lycius!*'" sets the bait, "so de*licious* were the words she sung" (249).

This sets the stage for the debut of the name "Lamia," done with lilting euphony, *Whither fled, Lamia, now a lady . . . ?* (171). The full stage is an inset sonnet-stanza (the only one in *Lamia*). Its first word, *Whither*, at once satirizes the Tritons, who *wither'd and adored* (16) to no end, and reverses the elegiac trope *ubi sunt* (whither?) for Lamia's embodied presence: *There she stood* (179), a woman in fine poetic form, punned by *stanza* (Italian: *stand*). The soundwave *Whither–There–Fair–wherein* has wafted her from Crete's forests to Cenchreas' shore. Keats coined *flutter* into a noun just for this visual measure, and just right for *flaunted with the daffodils*. The flower is a form of the immortal asphodel, famed in mythology as a remedy for poisonous snake-bites. Is Lamia's *full-born beauty* (172) this remedy? Like *Isabella*'s Pot of Basil and Madeline's Casement-window, Lady Lamia is meta-textual. As she scans herself, we scan her and the course of *Lamia*.

How are you doing? Interrupting Part II as it rolls toward its disastrous denouement, Keats suddenly turns to us, with a tricky quiz of judgment.

---

[1] The decadence reflects Milton's sole use of *bereft* in *Paradise Lost:* "Adam of short joy bereft" (11.628), after Archangel Michael slaps him down for his pleasure at a vision of fallen human arts.

Part II: "What wreath?"

> What wreath for Lamia? What for Lycius?
> What for the sage, old Apollonius?
> Upon her aching forehead be there hung
> The leaves of willow and of adder's tongue;
> And for the youth, quick, let us strip for him
> The thyrsus, that his watching eyes may swim
> Into forgetfulness; and, for the sage,
> Let spear-grass and the spiteful thistle wage
> War on his temples. Do not all charms fly
> At the mere touch of cold philosophy?   230
> There was an awful rainbow once in heaven:
> We know her woof, her texture; she is given
> In the dull catalogue of common things.
> Philosophy will clip an Angel's wings,
> Conquer all mysteries by rule and line,
> Empty the haunted air, and gnomed mine—
> Unweave a rainbow, as it erewhile made   237
> The tender-person'd Lamia melt into a shade.

A lot happens after Lamia lands in Greece. Fueled by "real" dreams during her prison-term, then setting herself on Lycius's frequent path, Lamia is ready for flirtation, including the skill of her words. He falls hard. She plays hard to get, then shifts to "playing woman's part" (I.337)—a role bawdy-spun for Keats's boy-to-boy winking. The couple heads to Corinth with a mysterious speed scarcely registered by love-blind Lycius. Evading the gaze of his tutor Apollonius, they come to a secret lodge, soon "their house" (393).

Part II is a surprise of switched tracks. The narrator is sometimes sarcastic. Lamia is anguished, Lycius a tyrant, Apollonius a sadistic demystifier. The lovers dally, with plush sibilance, in a *purple-lined palace of sweet sin* (31), sound-satirizing *sweets in.* Lycius's big mistake is ignoring this protected *in,* pushing for a big wedding in an outward display of his "prize," to awe his friends, be-dazzle the public, and "choke" his foes (2.57–62). Hearing her death knell in this exposure, Lamia wants none of it. At her resistance, Lycius metamorphoses from philosopher to a bully who could take on a serpent:

> Fine was the mitigated fury, like
> Apollo's presence when in act to strike

The serpent—Ha, the serpent! certes, she
Was none. She burnt, she lov'd the tyranny,
And, all subdued, consented to the hour   (2.78–82)

The narrator's real-time enthusiasm issues this full-throated *Ha!*, hissed along
serpent . . . serpent! certes, she. If *certes* is antique for *certainly* ("an old word,"
JnD), Keats gives it new poetic flair. It closely echoes *serpent* and *she,* then turns
the line to give *she* over to male-clubbed lore. Keats was pleased to gloat about
this to Woodhouse: "Women love to be forced to do a thing, by a fine fellow."[1]
In his dreams, women may think; but real are the dreams of men when they
have the pen.

No dreamer, Apollonius crashes the wedding with one of Keats's most densely
wrought analogies:

As though of some knotty problem, that had daft
His patient thought, had now begun to thaw,
And solve and melt:—'twas just as he foresaw.   (2.160–162)

This *knotty* problem is no Gordian test but something that a rhyme-wreathed
thought might assay, *And solve and melt,* a contracted *dissolve* before its syn-
onym *melt.* Having underscored Hamlet's wish that his flesh would melt, / Thaw,
and resolve itself into a dew (1.2; *DW* 7), Keats plays the chord here, with a
reverb from Lycius's feeling Lamia's *tender palm dissolve in dew* at their first sight
of Apollonius (1.370).

As the guests get hammered on free-flowing wine, they are invited to select
wreaths to *fancy-fit* their brows (2.220). *OED* gives Keats the coin on *fancy-fit.*
Now comes the reader's quiz, or trick quiz. The narrator's rhetoric of *What?*
solicits our agreement: his wreaths are pre-assigned. Keats's verbal wreathings
are more complex. If you are primed for Lamia to be exposed, you find some
of Keats's most affecting, humane poetry of doomed love. If you have pitied
Lycius's delusion, his morphing into braggart and bully may provoke your wish
for just deserts. If you are in cognitive alignment with master-detector Apol-
lonius, you've got a buzz-kill companion. How do you take this quiz—not quite
a final exam, but certes a pre-test?

Is the quiz-giver himself a character to read? His wreaths are rather over-
solicited. Lycius gets a nearly name-rhymed *thyrsus* (226), the Bacchus-wand
of intoxicated forgetfulness: best outcome for this sap. The willow "wreath for
Lamia" spells the end of her gambit with this emblem of mourning. But willow
is more than this. It is also herbal therapy (for headaches especially); so, too,

soothing *adder's tongue* (224). This is a shape-naming, but what do you make of a venomously undertoned *adder-stung*? Even *sage* Apollonius proves a puzzle. The double shafts of hostility, spear-grass and thistle (228), seem just right. Leslie Brisman reminds us of Milton's roll down the Devon hills, incurring thistles on his crown, which had Keats jesting about a natural muse for his piercing political polemics (7). Apollonius's coldly reasoned *just as he foresaw* (162), however, is not just his, but also our readerly foresight from Part I. His knowledge is ours, thorns and all. In herbal therapy, moreover, sage is famed for warding off evil. While the etymology is different from the epithet "sage," the phonics haunt about the word.

The rant against "philosophy" that begins at line 229 taps the imagination-vs-science debates of Keats's day (*Philosophy* is reasoned *science*). Keats shared Wordsworth's affection for the old mythologies against "the cold, narrow, lifeless spirit of modern philosophy."[2] He ended his essay on Kean for *The Champion* (21 December 1817) lamenting "the failure of our days! . . . the rainbow is robbed of its mystery" (*K* 76). Soon after, at that "immortal" dinner at Haydon's (Wordsworth also there), he and Lamb blamed Newton's science for "destroy[ing] all the poetry of the rainbow by reducing it to the prismatic colours" (Taylor 1:354). A couple of weeks on, Keats heard Hazlitt lay out an historical analytic in his inaugural lecture, *On Poetry in General:* "the progress of knowledge and refinement has a tendency to . . . clip the wings of poetry" (*Lectures* 18). *Conquer all mysteries by rule and line* could have come out of Keats's satire of neoclassical couplets in *Sleep and Poetry.* And there is no better, more bitter, critique of Enlightenment progress than *Empty the haunted air, and gnomed mine* (gnomes guard the gold). The rant in *Lamia* adds a gendered turn: a she-beauty battered by he-reason.

But so *Lamiated,* this polarizing yields no stable map. If *Philosophy will clip an Angel's wings,* Apollonius's clip of Lamia is certes uncertain. She was / is no Angel. But she was rainbow-sided. To unweave this thing of beauty is to cancel poetry in general (Latin *textus:* weave). This twist is related to a narratological shift at the end of this verse paragraph. Up to line 237 it seems nondiegetic discourse; then midline we meet a grammatically ambiguous "as": *as it erewhile made / The tender-person'd Lamia melt into a shade.* In the rant's slant, "as" is an analogy to what Philosophy does. But linked to *erewhile* it is a narrative temporality. Instead of *erewhile,* we may have expected a forecast ("in a while"); *erewhile* (a conspicuous archaism amid Keats's modern style) means "some time before," prior to the events told in *Lamia.* What *Lamia* does tell to us is word-history and rhyme-history:

> . . . if thou shouldst fade
> Thy memory will waste me to a shade:—
> For pity do not melt!

Thus implores Lycius of Lamia (1.269–271). *Fade, shade, melt:* the uncanny lexical past, returned to impending denouement. The disturbance of *erewhile* is one more twist of mystery, making an impending future also seem a folding back. Keats's labyrinthian wreaths weave from syllables, to words, to syntaxes, to large narrative fields, and beyond, into keynote texts that vex any certain score-keeping.

[1] Woodhouse to Taylor, *L* 2:164 (19 September 1819).
[2] As Hazlitt put it, on behalf of Wordsworth's meditation on the old mythologies (review of *The Excursion,* 556).

found and wound

> By her glad Lycius sitting, in chief place,
> Scarce saw in all the room another face,   240
> Till, checking his love trance, a cup he took
> Full brimm'd, and opposite sent forth a look
> 'Cross the broad table, to beseech a glance
> From his old teacher's wrinkled countenance,
> And pledge him. The bald-head philosopher
> Had fix'd his eye, without a twinkle or stir
> Full on the alarmed beauty of the bride,
> Brow-beating her fair form, and troubling her sweet pride.
> Lycius then press'd her hand, with devout touch,
> As pale it lay upon the rosy couch: 250
> 'Twas icy, and the cold ran through his veins;
> Then sudden it grew hot, and all the pains
> Of an unnatural heat shot to his heart.
> "Lamia, what means this? Wherefore dost thou start?
> Know'st thou that man?" Poor Lamia answer'd not.
> He gaz'd into her eyes, and not a jot
> Own'd they the lovelorn piteous appeal:
> More, more he gaz'd: his human senses reel:
> Some hungry spell that loveliness absorbs;

There was no recognition in those orbs. 260
"Lamia!" he cried—and no soft-toned reply.
The many heard, and the loud revelry
Grew hush; the stately music no more breathes;
The myrtle sicken'd in a thousand wreaths.
By faint degrees, voice, lute, and pleasure ceased;
A deadly silence step by step increased,
Until it seem'd a horrid presence there,
And not a man but felt the terror in his hair.
"Lamia!" he shriek'd; and nothing but the shriek
With its sad echo did the silence break. 270
"Begone, foul dream!" he cried, gazing again
In the bride's face, where now no azure vein
Wander'd on fair-spaced temples; no soft bloom
Misted the cheek; no passion to illume
The deep-recessed vision:—all was blight;
Lamia, no longer fair, there sat a deadly white.
"Shut, shut those juggling eyes, thou ruthless man!
Turn them aside, wretch! or the righteous ban
Of all the Gods, whose dreadful images
Here represent their shadowy presences, 280
May piece them to the sudden with the thorn
Of painful blindness; leaving thee forlorn
In trembling dotage to the feeblest fright
Of conscience, for their long offended might,
For all thine impious proud-hearted sophistries,
Unlawful magic, and enticing lies.
Mark how, possess'd, his lashless eyelids stretch
Around his demon eyes! Corinthians, see!
My sweet bride withers at their potency." 290
"Fool!" said the sophist, in an under-tone
Gruff with contempt; which a death-nighing moan
From Lycius answer'd, as heart-struck and lost,
He sank supine beside the aching ghost.
"Fool! Fool!" repeated he, while his eyes still
Relented not, nor mov'd; "from every ill
Of life have I preserv'd thee to this day,
And shall I see thee made a serpent's prey?"

Then Lamia breath'd death breath; the sophist's eye,
Like a sharp spear, went through her utterly,   300
Keen, cruel, perceant, stinging: she, as well
As her weak hand could any meaning tell,
Motion'd him to be silent; vainly so,
He look'd and look'd again a level—No!
"A Serpent!" echoed he; no sooner said,
Than with a frightful scream she vanished:
And Lycius' arms were empty of delight,
As were his limbs of life, from that same night.
On the high couch he lay!—his friends came round—
Supported him—no pulse, or breath they found,   310
And, in its marriage robe, the heavy body wound.*

*"Philostratus, in his fourth book *de Vita Apollonii,* hath a memorable instance in this kind, which I may not omit, of one Menippus Lycius, a young man twenty-five years of age, that going betwixt Cenchreas and Corinth, met such a phantasm in the habit of a fair gentlewoman, which taking him by the hand, carried him home to her house, in the suburbs of Corinth, and told him she was a Phœnician by birth, and if he would tarry with her, he should hear her sing and play, and drink such wine as never any drank, and no man should molest him; but she, being fair and lovely, would live and die with him, that was fair and lovely to behold. The young man, a philosopher, otherwise staid and discreet, able to moderate his passions, though not this of love, tarried with her a while to his great content, and at last married her, to whose wedding, amongst other guests, came Apollonius; who, by some probable conjectures, found her out to be a serpent, a lamia; and that all her furniture was, like Tantalus' gold, described by Homer, no substance but mere illusions. When she saw herself descried, she wept, and desired Apollonius to be silent, but he would not be moved, and thereupon she, plate, house, and all that was in it, vanished in an instant: many thousands took notice of this fact, for it was done in the midst of Greece."

Burton's 'Anatomy of Melancholy.' *Part* 3. *Sect.* 2. *Memb.* 1. *Subs.* 1.

For the foregone denouement, Keats sets Lamia and Apollonius in a cage-match. Just before elegizing the lost rainbow in his *Champion* review, he sighed that "romance lives but in books" (*K* 76). The book of *Lamia* kills it off.

This doom unfolds from the way the top of this last, long paragraph, moves *glad* from *her* to *Lycius*. Apollonius's assault is fatal reading, hexameter-fueled: *Brow-beating her fair form, and troubling her sweet pride* (248). No arrogance, her *pride* means splendor, in a vulnerable *fair form* and *sweet* affect. All this dies before Lycius's eyes and in his touch. For the first time, he speaks her name, three times. First in panic (as if realizing her identity in speaking it): "Lamia, what means this?" (254); next in despair: "'Lamia!' he cried—" (261), a dash of suspended breath; then in agony: "'Lamia!' he shriek'd; and nothing but the shriek . . . ," *shriek* echoing itself before the narrator's redundant supply of *echo* (269–270). The repeated *shriek* swallows the rhyme-partnered, off-tone *break* (270) into a suspenseful silence. What a stunning verbal wreathing from "no more *breathes*" to sickened "*wreaths . . .* faint *degrees . . .* pleasure *ceased*" (263–265)! Phonically and dramatically headed to *shriek,* the deadly silence step by step *increased* (266) as relentlessly in Keats's metrics as in Apollonius's piercing gaze. Keats arcs Lamia-namings across a horrific scene of her dying out of life. From "Poor Lamia answer'd *not*" (255), he cues the *knotty* problem about to unknot. At this grave denouement ("unknotting"), Lycius is gripped by sensations that Keats, with sharp sympathy, knew on the pulse of his own worst moments: he *press'd her hand . . . As pale it lay upon the rosy couch: 'Twas icy, and the cold ran through his veins* (249–251).

> You say you love; but then your hand
> No soft squeeze for squeeze returneth;
> It is like a statue's, dead,—

This is a lad's coy tease in an early Keats-lyric (*P* 98), returned with Ovidian severity to Lamia's finale, where her cold hand *sudden . . . grew hot,* with a midline rhyme *shot* to Lycius's heart (252–253). As his *human senses reel* at the sensation (258), we hear two things, the stress of *human* and a punned *real*. Lamia's eyes simultaneously go blank in grammatical disarray: *Some hungry spell that loveliness absorbs* (259). A loveliness with power to *absorb* is now spell-absorbed, hers (*that*) in particular, categorically all loveliness. More than a rhyme for *absorbs,* "tho*se orbs*" (260) echoes it with a phonic mimesis of ab*sorbs.*[1] It is also reciprocal to what Keats most feared in loving Fanny Brawne: "You absorb me in spite of myself," he sighed to her while writing *Lamia.* Line 259's *absorbs* is another unique instance in Keats's poetry, and it does not come into his letters until this one, 25 July 1818 (*K* 263), and another to her on 13 October: *You have absorb'd me* (*K* 277). Keats writes this with an intuitive Empsonian double-grammar, telling Fanny not only that she has *absorb'd* him, but that she owns an *absorb'd me.*

Woman-Lamia strangely absorbed, we're primed for her serpent-return. Instead, Keats metamorphoses Apollonius and Lycius. Lycius indicts the *juggling eyes* (a supernatural potency) of the real killer-snake at the feast: *his lashless eyelids stretch / Around his demon eyes!* (288–289), *demonize* hissed right into *demon eyes.* Apollonius counter-hisses, *And shall I see thee made a serpent's prey?* (298)—sounding a *seethe* in *see thee* and a *spray* of venom. Pressed in this word-war, *Lamia breath'd death breath* (299): reverse-inspiration, metrically choked, the very lettering a contagion of one word into the next. Completing this line, Apollonius's gaze levels a devastating simile: *the sophist's eye, / Like a sharp spear, went through her utterly* (299–300). Adverb *utterly* (completely) phantom-puns an adverb of speech action. It is a richly layered word, *utter.* In rare and obsolete usage, *utterance* is a publication; in legal terminology, it is forgery and fraud, and if used for transaction, a capital crime.[2] Keats's drama reaches its pitch in naming, in wordings. The sophist's *cruel, perceant* stinging (301) hellifies a passage of *The Fairy-Queen* that Keats marked: a Heaven-blessed blind old man, <u>wondrous quick and pierceant was his Spright, / As Eagle's Eye, that can behold the Sun</u> (I.9.47; Amy Lowell 2:570). Same eye, different spright. Keats hones *perceant* spear into a phonic anagram of the target, *Serpent* (305).

Yet again, Keats's word-work is narrative work. Finishing off Lamia, Apollonius also finishes off Lycius, who is ultimately his prey, not hers. Lamia vanishes into a *scream* (306), rhymed to the last uttering of *dream,* Lycius's *Begone, foul dream!* (271). Keats's five-line finale is a fine-tuned drama in lexical and grammatical poetics. The first two words of *And Lycius' arms were empty of delight* (307) sound the last contracted *d'licious,* then echo into its etymology-sibling *delight.* The rhyme-line, *As were his limbs of life that same night* (308), gives analogy (*as* his arms, so all his limbs) with a shade of causality: emptied *life* because of emptied *delight.*[3] From the complex perfection of this penultimate couplet, Keats closes on a tricky triplet, in rhyme and reason: *round–found–wound.* In the poem's last metamorphosis, a marriage robe *wound* into a shroud (by friends or its own mysterious agency) also spells a paronomasia of injury-wound (from spear-eyed Apollonius, from Lamia's frightful scream, from Lycius's detonated fantasy). The bottom line, alexandrine-spooled, is a wreath of loose ends. Lamia does not revert to serpent, and Lycius winds up in the body-form of the python smote by Apollo—and in Corinth, by the namesake-travesty Apollonius.

When Lycius cries, *Lamia, what means this?* (255), this could be a reader's question about Keats's *Lamia.* In 1917, Sidney Colvin confessed "bewilderment" about "the effect intended to be made on our imaginative sympathies." In 1978, Stuart Sperry, the first to theorize Keatsian irony into a mode of "perpetual *indeterminacy,*" still could not sort out the tone of *Lamia:* "a bitterness" verging at times on "self-mockery" has Keats writing against himself in no modal mastery. In 1979, Gene Bernstein made a premise of this effect: *Lamia* is a lamia, "deliberately indeterminate" in all its twists and contradictions. So, too, Garrett Stewart's brilliant explication of Keats's "new language of metamorphosis" (1976): a thematically vibrant phenomenology of compositions and decompositions worked through grammar, syntax, puns, phrases, and syllables.[4]

Keats's very last tangle comes on a curious textual turn. If Lycius's *wound* is the poetry's last word, it is not Keats's. He sets an asterisk to key a seemingly relevant account (source, even) in Burton's *Anatomy of Melancholy*.[5] Burton's "Apollonius" unmasks a fair gentlewoman as a *lamia,* but such lower-case identity is nowhere in *Lamia.* Burton's tarrier and marrier, *a young man twenty-five years of age* (Keats's as of 31 October 1820), is promised lifelong pleasure and leisure, and more: protection from other men's molesting. Or *Endymion*-Keats, prey for men's reviews. While the sense of sexual assault in *molest* had yet to develop, the germ is here: a male posse out to get Johnny Keats. Whose voice is sponsoring this script?

What's a reader to do? In a draft for the degraded public at the wedding feast, Keats implies degraded public taste—and he's willing to travesty his romance tropes in the bargain:

> *A Glutton drains a cup of Helicon,*
> *Too fast down, down his throat the brief delight is gone.*
> *"Where is that Music?" cries the Lady fair.*
> *"Aye, where is it my dear? Up in the air"?* (MsK 1.63.307)

Helicon, draft of vintage, brief delight, music fled, Lady fair, airy flights, echoing repetition: all debased. Finishing *Lamia,* Keats writes to his publisher Taylor on 23 August 1819 to seek an advance to settle some debts. Admitting his disdain of being *a popular writer,* he is determined to *get a livelihood* (MsK 1.60.293–294). The next day he repeats this accounting to Reynolds, with two parallel feelings: *I feel it in my power to become a popular writer—I feel it in my strength to refuse the poisonous suffrage of a public.* He had just finished writing, with an ambiguous comparative, *I am convinced more and more day by day that fine writing is next to fine doing the top thing in the world.* The preposition *next to* may mean *just below* or *alongside.* And so the theatrical alignment with Satan's determination to persist: *The more I know what my diligence may in time probably effect; the more does my heart distend with Pride and Obstinacy* (ALS Berg, p. 1; *PL* 1.571–572). He closes this tautened confession with a declaration that he is ready for *the best sort of Poetry - -that is all I care for, all I live for* (p. 1).

[1820, 1–46]

[1] This is too good not to credit Garrett Stewart, *CCJK*, 141.

[2] One crime for hanging reported in the *Examiner*, just below a review of *Lamia &c* (30 July 1820), p. 494.

[3] The doubled-down syntax is caught by Brisman (1975), 6, and Stewart's nearly simultaneous "Language of Metamorphosis," 35.

[4] Colvin, *Keats*, 408; Sperry, *Keats*, 245, 292; Bate, *Keats*, 547, on "as rapidly shifting an interplay of ambiguity as can be found in any narrative poem in the language" (versus an "original simplicity" in the fable that may tempt a reader "to pin the poem to an exclusive interpretation"). Bernstein (192) is sharp on the key tropes and cognitive consequences. Stewart's essay is a wonderful mini-epic on the lexical plays.

[5] From a section on "Love-Melancholy" (*Anatomy* 2:196–197). Keats's fair copy has an asterisk in the title to refer to this text (MsK 2.26.9). Instead of this "ground-work" (so Keats calls it), the end-supplement has a better effect in unsettling the ground.

Ending, Unending

TIME'S SEA ROBBED EVER-VARIABLE, ever-inventive Keats of the ten years he requested to glean his teeming brain. Editors make various decisions about a "last poem." A plangent nineteenth-century favorite was the love-sonnet, "Bright Star." Milnes closed *Literary Remains* with it, titling it *Keats's Last Sonnet* (*1848* 2:306), a logic from its final word, *death*. Other editors like *To Autumn*, an objective, serenely composed, gorgeous dilation of *soft-dying day* against inevitable endings. Still other editors prefer the broken-off existential epic of poetic vocation, *The Fall of Hyperion*. My experiment in *Formal Charges* (1997) took up Keats's late, private poems for, or about, Fanny Brawne. And then there is the eerie pre-posthumous fragment of imagination, "This living hand," a vividly present agent of writing bound for death. An ideal *Greeting of the Spirit* would host them all with a hypertext-technology open to readers' dispositions and experiments. I end with "This living hand," for reasons personally dear to me.

from *The Fall of Hyperion. A Dream*

Wordsworth, wrote Keats to Bailey back in October 1817, has *philantrophy enough to overcome the disposition* [to] *an indolent enjoyment of intellect,* staying *brave enough to volunteer for uncomfortable hours.* I read a canny Keats-slip in *philantrophy,* spelling a *trophy* for the effort.[1] Voluntering this way is for Keats intimate with vocation and professional credit, haunted by leaving medicine, a benefit to humanity, for poetry, uncertain of equal claim. Was it a revision, or a waking dream? The music had not fled. Keats returned to *Hyperion* in summer 1819, trying it out as poetic autobiography, with a new genre: *The Fall of Hyperion, A Dream.* In a new severity of *test* and *trial* (*ex-peri; to put to trial*), Keats heroically delivers his "boldest and most complex experiment in his own poetic idiom," remarks E. E. Bostetter (139). When in 1857 Milnes published "Another Version of Hyperion" in *Miscellanies of the Philobiblion Society,* it was taken to be a first draft. Almost two-thirds of the way into Canto I, we encounter the precursor: *Deep in the shady sadness of a vale . . .* (294). Before then, much happens.

---

[1] 29 October 1817; MsK 1.14.47 (*L* 1:173). I thank Chris Rovee for noting this spelling.

Canto I

"written for a sort of induction –"

> *Here is what I had written for a sort of induction—*
>
>> *Fanatics have their dreams wherewith they weave*
>> *A Paradise for a Sect; the savage too*
>> *From forth the loftiest fashion of his sleep*
>> *Guesses at Heaven: pity these have not*
>> *Trac'd upon vellum, or wild Indian leaf*
>> *The shadows of melodious utterance:*
>> *But bare of laurel they live, dream, and die,*
>> *For Poesy alone can tell her dreams,*
>> *With the fine spell of words alone can save*
>> *Imagination from the sable charm*
>> *And dumb enchantment –*

My Poetry will never be fit for any thing it does n't cover its ground well - You see he she is off her guard and does n't move a peg though Prose is coming up in an awkward style enough. Now a blow in the spondee with[ll] *finish her - But let*[it] *get over this line of circumvallation if it can. These are unpleasant Phrase[s]*

[The fine spell of words in Keats's hand has been lost. Woodhouse's copy continues]

> Who alive can say,
> "Thou art no poet; may'st not tell thy dreams"?
> Since every man whose soul is not a clod
> Hath visions, and would speak, if he had lov'd,
> And been well nurtured in this mother tongue.   15
> Whether the dream now purposed to rehearse
> Be poet's or Fanatic's will be known
> When this warm scribe my hand is in the grave.

I include Keats's "Prose" postscript because of its shift in register to self-satirizing. This includes the meta-poetic *fit*, the letter-punned *if it*, and some gender-play, as well as a jesting about Prose-ground incursions of awkward style (punning the manner into gated passage), with the arty Latinate *circumvallation* (a military siege operation). All this cuts into, and against, the scalings of the "induction" to privilege she-Poesy in the he-poet's penning.

But what a debut in the first word, especially for a dream-epic! *Fanatics:* Keats's sole use in poetry or prose. Its object is *dreams* and the reach into the master-genre, *A Dream,* leverages the mode into high privilege: *Poesy alone can tell her dreams.* Dream-wording is quite a gamble, a whole career's worth.[1] On such high-stakes, Keats launches his induction with two speculative rolls, one self-validating, another self-ironizing. The first, a *fine spell of words,* advertises poet-power, performed right here in the flow of *vellum—melo*dious—*laurel–tell– spell–well* nurtured–*will* be known. The second, on the value of the dream and the character of its mortal author, is deferred to unknown posthumous judgment. That's one temporality.

Another is the conundrum of the title. *A Dream* could indicate material to be unfolded. But it is called matter *to rehearse,* to retell in public voicing, even (though no etymology), *re-hear.*[2] This involute is quite a Moebius strip. Keats's poet and protagonist are temporally distinct but experientially continuous: an author who tells a dream and a dreamer seeking authority to tell it; poetry originating in a dream and poetry generating an originating dream; a severe testing of a dreamer who would be a poet and the severest poetry of *A Dream*. The strange tense of *purposed to* is part of the relay: it implies both a focused *purpose* and an open *propose*, with an archaic inflection of merely *fancied*.[3] Right from its induction, *The Fall of Hyperion* is Keats's most loaded laboratory of poetic temporalities, looping origin and consequence into ever-deepening convergence of dream-time, Moneta's history-haunted present, the dream-protagonist merging into her theater of memory, and the poet writing in the present. These routings traverse timescapes of textual history (*Hyperion*), of Keats's re-reading, redrafting, and inducting it—and not least, the projected time of posthumous reading.

In all these temporalities, forever deferred is the god of poetry, Apollo. He is named only in the dream-protagonist's cry to his absence—"Apollo! Faded, far-flown Apollo!" (1.204)—then once more, in a pathetic oath (286). For *The Fall*, human poet Keats coined an echo-word, *faulture*, to describe an epic ruin (1.70). No ruins at all are Keats's vibrant neologisms, with particular intensity in this last run at epic: poetry in essence, not just inventive language but language invented, pronounced, and charged with visionary resonance. The first ordeal, at Moneta's altar, threatens the very possibility of language, in a poetry of fiercely tensile wordings.

[For the first part of the induction, letter to Richard Woodhouse
(21 September 1819), MsK 1.64.313. Then MsK 3.2, f.165ʳ, sq.311.
MsK 3.2 is my basis, cited by sq., using Woodhouse's line numbers]

[1] Keats's poetry alone has 120 instances of *dream* or this syllable; dreams anchor many of his speculations, from the genetics of "Adam's dream" for imagination, to the grammar of "indolence," to a parsing with Coleridge of different "species of Dreams" (including "Nightmare"), to dream-talk with Fanny Brawne, to living a "dream among my Books," "dreaming over . . . Books," and a world of dreamers in Shakespeare's plays, whose words Keats often takes up as his own.

[2] Keats marked the performative sense in *Midsummer Night's Dream* 5.2: "rehearse this song by rote" (*DW* 2:63).

[3] *OED* (3): To represent to one's imagination; to imagine to oneself; to fancy, suppose. *Obsolete. rare;* and in the passive construction (8), *rare* and *archaic*.

From whose white fragrant curtains thus I heard
Language pronounc'd. "If thou canst not ascend
These steps, die on that marble where thou art.
Thy flesh, near cousin to the common dust,
Will parch for lack of nutriment—thy bones   110
Will wither in few years, and vanish so
That not the quickest eye could find a grain
Of what thou now art on that pavement cold.
The sands of thy short life are spent this hour,
And no hand in the Universe can turn   115
Thy hour glass, if these gummed leaves be burnt
Ere thou canst mount up these immortal steps."
I heard, I look'd: two senses both at once
So fine, so subtle, felt the tyranny
Of that fierce threat, and the hard task proposed.
Prodigious seem'd the toil, the leaves were yet
Burning, —when suddenly a palsied chill   122
Struck from the paved level up my limbs,
And was ascending quick to put cold grasp
Upon those streams that pulse beside the throat:
I shriek'd; and the sharp anguish of my shriek
Stung my own ears—I strove hard to escape
The numbness; strove to gain the lowest step.
Slow, heavy, deadly was my pace: the cold
Grew stifling, suffocating, at the heart;   130
And when I clasp'd my hands, I felt them not.

The dreamscape, after Keats's last, exhausted bower (19–55), comes to a wide wasteland. Far off, the protagonist-I discerns and proceeds toward a huge image, an altar at its feet, from which he hears *Language pronounc'd* (107). More than *pronounc'd*, the words come forth as an epic *fierce threat* and *hard task*, threatening utter annihilation, a *turn* into *burnt* (115–116). Keats redoes Lamia's dying on his own poet-pulses. Ten lines pace in harrowing agony (122–131)—*slow, heavy deadly was my pace: the cold*—from first thuds on, nearly insensate. Keats's medical literacy pairs with deep fluency in the poetry of death. He knows Ovid's horrid metamorphosis:

And gradual Death from Limb to Limb proceeds;
So does the Chilness to each vital Part
Spread by degrees, and creeps into her Heart.[1]

Such agony Keats underlined in Milton's (re)production for Adam on realizing
Eve's mortal fall:

Astonied stood and blank, while horror chill
Ran through his veins, and all his joints relax'd;
From his slack hand the garland wreath'd for Eve
Down dropt, and all the faded roses shed:
Speechless he stood and pale   (9.890–894; *KPL* II:100)

Adam, in liquid stone, is speechless. The only action is in the *wreath,* tuned
for *Eve,* then fallen in a thud of *d*'s: *Down dropt, faded, shed.* Keats spins the
dream into a nightmare of words dissolved into pained sound: a shar*p* an*g*uish
spelling out *pang* (caged in an action), *I shriek'd,* a sound soon all there is of
the self, *my shriek.* This, and Lycius's shriek in *Lamia* are the only times this
nominalized form appears in his poetry. The final agony imperils the warm
scribe of the hand—or both hands: neither can be felt nor feel, a truly devas-
tating feel of not to feel it.

   What awaits is a vision to see and the question that impends, no telling.

[sq. 317, 319]

[1] Book II; *Ovid's Metamorphoses* (London: J. Tonson, 1774), p. 70.

Moneta's globed brain

"The sacrifice is done, but not the less
Will I be kind to thee for thy good will.
My power, which to me is still a curse,
Shall be to thee a wonder; for the scenes
Still swooning vivid through my globed brain
With an electral changing misery
Thou shalt with those dull mortal eyes behold,
Free from all pain, if wonder pain thee not."
As near as an immortal's sphered words

252

Could to a mother's soften, were these last: 260
But yet I had a terror of her robes,
And chiefly of the veils, that from her brow
Hung pale, and curtain'd her in mysteries
That made my heart too small to hold its blood.
This saw that Goddess, and with sacred hand
Parted the veils. Then saw I a wan face,
Not pin'd by human sorrows, but bright blanch'd
By an immortal sickness which kills not;
It works a constant change, which happy death
Can put no end to; deathwards progressing   270
To no death was that visage; it had pass'd
The lily and the snow; and beyond these
I must not think now, though I saw that face —
But for the eyes I should have fled away.
They held me back, with a benignant light,
Soft-mitigated by divinest lids
Half closed, and visionless entire they seem'd
Of all external things—they saw me not . . .

Language pronounc'd insults this poet-pretender as no poet at all, just a fever of
himself, no use to the world. Asking who the prosecutor, whose altar, what
visage is half-buried in the sand (twin to Shelley's Ozymandias), dreamer-Keats
is answered by Keats's *disjecta membra:* the visage is Saturn's, long fallen. The
leveling voice is Titan priestess Moneta, sole guardian of his vast ruin.

Having inflicted visceral death-terror on the dreamer, she challenges his claim
to be a poet.[1] And so returns Keats's abandonment of medicine, with a hope
that poetry might be metaphysical medicine, even with physical comfort.

Majestic shadow, tell me: sure not all
Those melodies sung into the world's ear
Are useless: sure a poet is a sage;
A humanist, Physician to all men   (sq. 323)

Two utterances of *sure* are two too many for confidence. (Recall the Knight's
merely one *sure* about *La belle dame:* "sure in language strange she said"). The
petitioner has asked for it with a vengeance. His test (a cursed final examina-
tion) will be a real-time dream immersion in her nightmare of historical
memory.

The chiasmus of line 252, "*Will I* be kind to *thee* for *thy* good *will*," joins *I* and *thy* in volition and result, her will and his. The swerve is the escape-clause, *if wonder pain thee not* (258). An existential question, this *if*: it is not that wonder might be painful, but that *pain* exceeds all wonder. The very word rhymes with Moneta's *brain*. Keats could have written *memory* or *mind*, but he wanted brain-physiology. Her memory is her unrelieved re-experiencing, soon to be the petitioner's trial. The first *pain* Keats writes for him draws on a medically in-formed panic of a heart *too small to hold its blood* (264). Keats makes syntax a witness: *This saw the Goddess*, begins the next line, set up for a reciprocal in what she unveils, a visage to match the heart: *Then saw I a wan face* (266), a double intensification, a *shade veil'd* (204) in apparitional recession.

Shade and veil figure language about to materialize from phantom weav-ings. Keats propels dreamwords into a medical sublime: *an immortal sickness which kills not, ever deathwards progressing.* This is the only *deathwards* in his poetry, here interminable. At a limit of comparison to earthly things, beyond the lily and the snow, Keats breaks into the time of writing: *I must not think now* (272–273).[2] The dream-frame around this halt is a horrific meta-narrative chiasmus: *Then saw I wan face, / / I must not think now, though I saw that face—.* The aesthete of Melancholy, fancying he could feed on his mistress's *peerless eyes,* is mordantly rebuked by eyes beyond peerless. They do not see their be-holder, and may be vacant of the very thing he is after: a vision with a spell of words. Keats implies a Miltonic recompense in *visionless entire they seem'd / Of external things* (277–278): Milton's epic narrator speaks what is invisible to mortal sight. From here, *A Dream* opens into Moneta's theater of memory, not only to see what she sees, to hear what she knows, but to find words to re-hearse it all, some of them from Keats's abandoned *Fragment.*

[sq. 325, 327]

---

[1]Her assault and the dreamer's reply (147–210) are in *P* and *K.* Keats drafted this twice, starting anew at 187. On the basis of Woodhouse's note in his manuscript (sq. 322) that Keats meant to cancel the first try, Milnes published only lines 147–186. 187–210 were first published by de Selincourt in 1905 (separately, then in *Poems,* 518–519). Editorial practice since has been to present all of 147–210.

[2]"The Beautiful is the perfection, the Sublime the suspension, of the comparing Power," is a note Coleridge made as he was reading (Raysor 533).

Moneta's voice   310
Came brief upon my ear, – "So Saturn sat
When he had lost his realms" — Whereon there grew
A power within me of enormous ken,
To see as a God sees, and take the depth
Of things as nimbly as the outward eye
Can size &shape pervade. The loft theme
At those few words hung vast before my mind,
With half-unravel'd web. I set myself
Upon an Eagle's watch, that I might see,
And seeing ne'er forget. No stir of life   320
Was in this shrouded vale . . .

Long, long, those two were postured motionless,
Like sculpture builded up upon the grave   393
Of their own power. A long awful time
I look'd upon them; still they were the same;
The frozen God still bending to the Earth,
And the sad Goddess weeping at his feet.
Moneta silent. Without stay or prop
But my own weak mortality, I bore
The load of this eternal quietude,   400
The unchanging gloom, and the three fixed shapes
Ponderous upon my senses a whole moon.
For by my burning brain I measured sure
Her silver seasons shedded on the night
And every day by day methought I grew
More gaunt &ghostly – Oftentimes I pray'd
Intense, that Death would take me from the vale
And all its burthens – Gasping with despair   408
Of change, hour after hour I curs'd myself

Size and shape, words and web: Moneta's voice comes upon the ear as the text
of *Hyperion,* Keats rehearing, rehearsing it. In this reperception, the protago-
nist emerges as a Keatsian poet. A "power within *me*" spells his "the*me*" and its
textual figuring, the *few words* that unravel the web of history. It is here that

the *Dream* recovers its precursor-text, deep in the vale of Titan sorrows. Keats rewords the scene as *this shrouded vale* (321), immediate, and echoing in this new context Moneta's shaded *veil.* The worded web, half-unravel'd, is half revealed, and the dream-persona's entanglement impends as he sees and enters the text of *Hyperion.*

Keats's revised scene of Saturn and Thea immobile in the nighttime woods now involves the dreamer's witness, with excruciating camelion sympathy, without Moneta's support. By having her remain silent, Geoffrey Hartman observes, Keats adds her into "what must be borne" ("Spectral" 64). The simile at line 393 ("Like sculpture . . .") brings a new intensity, rewriting *Hyperion's* stilled tableau of "natural sculpture in cathedral cavern" (1.86) as a phased devastation of fallen deities, on a double antonym, "builded *up upon,*" the archaic *builded* finely sounding *dead* in its second syllable.

> Dante was the father of modern poetry . . . there is a gloomy abstraction
> in his conceptions, which lies like a dead weight upon the mind; a be-
> numbing stupor, a breathless awe, from the intensity of the impression;
> a terrible obscurity, like that which oppresses us in dreams . . . He is the
> severest of all writers, the most hard and impenetrable, the most oppo-
> site to the flowery and the glittering.

So Keats heard Hazlitt lecture early in 1818 (*Lectures* 34–35), and must have registered the antonym to his poetic spirit at that time. At the far end of 1819, Keats's Dantean dream bears dead-weighted effect with a difference. Oppressed in silence and slow time, the *Fall's* protagonist is far from stupidly benumbed: his burning brain fires a scene that nearly kills him in its intense impression. The paused weight / wait of words—especially *ponderous,* pressing down the mental burden—accrues lexical mass and density in temporal duration. For this intensity, Keats works the keyword *still* to deepest treachery. From the protagonist's having already *felt / What 'tis to die* in gradations of visceral agony on the steps of Moneta's temple (141–143), he now feels what he sees: *A long awful time / I look'd upon them; still they were the same* (394–395). The temporality of their *still*-stationing becomes the witness's durational *still,* in which he (not the gods of *Hyperion*) is the locus of action: *I looked, I bore, I measured, I pray'd, I grew more gaunt, I curs'd.* Every key of Keatsian poetics, his measures sure, comes to bear: the camelion poetics of being *in for—and filling some other body;* the *feel* of *the burthen of the mystery;* and not least, a *greeting of the spirit* in an intensity indistinguishable from self-cursing. Keats tautens his poetic measures into the *measure* of a burning brain, writing the dreamer into Moneta's brain, into the nightmare of her history, into her temporality, *every day by day* with no hope of *change.*

One of the most mysterious of semi-speculations is *that of one Mind's imagining into another,* Keats says of Milton's hell of dark imagination, then adds, *it can scarcely be conceived how Milton's Blindness might per vade the magnitude of his conception as a bat in a large gothic vault—* (*KPL* I:5).[1] Keats does not just imagine, but imagines *into* Moneta's brain with full camelion self-annihilation. The *dark secret Chambers of her skull* (1.288) are a vault of magnitude with no echolocation. And the entrant's eye is doomed to *pervade* (1.316) its dark terrain, the very verb Keats used for Milton's conceptions, and in his poetry only here. The Titans' *vale and all its burthens* may not even prove a vale of soul-making, just a spectral terror from which Death, personified, might grant the only mercy.

Any plan for fore-seeing god Apollo is pre-empted by this foreseeing protagonist, who, as a Keatsian poet, knows on his mortal pulses and from the script of *Hyperion* what's coming. Waiting in the wings is mind-felled Hyperion. Apollo struggling at the "gate of death" is ready to "take leave / Of pale immortal death" and become the poetry deified (*Hyperion* 3.126–128). The human poet has to find his poetry in Hyperion's coming death. The test was never about the fallen gods. It was always about mortal knowing and its poetic entanglements.

[sq. 329, 331, 335]

---

[1] For *per vade,* most editors follow H. B. Forman (3:21), reading *here ade* (i.e., *here aid*). Studying this script here and against Keats's other writings of *p,* I think *per vade* is plausible (Forman pauses over this, 21n1). It makes better lexical and grammatical sense, even.

                Moneta cried – "These twain   470
Are speeding to the families of grief,
Where roof'd in by black rocks they waste in pain
And darkness for no hope."— And she spake on,
As ye may read who can unwearied pass
Onward from the Antichamber of this dream,
Where even at the open doors awhile
I must delay, and glean my memory   478
Of her high phrase: perhaps no further dare. —
               End of Canto I.—

             — <u>Canto 2.</u>^d —
  "Mortal! that thou may'st understand aright,
I humanize my sayings to thine ear,
Making comparisons of earthly things;
Or thou might'st better listen to the wind,   4
Whose language is to thee a barren noise,
Though it blows <u>legend-laden</u> though the trees."

                [. . .]

"Hyperion, leaving twilight in the rear,
Is sloping to the threshold of the west.-
Thither we tend.-" Now in clear light I stood,
Reliev'd from the dusk vale. Mnemosyne   50
Was sitting on a square edg'd polish'd stone,
That in its lucid depth reflected pure
Her priestess=garments. My quick eyes ran on
From stately nave to nave, from vault to vault,
Through bowers of fragrant and enwreathed light,
And diamond paved lustrous long arcades.
Anon rush'd by the bright Hyperion;   57
His flaming robes stream'd out beyond his heels,
And gave a roar, as if of earthly fire,
That scar'd away the meet ethereal hours
And made their dove-wings tremble: on he flared
           +   +   +

From the protagonist's pulsating anguish in witnessing the Titans' agony, the name *Moneta* echoes through fourteen iterations of *moan* (412–443). Her report of the *twain* (Saturn and Thea) multiplies to a world of *pain* (470, 472), a conspicuous rhyme in the blank-verse. Keats's syntax for *Where roof'd in by black rocks they waste in pain/And darkness* (472–473) is exquisitely keyed. The first *in* is stationing; the second is a syllepsis of correspondent consciousness. The *darkness* of no hope arcs from the metaphor-laden *black rock* to the despair of wasting gods. Canto I, the only one Keats completed, closes with a pause in Moneta's return as the unsylvan historian, preceded by the poet's first direct address to his readers about our capacity to keep going in this intensity.

Keats used *unwearied* only twice before in poetry, tacit foils to the challenge here. One is the scene of dream-guaranteed poetic power in *Hyperion* Book III, as Mnemosyne tells Apollo that he has wakened from his dream of her into the "Unwearied ear of the whole universe," ready to hear his music (67). The other is the illusion of an *unwearied* melodist on the Grecian Urn. Keats's latest, and last, *unwearied* tests our capacity for epic endurance. The poet sounds our cue, *ye may,* into a subtle internal rhyme with his *delay,* and interweaves his station, *Where,* into a rhyme for us, *dare:* a dire synonym for its anagram *read* (476–479). Canto 2^{d} goes through the open doors, with dream-time momentum. After line 5, Keats is revising *Hyperion,* keeping to the mode of a dreamer's witnessing.

Moneta's accommodation for her high phrasing bears no guarantee of unwearied passages for what her memory holds, unrelieved, ever relived. Writing to Woodhouse on 21 September 1819, Keats underlined for his appreciation the "fine sound" of legend laden (MsK 1.64.311). *What leaf-fring'd legend haunts about thy shape/Of deities or mortals, or of both?* speaks a poet's curiosity about that Grecian Urn. Here it is for Goddess-literacy only. Writing *Though it blows* as its motion, Keats carries the fine sound of long-o assonance wafting forward to *though the trees* (6), even as he is thinking *through.* Editors (including Stillinger, *P* 490) like *through.* I keep Keats's accidental musical flow of sound over sense. Moneta's intent to humanize is on the same page as Raphael's affability to Adam in "likening spiritual to corporal forms,/As may express them best" (*PL* 5.573–574)—though a doubt about his simile-logic got Keats underlining at a pivotal though:

though what if Earth
Be but the shadow of Heaven, and things therein
Each to other like, more than on Earth is thought? (574–576; *KPL* I:133)

Another way to work the analogy is *what if fallen Earth be the shadow of Hell?* The grammar of guidance in Dante's dream vision of Hell comes with at least a promise of profit. Near the end of *Hell* Canto I (p. 4), Keats underlined dream-space shrieks on this score (Gittings, *Mask* 145):

> I for thy profit pond'ring now devise,
> That thou mayst follow me, and I thy guide
> Will lead thee hence through <u>an eternal space</u>,
> Where thou shalt hear despairing shrieks . . . (109–112)

Profit is a question lodged in the Keats-dreamer's guide. At Moneta's altar he *shrieks,* in despair of his life. Moneta now leads this recovering shrieker to the palace of yet unfallen Hyperion, along the lines of Keats's *Hyperion.*

The subtlest treachery of Keats's revision is wrought by a syntax that aligns mortal dreamer and soon to be mortal god. It happens in stages. First, in a text that Keats must have had in mind from Cary's *Purgatory,* dreamer-Dante sees himself reflected in the lowest stair to Purgatory's gates (p. 151):

>   so smooth
> And polish'd, that therein my mirror'd form
> Distinct I saw.   (IX.85–87)

Keats shifts the mirroring to (a now-named) Mnemosyne,

>   sitting on a square edg'd polish'd stone,
> That in its lucid depth reflected pure
> Her priestess-garments.   (2.50–53)

Keats gives the priestess this visual mirror, because the mirror of real consequence for his poetics of mortal sympathy is an imminent dream-psychology of recognition. This flashes in two formations, symbolic and syntactic. The symbolic one has "Mnemosyne" replace "Moneta." Maybe a slip; but the return of Mnemosyne, goddess of Memory and mother of the Muses, ripples with subconscious pressure from the project of reimagining *Hyperion.*[1] The syntactic mirror comes with a double-play in linear poetics that for Keats has become by now a fine-tuned skill. This is how it unfolds. The syntax-run from *My quick eyes ran on/From . . . to . . . from . . . to . . . Through . . . long arcades* (53–56) accumulates such momentum that the period at the end of line 56 scarcely halts the flow into the next line, soliciting a forward reading into *Anon rush'd by the bright Hyperion* (57). The word-order is so parallel to the verb / prepositions of the previous lines (*ran on* / *From . . . from . . .* / *Through*) that *rush'd by* seems to be carried by this sight-line. Only with the turn to line 58 is it clear that it is Hyperion who has *rush'd by* the dreamer's eyes, not the dreamer's eyes that *rush'd by* Hyperion. For the brief pause of line 57, in a superb drama of poetic syntax, Keats has dreamer's eye and dreamed object converge on the same words.

I don't think this effect accidental. Keats's double-loaded syntax compresses the pace and space of the last line of *Inferno* Canto I, which he triple-lined in the left margin: "Onward he mov'd, I close his steps pursu'd."[2] Carey / Dante makes the motions *he mov'd* / *I pursu'd* simultaneous. Keats's line 57 brilliantly conflates *he* (Hyperion) and *I* (dream-protagonist). He then discharges this double-packed syntax—an immortal about to become mortal, and a mortal experientially conflated with this immortal—into the analogical *as if of earthly fire*. Mortal dreamer and doomed god meet here, *earthly* absorbing a vanishing *ethereal*. While the fictive time of *on he flared* is past, long past in Titan time, the propulsion lives *on* in dream time, with no terminal punctuation.[3] Keats underlined Satan's voyaging through Chaos, <u>nigh founder'd on he fares</u> (2.490; *KPL* I:55), and recast its near sound for Hyperion's burst of ferocity. Knowing the sequel in *Hyperion,* Keats stopped, and by September surrendered.

He commented to George and Georgiana that Milton's meter *cut by feet* was a *vein of art,* and he was after *another sensation.* "Life to him would be death to me." Such high stakes suggest that more than meter determined his *guard against Milton* (*L* 2:212). It was about finding a way of writing about mortality without Milton's theology, without, too, his "artful or rather artist's humour," but with "a true voice of feeling," he said to Reynolds (*K* 267). This was Keats's challenge, the art of feeling and the feeling in art. It nagged at him, and reversing the surrender of September, he kept at it, off and on.[4] A few weeks after *Hyperion* was published in the *Lamia* volume (early July 1820), young Keats suffered a massive hemorrhage, to live what he had written for Hyperion: "the horrors that nerves and a temper like mine go through . . . The last two years taste like brass upon my Palate," he tells Fanny Brawne, knowing he had to leave England and her (forever), no hope of ease ever again.[5] Brass upon the palate—blood-taste, rust-metal sick—filled Keats, hemorrhage after hemorrhage. One of the last letters he wrote could have been script for Hyperion's throb of agony: "Shall I awake and find all this a dream? (*K* 429). Rereading *Hyperion* happened to him this way, too.

That's one *Fall.* Another is seasonal. By Keats's day, the British term was *Autumn,* but the lexically loaded name *Fall* was still current.[6]

[sq. 339, 341, 343. For 2.1–4 and 6: Keats's letter, 21–22 September 1819, MsK 1.64.31]

[1] Miriam Allott, noting the allonyms, sees Keats reverting from one to the other (672n); other editors tend to just gloss *Moneta,* as if Keats had lost track.

[2] Cary's *Hell,* p. 4; Gittings, *Mask,* 145.

[3] Edward Bostetter even misremembers the tense as *flares*—"forever triumphant and undefeated" (171).

[4] "In the evenings, at his own desire, he was alone in a separate sitting-room, deeply engaged in remodelling his poem of 'Hyperion' into a 'Vision'" (Brown, *Life of Keats; KC* 2:72).

[5] August 1820 (ALS, Berg, ff.1–2; see also *K* 423).

[6] *OED:* both names were common in British English in the sixteenth century; by the end of the seventeenth, *autumn* was primary, while in the United States *fall* won out by the early nineteenth century.

To Autumn

SEASON of mists and mellow fruitfulness,
    Close bosom-friend of the maturing sun;
Conspiring with him how to load and bless
    With fruit the vines that round the thatch-eves run;
To bend with apples the moss'd cottage-trees,
    And fill all fruit with ripeness to the core;
        To swell the gourd, and plump the hazel shells
With a sweet kernel; to set budding more,
    And still more, later flowers for the bees,
    Until they think warm days will never cease,   10
        For Summer has o'er-brimmed their clammy cells.

2.

Who hath not seen thee oft amid thy store?
    Sometimes whoever seeks abroad may find
Thee sitting careless on a granary floor,
    Thy hair soft-lifted by the winnowing wind;
Or on a half-reap'd furrow sound asleep,
    Drows'd with the fume of poppies, while thy hook
        Spares the next swath and all its twined flowers:
And sometimes like a gleaner thou dost keep
    Steady thy laden head across a brook;   20
    Or by a cyder-press, with patient look,
        Thou watchest the last oozings hours by hours.

3.

Where are the songs of Spring? Ay, where are they?
    Think not of them, thou hast thy music too,—
While barred clouds bloom the soft-dying day,
    And touch the stubble-plains with rosy hue;
Then in a wailful choir the small gnats mourn
    Among the river sallows, borne aloft

Or sinking as the light wind lives or dies;
And full-grown lambs loud bleat from hilly bourn;   30
    Hedge-crickets sing; and now with treble soft
    The red-breast whistles from a garden-croft;
And gathering swallows twitter in the skies.

To Autumn is probably the last poem Keats wrote for the *1820* volume. It is about ending, but it is no dark finale. It pauses at a rich interval between seasons, undeluded about mortality, yet suspending its weight, for this day. *How beautiful the season is now,* Keats writes to Reynolds from Winchester, 21 September 1819.

> *How fine the air. A Temperate sharpness about it . . . I never lik'd stubble fields so much as now – Aye better than the chilly green of the Spring. Somehow a stubble plain looks warm . . . this struck me so much in my Sunday's walk that I composed upon it*   (*K* 266)

While *stubble plain* is harvest's end, the sensation of sunlit warmth is Keats's Sunday inspiration, still with the feel of summer, unlike winter-cold spring. He is thinking again about Chatterton's native, *genuine English.* It helps him understand why he has *given up Hyperion.* The idiom for *The Fall* wasn't working for him.

Milton himself needed relief, Keats sensed. At the front of *Paradise Lost*, he wrote a note that while the *Genius of Milton* suited him for high argument—*rather to the Ardours than the pleasures of Song*—Milton also *had an exquisite passion for what is properly in the sense of ease and pleasure poetical Luxury . . . solacing himself at intervals with cups of old wine,* and this inspired many of *the finest parts of the Poem* (*KPL* I:ii). Keats knows the medical meaning of *interval:* a pause between fits of fever. And he knows the original military sense: between ramparts (*valla*), knows even Milton's single use of the word in *Paradise Lost:* "'Twixt host and host but narrow space was left, / A dreadful interval" (6.104– 105; *KPL* II:6). An *interval* is a pause pressed by known borders—in war, in sickness, or on vocational tracks.

Keats's ode is a qualified interval, a pause for enjoyment (winter is coming). He needed a vacation from his life-distresses, even from daily reading political outrages, especially at Manchester. Yet ever since Jerome McGann's "Keats and the Historical Method" (1979) indicted *To Autumn* as an evasion of the sociopolitical events of autumn 1819, the ode has been a textbook case of "false consciousness," pretending to a timeless meditation meant to "dissolve social and political conflicts in the mediations of art and beauty" (1017). I think *dissolve* is not right. Keats is taking a day off, not alchemizing.[1] He promised Woodhouse that *maturer years* would see him to a Miltonic mode, *ambitious to do the world some good—in the interval I will assay to reach to as high a summit in Poetry as the nerve bestowed upon me will suffer* (MsK 1.38.140–141). That was 27 October 1818, and the interval was about preparation. Tom's season was no soft dying, as Keats was laboring at the ardours of song. Vexed by *The Fall of Hyperion,* he wanted "to compose without this fever," he tells George on 21 September 1819, the same day he writes to Reynolds about the "temperate" season (*K* 275). To so *compose* might be to compose himself, for an interval. Keats was still healthy enough and not yet twenty-four. He might have time to turn the page. This is the day he wrote *To Autumn.*

Keats knows the traditions: harvest and death. Both are held off. From a sensation of infinite prolongation to quiet temporal signatures—to *bend and fill* rather than bend and fall—*To Autumn* is not a drama of corrected illusion, like *Ode on a Grecian Urn* and *Ode to a Nightingale.* Kin to *Ode on Melancholy,* it fills out what it knows. Keats extends the ten-line stanzas of the other Great Odes to eleven in *To Autumn.* This adds a rhyme, a penultimate couplet in the "sestet" phase: *abab cdedcce. Ode on Melancholy* issued a three-part argument (don't; do; here's why). *To Autumn* unfolds three simultaneous tableaux vivant, in sequentially wider scenes. Stanza 1 swells an apostrophe to the season's ripenings. Stanza 2 stations three personifications of autumnal slow time. Stanza 3 recalls Spring for a prelude to Autumn's vast auditorium. I love Stuart Sperry's remark that *adieu,* "the theatrical, slightly affected word that occurs in each of the odes of the spring," is absent here, though this is where you might expect it (*Keats* 284). Such is subtle perfection of Keats's double-plays, evoking but not distilling.

Stanza 1 begins, ode-wise, in apostrophe, and extravagantly: the syntax dilates through all eleven lines, strung on infinitives (*to load and bless, To bend . . . And fill, To swell . . . and plump*), present participles and gerunds (*maturing, Conspiring, budding more*), and additive conjunctions (*and* five times). The phonic score becomes hyper-harmonic in the last line's triple *mm: Summer–brimm'd–clammy.*[2] This last adjective, *clammy,* is for *cells,* a sound tuned all the way from line 1: *mellow–fruitful–fill–swell–hazel shells–kernel still more–flowers.* If sun and season conspire to load everything, Keats's mimesis is richly loaded poetry: words, syllables, sentences, syntaxes, rhymes, sounds. The period at the end of the stanza (as if the vocative syntax had forgotten itself) scarcely matters, absorbed by forward momentum of syntax into stanza 2, as if fainted into comma-pause in an interstanzaic enjambment.

Stanza 1's lexicon draws on a Keatsian core. His byword for dark passages, *mists,* comes here as a gentle atmospheric, alliterated *mellow.* How different from *we are in a Mist . . . We feel "the burden of the Mystery'* (*K* 130); from the quadruple-punctuated *mist* on Ben Nevis; from the strangling mist that ends Hyperion's Sun-days; and from Milton's simile for how the angels "descended" to evict Adam and Eve from Eden (Keats underlined this; *KPL* II:182):

> Gliding meteorous, as evening mist
> Risen from the river o'er the marish glides,
> And gathers ground fast at the labourer's heel
> Homeward returning.   (12.629–632)

Milton finely situates *as* for visual analogy and the coming temporality of post-lapsarian labor. The *mists* of *To Autumn* are all the more mellow for evoking and refusing these assignments. So, too, *Conspiring.* Keats deflects the sinister cast by going back to the etymology, "breathing with," to image a cooperative nurture of climate and sun, in the year's *maturing:* over its course, and with ripening agency.[3] His final touch is a wry diminuendo about bee-mindedness. The season's languor sets *still more, later flowers for the bees, / Until they think warm days will never cease* (9–10). This is the only *until* in all the 1819 odes. Bees don't *think;* it is deflected human-fantasy. The bee-mistaking *never cease* elicits a human thinker's positive knowing, with a soft echo of *cease* (Keats knows how to work this word) from the *Season* that all the while seems to be doing no such thing. If Keats can love Titania's conception of *the middle summer's spring* (*RS* 52), he can feel a sensation here of early Autumn's second summer, or even second spring.

The extravagantly accumulating, verbally loaded apostrophe of stanza 1 exhales into the start stanza 2: *Who hath not seen thee . . . ?* It is no question, except rhetorically. It is stage-setting for four personified labors, in slow-time: winnowing, reaping, gleaning, cyder-pressing. F. R. Leavis has finely appreciated the mimesis of slow-stepping in the line-break *keep / Steady,* where the syntactic pause and crossing from one line to the next evoke the steps "across a brook" (19–20).[4] In this scanned slow time, the temporal terms *Sometimes / sometimes* are factored out and "made prepositional."[5] Keats gives the poetry a deft mimesis, holding *find* at the end of line 13, to let its object-mission delay. And what to *find?* Nothing more than *sitting careless,* the muted rhyme at *wind* reverberating into *winnowing* (15). Copying the poem for Woodhouse, he spelled a letter-linked *winmowing wind* (MsK 1.64.310), as if wind had taken over the labor. An earlier manuscript had an even more cooperative (in sound and sense) *winnowing wing* (MsK 2.27.1).

This is a poetry of soundscape as much as visual imagination: Autumn *on a half-reap'd furrow sound asleep, / Drows'd with the fume of poppies* (16–17) echoes *reap'd* in *asleep, sound asleep* as "sound as sleep," interwoven with the *sound*-flow and *furrow* into *Drows'd*. Keats reworked his first draftings to achieve this effect: he first had *sound asleep in a half reaped field / Dosed with red poppies* (MsK 2.27.1). Those *last oozings, hours by hours* (22), sound-spun from *drows'd*, linger in slowest time over cyder-pressing, even gathering up the insistent *later flowers* of stanza I. Geoffrey Hartman writes a sentence to die for: "Time lapses so gently" that "we pass from the fullness of the maturing harvest to the stubble plains without experiencing a cutting edge." This is no "crisis" ode (126–127).

All these luxuries are subtly edged with temporal reminders, however: *store* tells of storing up for winter, *careless* is inflected by a consciousness of needed care; *half-reap'd* and *the next swath* are rests, not arrests; *like a gleaner* evokes the late season of stubble plains; the stanza's last line does say *last*. While Keats's draft has no punctuation at the end of stanza 2 (not even a dash, and the letter-draft only the briefest dash), stanza 3 interrupts to recall the season furthest away, past or to come: *Where are the songs of Spring?* (23). The alliterative lilt of *Where are . . . ?* is no idle musing. Its dactyl comes with dramatic stress, on a track loaded by *ubi sunt* tradition (keynote of elegy, private or communal). This is the crisis that blew up Wordsworth's "Intimations Ode" for a good two years.[6] Keats plays the elegiac tune (for the season, but also the genre), then retunes: *Ay, where are they? / Think not of them, thou hast thy music too* (23–24). The spondee *Think not,* replacing a long distanced *they* with a present *thy,* cues a "Song of Autumn": the ode's auto-mimesis. Keats sounds the notes from sky to plains to river to hilly bourn; its chorus joins lambs, gnats, crickets, red-breast, and swallows: *wail, mourn, bleat, sing, whistle, twitter.* By the time this orchestra gets to *whistle with treble soft,* Keats's poetry is part of it, the ono-matopoeia of *whistle* spreading its sounds and letterings to "*with treble soft.*"

Keats's music is more subtle yet in the way it plays spring tones without elegy. *O Bloomiest!* he had hailed Psyche in a draft (Morgan ms., p. 2). I'm glad he thought better of the gush. He kept the kernel, though, for a wonderful tran-sitive verb, revising his first draft's merely ornamental *gold clouds gild* (MsK 2.27.2) to *barred clouds bloom* the soft dying day. *OED* gives Keats unique ci-tation for this use of *bloom.* How finely this images clouds as sky-flowers, shining a *rosy hue* on the stubble-plains of harvest's end. Meanwhile, the mu-sical phrase *small gnats mourn* sounds *morn,* this tuned to a *borne* that evokes *born* (those lambs on the *bourn* might be *born* too).[7] The very sound of *swal-lows* flies off from the funereal *sallows* (willows). These harmonic intervals are pulses of thinking, through words, in words. You can hear this in the way the *or* of *borne aloft / Or sinking* (sounded first in b*o*rne) and the *or* of *lives or dies* image variations rather than temporal inevitability (the drafts actually read *lives and dies*). Keats's time-markers—*while, then, now*—are spatially equivalent infrastructuring, as prepositional as the placer-markers, *from, among, from.* He wanted to keep his verbs in motion, too. The copy he made for Woodhouse had the swallows *gather,* this canceled for his first thought, *gathering,* the last of the present participles, drawn through *soft-dying* and *sing.* Both drafts end on a long dash after the last word, *Skies,* suspended figurally on the page space.[8]

One English bird, the red-breast, will not migrate. *Stay, ruby breasted warbler.* It stays in the croft to whistle through the winter. Keats knows that Love's seasons may be otherwise.

[*1820*, pp. 137–139]

[1] It is distressing to me to see some academics prosecuting Keats's Sunday walk. The latest scold is Anahid Nersessian: she calls Keats out for willful sequestration, "tucked up in Winchester" while everyone else was talking about Peterloo. "'To Autumn' is perfect and unforgiveable" is her verdict (114–115, and throughout). In fact, Keats was intensely attentive, writing several pages to George and Georgina on 18 September with more than "a little politics" (his self-ironizing apology) about present turmoils and the turns of "tyranny" in English political history (*L* 2:192–194). Far better informed and more subtly considered and argued to me is William Keach's tracing of Keats during these very weeks (*Arbitrary Power* 55–59). Back in London, Keats joined the huge crowds that cheered Peterloo champion Orator Hunt's arrival there for trial.

[2] Only Tennyson might match this onomatopoetic, notoriously, with *bees* no less: *The moan of doves in immemorial elms, / And murmuring of innumerable bees* (Song in *The Princess*).

[3] *Conspiring* appears only here in Keats's poetry, in a sense quite opposite to its only sibling in the 1820 volume, the winter season when "the Night doth meet the Noon / In a dark conspiracy / To banish Even from the sky" (*Fancy* 22–24).

[4] Cited by Ricks, "A Pure Organic Pleasure," 2.

[5] Hartman, "Poem and Ideology," 130. See also Annabel Patterson on the dilated syntaxes.

[6] "Whither has fled the visionary gleam? / Where is it now . . . ?" didn't get answered until Wordsworth hit on a metaphysics of eternity (an immortal elsewhere). *Ode, Intimations of Immortality* concluded *1815* (2:345–355; the question and answer are on 349) and all subsequent lifetime volumes.

[7] Hartman indexes the springtime cues, 129. I used to love the spring-minded "full-grown lambs," until a Scotsman explained to me that this meant lambs ready for the meat-market. I don't think Keats knew this.

[8] For the letter's last stanza, MsK 1.64.311; for the earlier draft, MsK 2.27.2.

Late intimacies and sonnets still, still unstill

~~Sonnet~~ (1819): "I cry your mercy"

I cry your mercy — pity — love! — aye, love,
  Merciful love that tantalises not,
One-thoughted, never wand'ring, guileless Love,
  Unmask'd, and being seen — without a blot!
O, let me have thee whole, — all, — all — be mine!
  That shape, that fairness, that sweet minor zest
Of love, your Kiss, those hands, those eyes divine,
  That warm, white, lucent, million-pleasured breast, —
Yourself — your soul —in pity give me all,
  Withhold no atom's atom or I die,
Or living on perhaps, your wretched thrall,
  Forget, in the mist of idle misery,
Life's purposes, — the palate of my mind
Losing its gust, and my ambition blind.

8

Keats sent this sonnet to Fanny Brawne sometime in late 1819. Reading such private poetry can feel transgressive, an illicit wire-tap of intimate communication.[1] "I cry you mercy" (close to Keats's *your*) is a casual (British) idiom for "excuse me," or "pardon me," with a potential for sarcasm. You hear it in Othello's snarl at Desdemona's protest of her never-wand'ring love: "I cry you mercy, then, / I took you for that cunning whore of Venice" (*Othello* 4.2.90–291). Not Keats's tone, but the anguished negatives that advance his cry— *tantalises not . . . never wand'ring, guileless . . . without a blot*—have Othello-fuel, a miserable sense that she has not been whole and true, maybe a *belle dame sans mercy*, the poet begging for pity. Drawing on the archive in his poetry of female treachery (*mercy, wretched, thrall*), Keats joins the fraternity. He had Glaucus describe a *long captivity* as *wretched thrall* for trusting a heartless enchanter (*Endymion* 3.335–336). "Have mercy, Goddess! Circe, feel my prayer," cries an elephant-man to this same woman, the *mercy-Circe* rhyme a cruel touch on Keats's part (557), soon an actual couplet (622–623), and before this clinch, twinned with Glaucus's *groan for mercy* from Circe (604). Both *mercy* and *thrall* are rare words in Keats's poetry, so when he calls on them, it is with sharp sense. This sonnet is also the only time that the detractive word *blot* marks his poetry, as an aestheticized moral. The investments are as intense as they are rare. These are the words put to work in the first quatrain of this Shakespearean sonnet.

Yet the Shakespearean pattern is so submerged by the forward thrust and incremental expansion of Keats's syntax as scarcely to register as a discipline of form. There are only two sentences (1–4; 5–14) across which the opening *cry* courses from its resounded *I* to the final I-absorbing, faintly echoing, self-canceling *blind.* The sonic path surges from *aye*—the sound of *I* absorbed into the emphatic, with attachment to a now nearly personified *Love*—to *I die* (the true rhyme for *I cry*) to *idle misery.* The sentences splinter into fragments; ghost-conjunctions compact into commas; grammar contracts, compresses, and frays; meter ruptures into such a surplus of stresses and breath-fraught dashes (eleven in all) that any pattern-pace is a lost cause; and the formalism of end-rhymes competes with a ricochet of repetitions, of words, sounds, and syllables. The desire for *all,* cried three times, winds up (in sound and sense) in *thrall*—yet another recall from the devastating rhyme-revelation in the nightmare of *La belle dame:* "death pale were they all / They cried - La belle dame sans merci / Thee hath in thrall."

The agenda of the male blazon, argues Nancy Vickers about Renaissance instances, is to transform the beloved into a verbal representation that "safely permits and perpetuates" the poet's fascination and unifies his poetic self in "the repetition of her dismembered image." Yet a boomerang effect may result in "a collection of imperfect signs, signs that, like fetishes, affirm absence by their presence." The poet "speaks his anxiety in the hope . . . of re-membering the lost body, of effecting an inverse incarnation—her flesh made word"; but "successes are ephemeral, and failures become a way of life" (275). This is the throb in Keats's blend of blazon and apostrophe. All the effusive itemizing in the second quatrain (*shape, fairness, kiss, hands, eyes*), summed in the nearly parodic hyperbole of *million-pleasured breast* and the exquisite accounting of each *atom's atom*, could well serve the artistry of condensing "uncontrollable passion" into 112 words and 14 lines to perform "a breathtaking technical mastery . . . a virtuoso display as an end in itself." This is Stuart Curran's admiration, recognizing a pressure of crisis in the assured "artistic control": "Such a polished representation of frenzy, in which the polarities of plentitude and emptiness are discovered to be the same, strains the sonnet form to the utmost and bears intimations of decadence."[2] Such control, even strained with decadence, is as precarious as it is polished, a balancing act on active imbalancing: paradox or peril? Keats's alternatives, *or I die / Or living on,* are so intimately aligned (in conception and in the line's turn) that collapse into irresolution becomes the only resolution. The alliterated *mist of idle misery* is an existential dark passage (*We are in a mist*) that dovetails into the lover's life sentence.

Tautening this strain is a rhetorical mode, cry as apostrophe. Poetic invocation is a figure of vocation, a calling that performs and declares poetic capability.[3] When it doesn't produce, or even devolves into the loss of, *Life's purposes,* it delivers a *gust* (no *gusto*) and a blind future, in a dark parody of the call: *I cry* ending in *I die,* both summed in the weakly rhyming *idle misery.* And what of *love?* This keyword gets no partner, just a crying, almost bitter, repetition of itself (1, 3, 7). In the sonnet's close on *my ambition blind,* the adjective-grammar of *blind* intimates a verb of vocational self-cancellation. When Keats confesses to his "dear Girl" in August 1819, "it seems to me that a few more moments thought of you would uncrystallize and dissolve me" into no-self at all, he knew the antidote: *I must not give way to it - but turn to my writing again - if I fail I shall die hard – O my love* (MsK 1.59.292). He coined the negative *uncrystallize* for this sensation. Countering the looming dissolve into nothingness, crystalline sonnet-writing still beckons Keats to self-possession. He might capitalize on the negative, to compose this into a book of love—in another turn of intimate communication.

[Charles Brown's ms., p. 20]

[1] First published *1848* (2:305), from Charles Brown's ms.
[2] Curran, *Poetic Form,* 53–54, a virtuoso reading.
[3] Culler's argument, in "Apostrophe," and more elaborately Fry, in *The Poet's Calling.*

"The day is gone"

The day is gone, and all its sweets are gone!
   Sweet voice, sweet lips, soft hand, and softer breast
Warm breath, tranc'd whisper, tender semitone,
   Bright eyes, accomplish'd shape, and langrous waist -
Vanish'd unseasonably at shut of eve   5
   When the dusk Holiday, or Holinight
Of fragrant-curtain'd Love begins to weave
   The ~~texture thick of darkness~~
      woof of darkness, thick, for hid delight
        and all its budded charms
Faded the ~~flower of beuty from my eyes gaze~~   9
     sight   Beauty   ~~sad~~ eyes
   Faded the ~~voice~~ of ~~Love~~ from my ~~sad ears~~
Faded the shape of beauty from my arms,
   Faded the voice, ~~the Whiteness~~
      warmth, whiteness, ~~brilliance~~ paradise
   But, as I have read Love's Missal through to day,
   He'll let me sleep - seeing I fast and pray

In the dreamscape of Paolo and Francesca's Hell, "lovers need not tell / Their sorrows." Keats in love turns to poetry's telling to blend serenade, elegy, and Petrarchan ache. This sonnet may not even be addressed to Fanny, but instead be another of Keats's self-accountings.[1] It is as much about its formal resources as it is about the ache of a day's fading.

Pale were the sweet lips I saw is what CAVIARE writes (for publication) of a dream of Paolo and Francesca. Here, a beloved's sweet lips are gone from sight. This sonnet is one long sigh of exclamation and attenuating dashes. This lover is a poet, conjuring with words and signs, but finding predominant the trochee-pulsed anaphora of negative blazon: *Faded . . . Faded . . . Faded . . . Faded*. Brown's manuscript (p. 59) shows Keats working this out in the lyrical-lexical shade of *Paradise Lost*:

> Faded the voice, warmth, whiteness, paradise,
> Vanished unseasonably at the shut of eve   (8–9)

Contracting *evening*, the word *eve*, set just below *paradise*, is a schematic of Milton's fall on a vertical axis. Keats saw Milton punning *Paradise Lost* this way.

He underlined Eve returning to Adam "at shut of Ev'ning Flow'rs" (9.278; *KPL* 2:83).[2] What has not faded is literary memory.

Elsewhere Keats underlined and margin-marked Prospero's longing for "repose": "a turn or two I'll walk / To still my beating brain" (IV.1; *KS* 81), Shakespeare wresting *still* from perdurance to quiet, but only as an infinitive. Feeling this beat in his brain, in his meters, Keats drew vertical lines down the left margin. Shakespeare's Sonnet XXVII got marked, too (*KS* 40).

> <u>Weary with toil, I haste me to my bed,</u>
> <u>The dear repose for limbs with travel tir'd;</u>
> But then begins a journey in my head,
> To work my mind, when body's works expir'd:
> <u>For then my thoughts (from far where I abide)</u>
> <u>Intend a zealous pilgrimage to thee,</u>
> <u>And keep my drooping eye-lids open wide,</u>
> <u>Looking on darkness which the blind do see:</u>
> Save that my soul's imaginary sight
> Presents thy shadow to my sightless view,
> Which, like a jewel hung in ghastly night,
> Makes black night beauteous, and her old face new.
>   Lo thus, by day my limbs, by night my mind,
>   For thee, and for myself, no quiet find.

With such backing to lean on, Keats shapes a Shakespearean sonnet about his own nightly devotions. (Sonnet XXVII also haunts his sonnet *To Sleep*.)

The day is gone is a "record" (etymologically: known by "heart") figured with a Love-god author and a text called *Love's Missal* (13). The lovelorn markers, *gone / gone! / Vanish'd / Faded / Faded / Faded / Faded*, are surreally compensated by the present poetry. While *semi-tone* gets only a half-chime with *gone*, the second quatrain's rhymes are fully invested, in both sound and semantic linking. William Wimsatt shows how rhyme can "impose upon the logical pattern of expressed argument a kind of fixative counterpattern of alogical implication" (*Verbal Icon* 153). The effect gets complicated when the logical pattern is psychological, and the expressed argument is about being fixed, transfixed, fixated. Keats summons rhyme to counter-pattern loss. The weave of *Holinight / hid delight* (7–8) draws on *Bright, sight,* and *whiteness*. *OED* credits Keats with coining *Holinight* (reciprocal to *Holiday*). He worked at his wording for the full chord, changing *voice* (Brown's manuscript) to line 8's *sight*, and *tranc'd* to line 3's *light*. Personified *Love* is his collaborator: a writer, a weaver of texture and text (*textura:* Latin, *weaving*). Love passion becomes Love writing, Love-reading, and loving release into sleep.

Christopher Miller finely catches the oscillation of *holinight* between devotion and epithalamia, with a "mock virtue" of the devotion. This is done from "necessity rather than desire," *Love's Missal* rehearsed in the absence of the lover (174). Even so, *Love's Missal* does not balance the books. On such a ledger, moreover, the poet cannot but read himself as a text, and a genre: a cliché of Love-convention, its latest iteration of style. Keats knows this warp of the conventional loom, the paradox that the poet of "love" is pre-written by Love's missal. Another paradox, returning the sleepless poet to sonnet-writing, is the waking genre of writing to Sleep.

[Morgan Library autograph ms. MA 213.5]

[1] First published 1838; then, from Brown's manuscript, in *1848* (2:304).

[2] For the opening of *Hyperion*, Keats first wrote *Eve's one star* (3), then revised to lower-case e (BL f.1ʳ)—possibly, to avert Milton's first mortal sinner.

Sonnet to Sleep

O soft embalmer of the still midnight,
Shutting with careful fingers and benign
Our gloom-pleas'd eyes, embowerd from the light,
Enshaded in forgetfulness divine: 4
O soothest sleep! if so it please thee, close,
In midst of this thine hymn my willing eyes
Or wait the Amen ere thy poppy throws
Around my bed its lulling charities.   8
Then save me or the passed day will shine
Upon my pillow, breeding many woes.
Save me from curious conscience, that still hoards   11
Its strength for darkness, burrowing like the mole;
Turn the Key deftly in the oiled wards
And seal the hushed Casket of my soul
                                    John Keats -
                                    June 1820

Sleep is a sumptuous subject for poets, often titled as this sonnet is. Keats began it sometime in 1818, writing it on the flyleaf of volume II of his *Paradise Lost*, an apt site for sleeplessness as paradise lost (11). He may have had a full draft by April 1819 (*P* 646). When he made this later copy, he was quite ill and sensing no recovery, living on his own in London, broke, unsure that the new volume would succeed. A (re)call to Sleep in such days seeks more than rest. An embalmer promises an anesthesia more than half in love with easeful death. In *Isabella*, corpses are *embalm'd* (XIII); this sonnet is mortal poetics.

Keats's title is grammatically rich. As a dative, "to" Sleep issues a petition to a personified benefactor. At the same time, "to" layers an infinitive (Hamlet: *To die, to sleep*), even an aimed preposition, a hope "to" do so. Shakespeare's sleepless Henry IV feels all this:

> How many thousand of my poorest subjects
> Are at this hour asleep!—Sleep, gentle sleep,
> Nature's soft nurse, how have I frighted thee,
> That thou no more wilt weigh my eyelids down,
> And steep my senses in forgetfulness?   (3.1; *DW* 4:43)

Such a sad chime, *steep* for the *sleep* so futilely addressed. "Uneasy lies the head that wears the crown" is the last line of a double-sonnet's worth (28 lines) of poetry. Keats echoes the words, as Shakespeare in turn echoes Sidney's sonnet "Come Sleepe, o Sleepe, the certaine knot of peace" (*Astrophel* 39), this with a sadly punned *not of peace* for this sleepless one. These echoes acknowledge a shared genre, a literary echo-chamber of sleepless sighings. Macbeth's turn comes with a gothic wrench and amplification, in lines Keats marked in the margin (*DW* 3:21):

> Methought, I heard a voice cry, *Sleep no more!*
> *Macbeth does murder sleep, the innocent sleep;*
> *Sleep, that knits up the ravell'd sleave of care,*
> *The death of each day's life, sore labour's bath,*
> *Balm of hurt mind, great nature's second course,*
> *Chief nourisher in life's feast;—* (2.2)

Lady Macbeth rebukes this yammering, strung out on four iterations of *sleep*, with a dose of *sleave* and alliteration into *feast*. "So brainsickly of things," she says (*OED* credits the word *brainsickly* to Shakespeare), but she couldn't halt the genre, especially in sonnets. The tradition is so durable as to inscribe an "insomnia poetics": waking poems of sleeplessness.

By the time Charlotte Smith writes her Shakespearean sonnet *To sleep* (1780s), it is about the archive as much as the subject:

> Come, balmy Sleep! tired Nature's soft resort!
>   On these sad temples all thy poppies shed;
> And bid gay dreams, from Morpheus' airy court,
>   Float in light vision round my aching head!
> Secure of all thy blessings, partial Power!
>   On his hard bed the peasant throws him down;
> And the poor sea-boy, in the rudest hour,
>   Enjoys thee more than he who wears a crown.
> Clasp'd in her faithful shepherd's guardian arms,
>   Well may the village girl sweet slumbers prove;
> And they, O gentle Sleep! still taste thy charms,
>   Who wake to labour, liberty, and love.
> But still thy opiate aid dost thou deny
> To calm the anxious breast; to close the streaming eye.

The first quatrain gives a lover's complaint and petition; the next two quatrains complain of Sleep's partiality. The couplet restates the distress, sounding *still* only as duration, not silence or stasis, with a final hexameter of desperate petition.

Insomniac Wordsworth had all this beating in his head when he wrote no less than three sonnets *To Sleep* (1807 *Poems*, 1:107–109). The second, a rueful Petrarchan love-sonnet, bestows the very trope of sleeplessness, counting sheep, a rhymed antonym of *sleep.*

> A flock of sheep that leisurely pass by,
> One after one; the sound of rain, and bees
> Murmuring; the fall of rivers, winds and seas,
> Smooth fields, white sheets of water, and pure sky;
> I've thought of all by turns; and still I lie
> Sleepless; and soon the small birds' melodies
> Must hear, first uttered from my orchard trees;
> And the first Cuckoo's melancholy cry.
> Even thus last night, and two nights more, I lay,
> And could not win thee, Sleep! by any stealth:
> So do not let me wear to-night away:
> Without Thee what is all the morning's wealth?
> Come, blessed barrier betwixt day and day,
> Dear mother of fresh thoughts and joyous health!

The insomniac poetics triangulate *sleep* through those *sheep* to echo mercilessly in *Sleepless.* Even the assonated call to *thee, Sleep!* can't seal the deal.

Keats's *Sonnet to Sleep* joins the club, with its own lexical turns. *Enshaded* is his word (in no dictionary). He turns *sooth* (archaic: *true*) into a sounded sigh, a superlative (unique in his poetry) *soothest Sleep!* It is a lover's poem to the Big Sleep, Death: *soft embalmer, forgetfulness divine, seal the hushed casket.* Yet the paradox, as for all sleepless poets, is the wakeful poetry. Keats knows the deft turns on *still. The still midnight* layers its senses—quiet, temporally extended, unyielding—into *willing* eyes, the day that *will* shine upon the *pillow,* and a wakefulness of mind that *still hoards.*[1] It is a perverse auto-lullaby. Intent to sing himself to a sleep beyond song, poet-Keats stays busy with his wordings: *shutting, willing, lulling, breeding, borrowing.* The feel of not to feel it is long gone; *this thine hymn* (6) is the activated genre.

Two Shakespearean quatrains, *abab cdcd,* shape a Petrarchan sestet in which the *bc* rhymes repeat (*shine-woes*) and the *f*-chord (*mole-soul*) is so consonant with the c-chord (*throw-close-woes*) that the sonnet itself figures an intricate ward of Keatsian keys. Deftly done is Keats's spending an extra syllable for lines 11 and 12, and subtracting the last two lines equivalently. On this diminuendo, 13 and 14, though unrhymed, turn like a Shakespearean couplet-volta, with a meta-poetic wit figured by 13's first word, *Turn*, in line with 9's first word, *Then*. At its Petrarchan-shaded volta, *Then* is doubly charged, for another ironic contradiction. On the agenda for sleep, it is a time-plan: do this, then this. Poetically, it unlocks six more lines of petition. The final enjoining, *And seal the hushed casket of my soul*, would conjure sleep in these sleepy words, with a double-loaded metaphor: the body as the casket of the soul; the soul itself is the casket, and a word for an in-wardness beyond words.

But Keats (we know) is nothing if not a poet of words, working words, hearing others' words. A *key* turning *wards* echoes wording he underlined in Dante/Cary's *Hell* so closely as to reverberate an allusion.[2] The site is the seventh circle (Canto XIII), a place where suicides and self-injurers may never sleep. One report is from Emperor Frederick II's minister and confidant:

> I it was, who held
> Both keys to Frederick's heart, and turn'd the wards,
> Opening and shutting, with a skill so sweet,
> That beside me, into his inmost breast
> Scarce any other could admittance find. (60–62, p. 54)

This minister, disgraced by accusations of heresy and treason, was condemned to lose his eyes, and committed horrible suicide. Keats's sonnet—the form invented in Frederick's court, no less, and beautifully practiced by this minister—moves these words into his own still, ever-conscious midnight. Keats's sonnet-wording evokes the suicide in the form's origin.

Whether infinitive or dative, *To sleep* is wakeful. *Save me* . . . *Save me from curious conscience*, twice tolled (9, 11), calls out *rescue me* but also spells *except for me*, the addict to words. *Curious:* more than "peculiar," it denotes "scrupulous" (*DW* Glossary 3334). *Turn the key deftly:* that's what a sonnet is for.

[Keats's holograph; Berg Collection]

---

[1] Keats's letter-text has *lords* (1.53.267); so does *Brown* (p. 50). Woodhouse proposed *hoards* and Keats took it on board when he recopied the sonnet. Stillinger gives the textual history, *Multiple Authors*, 20–21.

[2] For the underlining, see Gittings, *Mask*, 151 and 32.

"Bright Star"

Bright Star, would I were stedfast as thou art -
　　Not in lone splendor hung aloft the night
And watching, with eternal lids apart,
　　Like nature's patient sleepless Eremite,
The mov ing waters at their priestlike task
　　Of pure ablution round earth's human shores,
Or gazing on the new soft-fallen masque
　　Of snow upon the mountains and the moors.　　　　　　8
No - yet still stedfast, still unchangeable
　　Pillow'd upon my fair love's ripening breast,
To feel for ever its soft swell and fall,
　　Awake for ever in a sweet unrest,
Still, still to hear her tender-taken breath,　　　　　　13
And so live ever - or else swoon to death -

"What is Keats?" asked Arnold, and stayed to answer: "A style and form seeker, and this with an impetuosity that heightens the effect of his style almost painfully" (*Letters* 100–101). Said in scorn, he still got the Keats-extremes. "I have two luxuries to brood over in my walks," Keats writes to Fanny Brawne during his last summer of vigorous writing, sequestered away from her (1819): "your Loveliness and the hour of my death. O that I could have possession of them both in the same minute." Absorbed by this passion "in spite of myself," he signs off, "I will imagine you Venus tonight and pray, pray, pray to your star like a Hethen." Celestial orb, goddess of love: he'll inhabit this astrology. "Your's ever, fair Star, / John Keats" (*K* 263): no *sever* in this *Yours ever.*

The summer before he met her, in June 1818, Keats conceived his sensual vision as such a star in the sublime vistas of the Lake country: "they can never fade away—they make one forget the divisions of life . . . and refine one's sensual vision into a sort of north star which can never cease to be open lidded and stedfast over the wonders of the great Power" (*L* 1:299). No better reader of this astrocopia than Stuart Sperry, with fine attention to the "strong idea of process" in *refine* (*Keats the Poet* 135):

The material elements within the poet's "sensual vision" are condensed and transmuted until they approximate, or rather are sensed as concentrated in, the higher, ethereal nature of the star . . . Yet the star is no cold idealization, no mere fixity. It both presides over and takes its being from the workings of "the great Power," an endless potential for creation, an ideal of beauty latent amid the elements of human perception.

Now in love with a woman whose constancy he vexed himself with doubting, Keats drafted the sonnet that begins in the apostrophe, "Bright star," an ideal constancy that could refine and concentrate a sensual vision into ever warm sensual intimacy.

Fanny Brawne copied the first draft (1818) on the flyleaf of Cary's *Hell* Canto V, a book they read together. Keats could imagine her voicing the octave-I as her pronoun, conceding her unsteadfastness and confirming his. *My dearest Girl,* he writes to her early August 1820, *I wish you could invent some means to make me at all happy without you. Every hour I am more and more concentrated in you* (Berg ALS f.1). *Every hour:* Keats feels time running out, not just away from her, but from England, from life. So *concentrated,* he can fantasize two surrenders: *I wish I was either in your arms full of faith or that a Thunder bolt would strike me* (f.3). He was bound for Italy, and this may have been his last letter, his almost last words, to her.

Even as he is *averse* to a painful last seeing of her, an instinct for *verse* still stirs.

> *If my health would bear it, I could write a Poem which I have in my head, which would be a consolation for people in such a situation as mine. I would show some one in Love as I am, with a person living in such Liberty as you do. Shakspeare always sums up matters in the most sovereign manner. Hamlet's heart was full of such Misery as mine is when he said to Ophelia "Go to a Nunnery, go, go!"*
>
> (ff. 2–3)

Tuned ever to what words can tell and spell, Keats's *full of such Misery* replays *full of faith,* both phrasings with an undertone (he knows how to do this) of *full love.* The *Poem* in his head is a pathos of parallel clauses: *some one in Love as I am, with a person living in such Liberty as you do,* his *Love* betrayed by her *Liberty.* The cue to Hamlet slants pathology into the tragic pathos. Hamlet's sneer about libertine Ophelia (3.1; a Nunnery is a brothel) voices Keats's grievance about Fanny's "Liberty," the enemy of his self-possession. *To be happy with you seems such an impossibility! it requires a luckier Star than mine! it will never be* (f.2). Trying for Shakespeare's *sovereign manner,* he revisits the sonnet, with an impossible star-sight, in a different temper, on his way to Italy, knowing he'll die there, faded from Fanny.[1] He wrote it on a blank verso opposite *A Lover's Complaint* in the volume of Shakespeare's *Poetical Works* (1806; see Figure 15)

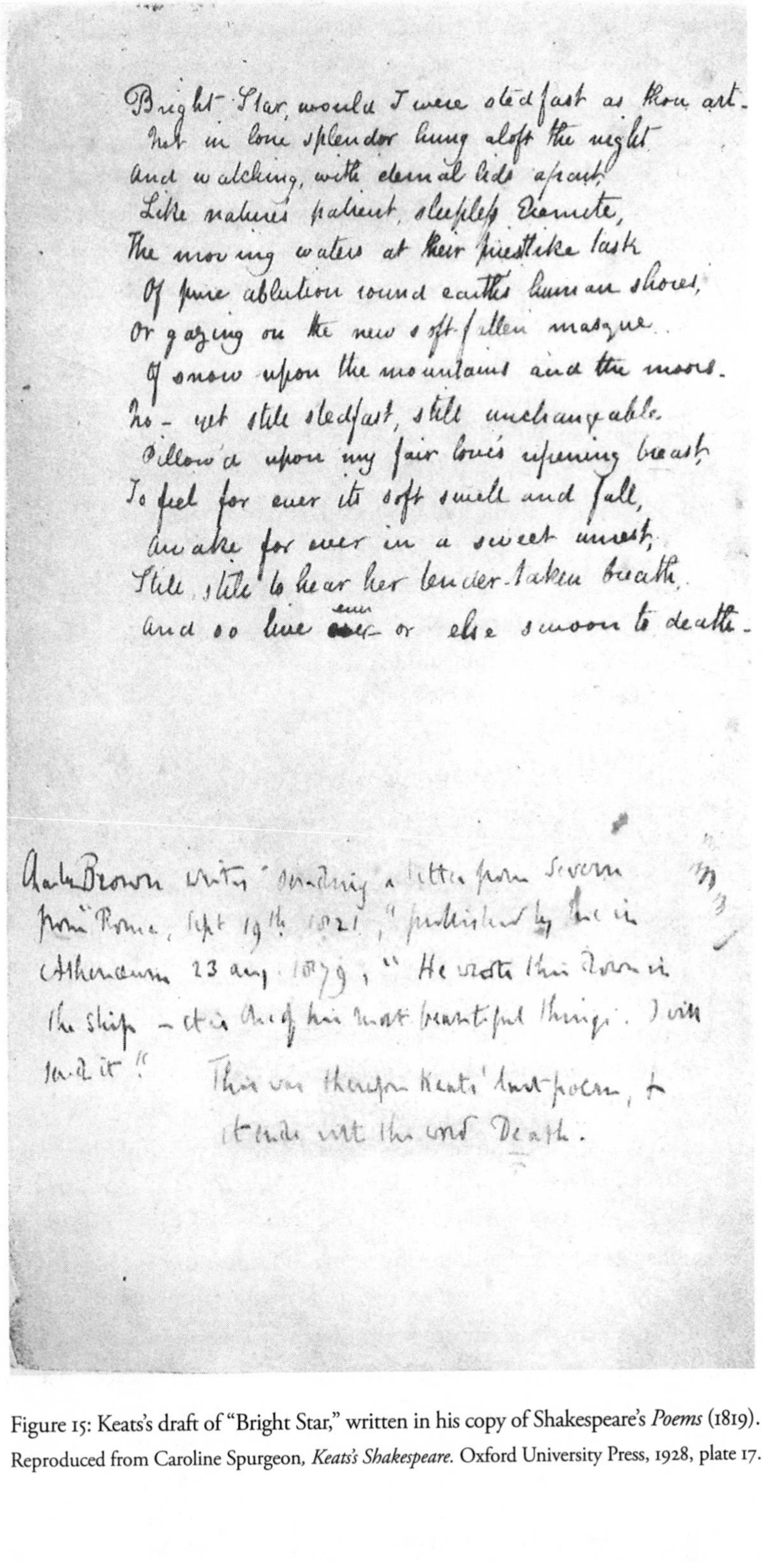

Bright Star, would I were stedfast as thou art—
Not in lone splendor hung aloft the night
And watching, with eternal lids apart,
Like nature's patient, sleepless Eremite,
The moving waters at their priestlike task
Of pure ablution round earth's human shores,
Or gazing on the new soft-fallen masque
Of snow upon the mountains and the moors—
No—yet still stedfast, still unchangeable,
Pillow'd upon my fair love's ripening breast,
To feel for ever its soft swell and fall,
Awake for ever in a sweet unrest,
Still, still to hear her tender-taken breath,
And so live ever—or else swoon to death—

Charles Brown writes "sending a letter from Severn
from Rome, Sept 19th 1821," published by him in
Atheneum 23 aug. 1879, " He wrote this down in
the ship — it is one of his most beautiful things. I will
send it." This was therefore Keats' last poem, &
it ends with the word Death.

Figure 15: Keats's draft of "Bright Star," written in his copy of Shakespeare's *Poems* (1819). Reproduced from Caroline Spurgeon, *Keats's Shakespeare*. Oxford University Press, 1928, plate 17.

that he took with him.[2] Reading the sonnet at increasing distance from one another, each could conceive the other reading it, a dovetailing that weights its full meaning.

In both versions, Keats summons a Shakespearean form, working a deathwards progress of desire to couplet clinch of *breath* finally closed in *death*. His keynote is Julius Caesar, on his way to death (in Rome, even).

> I am constant as the Northern Star
> Of whose true-fixed and resting quality
> There is no fellow in the firmament.   (*Julius Caesar* 3.1)

Keats evokes this icon of constancy and fixity as England recedes. Wordsworth may have summed up such matters in a more sovereign manner in lines Keats knew almost by heart, about looking for this kind of reference in a perilous world:

> Chaldean shepherds, ranging trackless fields,
> Beneath the concave of unclouded skies
> Spread like a sea, in boundless solitude,
> Looked on the Polar Star, as on a Guide
> And Guardian of their course, that never closed
> His steadfast eye.   (*Excursion* IV; p. 172)

This is a long-lost age for Wordsworth, evoked in elegy and nostalgia.

Keats opens in an apostrophe to this ideal, for life in time and history. It is a strong line, beginning with two stresses and resisting any lilt into iambic pentameter:

> *Bright star, would I were stedfast as thou art –*

Just about every syllable could be voice-stressed. The sound-work sharpens the entire line: *I* in the heart of *Bright*, the consonants of *Bright star* distributed into *stedfast as* (thou) *art*. In the heart of this overstressed line, *would I were* concedes what Robert Bridges calls "the irony of impossibility" (xc). The dash pauses the call, for seven lines of negative qualification. Such syntactic "apophasis" (the conjuring and lingering over what an argument has set for negation) is something Keats is so good at that by the time the sentence ends (8), who can remember the aching, anchoring *Not?*

Writing dramatically, Keats reboots. *No—yet still stedfast, still*. No fixity, *still* is a surfeit of sound, softly modulated into duration, *Pillow'd, swell and fall,* then its own doubled sigh, *Still, still.* Keats takes this to a perfect Shakespearean close of self-epitaphing: *breath/death.* Two brief dashes framing the final words give a typography of breath held, held in suspense, held forever. When Keats reread the sonnet, sea-tossed toward Italy, the lines come back with new immediacy. Writing to Brown (whom, like Fanny, he will never see again) of a *sense of darkness coming over* him as he sees Fanny *eternally vanishing,* he cries out, *Is there another Life? Shall I awake and find all this a dream?* (30 September 1820; MsK 1.87.401). He did not know, on his own pulses, how to answer "Do I wake or sleep?"

A late, enigmatic fragment of poetry shifts into an address from the waking dead to the living, and in this wrest of writing, there is no sweet unrest.

[Keats ms, in Shakespeare's *Poems, KS* plate 17].

[1] Joseph Severn said that Keats composed the sonnet onboard (Sharp, *Severn,* 54–55). Gittings thinks that Keats was rereading, not rewriting, it (*Keats* 600–601).

[2] An image of the verso-recto is in *John Keats at Wentworth Place,* unpaged (approx. p. 38).

"This living hand"

This living hand, now warm and capable
Of earnest grasping, would, if it were cold
and in the icy silence of the tomb,
So haunt thy days and chill thy dreaming nights
              heat
That thou would wish thine ^own dry of blood
So in my veins red life might stream again,
and thou be conscience-calm'd - see here it is ‡
       I hold it towards you-

This fragment (see Figure 16, next page) is a compact drama of rhetorical transmission, from speaker to recipient, from past to present, from substance to specter. How can we know the hand writing from the handwriting? "This living hand" is both somatic and scriptive, the agent of writing and writing itself, gothic twisted. Keats is the poet of manuphorics: the warm grasp of a welcoming hand; the nightmare of not being able to feel one's cold hands; the warm scribe my hand that writes for posterity.

Keats's single-sentence, blank-verse address metes out posterity in accumulating, relentless percussions. Only ten of 65 words have more than one syllable, with the positively *capable* the sole three-syllable stretch. The brief dramatic torsion is exquisite. A warm living hand morphs into a cold dead hand, then the agent of handwriting coolly handed forward, to its reader. A conditional-subjunctive *would, if it were* dilates to absorb its addressee in the conditional *that thou would,* with a semantically intensified *So* to convey the senses of *completely; in consequence.* As a proposed *if* becomes real—*see here it is*—the initial stagey eloquence turned startlingly colloquial, intimate: *I hold it towards you.* Twice-told, this *it* grabs all the referents in the field: living hand, cold hand, writing hand, handwriting. Chastening the syntax into these spare, unsparing monosyllables, Keats's lines conjure the present of writing into the future (or every present) in the time of reading. It was no dream; I lay broad waking. Red life to read life.

The measured plot of Keats's lines feels at once passionately uttered and calculated with a vampiric warp on the legal entailment called *mort-main:* the "dead hand" of the past on the living generation. Hazlitt's record of Edmund Kean performing Richard III's death may have haunted Keats's lines: "the attitude in which he stands with his hands stretched out, after his sword is wrested from him, has a preternatural and terrific grandeur, as if his will could not be

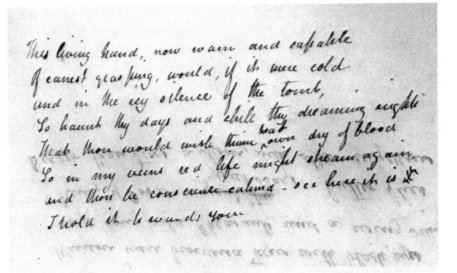

Figure 16: Keats's manuscript of "This living hand." This enigmatic fragment was first published in 1898 by H. B. Forman, in *Poetical Works of John Keats*, 6th edition, p. 417. From *John Keats: Poetry Manuscripts at Harvard: A Facsimile Edition*, ed. Jack Stillinger (The Belknap Press of Harvard University Press, 1990), p. 259, from the original manuscript in the Houghton Library, Harvard University.

disarmed, and the very phantoms of his despair had power to kill" (*Characters* 229–230). Keats is keenly tuned, even in agony, to writing as the stretch of a living hand: "I cannot bear the sight of any hand writing of a Friend I love so much as I do you," he wrote in his own hand, to Charles Brown, his last known letter (30 November 1820; *L* 2:360). Or Fanny Brawne: "to see her hand writing would break my heart" (1 November 1820, 2:351–352). Not handwriting so much as a hand writing, synecdoche (as in "Time's Sea") for the whole person, here in a horrible dark romance of heart-break.

I see nothing but thorns for the future, he laments in that last known letter to Fanny (mid-August 1820; ALS Berg, f.3). His first literary love, spectral twin Chatterton, is strangely conjured at the prick of the word *thorns*. Benjamin Bailey recalls Keats knowing by heart a famous stanza from *Minstrelles Songe* in *Ælla*.[1]

> Comme, wythe acorne-coppe and thorne,
> Drayne mie hartys blodde awaie;
> Lyfe and all yttes goode I scorne,
> Daunce bie nete, or feaste by daie.

This is a gothic turn with a glee worthy of Thomas Beddoes's *Death's Jest Book.* Keats relished the first line, where the call for the instruments of death vibrates with verbal life: *Comme* to *corn* to *coppe; acorne* to *thorne.* Keats's *chant* lived in Bailey's ear: "methinks I now hear him . . ." (*KC* 2:276). The metaphor, being pierced and bled, was the actual medical practice that tormented and exhausted Keats, time after time, in his last summer of life, and would be continued during his last weeks in Rome. It drained his heart's blood away, literally.

Chatterton again, as his ghost-twin. In the midst of his most productive season of writing (June 1819), Keats commented to a friend, "One of the great reasons that the english have produced the finest writers in the world; is, that the English world has ill-treated them during their lives and foster'd them after their deaths" (*L* 2:115). One fostering is continued reading. Always in Keats's writing-readiness, is his reading.

The last lines of "This living hand" make a literal grave from the trope of killing passion in *Sonet II* in Pierre de Ronsard's *Les Armours de Cassandre,* which Keats made his own in "a free translation" (*K* 200–202):

> When from the Heavens I saw her first descend,
> My heart took fire, and only burning pains
> They were my pleasures—they my Life's sad end;
> Love pour'd her beauty into my warm veins.

This was just after he met Fanny Brawne.

I return to Keats reading his favorite Shakespeare. The artful thrust of *This living hand* rivals Keats's sadly self-sentenced epitaph on his deathbed, "Here lies one whose name was writ in Water."[2] This is a last sigh of lifelong intimacy with Shakespeare: "Men's evil manners live in brass, their virtues / We write in water" (*Henry VIII* 4.2).[3] The idiom is "writ *on* water," dissolution imminent. More devastating, self-wasting, is *in water,* a disappearing ink. Keats's name would not mark his gravestone, but this dictation did. Oft writ, the phrase has a durable life; among its famous imprints, Keats's literary memory.

Keats drew double lines down the margin to the left of Sonnet XVIII, adding two more such marks next to 12 and 14, these also underscored (*RS* plate 16):

> <u>When in eternal lines to time thou growest</u>:
> So long as men can breathe, or eyes can see,
> <u>So long lives, this and this gives life to thee.</u>

Shakespeare's lines mattered to him more than 200 years on, as his eyes scanned the words and brought them to fresh life.

[*K* 286]

[1] *KC*, 2:276; Chatterton, *Works* (1803), 2:283. This is the song that Keats heard Hazlitt read in full in his lecture on "the old ballads" (*Lectures* 253).

[2] So Severn told their friend Haslam (*KC* 1:273; 1 June 1823); also in Hunt's *Lord Byron &c* (268).

[3] Has this been noted? The usual citation is Beaumont and Fletcher's *Philaster, or Love Lies A-Bleeding* (1611): "All your better deeds / Shall be in water writ . . ." (V.3). Fletcher collaborated on *Henry VIII*, performed in 1613. "To write in Water" is an old idiom, in *acqua scribis*, e.g., *In aqua scribis, hoc est, nihil agis* (Tilley's *Proverbs*, W113).

POSTSCRIPT

More than 200 years beyond Keats's imagining unknown readers for his lines, even as he has reanimated Shakespeare's lines, our eyes see and read his lines. Agonized out of life in February 1821, Keats survives in his vivid words, lives in our every reading. "Whenever you write say a Word or two on some Passage in Shakespeare that may have come rather new to you; which must be continually happening, notwithstand^g that we read the same Play forty times—," he writes to a fellow poet (Reynolds), on 18 April 1817 (*L* 1:133). He kept his *Word,* in his letters and conversation in the life of his reading. Let's say the same of Keats: ever new. To read Keats's words is to experience poetry animated. Animated in the way he reads poetry, audits it, attends to it; animated in the poetry he writes and rewrites—the formative energy in a continuously renewable greeting of the spirit. My greeting to Keats, and to you, has been a fresh engagement with this most rewarding of poets, notwithstand^g that I've read the same poems more than forty times, no end in sight.

Susan J. Wolfson, Princeton NJ
23 February 2022

TIME-LINES

JK: John Keats   GK: Georgiana) TK: Tom
George Keats (&G: Keats FK: Fanny Keats

1795   JK born London, 31 October to Frances Jennings Keats and Thomas Keats,
        chief ostler at the Swan and Hoop inn, owned by Frances's father.
        Famine (high prices, scarcity); Napoleon's army invades Italy.

1796   Robert Burns dies.

1797   GK born, 28 February

1798   Battle of the Nile; Irish Rebellion; *Lyrical Ballads* (Wordsworth /
        Coleridge).

1799   TK born, 18 November. Napoleon's *coup d'etat* installs him as First
        Consul. Parliament's Six Acts against political societies, Combination
        Acts against labor unions.

1800   *Lyrical Ballads* 2nd edition, with Preface; first collected edition of Burns.
        Union of England and Ireland.

1801   Edward Keats born, 28 April.

1802   December: Edward dies. *Edinburgh Review* founded; Peace of Amiens
        between England and France; France reoccupies Switzerland; Napoleon
        made First Consul for life.

1803   8 June: FK born. GK and JK board at Enfield Academy. England declares
        war on France; Lord Elgin brings sculptural fragments from Athens to
        England.

1804   16 April: father (age thirty) dies from a riding accident; 27 June: mother
        remarries; her parents, the Jennings, in Enfield take the children.
        Napoleon crowned Emperor, prepares to invade England; Britain declares
        war on Spain. Corn Laws (taxation of imported grain to sustain high
        prices at home).

1805   Grandfather Jennings dies; grandmother and the children move to
        Edmonton.
        Admiral Nelson dies in the battle of Trafalgar, against France.

1806	Scott, *Ballads and Lyrical Pieces;* Revd. Bowles's edition of Pope with a preface detractive to his character.
1807	Wordsworth, *Poems, in Two Volumes;* Byron, *Hours of Idleness.* France invades Spain and Portugal, with British opposition. England abolishes the slave trade.
1808	*Edinburgh Review* ridicules Byron's poems. Leigh Hunt edits *The Examiner.* Charles Lamb, *Specimens of English Dramatic Poets.* Uprising in Spain against Napoleon (May); Convention of Cintra sells out the Spanish patriots (August).
1809	JK's mother returns, quite ill; JK devoted to her care.
	Byron retaliates with *English Bards and Scotch Reviewers.* William Gifford becomes editor of *The Quarterly.* Napoleon suffers defeats. JK's future biographer and editor, R. M. Milnes, born in London.
1810	JK's mother dies from tuberculosis; grandmother Jennings appoints guardians.
1811	Guardian Richard Abbey removes JK from Enfield to apprentice under Edmonton surgeon and apothecary Thomas Hammond. GK and TK employed at Abbey's counting-house. George III deemed mad; Prince of Wales becomes Regent. Workers riot against the weaving frames. Elgin offers the British government his Marbles, with much controversy. Shelley expelled from Oxford for *The Necessity of Atheism.* Mary Tighe's *Psyche; or the Legend of Love* (1805) privately printed. Leigh Hunt, *The Feast of the Poets.*
1812	Byron's maiden speech in House of Lords opposes death penalty for frame-breakers. March: *Childe Harold's Pilgrimage* is an overnight sensation (Canto II berates Elgin). Britain declares war on United States; Napoleon invades Russia in June and retreats from Moscow in December, with catastrophic losses.
1813	Byron's celebrity blazes with new romances. Southey becomes Poet Laureate; Wordsworth given a government patronage position; Hunt's *The Prince of Wales v. The Examiner* (itemizing outrages) earns a prison sentence for libel. Shelley's *Queen Mab.*
	Austria joins the Alliance against France; Napoleon defeated at Leipzig.
1814	JK's first poems. December: Grandmother dies; Fanny moves to the Abbeys, who restrict contact with her brothers.
	Byron's *Corsair* sells 10,000 on the day of publication. H. F. Cary's translation of *The Divine Comedy;* Wordsworth, *The Excursion;* Edmund Kean's debut at Covent Garden theater.
	The Allies invade France; Napoleon abdicates and is exiled; Bourbon monarchy is restored. Percy Bysshe Shelley elopes to the Continent with Mary Wollstonecraft Godwin.

1815	February: JK writes sonnet on Hunt's release from prison; convinces Abbey to let him study at Guy's Hospital; enrolls on 1 October, moving to London; works as a surgeon's assistant. Buys Wordsworth's collected poems.
	Napoleon escapes Elba, defeated at Waterloo, exiled. French monarchy is restored. Parliament debates the acquisition of the Elgin Marbles.
1816	1 May: JK's first publication, *To Solitude*, in *The Examiner*. July: passes apothecary exam; July–August: with TK at Margate. September: JK, TK, GK living in Hampstead; October: JK meets Hunt; 3 November: JK meets artists B. R. Haydon and Joseph Severn, poet J. H. Reynolds. October–December: *Sleep and Poetry*. 1 December: Hunt's "Young Poets" article in *Examiner* prints *On First Looking into Chapman's Homer*.
	In *The Examiner:* Haydon defends the Elgin Marbles (March); Hazlitt, *On Gusto* (May) and defense of the Marbles (June); Wordsworth's tribute, *To B. R. Haydon* (also in *The Champion*). Published: Hunt, *The Story of Rimini;* Shelley, *Alastor &c;* Coleridge, *Christabel, Kubla Khan.* Byron leaves England after a scandalously failed marriage. At a sales dinner at the end of the year, his publisher sells 7,000 each of *The Prisoner of Chillon &c* and *Childe Harold III.* Elgin Marbles purchased by the government and exhibited in the British Museum.
1817	JK meets Benjamin Bailey, Charles Brown, Richard Woodhouse, dining often at Hunt's cottage in the Vale of Health. February: meets Shelley; Hunt shows JK's poetry to him, Hazlitt, and Godwin, and puts further sonnets in *The Examiner*. March: JK and TK move to Hampstead, north of London. Haydon takes JK to see the Marbles; JK's two sonnets on the occasion in *The Champion* and *The Examiner. Poems* published, praised by Reynolds in *The Champion.* April–November: JK writing *Endymion.*
	April: at Isle of Wight, JK reads Shakespeare, writes *On the Sea* (pub. *Champion,* August). June–July: JK sees Kean on stage. Hunt reviews *Poems* in *Examiner;* August: K finishes *Endymion II;* September: JK with Bailey at Oxford, writes *Endymion III*, perhaps contracts syphilis. October: JK visits Stratford-on-Avon with Bailey. November: reads Coleridge's *Sibylline Leaves* (1817), finishes *Endymion;* December: reviews Kean as King Richard III for *The Champion*, 21 December; sees Benjamin West's paintings at the Royal Academy; discusses "Negative Capability"; at Haydon's "immortal dinner" December 28, meets Lamb and Wordsworth. Writes "In drear nighted December."
	Byron, *Manfred;* Hazlitt, *Characters of Shakespear's Plays.* October: Z.'s first "Cockney School" paper in *Blackwood's* attacks Hunt, targets JK. March: Habeas Corpus suspended. December: William Hone tried and

acquitted of blasphemous libel for parodies of the liturgy. Princess Charlotte dies in the delivery of a stillborn child; death of JK's hero, Polish patriot Kosciusko, who also fought in the US Revolutionary War.

1818 January: JK visits Wordsworth in London, recites "Hymn to Pan" from *Endymion;* attends theater, dines often with Haydon, writes a sonnet about rereading *King Lear,* also "When I have fears," "Blue!," "Time's sea," "To the Nile." Winter: attends all but one of Hazlitt's eight Lectures on English Poetry; proofreads *Endymion;* writes "Dear Reynolds," *Isabella* (February–April), reads historians Voltaire and Gibbon. March: drafts a preface to *Endymion.* March–April: with very ill TK at Teignmouth. April: redrafts the preface; sonnets on the Elgin Marbles reprinted in *Annals of the Fine Arts. Endymion* published. Finishes *Isabella.* May: *Hymn to Pan* published in *The Yellow Dwarf.* Dines with Hazlitt at Haydon's; GK marries and emigrates to United States. June: harsh review of *Poems* and *Endymion* in *British Critic.*

June–August: tours Lake District and Scotland with Brown, visits Wordsworth's home and Burns sites, climbs Ben Nevis; reads Cary's translation of *The Divine Comedy;* sore throat and chills force a return to London, 8 August. Meets Fanny Brawne. September: JK ridiculed by *Blackwood's* and the *Quarterly;* writes *Hyperion* while nursing TK. October: *Examiner* prints Reynolds's praise of *Endymion.* 1 December: TK dies. JK moves in with Brown at Wentworth Place, Hampstead. Stops work on *Hyperion.*

Byron, *Childe Harold IV;* Mary Shelley (anon.), *Frankenstein;* Hazlitt, *Lectures on the English Poets.*

1819 January: *Eve of St. Agnes.* March: visits British Museum with Severn; his miniature of JK is exhibited at the Royal Academy. April: the Brawnes become neighbors at Wentworth place; JK meets Coleridge in April and talks of nightingales.

April: *La belle dame, Ode to Psyche,* maybe *Indolence,* "If by dull rhymes." May: Odes, *Nightingale, Grecian Urn, Melancholy;* life as "a vale of Soul-making"; burns letters and returns all borrowed books. July: *Nightingale* in *Annals of the Fine Arts.* July–August: at Isle of Wight, K writes *Lamia* and *The Fall of Hyperion.* September: at Winchester, writes *To Autumn* and abandons *The Fall.* November: resumes *The Fall.* December: JK's worsening sore throat; secret engagement to Fanny Brawne.

Cary's *Divine Comedy* republished by Taylor and Hessey. Byron, *Don Juan I–II; Childe Harold's Pilgrimage I–IV.* Reynolds's satire of *Peter Bell* appears in advance of Wordsworth's *Peter Bell,* reviewed by JK. Hunt launches *The Indicator.* August: "Peterloo Massacre," a militia charge on a peaceful workers' demonstration for Parliamentary reform, at which champion Henry "Orator" Hunt is arrested; the outrage plays for weeks in the London papers; September: K witnesses Hunt's triumphant entry into London for trial (and conviction). Goes with Brown to Winchester.

1820   January: GK in London to claim funds from TK's estate, depleting JK's share. *Ode on a Grecian Urn* in *Annals of the Fine Arts.* Seeing GK off at Liverpool, JK never writes to him again. A bad hemorrhage: "death warrant." March: revises *Lamia;* Haydon exhibits *Christ's Entry into Jerusalem* (JK in the crowd). April: *London Magazine* praises *Endymion,* JK proofreading *1820.* May: Brown rents his house; JK moves to Kentish Town. *La Belle Dame* in *The Indicator.* June: very ill, K moves in with the Hunts. *On a Dream* in *The Indicator.* July: *1820* published; *Nightingale, To Autumn,* and other poems also in *Literary Gazette; To Autumn* in *London Chronicle. Examiner* prints Lamb's praise of *1820.*

August: Hunt praises *1820* in *The Indicator.* When the Hunt household becomes impossible, the Brawnes take JK in, and for a month he has a caring family. Friends raise funds for him to winter in Italy; JK hopes Brown will accompany him but he can't be located; writes his will and assigns his copyright to Taylor for £200. September: *Monthly Magazine* and *British Critic* praise *1820.* With Severn, JK sails to Italy, arriving in Naples Harbor late October; after quarantine for ten days, they leave for Rome on JK's twenty-fifth birthday. November: at 26 Piazza di Spagna; JK's last known letter, to Brown. December: serious relapse.

1821   23 February: JK dies in Severn's arms; 26 February, buried in Rome's Protestant Cemetery. 17 March: news reaches London. In Pisa, Shelley publishes *Adonais,* an elegy that installs the fable of Keats as a sensitive poet undone by hostile reviews. It is generously quoted in several reviews, and ridiculed in *Blackwood's.*

1821   Byron drafts public letters defending Pope and attacking his detractors, with nasty remarks about JK; hearing of JK's death, he withholds these from publication.

1822   Shelley drowns.

1823   Byron's *Don Juan* Canto XI, with a soon famous line on Keats: "snuff'd out by an article."

1824   Byron dies in Greece.

1826   Fanny Keats marries novelist Valentin Llanos, born just weeks after JK.

1828   *Adonais* published in England, sponsored by Milnes and Alfred Tennyson. Hunt publishes some of JK's letters to him in *Lord Byron and Some of His Contemporaries.*

1829   *The Poetical Works of Coleridge, Shelley and Keats* published by A. and W. Galignani in Paris, presenting JK's lifetime volumes plus other poems, and a memoir based on Hunt's chapter. Several US editions based on this appear in the 1830s and 1840s.

1833   Fanny Brawne marries Louis Lindo (later Lindon).

1834	Ill since 1829, Woodhouse dies of tuberculosis.
1835	Hunt's closely attentive article on Keats's poetry appears in *London Journal*.
1836	Brown lectures on Keats.
1840	*Poetical Works of John Keats* (London: Taylor and Walton). Several US editions in the 1840s.
1841	*Poetical Works of John Keats* (London: William Smith). Brown gives his Keats materials to Milnes; GK dies on Christmas eve.
1842	Brown dies in New Zealand.
1843	Georgiana Keats marries John Jeffrey.
1844	Hunt's *Imagination and Fancy*, first chapter on Keats.
1845	Taylor sells his rights to Keats's poems and letters to Edward Moxon, Milnes's publisher. Jeffrey transcribes poems and letters for Milnes.
1846	Haydon commits suicide.
1848	Milnes, *Life, Letters, and Literary Remains* first publishes many letters and poems.
1854	Milnes, *The Poetical Works of John Keats*, with a memoir, handsomely illustrated: Keats's rebirth in Victorian literary culture.
1856	Milnes publishes *The Fall of Hyperion*, assumed to be the first draft of *Hyperion*.
1863	Severn, "The Vicissitudes of Keats's Fame," *Atlantic Monthly*.
1865	Fanny Brawne dies.
1867	New edition of *Life, Letters, and Literary Remains*.
1874	Charles Cowden Clarke's "Recollections of John Keats," *Gentleman's Magazine*.
1876	Milnes (now Lord Houghton), *The Poetical Works of John Keats*.
1878	H. B. Forman's *Letters of John Keats to Fanny Brawne* disgusts many, including Arnold and Swinburne.
1882	January: Oscar Wilde's lecture (published in the *New York Herald*) celebrates Keats's importance to English poetry.
1883	Forman's canonizing four-volume *The Poetic Works and other Writing of John Keats*.
1885	Milnes dies in Vichy, France.
1887	Sidney Colvin's *Keats* in "The English Men of Letters" series.
1889	Fanny Keats dies.
1898	"This living hand" first published in the sixth edition of Forman's *Poetic Works & c.*

WORKS CITED

NB: For eighteenth- and nineteenth-century publications, London is assumed to be the publisher's location, unless otherwise stated.

Editions of Keats

Allott, Miriam. *Poems.* Longman / Norton, 1970.

Arnold, William T. *Poetical Works.* Kegan Paul, Trench, 1884.

Bush, Douglas. *Selected Poems and Letters.* Riverside P, 1957.

Cook, Elizabeth. *John Keats.* Oxford UP, 1990.

De Selincourt, Ernest. *Poems.* 1905; Methuen, 1926.

Drury, G. Thorn. *Poems.* 2 vols. Routledge, 1894.

Forman, Harry Buxton. *Letters . . . to Fanny Brawne.* Reeves & Turner, 1878.

———. *The Poetical Works and Other Writings.* 4 vols. Reeves & Turner, 1883. Expanded and corrected, 1889.

———. *Complete Works.* 5 vols. Gowans & Gray, 1900–1901, for [Keats], "On Edmund Kean as Shakespearian Actor" and "On Kean in Richard Duke of York" (*The Champion* 21 and 28 December 1817), 3:229–240.

Forman, Maurice Buxton. *John Keats's Anatomical and Physiological Note Book.* Oxford UP, 1934.

Garrod, H. W. *Poetical Works.* Oxford UP, 1958.

Gittings, Robert. *The Odes of Keats & Their Earliest Known Manuscripts in Facsimile.* Kent State UP, 1970.

Rollins, Hyder E. *Letters, 1814–1821.* 2 vols. Harvard UP, 1958. Cited as *L.*

Sperry, Stuart. "Richard Woodhouse's Interleaved and Annotated Copy of Keats's *Poems* (1817)." *Literary Monographs* 1, U of Wisconsin P, 1967, 101–164.

Stillinger, Jack, ed. *John Keats: The Charles Brown Poetry Transcripts at Harvard.* Facsimiles. Garland, 1988. Cited as *Brown.*

———. *Complete Poems.* Harvard / Belknap, 1982.

———. *Endymion: A Facsimile of the Revised Holograph Manuscript.* Garland, 1985.

———. *Poetry Manuscripts at Harvard.* Harvard UP, 1990.

———. *Poems.* Harvard UP, 1978.

Wolfson, Susan J. *John Keats: A Longman Cultural Edition.* Pearson, 2006.

Williamson, George. *Keats Letters, Papers & c.* John Lane, 1914.

OPEN ACCESS

Harvard Keats Collection https://library.harvard.edu/collections/harvard-keats-collection

Keats's *Paradise Lost* http://keatslibrary.org/paradise-lost/

Keats Letters Project http://keatslettersproject.com/correspondence

An Electronic Concordance to Keats's Poetry, ed. Noah Comet. https://romantic-circles
.org/reference/keatsconcordance/u_unk.html

Mapping Keats's Progress, ed. Kim Blank. http://johnkeats.uvic.ca/

Chief Biographies, in chronological order

Hunt, Leigh. *Lord Byron and Some of His Contemporaries.* 2 vols. Henry Colburn, 1828.

Milnes, Richard M. *Life, Letters, and Literary Remains, of John Keats.* Edward Moxon,
1848.

Clarke, Charles, and Mary Cowden Clarke. *Recollections of Writers.* Samson &c, 1878.

Colvin, Sidney. *John Keats: His Life and Poetry, His Friends, Critics, and After-Fame.*
Macmillan, 1917. *John Keats,* Harper, 1887.

Lowell, Amy. *John Keats.* 2 vols. Houghton Mifflin / Riverside P, 1925.

Bate, Walter Jackson. *John Keats.* Harvard UP, 1963.

Ward, Aileen. *John Keats: The Making of a Poet.* Viking, 1963.

Gittings, Robert. *John Keats.* 1968; Penguin, 1979.

Woof, Robert, and Stephen Hebron. *John Keats.* Wordsworth Trust, 1995.

Motion, Andrew. *Keats.* Farrar, Straus and Giroux, 1997.

John Keats at Wentworth Place. Keats House, 2009

Roe, Nicholas. *John Keats: A New Life.* Yale UP, 2012.

General

CCJK	*Cambridge Companion to John Keats,* ed. Susan J. Wolfson, Cambridge UP, 2001.
KSJ	*Keats-Shelley Journal*
KSR	*Keats-Shelley Review*
PMLA	*Publications of the Modern Language Association*
SiR	*Studies in Romanticism*
UP	University Press

Addison, Joseph. [Genius.] *The Spectator* II:160 (3 September 1711): 459–464. J. and R. Tonson and S. Draper, 1747.

———. [On Pleasures of the Imagination.] *The Spectator* VI:411–413 (21–24 June 1712): 89–106. Tonson and Draper, 1747.

Amis, Kingsley. "The Curious Elf: A Note on Rhyme in Keats." *Essays in Criticism* 1.2 (1951): 189–192.

Arnold, Matthew. *The Letters . . . to Arthur Hugh Clough*, edited by H. Foster Lowry, Oxford UP, 1932.

———. *Poems*. Longman &c, 1853.

Arnold, William T., ed. *Poetical Works of John Keats*. Kegan Paul &c, 1884.

[Bailey, Benjamin], on Keats. *Church of England Quarterly Review* XXV (January 1849): 139–174. Attribution *KC*, 2:283–284.

Baldwin, Edward [William Godwin]. *The Pantheon: or Ancient History of the Gods of Ancient Greece and Rome. For the Use of Schools, and Young Persons of Both Sexes.* 1806; 4th edition, M. J. Godwin, 1814.

Barnard, John. *John Keats*. Cambridge UP, 1987.

———. "Keats's Letters." *CCJK*, 120–134.

Barry, Annabel. "– My Brother Tom is Much Improved: The Suffering Body at the Ends of Keats's Letters and Poems –." *KSR* 34.2 (2020): 118–137.

Barry, Elaine, ed. *Robert Frost on Writing*. Rutgers UP, 1974.

Bate, W. J., and James Engell, eds. *Coleridge's Biographia Literaria*, 2 vols. Princeton UP, 1983.

Bennett, Andrew. *Keats, Narrative and Audience: The Posthumous Life of Writing*. Cambridge UP, 1994.

Bernstein, Gene. "Keats's 'Lamia': The Sense of a Non-Ending." *Papers on Language and Literature* 15 (1979): 175–192 (alluding to Frank Kermode's *The Sense of an Ending*).

Best, Stephen, and Sharon Marcus. "Surface Reading." *Representations* 108.1 (2009): 1–21.

Bewell, Alan. "The Political Implication of Keats's Classicist Aesthetics." *SiR* 25 (1986): 221–230.

Blackwood's Edinburgh Magazine. Z, "Cockney School of Poetry." Vol. 2: "No. I." (October 1817), 38–41, and "No. II" (November 1817), 194–201. Vol. 3: "No. IV" (August 1818), 519–524.

———. 6.33 (December 1819): 235–247. A review of Leigh Hunt's *Literary Pocket-Book; or Companion for the Lover of Nature and Art.*

Bloom, Harold. "Keats and the Embarrassments of Poetic Tradition." *The Ringers in the Tower,* U of Chicago P, 1971.

Bostetter, Edward. "Keats." *The Romantic Ventriloquists,* U of Washington P, 1963.

Bridges, Robert. "Critical Introduction." *Poems of John Keats,* edited by G. Thorn Drury, 2 vols, Routledge, 1894, 1:xiii–c.

Brisman, Leslie. "Keats, Milton, and What one may 'very naturally suppose.'" *Nineteenth Century Contexts* 1.1 (1975): 4–7.

British Critic. 2nd series, 9 (June 1818): 649–654; on *Endymion.*

British Review. 3.6 (June 1812): 275–302; review of Byron's *Childe Harold's Pilgrimage.*

Bromwich, David. "Keats." *Hazlitt: The Mind of a Critic,* Oxford UP, 1983, 362–401.

———. "Keats's Radicalism." *Keats and Politics,* edited by Susan J. Wolfson. *SiR* 25.2 (1986): 197–210.

Brooks, Cleanth. "The Artistry of Keats." *The Major English Romantic Poets: A Symposium in Reappraisal,* edited by C. D. Thorpe, C. Baker, and B. Weaver. Southern Illinois UP, 1957, 246–251.

———. "Keats's Sylvan Historian: History Without Footnotes." *Sewanee Review* 52 (1944): 89–101.

———. Postscript. *Sewanee Review* 55 (1947): 697–699.

———, and Robert Penn Warren. *Understanding Poetry.* Henry Holt, 1938.

Brooks, Peter. *Reading for the Plot: Design and Intention in Narrative.* Knopf, 1984.

Brower, Reuben. "Reading in Slow Motion." 1959; introduction to *In Defense of Reading,* edited by Brower and Richard Poirier, E. P. Dutton, 1962.

Burke, Kenneth. "Symbolic Action in a Poem by Keats." *Accent* (1943); *A Grammar of Motives,* World Publishing, 1962, 447–463.

[Burton, Robert]. *The Anatomy of Melancholy.* 1621; 11th ed. (the one Keats read); 2 vols., (several printers), 1813.

Byron, George Gordon, Lord [anon.]. *Don Juan.* London, 1819.

———. *Letters and Journals.* Vol. 8, edited by Leslie A. Marchand, John Murray, 1973; cited as *BLJ.*

Caldwell, J. R. *John Keats' Fancy.* Cornell UP, 1945.

Chatterton, Thomas. *Complete Works,* edited by Robert Southey and Joseph Cottle, 3 vols., London, 1803.

———. *Poems, supposed to have been written at Bristol, by Thomas Rowley . . . in the Fifteenth Century.* London, 1777.

Clarke, Colin. *Romantic Paradox: An Essay on the Poetry of Wordsworth.* Barnes and Noble, 1962.

Coleridge, Samuel Taylor. *Biographia Literaria; or Biographical Sketches of My Literary Life and Opinions.* 2 vols. Rest Fenner, 1817. Cited as *BL.*

———. *Christabel, Kubla Khan, and The Pains of Sleep.* John Murray, 1816.

———. *Lectures on Literature, 1808–1819.* 2 vols., edited by R. A. Foakes, Princeton UP, 1987.

———. *The Notebooks.* 4 vols., edited by Kathleen Coburn, Princeton UP, 1973.

———. *Poems of Various Subjects.* London, 1796.

———. *Poems,* edited by E. H. Coleridge, Oxford UP, 1912.

———. *The Poetical Works.* 3 vols. W. Pickering, 1834–1835.

———. *Sibylline Leaves.* Rest Fenner, 1817.

Culler, Jonathan. "Apostrophe." *diacritics* 7.4 (1977): 59–69.

———. "The Language of Lyric." *Thinking Verse* 4.1 (2014): 160–167.

Curran, Stuart. *Poetic Form and British Romanticism.* Oxford UP, 1986.

Davy, Humphry. *A Discourse, Introductory to a Course of Lectures on Chemistry.* Royal Institution, 1802.

———. *Collected Works,* edited by John Davy, Smith, Elder, 1839, II:307–326.

———. *Elements of Chemical Philosophy.* Joseph Johnson, 1812.

De Man, Paul. *Selected Poetry of John Keats.* New American Library, 1966.

De Selincourt, Ernest. "The Warton Lecture on John Keats," edited by Williamson, 1920, 1–21.

Dickstein, Morris. *Keats and His Poetry.* U of Chicago P, 1971.

———. "Keats and Politics." *SiR* 25 (1986): 175–181.

Dineley, Penelope. *The Influence of Chatterton on Keats.* McMaster U Library P, 1975. CiteSeerX.ist.psu.edu.

Eliot, T. S. *The Sacred Wood: Essays on Poetry and Criticism.* Methuen, 1920.

———. *Selected Essays, 1917–1932.* Faber & Faber, 1932.

Empson, William. *Seven Types of Ambiguity.* 1930; new edition, New Directions, 1966.

———. "Thy Darling in an Urn." *Sewanee Review* 55.4 (1947): 691–697.

Encyclopædia Britannica. 8th edition, Edinburgh, 1857. A[lexander] S[mit]h, "John Keats." XIII: 55–57.

Ende, Stuart. *Keats and the Sublime.* Yale UP, 1976.

Examiner, 11 October 1818. "The Quarterly Review—Mr. Keats." 648–649.

Fairer, David. "Chatterton's Poetic Afterlife 1770–1794." *Thomas Chatterton and Romantic Culture,* edited by Nick Groom, St. Martin's P, 1999, 228–252.

Finney, Claude Lee. *The Evolution of Keats's Poetry.* 2 vols. Harvard UP, 1936.

Ford, George H. *Keats and the Victorians.* Yale UP, 1984.

Frost, Robert. *Collected Poems, Prose, and Plays,* edited by Richard Poirier and Mark Richardson. Library of America, 1995.

Fry, Paul. "History, Existence, and 'To Autumn.'" *SiR* 25 (1986): 211–219.

———. *The Poet's Calling in the English Ode.* Yale UP, 1980.

Garrod, H. W. *Keats.* Oxford UP, 1926.

Gittings, Robert. *The Mask of Keats.* Harvard UP, 1956.

Gregory, John. *A Father's Legacy to his Daughters.* A Strahan, 1793.

Hartman, Geoffrey. *The Fate of Reading.* U of Chicago P, 1975.

———. "Poem and Ideology: A Study of Keats's 'To Autumn.'" *Fate* (1973): 124–146.

———. "Spectral Symbolism and Authorial Self in Keats's *Hyperion.*" *Fate* (1974): 57–73.

———. "Reading Aright: Keats's *Ode to Psyche.*" *Centre and Labyrinth,* edited by Eleanor Cook et al., U of Toronto P, 1983, 210–226.

Haydon, B. R. "On the Judgment of Connoisseurs Being Preferred to that of Professional Men,—Elgin Marbles, &c." *Examiner,* 18 March 1816, 162–164.

———. "The Sacrifice at Lystra." *Examiner,* 2 and 9 May 1819; *Annals of the Fine Arts* IV (1820): 226–247.

Hazlitt, William [W. H.]. "The Drama No. XI." (Baldwin's) *London Magazine* 2.12 (December 1820): 685–690.

———[W. H.] [Gusto]. *Examiner*, 26 May 1816, 332–333.

———. *Lectures on the English Poets*. Taylor and Hessey, 1818.

———[W. H.]. "My first Acquaintance with Poets." *The Liberal* III. John Hunt [ca. 23–26 April] 1823, 23–46.

———[W. H]. On Wordsworth's *Excursion*. *Examiner*, 21 August 1814, 541–542; 28 August 1814, 555–558.

Hewlett, Dorothy. *Adonais: A Life of John Keats*. Bobbs-Merrill, 1938.

Hofkosh, Sonia. "The Writer's Ravishment." *Romanticism and Feminism*, edited by A. K. Mellor, Indiana UP, 1988, 93–114.

Hollander, John. *Melodious Guile: Fictive Pattern in Poetic Language*. Yale UP, 1988.

Homans, Margaret. "Keats Reading Women, Women Reading Keats." *SiR* 29 (1990): 341–370.

Hunt, Leigh. *Autobiography*. 3 vols. Smith, Elder, 1850.

———. "The Enchantments of the Wizard Indolence, and Exploits of the Knight Sir Industry." *A Book for a Corner: Selections in Prose & Verse*. 2 vols. Chapman and Hall, 1852, 2:9–11.

———. "The Eve of St. Agnes." *London Journal* 43 (21 January 1835): 17–20.

———. *Foliage, or Poems Original and Translated*. C. and J. Ollier, 1818.

———. *Imagination and Fancy*. Smith, Elder, 1845.

———. *Indicator* XXXI (10 May 1820), "La Belle Dame sans Mercy" (essay, with Keats's poem), 246–248.

———. *Indicator* XLIII–XLIV (2 and 9 August 1820): 337–352. *The Stories of Lamia, Isabella, The Eve of St. Agnes, &c., as Told by Mr. Keats.*

———. "On Keats's 1817 *Poems*." *Examiner* 497 / 498 (6 and 13 July 1817): 428–429 and 443–444.

———. *The Story of Rimini*. J. Murray, 1816.

———. "Young Poets." *Examiner*, 1 December 1816, 761–762.

Jarvis, Simon. "*Endymion*: The Text of Undersong." *Constellations of a Contemporary Romanticism*, edited by Jacques Khalip and Forest Pyle, Fordham UP, 2016, 142–166.

Jeffrey, Francis. Review of *1820*. *Edinburgh Review* 34 (August 1820): 203–213.

Jones, John. *John Keats's Dream of Truth*. Chatto and Windus, 1969.

Keach, William. "Byron Reads Keats." *CCJK*, 203–213.

———. "The Politics of Rhyme." *Arbitrary Power*, Princeton UP, 2004, 46–67.

Kelley, Theresa M. "Poetics and the Politics of Reception: Keats's 'La Belle Dame sans Merci.'" *ELH* 54 (1987): 333–362.

Kern, Robert. "Keats and the Problem of Romance." *PQ* 58 (1979): 171–191.

Kucich, Greg. "Keats and the Marking of Charles Brown's Spenser Volumes." *KSR* 3 (1988): 1–22.

———. *Keats, Shelley, and Romantic Spenserianism*. Pennsylvania State UP, 1991.

[Lamb, Charles]. Review of *1820*. *New Times,* 19 July 1820; *Examiner,* 30 July 1820, 494–495.

Lau, Beth. *Keats's Paradise Lost.* UP of Florida, 1998.

Lempriere, J[ohn]. *Classical Dictionary.* 1788; 8th edition, T. Cadell and W. Davies, 1812 (unpaged).

Levinson, Marjorie. "The Dependent Fragment: 'Hyperion' and 'The Fall of Hyperion.'" *The Romantic Fragment Poem,* U of North Carolina P, 1986, 167–187.

———. *Keats's Life of Allegory: The Origins of a Style.* Basil Blackwell, 1988.

Lewis, C. S. *A Preface to Paradise Lost.* Oxford UP, 1942.

———. "The Life of Keats." *Poetical Works of John Keats.* Little, Brown, 1865, 7–29.

London Magazine (Baldwin). September 1820, 2:315–321; review of *1820*.

———. April 1821, 3:426–427; "Death of Mr. John Keats" (sd. L).

London Magazine (Gold's). August 1820, 2:160–173; review of *1820*.

———. December 1820, 2:559–561; "An Essay on Poetry, with Observations on the Living Poets."

Lowell, James Russell. "Keats." *Among My Books,* 2nd series, Houghton Mifflin, 1876, 303–327.

Luke, David. "Keats's Letters." *Genre* 2 (1978): 209–226.

———. "Keats's Notes from Underground 'To J. H. Reynolds.'" *SEL* 19 (1979): 661–672.

Magnuson, Paul. *Reading Public Romanticism.* Princeton UP, 1998.

Manning, Peter J. "Keats's and Wordsworth's Nightingales." *ELN* 17 (March 1980): 189–192.

———. "Reading and Ravishing: The 'Ode on a Grecian Urn.'" *Approaches to Teaching Keats's Poetry,* edited by Walter Evert and Jack Rhodes, MLA, 1991, 131–136.

Marsh, George. "A Forgotten Cockney Poet—Cornelius Webb." *Philological Quarterly* 21.1 (July 1942): 323–333.

Maxwell, J. C. "Keats's Sonnet on the Tomb of Burns." *KSJ* 4 (1955): 77–80.

McDonald, Peter. *Sound Intentions.* Oxford UP, 2012.

McDowell, Stacey. "Shiftiness in Keats's 'Ode on Indolence.'" *Romanticism* 23.1 (2017): 27–37.

McGann, Jerome J. "Keats and the Historical Method in Literary Criticism." *MLN* 94 (1979): 988–1032.

Medwin, Thomas. *Conversations of Lord Byron.* H. Colburn, 1824.

———. *Life of Percy Bysshe Shelley,* edited by H. B. Forman, Oxford UP, 1913.

Miller, Christopher. "Fine Suddenness: Keats's Sense of a Beginning." *Surprise: The Poetics of the Unexpected,* Cornell UP, 2015, 199–222.

———. *The Invention of Evening: Perception and Time in Romantic Poetry.* Cambridge UP, 2006.

Milton, John. "An Epigraph on the admirable Dramaticke Poet, W. Shakespeare." 1630; in *Mr. William Shakespeare Comedies, histories and tragedies,* 2nd folio, London, 1632, 14.

Morely, Edith J. *The Life and Times of Henry Crabb Robinson.* Dent, 1935.

Mulvey, Laura. "Visual Pleasure and Narrative Cinema." *Screen* 163 (1975): 6–18.

Murry, John Middleton. *Studies in Keats.* Oxford UP, 1930.

Najarian, James. *Victorian Keats: Manliness, Sexuality, and Desire.* Palgrave, 2002.

Nersessian, Anahid. *Keats's Odes: A Lover's Discourse.* U of Chicago P, 2021.

New Monthly Magazine 4, 1822. Charles Brown's remarks on Keats and excerpt from *Lines written in the Highlands,* p. 52.

Patterson, Annabel. "'How to load and . . . bless': Syntax and Interpretation in Keats's *To Autumn.*" *PMLA* 94.3 (1979): 449–458.

Perkins, David. *The Quest for Permanence: The Symbolism of Wordsworth, Shelley, and Keats.* Harvard UP, 1959.

Pettet, E. C. *On the Poetry of Keats.* Cambridge UP, 1957.

Plumly, Stanley. *The Immortal Evening: A Legendary Dinner with Keats, Wordsworth, and Lamb.* Norton, 2014.

———. *Posthumous Keats.* Norton, 2008.

Prynne, J. H. *Stars, Tigers and the Shape of Words.* Birkbeck College, 1993.

Quarterly Review XIX; review of *Endymion,* 204–208.

Rajan, Tilottama. *Dark Interpreter: The Discourse of Romanticism.* Cornell UP, 1980.

Raysor, T. M. "Unpublished Fragments on Aesthetics by S. T. Coleridge." *Studies in Philology* 22.4 (1925): 529–537.

Read, Herbert. *English Prose Style.* G. Bell, 1928.

Rejack, Brian, and Michael Theune, eds. *Keats's Negative Capability: New Origins and Afterlives.* Liverpool UP, 2019.

———, and Susan J. Wolfson. "Murder'd Man." *KSR* 35.1 (2021): 11–29.

Reynolds, John Hamilton. *Letters,* edited by Leonidas M. Jones, U of Nebraska P, 1973.

Reynolds, Suzanne. "'Some Scraps of Paper': The Autograph Manuscript of *Ode to a Nightingale.*" *KSR* 33.2 (2019): 140–158.

Richards, I. A. *Coleridge on Imagination.* 1922; Routledge & Kegan Paul, 1935.

———. *Mencius on the Mind: Experiments in Multiple Definition.* Kegan Paul &c, 1932.

Ricks, Christopher. *The Force of Poetry.* Oxford UP, 1984.

———. *Keats and Embarrassment.* Oxford UP, 1976.

———. "Keats's Sources, Keats's Allusions." *CCJK,* 152–169.

———. "A Pure Organic Pleasure from the Lines." *Essays in Criticism* 21.1 (1971): 1–32.

Ridley, M. R. *Keats' Craftmanship.* Clarendon P, 1933.

Robinson, Henry Crabb. *On Books and Their Writers,* edited by Edith J. Morely, 3 vols., J. M. Dent, 1938.

Robinson, Jeffrey C. *Reception and Poetics in Keats.* St Martin's P, 1998.

Roe, Nicholas. *Fiery Heart: The Life of Leigh Hunt.* Pimlico, 2005.

———. *John Keats and the Culture of Dissent.* Clarendon P, 1997.

Rossetti, Dante Gabriel. *John Keats: Criticism and Comment.* Richard Clay; for T. J. Wise, private circulation, 1919.

Rovee, Christopher. "Trashing Keats." *ELH* 75 (2008): 993–1022.

Rzepka, Charles J. "Keats: Watcher and Witness." *The Self as Mind,* Harvard UP, 1986, 165–242.

Scott, Grant F. *The Sculpted Word: Keats, Ekphrasis, and the Visual Arts.* UP of New Hampshire, 1999.

Scott, John. "Poems by John Keats." [Baldwin's] *London Magazine,* September 1820, 2:319–320.

Sharp, Ronald. "Keats and Friendship." *The Persistence of Poetry,* edited by Robert M. Ryan and Ronald A. Sharp, U of Massachusetts P, 1998, 66–81.

Sharp, William. *The Life and Letters of Joseph Severn.* Sampson Low, Marston, 1892.

———. "The Portraits of Keats." *Century Illustrated Monthly Magazine* 71 (February 1906): 535–551.

Sheats, Paul. "Keats and the Ode." *CCJK,* 86–101.

Shelley, Mary. *Journals,* edited by Paula Feldman and Diana Scott Kilvert, Johns Hopkins UP, 1987.

Shelley, Percy Bysshe. *The Letters,* edited by F. L. Jones, Clarendon P, 1964.

Smith, Alexander. See *Encyclopædia Britannica.*

Sperry, Stuart M. *Keats the Poet.* Princeton UP, 1973.

Stevens, Wallace. "The Noble Rider and the Sound of Words." 1942; *The Necessary Angel: Essays on Reality and Imagination,* Vintage, 1951, 3–36.

———. *The Palm at the End of the Mind: Selected Poems and a Play,* edited by Holly Stevens, 1967; Vintage, 1972.

Stewart, Garrett. "*Lamia* and the Language of Metamorphosis." *SiR* 15 (1976): 3–41.

———. "Keats and Language." *CCJK,* 135–151.

———. *The Value of Style in Fiction.* Cambridge UP, 2018.

Stillinger, Jack. "Fifty-nine Ways of Reading *Ode on a Grecian Urn.*" *Romantic Complexity,* U of Illinois P, 2006, 201–207.

———. *"The Hoodwinking of Madeline" and Other Essays on Keats's Poems.* U of Illinois P, 1971, 67–93.

———. "Keats's Grecian Urn and the Evidence of the Manuscripts." *PMLA* 73 (1958): 447–448.

———. *Reading* The Eve of St. Agnes. Oxford UP, 1999.

Swann, Karen. "*Endymion's* Beautiful Dreamers." *CCJK,* 20–36.

———. "Harassing the Muse." *Romanticism and Feminism,* edited by Anne Mellor, Indiana UP, 1988, 81–92.

———. "The Strange Time of Reading." *European Romantic Review* 9 (1998): 275–282.

———. "Tracing Keats." *Lives of the Dead Poets.* Fordham UP, 2019, 29–52.

Taylor, Tom. *The Life of Benjamin Robert Haydon.* 3 vols. Longman &c, 1853.

Tennyson, Alfred Lord. In *The Golden Treasury of English Songs and Lyrics,* edited by Francis Palgrave, Macmillan, 1887.

Tennyson, Hallam. *Alfred Lord Tennyson, A Memoir.* 2 vols. Macmillan, 1897.

Vaihinger, Hans. *The Philosophy of "As if."* 1911; translated by C. K. Ogden, 1924; Routledge and Kegan Paul, 1949.

Vendler, Helen. *The Odes of John Keats.* Harvard UP, 1983.

———. "John Keats: Perfecting the Sonnet." *Coming of Age as a Poet,* Harvard UP, 2003, 41–80.

Vickers, Nancy. "Diana Described: Scattered Woman and Scattered Rhyme." *Critical Inquiry* 8.2 (1981): 265–279.

Waldoff, Leon. *Keats and the Silent Work of Imagination.* U of Illinois P, 1985.

Walker, Carol Kyros. *Walking North with Keats.* Yale UP, 1992.

Wasserman, Earl R. *The Finer Tone: Keats's Major Poems.* Johns Hopkins UP, 1953.

Wilde, Oscar. "Mr. Yeats's *Wanderings of Oisin.*" *Pall Mall Gazette,* 12 July 1889.

———. "Keats's Sonnet on Blue." *Century Guild Hobby Horse* I (July 1886): 1–86.

———. *Letters,* edited by Rupert Hart-Davis, Harcourt, Brace & World, 1962.

———. *The Picture of Dorian Gray. Lippincott's Monthly Magazine* 46 (July 1890): 3–100.

———. *Poems by Oscar Wilde and his Lecture on the English Renaissance.* Seaside Library VIII: 1183; George Munro, 1882.

Williamson, George C., ed. *John Keats Memorial Volume.* John Lane, 1921.

Wimsatt, W. K. "The Structure of Romantic Nature Imagery." 1949; and "One Relation of Rhyme to Reason." 1944; *The Verbal Icon,* U of Kentucky P, 1954, 103–118; 153–168.

Wolfson, Susan J. See author note.

Woof, Robert, and Stephen Hebron. *John Keats.* Wordsworth Trust, 1995.

Woolf, Virginia. *A Writer's Diary,* edited by Leonard Woolf, Harcourt Brace, 1956.

Wordsworth, William. "Essay, Supplementary to the Preface." In *Poems,* 1815, 341–375.

———. *The Excursion.* Longman, 1814.

———. *Letters,* edited by Ernest de Selincourt. *The Early Years, 1787–1805;* rev. Chester L. Shaver, Clarendon P, 1967. *The Middle Years, 1806–1820: Part 1, 1806–1811;* rev. Mary Moorman, Clarendon, 1969; *Part 2, 1812–1820;* rev. Moorman and Alan G. Hill, Clarendon, 1970. *The Later Years, 1821–1853;* rev. Hill, 4 parts, Oxford UP, 1978–1988. Cited as *EY, MY, LY.*

———. *Lyrical Ballads.* 1798, 1800, 1802. Cited as *LB.*

———. *Poems, in Two Volumes.* Longman, 1807.

———. *Poems.* 2 vols. Longman, 1815.

Wu, Duncan, ed. *New Writings of William Hazlitt.* 2 vols. Oxford UP, 2007.

Yeats, W. B. *The Collected Letters,* edited by John Kelly, Oxford UP, 1986–.

———. *Letters,* edited by Allan Wade, Rupert Hart-Davis, 1954.

———. *The Trembling of the Veil.* Private printing, 1922.

Z. See *Blackwood's.*

My books on or involving Keats

The Questioning Presence: Wordsworth, Keats, and the Interrogative Modes of Romantic Poetry. Cornell UP, 1986.

Formal Charges: The Shaping of Poetry in British Romanticism. Stanford UP, 1997.

Borderlines: The Shiftings of Gender in British Romanticism. Stanford UP, 2006.

Reading John Keats. Cambridge UP, 2014.

Romantic Shades and Shadows. Johns Hopkins UP 2018.

Cambridge Companion to John Keats, 2001, ed., with a chapter on the late lyrics. Also: chapters in *The Cambridge Companion to English Poets* (2011), *Keats and History* (Cambridge UP, 2000), and "The New Poetries," *The Cambridge History of English Romantic Literature* (2009). Essays include "Keats the Letter-Writer: Epistolary Poetics," *Romanticism Past and Present* 6 (1982); "What's Wrong with Formalist Criticism?," *SiR* 37 (1998); "The Know of Not to Know It: Teaching Keats's *Ode on a Grecian Urn,*" http://www.rc.umd.edu/praxis; "Keats's Thinking in Sonnets," *Front Porch Journal* (2012); "Yeats's latent Keats / Keats's latent Yeats," *PMLA* (2016); "Accidental Anthologies of 1818," *KSJ* 67 (2019). Four essays on Keats-letters at the Keats Letters Project (revised for *On he flared,* Keats-House, 2021). My work as teacher, textual editor, and critical interpreter shaped *John Keats: A Longman Cultural Edition* and "John Keats," *The Longman Anthology of British Literature: The Romantics and Their Contemporaries* (1998–2012).

ACKNOWLEDGMENTS

for foundational support and sustained careful attention

John Kulka, whose idea this was and got it launched
Garrett Stewart, who read this so often with care and encouragement

for editorial service and support at Harvard University Press: Emily Silk and
Emeralde Jensen-Roberts; and for alert copyediting, the mysterious KW

for various timely courtesies, generosities, and attentions along the way
Kim Blank, impresario of *Mapping Keats's Progress*
Brian Rejack, ace Keatsian, alert reader and resource
Brian Bates, encourager and research resource
Duncan Wu, for sage advice and steady support
Beth Lau, impresario of Keats's *Paradise Lost*
Stan Plumly, Keatsian extraordinaire, now in a finer tone
Seamus Perry, for timely advice and encouragement
Kevin Mensch, Manager of Computer and Technical Support, Princeton
     University, for vast material assistance
Timothy Young, Curator of Modern Books and Manuscripts, and the
     staff of the Beinecke Rare Book and Manuscript Library, Yale
     University
John Logan, Literature Bibliographer, Princeton University Library
Leslie Morris, Gore Vidal Curator of Modern Books and Manuscripts,
     Houghton Library, for tons of prompt and generous material assistance
Giuseppe Albano, Curator of the Keats-Shelley House, Rome
Julie Carlsen, Coordinator of the Henry W. and Albert A. Berg Collection
     of English and American Literature, the New York Public Library

Philip Palmer, Curator and Department Head, Literary and Historical
Manuscripts, and Sal Robinson, Assistant Curator, the Morgan Library
and Museum.
Joyce Oates, careful, imaginative correspondent
Starry Schor, cherished colleague
Ron Levao, always, for everything and more

INDEX

Keats's poetical works are indexed under *title* or "well-known first words." Excerpts from longer works are by first lines. **Keynote pages in boldface**

dreams, dreaming, everywhere in Keats's poetry (as documented in *An Electronic Concordance to Keats's Poetry,* ed. Noah Comet)

Edinburgh Magazine (not Blackwood's) on *Endymion,* 90
Edinburgh Review (Blackwood's). See *Blackwood's Edinburgh Magazine*
egotism and the "egotistical sublime," 14. *See also* Wordsworth: Keats on
ekphrasis, 162, 345, 349, 352n2
Elegiac stanza, 303, 305, 307n4
Elgin Marbles (Athenian Parthenon relief), 353n10; Byron on, 72; Haydon on, 57, 72; Keats on, **71–74**
Eliot, T. S., 21n11, 74, 309n2, 323, 353
embarrassment, 90–91, 103–107, 108n4, 108n6, 136, 182n9, 286, 358. *See also* blushing
Empson, William, on ambiguity, 348; on double grammar, 38n3, 380; on *Ode on a Grecian Urn,* 349–350, 353n8, 357; on *Ode on Melancholy,* 356, 360n3
Endymion, 20, **88–118,** 129, 153, 173, 237, 312, 341, 362
—Book I: "A thing of Beauty is a joy for ever," **92–95**; Book II: Adonis, **102–108,** 111, 264; Book III: Glaucus and Circe, 91, 283, 369, 407; Book IV: Cave of Quietude, **114–118,** 230; Dedication to Chatterton, 16, 31; "Pleasure Thermometer," **95–102,** 268; Preface, 13, 167; "slippery blisses," 366
—Keats's ambitions for, 9, 16, 21, 77, 88, 95, 138, 167, 301; his reflections on, 118, 281, 361; reception of, 10, 11, 31, 56, 88, 90, 93, 101, 109, 216, 287, 382; rhyme practices in, 90, 93–95, 98–99, 295; Shelley on, 238; Spenserian imprints in, 105, 113, 115–118; Wilde on, 192
See also "Oh Chatterton!": Spenserian diction in; "Hymn to Pan"; *Lamia:* Circe; "Romance"
Endymion and Cynthia, in *Endymion,* 91, 112
Eve of St. Agnes, The, 5, 10, 19, 215, **248–277,** 283, 286, 291, 308, 332–333, 340, 360n5, 361
—and Byron's *Don Juan,* 276; critical reception, 12, 249, 250–251, 263, 269; immodesty and obscenity, 264–266; Keats's drafts and revisions, 264–266, 274; the legend of St. Agnes, 248, 251–252, 257–259, 261, 266–268; and Milton's *Paradise Lost,* 261, 266, 275; its Spenserian stanza, 248
—episodes: casement window, 260, 262–263, 368; "hoodwink'd" Madeline, 248–249, 252, 257; Madeline's disrobing, 104, 260–261, 263–266; Porphyro's love-feast, 107, 256, 268–269, 270nn1–3; Porphyro's love-making, 271, 273–274
See also "Romance"; Spenserian stanza

Examiner, 26, 27, 33, 34, 57, 60, 61, 230, 343n23, 383; publishes Keats, 7, 24, 36, 52, 68–72, 75–76, 82; reviews of Keats's poetry, 3, 21n4, 37–38, 40, 47n2, 182n7, 207; "Young Poets," article in, 6–7, 50. *See also* Hunt, Leigh (editor of *The Examiner*)

Fall of Hyperion, The, 11, 343n17, 385, **386–400,** 403; and Dante's *Inferno* and *Purgatorio* (in Cary's translation: *Hell* and *Purgatory*), 398–399; first publication of, 385; the goddess Mnemosyne in, 396, 397; the goddess Moneta in, 388–395; and *Hyperion,* 392–398; Keats's "induction" to, 385–388; and *Paradise Lost,* 389–390, 399
Fame, 54, 87, 97, 129, 137–138, 202–205, 216, 218, 290, 292, **298–302,** 318. *See also* popularity as author
Fancy, 45, 83, 202, 290; and fetish, 140; and gender, 245–247, 340–341; Shakespeare on, 247
—Addison on, 242–244; Coleridge on, 244; Hunt on, 242; and James Bruce (discovering the source of the Nile), 145–146; and Milton, 243, 347; Milton (Adam) on, 243–244; Spenser on, 326; Wordsworth on, 236, 245
—Keats on: *The Eve of St. Agnes,* 249, 252, 257, 261, 266–267, 275; *Lamia,* 364, 375; *Ode to a Nightingale,* 332, 337, 340–341; *Ode to Psyche,* 321, 326
fetish and fetishism, 74–75, 140–142, 144n1, 269, 301, 408; Freud on, 142; in *Isabella; or the Pot of Basil,* 142, 176, 180
fever and poetry, in poetry, 10, 91, 109, 119, 166, 176, 180, 215–216, 229, 232, 253, 262, 278, 280, 283, 298, 301, 311, 317, 330, 336, 357, 391, 402–403. *See also* Burton, Robert, *Anatomy of Melancholy*
Fitzgerald, F. Scott, and *Ode to a Nightingale,* 337
Frederick II, Emperor, and the sonnet, 23; in *Inferno,* 416; Keats's "To Sleep," 416
Frost, Robert, on meter, 45, 53, 305; "The need of being versed in country things," 43; on word-soundings, 17
Fry, Paul, 307n7, 409n3

Garrod, H. W., 25n3, 124n5, 307n7, 329n11
Gittings, Robert, as editor of Keats, 25n1; on *Bright Star,* 421; on Keats's bawdy, 158n1; on Keats's Dante, 296n2, 398, 416; on *Ode to Psyche,* 329n11, 343nn6–7, 400n2
(Gold's) London Magazine, 238, 343n19, 372
Gordian knot and eponyms, 110, 112, 366–368, 375
"Great Odes," **308–360**; Keats's innovative 1819 genre, 5, 10, 19, 307n7, 308, 403